Creativity and Culture

Creativity and Culture

*A Psychoanalytic Study
of the Creative Process
in the Arts, Sciences, and Culture*

Daniel Dervin

Rutherford • Madison • Teaneck
Fairleigh Dickinson University Press
London and Toronto: Associated University Presses

Associated University Presses
440 Forsgate Drive
Cranbury, NJ 08512

Associated University Presses
25 Sicilian Avenue
London WC1A 2QH, England

Associated University Presses
P.O. Box 488, Port Credit
Mississauga, Ontario
Canada L5G 4M2

The paper used in this publication meets the requirements
of the American National Standard for Permanence of Paper
for Printed Library Materials Z39.48-1984.

Library of Congress Cataloging-in-Publication Data

Dervin, Daniel, 1935–
   Creativity and culture: a psychoanalytic study of the creative
process in the arts, sciences, and culture / Daniel Dervin.
      p.   cm.
   ISBN 0-8386-3366-8 (alk. paper)
   1. Creative ability.   2. Creation (Literary, artistic, etc.)
3. Creative ability in science.   4. Psychoanalysis and culture.
I. Title.
   BF408.D485   1990
   153.3′5—dc20   88-46150
                                                              CIP

Contents

To friends, colleagues, and officials
of Mary Washington College, this book is respectfully dedicated.

Acknowledgments

For their careful and enduring patience and expertise, I am deeply indebted to and grateful for the assistance of Lauren Lepow, Cynthia Crumrine, and Paul Rieder in preparing this manuscript.

Permissions have been granted for the following:

The reprint from *Musaeum Hermeticum Reformatum et Amplificatum* (Frankfurt: 1678), p. 393, by permission of the Houghton Library, Harvard University.

The reprint from Johann Daniel Mylius, *Philosophia Reformata* (Frankfurt: 1622), by permission of the Department of Rare Books & Special Collections, 443 Memorial Library, 728 State St., Madison, Wisconsin 53706.

From "The Ship of Death," in *The Complete Poems of D. H. Lawrence,* ed. Vivian de Sola Pinto and F. Warren Roberts. Copyright © 1964 by Angelo Ravagli and C. M. Weekley, Executors of the Estate of Freida Lawrence Ravagli. All rights reserved. Reprinted by permission of Viking Penguin, a division of Penguin Books USA, Inc.

From *Phoenix* by D. H. Lawrence. Copyright 1936 by Freida Lawrence. Copyright renewed © 1964 by the Estate of the late Freida Lawrence Ravagli. Reprinted by permission of Viking Penguin, a division of Penguin Books USA, Inc.

From Marcel Griaule, *Conversations with Ogotemmeli* (Oxford: Oxford University Press, 1975) by permission of the publisher.

The reproduction of *Bareback Riders* by W. H. Brown, National Gallery of Art, Washington D.C., Gift of Edgar William and Bernice Chrysler Garbisch.

The reproduction of *Upper Falls of the Reichenbach* by Joseph Mallord William Turner, R.A., by permission of the Yale Center for British Art, Paul Mellon Collection.

Permission to reprint my articles "Roland Barthes: The Text as Self/The Self as Text," "A Dialectical View of Creativity," and "A Psychoanalytic Approach to Language Acquisition and Literary Origins: Beckett, Joyce, and Wordsworth," is granted by *The Psychoanalytic Review,* published by the National Psychological Association for Psychoanalysis, Inc.

Permission to reprint my article "Breast Fantasy in Barthelme, Swift, and Philip Roth: Creativity and Psychoanalytic Structure," is granted by *American Imago.* However, in every instance, the original piece has been substantially modified.

Introduction: Of Marsupials and
the Mind's Means

About creativity almost everything has been said and almost nothing is known. Or, if that sounds too sweeping, consider the proposition that by definition creativity denotes an original vision, work, or breakthrough of a high order, so that achievements are distinguished not by what they share in common but by what endows each with the stamp of uniqueness. Therefore, the further we look for common features in creative work the further we remove ourselves from its nature. But perhaps this attitude is simply a residue of romantic nostalgia for a kind of individualism no more to be found, in which case we can construe creativity as part and parcel of our everyday experience in tackling the problems of living. But however helpful or even inevitable this consideration may be, going to the other extreme only reminds us that the term is easier defined and recognized than understood.

The results of creativity are easily recognized because they reside in that environment, natural to human beings, designated as *culture*. But if culture is natural to us, it also figures as nature's mirror, distorting or clear, but always changing, arbitrary, relative, and therefore radically subjective, because there are so many different cultures with so many diverse—not to say conflicting— value systems and versions of reality. Any culture that claims an absolute structure of reality is engaging in illusion, and it follows that the study of culture begins with the permanent existence of an illusion rather than the question of its future. It also follows that illusions are real enough in their own ways, and such realities should be taken into account when creativity is placed in its proper cultural context.

But that is not so easy. Most likely lodged in the recesses of our minds is the notion that creating, by analogy with a creator's or demiurge's primordial creation, partakes in divinity. Thus, at its peak of realization, creativity in the arts and sciences alike begets a vision of the world that permanently alters our sense of reality—an idea conceived or vision incarnated in such a way that the one cannot be unthought or the other disembodied. Homer, Dante, Shakespeare, Newton, Darwin, Freud, Einstein, Joyce—all have this in common. And to a greater or lesser extent, they can be included in the same discourse. But creativity must also take into account questions of gender (which is a psychocultural reshaping of everyone's biological sex), and already I have reeled off a list of male geniuses long enough to imply I have

9

inadvertently adopted a male model of who's who in the pantheon of greatness. Moreover, I slipped into a casual metaphor when I employed the verbs *conceived* and *beget* and so may have assumed a theory of creativity based on male parenting via cultural modes that would transcend biological strictures. This in turn assumes a mind-set of splitting gender along traditional lines of female = nature, male = culture, thereby giving women an advantage in life with one hand only to yank it away in culture with the other hand. These issues, which involve language, sex stereotypes, and abiding distinctions between men and women, will need to be addressed if any discourse on creativity is going to claim serious attention.

Tradition should also be taken into account. Science and particular sciences have their own traditions that make it difficult for outsiders to plug into them; the arts have their distinctive forms and literature its particular genres, all with bona fide traditions guaranteed to produce similar difficulties. All manner and degree of scientific or creative activity have kept alive these traditions. And although there has been continued overlapping, borrowing, and, more recently, synthesizing among them, it would be premature if not presumptuous to seek a common matrix in mental operations. That is not in the offing, but I am interested in setting out certain underlying features that characterize a great variety of mental activities. This enables me to begin asking questions about the likelihood that if the human brain has a consistent anatomy, could the myriad minds that operate through it have consistent properties—manifested especially in creative endeavors? But by invoking the brain, I am also evoking analogy. And while analogies cannot clench an argument, they are useful in relaxing rigid positions, in creating more mental space to move one's ideas around in, and in clarifying otherwise obstruse or abstract concepts.

With that in mind, I would like to say a few words about marsupials. Lay people like me look at them and see, for example, kangaroos. Scientists scrutinizing marsupials see different things: for some, furry little insectivorous mammals; for others, a most peculiar reproductive behavior; and for still others, evidence of continental drift theory, which it would seem has more to do with geology than with biology. But affinities between members of this order in South America and in Australia argue that the two continents were also once affiliated. Let it be said that the furry little creatures, unaware of their sizable contribution to scientific debate, go about their business of being marsupials as blissfully oblivious as nature and humankind will allow. Thus, while no one has ever seen the two continents combined, much less pulling apart, we affirm the plate theory through the marsupial. And the fact that the earth looks and feels firmly immobile under their feet—or for that matter under the more evolved feet of neocortexed *Homo sapiens sapiens*—is no argument against continental drift theory.

Marsupials, then, seem to be the visible and distinterested signifiers of an otherwise invisible hypothetical reality. Their discovery, their interpretation along with other supportive data, and their eventual role in a more ambitious enterprise of reconstruction cue the psychoanalytic methods I would engage. Thus, when skeptical readers point out that sometimes a marsupial is just a marsupial, I can agree, but will not feel alone in not accepting the position as final. Take the analogy one step further: to establish the validity of the plate theory as derived primarily from marsupial evidence, how many such creatures would be required to verify it, and in what kind of distribution? If intrepid marsupials had settled throughout Australia, that would certainly attest to their gamesomeness; or if they had diversified into countless subspecies, something would be made of that. But it would be neither the spread nor the mutations of the species that would lend support to the plate-drift theory, which requires their mere presence. Even a few marsupials could speak volumes of science. This, too—the apparent disproportion between cause and effect, between data and inference—while not an obvious asset does assert its place in reasoning. But I promise not to go so far as evolutionists who compare their labors to extrapolating all of *War and Peace* from a single page.

My basic analogy suggests that the mysterious, unseen movements of the continents are like unconscious mental processes that we never get to see directly but know about through certain visible products tossed up seemingly at random onto seemingly far-distant surfaces. For me (not extrapolating directly from clinical data), these products would have to be the cultural marsupials of art and science. Like the natural marsupials, these productions—seen in many different lights and sometimes more for what they mean to us than for what they are—are overdetermined: many different individuals attribute many different meanings to them. Thus to anticipate: If I should quote sources reasoning that Newton's arrival at his laws has something to do with fears of loss and anxiety over uncontrolled destructive rage, that does not mean I am repackaging the "real" scientific genius in (say, oedipal) guilt. But it may mean I am looking for confirmation of my own particular plate theory. It may also mean that the marsupials of our minds are overdetermined by our own preoccupations. It does not mean that marsupials are *caused* by continental drift theory any more than the products of art and science are caused by unconscious instinctual drives, although in both cases the various components are inseparably bound together.

No, psychic determinism is not being proposed, but psychic over-determinism? Very much so. In its own way, science is every bit as much a cultural invention as art—both being modulated through the contingencies of whatever society they emerge in. (I take art to address a meaningful representation of human experience; science to address verifiable versions of ourselves and our world.) Such an approach, by the same token, does not mean I'm cruelly reducing my mental marsupials to serve theoretical aims any more than the physical ones were absorbed into a scientific construct. And just as no marsupial has ever been harmed by plate theory, so would I hope that no harm would be inflicted on the enduring creative geniuses I am briefly appropriating as a data base. The only real harm would be in perpetrating a demonstrably false theory; as to its ultimate coherence, the reader is sitting in the judgment seat.

To consider all cultural products as overdetermined is simply to recognize that human beings operate out of complex motives. Which ones are important is affected by what we value most highly in the finished product as we extract its meanings. We often differ both with the originator of the given product and among ourselves about what that meaning really is—perhaps more extensively so in the arts. But even from the theory of evolution we extract many different meanings, partly because science is as much a creation of human culture as are literature and the arts. Beginning at opposite ends of the scale, motive and meaning may occasionally converge but should be distinguished from each other. Along with *motive* (something the producer brings to the work) and *meaning* (something the user takes out of it) is *structure*: something we experience in the product by reason of its content, ordering of parts, relation to other works, laws, and so forth.

To these distinct emphases, psychoanalysis lays its major claim through opening up and revealing a buried world of motives in everyone's psychic apparatus. But the field has more to offer than delineations of motive, though that may always be the starting point. What I hope further to establish through psychoanalysis are some congruencies in structure that range through scientific, literary, and artistic products. Accordingly, I am less interested in meanings than in their means. Moreover, as one of the shapers of meaning, motive is likely to deposit in the product such traces as may recur consistently and profoundly enough to acquire discernible structures. I will be content to locate and define these simple but wide-ranging structures without presupposing the nature or priority of motives, deep-seated or otherwise.

Psychoanalysis may be taken in a threefold sense as a: (1) clinical procedure; (2) body of theory about human beings and culture; (3) schema of individual development. Each of these opens a distinctive angle of vision into the cultural fields of art and science. Models derived from the clinical base are usually referred to as the *dream* or *conflict model*, but by reason of their primary emphasis on infantile disorders, these models run the risk of appearing regressive or reductive when applied to cultural subjects. Properly speaking, this is a disease model, likely to generate controversy when applied globally to unwitting subjects outside the clinic. Models derived from psychoanalytic theory, for example the interplay of eros and the death instinct, are currently favored by the French Freudians, who apply what may be called the *rhetorical model*. The third, or *developmental model*, which draws on observation as well as analysis and encompasses normal as well as disturbed processes, is the preferred approach here, though some overlapping can be expected, and no model magically unlocks the vault of certainty.

Creativity should be viewed within the range of normal development, yet seen widely enough to include primitive mental processes—highly charged wishes and emotions—that would dissolve any rigidly assumed boundaries between normal and abnormal. In other words, whatever severe underlying conflicts or disorders may crop up in the lives of creative individuals, creativity itself—be it psychoanalytically construed as reliving, re-presenting, mastering, problem solving, or working through—strives toward recovering or maintaining sanity, health, the inner sense of well-being and the like—or so I would hypothesize.

More particularly, what interest me are certain fundamental structuring processes emanating from one's early life that influence and shape creativity in both the arts and sciences. These processes are fundamental in both the sense of being widespread and being "deep," or largely unconscious. They can be discussed from different perspectives. As principles or regulators, they exist in the realm of theory; as poles, they reside within the creative processes and make themselves felt in the finished product in various ways. The term *poles* conveys both a sense of polarity (opposition or complementarity) and one of magnetic fields, drawing scattered and diffuse materials into concentric patterns. Depending upon one's emphasis, these poles may be either points of reference for analyzing creativity or organizing centers within creative activity. If this sounds hazy, I would plead for a measure of vagueness at the outset rather than a premature specificity of focus.

As these poles are construed psychoanalytically, they unfold and expand into something more like fueling stations or resource outlets that the creative mind has access to—entering and drawing from each in turn as cued by prevailing needs. These needs may include in a fluctuating balance: tension reduction, problem solving, conflict resolution, or truth telling, all of which serve to keep the mind focused along more-or-less conscious lines. But within a frame of deeper (i.e., less conscious) dynamic activity, I envision the mind moving back and forth between these poles and drawing on their distinctive resources at various stages of its task, just as (to reduce the analogy of supplies further) consumers may shop at the same two stores for basic needs—for example, food and clothing—over many years, but will seek out departments most responsive to their needs at various stages of their life cycle. The pattern of consumers' lives can then be seen as orbiting around these points or poles and leaving traces like the concentric lines of two magnetic fields.

What are the "goods" of either outlet center sought in the furtherance of creative activity? They have to do with creativity's associations with beginnings. Whether it be a scientific theorem or an aesthetic piece, to create means to originate. The extensive psychoanalytic literature on childhood theories of origins (which will be introduced piecemeal throughout) can be polarized into relatively subjective and objective versions. The more subjective group clusters around the family romance, for it offers a largely fanciful account of childhood origins constituted of orphans/foundlings and two sets of parents along exalted/humble lines. The more objective group clusters around the primal scene, for, as the actual begetting act of parental sexuality, it offers a truer account of origins—or would if it weren't ridden with anxiety and distorted by incomplete ideas and childhood fantasies of another stripe. Both versions create problems, which in turn may stimulate protocreative responses. The former removes the child entirely from sexual arenas, while imparting it with a heroic destiny. The latter tends to overwhelm the child, exposing it to more critical data than it can handle—knowledge too exciting, perplexing far beyond its capacities to assimilate—or else leaves it shielded in such a way that a mixture of semitrue "theories" are confusingly entertained and mingled with other sources from the animal world, movies, picture books, and the like.

If I could extend an analogy to distinguish between these two poles, I would say that although both structures are subjective enclosures, the family romance offers more skylights for idealizing origins and more subterreanean passages for indulging in romantic or gothic detours; the primal scene offers more doors that open onto ground-level realities. At one point in following the logical implications of these ideas, I concluded that the latter offered a preferable route for the creative process by leading to results of greater objective reality and emotional balance equivalent to the individual's achievement of maturity. But while there are works to support this view, and the energies that go into composing both art and the self may have similar reference points, the field is too complex for a consistent and, hence, predictable parallelism to emerge—which may be just as well. However, insofar as the fueling stations or polarities are not only reciprocal but potentially incompatible, they present possibilities for a dialectical theory of creativity and a model of creative conflict in its own terms.

Two other initial considerations need to be kept in mind. First, the creative energies shaping themselves at the more subjective pole are represented not only through primal fantasy—family romance or otherwise—but by other intensive and related activities having to do with self-reconstitution. Similarly, the creative energies at the more objective pole will often be concentrated on restoring or remaking beyond the self, with mastery or problem solving and assimilation. Second, because these polar features are being examined within the creative process, they may not be found in symmetrical balance in any given work. Many of those I have selected will in the interest of clarity, however, exhibit influences from both poles in order to bring out how frequently, harmoniously, and almost naturally they do operate in tandem. But there is no reason for the artist not to draw more heavily on one or the other to complete a particular work. A case in point: two novels Virginia Woolf wrote in close succession. *To the Lighthouse* (1927) concentrates heavily on reworking the parental relation with an artist-character on hand to pull things together into a higher synthesis; *Orlando* (1928) creates an imaginary and magical being whose many incarnations, adoptions, and encounters with queens, gypsies, and poets suggest a prevailing interest in reconstituting the self via a family-romance route.

From the looks of things so far, one could conclude either that the creative task activates an urge to resolve issues of origins or that the quest for origins activates the creative task. In the long run, this chicken / egg quandary doesn't matter, because both processes go forward hand in hand. What lies ahead is an exploration of these shaping influences on creativity, beginning on the firmer ground of my own field (literature)—expanding into other arts, delving into myth and language, until, like the intrepid marsupial coming to the edge, I may seem to leap onto another continent entirely—science—by attempting to find a common environment of the mind that nourishes both the arts and the sciences. But my method will be more similar to the actual and ancient marsupials, who made of Antarctica a bridge between the continents of South America and Australia. My conceptual Antarctica requires an examination of how a basic process called natural (self-) creativity operates in all of us in order to produce the human beings we are continually becoming. Since there is always a risk of sailing off into midair speculations, I shall, as far as possible, work close to my sources, letting the authors and their commentators speak through their texts in such ways that allow their relevance to arise within my contexts. Thereafter, they are free to return their natural habitats, and we to ours.

Creativity and Culture

1
A Dialectics of Creativity

"My mother was a royal virgin," Peterson said, "and my father a shower of gold. My childhood was pastoral and energetic. . . ."
—Donald Barthelme, "A Shower of Gold"

That night . . . you know . . . the night you got me . . . that night with Mum, what was it like? . . . And there's a lot of people my age that share that curiosity . . . about the true facts of that particular night—the night they were made in the image of those two people *at it*.
—Harold Pinter, *The Homecoming*

1. The Return to Freud

Freud in his early formulations about the artist was essentially correct, or at least on the right track, and his later disclaimers that the psychoanalyst must lay down his arms before the creative artist were both premature and unduly modest. That may be the primary thrust of this chapter; but its final justification hinges on extricating creative processes from models of pathological conflict within psychoanalysis, so that these processes may more clearly and legitimately stand out in their own right and be examined accordingly.

What were Freud's early formulations? They may be readily recalled from the 1908 paper on "Creative Writers and Day-Dreaming," the 1909 paper on "Family Romances," and the 1911 contribution to metapsychology, "Formulations on the Two Principles of Mental Functioning."[1] Here are the essential steps:

1. Unable to meet demands for instinctual renunciation, the artist turns away from reality;
2. In fantasy, like the child at play, the neurotic in conflict, or the adult in dreaming, he/she gives vent to erotic or ambitious wishes;
3. But unlike the child or the neurotic as such, the artist finds a way back to reality by molding his/her fantasies into a new kind of reality.

Having said this much, Freud is content to back off a bit, speaking of the artist's "special gifts" and his/her "innermost secret, the essential *ars poetica*," by which our feelings of repulsion are overcome by aesthetic transformations—and it is to this ability that the analyst bows in homage. One may wonder if Freud is not here being the Socratic ironist, who, despite his feigned modesty, succeeds in planting the clues to the baffling mystery's solution. And when in a 1912 postscript to his study of Jenson's *Gradiva*, he proposes going beyond character analysis to analyzing the creative process, yet does not pursue his own proposal, one may at least infer that he has opened up fascinating passageways down which he himself does not further wander.

My own wanderings have emboldened me to specify more precisely those formulations and apply them to the creative process. In so doing I am confident that the riddle of creativity will be kept alive and unsolved—only will it perhaps be better defined, not by tearing open its innermost secrets, but by tracing a few of its innermost springs. Implicit in Freud and explicit in Ernst Kris's formula of art, which comprises a "regression in the service of the ego,"[2] is the assumption that creativity entails a return to origins: to create, one must find a new way to begin. And since this is never a literal possibility, one draws on imagination and fantasy: *once upon a time ... in the olden days. ...*

A group of fantasies within psychoanalysis, designated as primal, comprise the child's repertory for dealing with its own origins and filling knowledge gaps. Ordered developmentally, the first one encountered is the (male) child's most primitive belief in the maternal phallus, a fantasy that maintains a narcissistic rapport with the mother by attributing to her the same features cherished within his early self-representations (the girl may make this attribution later and less momentously than was once maintained). In effect, the male infant assumes the mother, being perfect, has the same working parts as he. For him, a sense of dual unity and inner wholeness is thereby protected and may be enhanced by elated or oceanic affective states. Unspoiled by perception, the phallic mother is wish-fantasy at its purest. Monistic theories of origins, such as found in primitive peoples' belief in Tjurunga, the primal ancestor, or in Plato's myth of the Androgyne, may owe more than a little to this fantasy of ambisexual unity that either collapses at the castration complex or else survives to play a role in perversions, especially fetishism.[3]

More amenable to development is the family romance, which substitutes for the child's "lowly" and disappointing parents a lofty and ideally loving set. Here the attempt at correcting an experienced disequilibrium in the early dyadic relationship suggests a later stage of self/other awareness. [4] Defensive denial being less pervasive, the child senses that he/she must set right the poor fit between him/herself and the environment—if paradise lost is ever to be regained. A rudimentary self has formed to the extent that its esteem can be damaged by real or imagined slights, and the correction process that is called into play awakens imaginative solutions. In fact, psychoanalysis has located herein the genesis of the creative drive: in the myth of the birth of the hero begins the artist's creative romance with the world.[5] The blendings of myth and fantasy, however, are also attempts to overcome self-injury, narcissistic wounds, and the like, by repairing or reconstituting the body image.[6] Such healing processes are often manifested in fantasies about birth and rebirth; the work itself may become a vehicle for self-exalting aims that embody the fantasy of the self as orphan or foundling subsequently acquired by the audience, reader, or patron acting the part of the idealized adoptive parents. This may be one of the means by which the artist strives indirectly through his work, insofar as it is in part a remaking of the self, to find his / her way back to reality.

Since the psychodynamics of this process are complex enough to consume large sections, if not whole chapters, we may simply consider here how the process may be represented. Sartre, for example, who, at age nine, evoked the artist's family-romance sense of being both a "prince and a shoemaker," also fantasized that future work would comprise his remade, perfected self: "I discovered that in belles-lettres the Giver can be transformed into his own Gift, that is, into a pure object."

> I would start by giving myself an indestructible body and then would hand myself over to the consumers. I would not write for the pleasure of writing, but in order to carve that glorious body in words. Viewed from the height of my tomb, my birth appeared to me a necessary evil, as a quite provisional embodiment that prepared for my transfiguration: in order to be reborn, I had to write; in order to write I needed a brain, eyes, arms. When the work was done, these organs would be automatically re-absorbed. Around 1955, a larva would burst open, twenty-five folio butterflies would emerge from it, flapping all their pages, and would go and alight on a shelf of the National Library ... I sit in state ... I am reborn ... Hands take me down, open me.[7]

And so, one infers, lovingly adopt him.

In formulating the adoption fantasy, Freud distinguished an asexual stage, prior to the (male) child's acceptance of maternal origins, and a later sexual stage, in which the father is exalted while the mother is the impetus for make-believe "situations of secret infidelity and ... love affairs."[8] In addition, I have found that artists are often prone to represent a dark family romance, which appears to invert idealized images of the parents while retaining the allure of their magical powers. In this version a child is not adopted but kidnapped, not suckled but sucked, and the parent is not divine but demonic—for it turns out that the radiant moon goddess, Luna, has a dark twin. As Lamia, or Lilith, she projects versions of the midnight mother, who drains and ravishes rather than nurses and loves the children she steals. In Milton's epic (*Paradise Lost* 2. 11. 662–66), she is Hecate, the "Night-Hag, when call'd/In secret, riding through the Air she comes/Lur'd with the smell of infant blood to dance/With *Lapland* Witches, while the laboring Moon/Eclipses at their charms."

Prominent in literature of the Romantic period, she is the name of a poem by Keats. Her sisterhood ranges from valkyrie to vampires, and even among such moderns as James Joyce and D. H. Lawrence, she continues to exert a potent if latent influence. As the underside of Earth or the dark side of Luna, she does not so much bond the artist to a creative romance with the world as bind up dangerous oral aggressions that could impede the flourishing of the creative romance. While fascinating, she is more siren than sphinx, and her pursuit leads the creative drives deeper into subjectivity—into the macabre, morbid, masochistic, or decadent—rather than on to confronting the riddle of origins.[9] A surprising passage in a letter by Emily Dickinson suggests how a dualistic fantasy may inform a woman's creative work. She anticipates the prospect of missing out on the "Heaven I once dreamed" because "the Jesus Christ you love, remarked he does not know me," yet "there is a darker spirit will not disown its child."[10]

Other variants on the family-romance theme stem from the rescue fantasy, in which the individual (usually male) strives to gain control over his destiny by reshaping his origins one step removed. Freud singled out the child's desire to return the gift of life received from the parents by saving a life, either by rescuing the mother and thus "giving her a child or making one for her—one like himself," or else by rescuing the father as king or emperor and thus evening the debt of paternity by fathering oneself.[11] Invoking the myth of Perseus rescuing the bound-up Andromeda, Edoardo Weiss suggests that freeing the girl represents the male's externalizing and thus relinquishing earlier feminine identifications en route to consolidating his (heroic) masculine identity.[12] Consequently, rescue variants usually presume the more advanced triadic-level relationships and lend themselves to oedipal issues. The rescue fantasy may appear in the work of art as content as well as beyond it as motive, when the work itself becomes the life saved in the form of a love-gift offered in return for the original gift of life, to be caressed by the exalted hands of anonymous readers, as Sartre fantasizes (or as James Joyce does in offering his *Finnegans Wake* to an "ideal reader with an ideal insomnia"). "I spring from the pages into your arms," was Walt Whitman's unabashed way of addressing the reader.

While all of the above fantasies may be classified as primal, it goes without saying that they may be enlisted for and adapted to far-reaching and apparently unrelated purposes at virtually any stage of life. Yet in the framework of creativity they form much of the artist's subjective arsenal, chief among which is the family romance, with its many ramifications. Down this yellow-brick road, more than any other, the artist steps when either he / she cannot meet the demands of external reality or it does not correspond to his / her needs.

But what about the components of this external reality? Can they be specified in such a way as to suit the artist's development and complement the role of the family romance? A cautious yes may be given, for not only does the child have primal fantasies, but he / she is also involved, directly or indirectly, with primal scenes: representations of parental lovemaking.[13] And even though these events are on the side of objective reality, they, too, are subjected to the distortions of the child's developing mind and to those psychosexual phases in which he / she is most deeply enmeshed.[14] Nonetheless, while fueling primal fantasies, primal scenes are critical messages initiated by the world outside the child's mind. When interpreted correctly, they inform as nothing else can, not only of origins, but of something about one's emerging identity and future role in adult sexuality. They may enter the child's mind via a primal fantasy, such as the phallic mother, in which the phallus remains in place but reverses direction, so to speak, as its possession switches gender from mother to father.

The child's concern with origins and parentage establishes a common ground for the family romance and the primal scene. Since the answers each provides are so radically different, however, the two phenomena are properly treated as opposites; it is only by pursuing their polarity into the creative sphere that it will become possible to recognize their complementarity. The rescue of Andromeda by Perseus, for example, presupposes his confronting the snaky locks of Medusa: the romance with the lovely lady leads to the hero's confronting the monstrous sexual displacements of the primal scene. The opposing versions of origins suit each other so well in part because the "higher" is often a reworking of the "lower." Thus, the primal scene may best stand for the prototypal reality that the burgeoning artists turns away from in order to effect a "correction" via the realm of fantasy—and what fantasy could be more ideally suited to this task than the family romance? For here the child is not the excluded object—the orphan / outcast—but the royal heir or lovely princess; nor is the animalistic act of reproduction so terrifying or alienating once it is overshadowed by the Olympian heights of royal romance. But while the fantasy seals the child in safety, it also fosters illusion, splits the child's inner world, and, by nursing hurt feelings with a balm of reactive grandiosity, jeopardizes the same fragile self-esteem that was originally so vulnerable.

This means that the artist will come into his / her own only by finding a viable route back to reality. But if a thread of continuity—creativity, origins— can be sighted running through these experiences, some of the mist hovering over the artistic process has been dispelled. Critical poles between which the artist operates during early stages of the creative journey have been specified; operating as a dual anchorage between inner and outer reality for the artist, these poles variously regulate the formation of the work. If none of this thereby exposes any "innermost secret," it may yet tap into the same obscure world from which the secrets emerge.

2. At the Perimeters of Myth and Madness

> Pictor had scarcely set foot in Paradise when he found himself standing before a tree that had two crowns. In the leaves of one was the face of a man; in the leaves of another, the face of a woman. Pictor stood in awe of the tree and timidly asked, "Are you the Tree of Life?"
>
> —Hermann Hesse, "Pictor's Metamorphoses"

In subtle, obscure, often profound ways, polarities of origins survive in and intrude on the work itself, where they continue to exert an influence on form or content as well as on the response of a reader, who may also be reworking attitudes toward his/her origins within similar perimeters. The persistence of these poles within works widely separated in time and milieu encourages assigning them a priority within creative and mental processes generally. [15]

Their locus classicus is *Oedipus Rex*. Here is found the orphan-foundling, the child-hero, and two sets of royal parents: the real ones, who have abandoned him and with whom he returns to play out his incestuous/parricidal drama, and the adoptive ones, who die a peaceful, natural death. Otto Rank (1914) was the first to recognize family romance parallels, while Roheim (1934, 1952), Reik (1951), and others interpreted the Sphinx as the coitally combined, biological parents—an enigmatic primal scene resolved by the answer of Oedipus to its riddle: birth > a child > man, which is, in effect, himself in his progress from infant crawling on all fours, to upright king, to lame exile exiting on three legs into darkness with a staff.[16]

In his mythic capacity, Oedipus has been interpreted by Moloney as a sky god, crawling, then striding, and finally limping across the heavens: the name *Jocasta* deriving from "purple dawn" and *Laius* from "darkness."[17] Thus the sky god separates from his purple-dawn mother in the morning, slays father-darkness, and commits incest with her by his return in the evening (this same purple evokes the hues of royalty in the parent-rulers of the child's family romance as well as the artist's creative romance with the cosmos).[18] But the pleasures of gods are the taboos of mortals, and when myth is further humanized into art, in part by demystifying human reproduction, it also can become tragedy—at least it does in the case of Oedipus. But among many so-called primitive societies the primal scene is still enmeshed in an undifferentiated family romance with the cosmos, where there is no felt inconsistency between biological and mythical origins. To draw on a simple example, for the Indians of the Southwest, life originates from and continues to thrive between Sky-father and Earth-mother, the cosmic and tribal parents, and what the biological parents do under the bearskin nearby is not so awesomely threatening, given the other abiding, cosmic presence. The semiabstract designs on Indian pottery, depicting clouds, lightning, and rain, are a "sacred combination," which taboos restrict to formal, geometric arrangements, since they may otherwise reveal the weather-spirits (Kachinas) in their recent secret fertilizing labors, quite probably primal scene derivatives.[19]

Writing about the Zinacantan Indians of southern Mexico, Eva Hunt notes that the "top deity itself was a duality, the male and female principle combined, the pristine image of the reproducing heterosexual parents." She translates their names as "our flesh lord and lady," or "lord and lady of our sustenance." Even Christian saints and deities are incorporated into this schema: "the 'father-mother gods' are not a separate set of divinities, but simply the general name of the divine oneness of the parental divine duality."[20]

In this connection, one is reminded of Edelheit's (1974) formulation that "primal scene schema" may become mental structures and need not in all instances be accounted for by motive.[21] Thus when Emily Dickinson notes on an Edenic noon "how intimate the Meadows are with the Sun," a larger-than-life sexual scene is evoked without any specific latent content.[22] Edelheit's example of the heraldic figure of Gilgamesh separating two ferocious lions is also a mythic figure in Rank's family-romance motif. And Oedipus's fateful double, Teiresias, is fundamentally an internalized primal scence: having on two occasions thrust his stick between two "love-joined serpents" (as Ovid has it). As a signifier of primal-scene experience, he lives his life as both man and woman. This special bisexual ambience disposes Teiresias to a paradoxical family-romance episode. Called upon by the Olympians to settle a dispute over which gender enjoys sex more, he is blinded by Hera for his embarrassingly honest response that women do, and then, in compensation, given by Zeus the special gift of prophetic vision. Thus, Gilgamesh may represent the heroic aspect of these dual processes; Teiresias, the creative.

But these polar phenomena favor the mundane as much as the sublime. Ken Kesey, at a conference honoring Jack Kerouac, gave vent to a remarkable utopian fantasy. He speculated that out of complementary needs a political marriage between the United States and China, blending our technology with their wisdom, would eventually produce a Fourth World, "an alliance founded on the Beat Ideal of universal love and tenderness."[23] One need not adduce a hidden motive of self-regeneration in this exalted reverie in order to recognize that the writer has structured his dream for the future of mankind from a fertile union of opposites that inhere in everyone's past. The child to be born of this union (the Beat Ideal) is also drawn from the writer's past and projected forward; being an artist, Kesey expands primal fantasy material into a global family romance.

Before returning to works of literature, I would like to pursue the relationship of these phenomena a bit further in the primitive world, both of the self and of the species, because since embarking on this study another thesis locked within the original one has emerged. Appreciating the inherent difficulties in Freud's comparison between primitive humanity and the intrapsychic conflicts of modern man, I should like to draw a very limited analogy along similar lines, the basis for which is an archaic mode of thinking that tends to represent abstractions in spatial terms: precisely, through architecture. In an introduction to the religious cosmology of the Sudanese Dogon, Griaule describes a typical home as a symbolic setting. The ground floor represents earth, under which rests Lebe, the great ancestor; the flat roof above stands for heaven. Between these spirit domains various parts of the house correspond to various parts of the male and female anatomy:

> The vestibule, which belongs to the master of the house, represents the male partner of the couple, the outside door being his sexual organ. The big central room is the

domain and the symbol of the woman; the store-rooms on each side are her arms, and the communicating door her sexual parts. The central room and store-rooms together represent the woman lying on her back with outstretched arms, the door open and the woman ready for intercourse. The room at the back which contains the hearth and looks out on to the flat roof, shows the breathing of the woman, who lies in the central room under the ceiling which is the symbol of a man, its beams representing his skeleton; their breath finds its outlet through the opening above. The four upright poles (feminine number) are the couple's arms, those of the woman in labour is seated on a stool in the middle of the room, her back to the north, and is supported by women.

The infant is delivered on the ground and takes possession of its soul in the place where it was conceived. The earthen platform that serves as a bed, lies north and south and the couple sleep on it with their heads to the north, like the house itself, the front wall of which is its face. The man lies on his right side facing west, and the woman on her left side facing east, which are the positions they will occupy in the grave. Under the bed are put all the seeds for sowing except cotton seeds, which are placed on the lintel of the second door, symbol of the female sex. In sexual intercourse the man is sowing; he is like a Water Spirit causing fertilizing rain to fall on the earth and on the woman, on the sown seeds. Thus agricultural and conjugal acts are linked.

When the pair lie with a covering over them, as in death, the bed is also a grave; it is the grave of Lebe.[24]

Lebe is the primal parent / child, who resides in the earth and is reborn in the life span of the individual family. Such an elaborate cosmology is usually comprehended anthropologically in terms of agricultural fertility cults. But in the fusion of sexuality and ritual, there emerges upon closer examination a conflation of family-romance elements, both in terms of the cosmic parents and the divine ancestor / child of the primal scene. Rendered among cosmic forces, the house is both a microcosm and a representation of copulation encompassing birth, death, and rebirth. The village is likewise an extension of interlocking sexual and sacred space.

The village, which encompasses the primal scene of human reproduction as well as the setting for the symbolically sexual labors of the community, also depicts a human figure, probably Lebe, who is the source and product of these activities as well as their meaning. For when the environment has been so structured, there is no space left for—nor felt need of—individual initiative in better understanding the nature of human sexuality; as a result, these communities remain relatively static.

In biblical terms, this regular interpenetration of the divine and the human is life before the Fall, and, in Genesis, the primal act of sexuality—or rather some new understanding of it—puts an end to the cosmic family of man, woman, and God the father. Only in the aftermath of paradise lost does creative art as we think of it begin; only with the memory of paradise can a return to origins be stimulated. And as paradise ends in abandonment, family romances begin with adoption.

Thus—and here is the thesis within a thesis—the emergence of civilization

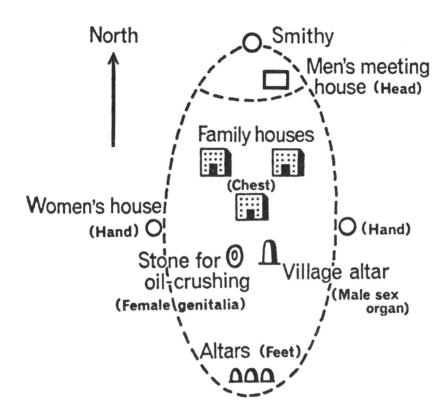

Diagram of village. From Marcel Griaule, *Conversations with Ogotemmeli.*

may in part be measured by the disengagement and relatively separate development of the family romance and the primal scene from a common matrix (i.e., the primitive, evolving mind of *Homo sapiens*). From an adaptational viewpoint the former may serve separation-individuation and the development of learning—especially, for example, the brand of philosophical wisdom that strives to accept man's existential situation as an orphan in a universe devoid of benign cosmic parents—while the latter may serve as a spur to scientific curiosity and mastery over origins displaced onto nature.

Later I shall return to the mind's tendency to deal with questions of origins through places of origins, but first I want to complete Freud's analogy between the primitive mind and mental disorder. His "case" analysis of the paranoid schizophrenic Schreber reveals a delusional system with its own striking religious cosmology. Family-romance elements may be embedded in his belief that the Schrebers belonged to the "highest aristocracy of Heaven" and bore the title "Margraves of Tuscany and Tasmania."[25] But this fantasy is appropriated by the delusional system and the notion that he has changed into a woman. In the hereafter, his and other souls enter a state of bliss spatially divided into the forecourts and the backcourts of heaven or God. The pleasures associated with these two areas are female voluptuousness and masculine penetration. As projections of Schreber's bisexuality, they also amount to a celestial primal scene.[26] For one in such a dedifferentiated psychotic state to be incorporated spiritually into the primal scene is also to achieve a fulfillment of the family romance through union with the almighty God, the ultimate idealized parent.

Although one is dealing here with primary process thinking, certain affinities with the mythical structure of primitive man's dwelling, whose rooms join male and female and whose sexuality partakes of the divine, may still be recognized. These constructs may be viewed on a continuum with what is ordinarily defined as the emergence of secondary process thinking in artistic creativity. In primitive society, life is organized around primal-scene patterns and larger-than-life cult figures embedded in the cosmos. In psychosis, the family romance and the primal scence have been truncated; either perversely libidinized or absorbed into primary narcissism, both polar structures, in effect, have been destroyed, and the struggle to reassemble them is part of the restitutive aim of the delusional system. While primitive and psychotic processes appear analogous to creative activity, they also predate or oppose it.

The truism of art as bordering on madness evokes the "case" of Hamlet. There the family romance comes unravelled by the queen-mother's remarriage, and the son's tragedy is intensified by his anguished pleas in her bedchamber that she remain both his loyal mother and his royal queen rather than pollute the sheets with an unworthy rival in the person of the sexual uncle. The sudden appearance of the ghostly father (saying, "leave her to heaven"!) at this point completes the personae of the primal scene, while dramatizing the failure of splitting that is essential to the family romance. In adult life as in mature art, the polar phenomena appear to be diametrically opposed, and their terrible clash accounts in no small degree for the tragedies of Oedipus and Hamlet. In other respects, however, the poles are dialectical and reciprocal.

Variations on creativity's magnetic poles abound throughout world literature, from classical to pop: from Perseus and the Medusa, Diana and Acteon, Cupid and Psyche ("Beauty and the Beast"), Tristan and Iseult, to Peter Pan and The Wizard of Oz.[27] Indeed, fairy tales often provide an uncanny directness and purity of treatment, while other forms of popular literature offer scenes of savagery, as Arabs, Indians, or pirates pillage a youth's home, murder his parents (or rape his mother), then carry him off for a series of fabulous encounters. True to form is the revival of Conan the Barbarian. In *Little Big Man*, following the family massacre, the young hero finds himself the adopted son of a Cheyenne chief.[28] In the popular and/or folk mode, these creative poles have been codified into conventions. And while they may, in fact, be affected by variables and conditions so far undefined, it is striking to see how closely associated they are in our minds and how frequently they are juxtaposed in scholarly writing without necessarily being connected. Herewith are five very diverse examples:

1. In his cogent analysis of *Who's Afraid of Virginia Woolf?* Blum shows how two childless couples engage in a series of games of a "striking sexual nature" that dramatize the "problems of primal scene and impregnation."[29] In the course of the games, in which sexual partners are exchanged, there is revealed a confusion of "origins of parental identity." And in the ensuing search for parental motives are "fantasies of an adopted child about his double parents."

> The mystery of parenthood and birth, origins and identity is heightened by the fact that the play takes place on the eve before the birthday of the child of George and Martha. Like Oedipus unraveling the riddle of the Sphinx, the two couples are engaged in the uncovering of a mythical son from a mysterious birth.

In this special family romance, if the adopted child were to find his biological, "real" parents, would he adopt them? Would they be preferred and idealized in fantasy compared to the adoptive parents? Or the adoptive parents might be idealized and chosen, as they chose the child who becomes "chosen" as well as abandoned. In this play, all four "parents" are finally aggressively devalued.

2. What happens to an individual with one set of white parents and one set of black is analyzed by Stephen Weissman in "Frederick Douglass, Portrait of a Black Militant," subtitled "A Study in the Family Romance."[30] In the first of the subject's three autobiographies, Weissman finds embedded in the account of slavery, revolt, and escape "classic features of the unconscious hero myth: the extraordinary perceptiveness of the child hero, the extraordinary feats of the young hero, and the sense of being specially chosen by fate with signs of divine favor." Douglass's precipitating trauma was his separation from his grandmother at the age of five and his being sent to live with the white master who was his biological father. The sense of abandonment and belief in dual parentage led to feelings of being "alone and stranded," as well as to counterbalancing fantasies of being a heroic figure "who will go it alone and singlehandedly obtain revenge and secure his personal independence." The fantasies here, as will be seen for the artist, serve an adaptive function—"a heroic sense of identity" along with "personal courage and strength" in the service of survival. Gradually, as Douglass attains his ideals, his subsequent autobiographies decline in melodrama and the heroic: the family romance becomes less functional as a superstructure.

However, the earliest version also lets us into the child's world of "darkness, nighttime, ignorance, mystery, whispered secrets, and nightmarish awakening." The accounts of waking up "in terror at dawn to a scene of thinly disguised sexual brutality in the form of a passionately jealous whipping of his aunt by his father" are interpreted as "screen memory" because there are "no concrete memories of the first five years." Thus "the unconscious organizing themes in the imagery are a mixture of separation anxiety and primal scene terror." In subsequent versions, "this perspective will shift dramatically." And thus while the two phenomena under consideration, in this instance, appear to follow a somewhat parallel development, it is still very possible that the one (primal scene) had intensified the other (family romance).[31]

3. Noting in his study of Mary Shelley's novel *Frankenstein* that the primal scene imagery is "pervasive and unmistakeable," Marc Rubenstein continues: "The scene of the monster's reanimation speaks for itself, but the spirit of primal scene observation penetrates into the very structure of the novel and becomes part of a more deeply hidden search for the mother."[32] It may be recalled that the mother was the prominent feminist, Mary Wollstonecraft, who died in giving birth to her daughter. This search is embellished, as Rubenstein points out, by a family romance involving a quest for the famous, absent parent.

4. Leslie Fiedler has referred to Tarzan as the "immortal myth of the abandoned child who survives to become Lord of the Jungle."[33] In this "pop Darwinian jungle," Fiedler is struck by the astonishing frequency of (usually unconsummated) rape that threatens Jane and every other woman who wanders into the jungle. Tarzan, too, at times is in danger of sexual assault: "But more customarily, he watches from concealment, like a child at the bedroom door, convinced that the groans of his beloved mother mean she is being forced by his hairy father. In Burroughs' Primeval Forest, Freud's Primal Scene is eternally reenacted."

5. In Virginia Woolf's *Between the Acts*, Giles Oliver stumbles upon something very like Ovid's "love-joined serpents," when on a country path he notices a snake "with a toad in its mouth."[34] It is an act of both copulation and birth perversely distorted: "The snake was unable to swallow; the toad was unable to die. . . . It was birth the wrong way round." Smashing them and staining his shoes, Giles becomes a latter day St. George, an ironically modern hero to the mysterious Mrs. Manresa ("I am the queen, he my hero, my sulky hero") and something less so to his wife, Isa ("Silly little boy, with blood on his shoes"). Gilea's seemingly inconsequential act is one of many that take place between the acts of a village pageant, whose summer of 1939 festivities occur between the more bellicose acts of European history. Merciful rain and foreboding aeroplanes alike interrupt. The artist presenting the collage of dramatic pieces is Miss La Trobe, a perennial misfit and "outcast." Her production operates both to divert the populace from the ominous but imminent acts of warfare and to delay the more intimate but inevitable combat between the Olivers, who face each other at day's end grimly aware that

"before they slept, they must fight." Then "they would embrace . . . and from that embrace another life might be born." Concurrently, another character has returned to reading her *Outline of History*, which is really a book of origins centered in England: "Pre-historic man . . . half-man, half-ape, roused himself from his semi-crouching position and raised great stones"—an act of nature that becomes an act—perhaps the first act—of art, while the pageant may be the last act of art for sometime. Yet the book ends in anticipation of the one human act that makes all the other acts possible.

Among those troubled individuals cited within psychoanalytic studies who neither go outright psychotic nor succeed in a creative-arts resolution to conflicts over origins, the family romance has often been invoked as a defensive solution to primal-scene hazards. Alice Miller captures the gifted child's grandiose tendency to reverse early injuries: "I am in the centre, my parents are taking notice of me and ignoring their own wishes (fantasy: I am the princess attended by servants); my parents understand when I try to express my feelings and do not laugh at me; my parents are rich in talents and courage and not dependent on my achievements; they do not need my comfort nor my smile (they are the king and queen)."[35]

Ernst Kris has written of those whose "biographical self-image is particularly firmly knit and embraces all periods of their lives from childhood on" as creating not an artistic myth out of cultural traditions but a "personal myth" out of neurotic symptoms.[36] During the latency of one patient, after a period in which the father has been absent from the family and involved with various women, the original family was reunited and temporarily crammed into a tiny apartment. The patient slept in an alcove off the parents' bedroom, where he was exposed to their marital intimacies. In his autobiographical self-image he had started college at fourteen and had gone on to achieve notable success at an Eastern university as a scholar and ladies' man. In the course of analysis, however, many of these facts dissolved (his age was sixteen and his prized German girl turned to a rival) and were interpreted as reinforcing a fantasy in which the "intellectual superman wooed the German princess." While both parents were immigrants, his father was an unsuccessful Polish shopkeeper, although his mother came from educated German stock—the stuff of a family romance start for an artist, but put to a strictly personal use here. Kris sums up his clinical vignette as follows:

> Living arrangements forced him into a proximity with the parents' sexual life, presumably not experienced since earliest childhood. This proximity renewed the early infantile conflict and reawakened the fantasy of his earlier periods of life.
>
> The traumatic nature of the experiences during the early part of the phallic phase has a specific bearing on our subject. We are inclined to attribute to the nature and timing of these experiences some of the importance which fantasies have gained for the patient's life. At an unusually early age these fantasies have been edited in various forms, all more or less loosely connected with the theme of the family romance.

3. James Joyce

Around the turn of this century, both James Joyce and D. H. Lawrence rose dramatically from the lower classes by means of their literary ability. Their winning of prizes or scholarships, which quickly distinguished them from their peers and their drab backgrounds, also fostered exile from their native soil and set them on a quest for creative fulfillment elsewhere. Sons of discredited fathers, they were close to their religiously devout mothers and went on to create in Molly Bloom and Connie Chatterley two of the most memorable women in modern fiction, for which the two authors would be celebrated as well as censored. Yet their affinities with the feminine are highly ambivalent. Joyce depicts in his alter ego, Stephen Dedalus, refusing to pray at his mother's bedside shortly before she died—a 'covertly matricidal act,'' as it has been called by Schechner;[37] and Lawrence actually has his stand-in, Paul Morel, slip his dying mother a lethal dose of morphine. Moreover, both of their coming-of-age novels, *A Portrait of the Artist as a Young Man* (1914) and *Sons and Lovers* (1913), were composed in the aftermath of maternal loss. Quite possibly the principal root for the compound of hostility and devotion that culminated in creative identifications is the fact that before these sons had reached their second year the mother had already conceived and given birth to a younger sibling. In Joyce's case this process was to repeat itself many times over: he was the oldest child among ten; hence the theme of fraternal betrayal running through his works.[38]

In Lawrence's case there was only the one younger rival, but issues were complicated by his early illness and the mother's infecting her children with her unregenerate hatred for her spouse. It is also interesting that both young men, having lost their mothers at the close of adolescence, attached themselves shortly thereatfter to women with whom they eloped to the continent and loved faithfully throughout their lives, although Joyce did not marry Nora for thirty years and Lawrence wrenched Frieda away from her children. But in spite of all their difficulties, Joyce would insist that Nora had made a man of him, and Lawrence, that his relationship with Frieda was the one thing that really mattered. It is clear from letters that their wives permitted all their polymorphous-perverse, component sex drives to be expressed, assimilated as far as possible into consciousness, and made available for creativity. "It is astonishing how barbaric one gets with love," Lawrence wrote following his elopement with Frieda (11 June 1912). "One finds oneself in the Hinterland der Seele, and—it's a rum place. I never knew I was like this."[39] And Joyce wrote Nora (2 December 1909), "side by side and inside this spiritual love I have for you there is also a wild beast-like craving for every inch of your body, for every secret and shameful part of it, for every odour and act of it."[40] The fact that each disparaged the other's work may derive in part from vestigial sibling jealousy.

The authors' biographical congruities prompt one to wonder about other similarities—on creative and emotional levels—of the complementary phenomena presently under discussion. In several respects there is a remarkable congruity: for both, the question of origins is treated via a place of origins; and the family romance, after splitting into positive and negative forms, is eventually integrated into a viable form of adult sexuality.

The two masterpieces that Joyce wrote midway in his career may be seen as concentrating respectively on the two phenomena: in *A Portrait* the family romance comes into full bloom, as Stephen is endowed with a host of religious and mythical identities, including Achilles, Icarus, Lucifer, and Christ. Just as Oedipus must correctly "interpret" the meaning of the Sphinx, so must Stephen work through the religious layers of the Holy Family, with its Immaculate Conception, Virgin Birth, Communion of Saints, and Mystical Body to the essential meaning of human sexuality, in Stephen's words, *"secundem carnem"* (according to the flesh).

A Portrait opens with Stephen's father telling him a story, presumably in answer to his question, Where did I come from? The father, with his patriarch's "hairy face," tells of a "moocow coming down the road," meeting a "nicens little boy named baby tuckoo," and passing by "where Betty Byrne lived ...." Close examination of this passage has established connections between the moocow as Mother, Mother Ireland, and Mary the Mother of Jesus, and between Betty Byrne as Elizabeth, the mother of John the Baptist—in effect, a family-romance scheme of origins woven into the very beginning of the novel.[41] Moreover, primal fantasies determine the course of Stephen's future artistic development. When he awakens from a euphoric (possibly orgastic) dream and feels inspired to compose a poem, the "instant of inspiration" is portrayed as a spiritualized primal scene fertilizing his imagination. "In the virgin womb of the imagination the word was made flesh. Gabriel the seraph had come to the virgin's chamber" (*Portrait,* 217). The religious analogy makes artistic conception a sacred act—perhaps homoerotic wish-fantasy as well—but certainly, with the "seraphim themselves breathing upon him," a family-romance version of artistic origins, which Joyce frames in delicate irony.

In the earlier and more transparently autobiographical *Stephen Hero*, he turns his mother's religious attachment to Jesus into an occasion for venting his rage and resentment, as if her religion were a betrayal and Jesus an unwelcome intruder in the relationship, though the divine child is probably a stand-in for the series of younger children the mother had after her firstborn. By the revisions of *A Portrait*, Stephen has effected an identification with Christ, both as chosen son and outcast-scapegoat, casting his Jesuit teachers and his peers into the role of betrayers. Thus does identification strive to overcome ambivalence.

But if the Christ identity threatens to lock Stephen into a religious family romance, his classical Icarus identity offers problems of its own. In fleeing the Cretan maze with the wings of his father-artificer, Icarus is also escaping the

Minotaur, only to plunge into the sea. The Minotaur is a composite monster born of the union between a sacred white bull and Pasiphae, queen of Crete— in other words, like the Sphinx and other mythic mixes, possibly a disguised primal scene. Hence the logic of the Icarus flight. Stephen is not altogether free from that which he would escape: his friends allude to his Minotaur side in calling him "Bous Stephanoumenos," and he suffers from "monstrous reveries" (90), becoming a veritable "den of monstrous images," which may warn against incest but which more broadly suggest unassimilated images of parental sexuality as bestial.[42]

Trying to assimilate these feelings by confiding them to a friend, he is rebuffed and blurts, "You mean I am a monster." He ponders the word *Foetus* carved on the desk in his father's anatomy theater, as he tries to come to terms with his own biological origins (89); unable to integrate his lowly begetter with his exalted spiritual revision, he asks himself during a religious retreat, "Who made it to be like that, a bestial part of the body able to understand bestially and desire bestially?" (140). His attempted solution is to recreate himself spiritually (though outside the Church). When the "soul is born," he tells a friend, it "has a slow and dark birth, more mysterious than the birth of the body" (203). And a patchwork self of mythic, religious, and literary identifications is what Stephen in *Ulysses* literally wears in the tattered black mourning attire of a latter day Hamlet and defrocked cleric. Moreover, his family romance has now also turned black, less a fantasy than a nightmare, with primal scene terrors impinging.

In order to extricate himself from his no longer serviceable Christ image as well as from the *mater virgine et dolorosa* embedded in the "reproachful" image of his own dead mother ("her wasted body within its loose brown graveclothes"), Stephen must extricate himself from the family romance contained within the religion of Christ. And before he can hope to forge in art the "uncreated conscience of his race," he must plumb the hidden regions of human sexuality, because art for him is "essentially a sexual and reproductive activity."[43] Moreover, since he associates "creativity with paternity," as Cheng, only the latest of many Joyceans, has shown, he can appropriate this paternal power only by grasping the paternal sexual role in the primal scene. But it must be distanced from his own family; hence he will anatomize the family romance of his faith.[44] Accordingly, in *Ulysses* (Oxen of the Sun section), he applies his mental ingenuity prior to his encounter with the Blooms. Either "she [Mary] knew him [Joseph], that second I say, and was but creature of her creature," Stephen drunkenly discourses in a mockery of the Last Supper among the medical students at the maternity hospital where Mrs. Purefoy is giving birth, "or she knew him not ... A pregnancy without joy ... a birth without pangs, a body without blemish, a belly without bigness. Let the lewd with faith and fervour worship" (*Ulysses*, 391–92). So proceeding, Stephen exposes a central dilemma of his faith. Either Mary had carnal knowledge of God (in which case God is all too human) or of a mortal man (in which case she lied to Joseph in saying, "I know not man"); otherwise her conception came about noncarnally, through the sacred pigeon via the ear (a displacement upward of coitus that children sometimes make).[45]

Whichever way, the sexual distortions of the Holy Family can be "interpreted" as disguising a primal scene. And to the extent that Stephen can recognize that the primal scene of human origins has been shielded by the fig leaf of religious dogma, he will be free of the gnawing guilt ("agenbite of inwit") of his Catholic conscience for not kneeling at his dying mother's beside, or, as was the case of Joyce, not fulfilling his Easter duty. The threefold enigma of "Bridebed, childbed, bed of death" may become less obsessive and history less a nightmare from which he is trying to awake.

However, just as the Minotaur of Stephen's monstrous sexual fantasies was his own creation in *A Portrait*, so is the reproachful mother's ghost his nightmare production in *Ulysses*. Both are representations of the dark side of the family romance, its negation or contamination by primal-scene intrusions. The sources for the morbid mother imagery are not located in classical antiquity but more proximately in the nineteenth-century's versions of myth to be found in the Gothic. Reflecting on Hamlet as a ghost story and brooding on his mother's ghostly presence, Stephen, out on the beach at Sandymount, begins designing a gothic tale and weaving his mother's image into a vampire narrative.

Across the sands of all the world, followed by the sun's flaming sword, to the west, trekking to evening lands. She trudges, schlepps, trains, drags, trascines her load. A tide westering, moondrawn, in her wake. Tides, myriad-islanded, within her, blood not mine, *oinopa ponton*, a wine-dark sea. Behold the handmaid of the moon. In sleep the wet sign calls her hour, bids her rise. Bridebed, childbed, bed of death, ghost-candled. *Omnis caro ad te veneit.* He comes, pale vampire, through storm his eyes, his bat sails, bloodying the sea, mouth to her mouth's kiss. (*Ulysses*, 47–48)

The vampire god as the concrete manifestation of the *"dio boia* (hangman god) ruler of things material," may be, according to Schutte,[46] one of three forms of the god of the universe, the others being Jehovah and the god of art. And thus the son's lineage from the vampire mother is both divine and dyadic, equally an inverted family romance and a deficient account of origins. Indeed, later in the day Stephen will propose a theory of procreation "by potency of vampires mouth to mouth" (*Ulysses*, 390).

A clue to the psychosexual basis for the elaborate vampire fantasy material occurs in his childhood when he hears one of the older boys tell another, "You are McGlade's suck," and Stephen reflects, "Suck was a queer word," which he associates with the unpleasant sound of water escaping down a drain (*Portrait*, 11). Later, as an adolescent, he surrenders himself to a prostitute, who joins her mouth to his with the "dark pressure of her parting lips ..." (*Portrait*, 101). Although this fall into sinful lust will occasion his abject repentance, he will not begin to surmount these regressive impulses until he can translate them into that Fortunate Fall necessary for the artist to rise with the hawklike man, "his ghostly father Daedalus, a winged form flying above the waves and slowly climbing the air"—the antithesis of both the vampire's lowly "bat sails bloodying the sea" in *Ulysses*, and the "batlike soul" of the Irish peasant woman unable to aspire to, or soar into, the heights. In *A Portrait* the hawklike artist thus escapes from the batlike female; in *Ulysses*, the artist is grounded ("You flew. Whereto?" is Stephen's ironic self-reflection). And so the twofold threat of the vampire emblem of regressive, passive wishes, involving oral/incestuous fixations on the one hand and homosexual dangers on the other, is revived and continued.

In an incisive study of Stephen's boozy and enigmatic response of "Black panther vampire" to first meeting Bloom, as he bends over Stephen in the Dublin night to give assistance, Seidel explores the implicit homosexual threat in the man who seems too willing to share his home and wife with a young stranger.[47] While this may explain Stephen's reluctance to spend the night, Bloom is an unlikely pederast in his desires to find a replacement son for his bereaved Rudy.[48]

The thematic shaping provided by the homosexual leitmotiv relates to the larger motif of Stephen's inability to complete the mourning process and separate from the reproachful figure of his mother as she survives in his nightmare. In both instances, something primitive and violent is projected: the vampire onto mother, the panther/vampire onto Bloom. These projections are also internalized by Stephen when he designates his painful remorse as "agenbite of inwit," that is, the inward gnawing of conscience. The drives that interrupt his self-development and disrupt his relationships are those associated with oral aggressiveness.

In response to his students' begging a ghost story from him (in Nestor), Stephen gives them instead a cryptic riddle; but in briefly assuming a teaching role, he may be identifying with the nurturing mother. He sees himself as still a child in the "misty glasses weak eyes" of a lad looking up to him pleadingly; bending over the boy, Stephen assumes both a maternal posture and a vampire one, as well, when he plays a bad-mother role with the boys by frustrating their wishes and leaving them in dismay as he nervously laughs and explains the riddle in even more cryptic terms: "The fox burying his grandmother under a hollybush." The meaning apparently has more to do with Stephen's inner state than with anything else. He may be, as noted by Benstock, "the fox, as artist," who in his theories of art "buries his mother-grandmother in literature."[49] But the self-image of the fox recurs as Stephen reverts to his reveries over his "mother's prostrate body" and her burial: "A poor soul gone to heaven: and on a heath beneath winking stars a fox, red reek of vampire in his fur, with merciless bright eyes scraped in the earth, listened, scraped up earth, listened, scraped and scraped" (*Ulysses*, 28). The fox embodies the early ruthless state of oral aggression in infancy, which the mother's death reawakened and which now blocks the mourning processes, provoking the violent projections. These, to return us to our original point of departure, are represented through the fantasy material of a black family romance.

An additional gothic source for Stephen's nightmares may stem from his recollection of the scene where Dr. Frankenstein is disturbed by the wildest dreams on the night he has animated his monster. He dreams of embracing his beloved "cousin" Elizabeth:

> I thought I saw Elizabeth, in the bloom of health, walking in the streets of Ingolstadt. Delighted and surprised, I embraced her; but as I imprinted the first kiss on her lips, they became livid with the hue of death; her features appeared to change, and I thought that I held the corpse of my dead mother in my arms; a shroud enveloped her form, and I saw the grave-worms crawling in the folds of the flannel. I started from my sleep with horror ... I beheld the wretch—the miserable monster whom I had created. ... His eyes ... were fixed on me.[50]

Stephen's account is comparable:

> In a dream, silently, she had come to him, her wasted body within its loose graveclothes giving off an odour of wax and rose-wood, her breath bent over his with mute secret words, a faint odour of wetted ashes.
> Her glazing eyes, staring out of death, to shake and bend my soul. On me alone. The ghostcandle to light her agony. Ghostly light on the tortured face. Her hoarse loud breath rattling in horror, while all prayed on their kness. Her eyes on me to strike me down. (*Ulysses*, 10)

And after his vampire daydream, he thinks, "mouth to her mouth's kiss," as "his lips lipped and mouthed fleshless lips of air: mouth to her womb." She is his monster, that is, the monster created by his early drives, both oral and incestuous, which returns to him as Frankenstein's monster to its maker. Joyce's foxy resolution may be to bury the early mother-relation in the book, or, perhaps, better: to create a living being beyond the Frankenstein monster, in the form of a book with a human organ assigned to each section, and described by Ellmann as a "portrayal of an archetypal man who would never appear and yet whose body would slowly materialize as the book progressed, linguafied as it were into life."[51]

While those darker currents of psychic life revealed through gothic conventions may carry Stephen beyond the veil of an idealized family origin, they, too, lead deeper into subjectivity. The quester must discover a human form of sexuality that alone can banish his morbid fantasies and bestow a basis for identity. Consequently, Stephen's grandiose self-sufficiency begins to lessen as the Blooms' marriage begins expropriating the narrative. The stage is set for a rebalancing of self and world in a famous passage (in Proteus): while walking along the beach, he performs a little test to see if matter is contingent on mind. Closing his eyes, he wonders: "Has all vanished since?" Can the world be omnipotently manipulated by magical thinking (does mother come and go at the blinking of the eye)? No, he learns. "See now, there all the time without you: and ever shall be world without end." What he sees is also significant. Two midwives, who had apparently attended his own birth, cross his line of vision, and in the ensuing meditation, "Wombed in sin darkness I was too, made not begotten," he distinguishes his own origins in "They clasped and sundered, did the coupler's will" from the savior's: "begotten not made." So far, it is a conclusion more injurious than liberating.

But at least Stephen's quest begins moving away from the no-longer-tenable grandiose self-images and the conflict-ridden beds of his own past to the complex humanity of Molly and Leopold Bloom. In the brothel around midnight, Stephen sees what the dreaded Sphinx ("the beast that has two backs") signifies: "Married" (Ulysses, 560). So disposed, he will shortly encounter the Blooms' marriage, and the reader will pass on to their bedroom of love, loss, betrayal, and odd reconciliation where Bloom, "the childman weary, the manchild in the womb," returns late at night to rest head to foot with Molly.

Paraphrasing and altering Stephen's threefold enigma, Bloom (in Ithaca) enters "reverently, the bed of conception and of birth, of consummation and of marriage, of sleep and of death." This bed has a peculiar archetypal life of its own, echoing that of its occupants. The "snakespiral springs" are very old, the "pendant viper radii loose"; and it is entered as a "lair or ambush of lust or adder." The man, the woman, and the serpent take us to the original betrayals of our original parents—the primal scene of humanity in Genesis. The three serpent references underscore not only the threefold enigma of sex, birth, and death, but also the three parties involved: man, woman, rival (as lover, snake, or child). The "snakespiral" may signify the human family's coming into its own after the Fall, which becomes for Joyce a winding ascent into humanity.

The spiral's ambivalent line also represents the ambiguity of Bloom's position. The abode he enters is "his own or not his own"; his extended limbs encounter "new clean bedlinen, additional odours, the presence of a human form, male, not his. . . ." And, finally, "if he had smiled why would he have smiled?" the anonymous narrator wonders. The answer is that Bloom would smile at the recognition of his own belatedness, but also—and here the ambiguity twists both life and the resolution of the oedipal conflict into the narratives of art—at his acquiescence in his betrayal. He reflects "that each one who enters imagines himself to be the first to enter whereas he is always the last term of a preceding series . . . repeated to infinity." Or to Adam. But unlike Adam, Bloom in his belatedness knows about the serpent in the bedspring.

Thus the conjugal bed and the primal scene are both affirmed and mysteriously altered: Bloom is beside Molly, but is pointing away from her in the direction of the emerging newborn. Moreover, they form not a closed-off, exclusive couple but a more open, wheellike configuration, which is opened up by the artist's creative powers, so that their lived experiences may turn like the seasonal patterns and cycles of life and thereby be widely shared. Implicitly they also recall the ecstatic episode on Howth Hill when they first swore their love. There, a reciprocal action was performed: as Bloom's fertile seed leaps in Molly's womb, she passes the moistened seedcake from her mouth to his—another circular process that the novel also affirms with its last word, "Yes," backing into the first word, "Stately."[52]

These verbal and sexual recirculations, or miniodysseys, recapitulate the larger structure of mythic return around the bed of birth, conflict, death, and renewal.

Thus, although the family romance is brought down to earth at 7 Eccles Street in "dear dirty Dublin," Molly is enlarged into "Gea-Tellus, fulfilled, recumbent, big with seed," and Bloom is both a Eucharistic Host and a Moses, not quite connecting with Molly's land of milk and honey. In her "bedsteadfastness," Molly is Earth; in his wanderings and return, Bloom is the longed-for "homerule" Sun. They are the cosmic and carnal parents of myth and fact. Combining sacred and secular, they make creativity possible; more than a little of the artist's "innermost secret" may well arise from the wedding in them of the family romance and the primal scene.

Between these poles, the theme of betrayal, so prominent in Joyce's work, provides a necessary link, for the real-life occupant of 7 Eccles Street was once Joyce's closest friend, John Byrne ("Cranly"), who is cast as ambivalent peer, both disciple and betrayer, in *A Portrait* (Judas to Stephen's Christ). And, to drive the connection home, Joyce scholars have determined that Bloom's height and weight coincides precisely with John Byrne's. Thus the Blooms' occupancy of the same address strongly implies a reworking of the original feelings of betrayal—though now more parental than fraternal. Bloom is both betrayer and betrayed in his respective roles as parent and cuckold. Also psychically impotent due to the crib death of his son, he harmlessly masturbates during his wanderings; and while Molly betrays him with a lover, she does not betray him with a pregnancy: Joyce sees to it that Molly gets her period the morning after Bloomsday. The primal scene of this "fabulous artificer" will produce no new siblings.[53]

4. D. H. Lawrence

> I think the only re-sourcing of art, revivifying it, is to make it the joint work of man and woman. . . . Because the source of all life and knowledge is in man and woman, and the source of all living is in the interchange and the meeting and mingling of these two: man-life and woman-life.
>
> —D. H. Lawrence, *Collected Letters*

D. H. Lawrence also drew on religious archetypes for self-representation. In *The Man Who Died* the Christ figure awakens in the tomb to learn "I have outlived my mission"; the "teacher and the saviour are dead in me now." The "burning purity" of the "rapt youth" is gone; his virginity had been a "form of greed"; his being crucified is the price for having sinned against the body.[54] And so his resurrection aims at returning the family romance to the perplexities of mortal flesh in this life: "Strange is the phenomenal world, dirty and clean together!" With the peasant's gamecock, which had called him back from the grave, he embarks on a quest that will take him to the temple of the priestess Isis in Search. And there, as his wounds are healed, he builds his renewed life on the "soft white rock of life ... the deep-folded, penetrable rock of the living woman!" This is also a conception *secundem carnem*. And the new cycle of life generated by it is on a par with the unraveling of the mystery of human origins that is represented by that other rock of fertile life, the Sphinx.

Lawrence wrote this parable of rebirth late in his life, when he desperately needed healing from his afflicted lungs, and after he had come to recognize that his own ambitious strivings were futile, and that his bond with Frieda, like Joyce's with Nora, was what he valued above all else. Human sexuality, albeit redefined and tinted with mythic hues, is the Lawrencean as well as the Joycean solution to the messianic excesses of the family romance and the felt betrayals of the primal scene.

But for Lawrence, creativity was not always sufficient to bind the hallucinatory hopes of his grandiose fantasy: he set out literally to implement his dreams, to father a utopian colony, perhaps in Mexico or near Taos, for "a select few" who would "add together their little flame of consciousness to make a permanent core ... a holy center" (*Letters,* 1030). He called this his "Rananim" project, born in large part out of the apocalyptic experience of World War I and the earlier death of his mother. He and his disciples were to be "sons of God who walk here on earth," a "body of chosen patricians," or, again, "princes, as the angels are ... new born on the earth." Throughout this difficult time, Lawrence oscillated between states of feeling buried inside a dark tomb and being "born afresh," like a "seed that falls into new ground."

His only actual convert to this enterprise was Dorothy Brett, who accompanied the Lawrences to the New World in 1923 and captured on canvas the negative and positive images of her hero's family romance when she painted a crucified Christ being offered a bunch of grapes by a fawnlike Dionysus—both gods unmistakably Lawrencean. But Brett herself became the occasion of so much jealousy and divisiveness that Lawrence ruefully concluded, "A life in common is an illusion, when the instinct is always to divide." And later when she showed him her painting he returned to Frieda and sent Brett packing;[55] whereupon he composed his parable of the self-important savior who dies and, being reborn a man, spurns Mary Magdalene's idolatry for its life-denying spirituality.

If Lawrence's utopian dreams did nonetheless remain fervent, they thrived ultimately only in the creative enterprise; their most memorable incarnation was the pastoral world shared by the lovers in *Lady Chatterley's Lover,* with its pristine Adam and Eve–like, family-romance, rescue-fantasy features balancing the explicitly modern sexual scenes, in which Mellors assumes the paternal function along with the paternal dialect. On this level, the Joycean affinities are close.

And although the authors tend to diverge in other family-romance features, their affinities are evident also in the intimate link of creativity to aggression. Greenacre writes that family-romance "fantasies of a well-organized nature seem to emerge most clearly in the early latency period," but she emphasizes their preoedipal sources and the powerful libidinal and aggressive drives bound up in them and transmitted to creativity.[56] Along with the artist's heightened sensitivity to intrapsychic and environmental phenomena, she continues, is the ability to invest "peripheral objects" with intense emotional cathexis. This neutralizes to some extent the force of the instincts and also forms the basis for the artist's "creative romance with the world." Two examples bring out how this may extend to both the human and extrahuman world. "One may always scatter the seeds of one's secret soul out to a stranger," Lawrence wrote in his late adolescence to a female acquaintance, "hoping to find there fertile soil to replace the exhausted home earth." And in a perfectly casual way he remarks in another letter: "We found some lovely big cowslips, whose scent is really a communication direct from the source of creation—like the breath of God breathed into Adam. It breathes into the Adam in me" (*Letter*, 570).[57]

In addition, his mother, frustrated in her marriage, libidinized the filial tie. Endorsing a piece of family mythology that he was born hating his father, Lawrence opened the realistic narrative of *Sons and Lovers* to include a mystical-lyrical scene in which Mrs. Morel finds herself locked out and cast into the moonlight of her kitchen garden by her drunken husband. At first the child she is carrying "boiled within her," since it is at this point the hated father's doing. But among the "tall white lilies" another part of her being awakens. She reaches into the flower bin and streaks yellow pollen over her face, drinks in its scent, and slips into a swoon. "After a time the child, too, melted with her in the mixing pot of moonlight," and she is able to resolve her hatred by reclaiming the child as her own through a brand of mythic reconception, or pollination, which also restores her to membership among the virgin goddesses of Earth. The "re-sourcing" of origins could not have taken place in Lawrence's own place of birth, which had no back or side garden, and so he shifts forward to the second home, where he actually moved in his second year. In this way, Lawrence, like Joyce, revises origins by rearranging the place of origins—no minor alteration, since it renders him the special child of the mythical parent and allows a "creative romance with the world" to unfold.

It also excludes father and sets the stage for him to play his part of son / lover in the family oedipal drama. Before having read any of Freud or heard of complexes, he wrote a friend during the period of his mother's final illness (1910) that his parents' marriage had been "one carnal, bloody fight," and that there has been a "kind of bond between me and my mother ... We have loved each other, almost with a husband and wife love." But he further specifies their love as a "peculiar fusion of soul" and concludes, "nobody can come into my very self again, and breathe me like atmosphere" (69–70). Only objects in nature can do that. The Adam in him, which the cowslips awaken fleetingly, recaptures the unfallen self still in the garden of Eden with his maternal Eve.

But he, too, had to deal with ambivalence stemming from early childhood, and not only is an extensive, negative family romance found unfolding in his first decade of writing, but there is also a more severe split in the self-and-mother representations underlying the positive and negative fantasies of origins. A host of Lawrenceans have discovered abundant material clustering around the central image of the "devouring mother," a term Lawrence applied to Frieda in a 1918 letter (*Letters,* 565). This aspect of the mother is variously cited as the "mother-ogress, who destroys her son or daughter" (Miller); as a "maternal cannibal" conveyed by "psychologically murderous parasitism" in "Paul's [Morel] fantasy life," as it is displaced from his mother onto Miriam and Clara (Klenbard); via the Lawrencean "fox, the devourer of chickens [which] symbolizes the 'devouring' mother" (Bergler); through the dominating males in the leadership novels, who in overreacting to the threat of being destroyed by the devouring mother turn into devouring mothers themselves (Ruderman); and finally the prevalence of vampire imagery in depicting the male / female relationships in *The Rainbow* and *Women in Love* (Twitchell).[58]

Other critics have drawn attention to the mythic dimensions of Lawrencean females as Circe, Persephone, Magna Mater, Hecate, and Astarte, to encompass the procreative and destructive, the child-bearing and child-sacrificing aspects of woman.[59] As for Joyce, classical myths along with fairy tales, animal fables, and gothic fiction provide a preexisting medium for Lawrence's fantasies of destructive motherhood to attach themselves to and thereby allow him to initiate the complex reshaping processes of art. Although Ruderman judiciously reminds us that the "devouring nature of the mother actually inheres in the mother herself" and credits Lawrence's adult observation of his sisters "who have jaguars of wrath in their souls, however they purr to their offspring," the devouring urges nonetheless find their counterpart within the child, whose oral aggressiveness and wishes for merging are instinctually rooted and only made more difficult by similar unresolved forces within the mother.[60]

Under the intensified conditions of a childhood such as Lawrence's, the results are likely to include conflicted identifications. In *Sons and Lovers*, Mrs. Morel's tendency to seek emotional nourishment from her children, especially Paul, is expressed as the "two knitted together in perfect intimacy," and her "life now rooted itself" in his.[61] Following her death, we read that for Paul "the realest thing was the thick darkness at night," and that he would talk to "barmaids, to almost any woman, but there was that dark, strained look in his eyes, as if he were hunting something" (*Sons and Lovers*, 410). Here are the first signs of that vampirism that will condition the relationships in the two novels to come, and it is in the male/son rather than in the female/mother that they first appear. But in his careful reading of *The Rainbow* and *Women in Love*, Twitchell traces the evolution of the "female as vampire" from "Gertrude Morel to Miriam Leivers, then to Anna, Ursula, Hermione, and finally to Gudrun."[62] In subsequent works, he concludes that this figure disappears, and a healthier image of woman eventually appears, after a middle period of predatory maleness.[63] "Don't you think I get people in my grip?" Lawrence could ask his publisher in 1913 (*Letters*, 186); but the future direction of his prose is toward a loosening of that grip, as he ripens into the insouciance of his final period.

Twitchell also notices throughout *The Rainbow* and *Women in Love* that "Lawrence repeats again and again" a scene in which "two young people meet and enter into what is described as a 'battle for life itself.'" Vampire imagery intensifies the drama therein, and, in most instances, the males are the weak ones: "praying mantises waiting to be devoured by the female after she has used them." The female vampire as Lamia may be blatant in these works because the instinctual drives are still displaced and supported by traditional fantasy, but as the insistent fantasy fades in the male-leadership novels, the conflict gradually becomes internalized as the men become cruel, predatory, and devouring in their own right.

"The world is a great and foul beast," he wrote in 1916, (*Letters*, 476), that has got him and his friends in its grip, "but with subtlety we can get round the neck of the vast obscenity at last and strangle it dead." Here the devouring object appears to be a dragon. "Now is the time for the wisdom of the serpent," he wrote at the same time in anticipation of his Mexican novel's revival of Aztec savagery. "Away with the turtle doves, in with the asps. Secretly, the heart must be bitten out of the old body." The allusion here may be to Shakespeare's Cleopatra, whose poisonous, sharp-toothed asp at her breast is treated as a baby "that sucks the nurse asleep." But the Lawrencean serpent in its "strange sapience" goes further and, like a knife-wielding Aztec priest, bites the heart out of its victim for the "chance to reconstruct according to one's heart's desire." Though not yet fully born from the mystical dark gods of the solar plexus and phallus, this serpent's functions are still largely defined and circumscribed by the devouring object it aims to attack. Yet it points to a psychosexual stage beyond the maternal grip of early childhood.

In marriages where the husband is unable to hold his own, Lawrence writes,

the unhappy woman beats about for her insatiable satisfaction, seeking whom she may devour. And usually, she turns to her child. Here she provokes what she wants. Here, in her own son who belongs to her, she seems to find the last perfect responses for which she is craving.[64]

Taken as an analogue to his family or to the plot of *Sons and Lovers*, this passage also shows how the devouring, oral-stage mother becomes the incestuous object for her child. Before he would develop his alternative theory of psychosexual development, Lawrence, in 1918, acknowledged, "it seems to me there is much truth" in "this mother-incest idea":

> that at certain periods the man has a desire to return into the woman, make her his goal and end. In this way he casts himself as it were into her womb, and she, the Magna Mater, receives him with gratification. This is a kind of incest. (*Letters*, 565)

But even here Lawrence is thinking in a context of adult sexual relations, and when he sets forth his own pollyanalytic system, he asserts that "there is no real sexual motive in a child," for the "great sexual centres are not even awake."[65] The real danger, then, is the bond of spiritual, sympathetic love that parents draw their children into, and this stumulates the thought of incest, leading to that morbid form of mental consciousness Lawrence loved to harangue as "sex in the head."

But the point remains that he had earlier connected the sexually frustrated wife with the devouring mother. And when this threat is represented in the child's mind, we are likely to encounter the classic, downward displacement of the devouring mouth, via lamia's fangs, to form the dangerous and prohibitive *vagina dentata*.[66] This image is adaptive for the child insofar as it reinforces the incest taboo with threats of castration; it is not adaptive if the vaginal teeth are assigned to all future love objects. But it is precisely the nature of the threat to "Aaron's rod," in the novel of that title, when he portrays his wife as using her harpy's beak against him. It is, so to speak, a bad oedipal marriage. And so was the first marriage of the gamekeeper Mellors, who "had a big wound from old contacts."[67] His first wife "would tear at me down there, as if it was a beak tearing me."[68] But while Connie has been sexually frustrated, her appetites are not devouring, her mouth is not fanged, and her vagina is not a beak, so she can offer the prospect of mutuality and the peaceful stillness that presumably succeeds vaginal orgasm rather than the excited friction of clitoral sex that had formerly stirred castration fears in the son who aspires to become a lover.

The mother-ogress, the Persephone-Circe figures, and the Lamia fantasy-material may now be more clearly recognized as the obverse side of the family romance, in which the fantasy of divine origins is offset by a reversal: the life-giving goddess is replaced by a child-stealing witch in order to compose a demonic version discernible in the pale, sickly son of Lamia, his vampire-mother. A black family romance, it remains a dyadic version of origins with no paternal sexual role assigned; but hints of something self-damaging from a wounding relationship lessen the force of denial, upheld in the white version. The death of Lawrence's mother, coming as it did in his late adolescence, when his writing had hardly begun to mature (so similar to Joyce's situation), suggests that henceforth the creative task will entail a "re-sourcing," that is, a remaking of the self and the early object-world. For this remaking project, he will draw on self-constructs born from the family romance, which will in turn immerse him in a struggle to straighten out the human sex relation. This requires that he recognize his original humiliating position between the carnal parents ("We were the in-betweens / little nondescripts . . .[69]), because the acceptance of his sexuality comes down to an acceptance of their sexuality and the sacrifice, as well, as of the virigin mother. The cost is dear for the simple, homey truth of a late poem to remind us, ". . . you and I / were both begotten / when our parents felt spry / beneath the cotton—"[70]

But Lawrence had to contend not only with the interface of his childhood needs and his mother's unmet desires, he also had to come to terms with a coarse and violence-prone father as his primary model of male sexuality. That he identifies partly with the father is evident by his trouncing and then burning of a favored doll via his self-character, Paul, in *Sons and Lovers*, as well as his allowing Miriam to be a sacrifice to his adolescent passion. But Lawrence's lifelong, self-declared mission to set straight the adult sex relation (*Letters*, 200) encompassed working through his own hostility toward an outwardly hostile father; the means of accomplishing this was to return again and again to the scenes of family violence and sex for constant revision, until there emerges in *Lady Chatterley's Lover* a male who speaks in both the father's dialect and in the son's English the words of tenderness and sensuality to a woman of incomplete sexual experience.

Let this chapter close with two final comparisons of the two artists. Addressing himself to the paradox that *Lady Chatterley* "was written by an impotent man" dying of tuberculosis, Mark Spilka perceives in the creation of Connie Chatterley a "sustained act of sexual sympathy," which must have come about because he "could still appreciate the sensual otherness of a woman much like Frieda."[71] And in her study of *Ulysses*, Marilyn French detects a strong feminist current in Bloom's noncapitalist, that is, non-proprietary, mode of relating to Molly, even to the point of nonintervention in her taking a lover.[72] Both Lawrence and Joyce appreciated the physical side of their wives without downgrading the personal dimension (Joyce believed he wrote *Ulysses* in part for Nora's approval; Lawrence made Frieda his collaborator); and both cultivated their spouse's independent sensuality: Joyce once set up Nora for a lover, and Lawrence conceded to Frieda's affairs. While these arrangements, which may indeed be colored by masochistic or homoerotic traces, need not be idealized, there at least may be found in them the male artist's recognition that if he is to stay in touch with the sources of his art he must also stay in touch with the sources of life that make creativity possible.

For Lawrence's Paul no less than for Joyce's Stephen, the artist comes into his own by engaging the family romance to retain the mother and remove the father from his sexual role. Then by freeing themselves from the fetters of early fantasy, the authors use its powers creatively to blaze a trail toward selfhood in a distinctive art that replaces the father's world with new visions of adult sexuality. While brightened with the golds of fantasy, this yellow brick road also rests on the common clay of parental sexuality. Both *A Portrait* and *Sons and Lovers* are concerned with presenting origins—personal as well as artistic—as these are constituted within the by-now-familiar polar network. The manner in which the fanciful and the real become synthesized is but one way of addressing the question of maturity in works of art.

As artists, both Lawrence and Joyce drove creativity to its utmost limits and beyond. For Lawrence this meant founding a literal utopia when the work of creative transformation could not contain his energies. For Joyce it meant yielding to the temptation to make language replace reality and, then, to make up his own language to replace that of his racial inheritance. These dangerous swerves away from mastery toward acting out, away from established traditions and deeper into subjectivity, almost to the point of psychosis, testify to their authors' radical re-creations of origins (personal and cultural) as well as to their eventual triumphs, when they returned with new visions that held human reality in a dynamic equilibrium.

2
The Subjective Phases of Creativity
in Emily Brontë

> For a quite specific form of imaginative activity is one of the
> essential characteristics of neurotics and also of all comparatively
> highly gifted people. This activity emerges first in children's play,
> and then, starting roughly from the period before puberty, takes
> over the topic of family relations.
>   —Freud, "Family Romances"

To say that the family romance arises from the child's disappointment with
the parents, experienced as a wound to fragile self-esteem, is to cover an
enormous amount of ground. The precipitating "event," which can actually
be a series that coalesces and crystalizes around one occasion, may take place
between the first and second years of life; but the lineaments of the
compensating fantasy with a "well-organized nature seem to emerge most
clearly in early latency," according to Greenacre.[1]

First, no parent can, nor need aspire to, perfectly mirror and meet the
child's needs in order to protect the child from ever suffering loss or
disappointment. The concepts of "optimal frustration" and "good-enough"
mothering favor a pragmatic course of events. Many children suffer severe
early damage to their self-image and esteem yet never become artists; by the
same token, artists need not suffer unique early blows to their narcissism in
order to develop the way they do. In other words, the narcissistic wound is not
a theory of creativity but an "unconscious stimulus,"[2] an almost inevitable
given to which the artists-to-be respond in ways that are special to them and
premonitory of their art. So even if the family romance has been one way of
conceptualizing an adaptation with a built-in promise for later creativity, it
still may only occupy a place in everyone's inner world without further
blossoming into what Greenacre and others call the artist's creative romance
with the world. It should be valuable to examine in relative isolation how such
subjective phenomena may develop before being set off against relatively more
objective phenomena subsumed under the primal scene (the notion of time
may be deceptive here, unless we take into account that primal-scene material
requires more developed personality structures for representation). The
consistency in which the family romance and the primal scene interact in the
sphere of creativity has led me to formulate the present theory about them as

poles and shapers, even organizers or regulators, of creative endeavor. The better they are generally recognized, the less need there will be to summon psychoanalysis to highlight exclusively anomalous, pathogenic, or defensive blemishes.

With these views in mind, I shall explore five specifically subjective steps in the development of one artist's creativity. Perhaps the study of no other artistic genius is more sobering or better calculated to grind down one's generalizations and lofty idealizations of art than that of Emily Brontë. The present reconstruction of her early development relies on the careful scholarship of Winifred Gérin's biographies.[3] Through it one may come to see how Emily Brontë, if exceptional, is also exemplary. Her father, Patrick Brontë, was a country clergyman with a "keen love of nature," who "walked and talked with his older, astoundingly perceptive children, treating them as equals with interests like his own, teaching them to watch the moods of nature, to see God everywhere." He read widely and wrote poetry. He had married an "intrepid young woman with high ideals, who regarded poverty as a positive advantage in the pursuit of perfection." From 1814 to 1821, she gave birth to six children, before her death from cancer at thirty-eight. In 1820, the family moved a short distance to the parsonage at Haworth, where they would live out their lives.

When the eldest daughter was four and a half, Mrs. Brontë gave birth to her fifth child, Emily (30 July 1818), and, eighteen months later, to Anne. Each new arrival was greeted warmly and cared for by the others. The children began their lives surrounded by love and security, as Gérin rightly stresses, with toys and dolls and books, with yards to play in and moors to explore, although it is difficult to know how available such a constantly expectant mother could have been. In any case, another pattern also quickly emerges, one of successive, premature, and cruel losses. Emily was eighteen months old when she lost something of her mother to Anne, and forty months old when her mother died. The older girls had apparently developed strong maternal feelings and assisted in care giving. But the arrival of a tyrannical older, unmarried sister, Miss Elizabeth Branwell, left all of them unhappy and precipitated the marriage of the two servants, one of whom had been especially devoted to Emily. They were replaced by an elderly woman, whom the children affectionately cited in their writings as "Tabby." Yet it seems doubtful that the accumulation of auxiliary mothers could ever occupy the real one's place, even as compromised in her care as she must have been.

Separation was soon imposed from a different angle when, in 1823, the girls were schooled out. This precipitated a second family tragedy: the loss of the two oldest to a typhoid epidemic and tuberculosis in 1825. Emily had been away from home for the first time for six months and, along with her older sister Charlotte, managed to escape the disease. Subsequently, as the two girls grew closer together, the aftermath of these traumas began to show up in Emily. Gérin at first claims that Emily had not been affected by the unsavory Aunt Branwell, but later notes that the child was "driven in on herself." From this withdrawal, one could reasonably infer that successive losses made it difficult for her to trust anyone (with the exception of Charlotte) beyond herself, her pets, and her physical surroundings, from which she never parted. In fact, Charlotte alone of the six effectively broke from the parsonage and formed outside relationships.

Therefore, in charting through Emily Brontë, a subjective sequence in creative development, I postulate as a preliminary stage in the creative process: (1) the cluster of early losses that deeply affected Emily, both in the sphere of object-relations and in the area of self. I shall outline step by step how the pain from these injuries might evolve through successive phases of development and ultimately achieve a transformed expression.

When Emily was eight, Charlotte records the following event:

> Papa bought Branwell some wooden soldiers at Leeds. When Papa came home it was night, and we were in bed, so next morning Branwell came to our door with a box of soldiers. Emily and I jumped out of bed, and I snatched up one and exclaimed: "This is the Duke of Wellington! This shall be the Duke!" When I had said this Emily likewise took up one and said it should be hers; when Anne came down, she said one should be hers. Mine was the prettiest of the whole, and the tallest, and the most perfect in every part. Emily's was a grave-looking fellow, and we called him "Gravey." Anne's was a queer little thing, much like herself, and we called him "Waiting Boy." Branwell chose his, and called him Buonaparte.[4]

This is the latency period of the Brontë children and, also, well into Winnicott what calls the sphere of transitional phenomena. These toy soldiers, as Gérin writes, "fill their imagination to become adventurers, epic writers, chroniclers . . ." What is remarkable about this whole episode is the children's collective readiness to infuse this intermediate space of play with hitherto unspecified and probably unconscious idealized self-images. It appears to be a lunging forth of primary-process ideation into the human sphere, and so may be richly revealing of inner reality. For example, Emily's soldier was originally named Parry, after Captain Edward Parry, the Arctic voyager she had already been reading about and had become attracted to. Parry's significance to Emily, who would never become a voyager, was that his adventures dated from 1818, the year of her birth, and, accordingly, his sojourn in those "death-white realms" assumed special significance.[5]

The children not only played games with their soldiers but also began spinning tales around them, some of which eventually were written down and one of which, at least, found its way into print. In it, Sir Edward and Lady Emily Parry entertain guests in their modest palace. They have a child named Little Peter, whose soiled clothes and brattish manners evidently echoed those of the younger Brontës.[6] Following dinner, Anne's hero, Captain Ross, is taken seriously ill, and is cured by an incantation from "Genius Emily." "Magical powers, as daily displayed in 'making alive again' the casualties among Branwell's soldiers," writes Gérin, "became the common attributes of the four young Genii as their complex Glasstown chronicles evolved."

Three themes from these endeavors have begun to emerge: (a) the children's dawning awareness of their own creative powers; (b) the communal effort arising from shared interests; (c) the important concern with making-alive-again as it points to the need to restore to life lost relationships, experienced so early as to be self-losses. The soldiers serve first as reborn, magically strong, self-objects, then are enlisted in the effort to undo object-losses. This area of focused play then, with its discernible needs for mastery, comprises the second, or making-alive-again step (2).

From play with wooden toys, the children progressed to playing the same parts in their dramatizations. Playing with toys seems to have encouraged the "play of fantasy."[7] And then, with Charlotte initially acting as the communal scribe, the chronicles gradually assumed a permanent life of their own. Elements of childish grandiosity came to the fore. "They saw themselves not circumscribed by the narrow limits of their home, but as carrying within themselves powers that made them 'more than conquerors.'"[8] And "they began to call themselves Kings and Queens," with Branwell the "'Little King'—his sisters serving in his suite as his attendant Queens." This fanciful arrangement actually tended to mirror the father's singling out of his talented son to advance the family's fortunes (hopes that were tragically misplaced and short-lived). The universe of the Glasstown Chronicles is accordingly masculine and militaristic. What can be recognized as more fully developed family-romance themes come to the fore in these imaginary histories of exalted lineage.

They are molded within a framework of loss and ongoing personal hazards. The "advent of their aunt brought all the children together in one common gesture of self-preservation," and their characteristic interdependence "sprang from this double need for love and for union against a common 'menace.'" Their father's "increasing oddity," in Gérin's words, would only strengthen these bonds and collaboration in an alternative reality.[9] The elderly Tabby simply thought them mad.

Already relatively isolated in their Yorkshire village, the children raised further barriers against the outside world in order to preserve and nourish what was still intact in their lives. Among their fanciful realms was the Palace of Instruction on a fictitious island in the Atlantic. What they formed in general may be akin to a phenomenon known in psychoanalysis as the Academia: a "special type of peer group" involved with the "reorganization of psychic structures during adolescence."[10] It functions as a "way station" to "more mature self-structures and self-objects." This interpretation suits the Brontë children's activities, if we add that creativity was also being nurtured.

(3) Their collective enterprise comes into its own toward the end of latency and the start of adolescence when members of the family, including both those lost and remaining, are magically restored and idealized into a shared, unified whole, which becomes known in time as the Gondal Chronicles, supplanting the Islanders and Palace of Instruction. These newer tales were largely Emily's

contributions from around ages eleven to fourteen, when Charlotte was away at school, and they thus coincide with Greenacre's statement about the consolidation of family romance material. Likewise, Emily's attachments to her locale—its landscape and animal life, whether wild or domesticated, were widening extensions of transitional phenomena that served her ambivalently by fostering creativity while discouraging her involvement in persons beyond the Brontë parsonage. As her play became more artful, its elements also became more firmly internal.

While its thrust and shaping may have derived from intrapsychic sources, the mythical Gondal also incorporated material from the real world. Its dungeons had their counterpart in the family cellarage; its landscape was borrowed from Sir Walter Scott; and Emily's Augusta derived from Princess Victoria, the heir to the English throne. The Queen was born only nine months after Emily, and the former's career is mirrored by the lords and ladies of Gondal. She was a "feminine symbol of power" for Emily, "an emancipated woman," writes Gérin, both "a queen and a rebel."[11] Her 1838 coronation found its mirror image in a Gondal crowning of joint heirs to the throne. These chronicles then become more and more royalist and feminine.

The Brontë children's monitoring and absorbing of historical events may be seen as precursors for the eventual return to reality at a time when the creative imagination has matured and been able to find a suitable means.

(4) Meanwhile, the children stumbled onto Lord Byron, and without intending for anyone ever to see them, Emily begins selecting and revising the Gondal prose narratives into finely wrought, interrelated poems. This step entails the application of aesthetic skills and values to a preexisting body of poetry as well as to their own materials that had served as a means of rebinding their lives both to one another and to the original maternal matrix from which they had been torn. Most important, the fantasy elaborations had been legitimized by connecting them with a literary tradition, and now by concentrating on her medium, Emily begins her apprenticeship in earnest. Her earliest extant poems date from her eighteenth year, and she worked intermittently until her death on the Gondal materials, keeping them alive after the others had lost interest. One critic is convinced that all her verse, including her fine poem, "No Coward Soul Is Mine," though "accepted as her own sentiments, voiced in her own person," was "spoken by a Gondalan facing a crisis incident to the civil war."[12] In this case Gondal serves as the substratum of Emily's creativity, her private myth system.[13]

But in another sense, as well, it served her creative development, for in this self-controlled universe there was sufficient space to allow many of the early painful experiences of loss to reenter, to be relived and worked over and over again, not necessarily until they were worked through, but at least until a certain distance and modification could be achieved. "But thou are now on a desolate sea—/Parted from Gondal and parted from me," runs one stark stanza: "All my repining is hopeless and vain,/Death never yields back his victims again."[14] Other poems depict mystical states of ecstatic fusion in which the "inner self ('essence') leaps to commune with a being which can only be described in terms of negatives—the invisible, the Unseen."[15]

From the Gondal materials critics have traced prototypes of the principal characters in *Wuthering Heights*—"weaving through all was a dark boy of sorrow ('child of dust') whose full name and identity never become clear."[16] Certainly there is a thematic continuation of tenacious, passionate longing and irremediable loss. But the novel is so well grounded in the four-square world of observed life that one can only conclude that the new work made a quantum leap. It would be tempting to examine how Emily developed so well her powers of outwardly mirroring inner reality in the Gondal never-never land that she was at last empowered to deflect the mirroring powers of her art onto the external world of her own time and place—were it not that theoretical points would be raised that can be more adequately explored in the next section.

Whether or not it was necessary for Emily to have more life experiences before her art could ripen under the conditions of ordinary sunlight and rain, or whether the fruition was inevitable, the fact is that several events further shaped her personal life and no doubt the life of her imagination as well.

Apart from a brief outing with Anne to York, Emily was to make three more forays into the world beyond Haworth, all of them relatively short-lived and disastrous. On her seventeenth birthday she left home for the first time in ten years to attend a school Charlotte had attended earlier and had since joined the faculty. Emily did not adapt well to the regimented environement. Her "need for solitude, her obsession with her imaginary world," and "her distress at being severed from the sources of invention" were all greater than Charlotte's and, unlike her sister, Emily saw no necessity "for submitting to the practical necessities of life." She lasted three months.[17] Two summers later she abruptly took a teaching position at nearby Law Hill, where she stayed for six months. Finally, four years later, in order to secure an education to start their own school at home, Emily and Charlotte traveled abroad to Brussels. Although they were to be summoned home after nine months due to Aunt Branwell's grave illness, Charlotte eventually returned to Brussels alone.

Along with the aunt's death, Emily was to undergo the specter of Anne's breakdown from tuberculosis, the moral and physical deterioration of Branwell as he succumbed to various addictions, and their father's faltering into blindness. Writing that the burial of Branwell on 1 October 1848 was the last time Emily went outside, Gérin raises the question of whether Emily willed to die. The cold she caught on that day infected her lungs; she grew incommunicative and listless, refused medical help, and died in the parsonage on 18 December 1848. Five months later Anne followed her to the grave.

Some months before she died, Emily had stopped writing. *Wuthering Heights* had come out the year before, as had some of her poems, and their disappointing reception could only have closed off whatever few paths into the future she felt were remaining to her. Yet that work has turned her life into a triumph and transformed her parsonage into a world-famous shrine.

After a period of hostility and neglect, *Wuthering Heights* gradually gained acceptance, but only amid continuing misapprehensions. In "The Originality of *Wuthering Heights*," Keith Sagar points out that the formidable F. R. Leavis excluded it from the Great Tradition and considered it, along with George Saintsbury, a kind of "sport."[18] Americans, removed from the social conditions of England as well as from the plight of the Brontës, have tended to view it as a New England gothic.

One of the great virtues of Gérin's biography has been to demonstrate that, far from springing full grown from Emily's fertile brow, (5) the work is firmly grounded in her total milieu. This includes not only architecture and locale, but characters and situations that first may have reached Emily through her father's dinner-table tales or from her own experiences at Law Hill. There, for example, she learned about Jack Sharp, an adopted son of a landowner, who exploited his good fortune to take over the family wool business, only to be later thwarted by a legitimate heir.

Since this bit of local history evidently entered into some stage of the formation of Heathcliff, I would like to stay with him rather than attempt a more thorough analysis of the whole work. Counteracting the Romantic attitudes toward Heathcliff as an elemental force of nature, a creature born of the storm, and so forth, Arnold Kettle perceives him realistically in the revenge-hero tradition.[19] As one of many waifs from Irish or other immigrants cast aside by the upheavals of the Industrial Revolution, Heathcliff is rescued from the Liverpool slums by Earnshaw and brought to Wuthering Heights.[20] There, his orphaning is once more reenacted, as Nelly "put it [him] on the landing of the stairs, hoping it might be gone by morning," and there his association with loss is confirmed as he is named after a "son who died in childhood."[21] (The connection between the replacement child and renaming the toy soldier may be noted.) Thereafter, the legitimate son, acting out of jealousy and self-interest, thwarts Heathcliff's prospects. After a period of absence on the continent, Heathcliff returns with financial means and worldly knowledge. He then proceeds, as Kettle says, to use "against his enemies with complete ruthlessness their own weapons, to turn on them (stripped of their romantic veils) their own standards, to beat them at their own game. Thus he "gets power by the classic methods of the ruling class, expropriation and property deals."[22]

The novel, in other words, is based on an accurate knowledge of the workings of society; far from displaying a randomness in its narrative, the structure is quite the opposite: tightly knit in a carefully worked-out time frame. These viewpoints are important because they help to correct a previous psychoanalytic reading of the novel, which asserts that when "she gives herself to self-expression in writing" her unmodified "simple, strong primoridial emotional attachments and repulsions of early life" pour out "with the force and power of an ice-cold torrent suddenly released." The part about early attachments may be tenable, but hardly the inference about lack of control and mastery. Even less so are the following assertions: "the ego is scarcely present. The unchanged unconscious self speaks with as much freedom, almost, as it speaks in the psychotic."[23]

Of course, there is much more to Heathcliff than local color and revenging-hero motifs. Closer at hand than Jack Sharp was Emily's own doomed brother, Branwell, with whose unhappy, passionate nature she was more intimate than anyone else. He once declared "he heard Maria's voice crying outside the windows at night," as Catherine would perceive Heathcliff in the novel. For literary anchoring, there were Milton's Satan, Shakespeare's avengers, and Sir Walter Scott's "Black Douglas," who all "contributed vital characteristics to Emily's 'black-browed' hero-villian of Gondal," but for Gérin "Heathcliff is the Byronic hero par excellence."[25] And it is here in the mainstream of literary tradition that the final step in this process is consolidated. Heathcliff joins the company of an illustrious line of hero-villains, validated by the public by reason of his affinities with contemporary social conditions; through him and his relationships the artist finds her way back to reality.

Of all the sources that went into his making, it is the distinctive features of Byron himself that bind the creation of Heathcliff to the very first step in this sequence, namely that of narcissistic injury. "There was," writes Gérin, "an incident related by Moore in his *Life of Byron* (1832) which left a recognizable trace in Emily's work. At the height of Byron's infatuation [for Mary Chaworth] when he visited her daily and believed she returned his love, he overheard her saying to her maid one evening: 'Do you think I could care for that lame boy?'—a speech which Byron himself described as hitting him 'like a shot through the heart.'" Byron "instantly darted out of the house scarcely knowing whither he ran, and never stopped till he found himself at Newstead," three miles away. According to Moore, he became embittered for life. "The relevance of this incident to the scene in *Wuthering Heights*," according to Gérin,. "takes place when Heathcliff overhears Catherine telling Nellie Dean that it would degrade her to marry him, whereupon he runs away and is not heard of for three years."[26]

Byronic Heathcliff is doubly wounded: cheated by Hindley the loyal son and betrayed by Catherine; and while these motivate his rage of revenge, they also link him more closely to the inner workings of the creative process, especially as we have defined its concerns with origins. For Heathcliff also embodies the essential themes of this study.

Like Emily Brontë, artists know their origins, but they remake them as they create new forms. In her Gondal, the birth of the princess Augusta takes place when Venus sees her starry reflection in a lake's waters.[27] This family-romance version of origins conveniently relates the "psychological birth of the individual," in Margaret Mahler's phrase, to the all-important mirroring transactions, and deserves to be explored independently. Gondal has already been seen to be a subjective creation within a secondary, corrective realm of experience, and "in her poetry," according to Stevie Davies, she "had constantly reverted to the theme of the rejected child handicapped throughout life because of rough early conditions: 'bred the mate of care, / The foster-child of score distress.' "[28] Accordingly, we may be entitled to a more objective account of origins in the spatially finite and time-bound world of *Wuthering Heights*.

Yet Heathcliff's origins appear wrapped in mystery: in true family-romance fashion he is the orphan / foundling, gypsy child (whose real parents are never known), adopted by a more worthy family. Here already, though, Emily had begun to work her revision: to be consistent with the fantasy, Heathcliff would have had to have been born to the Lintons, country gentry who live in Thrushcross Grange, and into whose elegant world Heathcliff can only peer disinterestedly through the windows until Catherine decides to move inside, whereupon he turns envious and vengeful. So we do have within the novel two houses, two sets of parents, one lowly and one lofty, but the family romance serves only to tantalize the characters, to open narcissistic wounds and rub in salt until the clearly defined motives of revenge take over. To this extent the novel "critiques" the family-romance construct while at the same time using its features (not an unusual strategy, when we reconsider Joyce or Lawrence, or come to Dickens). So far we can state that Heathcliff owes something of his origins to his creator's narcissistic wounds, which can be offset only so much by either the balm of fantasy or the spite of revenge.

Heathcliff's literal origin in the book, his earliest appearance, is also remarkable. "One fine summer morning," Nelly Dean recounts, "Mr. Earnshaw, the old master, came downstairs, dressed for a journey." He is about to walk sixty miles to Liverpool, though for what reason, we are never told. Like the father in "Beauty and the Beast" (which Emily Brontë may have had in mind), he offers to bring Nelly and the children back a gift (for Hindley, a fiddle; for Cathy, a whip); but he returns with something else—"a gift of God, though it's as dark almost as if it came from the devil." And "opening his great coat, which he held bundled up in his arms," a "dirty, ragged, black-haired child; big enough both to walk and talk" appears.[29]

This appearance of Heathcliff raises again the whole question of origins, and it is intriguing to wonder why the author stages such a birth-from-the-father scene for her readers. Does it represent a shift from the lost maternal object to the living paternal one as a second source of life? Is it patterned on the second birth of Dionysus, from the fertile thigh of father Zeus? Is it a variation on the making-alive-again theme of the children's games? If so, it is certainly an advance over the magical formulas of childhood, since Heathcliff becomes one of the most captivating characters of literature.

Perhaps we are witnessing in this apparent primal fantasy the power of literature to reproduce alienated parts of the self that have been orphaned and abandoned by early loss and injury but are given a second life through the imagination. Heathcliff is the injured self, who must revive and relive his injuries in hope of a remedy (behind him and within the most secret recesses of the creative process, one may expect to find technical processes of projective identification, reintrojection, and externalization, about which one can do little more than speculate).

In this light, Heathcliff's character incorporates all the elements mentioned earlier, including those drawn from the ego's advanced functions of synthesis and reality testing, but he is also absolutely consistent with his creator's innermost development. On one deep level, he may be Emily's second birth from the father, arising out of the death of the mother and the part of the self still in symbiotic rapport with her at the time. On another deep level, Heathcliff is the child of storm, an elemental product of uncertain lineage ("gift of God" or "from the devil"), born of the tumultuous union of opposites on the heights when rain and wind render them wuthering; hence his name, and the possibility of primal-scene fantasies displaced onto the physical environment. So, if he arises parthenogenetically from paterfamilias, he also embodies images of stark contrasts, which lend themselves to various interpretations. Often he merges with the terrain: "an arid wilderness of furze and whinstone"; or with, as Sagar shows, the architecture: the image of "narrow windows . . . deeply set in the wall . . . the corners defended with large jutting stones" is akin to "his black eyes withdrawn so suspiciously under their brows."[30] And his revenge drive, too, is depicted naturalistically: "we'll see if one tree won't grow as crooked as another, with the same wind to twist it."

Collectively, these images of furze, stone blocks, and trees serve as a reminder that Heathcliff is very much nature's child, as every child is a product of biological forces that may remain otherwise invisible to him as he is growing up. He could be the "Emperor of China's" heir, or, as Charlotte speculated, "an Afreet, a Ghoul";[31] or even, as Nellie tells him, "fit for a prince in disguise." So Heathcliff's origins remain mysterious, mingling nature and romance as well as signifying the poles of the creative process.

At the same time he is closer to the symbiotic matrix that for every child once encompassed the natural world. To Cathy, Heathcliff is as "necessary as the eternal rocks beneath," and Sagar agrees with her that she is Heathcliff, since to be separate from him "is to be cut off from part of herself, that part on which her health, sanity, and capacity for fulfillment depends," as well as "the ground in which that capacity can flourish most freely." Their embraces are more akin to a symbiotic fusion of one melting into the other than of growing sexual interest; and Sagar is also right, following Dorothy Van Ghent, to suggest that they could never marry, since "marriage implies a union in otherness," and the union of "like with like is obscene." This last point might be better stated: Heathcliff is constituted from the unassimilated good part of the self that has been diverted into hatred through injury—which may sound awkward, even if it approximates Emily's deeper aims.

What she tells us is that they are one: "Nelly, I am Heathcliff," Catherine cries; and on the night of her death, he cries out, "I cannot live without my life. I cannot live without my soul." As children they shared an oak-paneled bed, which Heathcliff will eventually die in and where Lockwood will later dream of Catherine's ghost outside his window trying to get back in. In another bed in Thrushcross Grange, Catherine will die giving birth to her infant Cathy, while Heathcliff bloodies his head against a tree outside. In an interesting Jungian analysis of the wood images of bed and tree, to which are added the table Catherine swoons under and her coffin (from which Heathcliff knocks one side loose in order to rest beside her), Joan Carson believes them to be "traditional symbols of the womb."[32] And she discusses Heathcliff/ Catherine as the complementary pair Jung designates as animus/anima.

This reading is enhanced by Dorothy Van Ghent's fascinating analysis of the shifting dark-child/golden-child (male/female) imagery in Emily Brontë's poems: "What really seems to be implied by all these shifts is not a mere exchange of characteristics but a radical identification of the two children, so that each can appear in the mode of the other, the bright one in the mode of darkness and the dark one in the mode of light."[33] Van Ghent was also the first critic to analyze in detail the boundary images. Extrapolating from Catherine's bloody wrists being rubbed against the broken pane in Lockwood's dream and from Heathcliff's removal of her coffin panels, she proceeds to an extended exploration of the windows as the "medium, treacherously transparent, separating the 'inside' from the 'outside,' the human from the alien and terrible." After her death, for example, Catherine "can look through the treacherous membrane that separates her from humanity."

At this point, while the window imagery still functions within a two-character bond that, for purposes of convenience, can be connected with the mother-child dyad, a few interpretative comments may be made before taking into account how the window may function at the triadic level. The bond of Heathcliff and Catherine represents the child's important sense of oneness within the symbiotic matric before it splits apart by inevitable loss. It may also build on double identifications with both parents, a representation of childhood bisexuality, the Freudian complement to Jung's animus/anima. It is clear that their separation is associated with the membrane image of glass and with the wood image of panel (bed, coffin). The bed in which the two children are at one is also the bed in which Heathcliff dies. While writing this I am reminded of the threefold bed referred to in *Ulysses*—"Bridebed, childbed, bed of death"—and recall that while the earlier novel rules out a shared bridal bed for Heathcliff and Catherine, they are each bedded with separate spouses. And it is in Catherine's room at Thrushcross Grange that the threefold bed is fully rendered. For there in her bridal bed she dies after giving birth to Cathy. Heathcliff's agonized exclusion from this tragic episode suggests that Emily's traumatic separation from her mother occurred not at forty months but at eighteen months, when the emotional betrayal of a younger sibling's birth occurs (in Gondal the younger heroine Angelica [Anne with supernatural powers?] brings about the downfall of the central heroine,

Augusta [Emily]). But either loss could be represented in the shattered symbiotic membrane that cuts and injures the child as she tries to get back inside.

From the later triadic viewpoint, Catherine and Heathcliff are made out to be each other's primary love objects, and through this interlinking remain each other's final love objects as well. Here are those "simple strong primordial emotional attachments," which the psychoanalyst noted. Others have suggested that "*Wuthering Heights* is essentially a novel about children";[34] the "portrayal of childhood ... identified chiefly with the children";[35] more paradoxically, "we always are, in Emily's mythology, the child we were";[36] or that "Emily Brontë cast a vague incestuous aura over the entire plot," the libidinal drives and marriages being but at the most one step removed from the original family: "Heathcliff marries his lost love's sister-in-law, his wife's son marries her brother's daughter, Cathy's daughter marries her brother's son."[37] Other, more primitive drive patterns have persuaded Michael Reed that the "core fantasy" of the novel is one of "agressive oral fusion."[38]

It is fair, then, to ask whether Emily reworked her origins in the direction of adult sexuality, where she had so far no direct experience, or whether parts of the novel remain stunted by childhood traumata. In fact, either possibility could cast a shadow over the masterpiece.

Heathcliff departs from the novel while still in the innocence of his childhood; when he returns, several years later, he is a grown man, fully equipped to marry and beget a child, which he does. But the libidinal and aggressive drives in his personality remain unfused; he displays no affectionate tenderness for his wife, and his love for Cathy is so unqualified that it quickly turns to hate at its betrayal. In other words, his absence from the novel during his adolescence is equivalent to a scomotizing (or blanking out on the author's part) of his genital sexual development. Emily, who seems to have bypassed her own adolescence, may not have been able to imagine that of a male. The question of origins is now raised from the other end of the line, as it were, for in order to come to terms with his or her own beginnings, a child must learn about the sexuality of both parents, of both sexual partners.

A closer examination of the window motifs may be helpful here. The ghost of Catherine attempting to reenter the bedroom window of Wuthering Heights has been interpreted as the child's wish to recover the security of the symbiotic bond. But what are we to make of the fact that it occurs as Lockwood's dream, in which he now occupies the bed and grinds her wrist against the broken plane? It seems that the dyadic view of maternal loss through childbirth must open the way for a male element to be involved as well. On this level of triadic relationships, Catherine's shedding of blood on "bedclothes" may signal the onset of the girl's menstrual cycle, which makes possible another cycle of conception, pregnancy, and birth.

Catherine, in fact, gave birth at Thrushcross Grange. As children, she and Heathcliff had peered into the windows there, and "we saw—ah! It was beautiful—a splendid place carpeted with crimson, and crimson-covered chairs and tables, and a pure white ceiling bordered by gold, a shower of glass-drops hanging in silver chains from the centre, and shimmering with little soft tapers."[39] They do not see anything so stimulating to childhood curiosity as sexual activity: "Old Mr. and Mrs. Linton were not there." Instead, Catherine sees an idealized double of herself and Heathcliff. "Edgar and his sister had it entirely to themselves. Shouldn't they have been happy? We should have thought ourselves in heaven!" Influenced (one could say dazzled) by her adoption fantasies, Catherine does not see a primal scene (the reader might say none was there). But when she does enter this idealized world, by marrying Linton and hoping to leave behind Heathcliff, she encounters something other than her ideals. Her unhappy married life and premature death in childbirth may be taken as the child's early awareness of sexuality, with or without specific primal scenes, as an alienating, destructive force—more as a sadomasochistic primal fantasy than as mutual pleasure. Does the novel then bring about a more mature revision of sexuality, or does it remain bound by the issues of childhood?

Toward the end of this novel, which manages to encompass three generations, Heathcliff enters a phase of self-bafflement, which he at one point refers to as "moral teething," as clear a description as one could ask for of that period of drive-fusion and object-harmonizing that Winnicott names the "stage of concern." He is now in a position to observe the coming of age of another Cathy and her growing love for Hareton. Through this, he "comes to understand something of the failure of his own love," in Arnold Kettle's view. The others "symbolise the continuity of life and human aspirations, and it is through them that Heathcliff comes to understand the hollowness of his triumph."[40] This is both beautifully and truthfully stated. The young pair introduce for the first time in the novel not only the rebudding of nature but the normal budding of male / female sexual feelings. They may not be stronger than Heathcliff's malice, but they render it irrelevant in their new perspective.

They therefore represent stages of development elided by Heathcliff, and their inclusion in the novel does not so much suggest a mastery of heterosexual drives or assimilation of adult sexual relations as their recognition and inclusion in a creatively imagined whole. The new pair are also Heathcliff and Catherine repeated and modified, reborn from the working-through process, to whatever extent it succeeded. To emphasize the youngster's importance is to assert a realistic reading of life's passionate vicissitudes over a romantic one. The romantic reading is attached to Heathcliff's undying attachment to Catherine and it is reinforced by his instructions to be buried adjacent to her remains, as though their decomposed parts mingling below earth or their shades floating over the moors somehow surpass—rather than by-pass—human love. Perhaps Emily did the right thing by keeping the two strains in poised tension, not letting us forget the tenacity of early drives, even amid other maturation forces, for the manner of Heathcliff's dying is most revealing. It is by self-starvation. But, finally, readers will best decide for themselves if the novel reveals a serious vision of reality unavailable to children or, for that matter, to most adults.

The five stages of creativity we have explored may now be restated:

1. The suffering of object-losses and narcissistic wounds in early childhood;
2. Creative play in the transitional sphere aimed at making-alive-again;
3. Continuation of play into the realm of imagination via the family romance, where an alternate world is created to allow for rebinding lost objects and mending damage to the self via reliving and mastery;
4. Emergence of cultural traditions and aesthetic interests, directed to forming aesthetic works from the whole cloth of developed fantasy;
5. Reintegration of early losses and self-damage with realistic observations of society and adult relationships in a space-and-time-bound setting.

In closing, I would like to mention one of those curious details that neither quite fits in nor quite remains still. It consists in a similarity between Heathcliff and the novel. Both mysteriously seem to originate from nowhere. One day, they are just there, and readers or adopted family are compelled to find a way to adapt. The literary parentage of the novel has never been established; its originality, as we have seen, placed it outside the Great Tradition, the English bloodline of legitimacy. It looks Romantic and Gothic but pops out squarely in the Victorian period, and is, as that age is not, utterly uncompromising. It first appeared to be as disordered and unruly as Heathcliff had appeared disheveled and rude. And, like Heathcliff, it embodies such elemental vitalities that we end up adopting it as our own. It all makes for a strange new episode in the family romance of culture.

3
"Precious Seeing":
Mirroring as a Humanizing Process;
Self-Remaking as a Creative Process

... for the eye sees not itself / But by reflection, some other things.
—Shakespeare, *Julius Caesar*

... the 'self' may be seen as an artistic creation like a family romance, or transitional object. ...
—Sheldon Bach, "On the Narcissistic State of Consciousness"

1

To continue examining more closely what passes through the subjective pole of creativity is to follow the family romance deeper into the area of the self and the dynamics of self-remaking as cued by Yeats's verse, "Myself Must I Remake."[1] The child's mimetic transactions with the mother equip it with the primordial personal base for future mimetic transformations of art; but mirroring can also operate as a fatally deceptive and seductive magnet to undermine other necessary steps of self-remaking that underlie creativity.

Throughout this section my debt to the psychoanalytic writings of William Niederland and Heinz Kohut is pervasive. The former's correlations between early self-injury and reparative creativity lend themselves to a family-romance conductor / transformer of energies; the latter's concept of the bipolar self, composed of grandiose and idealizing features, also addresses the need in the creative individual to get beyond damaged self-esteem and reactive grandiosity via the preliminary regulators available in the adopted child of exalted parentage. The authors' joint contributions provide optimal distinguishing lenses by which to examine the operations within the creative self.[2] If, for instance, those early mirroring transactions between mother and infant, in which self and world are first seen in the mother's eyes and her smile, and deemed essential for the grounding of a nuclear self, it is only fitting that they should also form the nucleus for this inquiry. For the poet has already taught us that "love first learned in a lady's eyes, / Lives not alone immured in the brain," but "Courses as swift as thought" throughout one's being and "adds a precious seeing to the eye."[3]

The example of Emily Brontë focuses the three steps in the mirroring process crucial for art: (1) the psychological birth of a sense of self serves as the basis for birth of the artist; (2) image of self and other derived from the early family environment suffer disruption and reparative development in play and fantasy; (3) their further molding and gradual assimilation into a cultural tradition. The first step in Emily Brontë's creative remaking may be illustrated at the point that "Venus, the brilliant morning star, looked down on her own image mirrored in the dark waters of nearby Lake Werna."[4]

> Cold, clear, and blue, the morning heaven
> Expands its arch on high;
> Cold, clear, and blue, Lake Werna's water
> Reflects that winter's sky.

The finding of the star's watery double beautifully signals the awareness that internalizing the mother's responses is the child's primary means of becoming human; as this occurs within a family romance ambience we have, in addition, the seeds of the artist's creative romance with the world. The mother is a starry goddess; her daughter, the powerful princess Augusta, will be "worshipped of all men" and bring "tragedy to those upon whom her amorous light shone"[5]—these being mainly rival powers, siblings, no doubt, including another virgin heroine, Angelica (Anne?), who conspires in the undoing of Augusta. As an extension of the first mirroring period, Gondal's world reflects and binds other constellations of needs, conflicts, and relationships in the larger family galaxy.

A later, or third, phase of mirroring, more in the service of art than in the reconstitution of the self and early world, occurs in the later, relatively mature reflections of experience in *Wuthering Heights*; yet, here too, Sagar gets at the more fundamental processes when he says, "Emily Brontë's own nature led her to wild nature as its mirror, subsuming Heaven and Hell."[6] At the age of six, for example, she was out on the moors during the "Crow Hill bog burst," a minor earthquake that Gérin reports was "a terrifying ordeal" to everyone except Emily, who found it "delightful."[7] Could it have been felt as an amplification of her own feelings? The novel also suggests an underlying mirror-image identification between Heathcliff and Catherine, which maintains their interdependence as both desired and dreaded. Severed from Heathcliff, Catherine in Thrushcross Grange is haunted by her own frightening image in the mirror; such apparitions in dreams or as shades hovering about the moor suggest free-floating mirroring images that have not adhered to the author's evolving nuclear self (or her gender identity) and, so, being alien, are designated "supernatural."

A direct link between the mirroring transactions of mother and child need not be presumed in order to explore the many affinities between them. Perhaps it is accidental that the earliest humanizing events in the individual's development are paralleled by the humanizing functions of art in the development of the race. But it is auspicious to find that the earliest literary work appears to be molded out of the earliest psychological processes. The ancient Sumerian epic *Gilgamesh*, dating from around 3000 B.C. in written form, may be seen as a portrayal of early human existence in a cultural sense; but by reflecting early life stages in the individual sense as well, it serves not only as a valuable literary document but as a timeless vision of our human condition.

At the outset Gilgamesh ruthlessly exploits his power over his people: he leaves no daughter to her father, no virgin to her lover; he lets his people work half to death on city walls only to lose interest and let their work decay. Lacking any sense of others, he also lacks a sense of himself. His body image is ambiguous: two-thirds god, one-third man. Though powerfully alive, he is not humanly so. Events conspire to bring him face to face with Enkidu, who happily has dwelt among animals and grazed with gazelles. His whole body is covered with hair, and the hair of his head is like a woman's. They meet and wrestle to a draw; their dreams and their adventures are then recounted, as "their becoming human together."[8]

At the close of their battle, Gilgamesh "turned to Enkidu who leaned / Against his shoulder and looked into his eyes / And saw himself in the other, just an Enkidu saw / Himself in Gilgamesh" (*Gilgamesh*, 24). This is indeed a modern interpolation, expanded from—and I believe warranted by—original lines, which have the two only resembling each other and likened to brothers. Clearly, if they are not twins, they are complements. Each can love something of himself in the other, and something more as well. Both have had nominal relationships with women: Gilgamesh with his mother, in whom he confides his dreams; Enkidu with a prostitute, who uses her sex to separate him from his life with beasts. But if the two heroes' feelings for each other define a special stage of individual affection, the quality of this love is such that its portrayal between two fully grown males strongly suggests a displacement from an earlier phase. In effect, each one performs as the ideally loving / responding other; together they form a whole, a dual unity. Thus their self-recognition through each other's presence reproduces the kind of mirroring that marks a crucial step in becoming human.

That their bond is still largely narcissistic is evident from its exclusiveness and susceptibility to suffering from changes in circumstances. The inevitable collapse of this otherwise perfect bond is precipitated by the willful battle with Humbaba, a tyrant or ogre in the cedar forest, who stands for death, and by the killing of a bull sacred to the jealous goddess Ishtar. The mortal wounding of Enkidu suggests that in ancient societies, Sumerian or Homeric, it is the loss of the warrior-comrade that triggers the acute grief reaction leading to protracted mourning. In any case, it is the loss of the idealized, mirroring object that forms the second stage in this porcess of becoming human.

That Gilgamesh's search to recover his lost companion also entails a quest for immortality implies (technically speaking) that an object-loss is felt as a self-loss. As he draws near to hear his companion's final utterances, the change in the one appears through sighting the other. "Your eyes have changed," Enkidu murmurs. "You are crying. You never cried before." And then he poses the question that will occupy the remainder of the poem: "Why am I to die,/You to wander alone?/Is that the way it is with friends?" (50).

In wrestling with these issues, which accompany the third stage of becoming human, the poem enters the company of such other literary masterworks as the *Iliad*, the Book of Job, *King Lear*, and the great elegies. Traditionally, the loss of someone loved is replaced by the discovery of meaning: it is poetry's contribution to resolving the mourning process. The meaning this poem discovers is depicted with deft irony, when the snake steals the magical plant of immortality before Gilgamesh can incorporate it. Thus is the individual made aware of his mortality and separateness from the rest of nature. But Gilgamesh himself does not achieve wisdom so much as something else brought about by his return to his city. "He looked at the walls,/Awed at the heights/His people had achieved" (90). What he acquires is what the child also acquires through the mirroring process and its aftermath: the sense of a bounded self.[9]

The survival of this most ancient of poems reminds us, however, of another truth: works of art are uniquely equipped to replace the original lost object-relation, because by continuing to mirror ourselves and our world, they keep something of the original experience alive as well. Thus the power of art outshines its mortal flickers. That art also, in indirect and non-specific ways, continues in cultural modes the early mirroring transactions which first ground our humanity is the hypothesis to be extracted from the Sumerian epic and to be developed more fully among later works with supportive data.

By way of rounding out this introduction, I would show more precisely how the early mirroring relationship may extend into the creative sphere. Shakespeare's verses cue our inquiry. The "love first learned in a lady's eyes" signals our emergence into human consciousness; the "precious seeing" added to the eye signals our capacity to create and/or respond to beauty and art. James Hamilton has noted a passage of experimental prose from Picasso which both captures the mirroring transactions and demonstrates their adaptability for creative explorations of the early environment:

> Listen in your childhood to the hour that white in the blue memory borders white in her very blue eyes and piece of indigo of sky of silver the white glances run cobalt through the white paper that the blue ink tears away blueish its ultramarine sinks so that white enjoys blue rest agitated in the dark green wall green that writes its pleasure pale green rain that swims yellow green in the pale forgetfulness at the edge of its green foot the sand earth's song sand of the earth afternoon sand earth.

This child-artist first finds the mother and himself through certain color tones—blue eyes and blue memory, white glances and white hour. Through them he finds the environment—indigo sky, silver traces—and then the means of reproducing the mirroring experiences in the blue ink on white paper.[10] Because mother is rediscovered in the environment, the artist's creative romance can thrive; because he can make these connections and continue them in the creative sphere, he has entered culture.

2

The life of Pope (1688–1732) is instructive because it not only combines two of the more useful modalities in understanding the formation of creativity but presents them in extremely sharp relief. The first involves questions of parentage and sources of artistic gift. "Endless mystifications have been cast round his ancestory," according Edith Sitwell. "For the small enchanter lived, and still lives, in an atmosphere of spells, enchantments and fairy tales"— some woven by him, some by others.[11] More willing to "show what his father was not, than what he was," as Johnson reports, Pope was indeed the son of a London linen merchant who converted to Catholicism and, after burying his first wife, married the daughter of a small landowner.[12] To these devoted, middle-class parents was born Alexander, and out of something more than gratitude he elevated their line in his fantasy to aristocracy and romantic heroism. Here in what Sitwell terms "fables about his father's ancestry" and "romantic feelings about noble birth" are emergent signs of the family romance.[13]

Obviously Pope knew who his real biological parents were, but his knowledge was complicated by at least two unrelated factors that became entangled: his talent and his deformity. The former was precocious: "As yet a child .../I lisped in numbers, for numbers came."[14] But as with his parentage, the precise facts of his poetic development as well as the details of his lifelong relationships have been falsified and doctored—altering his correspondence and back-dating his poems to give him the aura of a prodigy, born of more than ordinary mortals. He also had the perplexing habit of "planting" his letters, poems, and other manuscripts in the libraries of his "betters," as if his writings must play out the role of the foundling on the stranger's doorstep in order to validate the family romance, one step removed (à la Sartre).

The idealized father of the young poet's imagination was the aging John Dryden: "Had I been born early enough, I should have known and loved him."[15] Pope's seeing Dryden would be like "the dream of seeing poetry in some bodily form," and at twelve he prevailed on friends to meet Dryden at his favorite coffeehouse, though little came of the visit.[16] Later Pope would attach himself as editorial apprentice to the aging Restoration playwright, William Wycherley, and over the long haul the poet's life has been seen as patterned on Horace.[17] But the acquisition of idealized figures or classical models could not substitute for the journey of creative self-remaking that would lead to the discovery of his own voice.

Pope's earliest writings were translations and imitations of the classics, and in these endeavors lies a clue to the darker side of creativity. "My first taking to imitating was not out of vanity but humility. I saw how defective my own things were and endeavoured to mend my manner by copying good strokes from others."[18] The awareness of defects in his "own things" is a reminder of the congenital deformities in "this imp of a poet, grotesque and sinister."[19] About four and a half feet in stature, he apparently suffered a "tubercular infection" between the ages of seven to ten.[20] He has been described as "protuberant behind and before," and likened himself to a spider.[21] He dressed in a stiff canvas bodice and wore three pair of stockings, either for warmth or to fill out his spindly legs. His dress, according to one critic, "concealed his physical malformation as much as possible," and a "series of carefully staged portraits . . . concealed it altogether."[22] Indeed, his poetry mediated a prolonged struggle between his own self-image and those portraying him as a "toad, spider, wasp, monkey, and general enemy of mankind."[23] No wonder, he suffered from delicate health and prolonged headaches throughout "this long disease, my life."

> There are, who to my person pay their court:
> I cough like Horace, and, though lean, am short,
> Ammon's great son one shoulder had too high—
> Such Ovid's nose, and 'Sir, you have an eye.'
> Go on, obliging creatures, make me see
> All that disgraced my betters met in me.[24]

These lines play with his anomalies, which, through wit, may be assimilated into consciousness; but long before then their influences must have been far more painful. Sitwell raises the possibility of some hereditary link with Pope's father who "suffered from a slight curvature of the spine."[25] Maynard Mack, however, attributed the son's "double curvature of the spine, lateral as well as backward," to a tubercular bacillus transmitted by his wet nurse.[26] In any case, the poet's awareness of such anomalies may well have fueled his quest for the ideal poetic father in Dryden, who had been observed "very particularly" when Pope was twelve.[27]

For although physical deformity per se need not have anything to do with the development of creativity, how a given anomaly is internalized and represented in the mind may well have. As a youth Pope apparently did not behave as though he were physically handicapped, but it is hard to believe that this did not set him apart to some extent and foster a sense of being an exception, the fertile soil from which the family-romance fantasy may grow. His older half-sister recalled him as a "pretty boy, with happy laughter, clear eyes, and round rosy cheeks that healthy children have"; Sitwell adds that along with a "gentle and affectionate disposition," the "sweetness of his voice earned for him the loving name of 'the little nightingale.'"[28] Excessive attention by others more cognizant than he of his anomalous frame may have fostered the very exception-image they sought to surmount; in any case, he seems to have maintained a certain narcissistic disposition manifested in the ways in which he compelled his servants to cater to him, dressing and undressing him, and running petty errands for him at all hours of the night. "He expected that everyone should give way to his ease or humour," writes Johnson, "as a child whose parents will not hear her cry, has an unresisted dominion in the nursery."[29]

But whatever the effects of organic factors in his development, they must have been exacerbated by an accident in early childhood. He was struck, trampled, and cut in the neck by the horn of a runaway steer. Whether this accident would be later invoked to account for the peculiarities of his physique, while possible, is not known. What does seem more likely is that writing beautiful poetry offered the prospect of mending the self into a new shape of wholeness and perfection. Art must correct nature, for "*True Wit* is *Nature* to Advantage drest."[30]

The evidence for this position must remain indirect, but a good case may be drawn from a series of events that took place as the young poet was just beginning to establish a name and reputation for himself as one of England's sons of Virgil. This time he was attacked not by a so-called "wild cow," but by a bullish old critic named John Dennis, and the attack was not entirely by accident—there had been a provocation.

On the face of it, Pope's satirical verses looked mild enough in skewering Dennis as someone who "stares tremendous, with a threatening eye, / Like some fierce tyrant in old tapestry."[31] But a sensitive nerve was evidently pressed, and his counterthrust hit Pope in his two most vulnerable areas: lineage and body image. Dennis maliciously suggested that if Pope had been born of proper Greek parents, he would not have lived half a day; and if his outward shape be that of a "downright monkey," his "inward man is ten times more ridiculous."[32]

Sitwell believes the immediate effect of this attack was Pope's suspending his courtship of Martha Blount, and then of a black poison slowly working its way into his warm-hearted and compassionate nature. His subsequent behavior does indeed reveal how traumatically disruptive Dennis's assault had been. Pope managed to entangle himself in the affairs of two seemingly ill-wed women only to bring upon himself the resentment of their husbands as well as the disapproval and ridicule of the community. Although the story is complicated, it does appear that Pope, in making a fool of himself, revealed an unmet sense of guilt via a need for humiliation. And so there may have been more than a little oedipal hostility and anxiety in his mocking the "threatening eye" of the critic, because when that eye found him out, he was most painfully exposed. He may then have tried to minimize the damage by dramatizing his own ineptness, as if to say I could not want to discredit father's powers of vision in order to possess mother, for look at the "harmless little creature" others "pull ... into pieces."[33]

But damage to self may have been greater than a thwarted oedipal scenario would indicate. Pope apparently turned temporarily away from writing as if somehow it had failed him; and, indeed, insofar as it was a defense against being seen as deformed, it had. He began to take lessons in painting, and for some eighteen months resided at the home of a fashionable London portrait painter. Although this interest was not to last, one of the sketches Pope completed and later used as frontispiece for his "Essay on Man" is remarkable for externalizing a felt injury to self. It is a collage of images, all of them commonplace, yet chosen and arranged on the theme of *sic transit gloria mundi*. They include a ruined Roman wall, broken pillars, a death's head with a laurel wreath, and a philosopher, sitting by idly blowing soap bubbles. In the foreground on a pedestal marked *viro immortale* rises the statue of an Adonis, but it is broken in half at the trunk, and scattered on the pavement are its upper parts—torso, hand, head, arm—each disconnected from the whole. This may be the sundered bodily self—literally pulled into pieces. By rendering it in another medium, perhaps Pope could separate it from himself and especially from the medium he was most able adequately to realize and reconstitute himself through.

Nonetheless the "inward man" behind the diminutive hunchback's verses continued to draw hostile fire, which at times impugned his moral character through physical defects: "the emblem of thy crooked mind / Marked on thy back, like Cain."[34] In his reply Pope would attempt to separate the character of his writing from that of his conduct and both from the unfortunate shape that proceeded from the creator who fashioned perfect forms. He would willingly be judged by literary or moral standards but not by unChristian exposure. Verbally assaultive as he may seem, a little devil he was not.

Pope's deep involvement in his vocation soon made writing coextensive with living, a prospect he came to view ambivalently: "Heavens! was I born for nothing but to write?" And thus his gift is also like a curse: "Why did I write? What sin to me unknown / Dipt me in Ink, my Parents', or my own?"[35] In the darker regions of his mind may be encountered primal-scene allusions polarizing his family romance of high birth. For here he comes close to suggesting that the act of parental coupling itself, his own begetting, low and bestial as Iago's "beast with two backs," and morally deformed by man's fall, may have contributed to his own deformity. And it is here also that may be found the sense of self as exception that Freud noted in Richard II the crookback king. Elsewhere he pondered how "Extremes in Nature equal ends produce, / In Man they join to some mysterious use."[36]

However, taking the idea that Pope's satirical art was intended as a clear and faultless mirror to be turned away from the self in order to reflect the literary and moral deformities of his society heads this inquiry in a new direction: toward the present mode of examining creativity within the area of self. The assumption would be that in reflecting the anomalies of his fellow men, Pope was both shifting the focus away from himself and exhibiting a

Frontispiece to *The Essay On Man* **by Alexander Pope. From an engraving after a drawing by Pope, used in the 1745 edition of** *The Essay On Man*.

perfected version of himself in the body of his art, though to what extent cannot be specified.

It may also be assumed that society will reciprocate and that gradually deflected images of the real self may be integrated into the art as well. The danger arises when someone in society sees past the reflections to the deformities of the injured self as when Dennis's critical mirror revealed the "downright monkey" behind it all. Facing this threat, the poet may have regressed to negative self-exhibition and also taken temporary refuge in the visual medium of emblematic painting, so enabling him to depict a failure of grandiose ambitions and a kind of self-ruin. Presumably, these fragmented or scaled-down self-images could then gradually be reassimilated into the total personality, rendering the poet less vulnerable to future attacks as indeed he proved himself to be by holding his ground and fighting with his pen: "the only method of self-defense or retaliation, that is left me against a person of your quality and power," he wrote in "A Letter to a Noble Lord."[37] But more than a defense, "his word alone," so penned a contemporary, "gave Infamy or Fame."[38]

But certainly the most moving effects of Pope's diminutive body image were his attempts to scale down his environment equivalent to his own proportions. Satires like his "Dunciad" may be seen as an obvious dressing-down, cutting other poets down to size, just as his "Rape of the Lock" was a mock-heroic reduction of inflated verse styles and the excesses of fashion. But when his earnings from the translations of Homer enabled him to acquire a house at Twickenham near London, the "Lilliputian scale of the poet's domain" reflected "his own proportions," as Maynard Mack notes: "A House, with Trees a-row, / And like its master very low."[39] In effect, by correcting the mirror of nature to match his dimensions, he turned it into a work of art or, more precisely, into an intermediate stage of creation that was "not an entirely new environment but a transformation of that which already exists"[40]—a transitional object, the continuation of the "child's first not-me possessions" or "subjective-objects," as construed by D. W. Winnicott.[41]

If the house was a correction of self and surround, the total estate functioned as the restoration of a lost personal relationship. Pope, who never married, did not lose his mother to death until he was forty-five; so it is safe to speculate that the real sense of loss was related to emotional factors, especially to the period of his childhood illness. "Passing through the gloom from the grotto to the opening day," wrote Horace Walpole, "the retiring and again assembling shades, the dusky groves, the larger lawn, and the solemnity of the termination at the cypresses that lead up to his mother's tomb (actually a memorial obelisk) are managed with exquisite judgment."[42]

In a gloss on this passage, Mack draws analogies with the effects of Pope's verse, but for our present interest the more important point is that the obelisk "was in fact the point of visual and emotional climax in the garden" and the "principal point of rest in a garden of memory and meditation."[43] But of equal interest was Pope's place in the garden, his own center of creativity, the grotto, traditionally a "place 'sacred' to poetry, the dwelling place of his Muse."[44] The grotto contained a spring that Pope turned into a waterfall and then by an ingenious placing of mirrors, "every Object is multiplied, and its Position represented in a surprising Diversity." The grotto balances the real and the illusory, so that "by a fine taste and happy management of Nature, you are presented with an indistinguishable Mixture of Realities and Imagery."[45] In this way, being no less genuine for being actual, the artist's creative romance with the world flourishes from the family romance seedlings. The grotto became a "shrine for great Nature—Pope's metaphysical Goddess."[46] Consequently, the psychoanalytic view of the early mother as environment, which underlies Winnicott's elaboration of transitional space, can be studied in a marvelously concrete way, thanks to the imaginative researches of Maynard Mack. They reveal how the cultivated surroundings do not precisely reflect Pope or his mother, but his ideal fantasy of both.

By means of these acts of self-reconstitution and object-recovery, which may generally operate within or alongside what is considered artistic creativity, crucial intermediate stages of creative processes can be investigated. If the altered natural surroundings revealed a revision of maternal boundaries, the poet similarly embedded himself in a preexisting poetic convention and tradition, principally Horatian, a less tangible but no less genuine reaching-out to the nonself via the transitional spheres of culture. At his Twickenham villa, Pope was able to realize the role of the philosopher-king, "the recluse whose kingdom is in his mind or lies about him in nature," who could introduce others to the "marvel of his realm." Finally, his estate could serve as an imagined "ideal community of patriarchal virtues and heroic friends," a perfected reflection of the ill-shaped society he would attack and set about correcting.[47]

3

> My face in thine eye, thine in mine appeares,
> And true plaine hearts doe in the faces rest,
> Where can we find two better hemispheares... ?
> —John Donne, "The Good-Morrow"

We tend to think of art as more than mirror—merely reflective of self and society—and properly so; on the other hand, the mirror is more than a metaphor of art. It has always been associated with magical powers, often demonic or taboo as in the shield of Perseus or the truth-telling mirror-mirror-on-the-wall in Snow White. Seldom does it merely reflect surfaces; more likely it reproduces a persecutory double or reduces one to stone. Or it concentrates tragic insight as when Richard II says, "Give me the glass, and therein will I read." At first it seems to flatter him, then:

A brittle glory shineth in this glass:
As brittle as the glory is the face.[48]

As "face" fails to catch the rhyme with "glass," so the one does not quite reflect the other. He smashes the glass and rebuts the facile lie that the glass is mere shadow, for he is thus reminded of the "unseen grief / That swells with silence in the tortured soul." The mirror that reveals the inner self is at the opposite extreme from the mirror image that the Grecian lad felt entranced by and has bestowed on posterity as the unlovely condition called narcissism.

One reason for the inexhaustibility of the mirror is that it is bound up with the earliest transactions between infant and mother. The mother's mirroring response to the infant's earliest facial expressions and gestures are in turn reflected by its smiling responses, which are gradually internalized into a cohesive self, as visual reflections breed mental reflections. The devil's image casts no reflection because the devil has no mother. Both thinking and creating in play or, later, in art draw upon the first interpersonal reflecting processes as the reflecting mirrors of the self acquire the ability to hold images of the original object (mother) who is receding into an absent object and being re-created as an internalized object. In contrast to the discredited notion of maternal bonding, mirroring addresses the means through which the child gradually separates those qualities belonging to the mother and those proper to the self—those felt to be outside and those within, those good and those bad. Through these operations the child forms what Stephen Weissman has termed the "visual ego," which we use as adults in an overseeing capacity: we "look after" ourselves as adults who once were looked after as children.[49]

As both a flattering narcissistic instrument and a sometimes harsh reminder of the outside world so alien to the self, the mirror retains a reflective ambiguity. The aim of dreams for Freud was attaining an "identity of perception" between seeing and the seen as a way of stating the goal of reattaining the ideally mirroring object of the self.[50] Such was the power of the Great Gatsby's smile: "It understood you just so far as you wanted to be understood, believed in you as you would like to believe in yourself, and assured you that it had precisely the impression of you that, at your best, you hoped to convey."[51] On the other side is the notion contained in the late medieval work, *Mirrour for Magistrates*, a series of cautionary tales rulers might scrutinize for models of virtue and tales of vice that would serve as self-warnings or admonitions to look after oneself, or else. The mirror may emanate from the id or the superego.

Art becomes a mirror neither for its flattering feedback nor for its faithful verisimilitude alone, but for its powers of both clarity and ambiguity. To modern minds, the wasteland image is both clear and ambiguous, even when it is called an image of our cultural condition; and nothing could be more clear or more ambiguous than the cockroach that Kafka's Gregor Samsa turns into. Yet both of these are telling reflections of the self and its milieu.

4

> What ever dyes, was not mixt equally;
> If our two loves be one, or, thou and I
> Love so alike, that none doe slacken, none can die.
> —John Donne, "The Good-Morrow"

An interesting manner in which the mirror preserves the ambience of self and other occurs in Tennyson (1809–92). In "The Lady of Shalott" he invokes the most famous mirror in Western thought: from Plato's myth about the shadows of images in the cave of humanity and their bearing on reality. The cave wall serves as a sort of dusty mirror or screen for reflecting carved figures carried over the heads of a procession, and these figures are themselves but copies of a reality, which consists for Plato of ideal forms. Similarly isolated from reality, Tennyson's lady "weaves by night and day / A magic web with colors gay," which she observes in a "mirror clear."[52] And so her art too is but a reflection, and after seeing "two young lovers lately wed," she becomes "half sick of shadows" (ll.70–1). When the sun "flamed upon the frozen greaves / Of bold Sir Lancelot" and flashed into the "crystal mirror" (ll.76–7), she looks down to Camelot: her vision cracks the mirror of herslf apart, and she floats toward extinction.

Here the mirror serves as a protective device to permit the making of art. The artist may be construed as Tennyson's feminine persona, or Jungian anima, as one critic has it,[53] and it is significant in this connection that his she-side is destroyed by the instrusion in her shadowy world of a masculine and, hence, sexual reality. But the loss is neither to Tennyson nor his art insofar as the poem stands as the record of this clash. Nonetheless the association of mirrors with feminine, combined elsewhere in that celestial reflector, the moon, tells us something about mirrors' defensive uses. It is also apparently a mode of perception, for Tennyson would explicitly invoke mirror imagery to present the encounter with the person who was to make the deepest impression on the poet's personality, his close friend, Arthur Henry Hallam:

> So, friend, when first I looked upon your face,
> Our thought gave answer each to each, so true—
> Opposed mirrors each reflecting each—

That this special moment resonates in part from past relationships is evidence in the *déjà vu* sense of the following lines:

> Altho I knew not in what time or place,
> Methought that I had often met with you,
> And each had lived in the other's mind and speech.[54]

One may infer that some of the intensity of this mutual bond was lessened by Hallam's subsequent engagement to the poet's sister. Intensely emotional, certainly narcissistic to a degree, their relationship when cut short when Hallam's early death compelled Tennyson to gather the fragments of his lost friendship and reproduce them after seven years in his long, brooding elegy, "In Memoriam A.H.H."

More often ruminative than moving, this poem has a peculiar sort of androgynous softness in the mellifluent verses where the poet portrays himself as both "widower" and "widowed." Here the deeper sense seems to be that the glass divider has melted down, yielding to a merger between complementary segments. Early on, there appears an arresting scene that is central to this inquiry, if not necessarily to the poem. The poet is illustrating the suddenness of death, and draws a girl awaiting her beloved and preparing herself before a mirror:

> And, having left the glass, she turns
> Once more to set a ringlet right;
>
> And, even when she turn'd, the curse
> Had fallen, and her future lord
> Was drown'd in passing the ford.[55]

Here the briefly vanishing self-image from the mirror is associated with death, and by inference with loss of the mirroring object (*ford* does not quite reflect *lord*).

It was T. S. Eliot who objected to Tennyson's endless ruminations, and that response does get at the sense one has of the bereaved poet recovering his lost love memory by memory, masticating and digesting it as part of the mourning process. It is in part a regressive process, and Tennyson introduces this thematically when he contemplates the infant at the preobject stage:

> The baby new to earth and sky,
>   What time his tender palm is prest
>   Against the circle of the breast,
> Has never thought that "this is I";
>   (stanza 45, 11.1–5)

Soon he learns, "I am not what I see, / And other than the things I touch." Parting from the breast as self or mirror of need, "So rounds he to a separate mind" (11.7–9). And in so rounding out this process, Tennyson manages to suggest by the curve of growth the importance of early experiences between child and mother as being formative in a very precise sense. His lost friend, like the infant's mother, recalls a blissful state of perfection, and in stanza 52 the poet freely admits, "I cannot love thee as I ought, / For love reflects the thing beloved" (11.1–2). The poem then proceeds with its work of renunciation and reconciliation toward its ultimate goal of replacing loss with meaning.

The poet's having been gradually made "kindly with my kind" (stanza 66, 1.7) conveys in its word-pairing a transformation of the mirror relationship in the shifting from the early objects toward humanity at large. Rhyming also offers opportunities to echo—by analogy with mirroring—the same, yet with a difference.

In the final stanzas a reversal of time is brought about: the friend of the past is turned into an ideal of the future. Hallam becomes both a kind of ego-ideal for the poet and a cultural ideal for his public, an intimation of perfection achieved through creative evolution: "the man that with me trod / This planet was a noble type / Appearing ere the times were ripe," who now "lives in God ... / To which the whole creation moves" (stanza 131, 11.137–44).

5

If an analogy can be drawn between the fusion of dreamer and dream in Freud's identity of perception and the mirroring phenomena between infant and parent, is there a counterpart in literature? Dreaming is unconscious mental activity that becomes partly conscious, whereas mirroring is conscious mental activity that undergoes repression or transformation into psychic structure and so qualifies as a primitive stage of the developing self. Dreaming may then be regressive attempts to recover (or attain) the pleasurable states of fusion once enjoyed (or sought) in mirroring. Literature necessarily encompasses much later, far more complex stages of development and thereby empowers us to ponder with Yeats, "How can we know the dancer from the dance?"[56] Yet the earlier mirroring phenomena need not disappear entirely and may indeed offer important clues to the mimetic nature of representative forms or even unfold a basis for them.

The earliest literary forms in ancient Greece turned on a device that became most fully developed in drama and was singled out by Aristotle in the *Poetics* as the *anagnorisis*, or scene of recognition. This moment in the action usually involved discovery of persons, as, for examples, Orestes of his sisters Electra in one play, Iphigenia in another. The *anagnorisis* could be promising or despairing, depending on whether it occurred within a comic or a tragic framework. But regardless, the recognition was precisely that: a re-cognizing of a formerly familiar and significant other. This suggests an adult analogue to the child's recovering a perception of the mother during those rap-prochement moments that occur after she has already been experienced as absent. While occurring in the cultural space of the theater, the newly found (or reperceived) other reinstates, if only temporarily, the original mirroring object, in something akin to the wish-fulfillment achieved by an identity of perception in the dream.

Literature is built out of such experiences, not only in classical drama but in the many recognitions of disappearing and returning characters, especially in picaresque novels of traditional plot-making. Moreover, the techniques of coinciding opposites or correspondences draw on the same capacities within the reader to recognize subtle patterns of identity. But literature is also built out of departures from the above paradigm. For example, the discovery of the right object in the wrong place, that is, the child's parent in a sexual relationship, as in *Oedipus Rex*, combines the *anagnorisis* with the *peripateia* or reversal, and was, as Aristotle notes, Sophocles' great contribution to tragedy. This combination also leads to a phenomenon that both literature and psychoanalysis both share an interest in: namely, insight.

While insight may stem from one's mirroring and reflecting on mental images, it is committed to meaning, even at the cost of painful emotions. James Joyce, for a time, raised insight to a structural principle in his interest in the epiphany as a "sudden spiritual manifestation, whether in the vulgarity of speech or gesture or in a memorable phrase of the mind itself."[57] This interplay between self and reality endows the environment with radiant meaning and, at least for Joyce, begins to make art possible. The Greek words *epiphanos* (showing-forth) and *theophanos* (showing-forth of divinity) also occupied a structural element in the drama, sometimes involving the actual descent from Olympus and onstage materialization of such goddesses as Athena or Aphrodite. This showing-forth of ideal perfection may be associated with the original exalted image of the parent as coextensive with life, the eidetic as divine, and fit into a developmental sequence of literary recognition that will later settle on more mundane figures—long-lost relatives, siblings, and spouses reuniting.

Additional derivatives from the mirroring process may be distinguished along lines of self-images and representations of others. "Bad" images, derived from felt deficiencies in the mother or from projections of rage from need-frustration, may show up in popular forms as ghouls, witches, monsters, Mr. Hydes, and other persecutory objects, as the mirror turns ugly.[58]

It is even more threatening when the mirror captures not mother but a stranger instead. Herein may lie the basis for what has come to be called existential states of dread, alienation, and aloneness. The Theater of the Absurd may best present the myriad forms of this condition. One recalls, for example, the strangers who come for Stanley in Pinter's *The Birthday Party*. When they destroy his glasses, he must adapt to their alien vision of what appears to him as a meaningless reality. Or consider in *The Stranger* Camus's Meursault, who kills an Arab, a stranger whose humanity is not recognized, due to the hero's own self-deficiencies. Socially, this hero is an antihero, who is tried and found guilty—less of murder than of impiety at his mother's funeral. But through this ordeal he becomes familiar and achieves selfhood, while the functionings of society ironically turn alien and its members become strangers. In such ways, the mirror of the self manages brilliantly to reflect an absurd world, for by not condemning his hero, by not accepting the antihero label, Camus has mirrored through him the dark face of society.

The obverse occurs in Oscar Wilde's *Picture of Dorian Gray*, where the true self is figured in traditional moral values. Bernard Green suggests, however, that Dorian Gray finds himself trapped by the discovery that, along with his features projected and idealized on the artist's canvas, his self has also become something external. His hedonism becomes an attempted "cure for living encompassed within skewed and one-sided images of oneself."[59] When all else fails he desperately tries to free himself by murdering the artist and stabbing the painting, only to be found fatally stabbed, his own features assuming the portrait's horrible face. *Sic transit gloria mundi*, with a vengeance. Wilde's immortal comedy, *The Importance of Being Earnest*, manages both to handle the adoption theme playfully and to mock the biological base of origins. The earnest man is society's ideal of the duty-bound heterosexual husband; the playful alternative to this seriousness is the Dandy (the Uranist), who is gay in more senses than one. But to be socially acceptable he must mirror social values with his "earnest" mask.

The failure of the mirroring object to instill a firm core of self-images or the intrusion of the stranger may be further related to distorted self-representations such as Pinocchio (and its more literary forms, Cyrano and Gogal's character); Kafka's Gregor Samsa, who woke to find himself a cockroach; Philip Roth's David Kepesh, who turned into a female breast; as well as the more subtle manifestations, such as Dostoevsky's underground man who feels himself to be at times a mouse or a saint. Phyllis Greenacre has studied distorted body-image phenomena and maternal deprivation in her book *Swift and Carroll* (1950).

Other apparent deviations of self-images that occur in the psychoanalytic context of narcissism are variously represented in myth and literature by such motifs as the twins or the double, a fascinating phenomenon studied by Otto Rank *et al.*[60] The dandy, as a social or a literary type, may be said to be his own double or love-object by living out his own grandiose self-image through his extravagant and exhibitionistic lifestyle. Such was Oscar Wilde when he wasn't accommodating his readers' conventional morals. In contrast to his Restoration predecessor, the fop who turns himself into a mirror of society to the improverishment of his inner being, the dandy mirrors a brighter image of possibility than is found among his colorless middleclass peers.[61] But for Wilde, this succeeded only so long as the surface of the mirror was not questioned: the dandy then became for him a "brilliantly cohesive" image, writes Beckson in a Kohutian mode.[62] His analysis suggests that Wilde had consciously come to rely on the grandiose power of his mask to such an extent that he mistook the permissible lies of art for the impermissible ones of life and believed his mask would conceal the sodomitic behavior for which he was put on trial just as it would shield him from his own self-destructive urges. In both he was mistaken.

The motif of the double recalls another Platonic myth: that of the original unisex state of mankind, figured in the Androgyne and followed by the splitting into sexual halves and the quest for one's other part, which is, at bottom, narcissistic, if, as Freud affirmed in his first application of the term, mankind is on a lifelong quest to recover his original but illusory sense of wholeness.

6

> Whatever I see I swallow immediately
> Just as it is, unmisted by love or dislike.
> —Sylvia Plath, "The Mirror"

One of the afflictions of our own self-regarding age appears in our self-regarding literature; but early in the modern period the complete narcissist had already been rendered in definitive dramatic form. He is Ibsen's Peer Gynt, who, late in his circular career, peels an onion to reach its "innermost filler," only to realize that, like him, it has none: "nothing but layers—smaller and smaller."[63] Peer's nuclear self had never been established, and so lacking this inner compass, he traveled in circles, never achieving a sense of identity or a stable relationship (unless he integrated his belated awareness at the very end of the play when he cries out in Solveig's arms, "My mother—My wife! You innocent woman—!" [*Peer Gynt*, 240]).

With astonishing lucidity, Ibsen established Peer's basic character and its dynamics at the outset of the play. In what is otherwise a tall tale told to impress his mother, Peer reveals much of his inner reality. He fires upon a buck only to find himself borne away by the animal, riding atop its antlers Centaur-fashion, with the animal or Peer's lower self in control. At last the two tumble over a high ridge toward a glassy-clear lake below:

> Downward, endlessly, we go.
> But in the depths something shows
> Dim white, like reindeer's belly fleece.
> Mother, it was *our* reflection
> Shooting upward through the lake from
> Silent darkness to the glassy calm
> On top with the same breakneck
> Speed as we were hurtling down.
>
> (34)

Peer and buck splash together in an orgastic foam of narcissistic coupling. But it is not so much Peer's bestiality that has run away with him as his grandiose self which defies boundaries. The failure in this area of the self is hinted at in the mother's responses to him. The play had opened with her taunt, "Peer, you're lying," and throughout their exchange she either overvalues or devalues him. "If only you had put your mind to it / You'd be a splendid bridegroom now—/ Instead of a filthy ragamuffin."[64] Whether her savior or a "beast," Peer sees that "win or lose, it doesn't matter—/ You boil me in the same hot water" (39).

This double bind points to possible defects in the earlier mirroring process which have perpetuated a defensive grandiosity: "I will be a king, an emperor!" (40). Later he will boast, he can fly and adopt the troll motto, "To yourself—be enough" (85). Consequently, the symbiotic tie to the mother has been protracted, for in the same scene he reenacts the tale of the buck by hoisting his mother onto his shoulder and prancing about the yard until she is dumped on the mill-house roof. That the mother wants to be excited and seduced by her son but also fears it is confrimed not only by her inconsistency of response, but in her past relationship with Peer's father, who drank to excess and deserted his family. Peer inherits both the mother's unrequited eroticism and her unappeased rage, but he lacks the basic centering that would circumscribe grandiosity and foster degrees of self-acceptance. Wary of trolls who demand nothing as well as of humans who pose threats of intimacy or commitment, he acts out his ambivalence through attraction-withdrawal motifs to avoid the felt dangers of symbiotic engulfment. He therefore runs in a wide circle, unable to meet the elusive "Great Boyg" of integrated selfhood. He marries and abandons Solveig for no apparent reason; but in the course of time her fidelity to him and his anxious encounters with the button-maker, who would melt him back to nonbeing for failing to become a "button on the vest of the world," lead him round and round back to her abiding presence.

To his question, "Where was I, as myself, as the whole man, the true man?" she answers, "In my faith, in my hope, and in my love."[65] The image of wholeness which he had missed from his ambivalent mother is now at last mirrored in Solveig. He sees that all women are mother, Solveig included: "You're mother even to the boy inside?" (239). In so doing he appears to acknowledge the fear of incest, the recognition of which is singled out by Freud as a prerequisite for mature love. But because he can also now recognize Solveig as separate and harmless, he may be able to remain with her as the child-man he finds himself to be.

Inside his top hat Ibsen kept a mirror whose reflections of his own countenance gave him pleasure. Though this may sound like mere vanity and narcissistic indulgence, it may have also been a means of keeping alive a good mirroring relationship beyond the vicissitudes of a troubled childhood, which included several younger siblings, his father's bankruptcy, his mother's withdrawal, and his own early departure from home to serve as an apothecary's apprentice. Away from home young Ibsen played out his own troll's impulses and fathered an illegitimate son with the young maid at the apothecary's lodgings. Unlike Peer, he did not run away, but like Peer, he was haunted by the troll queen and her bastard son; and it is not surprising that having put so much of himself into the play, he reacted with extreme rage at one hostile review.[66] Here the mirror of the inner self reflected through art is experienced as rejected, thus placing his very identity in jeopardy. In anger Ibsen wrote, "if I am not a builder, I am at least capable of destroying"; "if

I am no poet ... I shall try my luck as a photographer.''[67] Like Pope in this regard, he revises his medium downward, but this change is a calculated and lasting strategy that achieves the breakthrough into modern drama.

Henceforth, he turns his mirror into a camera lens focused on the external world, and it is following *Peer Gynt* that Ibsen entered his iconoclastic period of social realism with such works as *Pillars of Society* (1877), *A Doll House* (1879), and *Ghosts* (1881). In fact, Ibsen did quite literally what I described. He sat in public places, his back to society, but observing its members as well as himself most carefully in his hat mirror. It is their world that his art then mirrors on the European stage—and it is not a pleasing image.

7

In Sartre's *No Exit*, there are neither doors nor mirrors: the characters can only hope to have their identities affirmed through the reflections of themselves in the others. "Hell is other people" when failure to achieve existential selfhood is reflected by the others, and past betrayals and self-deceptions are merely repeated in this drama of the damned.

In his *Saint Genet*, Sartre views the lack of the mirroring response in the early development of the adopted and apparently abandoned French playwright Jean Genet as accounting for the origin of his perverse creativity:[68]

> The child was playing in the kitchen. Suddenly he became aware of his solitude and was seized with anxiety, as usual. So he "absented" himself. Once again, he plunged into a kind of ecstasy. There is now no one in the room. An abandoned consciousness is reflecting utensils. A drawer is opening; a little hand moves forward.
> Caught in the act. Someone has entered and is watching him. Beneath this gaze the child comes to himself. He feels that he blinding, deafening, he is a beacon, an alarm that keeps ringing. *Who* is Jean Genet? In a moment the whole village will know. ... The child alone is in ignorance. In a state of fear and shame he continues his signal of distress. Suddenly ... A voice declares publicly: "You're a thief." The child is ten years old.

"That was how it happened, in that or some other way," concludes Sartre's justly famous passage; his exposition of this paradoxical metamorphosis from undifferentiated "innocence" to negative existence is unexcelled. Quite clearly Sartre perceives the impact of maternal deprivation on a child brought up by the National Foundling Society and placed at seven in the care of Morvan peasants, but Sartre prefers to focus on the social question of illegitimacy which contradicts Genet's inner sense of innocence and prepares him for his role as thief.

> He is a fake child. No doubt he was born of woman, but his origin has not been noted by the social memory. As far as everyone and, consequently, he himself are concerned, he appeared one fine day without having been carried in any known

womb: he is a synthetic product. He is obscurely aware that he belongs legally to administrative bodies and laboratories, and so there is nothing surprising in the fact that he will later feel elective affinities with reformatories and prisons. Being a fabricated creature, he will find his truth in sophism; being a child of miracle, he will be mineral or spirit; but he does not belong to the intermediate kingdom: to life.[69]

While the missed mirroring response may be but one element amid massive deprivation, it is a crucial one for Genet, as well as a clear basis for the impoverished inner self and the power of others to define its essence for him. He records feeling that a young Italian he overhears could turn him by a "simple wish, even unexpressed, into a jackal, a fox, a guinea fowl." This is perhaps the obverse side to the more benign, protean self that Robert Jay Lifton describes among contemporary youth, for Genet's susceptibility, as Sartre points out, stems from an inner deadness.[70]

Thus deprived of an available mirroring object, Genet's inner mirroring fails to grow into life; he manages to achieve objective status in the world only through being a homosexual outlaw, the reverse image of social normality, and he creates an art based almost entirely on mirrors as reflections of nonbeing. In *The Maids*, his maids are defined by their Madame—are in fact summoned into existence by Madame. She is the eternally absent object, who, even when she is present is present only for her own needs (which the maids are constituted to reflect). Not only are the maids deprived of humanness, they are to play at being Madame and each other; they are to be played by male actors, rendering them fake maids, and these male actors are not real, that is, heterosexual males, but fake boys, homosexuals, which distances the spectator even further from substantial reality. And it is only by his endorsing this perversely Platonic world of shadows in mirrors, by an extreme willing suspension of disbelief, that this art can hope, along with its creator, to achieve a degree of reality.[71]

For in Genet's extremely demanding theater, the spectators acquire the missing power of the original mirroring object; only they can endow the perverse artist, through his shifting and receding chamber of mirrors, with authentic, if only momentary, selfhood.[72] In Kohutian terms, the audience is the idealized other who alone can bestow legitimacy on the deficient/grandiose self. But even this would amount to a miraculous metamorphosis, and it is perhaps here that similar processes in art—otherwise overlooked or too readily accepted as normal—are operating. For this inquiry began with an example of physical deformity corrected through an artform and is now ending is with an example of emotional deformity. Both are encompassed by the self and needs specific to it rather than by what is included within a traditional framework of drives and defenses peculiar to creativity, such as displacement, denial/fantasy, and sublimation. True, these may still play a part in the total, but their formerly held primacy in psychoanalytic criticism should yield ground to an approach that aims both to maintain a measure of scientific objectivity and to move closer to the actual concerns of art as mimesis.

As far as the dynamic polarities go, they are negatively affirmed in Genet's inverted and paradoxical art. Within the play, Madame is the idealized parent by reason of her power over the narcissistically incapacitated maids. If their playacting in Madame's absence can convert the audience into believing they are real, then their playing at the murder of Madame will also be validated, and they will be reborn into their own family-romance ideal of the eternal couple—the criminal and the saint, to be lovingly welcomed and adopted by the audience. Their newly won completeness will replace the hated primal scene of Madame and Monsieur, from which they have been excluded.

8

Art is more than reflection. Pools and lakes may reflect beautiful forms in beautiful ways, yet we do not consider them works of art. Is it simply because they have not been made? These natural mirrors may replicate and even distort objects in the real world, including ourselves, but not being made by us they do not confirm the power of our presence. The results of creativity may be analogous to such reflections but actually are something far different, about which we say very much and know fairly little.

The child who is pleased to find in pools and plants, in rocks and trees, continuations of the mirroring and holding relationship with the mother is on the way either to conducting the artist's creative romance with the world or to responding to the results of it from the hands of developed artists. But if the child seeks and finds in the mirroring capacities of nature only his own self-image, then the process has been cut short. To rephrase Mickey and the milk from Maurice Sendak's *In the Night Kitchen*, the growing self must be able to say, "I'm not the mirror and the mirror's not me." But the mirror participates in being both self and nonself and thus exists in Winnicott's transitional space of experiencing. And since both natural and manufactured mirrors depend on observers to validate their reflections, we have here but one of the many ways that the self bridges its surroundings and that creative processes are enmeshed in developmental ones. These will be examined more minutely later on, but for the present we can explore what happens when developmental steps do not foster creative ones.

Or perhaps it would be better to say that apparent developmental impasses foster creativity of a certain kind only. The surface aspect of the self that Narcissus becomes so taken with may be called the "I" to distinguish it from the more complicated systems in the self referred to as the ego, superego, and id, with all of their distinctive functions and representations. The "I" often stands for, but seldom adequately, the whole personality. If we recall Freud's observation that the ego is not master of its own house, then we could take it one step further and say the "I" is not master even of the ego. And if the

"I" can reflect only the "I" and not the larger self and body of experience, then it goes without saying that it is too impoverished to reflect the larger environment. Narcissus, unaware of the water he peers into, feeds on himself, that is, on his I-self, becomes self-narcotized, and starves to death.

Self-regard has been the perennial problem of artists and writers, but not until recently has it been instated as an ideal. In the past, ingenious strategies were employed to overcome what has been variously understood as the egotistical sublime, solipsism, and the cult of sincerity. There have been, for example, choruses in Greek drama, reflectors and refractors of character in Shakespeare, as well as contrasting plots, doubles, masks, and personae throughout fiction. These boundary indicators that presume aesthetic judgments by objectifying and surpassing the subjective "I" have constituted much of both the pleasure and sense of truth in art. It took Joyce ten years to draw a portrait of the young artist from his own self-experience. At the end of that book, as Stephen appears to be on the threshold of maturity, Joyce has him inscribe in a diary—that most narcissistic of literary forms—a comment about Stephen's mother: "She prays now, she says, that I may learn in my own life and away from home and friends what the heart is and what it feels."[73] And at once a new perspective on Joyce's self-character and what is missing in it is revealed.

When Joseph Conrad wrote about someone listening to someone else (Marlowe) tell a story about someone else still (Kurtz), he demonstrated that framing and distancing intensifies rather than dilutes. Some may write from a first-person to dramatize an "I" overwhelmed by history or circumstances (e.g., Twain, Dickens, Hemingway), whiled still others may tell a story from several points of views (*Wuthering Heights, The Naked and the Dead*), or in several voices and styles (*Ulysses*).

Since these examples from the past are axiomatic for establishing a perspective—indeed, a frame—for recognizing the difficulties in the present, the reader may permit a few more recent instances. Whether it is a classic of adolescence or of maturity, Salinger's *A Catcher in the Rye* has been enormously influential on later writers. Here is the first-person-narrative voice at its purest, most narcissistically self-absorbed form, that of a male adolescent. But what saves it, along with the particularization of voice and the poignant filtering of experience, is that far from being a case of self-celebration, Holden has suffered a breakdown of an unspecified nature and is telling his story to a psychotherapist. This frames the self in a perspective different from that of an expressive / performing "I." Similarly, Philip Roth's Portnoy tells his story with narcissistic abandon until he is interrupted at the end by Dr. O. Spielvogel, with his famous, "Now, perhaps we begin?" Bruno Bettelheim actually took the cue and published therapy notes on the Portnoy case, wherein he touches on the implicit dangers in this kind of writing, dangers that have become more widespread.[74] Portnoy's sickness is that he "cannot relate to other persons"; cannot "give of himself"; and has no "realization of his sickness," since "all he sees of the world are his own projections which he is certain are true pictures of reality." His narcissism is seen as covering self-loathing, his verbal displays as a reaction to emptiness. This thoroughly devastating reflection (not without its countertransference shadings) of the inner Portnoy actually fills in the projected "I" of Roth's text and completes the novel by means of framing and including the larger self and early environment in more rounded terms. It is not that the reader expects a built-in analysis, but at least enough gravity to hold the object in our own atmosphere and protect it from its own manic flights or exhibitionistic displays.

As if in revenge, Roth's later novel, *My Life as a Man* (1974), also composed in the first person, is about a writer battling it out with his psychoanalyst, who this time around will not be given the last word. What saves the manic flight here from taking over completely is the device of a fiction within fiction. When Roth published *The Facts* (1988), a version of his life as a writer, he enlisted his own fictional creation, Zuckerman, to critique the author by way of preempting more objective strictures. The inevitable follow-up interview managed to cast doubt on both voices.[75]

The novel of manic flight and, it seems, the recent Jewish novel in general (including those of Bruce Jay Friedman, Saul Bellow, and Normal Mailer) have been seen as male-centered and misogynist.[76] In the same company belong the bohemian sex novels of Henry Miller and the beat generation outpourings of Jack Kerouac, Ken Kesey's *One Flew over the Cuckoo's Nest*, and others. But if women have been poorly represented in these works, some recent women writers have not fared better in moving beyond their own self-experience. Rita Mae Brown's Molly Bolt in *Rubyfruit Jungle* (1973) is a sort of female Huck or Holden, whose self-serving distortions make it appear that everyone is demented, exploitive, or perverted, except the yours-truly narrator. We are expected to believe that the only undistorted mirror reflects the heroine. Erica Jong's *How to Save Your Own Life* (1977) similarly projects the I-perspective through a self-character who completely controls the reader's response to her experiences as well as to all other characters. In reviewing trends in American women's fiction, Elinor Langer notes the absence of society or of any palpable outside world in cozy works where the "heroines of the novels of contemporary white middle-class women tend to be other white middle-class women like their authors."[77]

These trends advance a two-dimensional fiction in which the self-character has both the first and the last word, and the story is bound only by the books' covers, while the advantages that can accrue only from framing and distancing are missing. "The aim of my writing is to utterly remove the distance between author and reader," write Erica Jong, "so that the book becomes a sort of semipermiable membrane through which feelings, ideas, nutrients pass."[78] They pass apparently to a reader reduced to a symbiotic stage, as totally dependent on an omniscient author as the infant is on an all-important mother.

Little if any space is allotted for free and varied responses; almost no possibility of separation or loss is permitted—denied, in fact, by the incessant manic tone. Erica Jong's 1977 novel is about a woman writer in her thirties separating from a bad environment (husband, lovers, New York) and asserting her own autonomy. But the expanded spaces allotted for Isadora Wing's individuation is denied the readers, who have no place to fit in, apart from relinquishing their own independence and becoming a positive reflector of the character's aspirations. Thus the reader's role is to passively admire the performance or to pity the character's plight, but not to raise questions, for then, like the analyst or spouse or parent before him, the reader may become the "bad object," the obstacle to manic fusion or symbiotic merging.

But there are many other sexually explicit novels whose only aim is to seduce the reader into passive participation and eventual engulfment. And there are many readers who seek no more than this in fiction. At this point the author's work adequately mirrors the reader's regressive needs. Seduction, the hapless reader may feel, is preferrable to neglect or abandonment.

The seductive powers of the first-person narrator were duly recognized and indiscriminatingly embraced by Philip Roth in an interview:

Q. What about writing in the first person, are you most comfortable with that?
A. I seem to be doing it mostly. It's for me a way of gaining stylistic freedom. I'm able to use conversational tones and rhythms that have great expressive value and appeal for me. I can turn the volume up and down within a single sentence. I can slip in and out of the kind of colloquial talk and the kind of formal talk I'm partial to. And of course it's the "I" who can be most intimate, who speaks in confidence, who tells us secrets—sexual secrets, hate secrets, love secrets, family secrets, tribal secrets, the stuff of shame, embarrassment, humiliation and disgrace. If I said to you, as shame-ridden adults and small children sometimes do, "I have this friend, and a strange thing happened to him on 42nd Street last night, and now he says he needs to see a doctor," you might or might not pay attention to the plight of my dear friend. But if I say, "Look, Sara, we don't know each other too well but something rather strange happened to me last night on 42nd Street, and I've got to tell somebody ..." well, I think I'd be in business ... Of course using the first person in this way obviously accounts for the confusion in some of my readers as to just whose experience I'm talking about and where I would like their attention to be focused. I have been told that I ought readlly to be flattered to be taken for the speaker instead of the ventriloquist. But suppose you were Edgar Bergen and you went out into the street and somebody tried to drive a nail into your head because they thought you were Charlie McCarthy and your head was made of wood. You wouldn't like it.[79]

Obviously, the aim is to abolish the enemy distance, the specter of separateness: to seduce the reader with the promise of intimacy and, finally, to see it only in terms of authorial convenience ("stylistic freedom").

Similarly, Erica Jong prefers first-person closeness: "the books I read with most pleasure and most avid attention were often memoirs or novels that had the immediacy of memoirs ... I tended to prefer the first-person novels to the third-person ones. ..."[80] Referring to the "perilously thin" or "wholly irrelevant" distinctions between autobiography and fiction, she cites Colette as writing "mock memoirs."[81] "I loved the novel," Jong continues, "that pretended not to be a novel, in short—the novel that made you believe it was all spilled truth."[82] Contrariwise, the "perfectly wrought novels of E. M. Forster and Elizabeth Bowen" are not suitable frames "for my experience of life." The affirmation of spontaneity and inclusiveness, while potentially as valid as any other strategy, does not appear to be actually employed in her own celebrated *Fear of Flying* (1973):

> I spent months writing chapters which never found their way into the book at all. The ending was rewritten at least seven times. The last chapter, which is now about six pages long, was rewritten so many times you wouldn't believe it.[83]

If not highly wrought, Jong's prose is highly wrung, and as deliberately calculated as any other modern perfectionist. Here the avowed aim is for an "indeterminate feeling," but the effect might be quite otherwise, since the writing throughout is carefully managed within the I-perspective. The danger for the writer is that when the projected self-character is widely admired by the public, it is virtually impossible to let go. Thus it was almost inevitable that the acclaim of *Fear of Flying* dictated a second command performance of the same heroine, in *How to Save Your Own Life*, and another return, in *Parachutes and Kisses*. Authors who manage to seduce the public into admiration one step removed—a concern expressed by the Jong character— may find the next time around that it is the public who has seduced them.

When the aim in much contemporary fiction becomes symbiotic merging or manic fusion over distance and perspective, when it becomes self-display over self-objectivization, then we are entitled to examine the function of mirroring and to expect that the inner workings of creativity—self and object-world remaking—may have been detoured. Otherwise we would be drawn into mistaking an early phase of human development for the aim and ideal of art (if not also of life). What happens when the self-remaking process does not occur within its own hard-won creative spaces is that the public takes over and dictates the way in which the remaking will come about. When the public remakes the artist in its own image, the artist suffers the slow death of creative vitality. This happens more dramatically in show business and is amply documented by a cemetery of stars. One reason the Beatles gave for their collective death was to permit the members to live. But if we ask only an idealized reflection from artists, and if we should be content to be enveloped or seduced, to repeat instead of to discover, then we, too, will become hooked on the *narco* in narcissism. Not that getting high or feeling good in the short run is to be avoided: it is simply unrelated to truth, as art is.

But since the making of literature is not an exclusively intrapsychic process, cultural analysis may also be in order. Here the same phenomena may be reexamined as part of a more general overvaluation of immediacy, largely promoted by movies and communications media. These collaborative, technological enterprises have succeeded most amazingly in virtually abolishing distances of both time and space. For example, it took Mailer and Heller, respectively, four and fifteen years to write what are probably the two best treatments of World War II. What they made evidently made them. Thereafter, celebrityhood seems to have accelerated the production, if not the quality, of their work.

Mass media dictate that all roads lead to the close-up, and the close-up is finally a dead end. Against such electronic magnetism, the contemporary imagination manages little more than compromises. The relative success, for example, of Erica Jong's *Fanny* (1980) may be gauged by the author's strategy of distancing. While situated in eighteenth-century England, the fiction's heroine divides her time between raunchy sexual escapades and uplifting feminist homilies. Both a realized character and an authorial mouthpiece, she effects an agreeable compromise between narcissistic exhibition and cultural relevance. This novel also draws some of its energies as well as its appeal from the creative polarities these pages have been elucidating. For the titular heroine, Fanny Hackabout Jones, is the conception of a remarkable literary marriage between John Cleland's eighteenth-century pornographic narrative, *Fanny Hill*, and Henry Fielding's *Tom Jones*. The child who emerges from the pages of this primal scene of literary forbears provides both author and reader with a family romance of sufficient remoteness and mythical aura to flourish.

9

Writers these days are hard put to survive, much less compete, and it is possible that Roth and Jong represent certain adaptive strategies for the sake of sheer survival. In the past, writers coped with either a slow maturation of talent or a lag in public acceptance by forming supportive sub-cultures—cultural oases within the larger society. They endured not only neglect but deprivation, and in the early modern period took the long view. Ezra Pound is recalled as saying that his peers should not count on being read or understood by more than a handful during their lifetime. But the literary life has not retained the prestige it once enjoyed, even in his day.

And so it is possible to interpret the self-regarding tendencies among writers as a sort of identification with the aggressor (the media) for purposes of survival. This is both understandable and unfortunate. The intimacy afforded by television is obviously ersatz; only a small portion of the person is ever visible, and marketing research driven by advertising priorities creates an increasingly closed circuit of programming designed to mirror viewer tolerance. Positive feedback that dictates these media cannot help but influence other disciplines. Both in her interviews and through her self-character, Erica Jong is continually mindful of this interaction; no sooner has Isadora Wing had an orgy than she tries to answer questions she imagines her friends will be asking her. The communications aspect of the experience becomes the overriding one, the instant replay over the painstaking reconstruction, self-presentation over self-remaking, canned applause over soul-searching.

Distancing in this context is considered dangerous by the celebrity-author, because while it allows for a sense of wholeness in the subject, with diffuse and varied responses in the reader viewer, it also runs the danger of being lost sight of as center of interest. The close-up, where there is no mistaking who counts, guards against this risk taking. Writers have also gotten the message. The television image always has a center and a periphery. Paradoxically, the closer the close-up comes the less we see, and when at last it is nothing more than an enveloping mass, we hear its message, which is a simple one and often the same: love me. When literature adapts or copies this perspective, the loss of the sense of otherness in human relations as well as the sense of depths in the self is considerable. But the media in the capacity of an idealized other have conditioned us into believing that what it can offer is what we want, that a blissful "identity of perception" is possible between our deepest wishes and its products.

But that the love-me / love-yourself trends of the 1970s Me Decade, as Tom Wolfe names it, were not all-pervasive is evident in another widely acclaimed work of the period, Lisa Alther's *Kinflicks* (1976). Her heroine, Ginny Babcock, qualifies for the present context as a self-character. She grows up in a small Southern town in the sixties, attends college in the North, lives in a commune, marries, but never settles down. Her many adventures comprise a microcosm for reexperiencing the cutting edge of American social history during the last decades. Thus after her cheerleader / athlete-hero phase, she goes through the civil rights, the peace and the women's movements as well as delving into suburbia and the sexual revolution. Many of these episodes are rapid action, Keystone Kops comedy, which lends them a manic, absurdist quality. But we would not want to overlook how Alther has managed to expand Erikson's notion of "identity diffusion" and Lifton's "protean self" to unimagined proportions in filtering so many diverse and apparently contradictory experiences through one character.

Yet the novel's interests lie beyond its exceptional virtuosity. In fact, having read it with entering college classes for several years, I have been impressed (allowing for social amnesia) by how the students respond to the cultural vignettes with less interests than they do to another dimension of the novel entirely. Ginny periodically returns to her roots; and increasingly during the latter part of the novel, these counterbalancing episodes weigh more and more heavily. Upon each return visit, Ginny appears in one of the culturally tinted images of her ever-changing life-style—for example, New England scholar, salt-of-the-earth ecologist, radical lesbian, hausfrau, and so forth. Each of these gives way to the next—sometimes her mother scarcely recognizes her. Ginny, on the other hand, has but scarcely known her mother. One senses that the mirroring transactions leading to identification and the completion of Mahler's separation-individuation phases have been somehow diverted.

Ginny's identity diffusion—and perhaps much of her generation's as well—has not assimilated that nuclear core in the self, the inner mother that would allow her to conduct a meaningful separate existence.

At this point the love-me character might turn to the readers and seduce them into a symbiotic merger, thereby postponing indefinitely the need for a break. But Alther shifts her story into another direction. Mrs. Babcock is dying, and as Ginny faces her failure to form any lasting tie, she recognizes the emptiness of her life and attempts suicide. Failing, she recognizes herself as a survivor. This is made convincing because Ginny and her mother begin spending time together, sorting out their differences, acknowledging their mutual expectations and disappointments. At the end Ginny takes with her, as she contemplates returning to the larger world, the family clock that her mother had sent for in her hospital room and then passed on to her daughter. The clock imparts a sense of family continuity, but also, after all her flights and descents, it will begin anchoring Ginny in time. This novel recognizes as others fail to, that even in our most culturally distracted states, there is an inner dimension to experience, a uniquely personal sphere, which is not swallowed up by narcissistic interests, and so may just be worthy of serious attention.

"Myself must I remake," writes the poet, who must return to sources if he is to create life anew.[84] Some manner of early "narcissistic injury," writes the one psychoanalyst, leads the creative individual "to repair the deformed and unsatisfactory body image, to restore its disrupted self-representation to a unitary whole."[85] "The rudiments of the nuclear self," writes the other psychoanalyst, emerge in part from the mirroring relationship with the mother.[86] Artistic technique itself remains the artist's "innermost secret," writes Freud.[87] Is it possible that as these explorations have elucidated certain aspects of creative processes, they have also afforded a looking-glass glimpse into one of art's oldest secrets?

4

Roland Barthes: Self-Remaking *à la Française*

> There really does exist in the mind a compulsion to repeat which
> overrides the pleasure principle.
> —Freud, *Beyond the Pleasure Principle*

In March of 1980 Roland Barthes died from injuries incurred a month earlier in a Paris traffic accident. Returning from lunch with friends and stepping off a traffic island, he was struck by a laundry van. He suffered injuries to the limbs and head but actually died of pulmonary complications. He was sixty-four. Additional biographical nodes: the previous year, his mother, with whom he had been living, died; his friends felt he was foundering in depression. As an adolescent and intermittently through his thirties he suffered from tuberculosis. During his first year of life, his father died in a naval battle. His exceptional career as man of letters and founding genius of semiology is well known. In the 1960s he attended the seminars of Jacques Lacan. Barthes was personally gentle, kind, retiring, a lifelong bachelor whose subtle attacks on bourgeois capitalism and the literary academy gradually yielded to the cultivation of an erotics of the text. The ways that these mostly familiar details may fit into an interpretive context will grow clear as we examine how the psychoanalysis *in* Barthes's later texts yields a psychoanalysis *of* them.

The three texts I will be drawing on (*The Pleasure of the Text* [1975], *Roland Barthes by Roland Barthes* [1977], and *A Lover's Discourse* [1978]) are as modernist and eclectic as are his appropriations of psychoanalysis. Nonetheless, the figures that clearly dominate are the French Freud, Jacques Lacan, the English analyst D. W. Winnicott, and Freud. Lacan's influence is most evident in *Roland Barthes by Roland Barthes* (hereafter cited as *RB by RB*), while Freud and Winnicott serve as useful referents for the other two texts.

1

That *RB by RB* was influenced by Lacan, especially his seminal essay on the mirror stage, there can be no doubt. This "event" occurs when the infant (six-to-eighteen months) perceives his "specular image" in the mirror. "Unable as yet to walk, or even to stand up, and held tightly as he is by some support [human or artificial], he nevertheless overcomes, in a flutter of jubilant activity, the obstructions of his support and, fixing his attitude in a slightly leaning-forward position, in order to hold it in his gaze, brings back an instantaneous aspect of the image."[1] For Lacan, this psychic event represents a turning point in early development. It occurs before the acquisition of language, and, because the specular image is both a true identification and a false picture of unachieved physical integration, it is both the prototype for subsequent identifications and the source of self-alienation. The specular image is internalized as the "ideal-I," *le moi*, and it initiates by concealment a dialectic with the actual disorganized self (*le corps morcelé*), the fragmented body. The ideal-I, meanwhile, mediates between the organism and the environment. As the "statue in which man projects himself, [or] with the phantoms that dominate him," this psychic agency constitutes the Imaginary, one of three categories, along with the Symbolic Order and the Real, of psychoanalytic data.[2] Clément detects a rough correspondence between ego (Imaginary), supergo (Symbolic Order), and id (Real).[3]

Be that as it may, it is between the mirrored "I" and the fragmented body—between, that is, images of delusional omnipotence and de facto helplessness—where Barthes must create himself as his own self-subsistent subject; but *le sujet*, as John Sturrock writes of Lacan, "is no thing at all and can be grasped only as a set of tensions, or mutations, or dialectical upheavals within a continuous, intentional future-directed process"—which is a fair description of Barthes's text, or at least of the reader's experience of it.[4]

Barthes rephrases, Lacan's Imaginary as the "image-repertoire" or "image-system" concretely displayed through the forty-page family album introducing his autobiography and maintained as his subjective self-representations. The image-system leads to fictional versions of the self, the "fatal substance of the novel, and the labyrinth of levels in which anyone who speaks about himself gets lost" (*RB by RB,* 119–20). His text "must be considered as if spoken by a character in a novel or rather by several characters"; it is not about his ideas but about his resistance to them or his nondirective playfulness toward them, a "*recessive* book . . . which may also gain perspective thereby" (119). As the specular title tells us, he is to start with himself as his own subject matter, the signifier fused with the signified and framed in the Lancanian mirror.

To drive the point playfully home he includes a photo of his mother holding him forward, exactly as Lacan prescribes, with the caption, "The mirror stage: 'that's you' " ("*Le stade du miroir: 'tu es cela,*' ") as if the mother were holding him before an actual mirror to perceive his ideal double. Yet we are being deceived, intentionally or not, for the infant is not looking at his specular or any other self, but at someone's camera, and it, to add another worry, does not reflect an inverted (and hence alien) image but a correct copy of our visual image. Thus, Barthes may be playing as much with Lacan's theories as with his own in this revealing yet oddly impersonal work that

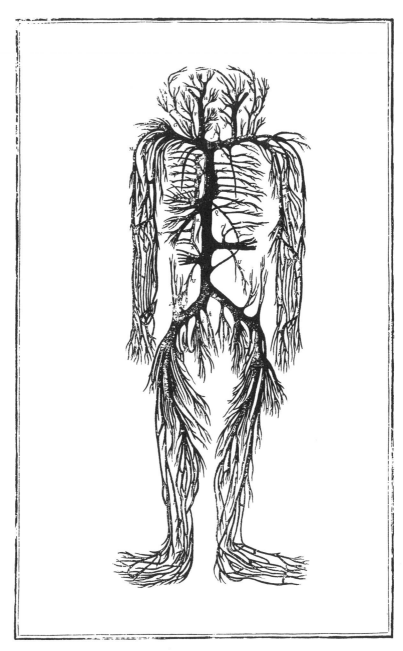

Anatomie. **From** *Roland Barthes by Roland Barthes.*

The mirror stage: "That's you." From *Roland Barthes by Roland Barthes.*

resolutely resists pursuing any content outside the frame of the self as subject. And yet, paradoxically, the effect is the opposite of self-idealization, for by offering "his discourse in fragments" and risking aphorisms along with arrogance (152), he aims to include the ideal-I's opposite: the fragmented body, or at least its equivalent in the disassembled text. The ultimate container is then the reader, who will be converted into the self-bestowing mirror/camera/mother and more besides, for the reader is being given the means to endow the subject with authentic selfhood by recreating a whole person from the textual fragments that serve as the image system. As the Other, the reader is also the source of desire and allied to the Real.

Such are the psychic dialectics that organize the text and determine its perimeters. On the last page appears the partially reconstituted body in the shape of an anatomical drawing of the circulatory system (*Anatomie*). In effect, it is the shape of his text, a self-circulating "writerly" text (118) with many silences, spaces, or simply other systems left out, which the aroused reader fills in according to the modernist mode that accepts all works as incomplete. Opposite the drawing appears the book's aim: "To write the body. Neither the skin nor the muscles, nor the bones, nor the nerves, but the rest: an awkward fibrous, shaggy, raveled thing, a clown's coat" (180). If the reader, *in loco parentis,* cooperates, Barthes will be remirrored and reproduced—in effect, reborn, this time into a more integrated state of wholeness.

The how and whereby is found in Lacan's second category, the Symbolic Order, constituted by language and marked by the child's entrance into the father's society of morals and laws via castration anxieties and oedipal conflicts. We may then puzzle over how Barthes, who never saw his own father, can claim that he sees language (161), unless it is by seeing language that he also sees, that is, constructs, the father. For it is in those cultural zones where the paternalistic *Doxa* (his term for bourgeois stereotypes, platitudes, and pieties) can be opposed with his paradoxes, inversions, and semiology that he may score oedipal triumphs and gain an impressive following.

However, these achievements are all the more unusual by reason of his resorting to cultural displacements in the absence of an actual father to slay in fantasy and reproduce internally. Unable to contend with the author of his own life, he contrives in "The Death of the Author" to establish the author's death by reason of irrelevance.[5] Moreover, as the "destruction of every voice, of every point of origin," the act of writing murders previous acts and conceals its traces. Storytellers are mediators: the notion of an author is merely a modern, self-limiting contrivance. The life is in the narration, the tale, or the text. Far from any "relation of antecedence to his work as a father to his child," the "author is absent." He is "never more than the instance writing."[6] Accordingly, as the "voice loses its origin, the author enters into his own death, writing begins."[7] Without the author, the text is no longer authorized, its meanings no longer dictated by its sources—its authority is cancelled. Thus does the fatherless son pay his debt to paternity. Possibly to allay guilt, the son, as author, authorizes his own death, but not so much authoring his text as dying into it that he may be reborn through it. The text is not his: he is the text's. There, he awaits the reader's discovery. As the reader can proclaim, I read, therefore I am, so Barthes can claim, I am read, therefore I exist—except that it is not his voice, but his text's.[8]

But for him to be more adequately read, so his autobiography implies, readers must assimilate his ideal-I, his image system, and his fragmented body, that is, the total text. The series of photographs that begins with his mother as a young woman alone can be rounded out by his emergence as a complete person: from the Real (mother and wellspring of desire) via the Imaginary (mirror versus fragmented body) and the Symbolic (father's language, Lacan's theories, society's signs), he aspires to self-integration, but only providing that the reader performs a corrective and more inculsive mirroring role. For just as the actual mirror and unacknowledged camera are signifiers of the mother, so the reader (container, bestower) is a replacement for, and almost magical restoration of, that lost signified, the mother. But more than this, the reader must also concur with Barthes's personal semiotic code as idiosyncratic alliance with the Symbolic Order (Lacan's *le nom du père*). In effect, the reader creates Barthes along lines laid down by Barthes himself.

So much for a psychoanalysis governing the text; from it I turn to a psychoanalysis governing the self.

2

While Barthes's autobiography alludes to "a not unhappy youth, thanks to the affection which surrounded me, but an awkward one, because of solitude and material constraint," he is more explicit about the consequences of his unhappiness in *A Lover's Discourse*, where, by way of Winnicott's investigation of maternal loss and creative play, the frame of reference reverts eventually to Freud. His *Beyond the Pleasure Principle*, with its introduction of the death instinct and its paradigmatic anecdote of the *fort-da* game, has been the most cherished text in France's rediscovery of psychoanalysis. But readers emphasize different aspects of that play episode. For Lacan it is the "murdered" object's reappearance in the symbol that sets in motion the "eternalization of desire."[9] For Winnicott it epitomizes the child's discovery of potential space, an "intermediate area of experiencing," wherein play with transitional objects continues into cultural spheres, where reality and illusion must continually be sorted out.[10] For Barthes (and Lacan) it reveals the capacity of language to arbitrarily fill the void of (maternal) absence or death. The game, it may be recalled, was performed by Freud's grandchild in the mother's absence and was aimed at his mastering the weaning process. He would cast out a spool on a string, crying o-o-o, which Freud extrapolated to *fort* (gone); then the child would pull the spool back, to the cry of *da* (there)!

For Freud it exemplifies the tendency to repeat, whereas for Barthes it means that "miming the mother's departure and return" becomes "a staging of language [that] postpones the other's death."[11] To "manipulate absence," therefore, is "to extend the interval when the other might topple sharply from absence into death." This paradigm is applied to Barthes's childhood memories when "I was very early accustomed to be separated from my mother" (*Lover's Discourse*, 14). Specifically, "there were interminable days, abandoned days when the Mother was working far away; I would go, evenings, to wait for her at the Ubis bus stop, Sèvres Babylone; the buses would pass one after the other, she wasn't on any of them." At least not on any of them was the all-good mother who would never have deserted her child in the first place: she left never to return. Unable to recall her or draw her back as the child would with the spool on a string, he construes the paradigm to signify helplessness.

Other differences notwithstanding, both Freud's paradigm and Barthes's memory favor emotional displacement onto an arbitrary sign system. For the one, mother was signified by the spool; for the other, by the bus. But Freud's grandchild, who threw the spool and pulled the string, magically controlled the absent object; while Barthes, who looked for mother when he saw her signifier approach, was undoubtedly humiliated by the failure of his magical control. What had at first seemed to his young mind a natural sign (bus = mother) becomes after painful reflection an entirely arbitrary connection that can include its opposite. But as the bus comes to signify no-mother, the absence experienced as something missing is then likely to take on for the growing boy the additional significance of castration. In his autobiography he describes a white streetcar (a bus, from the look of the photo) that ran from Bayonne to Biarritz, on which he would ride to the beach with his mother, as other photos reveal. To this a caboose was added, which also increased their enjoyment. Now, with both of these subsequently vanished, Barthes laments that "the pleasure which vanishes vanishes for good, there is no substitute for it. Other pleasures come, which replace nothing" (49–50). Other buses, other passengers. But the important bus is the vanished bus, just as the important object is the mother who does not reappear at the expected time; and so the child who is the mother's phallus in Lacan's theories also disappears to be replaced by the more elusively signified sense of castration.

Not so elusive is the association of female with castration, which helps account for the hostility toward mother, in Lacan's reading of the spool episode, as the child's aggressive destruction of her; for Barthes, however, the accent falls on the child's sense of abandonment and his incapacity to recall (recover) the mother. Yet Lacan's more aggressive text is Barthes's subtext, its latent content; moreover, within Barthes's context of loss and lack of any *père de famille* for a fully realized oedipal drama, a secondary association of mother with castration seems all the more probable. Maternal hostility and filial resentment in fact originate in Lacan's mirror stage, when the mother's "that's you" only deceptively endows her child with selfhood while actually keeping him for herself as the longed-for phallus (Lacan eschews normal development, and the fact that he construes femininity as a phallic masquerade has not endeared him to feminists). This apparent Lacanian animus toward the female underlies negative aspects of the ambivalent tie to mother in Barthes's text. For Lacan, the "eternalization of desire" that fuels psychic life is hopelessly narcissistic insofar as it is predicated on the child's desire to fulfill the mother's desire for a phallus, a vicious circle that preempts independent phallic aspirations. Such presuppositions of envy and desire hovering around castration manage simultaneously to render all women suspect and to arouse endless desiring for what can never be.

These desires growing out of an absence take on a life of their own and spread into the arbitrary sign systems of culture, where the lover uneasily awaits an ideal fulfillment. Indeed, the condition of waiting, no matter how short or how long the interval between absence and arrival (or nonarrival and death), becomes the condition par excellence for Barthes's lover. At such times, all signs—the earlier periodical buses, the later telephone ringing in the bar—may signify the beloved's arrival (or the antithesis). At this point Barthes invokes both Freud's paradigm and Winnicott's concept directly: "No doubt I try to deny separation by telephone—as the child fearing to lose its mother keeps pulling on a string; but the telephone wire is not a good transitional object," though it is one charged with meaning—distance and the power of the absent object over the waiting subject (115). And several pages later he connects language with the mother present in the mirror stage ("that's you") and silence with her absence, followed by the subject's painfully drifting "without existence" (168). But the mirror that endows the infant with an early sense of selfhood by reflecting its own sense of well-being, especially during nursing, is no longer Lacan's deceptive-alienating mirror, but the mother as emotionally responding mirror in Winnicott's theory.

This divergence between Lacan and Winnicott in conceptualizing the beginnings of self needs to be clarified because it is truly radical, and, while it is not taken up by Barthes, it must be taken into account by a study concerned with how the self makes itself over by inscribing the text of oneself. Moreover, the astronomical rise of Lacan's authority as a guide in analyzing literary texts prompts a brief digression, for the French Freud has reputedly bridged the gulf between classical psychoanalysis and modern linguistics. But his famous apogem that the "unconscious is structured like a language" may be more convenient than true.[12] Moreover, it is impossible to know how this provocative writer is to be read, for he fools with language so perversely that it is by no means clear whether he is the wise fool and superb ironist or merely sophomorically fooling us. At the very least the skepticism within contemporary psychoanalysis should circumscribe the indiscriminate enthusiasm Lacan has received in literary circles.[13]

Having had my go at Lacan in other pages, present purposes can best be served by referring to an incisive and judicious comparison of Lacan and Winnicott by Michael Eigen.[14] Since Winnicott emphasizes the self-confirming aspects of the mirroring exchanges for the child who not only sees his pleasures reflected in the mother's face but can also feel, "when I look I am seen, so I exist," Eigen recognizes that the movement is one of dramatic unfolding rather than of traumatic rupture.[15] This assumes that the mother's face is not a blank to conceal her own distracted reveries nor that her smile is controlling and manipulating, but that she is a nonintrusive, empathic presence. But, as was suggested earlier, the mother in Lacan is a continuation of the deceptive mirror, and, so, by her smiling response she only reinforces a "quasi-spurious sense of self-sufficiency," which mesmerizes and alienates the child from himself. He becomes an "imitation of himself"; or, more disturbingly, in Juliet Mitchell's gloss, the "self is always like another."[16]

Since Lacan does not distinguish these processes from normal development, or from what Winnicott terms good-enough mothering, pathology becomes universal and normative by default. From a severe reading of Lacan's mirror stage, one could infer that the mother/mirror sets up a narcissistic deficiency in the child and then sets it off on a foredoomed homosexual quest for its ideal (but illusory) double. Because of Lacan's "basic mistrust of the visual," Eigen writes, the child's experience with the mother's face is "paranoid-seductive," and the only recourse lies in the symbolic mode of language; on the other hand, Winnicott's approach, which locates a "matrix of true feeling" in those processes, allows for a "fundamentally fertile symbiosis between word and vision."[17]

It was my (1980) conclusion that Lacan, without sound data from infant observation, ethology, or clinical experience, had reversed the normal sequence, since infants are nursed before they play with their image in a mirror; in so doing he imposed adultomorphic concerns on early childhood phenomena, thereby overlooking Eigen's succinct view of the primary smile as "the home base of the human self." For him the smile introduces a "radically new sort of consciousness," and expresses "all out, spontaneous living through faith."[18] By rendering the visual alien to oneself, Lacan would undermine the child's capacity to face his expanding environment and, by investing it with the primordial aliveness of the mirroring period, to embark on his creative romance with the world, whether or not he/she eventually becomes an artist. Consequently, if Lacan possessed Plato's logical consistency, he, too, would ban artists from his commonwealth for their cultivation of those disturbing images that are faint, distorting shadows of reality.

Lacan's and Winnicott's radically divergent readings of early childhood experiences focus the unresolved tensions in Barthes's work. For him, signs like *bus* and *telephone* are both arbitrary and significant—their ominous meaning for him differs from that assigned by others. He implies a psychic determinism operating through his semiological method. For as mother becomes associated with her absence, and as absence is associated with loss/castration, so may any woman inherit those dangers that can best be avoided by avoiding her whole sex: mother's signifiers attached to a newly minted beloved also signify the original traumas. Accordingly, eschewing all received ideas, the Barthian lover-turned-semiologist will take nothing for granted, nothing on faith—everything is to be read and decoded afresh. For it is both logical and fitting that his fascination with semiotic codes should derive from undoing and avoidance.

If for another person the bus signifies to-work or to-home-from-work, for him it spells the all-important other, and, after childhood, always in an ambience of absence. "I take a seat, alone, in a café; people come over . . . But the other is absent . . . let the other appear, take me away, like a mother who comes looking for her child"(17). Just as the *fort-da* game has been construed as a metonymy of loss and recovery, of mastery through play/symbol-formation/language, so I think Barthes's paradigm of waiting and seeking signifiers of the absent other in the cultural environment can be taken as a paradigm for his semiotic system, which ideally traverses the arc between brilliant originality and sheer contrivance.

What, for example, better epitomizes the artificial rituals of bourgeois capitalism than the bus that hauls one to and from work? But Barthes's lonely presence at the bus stop renders the signifier both arbitrary and ominous as the conveyor of hidden meaning (mother/no-mother; phallus/no-phallus, etc.). Because words are rooted in desire, thriving uncertainly in the void left by his mother/mirror, Barthes "sees" language ("that's you") or, more precisely, its terrain of signifiers that may help him construct a new system of desire for the father hidden in the Symbolic Order. Language thus allows for the possibility of a change in the object of desire; its arbitrariness permits a freedom in interpreting. And however overdetermined, the sheer visual presence of print reassuringly counters the felt absence of the mother, and semiology yields to, or rather is fulfilled by, an erotics that seeks a nonspecific joyous bliss in the text.

And if the bus-missing mother finally cannot be controlled in order for painful loss to be avoided, then at least the world he has lost her to can be controlled when its meanings are rendered arbitrary and compliant to his readings. The mastery is impressive, if displaced; yet anxiety persists. The unpredictability of experience is replicated by the uncertainty of once-familiar textual signifiers, and to readers of his own texts Barthes becomes himself a kind of felt absence. Texts, like mirrors, may reverse or affirm an opposite when they reflect; thus, as ideal-I or self-mirror, his text "reflects" the mother's absence; as segmented body or phallus, his text "reflects" castration.

Similarly, as the child, Roland never quite surmounted maternal absence, so the mature Barthes succeeds only in reversing the roles from passive to active. Thus his later years are lived with his mother as he travels between Paris and Bayonne, between work and holiday, while she presumably is the one who awaits the trains or buses that will signify his arrival. Other graver intervals of tuberculosis evidently complicated the processes of loss/recovery and separation/individuation. One speculates that the actual or felt presence of the mother served him as an important mirror of self-continuity and made possible the repeated acts of self-reconstitution, whether it be during her absence or following his illnesses. In a difficult passage late in his autobiography, Barthes wonders how the writing of his book should be possible only from the mirror's rays that reverberate in him. And he concludes that "all this happens ... through the Mother, present next to the mirror" (153).[19] Here, the child as mirror becomes real in the mother's presence (as her reflection), but then goes blank in her absence. That is finally why he must constitute himself in the Lacanian mode through his own sign system, and that is also why such an act of self-begetting becomes the deeper meaning of his beguiling title, *Roland Barthes by Roland Barthes*. To mirror himself he must appropriate the mother's mirror without becoming her. He is to become not the parent but the mirror that produces the child's image and the writer who portrays its segmented body. The parent is now that indeterminate reader, whose act of reading best reconstitutes him. But for this to happen, the desired reader must exhibit Winnicott's good-enough mothering in the empathic responses that correct the cracks and distortions wrought by Lacanian mirroring.

3

Returning to the peculiar circumstances of his fatal accident, we recall the previous death of his mother and his own decline toward apathy and depression. The laundry van arrives on the scene as a signifier of something more terribly arbitrary than absence or loss, something like the death instinct itself. With the mirror/mother as container of self recently deceased, the body is once more reduced to *le corps morcelé* and the need to effect a reconstitution of self is revived, but now there is no mirroring object for *le moi* to find itself through. Perhaps a long-deferred fantasy (suggestive of a fusion of the self with the female other) is reawakened: "Keats, half in love with easeful death," he had quoted, adding, "then I have this fantasy: a gentle hemorrhage which flows from no specific point in my body, an almost immediate consumption" (from "I am engulfed, I succumb" (12). And so a month after the accident, after release from intensive care, the obituary merely states "pulmonary complications."

After Lacan's dialectics have been played off between self and double, between ideal-I and fragmented body, and after Freud's repetition model of loss and recovery in the *fort-da* game overrides Winnicott's more hopeful scenario of transitional phenomena, we revert to that most paradoxical of Freudian texts from *Beyond the Pleasure Principle*: "*the aim of all life is death*."

5
Pip and Peer

What we call the beginning is often the end
And to make an end is to make a beginning.
—T. S. Eliot, "Four Quartets"

1

The unique place occupied by art in human life consists in the fact that it belongs neither to mind nor to nature, yet represents both. D. W. Winnicott, in a classic paper whose depths are still being plumbed, traces art and cultural products generally as emerging from an intermediate zone of transitional phenomena in the emotional spaces between infant and mother, which expand during the first phases of separation and continue throughout life as inner and outer reality are continually being sorted out.[1] Within this framework, I have been examining various specific processes—most prominently those subjective and objective poles or regulators to which I now return in order to trace their operations in two works of the mid–nineteenth century.

In Charles Dickens's *Great Expectations*, the question of origins haunts the life of Pip, although it appears as if the issue had been irrevocably settled on the first page.[2] "As I never saw my father or my mother ... my first fancies regarding what they were like, were unreasonably derived from their tombstones" (1). His own name, by which he will be known throughout his life, is what his "infant tongue" could make of Philip Pirrip, the father's name passed on to him. But one's parents, and the "five little stone lozenges" of his siblings, are not so readily buried. Pip has been raised "by hand" by a surviving older sister (Mrs. Joe) and her simple-natured and decent spouse, Joe Gargery, a blacksmith, who treats Pip like a dear friend. Called Dickens's "grimmest attack on the maternal image," Mrs. Joe is generous both with the infamous cane, euphemistically known as the Tickler, and with the heavy coating of guilt with which she plasters the family bread.[3] Since hunger in all its ramifications will figure prominently in the story, it is not accidental that on Mrs. Joe's "coarse apron" was a "square impregnable bib in front, that was stuck full of pins and needles." Holding the bread against her bib to cut it, she sometimes left a pin or a needle in the slice that young Pip or poor Joe got in their mouths.

And so with Pip virtually orphaned twice over, the ground is seeded for a robust family romance to spring into bloom, for he soon learns, contrary to his bleak origins, that he has great expectations. Miss Havisham, "an immensely rich and grim lady who lived in a large and dismal house," has sent for him; and "for anything we can tell," Mrs. Joe exclaims, "this boy's fortune may be made by his going" there (48–49).

The sham lurking in this lady's name does not conceal any lack of great wealth—she is heiress to a brewery fortune—but rather the inner poverty of a life built around wealth. She receives Pip in the white satins, lace, and silk of her wedding dress, worn for a day that never arrived: she was jilted, and many years have passed, despite her efforts to arrest time. All of this Pip sees quite clearly: "the bride within the bridal dress had withered like the dress, and like the flowers, and had no brightness left but the brightness of her sunken eyes" (54). He is made to play cards with the lovely girl, Estella, and later is teased and humiliated by her, though smitten in love at the same time. More important, this other world that has revealed itself to him also reveals the humble nature of his own; after relieving his "injured feelings" by kicking the brewery wall and twisting his hair, he returns home, now aware that he is a "common labouring-boy" in a "low-lived bad way."

Forced to speak of his visit, he draws a fine picture of having "cake and wine on gold plates." But having lied to Mrs. Joe and Mr. Pumblechook, he will, in keeping with his illusory expectations, next lie to himself. And when he soon finds that a wealthy, anonymous patron has taken a keen interest in his advancement, he extrapolates more from his golden fantasies than from his sparse knowledge of either Miss Havisham or her adopted daughter, Estella, that they are the ones. Taking leave of the embittered old woman, he attributes her magical powers to the "crutch stick" playing around him, "as if she, the fairy godmother who had changed me, were bestowing the final gift" (152). Here is the fiendish Tickler once removed and transformed by Pip's hungry fancies into a magic wand.[4]

Thereafter, Pip's "golden fantasy" takes on the lineaments of the classical family romance:[5]

> She had adopted Estella, she had as good as adopted me, and it could not fail to be her intention to bring us together. She reserved it for me to restore the desolate house, admit the sunshine into the dark rooms, set the clocks a-going and the cold hearths a-blazing, tear down the cob-webs, destroy the vermin—in short, do all the shining deeds of the young knight of romance, and marry the Princess. (223)

The very trappings of the house made up for him a "rich, attractive mystery, of which I was the hero." First he must become a gentleman and learn to spurn his lowly beginnings; meanwhile Estella will be transformed into a "brilliant and beautiful" woman. They walk together in the "ruined garden" now magically "all in bloom" for Pip, with Estella's hand on his shoulder. As Pip drifts into "stronger enchantment," he listens to Mrs. Havisham feverishly egging him on—"Love her, love her, love her. If she favours you, love her. If she wounds you, love her. If she tears your heart to pieces"—and he cannot avoid thinking that the words pouring from her sound like a "curse" (231).

Could the fairy godmother be a witch after all? She places "some of the most beautiful jewels from her dressing-table into Estella's hair, and about her bosom and arms"; but later, when all the secrets are known, and Pip's disillusionment is complete, she will claim, "You have made your own snares. I never made them." But the truth is not so simple: he made his own snares when he invested in his elaborate fantasies, or at least blinded himself to those of others, for the vindictive old woman was clearly out to snare him, too. And it is to the credit of Estella, the snare itself, that far from luring Pip on, she consistently warned him and mocked those grandiose expectations he would eventually call his "poor dreams." That he was undeterred, nonetheless, only magnifies the power of a golden fantasy such as the family romance to determine human destiny.

But the power of great fiction over the golden fantasy also manifests itself when the midnight side is given equal due, and the decisive theme of poverty, be it Pip's low birth, Estella's deprivations, or Miss Havisham's emotional impoverishment—all with their distinctive accompaniments of self-hatred, guilt, and aggression—erupts through the flimsy texture of romance.

As the fairy godmother is more and more reduced to the sham-parent, another possibility, hitherto minimized through shame and guilt, comes to the fore and returns us to the question of origins, to the graveyard, and to the origin of Pip's adventures. "My first most vivid and broad impression of the identity of things, seems to me to have been gained on a memorable raw afternoon towards evening." He is near the tombstones of "Philip Pirrip, late of this parish, and also Georgiana, wife of the above," and of their several infant children. In the sense that these are the good, original parents of early memory who might have offered an alternative to Pip's poverty, and in the sense that they are also the bad parents who have abandoned him, they set the stage for the family romance to be played out in the social sphere of low and high, and in the affective sphere of hate and love, though the former is largely disavowed.

For Pip at this moment is only feeling a sense of abandonment: "The small bundle of shivers growing afraid of it all and beginning to cry." And strangely, this original need to be rescued is answered not by the family romance already sketched in, but by another kind entirely, one that will indeed underwrite his great expectations and lead him ultimately back to reality. It is worth noting whence this second version arises:

> "Hold your noise!" cried a terrible voice, as a man started up from the graves at the side of church porch. "Keep still, you little devil, or I'll cut your throat!"
>
> A fearful man, all in coarse grey, with a great iron on his leg. A man with no hat, and with broken shoes, and with an old rag tied round his head . . . who limped and shivered, and glared and growled.

The man turns him upside down to shake out his pockets, and, in so doing, reverses Pip's field of vision, the church steeple now under his feet. This odd epiphany, a critic observes, ironically changes the viewpoint, "reversing the accepted senses of innocence and guilt, success and failure."[6] It also prepares us for a reverse version of the family romance, because the convict, out of gratitude to Pip for stealing him food, remembers the episode in later life, when he is freed and becoming a man of wealth in Australia. It is the convict Magwitch who has adopted Pip and set his great expectations astir. And it is this discovery, when Pip has become a gentleman, that effectively destroys the other family romance, the golden one involving Miss Havisham and Estella. But it is also through his finally coming around to accepting the lowly convict as his genuine father and committing himself to the other's survival and well-being, even when it comes down to humiliation and further imprisonment, that Pip succeeds in weaning himself from the golden fantasy and reconciling himself to his fellow human beings.

The process is so painful that it literally scorches him. He returns to the rooms of Miss Havisham, having earlier cleaned up his mistaken notions of her grandiose plans, and finds her at the fire, where her old wedding dress suddenly catches flame. She runs toward him, and in subduing her his arms are badly burned, though to Miss Havisham the accident will prove fatal.

While having his burns dressed by his friend, Pip is exposed to more searing truths, not about his origins but about those of the shining princess, Estella, adopted by Miss Havisham but brought up as a lady for unalloyed motives of revenge. She was originally brought to the old woman by the lawyer Jaggers, who had represented Estella's mother in court. This woman, visible in the novel as Jaggers's cook, Molly, had murdered another woman out of jealousy over a man she had been having an affair with, and that man turns out to be none other than Magwitch. Thus is Estella born of a convict and a murderess.

Within the narrative these revelations do several things: they advance the theme of "the dark origins of even the most respectable fortunes";[7] they draw Estella, via Pip's adoptive father, Magwitch, into the family orbit as an incestuously tinged libidinal object; and they complete the criss-crossing pattern of origins in which one family romance adoption is unraveled by another. The former lifted Pip upward via a vision of the female as fairy godmother; the latter dragged him down via the male as convict-benefactor. But the second one also introduces the image of the sexual father, easily connected in the child's mind as well as in prudish Victorian sensibility with "criminal" behavior, either as perpetrating an assaultive act or an illicit sexual one. In other words, the true version of Estella's origins involves a primal scene, and it is this ineluctable condition of human origins that plays off against the family-romance versions of noble adoption. Moreover, this process of inner discovery is woven into the novel's narrative structure.

But at this point in the revelations of the novel, both Pip and his reader are still adrift between the devil and the deep blue sea. The high version of origins has been demolished along with Pip's great expectations, but the lowly version is hardly more satisfactory, for while its elements of violence and illegitimacy touch on the darker side of Victorian England, the novel is more than a social document, and the narrative does not stop there. A further version of origins is attempted, one that modified the other two. First it would be helpful to explore some of the darker elements in Pip's character, those that connect with the sinister Magwitch version of origins and thus enable it to be recognized as colored by primal-scene fantasy: distortions that can no better foster Pip's emancipation from his past than could the opposite fantasy, involving sexless idealization.[8]

Accurately perceived, the terrifying primal scene of childhood becomes the act of tender / sensual copulation calibrated for conception. So comprehended, it serves to clarify the child's often primitive distortions and fanciful theories about sex. While both of these extremes often remain on the periphery of the story, they also impinge on Pip's anxious consciousness.

Consistently, they point to the general role of aggression in the novel and to Pip in particular, both as innocently victimized and as ambiguously guilty. Clearly he is the victim of Magwitch's desperate assault, as he is of Mrs. Joe's maternal aggression. But in two other episodes his participation is more uncertain: one involves the burning he receives form his sham-patroness; the other a roughing-up at the hands of the mean-spirited Pohick, whom Pip had had removed as porter at Miss Havisham's. Pohick, in fact, confesses to the murderous attack on Mrs. Joe with the leg iron that Magwitch had removed with the file stolen for him by Pip. The connecting line may be thin, but not so thin that it cannot be traced by Pip's never-admitted aggression toward the woman armed with pins and needles across the unassailable apron over her breast.[9] In his fistfight, provoked by the "pale young gentleman" who will become his dearest friend, Pip finds he had "never been so surprised in my life, as when I let out the first blow, and saw him lying on his back" (87).

But if outward aggressiveness is displayed only to be disavowed, the self-torments of inward aggression are pervasive. Pip never tires of detailing the agonies of guilt, both deserved and undeserved, which he suffers from his conscience and the world. The oral component is evident both in Mrs. Joe's repelling breast and in Magwitch's desperate hunger, for which Pip feels responsible. Miss Havisham's morbid speculations contribute to this theme when she pictures herself dead and spread on a large table, with her acquaintances gathered round to devour the corpse (rescued from the fire, she is laid out half-cooked on the same table); and Pip has a vivid hallucination of Miss Havisham "hanging . . . by the neck" from a "great wooden beam" in the abandoned brewery (60). These fragmentary images of mutilated maternal figures, especially in view of the fact that Estella's conception is surrounded by the murder of a woman, suggest primitive fantasies interfering with coming to terms with origins.

There is, in addition, much uncertainty in Pip's mind as to whether Estella is real or unreal: a celestial "star" of fancy, as her name signifies, or a flesh-and-blood woman. For how can human life emerge from an act of violence? Lacking sexual awareness and models, Pip is in a quandary. Nonetheless, the route to mastery of fears allied to disavowed aggressions lies along the road of recognizing and identifying with the lowly but potent father. That Dickens saw his own father enter a debtors' prison and suffered the abandonment and humiliation of drudgery in a blacking factory may serve as a reminder that while the world of Pip is invented it is also close to home. But the fact that the novel's ending forks in two directions—one in which he gets a sadder-but-wiser Estella, the other in which he accepts lifelong bachelorhood—indicates the power of fantasy to vie on equal terms with the sense of reality.

Pip's more subtle forms of aggression involve his treatment of the faithful friend and protector, Joe Gargery, and the sweet and honest girl, Biddy, when he deserts them for his great expectations in London. His final disillusionment comes after he deceives himself into believing that he can go home again and recover those good familial objects he had mistreated and neglected. Here Dickens atones for a great deal of his sentimental reputation, for Pip, after a long illness, returns on the very day that Joe weds Biddy. Overcome at first, he nevertheless blesses their union. Returning eleven years later, he makes the final important discovery both for himself and for this study, when, looking in on the Gargerys, he discovers—himself.

> There, smoking his pipe in the old place by the kitchen firelight, as hale and as strong as ever, though a little grey, sat Joe; and there, fenced into the corner with Joe's leg, and sitting on my own little stool looking at the fire, was—I again!
> "We give him the name of Pip for your sake, dear old chap," said Joe, delighted when I took another stool by the child's side." (466)

Finally, then, the real (as any) parents in the loving pair of Joe and Biddy are found, human procreation is affirmed, and, with those accomplishments plus the dissolution of Pip's "poor dreams," he can be born at last. The new edition of Pip is the reconstituted self brought about by the delayed psychological birth into individuation.

The novel effectively reproduces what Freud's paper described as "the passing of the Oedipus complex." The paternal function has been recognized, modified, and assimilated; early libidinal objects have been relinquished, and Dickens is surely exercising mature artistic judgment as well as psychological insight when, in his original ending, he has Pip return to his foreign business enterprises and prospective bachelorhood. The ill-advised, altered ending, in which Pip reclaims a mellowed Estella on the old brewery grounds, must strike the reader as both artistically sentimental and psychologically dishonest, if only because of Estella's link with the sexual father and the lingering sense one has, despite Pip's progress, that sexuality remains a bit too closely associated with aggression.

2

In *Peer Gynt*, as in *Great Expectations*, the pattern of the character's life shapes the pattern of the work itself, being in both cases a circular one of departure, extensive travels, and eventual return. The center around which Pip and Peer gyrate is not only home but woman. Peer's Aase, the "bad" mother, like Pip's Mrs. Joe, eventually gives way to the plain but devoted, Biddy-like love-object, Solveig, whom Peer marries, abandons, and returns to; he finds her still waiting, unlike Pip, who returns too late. Nonetheless, both women provide essential insights for the wandering heroes to integrate. Both Pip and Peer suffer damage to their emerging sense of self. Now that Pip's great expectations have been explored, the distinctive features about Peer's can be foregrounded.

His defects stem from lack of father and from ambivalence in a mother who praises him as superior in one breath and denigrates him as a "beast" in the next. His seductive and grandiose tall tales, which the mother finds herself excited by, are also rejected by her as lies, and it is in his impacted lying that Ibsen offers clues to what we might now term superego defects and impaired ego boundaries. "I could be a king—an emperor!" Peer asserts; and later, "I can ride through the air like the wind."[10]

As this expansive grandiosity is played out, Peer finds himself sinking lower and lower among the orders of life, until in the troll realm he tells the King of Dovre's daughter that he is no less than a king's son himself. The trolls proceed to adopt Peer as one of their rulers, and he proceeds to adopt their motto: "to thine own self be all-sufficient." Thus, in this alternate reality a family romance is projected and, also (as in the case of Pip), critically examined. Peer can realize his great expectations of a "troll bride and a well-run kingdom," but only at the negation of his human potential. When the trolls turn on him, it is to pluck out his eyes; he narrowly escapes, only to encounter the voice of the enigmatic Great Boyg, which appears to represent an answer to the very question of self-identity that Peer consistently has circumvented.

We are briefly back in the area of self explored earlier. The Gyntian self becomes known as the "regiment / of wishes, appetites, and desires . . . / the sea of ambitions, needs and demands." Thus Peer seeks gold to "make myself an Emperor," and hence become the central object of his own family romance, his own ideal mirror image. But before he has discovered that there is no core to the onion rings of his personality, his quest takes him deeper into the maelstrom of self-centeredness where:

> . . . a man's himself with a vengeance;
> Himself, and nothing else whatsoever;
> The self full sail, full speed ahead.
> Each one shut up in the cask of self,

Immersed in a fermentation of self,
Hermetically sealed with the being of self,
The barrel pickled in a bath of self.[11]

There in the asylum he is hailed a hero and crowned Emperor of Self by the lunatics. Shortly before this climax, Peer had encountered the second enigmatic representation of the self in the great Sphinx, whose riddle Peer responds to as though it were also a concretization of the great Boyg. Yet the riddle is not posed by the Sphinx, but by the German behind it, who will conduct Peer to the asylum; and it is not the Sphinx's riddle, either, that is posed, but the same one asked of the Boyg earlier: Who are you? The Boyg answers, "Myself," and Peer, who cannot answer in kind, must go round and round. But the Sphinx's riddle is, What goes on four legs, then two, and then three? To which the answer is man, that is, the cycle of human life, which is also solar or circular (from womb to tomb) but can be a progression. The Sphinx, in its composite form of lion and woman, has been interpreted as a primal scene, that is, a disguised adult sexual relationship, and the correct perception of it is not only copulation / birth, but a new step in the direction of self-awareness for the child. However, since, in the play, both Boyg and Sphinx address different aspects of the self, some further clarification is called for.

Other composites of human and beast were introduced at the outset of the play. The first occurs when Peer makes up a tale of wounding a buck, only to be carried off on the beast's antlers and pitched into a lake, out of which their combined image swells up, narcissistically, to greet them. Peer then acts out the tale of Peer and the buck, with his mother borne aloft on his shoulders and swung about in an exciting, dizzying way until they are out of breath. Both the tale and the replay may evoke defective or revised primal scenes in which Peer's bodily (animal) self is his own sexual object, in the buck episode, and then is employed as a composite in order to usurp the role of father with the mother, in the reenactment of the buck episode with his mother. So doing, he makes himself, rather than the parents, the key to sexuality. But both Peer / buck and Peer / buck-with-mother are deficient as sexual composites, and he travels in circles, celebrating the marvelous Gyntian self repeatedly exposed as a grandiose void. Only with the prospect of death at the next crossroads does he manage to find his way back to Solveig, who has preserved a favorable image of him.

If the Boyg stands for the missing nuclear self, which can lead to the consistency and commitments of a self-identity, the Sphinx stands for early object-relations, which must also be acknowledged before they can be internalized and consolidated as part of the self. Both self-representations and object-representations combine in forming the whole person. An absent father plus an ambivalent mother add up to narcissistic damage, which handicaps Peer's development and fosters the grandiose expectations embedded in the family romance. This extreme investment in the subjectivity of an as-if self and an alternate reality, Ibsen shows, leads to the madness of the asylum, where neither the riddles of self nor the mysteries of the world can be resolved. Still, Peer, like Pip, is given a certain reprieve as he returns finally to the place of origins. His mother has long since been buried; and while Solveig retains an image of his potential wholeness within her, it remains for Peer to realize that the bad-mother image does not reside in every woman. This Ibsen grants him when he cries out before Solveig, near the end, "My mother, my wife—you innocent woman!" Clearly, a personal riddle, involving the self and other, has been resolved. The light of dawn breaks over them, as Peer is stretched is Solveig's lap, still the eternal son, but no longer in constant flight, and, if mortal, also human.

The patterns uncovered in these two works support the larger patterns traced in the creative development of Joyce and Lawrence. A family romance in its positive, radiant form is inaugurated but soon collapses into its opposite, as presumably primitive aggressive drives or festering injuries to the self cannot be contained within an idealized version of origins. The dark side of the family romance reveals the vampire, the witch, or the demonic visage of the mother-goddess. From these two works, this darker aspect apparently may also reveal the criminal underside of society or the troll underworld of nature. Within this darkness are intimations, as well, of the primal scene, as a source of childhood fears but also as a clue to adult sexuality, the dawning recognition of which carries creative processes to their final stage.

6
Dialectical Creativity and the Self:
Thomas Hardy's *The Mayor of Casterbridge*

This 1886 novel begins with what has come to be called the crime of Orestes or the primal crime, to distinguish it from the crime of Oedipus.[1] Michael Henchard, a young, out-of-work hay trusser, takes his wife and their infant daughter into a country-fair tent where he proceeds to get drunk on "furmity," a grain mixture laced with rum, in which state of intoxicated desperation he auctions off his wife and child for £5. Waking in cold sobriety, he takes an oath of abstinence for as many years as he has lived. Irascible, impulsive, and driven, he nonetheless manages to discipline himself like an alcoholic on a dry drunk to such an extent that he rises in the corn trade to become the leading citizen of Casterbridge and, eventually, its mayor. Although believing that Susan has perished in some foreign place along with her sailor benefactor, Henchard does not take another wife, having, as he later comes to see, traded love for ambition on that fatal night in the tent.

While still at the peak of his manly power, with its supports just cracking before an inevitable if unforeseen collapse, he encounters three newcomers to Casterbridge. These are his abandoned wife, Susan, who mistakenly believes that her second "husband" has been lost at sea; her daughter, Elizabeth-Jane, whom Henchard will try to claim as his own, though she is, in fact, his stepdaughter, named after the original child, who died soon after the auction; and Farfrae, an open-hearted and capable young Scot, whom Henchard persuades to become his business partner.

Henchard reclaims Susan by remarrying her in order to avoid any trace of former scandal, and, while thwarting Farfrae's courtship of Elizabeth-Jane, he does not succeed in preventing the Scot from succumbing to the charms of his own former mistress, Lucetta, recently settled in town. Susan dies shortly after their remarriage, and Henchard belatedly turns to Lucetta, who recoils from him upon learning of his past. Farfrae then marries Lucetta. Henchard follows poor advice on the harvest and, in a series of deals, soon goes bankrupt.

The two men's futures can be symbolized by the turning of fortune's wheel or by another Shakespearean image, that of the two well-buckets: as one dips down, the other heaves up. For Farfrae not only marries Henchard's mistress but also takes over the corn business, moves into the other's house, and, before long, is chosen mayor of Casterbridge; meanwhile, Henchard rents a room in a squalid section of town and gets hired back as a common laborer. Around this time his oath of abstinence lapses, and he returns to his former drinking habits. But though wet or dry, his character remains constant, and his schemes of revenge turn out to be as futile as his other endeavors.

Nonetheless, the damaging secrets of his affair with Lucetta leak out and draw to a climax on the evening following the visit of a "Royal Personage" to Casterbridge. This event is the zenith of Lucetta's social ambitions as the new mayor's wife, but it is Henchard's nadir, for he intrudes, in his soiled and ragged condition, into the ceremonies, thereby compelling Farfrae to forcibly remove him from the assemblage of citizenry and embarrassed royalty. But on that same evening, Lucetta will suffer her downfall, and Farfrae will receive a shock to his complacency. The love letters of Lucetta to Henchard have fallen into the hands of the townfolk, and they decide to make sport of her shameful past by exposing her to a "skimmity-ride." They mount "two images on a donkey, back to back, their elbows tied to one another's." These are effigies of Henchard and Lucetta: "She's facing the head, and he's facing the tail."[2] They are driven in a procession through the streets of town, passing under the windows of the mayor's house. Farfrae has been conveniently called out of town, but Lucetta cannot help seeing the "procession—a scandal—an effigy of me, and him!" (*Mayor of Casterbridge*, 273). This witnessing breaks her spirit. She suffers convulsions, grows delirious, and dies before morning—not, however, before confessing to her distraught husband, returned too late to save her. These two episodes—the visit of the "Royal Personage" and the fatal skimmity-ride—are both explicitly linked by Hardy's narration and the climactic "multiple catastrophe," toward which he pitched the novel.[3] They are also linked in time—as ceremonies of daytime and nighttime. Is it feasible, then, to expect them also to be linked through the creative process?

The sexual pair mounted on the donkey and driven through the night streets clearly recreates a flagrant sexual scene, but, as implied by its lethal power, more than a simple one. Given the circumstances of the times, it may be argued that the social motive would be sufficient to account for the devastating effect, and while I don't believe that social motives are ever exhaustive, I am not sure that such a viewpoint can be countered directly, especially here. But I can proceed indirectly by taking note of voyeuristic motifs in the novel in respect to Henchard, who spies on Farfrae, first with Lucetta and later with Elizabeth Jane. Equally suggestive is the novel's inherent concern with origins, not on the part of Henchard and Farfrae, who suddenly just appear without personal histories, but on the part of Elizabeth-Jane.

To be sure, her quest is muted. For a good part of the novel she is kept in the dark—actually misled—about the identity of her father. Only near the end is the question resolved for her, when the wandering sailor, Newson, returns and persists, against Henchard's deceits, to reclaim his daughter. This event is associated with her liberation from the false hold on her by Henchard and with the courting of her by the widowed Farfrae. The novel closes shortly after their marriage, which signifies a renewal of life in keeping with the Novel's affinity for future-oriented pairings in the comic mode. But the stronger interest by far is in the tragic story and in how the origins of Henchard's character that stem from the primal crime determine his downfall.

The sexual pair on the donkey evoke a primal scene depicted in terms of the infantile distortions that have accompanied it historically ever since the Sphinx represented male and female joined in a monstrous composite. The donkey clearly conveys the bestial side of the act, as well as a sort of dumbness of purpose, or the child's uncertainty, since the figures are not genitally joined, but facing away from each other and connected by their elbows. Yet it is terrifying, nocturnal, and produced, as it were, from below, by the less socialized common folk. In doing so they are able to vent their rage against both the gentry for keeping them down and the parents for excluding them as children from scenes of imagined pleasure.

Yet for all its distortions, the import of the message is clear. Perhaps this brutally painful version of human origins can become as destructive as it does because the hapless characters astride the sexual donkey have implicitly endorsed another, more agreeable version. Lucetta has risen through coquetry and marriage to the pinnacle of her society and had earlier in the day entertained hopes that her husband would be knighted, making her a lady. This bit of fairy-tale magic did not come about: she did not receive a family-romance adoption by title. And Henchard, who had risen from the humbled orders to become mayor, realizes how illusory his career has been all along when he attempts to impose himself like the childish emperor in his not-so-new clothes before the Royal-Personage. Here is a stark glimpse of Henchard's aspirations for acceptance, if not quite literal adoption, by the aristocracy.

But both the family romance flamed by eros as well as the family romance spurred by ambition are thwarted, and the debased sexual couple on the donkey parading through the evening streets offers a grotesquely objectified counterpart to Lucetta's and Henchard's grandiose fantasies. One does not so easily escape origins, the commoners remind them. In some obscure fashion, beyond the scope of this study to investigate, the aggressive nature of this primal scene depiction may be related to the fact that Lucetta is with child at the time. In effect, the donkey effigies operate as an attack on the maternal image, similar to Henchard's betrayal by the auction of Susan. Perhaps the idealized mother is being reproached by a reminder of her "lowly" sexual functions.

Where the self fits into this framework can now be clarified by returning to the primal crime that precipitated the events in the novel. What Michael Henchard did in auctioning his wife and daughter was to destroy vital ties that he would struggle in vain to restore throughout his life; but he also simultaneously affirmed self-autonomy. Having spurned the essential components of love and trust as the basis for lasting human relationships, he asserts the primacy of the grandiose self to be implemented by ruthless ambition (perhaps made acceptable to consciousness only via a family-romance fantasy of ultimate moral legitimacy and justification through recourse to a higher, benevolent power).

The instinctual mode by which his actions may be most clearly understood seems to be primitive orality. Henchard's dependency on the woman for nurture—be it physical or emotional—is denied at the auction, where the rum-laced furmity warms him into an all-too-brief illusion of heroic self-sufficiency. And his subsequent rise to power can be attributed to the same oral drives displaced onto acquiring domination over the production of the grain that is the essential substance of life. But, since the drive is no longer mediated by a human object, it remains blind, growing more ruthless and more self-alienating.

Thus, in his desolation, Henchard turns to the warmhearted Scot, Farfrae, whom he loves with such intense ambivalence that critics have wondered about the latent homosexuality in his character; indeed, this is part of the inheritance of the crime of Orestes.[4] Destruction of the tie to woman raises the prospect of male libidinal ties, and Henchard loves Farfrae too much to press his revenge to the end.

But it does seem inadvisable to psychologize characters too far in terms of their latent propensities, especially when there is a clearer field to explore. A psychology of the self would shift the focus away from the drive aspect of a relationship to the question of whether certain drives may not function in order to maintain a sense of cohesive aliveness within the nuclear self. Certainly, Henchard's ruthlessness suggests that his perception of external reality is conditioned by a sense of inner deadness. This elusive state is dramatized in one of the most powerful episodes of the novel. It takes place following his scene of humiliation and the death of Lucetta. He has been driven to the literal edge of suicide, and gazes in despair over a pool of water:

> There slowly became visible a something in the circular pool formed by the wash of centuries; the pool he was intending to make his death-bed. At first it was indistinct by reason of the shadow from the bank; but it emerged and took shape, which was that of a human body, lying stiff and stark upon the surface of the stream . . . he perceived with a sense of horror that it was himself . . . his actual double was floating as if dead. (290–91)

Here is, of course, the mirror of Narcissus externalizing the inner deadness that Henchard has for so long denied and displaced onto his relationships, for the destruction of the primal tie with his wife and all she stands for as woman can now also be seen as a destruction of part of the self, which he vainly hopes will be restored through fantasies of power, rebirth, and bonding with Farfrae. The reflection also suggests his debased sexual drives as well as a warded-off wish to merge with an all-enveloping object. But at first he believes a sort of miracle has saved him, though in this, as in almost everything else, he is deceived.

If the "drowned" effigy is one double for Henchard, then Farfrae is clearly another: as the good, disavowed components of the self, Farfrae relives Henchard's life as a true mirror of self-development. He is decent, considerate, and fair in his business dealings, warm and sincere in his private affairs, not in his own right a perfect or ideal self, but a true one, such as might have prospered within Henchard had he not violated both Susan and himself at the outset.[5] Paradoxically, the mirror of Farfrae's own natural goodness reflects Henchard's incorporative and aggressive orality. At the wedding party for Elizabeth-Jane and Farfrae, which signals the end of any hope of a loving object-relation for Henchard, he appears at the back door with a gift. It is a caged goldfinch that, going unnoticed, is allowed to starve. This ill-fated gift of self both contrasts with the singing Scot and anticipates Henchard's imminent death by refusing any further interest in nourishment. It is the death of Narcissus, who stared into his image until he, too, died of starvation, but the classical myth is only emblematic of a fully fleshed-out human tragedy.[6]

The theme of narcissisitc injury as impetus to creativity may make readers wonder how Dickens and Hardy, while operating out of a rigid nineteenth-century, class-bound society, nonetheless implicitly observed later psycho-analytic principles. That they do suggests a measure of transhistorical validity to this approach, although many English readers of their traditional authors are content to take self-injury as a symptom of class oppression and proceed to either moral resolutions or Marxist revolutions. The Freudian reading, then, threatens or trivializes the more valued social interpretation. But it need hardly be said that one reading does not cancel out others, and that every culture is likely to represent the narcissistic injury as well as the healing agencies of the family romance in what is perceived as the most relevant context, even if to others it appears mostly relative. By the same token, despite its biological ubiquity, the primal scene may also be represented in a host of culturally meaningful disguises. For example, the effigy of the sexual couple astride the donkey may suggest to Christians a perverse parody of the Holy Family.

7

George Eliot and the Paradox of Maturity; August Strindberg and the Pathology of Creativity

> As Kohut has shown, the outcome of premature disillusionment in the parents is a driven search for idealizable objects.
> —John Gedo, "On the Psychology of Genius"

1

For Virginia Woolf, *Middlemarch* is "one of the few English novels written for grown-up people," though she does not address the question of maturity more fully in her elegant tribute to George Eliot than to mention her "spirit of sympathy," her tolerance, and "wholesome understanding."[1] But most critics and readers would heartily second this endorsement. The novel, in its evenhanded, almost scientific portrayal of early nineteenth-century provincial society, is mature, even if part of its subject matter is immaturity. And if ever a work of art should serve to call into question many an early Freudian hypothesis about art being analogous to dream, art being at best a compromise with the pleasure principle, *Middlemarch* should eminently qualify, for it resides firmly on the far side of the id.

Or so the reader would be led to think by the author's measured judgments delivered on all manner of human striving, the balancing of conflicts, the realism of observation, the breadth of sympathy, and so forth. Yet, even before finishing the Prelude, the reader trips over a family romance and plunges into the depths of its fantasy, not to reemerge until the final pages. As already seen, the earliest allegiances of the imagination are so tenacious that many otherwise safe assumptions about maturity can no longer be taken for granted. Yet if *Middlemarch* should prove to be less than an all-out novel for grown-ups, what *is*?

Virigina Woolf contends that the "troubled spirit, that exacting and questioning and baffled presence who was George Eliot" is ultimately found only in her characters.[2] In *Middlemarch*, she is found especially in Dorothea Brooke. A woman of great capacities and strengths, Dorothea does not "look at things from the proper feminine angle,"[3] and yet finds herself in a society of severely limited options for women.

No emancipationist, Dorothea is an idealist of a peculiar stamp, caught between two worlds, two visions of women. Moreover, this very desirable and very lovely "pre-Raphaelite Madonna"[4] is not really like her homely creator, who escaped from the Midlands and married a much younger man after having been for many years the mistress of Henry Lewes. Yet if Dorothea shares her author's ideals without fulfilling the intellectual commitments they incur, Dorothea's "powerful, feminine, maternal hands" also describe her author's. A continuum is apparent, and the necessary inner link may be in the family-romance theme announced in the Prelude and subsequently submerged.

In it, we are invited to consider how the "mysterious mixture" of human history "behaves under the varying experiments of Time." The life of Saint Teresa of Avila (1515–82) is evoked, and the "thought of the little girl walking forth one morning hand-in-hand with her still smaller brother, to go and seek martyrdom in the country of the Moors," is entertained. This saint's "passionate, ideal nature demanded an epic life":

> What were many-volumed romances of chivalry and the social conquests of a brilliant girl to her? Her flame quickly burned up that light fuel; and, fed from within, soared after some illimitable satisfaction, some object which would never justify weariness, which would reconcile self-despair with the rapturous consciousness of life beyond self. She found her epos in the reform of a religious order. (*Middlemarch*, xiii)

Girded with faith, saints renounce their worldly parents for celestial ones, to be reborn as sons and heirs to heaven or brides of Christ. But for the "later-born Theresas" there is "no coherent social faith and order which could perform the function of knowledge for the ardently willing soul."[5] As a result, the family romance comes unshackled from religious structures and is cast into the disordered secular world. Though not quite known to her, it is Dorothea's lot to strive for a semblance of secular sainthood. She is the saint reborn as a historical revision of an ideal that transcends history. To underscore the family-romance theme, Dorothea is an orphan, having lost her parents at the age of twelve, and is raised by a beneficent but altogether worldly uncle.

Long before she is to discover her calling in marriage to Will, he twits her for having a martyr complex rather than a saintly vocation: "I suspect that you have some false belief in the virtues of misery, and want to make your life a martyrdom" (153). A martyr in late Roman times, Dorothea's saintly namesake sends an angel with a basket of apples and roses to a lawyer who had mocked her en route to her beheading, and he is converted to her ideals of love. The parallels with the novel, according to Gillian Beer, is that the lawyer is Casaubon, her first spouse; the angel is Will, her second.[6] And in accord with another legend (also traced by Beer), Dorothea is associated with Ansker, whose "martyrdom was not to be a martyr." Her family romance is not so much literally played out in terms of a quest for the ideal parent (except to some degree in her first marriage to Casaubon) as it is developed and mastered in its affective aspects: grandiosity in the self giving way to idealization of the other. These are the links that join the creator with her character (or self-character, like Lawrence's Paul and Woolf's Lily Briscoe). Probably the author's omniscience of viewpoint, which allows her to sail from one habitat to another, to enter her characters' minds at random, to look beyond their present, and so forth, is, despite its reinforcement as a convention, a vicissitude of the same grandiosity which is being examined from another angle. On the other hand, the realistic conventions of the novel function to reduce self-grandiosity. That ardent flame allowed for the saint, which "quickly burned up" the light fuel of her society, and, "fed from within, soared after some illimitable satisfaction," is dampened by such sober observations in the novel as "we are all of us born in moral stupidity, taking the world as an udder to feed our supreme selves" (146).

"From that stupidity," Eliot's measured prose informs us, "Dorothea had begun to emerge." Yet when she is faced with a choice of men to marry, she turns down the rural aristocrat, Sir James Chettain, who is conventional though sexually mature, as he shows by marrying and forming a family with Dorothea's sister. The preferred man is Casaubon, an aging, sexless pedant, who has wrapped himself up in a grandiose project to write a "key to all mythologies," to which he must devote all his energies and still will never complete. An exacting man, he will at least be allowed the decency of a punctual demise in Dorothea's prime.

Ellmann has taken Casaubon as highlighting the "narcissistic sensuality of her adolescence,"[7] which she must overcome and bury, whereas the narrative voice inists that she was "open, ardent, and not in the least self-admiring," but for "all her eagerness to know the truths of life, retained very childlike ideas about marriage" (3–4). Ellmann is no doubt nearer the mark, and Eliot may be working too closely to her self-character at this point to identify Dorothea's blind admiration for Casaubon as her own displaced wishes and ambitions. However, a saving dose of irony is shortly injected when we hear that the "really delightful marriage must be that where your husband was a sort of father, and could teach you even Hebrew, if you wished it." And the Reverend Casaubon is seen not only as a scholar of "profound learning" but also as a "man of wealth enough to give lustre to his piety." But Eliot's irony does not put the brakes on Dorothea's family-romance aspiration (as Dickens's does with Pip's). Modified as hers might be to sustain a vital self-balance, it cannot contribute to genuine self-fulfillment. Dorothea's saintly prototype could become a mystical bride of Christ and devote herself entirely to a religious calling; but Dorothea must settle for a more modest equivalent: spiritual bride to "a modern Augustine who united the glories of doctor and saint." Hers will be a higher kind of marriage:

There would be nothing trivial about our lives. Everyday things with us would mean the greatest things. It would be like marrying Pascal. I should learn to see the truth by the same light as great men have seen it by. And then I should know what to do, when I got older: I would see how it was possible to lead a grand life here—now—in England. (18)

Perhaps it is Eliot's imaginative allegiance to the powers of the family romance that blinds her to the obvious modern perception—unfair as it is: Dorothea is merely running away from a sexual encounter. Not that the one cancels out the other, for Dorothy must be doing both, though her behavior would have us believe that she was rather more surprised than relieved by Casaubon's predictable impotence. Barbara Hardy maintains that Eliot's sexual reticence is not excusable on the basis of either historical necessity or convention, since more sexual substance is included in her other works.[8]

This sexual hiatus, to hazard little more than a guess, stems in part from the author's priority of interest in dealing with those earlier conflicts centering on grandiosity and idealization, already alluded to. And if expectations for Dorothea in the sexual zone turn out as disappointing as they do in the feminist area, they will not disappointing in this one, which is, after all, no less centrally human.

The theme is egocentricity, and it is developed in the familiar images of mirrors and reflections, light and dark, blindness and vision. Casaubon is seen as "the centre of his own world" (57) before he becomes the center of Dorothea's. She sees reflected in Casaubon's mind an extension of "every quality she herself brought"; "he thinks a whole world of which my thought is but a poor twopenny mirror ... what a lake compared to my little pool" (15). Casaubon's own gloss on these images quickly turns that lake into a dry bed (in more than one sense): "As in droughty regions baptism by immersion could only be performed symbolically, so Mr. Casaubon found that sprinkling was the utmost approach to a plunge which his stream would afford him; and he concluded that the poets had much exaggerated the force of man's ruling passion" (42).

At least they did in his case. And Dorothea has had to experience this aridity of both spirit and body. Upon reading his letter of proposal, praising her for an "elevation of thought and a capability of devotedness," she trembles and undergoes a "rush of solemn emotion in which thoughts became vague and images floated uncertainly," and "she could but cast herself, with a childlike sense of reclining, in the lap of a divine consciousness which sustained her own" (28). This voluptuous, quasi-religious ecstasy marks Dorothea's fusion with her ideal, but it will be her only sensual experience until Will Ladislaw makes so bold as to kiss her on the mouth after Casaubon's death, by which time she has already begun weaning herself from her grandiose attachments.

With Dorothea briefly but blissfully fused with her ideal, the reader may consider how the theme of narcissism is diffused throughout the novel. In an attempt to rescue "poor Mr. Casaubon" from being the "mere occasion which had set alight the inflammable material of her [Dorothea's] youthful illusions,'' as well as from the denigrations of other characters, the omniscient narrator reminds us that no great man can escape ''unfavourable reflections of himself in various small mirrors; and even Milton, looking for his portrait in a spoon, must submit to have the facial angle of a bumpkin'' (56). This judicious sympathy also serves to place a very distinctive, indeed witty, frame around grandiosity in general. All the same, Dorothea is to be no more than a ''little moon'' to ''adorn the remaining quadrant'' of Casaubon's solar course (64).

A more elaborate use of the mirror image as a perspective on narcissism is developed in a parallel plot dealing with the marriage between the gifted, idealistic physican, Lydgate, to the romantically shallow Rosamond. While Lydgate can be viewed in key ways as Dorothea's male counterpart, Rosamond is a stereotype and female foil from the outset. A man of medical— and hence, as we shall see, sexual—knowledge, Lydgate views ''plain women'' as ''the other severe facts of life,'' but places Rosamond ''above his horizon'' as ''grace itself,'' perfectly ''lovely and accomplished,'' having ''the true melodic charm.'' Rosamond would, likewise, rather see herself in this richer light than be reminded of her vulgar heritage as the ''daughter of a Middlemarch manufacturer'' and innkeeper. The narrator captures her narcissism when Rosamond pauses before a mirror to touch up her ''hair of infantine fairness'' and we are shown ''two nymphs—the one in the glass, and the one out of it, who looked at each other with eyes of heavenly blue'' (76). It is clear that she would only see—and only have the world see—her idealized self-image: her majesty the Infanta. And Lydgate cooperates—until well into their marriage, when her ''shallow nature'' and inability to love are painfully driven home: the Infanta, alas, is infantile.

But if, in contrast to Dorothea, it turns out to be too late for Lydgate to come to his senses, it should not be too late for the reader, for we have been amply forewarned throughout, but most compellingly by the extended metaphor that opens chapter 27 in book 3:

> Your peir-glass or extensive surface of polished steel made to be rubbed by a housemaid, will be minutely and multitudinously scratched in all directions; but place now against it a lighted candle as a centre of illumination, and lo! the scratches will seem to arrange themselves in a fine series of concentric circles round that little sun. It is demonstrated that the scratches are going everywhere impartially, and it is only your candle which produces the flattering illusion of a concentric arrangement, its light falling with an exclusive optical selection. These things are a parable. The scratches are events, and the candle is the egoism of any person now absent—of Miss Vincy, for example. (182)

Later, when the narrator with her gentle, and not so gentle, irony informs us that Casaubon, ''like the rest of us, felt how soothing it would have been to have a companion who would never find'' out that one is not ''unmixedly adorable,'' she asks, ''will not a tiny speck very close to our vision blot out the glory of the world, and leave only a margin by which we see the blot? I know no speck so troublesome as self" (289). It should not be difficult to agree, up to this point that many persisting features have been both keenly and gracefully captured from the vantage point of maturity, and so far Virginia Woolf's observation about this being a novel for grown-up people seems to be confirmed. The three aspects under which narcissism has come into focus: (1) the family romance, (2) the grandiose self-image and idealized other, and (3) authorial omniscience, have each been subtly interwoven into a superb whole.

Or so it would seem. For on the other hand, the balancing pole and presumed regulator of creativity, which is adult sexuality as initially represented by the primal scene, has not yet been considered. If wholeness is implicit in maturity, then one might expect, if only obliquely, references to or derivatives from this fundamental image of origins that must inhabit some region of everyone's mind and often serve in art as a corrective to the family romance.

Dorothea's saintly model is depicted as having an unspecified hunger that carried her beyond "many-volumed romances of chivalry" to subside ultimately in the "reform of a religious order." The primal scene focuses the quest for knowledge of both one's origins and one's sexual destiny. Dorothea, one recalls, "with all eagerness to know the truths of life, retained very childlike ideas about marriage." She daydreams about a patriarchal spouse who would teach her Hebrew, as if that language might fill gaps in her understanding or hold a key to an exalted past she is cut off from by the loss of her parents. But it is only a family-romance type of solution that leads her into a maze of greater subjectivity.

Her evenings are spent reading Casaubon's manuscripts back to him and marking little crossees at his cues, but as the couple shifts from library to bedroom to bed, he drifts off to contented sleep while her thoughts prevent her peace. She finds herself no longer believing in the "trustworthiness of that key"; and, having earlier foreseen a life "in a virtual tomb, where there was the apparatus of a ghastly labour producing what would never see the light," she now pictures for herself the consequences of their conjugal efforts: "a theory withered in the birth like an elfin child" (329).[9] Conceived through a kind of perverse mental incest, their unnatural offspring signifies the mind's deviation from sexual understanding.

Dorothea's lack of parents is one ground for inferring sexual ignorance, and the direct outlet of her sexual curiosity is denied or inhibited by idealizing fantasy. No doubt the intrusion of grandiose aspirations would carry her further afield. In short, Dorothea would rather wed and take shorthand from her Sphinx than solve its riddle. But when she has "looked deep into the ungauged reservoir" of Casaubon's mind, she finds only a "vague labyrinthine extension" of her own questions. And while he has attempted to show "that all the mythical systems or erratic mythical fragments in the world were corruptions of a tradition originally revealed" (14), he has learned nothing of origins, and she can learn nothing from him. The bankruptcy of this grandiose system is the inner analogue to his sexual impotence. And Dorothea finds herself in marriage literally abandoned in the dark, labyrinthine chambers of Casaubon's castle.

This is surely the nadir of her family romance—to be locked in an effete version of Bluebeard's castle (a female counterpart to those negative male versions encountered earlier). But the key to release her from its dungeons had already appeared on the estate one day in the person of Casaubon's virile young cousin, Will Ladislaw. Will introduces what Barbara Hardy calls the rescue-into-love theme, but he also represents the larger world of art and politics. It will take most of the novel, however, for Dorothea to stir herself from the stupor of ideals and wifely duties in order to recognize him as a legitimate sexual partner. Her choice, as will be seen more clearly later on, is tantamount to interpreting the Sphinx's riddle.

If Dorothea is nonetheless sidetracked on her explicit quest for knowledge, the quest itself is conducted at a safe distance through the physician, Lydgate, who is fittingly an orphan also, and so, by implication, distanced from his origins as well as from sexual knowledge. In his youth he is described in a flashback as a "vigorous animal with a ready understanding, but no spark had yet kindled in him an intellectual passion." On a wet vacation afternoon he glances through an old Cyclopaedia; and under the heading of Anatomy, the "very first passage that drew his eyes was on the valves of the heart." Since the passage immediately following describes the awakening of an intellectual passion that would lead him into the medical profession, it may be quoted in full, but it is also a curious specimen in itself—illogical, cryptic, oddly evasive yet revealing:

> He was not much acquainted with valves of any sort, but he knew that *valvae* were folding doors, and through this crevice came a sudden light startling him with his first vivid notion of finely-adjusted mechanism in the human frame. A liberal education had of course left him free to read the indecent passages in the school classics, but beyond a general sense of secrecy and obscenity in connection with his internal structure, had left his imagination quite unbiassed, so that for anything he knew his brains lay in small bags at his temples, and he had no more thought of representing to himself how his blood circulated than how paper served instead of gold. But the moment of vocation had come, and before he got down from his chair, the world was made new to him by a presentiment of endless processes filling the vast spaces blanked out of his sight by that wordy ignorance which he had supposed to be knowledge. From that hour Lydgate felt the growth of an intellectual passion (98).

Logical consistency compels one to ask, what is the connection between a dry desciption of the valve system in the heart and the "indecent passages in the school classics"? The link is not obvious. One would have to think there was something indecent about the pumping operations of the heart, which a liberal education somehow braces one to come to terms with. Surely the whole internal anatomy of the human body cannot be sexualized? The only truly logical explanation is psychological: that *valvae* is a substitution for (or, like the brain reference, a displacement upward of) an organ that sounds as well as functions somewhat similarly, the repressed word then being *vulva*, literally meaning covering, though here it has itself been covered by its close cousin, *valvae*. And one would have to trace the two words pretty far into the Indo-European language tree to find a common branch, although a consultation with Eric Partridge's *Origins* does note a certain kinship. To discover the vulva is certainly far more momentous than to find oneself excited by the folding doors of the heart, because through those other folding leaves and from the crevice beyond, life itself emerges: it just might be the meaning of his own origins that he discovers in human anatomy, perhaps euphemistically signaled by that "sudden light startling him with his first vivid notion of finely-adjusted mechanism in the human frame."

Incidentally, in reviewing Erica Jong's *Fear of Flying*, Paul Theroux refers to the heroine's "cherished valve," thereby making explicit, at least for modern readers, a connection this novel obscurely hints at.[10] The relative difficulty of the sexes' coping with, in Freud's phrase, "the psychic consequences of anatomical differences" and the Victorians' obsessesion with genealogical legitimacy, which often couched the inexpressible functions of nature behind the fig leaf of Latin (including Freud himself, who wrote of an early memory of seeing *matrem nudam*) would be an interesting digression. The point is that there is something feminine and sexual about Lydgate's discovery, and what it tells him of his origins is depicted in terms of his destiny. He will master the origins of life through the practice of medicine, but, personally, he will prefer higher love-objects over "plain women."

Perhaps beyond these textual artifices and ambiguities, with their discreet veilings and distancing techniques, is the notion that sexual knowledge is something men may enjoy, but not women—not ladies, at any rate. And it is fascinating to watch how the plot allows the paths of Dorothea and Lydgate to cross back and forth without bringing them together at a point when each may take a healthy sexual interest in the other. *Why* they are kept apart is revealed, nonetheless, when we recognize *how* they are further linked.

Dorothea, we recall, is linked to sainthood by her name and by Saint Theresa in the Prelude, and, while I have emphasized these as family romance signifiers, there is a further dimension that makes one wonder if the saintly linkage isn't Eliot's intuitive means of endowing her heroine with an unconscious, or at least of hinting at her otherwise unexpressed sexual depths. Hilary Fraser has demonstrated that Eliot had seen Bernini's "The Ecstasy of St. Teresa" on a recent trip to Rome and had very likely read her *Life* as well as Richard Crashaw's poems in her honor.[11] Together they form a powerful portrait of repressed sexual desire and religious displacement. The angel who appears to her was

> very beautiful, his face so aflame that he appeared to be . . . all afire. . . . In his hands I saw a long golden spear and at the end of the iron tip I seemed to see a point of

fire. With this he seemed to pierce my heart several times so that it penetrated to my entrails. When he drew it out, I thought he was drawing them out with it and he left me completely afire with a great love for God. The pain was so sharp that it made me utter several moans; and so excessive was the sweetness caused me by this intense pain that one can never wish to lose it.[12]

In Crashaw's tribute, "How kindly will thy gentle HEART / Kisse the sweetly-killing DART! / And close in his embraces keep / Those delicious Wounds, that weep / Balsom to heal themselves with."[13]

By coincidence or by design, the heart is the organ penetrated by the sharp pain of love, creating such an intense ecstasy as to be deemed divine, and, so, forbidden to mortals. When Lydgate, portrayed in a similar displacement upward, discovers this organ of female ecstasy, he, too, becomes a forbidden love object and is dispatched in haste to an unworthy wife, lest he appear to Dorothea as the sword-bearing angel. But what is forbidden for its evident incestuous aura in practice endures as an ideal in fantasy; draped in religious attire and relegated to an ancient past, it is alloted reentry into consciousness as a distant ideal. The voluptuous merger with an exalted love-object that would effect a libidinal climax to the family romance is in any case repressed, sublimated, or otherwise handled by available psychic accommodations. Finally, in the distortions of the forbidden sexual couple of angel and saint, traces survive of the primal scene's attraction / repulsion excitement. But the unconscious in the novel, as in the individual's life, burns around the periphery and only rarely singes the text. When the repressed eventually makes its return, it is disguised beyond recognition—or almost.

In the long run, Dorothea's idealism, eagerness to learn, and sense of duty are all deflected onto questions of Will Ladislaw's character and his suitability for marriage. The brilliant comedy of wit and satire on manners in the first half of the novel is largely exchanged in the second half for intrigue and melodrama, but perhaps this is the only way the author can consciously work beyond the surfaces of society to explore the deeper springs of character and desire. At any rate, Dorothea undergoes a severe testing and ordeal of radical doubt before achieving any mature self-realization. These comprise the novel's central crisis: her subsequent marriage to Will and her projected motherhood are dealt with summarily.

Dorothea is temporarily separated from Will by a clause in her husband's will that she not remarry and by Will's own apparently unstable character: there are rumors about his lowly genealogy as well as about his interest in Rosamond, now Mrs. Lydgate. However, Dorothea has been persuaded that he is blameless by the sincerity of his love for her. By her trusting simplicity, Dorothea becomes "an ideal for others in her believing conception of them" (532). She is, in the conventional imagery applied earlier to her, "the mirror of women" (61). But she is also the mirroring object, in a deeper sense, for Will, who "felt that in her mind he had found his highest estimate" (532). For her part Dorothea views their relationship as being "inwardly whole and without blemish" and entertains "no vision of their ever coming into nearer union" without, however, "taking any posture of renunciation" (533).

Such is their emotional state when, on a visit to the Lydgates, Dorothea accidentally stumbles onto the following scene:

> She found herself on the other side of the door without seeing anything remarkable, but immediately she heard a voice speaking in low tones which startled her as with a sense of dreaming in daylight, and advancing unconsciously a step or two beyond the projecting slab of a bookcase, she saw, in the terrible illumination of a certainty which filled up all outlines, something which made her pause motionless, without self-possession enough to speak.
>
> Seated with his back towards her on a sofa which stood against the wall on a line with the door by which she had entered, she saw Will Ladislaw: close by him and turned towards him with a flushed tearfulness which gave a new brilliancy to her face sat Rosamond, her bonnet hanging back, while Will leaning towards her clasped both her upraised hands in his and spoke with low-toned fervour. (534)

Obviously this need not be treated literally as a primal scene in order for it to function as one on certain deep levels. In includes the excluded third party in a suitably Victorian scene of sexual intimacy, betrayal, and guilt. It is powerful enough to nearly demolish Dorothea, whose ordeal follows fast upon her abrupt departure. Her anger with Will demands that she face up to her unacknowledged desire for him, and she wrestles with her emotions through the night, until she has sobbed herself to sleep on the cold floor by her bed. Her agonies approximate the saint's dark night of the soul and the individual's mourning process, though they are far more concentrated; by morning she is able to sit down with her grief and compose herself enough to make it a "lasting companion" and "sharer in her thought" (543). She breaks out of the Rosamond-type of self-centeredness and masters her narcissism, first by retracing the previous day's events and her own hasty reactions. She "had enveloped both Will and Rosamond in her burning scorn," and she realizes that her emotional responses do not determine the nature of the scene that excited them: "this young marital union . . . like her own, seemed to have its hidden as well as evident troubles" (544). She enlists reality testing to modify her narcissistically colored perceptions and recalls her original mission of mercy with a new sympathy, pondering how she might still be of help to the Lydgates. She does not yet know with any accuracy the nature of the transaction between Will and Rosamond (as it turns out, Will was confessing his love for Dorothea and only consoling the jealous Rosamond); and, while Dorothea is sorting out her morning thoughts, she opens her bedroom curtains and witnesses another scene, this one on the outside; a "man with a bundle on his back and a woman carrying her baby" (544). Is this the radiant meaning of the primal scene as seen by eyes open to the otherness of experience? Not the grandiose, but the lowly "key to all mythologies" that Casaubon sought? Not, of course, if one wants important revelations, but the influx of light suggests an advance in cognition similar to the light that accompanied

Lydgate's discovery of *valvae / vulva*. It is finally this vision of unexceptional adult sexual relations that allows her to feel a "part of that involuntary, palpitating life" which she can no longer hide from or evade by "selfish complaining" (544). In addition, "palpitating" may cue us to the ordinary heart of human affection, in contrast to that other organ of forbidden ecstasy.

As a transition to a sense of otherness, that illuminating moment also enables Dorothea to accept the truth when she hears it later on from Rosamond; but in a larger sense it prepares her for a sexually mature, though not necessarily sexually liberated, life with Will. She becomes in "her full nature" a "new Theresa," who obscurely contributes to the "growing good of the world." Specifically, she has children.

Finally, additional clues suggest that concurrent with her idealism have also been deeply based fears of a sexual nature. It is Will who voices these notions, when in a passage noted earlier he questions Dorothea's affinities with martyrdom and continues, "You talk as if you never had known any youth. It is monstrous—as if you had had visions of Hades in your youth like the boy in the legend. You have been brought up in some of those horrible notions that choose the sweetest women to devour—like Minotaurs" (153). The boy in the legend is Eros, who had a vision of Hades, according to a note in the text. The rapid associations in Will's outburst, so deftly rendered by Eliot, indicates that he is groping for some clearer image or deeper perception of Dorothea than he is able to verbalize. "Monstrous," a global response, leads to a fleeting image of a youth (Eros, Anskar) who had a vision of Hades, and this becomes associated with "horrible notions," which become more distinct as the Minotaur, the half-human and half-bull monster which fed on young virgins. The suggestions are of seeing something terrible as a youth, something that interrupts and forecloses that period, something from below, the underworld, something monstrous, the sort of composite creature who swallows up virgins as the Sphinx does to those failing to decipher its riddle. In other words, albeit faintly and obliquely, there are suggestions of primal-scene terrors of childhood, connected with fears of being devoured by the combined pair and that are handled by identification and idealization processes which reappear as a wish for saintly martyrdom. It is implicit in the saint's vision of spiritualized sexual pleasure as a form of disembowelment. It is proper that Will should dimly recognized these hidden dimensions to Dorothea's character, its inner scaffolding, as it were, through which she has built up herself, because in due time he will be the one to offer in an adult sexual relationship an alternative to primitive sexual fears, providing she can relinquish some of the narcissism and incest aversion that bind together her family romance.

As Dorothea's conflicts in the area of the self are resolved she moves on to a (by most standards) mature relationship, and so closely does she approximate traditional psychoanalytic views, including Karen Horney's, of genital maturity that one is almost content to leave matters at rest there. Certainly a humanizing process is traceable through her character, but there may be slight discomfort with the adroitness of this process, as if some application of idealization were still lubricating things. This vague sense becomes more sharply defined if attention is shifted to Will, who has also undergone ordeals of trust and constancy to prove his worth to Dorothea. But, then, does that mean she will always be the idealized object he held her up as during his crises, that he need never fear any disillusionment, never undergo the stresses and strains of lowering such an ideal to a flesh-and-blood sexual equal?

Before he has attained his ideal, the author carefully scrutinizes his mind. "He was both exasperated and delighted by the calm freedom with which Dorothea looked at him and spoke to him, and there was something so exquisite in thinking of her just as she was." He "could not bear the thought of any flaw appearing in his crystal," even though it is resting in another man's cupboard. Eliot realizes he cannot merely remain in love with his love, and asks, "Do we not shun the street version of a fine melody?—or shrink from the news that some rarity . . . which we have dwelt on even with exultation . . . is really not an uncommon thing, and may be obtained as an every day possession?" (325). The sexual implications of these similes are easy enough to read, and Barbara Hardy wonders whether Eliot's irony has not deserted her in reworking these "troubadour images."[14]

Despite the transformations of the couple as they emerge into the ordinary world, it is apparent that Barbara Hardy is uncomfortable also with the "later passages describing their farewell and final union [in which] George Eliot still surrounds the lovers with a dazzling halo." But perhaps the saint's halo now shared by a sexual couple is a significant enough modification of that dangerous ecstasy and narcissism arising at the outset and of the attendant fears that arose along the way. Of course, it's a book for grown-ups, especially for Freudian grown-ups.

2

From the cultivated sanity of George Eliot no one seems further removed than August Strindberg, whose apparent insanity, cultivated or conditioned, is deeply entangled in his creative enterprises. Unlike D. H. Lawrence, who could say with a good deal of truth that "one sheds one's sicknesses in books—repeats and presents again one's emotions, to be master of them," and unlike K. R. Eissler's cautious statement about Goethe, "that creativity might under favorable conditions avert the outbreak of a psychosis, or heal a psychosis, or unfold instead of a psychosis," with Strindberg we are in a terra incognita, where creativity and schizophrenia go hand in hand, but not happily so; rather, each appears to feed off the other.[15] His works may be lucid and beautifully organized, but they contain a bleak vision of paranoid despair, and so the paradox of creativity and maturity widens to reveal a frightening abyss when we turn to The Ghost Sonata (1907).

This most seminal of modern plays has been depicted as Expressionistic, Absurdist, and, by Maurice Valency, Surrealistic, putting "fantasy and reality on an equal footing."[16] All of these views are defensible. As in Absurd drama, metaphors, such as the Mummy in the cupboard, are concretely mounted on the stage. As in Expressionism, subjective states are projected onto the surfaces of reality, twisting and distorting them. And as in the dream, it is possible to speak of condensation, decomposition, and the like, but in a peculiarly schizophrenic style in which manifest and latent thoughts freely intermingle.

It is also one of the most difficult of modern plays, and how far the approach via creative regulators may hope to clarify its purport can soon be decided. Strindberg constructed this chamber work on musical principles, emphasizing "theme and mood" and symbolic setting, and concentrating on ultimate realities—the illusion of happiness, evil, guilt, the meaning of life, the prospect of death.[17] And here, as in other creative works, questions of ends are dealt with in terms of origins: to comprehend the one is to foresee the other.

Closely allied with these issues are Strindberg's other experiments in the drama. These were precipitated in part by the work of Maeterlinck, who, basing his theories on the cycles of medieval station drama, wanted to create an intimate modern equivalent in plays depicting "soul states." Strindberg's chamber works, written for an Intimate Theater, were an expression of this interest, but, as will be seen, a far more radical one than could ever have been intended, for his dramatized soul states replicate with uncanny aptness everyman's phases of psychosexual development.

The hero of this unique station drama is simply the Student, and a consideration of his origins begins to encompass our now familiar creative regulators. On the family romance side we learn that he has made his "debut last night as the brave rescuer," who by tomorrow will be famous and bear a "name worth something." That this does not come about may suggest a subverting of the fantasy in its rescue variant. Meanwhile, he is allowed the family-romance prerogative of two sets of parents, or at least two fathers. His original father had been a merchant and was ruined by the old man (Hummel, the second father), whom the Student finds himself chatting with on a street corner by a water fountain. Hummel, who knew the Student as a infant, will only comment enigmatically that the paths of fate are strange, that he takes an interest in human destiny, and so forth. Before long, however, Hummel has struck a Mephistophelean bargain with the student, who will be allowed entry to the nearby house, where he hopes to court Adele, the hyacinth girl, if he will only do Hummel's will. Their handshake nearly freezes the life out of the student, for it soon develops that the old man is of a family of vampires preying on the very house the Student aspires to join. By now we sense that the hopeful rescue of the family romance has been derailed and rerouted in a demonic direction.

At this point in the play it is possible to see the Student as poised within (or surrounded by) four images of ruin. Hummel himself is something of an eighty-year ruin, crumbling in his wheelchair and responsible for the downfall of the Student's first father. The ruin of the house that the Student is about to enter can be anticipated, and the Student has only just emerged from a house that literally collapsed the previous night. His efforts at saving some of its members establish his heroic side, although the rescue operation is ambiguous: "I dashed over and picked up a child that was passing under the wall. . . . The next moment the house collapsed. I was saved, but in my arms, which I thought held the child, was nothing at all" (*Ghost Sonata*, 275–76).

This incident functions as either a screen memory or a dream fragment. Its import is an account of self-rescue, the child fusing into the student. The collapsing house symbolizes origins, either derivative of the infant's fantasy that being born is an aggressive assault against the mother's body, or of a violent scene from which the child discerns the emergence of babies. Most likely both meanings are herein condensed.[18] Either way, the emergence of the Student from the collapsed house is the first stage of his symbolic progress through life. Moreover, the play begins with his appearance on a Sunday morning, the day of his birth; and as a "Sunday child" he has second sight, an ability "to see what others can't." These considerations begin to anchor the unfolding drama at the sexual pole of origins.[19]

Arriving at the fountain, the Student reaches his next stage on the psychosexual scale. With his second sight he perceives a Milkmaid, from whom he begs a cup of water; because his eyes are "inflamed" from being up all night (also from what they saw), he beseeches her to bathe them for him, since his hands have been in contact with wounds and dead bodies. These services seem quite proper for the newly born, but they send another signal—if the collapsed house is taken as the first—that life has been undermined at the source, for the reason that the student alone can see the Milkmaid is that she is already dead, murdered by Hummel.

The third stage of Student's progress entails his encounter with Hummel and the awakening of oedipal striving. Looking toward the house, the Student has "imagined all the beauty and elegance there must be inside" and imagines "living up there in the top flat, with a beautiful young wife, two pretty little children, and an income of twenty-thousand crowns a year" (274). These wishes seal the bargain with the Mephistophelean father, and the Student has been launched into the greater world of love, ambition, and triangulated relationships.

For the house that he enters in the next scene is a microcosm of nineteenth-century European society. It is a "house of horrors and . . . world of deceit,"[20] entirely predatory and presided over by the vampiristic spirit; as the characters take turns stripping one another bare, there is finally nothing left but their garments or the pile of bandages that were wrapped around the decaying mummy's body. It is a ghosts' supper in the round room of our world. And when it is finished nothing remains: life has been sucked dry and denuded in this macabre variation on the way of the world. Nothing substantial remains: Hummel himself is destroyed.

This nightmarish vision has been described in various ways, but the clinical concept that most succinctly suggests the inner state behind it may be Minkowski's depiction of the schizophrenic process as "loss of vital contact with reality."[21] Such a person "sees the external world in terms of the internal model that he carries with him. Thus, what he lacks in himself he experiences as lacking in the world." Applied to the artist in Strindberg, this statement suggests that the mirroring function of art has been appropriated by a morbidly schizophrenic reverie or image of the world that depletes it of vitality. This mechanism Minkowski calls *denudation*; it schematizes and reduces, perceiving, for example, the skeleton as more real than the flesh-and-blood person, and so may lead the Strindbergian variety of artist toward highly concentrated modes of expression. (Although the supposedly naturalistic play *Miss Julie* [1888] reveals no less a paranoid picture, the more subjective form adapted later allows for a greater exploration of disturbed mental states.) [22] But Strindberg also seems to have the creative integrity to reflect not only the morbid elements of his inner world, but to discover or locate recognizable processes of morbid corruption in his environment: he is not merely reflecting his own psychosis, but also using it to express the deeper disturbances in society.

For a while it appears that the Student may be exempted from the cannibalistic feast. He turns up only at the end of the scene with Adele, the girl glorified in his oedipal dreams, in the Hyacinth Room, where he is now ready for the final stage of his progress. The third and final scene takes place there, and the progression from outer to inner, which has accompanied the Student's progress through the vital stages of life, now intersects his scene with Adele. The sexual symbolism here is most transparent: Adele is the hyacinth girl and her room filled with hyacinths is the Hyacinth Room, so that by entering the room, the Student enters the girl. Strindberg has placed the act of sex on his stage in the only way available to him (and one far more evocative than the out-front theatrics of later decades).

This has been necessary because the question of the possibility of human happiness in this world must ultimately be decided by the one act that humans most highly prize, that of physical union with one's beloved. Ostensibly, the Student is standing over Adele with her harp, but their dialogue is highly symbolic. She invites him to sing to the flower of her soul, the hyacinth. The Student proclaims this love in thinly disguised sexual terms:

Student. I love it above all other flowers—its virginal shape rising straight and slender out of the bulb, resting on the water and sending its pure white roots down into the colorless fluid. I love its colors: the snow-white, pure as innocence, the yellow honey-sweet, the youthful pink, the ripe red, but best of all the blue—the dewy blue, deep-eyed and full of faith. I love them all, more than gold or pearls. I have loved them

ever since I was a child, have worshipped them because they have all the fine qualities I lack.... And yet ...
Girl. Go on.
Student. My love is not returned, for these beautiful blossoms hate me.
Girl. How do you mean?
Student. Their fragrance, strong and pure as the early winds of spring which have passed over melting snows, confuses my senses, deafens me, blinds me, thrusts me out of the room, bombards me with poisoned arrows that wound my heart and set my head on fire. (296)

The sexual commentary here is fairly straightforward, expressing explicitly a conflict of ambivalence that plagued Strindberg throughout his life and appeared continually in his writing. The sources of this ambivalence may, however, be more clearly seen. In the dualism of the alluring virginal bulb of woman and the bombarding poisonous arrows she emits is something very nearly akin to what Freud designated as the attracting / repelling force of the incest taboo toward what is both "sacred, above the ordinary and at the same time dangerous, unclean and mysterious."[23]

The arrows that the Student discovers in Adele's sexual flower suggest the prior phallic penetrations of his prized oedipal object; the fact that the arrows are poisoned reiterates the earlier, more primitive fears at the oral stage, foreshadowed by the slain Milkmaid; the fact that they set his head on fire suggests a tortured ambivalence that can lead to the collapse into madness or to an equivalent self-destructive blaze.

Together, alien arrows and virginal bulb suggest a primal scene that in the total context may be interpreted as an act of vampirism, that is, a primitive oral attack. Now the meaning of his second sight becomes clearer: the Milkmaid he had earlier encountered was a ghost of the good, oral-stage mother murdered by the bad mother, disguised as vampire Hummel. Hence, the vampire version of the primal scene is dictated by the infant's aggressive orality: he is the vampire also.[24] This is why the disillusioned Student can tell Adele after their sexual exchange, "Your flowers have poisoned me and I have given the poison back to you" (303).

By adapting a dramatic form that concentrates on soul states, that is, inner reality, Strindberg is able to expand the continuum of sexuality to include the infantile period (as Freud had done conceptually two years previously in *Three Essays on the Theory of Sexuality*); and by insisting on the universality of the vampire process—mingling, as critics have pointed out, the horrible and the commonplace—he is able to defuse somewhat his painfully intense paranoia, even to rationalize it through a combination of art and Eastern religion.

Strindberg's soul states, then, encompass origins: life is seen as poisoned at its very sources and unable to heal or purify itself at later stages. Despite our strivings toward happiness, despite our compromises and bargains with worldly powers, our actions are predetermined. There are profound psychoanalytic insights to be found here in the recognition that early damge to the self is often irretrievable, that it often persists to affect all future stages of development. The schizophrenic process has been "worked through" to reveal its own terrifying reality; this we may accept as valid. What may invalidate the experience for us on another level is the negation of any kind of trust, the absence of which violates our reality-sense or our living through faith (in Eigen's concept quoted in chapter 4).

But in this play the positive family romance twines around those very emotions of trust and hope, strangling them; to underscore the hopelessness of striving in this world, the Student must undergo a double disillusionment. Hummel is exposed as a "false benefactor," and the real father, whom Hummel had allegedly ruined, is later revealed by the student as a madman who had arranged his own ghosts' supper to retaliate by exposing all his acquaintances by whom he had felt betrayed. Adele is ultimately seen as the child of malicious, vengeful coupling, growing out of the predatory relationships of the Round-Room. She is the daughter of Hummel and the Mummy, whom the Colonel has married after Hummel has seduced the Colonel's fiancée. It is that kind of world. And even though Hummel is no longer a threat, Adele begins to waste away, having been gradually starved by the gigantic Cook, who reveals herself to be a member of the "Hummel family of vampires."

But then so are Adele and, ultimately, the Student; everyone is situated at some point on the microcosmic web of humanity that revealed itself in the round room. To pull on one corner is to influence all the other sections. To reverse the hierarchy by drawing Hummel down and lifting the Cook to the top is to change nothing. No one escapes from the skein of malign influences by which Strindberg schematized the world. Its meaning appears to be the negation of meaning, the hollowness of hope. The play draws to a close as the Hyacinth Room disappears and is replaced by Böcklin's painting of "The Island of the Dead," with a forlorn ship nearing its shores as the last earthly soul state. The abandonment of the pleasure principle seems dictated not by the reality principle but the death instinct. And, so, it also seems that the two governing polarities of creativity are also extinguished by this profoundly pessimistic work.

But for this to be true, one would have to think of Strindberg himself subsisting in his final years—he died five years later of stomach cancer—as a burned-out hull, whereas he went on creating and struggling, with all his ambivalence toward women and life in general still unresolved. A clue to the persistence of his own vital processes appears in the lifeline he found to pull himself out of his inferno. At the other end of it was another madman, the eighteenth-century mystic, Swedenborg.[25] "A significant step towards restitution appears," according to Lidz, "after he [Strindberg] found that Swedenborg had experienced almost identical delusions and hallucinations."[26] The pervading sense of evil and suffering could be rationalized if earthly life were hell and he was being punished in "preparation for a future life.'' This also helped to make sense of his earlier identification with Christ, whose passion and death were, paradoxically, signs of divine favor. It was not easy being a son of such a heavenly father, but it perhaps helped to overcome the double-binding experiences of his childhood, emphasized by Lidz. It is interesting in this context that the term adapted in the literature of psychoanalysis to describe the effects of double-binding parents on the child is "soul murder." Given classic formulation in Freud's first analysis of homosexuality and paranoia in the Schreber case (1911), it also hints at the suitability of Strindberg's selecting a drama of soul states, wherein the inner contradictions of self-experience can be explored, fragments reconnected, and a degree of self-remaking undertaken.[27] Such a project becomes feasible because of Strindberg's suggestibility to the thoughts of his alter ego, Swedenborg, for through him the notion of another life or soul state beyond, and of another birth for the self, began to take hold. This possibility returns us to the family romance and its connection with self-reconstitution.

But any such creative enterprise for Strindberg takes place within a schizophrenic ambience. Minkowski refers to schizophrenic "attitudes," in which the individual foundering in a void clings desperately to any fragments of vital reality, internal or external, past to present. This is R. D. Laing's paraphrase, and he continues, "the tenacious clinging on to something 'real,' be it an image, a memory, an emotion," comprises the "attitudes," "psychic stereotypes," or "morbid reveries."[28] The schizophrenic artist's morbid reverie is analogous to the poet's daydreaming in Freud's (1908) paper; yet it is apparent that the former will have a much greater difficulty bringing his subjectivity back to reality. It helps, of course, if he is a genius like Strindberg, but it also begs the question. What is evident from the present context is that a greal deal more effort is required on the reader's part to reach the schizophrenic artist.

With this in mind I would return to the Hyacinth Room, where inner and outer realities have merged, where objects like flowers stand for parts of the body or self, and where the verbal exchanges between the Student and Adele stand for sexual intercourse. When they are nearly finished with this split-level discourse, Adele claims that the Buddha statue is their baby: "We have given birth to it together. We are wedded" (297). (And it is worth noting that during this symbolic coitus, Adele's parents are mentioned, by way of reversal, as voyeurs sitting silently in the next room.)

The student and Adele have given birth to an inanimate object, one that has been present all along and has drawn their attention consistently away from each other. The sitting Buddha seems to me to be an equivalent to a schizophrenic "attitude," in the god's striking a pose of immobile calm. His ability to stimulate the imaginations of the couple suggests an attempt by Strindberg to bring to life this "attitude"—poised as it is somewhere between highly condensed artistic symbolism and catatonia. And, indeed, on one level the Buddha as their baby is fittingly a stillborn child, because all the potency and fertility have been sapped from their lives. It is for them only a children's miming of adult sex, with a doll substituting for a baby.

But the figure is also imbued with its own meanings, which the Student and Adele extract from it. This "large, seated Buddha" is described as placed on top a stove, and on his "lap rests a bulb from which rises the stem of a shallot (Allium Ascolonicum), bearing its globular cluster of white, starlike flowers." For the student, it is an "image of the Cosmos."

> *Student.* . . . This is why Buddha sits holding the earth-bulb, his eyes brooding as he watches it grow, outward and upward, transforming itself into a heaven. This poor earth will become a heaven. It is for this that Buddha waits.
> *Girl.* I see it now. Is not the snowflake six-pointed too like the hyacinth flower?
> *Student.* You are right. The snowflakes must be falling stars.
> *Girl.* And the snowdrop is a snow-star, grown out of snow.
> *Student.* But the largest and most beautiful of all the stars in the firmament, the golden-red Sirius, is the narcissus with its gold and red chalice and its six white rays.
> *Girl.* Have you seen the shallot in bloom?
> *Student.* Indeed I have. It bears its blossoms within a ball, a glove like the celestial one, strewn with white stars. (297)

It is therefore meant to be taken as a unitive symbol, drawing together earth and heaven, male and female, as well as fragments of the self, into a higher unity. The Buddha, moreover, can be trusted and need not be tested. But it is also a symbol of sexual fusion and, therefore, owes something to the primal scene, especially as it soon turns into the couple's love child.

As a self-representation, as well, its serene aloofness certainly bespeaks an enviable alternative to the fiery anguish of paranoia. And, as suggested by the shift from the sexual object implied in the hyacinth to the self implied in the narcissus, the final soul state may entail a blissful fusion with an idealized object from which ideas of rebirth or reincarnation radiate into a higher, conflict-free state. For, finally, as the brooding Buddha is also a god, presiding over the totality of life, with the power to bestow life as well as to transform it, he functions as the idealized parent of the family romance, into whose cosmic family, or out of whose fertile lap, the Student may hope to be reborn. Such a divine parent cannot act as a false benefactor or ever be subject to ruin and madness. At this final stage we reach the culmination and interfusion of the creative poles that have been traced as the family romance and the primal scene.

3

Both *Middlemarch* and *The Ghost Sonata* telescope bourgeois nineteenth-century society, though in ways that at first bear little, if any, resemblance to each other. Although Eliot's art reveals a self-weaning from golden fantasy, while Strindberg's is nourished by it, the highlighting of the one's sanity and the other's madness, while justifiable, may falsely polarize things. David

Carroll's study of the novel, for example, has brilliantly demonstrated a series of predatory, paired relationships.[29] The prototype involves the banker-methodist Bulstrode, whose shady past leaves him vulnerable to backmail by Raffles, until Bulstrode finds a way to murder his former companion. In a sense, each creates the other: "they have become the other's threatening extension," and together constitute a unit. Similarly, Casaubon marries Dorothea out of vanity and fear, while she is carried along by hardly more savory motives; even after his death he tries to continue feeding on her life by the conditions in his will. And the Lydgate-Rosamond pair, too, are locked into mutual exploitation. The overall effect is of "vampires feeding off each other," a decidedly Strindbergian image.[30] But in Eliot's world there is a true hierarchy of mental functioning, while in Strindberg's the pattern is circular, at least until the deliverance of death. Both use the dangerous love arrows and the web image in their writings, but here is where their differences are most apparent: Eliot sees Middlemarch, "this particular web," as the "combination of all intermingled webs spun between the mind and the external world";[31] and, as omniscient narrator, she becomes interested "in unraveling certain human lots, and seeing how they were woven and interwoven," without extending herself to "that tempting range of relevancies called the universe" (*Middlemarch*, 96). Strindberg offers the inner perspective of a species trapped in a web that expands to the limits of our world. It is the same image but viewed from so radically different a perspective that one wonders how they could have anything in common.

A third distinguishing image is the mirror itself. Eliot's narcissist believes that all the random scratches are a "fine series of concentric circles round that little sun" of his ego. Strindberg's paranoid believes that those scratches are evil fingers pointing at him, that all thought is composed of "ideas of reference." Moreover, the pattern on the surface is actually his own efforts to reconstitute a destroyed inner world, to shore up fragments of the self, but beyond the restored mirror, the design of the malevolent concentric web is still visible. Eliot's art also goes beyond the narcissistic-mirror danger to reveal how characters can reproduce their antiselves, morbid projections of their inner malaise.

Such similarities obtain because, in a general way, the mirror is based on, or built up from, early positive object reflections (the good-breast image, the smiling response, etc.), which are molded into part of the self and serve artists as the sustaining blank surface or dream screen onto which they can begin projecting their vision (see appendix A). But behind this supportive surface may be a less stable self and the more primitive drives and representations of Melanie Klein's paranoid/schizoid stage, in which others are determined solely by libidinal and aggressive drives.[32] Such material also makes itself felt in the creative process and, eventually, as we have seen, in the work itself.

8
The Dualistic Mode in Virginia Woolf's
To the Lighthouse

> Some collaboration has to take place in the mind between the woman and the man before that act of creation can be accomplished. Some marriage of opposites has to be consummated. ... The curtains must be drawn. ... The writer ... once his experience is over, must lie back and let his mind celebrate its nuptials in darkness.
>
> —Virginia Woolf, *A Room of One's Own*

Just as the lighthouse of Virginia Woolf's vision casts double shadows, so has the light cast on her genius evoked divided responses. At times she emphasized the special virtues of sexual separatism and attacked the masculine sentence as artifical; at other times she conceptualized a sexually neutral ideal of objectivity and impersonality, which Marilyn Farwell has shown is derived from her male peers, notably T. S. Eliot.[1] And as she once called for the murder of that deadly ideal, the Angel of the House, so for the feminist critic she is cast as the inimical angel herself.[2] At the source of this dualism is Virginia Woolf's own sense that due to differences between her parents, "she was the heiress to two very different and in fact opposed traditions," which were like "two rival streams [that] dashed together and flowed confused but not harmonized in her blood."[3]

It is intriguing to consider her duality in light of polar creativity. How, for example, might she opt for a family romance (with its lowly, disappointing parents to be discarded for a more suitably noble pair) when her real parents could hardly be deemed lowly, although disappointing in sharing the child's intense need to be loved, any parents, Olympian or otherwise, could be, as hers indeed were. Nonetheless, for this young artist to adopt a fantasy of exalted origins would be no simple matter, given a father who "was the dominant English man of letters of the second half of the nineteenth century"[4] and a mother of universally acclaimed beauty and grace.[5] The family romance seems redundant.

Her strategy, insofar as one can be inferred from *To the Lighthouse*, presents a peculiar variation on the adoption theme. This 1927 novel, based on childhood holidays at St. Ives on the North Cornwall coast in the late 1880s, shifts the setting north to Scotland and the time ahead to the pre–World

War I period. With the Ramsays are their eight children and various acquaintances. There is little overt action. In the first section, a trip to the lighthouse is cancelled early in the day, and, a while later, two of the young guests become engaged. The second section marks the passage of time and the abandonment of the summer cottage. Counterpointing the greater catastrophe of the war are individual tragedies. In the third section, a few of the survivors return to the cottage, and the trip to the lighthouse is finally completed.

Throughout these sections the adoption theme is subtly interwoven. Instead of changing lowly parents for more suitably lofty ones, Woolf keeps the real ones and gives their aura of fame and beauty ample development: Mr. Ramsay is an eminent philosopher of heroic aspirations, and Mrs. Ramsay is a woman of such searing beauty and charm that no one can remain unaffected by her presence. Granted that as much irony slips into the one portrait as ambivalence into the other, both are still endowed with a magnificence that lifts them, for a time, above mere mortals. Since "theirs is a primordial world of Titans,"[6] they are perceived with the radiant vision of childhood as well as with the cool scrutiny of maturity; yet something of the idealized original parents remains in the thinly fictionalized Ramsays, empowering them, as it were, to play themselves in the unfolding family romance.[7]

But this is not to take place with their own children (named "after the Kings and Queens of England—the Red, the Fair"), for the family romance serves to circumvent literal incest. That is why an orphan/foundling must be called into being. And there is one character in the novel who, suitably, is not only lacking in parents but is also lacking in sex. This is Lily Briscoe, who is primarily an artist, for now the adoption fantasy can unfold into a creative romance with the world. Like the outcast artist, Miss LaTrobe in *Between the Acts* (1941), she is the "familiar visionary figure who emerges at the end of every one of the major novels."[8] Moreover, she is intensely involved with the Ramsays as the inspirational subject matter of her painting and continually strives to transform her emotional responses to them into aesthetic strategies. She contemplates Mr. Ramsay as a "generous, pure-hearted heroic man" beyond praise, and she observes Mrs. Ramsay, bowed over her book, as the "loveliest," the "best of people, but also different" (*To the Lighthouse*, 76).

At this point in the novel Mrs. Ramsay, not destined to live out the year, is fifty; Lily is thirty-four. She remembers an earlier night, apparently on the same holiday:

> Sitting on the floor with her arms round Mrs. Ramsay's knees, close as she could get, smiling to think that Mrs. Ramsay would never know the reason of that pressure, she imagined how in the chambers of the mind and heart of the woman who was, physically, touching her, were stood, like the treasures in the tombs of kings, tablets bearing sacred inscriptions, which if one could spell them out, would teach one everything, but they would never be offered openly, never made public.
> What art was there, known to love or cunning, by which one pressed through into those secret chambers? That device for becoming, like waters poured into one

jar, inextricably the same, one with the subject adored? Could the body achieve, or the mind, subtly mingling in the intricate passages of the brain? or the heart? Could loving, as people called it, make her and Mrs. Ramsay one? For it was not knowledge but unity that she desired, not inscriptions on tablets, nothing could be written in any language known to man, but intimacy itself, which is knowledge, she had thought, leaning her head on Mrs. Ramsay's knee.

Nothing happened. Nothing! Nothing! as she leant her head against Mrs. Ramsay's knee. And yet, she knew knowledge and wisdom were stored up in Mrs. Ramsay's heart. (78–79)

Out of similar great expectations and promises of the key to all mythologies is the family romance articulated. Like so many reflectors, other characters reinforce Lily's enthusiasms. Mr. Bankes see "her at the end of the line very clearly Greek, straight, blue-eyed," the Graces having "joined hands in meadows of asphodel to compose that face." The omniscient narrator's voice also proclaims her "royalty of form"; and reading to her son James, she wore in Lily's eyes, "an august shape; the shape of a dome" which is rendered in part on canvas, in Mr. Bankes's eyes, as a "purple shadow without irreverence" (80–81). Thus proceed—as royalty is shaded by purple, as the sacred is figured by the dome—through Lily's artwork the intricate transformations of Viriginia Woolf's imagination.[9]

To a certain degree, Lily's creative drive siphons off her intense love for Mrs. Ramsay, ameliorates it, renders the pain barely tolerable when Mrs. Ramsay is dead, but never leaves Lily quite at peace. The specific way in which creativity makes her conflicts bearable is through the diffusion of the child's family romance into the artist's creative romance with the world. "What," Lily asks herself, "could one say to her? 'I'm in love with you?' No, that was not true. 'I'm in love with this all,' waving her hand at the hedges at the house, at the children. It was absurd" (32). But it isn't really, since she does embrace these objects eventually on her canvas, for in the end her art is all she has.

If readers sense that the emotional relationship between Lily and Mrs. Ramsay is the supremely important one of child and idealized parent, they need not be dissuaded by Lily's nominal maturity or her tie to a father she keeps house for during the rest of the year. Such details exist outside the narrative and pose no threat to the emotional realities that constitute her life with the Ramsays. Nor does the fact that, literally speaking, Lily is no orphan impede her from playing an adopted-child role with the Ramsays or from playing out through them her creative romance with the world.

"Only Lily Briscoe," thinks Mrs. Ramsay, both relieved and patronizing: how Lily appears in the eyes of Mrs. Ramsay will draw attention to the next stage of inquiry. What we see of Lily through the gaze of the woman she idealizes is "her little Chinese eyes and her puckered up face," and we are left with the unkind observation that "she would never marry" (29). To Mr. Ramsay, she is "skimpy."[10] At dinner that evening she contrasts Mrs. Ramsay's "abundance with her own poverty of spirit," and feels herself "solitary, left out." And after the ten-year gap, the omniscient narrator in the third section depicts her as a "skimpy old maid, holding a paint brush" (269). Mrs. Ramsay's death has left her with the "pain of want . . . bitter anger" and feelings of helplessness and emptiness. Counterpointing a moment when she bursts into tears and cries out for Mrs. Ramsay is the following laconic report from the Ramsay party en route to the lighthouse:

> Macalister's boy took one of the fish and cut a square out of its side to bait his hook with. The mutilated body (it was still alive) was thrown back into the sea. (268)

To Lily the loss of Mrs. Ramsay is indeed like tearing off a part of herself.[11] The careful juxtaposition of Lily's tears and the mutilated body, the indirect associations with Mrs. Ramsay as waves and sea and Lily as a little fish in this greater element, her salt tears, and so forth, strongly suggest a reciprocity between the two figures along the lines of deficiency and completeness, of poverty and bounty. And, therefore, it is probable that from the outset Mrs. Ramsay's part in Lily's life is meant to be a corrective and restorative one carried out through creative processes. In other words, the artist is both remaking herself, that is, correcting a deficient self-image, and restoring a lost, idealized object. As more than a personal wound, the action symbolizes the "sudden wounding of the artist's consciousness which stimulates creativity."[12]

To summarize what has been set forth so far about creativity: the family romance, which deals with disappointment in the sphere of early attachment, also functions as a step in the direction of separation. In the imagination, new parents are concocted, and one's self is endowed with the ambivalent freedom of the orphan / foundling. This transformation and displacement of emotional conflicts into creative fantasy is parallel to Lily's tendency to redirect emotional conflicts into aesthetic areas. This transfer effectively diffuses the artist's creative romance throughout the world of experience. At the same time, due to the early (so far, hypothesized) disappointment, as well as to other nonspecific factors, the damage to self-esteem must be repaired, the loss of self recovered. And it is in the spaces created by the family-romance fantasy that the remaking of the self, along with the original family and environment, gets underway. These processes appear to be fundamental components of creativity, but rarely are they so clearly on view as in *To the Lighthouse*.

Scarcely less distinctive are the means by which the next stages in creativity will be implemented. Before attempting to understand how Lily will deal with Mrs. Ramsay as an absence, we must understand more of how she is dealt with as a presence. The opening section of the novel is called "The Window," and Lily is introduced painting "Mrs. Ramsay sitting in the window with James." In the second section, called "Time Passes," the holiday cottage is abandoned; Mrs. Ramsay dies; her son Andrew is killed in the war; her daughter Prue dies in childbirth. In the third section, called "The Lighthouse," Mr.

Ramsay and others, including James and Lily, return to the cottage after ten years and make the voyage across the bay to the lighthouse while Lily continues with her painting. James is now sixteen and still remembers with bitterness that morning ten years ago when his mother had promised him a trip to the lighthouse only to have his father peremptorily veto the outing on account of the weather. And so now, when he at last reaches the lighthouse with his father, whose belated words of praise for his steering soften his earlier resentments, James thinks, "So that was the Lighthouse, was it?" And he answers himself, "No, the other was also the Lighthouse. For nothing was simply one thing. The other Lighthouse was true too." This other lighthouse was the one he had seen and still remembered from sitting with his mother while she read him a fairy tale.

> "And that's the end," she said, and she saw in his eyes, as the interest of the story died away in them, something else take its place; something wondering, pale, like the reflection of a light, which at once made him gaze and marvel. Turning, she looked across the bay, and there, sure enough, coming regularly across the waves first two quick strokes and then one long steady stroke, was the light of the Lighthouse. It had been lit. (94)

Thus, before Mr. Ramsay is to be associated in the third section with the lightouse as male edifice, a mental structure that rises above the elemental world of sea, land, and natural light, Mrs. Ramsay has been associated with the lighthouse to her son and as a magical promise of fulfillment, to others as a radiant source of beauty, and, more immediately, to Lily Briscoe as a light source through the window, which she attempts to render on her canvas, if she could only match her emotions to the appropriate colors and shapes. Mrs. Ramsay is consistently depicted as illuminating her immediate surroundings. "With the stars in her eyes and veils in her hair, with cyclamen and wild violets," thinks Mr. Tansley in spite of himself. Her presence turns her house into a lighthouse: "lights moving about in the upper windows . . . the house was all lit up·. . . Lights, lights, lights" (119). Around her at the dinner table, "all the candles were lit up, and the faces on both sides of the table were brought nearer by the candle light, and composed, as they had not been in the twilight, into a party round a table, for the night was now shut off by panes of glass" (146–47). It is her power then, so these passages imply, to endow others with her wholeness and to quicken their environment with her felt life. She is a "beacon of orientation"[13] and functions like the mother as mirroring object to her children, for it is in just such ways that they begin acquiring that nuclear sense of self that unfolds into a sense of wholeness, through which they become aware of the environment around them as also being radiant with life. Thus Mrs. Ramsay, who often pauses before a mirror for self-appraisal ("When she looked in the glass and saw her hair gray, her cheek sunk, at fifty, she thought, possibly she might have managed things better" [14]), functions for the others as both mirror and window. Through her they see what they are—unhappily, for Lily—or what they might become: "a fellowship, a professorship," thinks Charles Tansley, who, in her presence, "felt capable of anything"; or what kind of place the world might be.

Yet Mrs. Ramsay does not exist solely through her own or other characters' reflections. Mitchell Leaska observes that she, for all her catalytic function in bringing people together, is herself an "extremely isolated person ... unable to share her deepest feelings with anyone." And, he adds, "how necessary it is for her always to be at the centre of things, to have a kind of spiritual immortality."[14] So she is a complicated, rounded character in her own right, one who seeks as well as emits reflections from her surroundings. Interestingly, she is also literally shortsighted.

All the same, it is not surprising that her loss is felt in the second section as the disappearance from the world of a familiar power of self-affirming relfection:

> "Well, we must wait for the future to show," said Mr. Bankes, coming in from the terrace.
> "It's almost too dark to see," said Andrew, coming up from the beach.
> "One can hardly tell which is the sea and which is the land," said Prue.
> "Do we leave that light burning?" said Lily as they took their coats off indoors.
> "No," said Prue, "not if everyone's in."
> "Andrew," she called back, "just put out the light in the hall."
> One by one the lamps were all extinguished, except that Mr. Carmichael, who liked to lie awake a little reading Virgil, kept his candle burning rather longer than the rest. (189)

"Nothing, it seemed, could survive the flood, the profusion of darkness which, creeping in at keyholes and crevices, stole around window blinds," continues the next segment, suggesting that the once-radiant window is now dark and blind. Time passes, everything changes, nature encroaches on the human world. And then a drab, old cleaning lady is sent to initiate the process of restoration, "to open all windows, and dust the bedrooms." But the windows will no longer reveal the same scene, nor the mirrors reflect the same images. Yet light returns: "some channel in the depths of obscurity through which light enough issued to twist her face grinning in the glass" (197). Her somber, worn, slightly grotesque image replaces Mrs. Ramsay's and no longer reflects life, beauty, or one's former best self.

Consequently, the self, as such, is largely missing from this section. There is instead a neuter, anonymous self in search of some individuating sign, some reflection of self in what another character in another work describes as "the world seen without a self."[15] "The mystic, the visionary, walking the beach on a fine night, stirring a puddle, looking at a stone, asking themselves, 'What am I,' 'What is this?'" (197–98).

Just how explicit the novel is about the loss of Mrs. Ramsay as mirroring, self-integrating object occurs a few pages later.

That dream, of sharing, completing, of finding in solitude on the beach an answer, was then but a reflection in a mirror, and the mirror itself was but the surface glassiness which forms in quiesence when the nobler powers sleep beneath? Impatient, despairing yet loth to go (for beauty offers her lures, has her consolations), to pace the beach was impossible; contemplating was unendurable; the mirror was broken. (202)

Without this organizing presence, the natural resurgence of life in the spring is meaningless.

But the stillness and the brightness of the day were as strange as the chaos and tumult of night, with the trees standing there, and the flowers standing there, looking before them, looking up, yet beholding nothing, eyeless, and so terrible. (203)

Yet this chaos surrounding and invading the deserted house, "left like a shell on a sandhill to fill with dry salt grains," is not final, but rather preliminary to a human return and a creative regathering. For creativity can only follow loss, can only build within an emptiness; so long as the object—the source of nurture and inspiration is present—one remains dazzled and distracted by it. But once it is removed, it can be created. "She has never finished that picture. She would paint that picture now" (220).

And that is what Lily, out of her anger, want, and emptiness, proceeds to do. How she proceeds to do it is in keeping with her character. The desire for a person must be actively transformed into a desire for making. The anger passes into "her first quick decisive stroke," which, in emulating the "stroke" from the lighthouse, connects her symbolically with her lost love object. "The brush descended. It flickered brown over the white canvas" (235). Her gesture also cues the shift from passive absorption of pain to active mastery. And, most significantly, the emptiness within her is transferred onto the blank canvas. The others have left for the lighthouse. She is both relieved and disappointed, and confronts "her canvas as if it had floated up and placed itself white and uncompromising directly before her" (234). She briefly becomes aware of the "emptiness" of her surroundings and looks "blankly at the canvas, with its uncompromising white stare." The canvas has come alive, not as a person, but as part of a person, reflecting Lily's own emptiness and suggesting her regression to a preperson stage of early childhood, as prerequisite for creativity.

The recurring images of white and blank give clues to this regressed emotional state stemming from want, emptiness, and rage, and one that, in addition, is necessary for the artist's "disorderly sensations" (254) to link up with the preceding account of chaos and tumult in nature. Further clues turn up when the canvas is felt "looming out at her" as she attacks it "with brown running nervous lines" (236). She is nearly swallowed up and drowned by the intensity of this process and by the threat it represents.

What that threat amounts to is further hinted at by this remarkable passage:

"For the mass loomed before her; it protruded; she felt it pressing on her eyeballs" (237). By way of relating her experiences to psychoanalytic phenomena, I would like to quote two passages of clinical material reported by patients who have had an impression of "something shadowy and indefinite, generally felt to be 'round,' which comes nearer and nearer, swells a gigantic size and threatens to crush the subject." These sensations are hypnagogic states, or Isakower phenomena: "mental images of sucking at the mother's breast and of falling asleep there when satisfied."[16] From Lewin derives the concept of the dream screen, "the background or projection drop for the dream picture," from the survival of the "baby's vast picture of the mammary hemisphere." Roughly equivalent to the dream screen is the artist's blank canvas, notably so for Lily, whose canvas protrudes and presses against her eyeballs like the looming mass of the mother's breast. Against the infant's dread of being swallowed up by this object, Lily's defense is the counterattack of her brush striking back and beginning by color to alter the nature of the threat. Simultaneously, the hallucinated breast gratifies her needs, and its fluids almost magically stimulate the flow of Lily's paints: "Then, as if some juice necessary for the lubrication of her faculties were spontaneously squirted, she began precariously dipping among the blues and ambers" (237). A little later, "she seemed to be standing up to the lips in some substance, to move and float in it" (285).

It amounts to a process of breast recovery (the positive maternal image) and breast mastery (symbiotic dual-unity) that Lily is so far conducting along creative lines. She has "had a few moments of nakedness when she seemed like an unborn soul" (237), and as she paints she loses "consciousness of outer things, and her name and her personality and her appearance" (238). It is here that self-remaking also begins, and a "good breast," in Melanie Klein's sense, is reinternalized and functions creatively, for Lily, "like a fountain spurting over that glaring, hideously difficult white space" occupied formerly by the self and all-important other (238). "She began to model her way into the hollow there" (255).

Simultaneously, she is "sitting beside Mrs. Ramsay on the beach." The whole object or person does not disappear but is maintained by elusive mental activities similar to those described by Weissman as "dissociative" or by Rothenberg as "Janusian."[17] Soon Lily begins recovering memories of Mrs. Ramsay alive, which are counterpoised with acute grief reactions to her death, as Lily goes "on tunnelling her way into her picture, into the past" (258). And here the creative process greatly resembles the mourning process, in which a relationship with a lost object is relinquished even as it is revived bit by bit, until Lily actually hallucinates Mrs. Ramsay's return as a "wave of white went over the window pane" (300). But by now, although the associations of wave and white persist, the long-sought sense of separateness has also been achieved: "so much depends . . . upon distance," is her way of putting it (284). The object has both been internalized, as Lily finds the powers to endow her canvas with life, and reexternalized, as Lily discovers it in its former setting in the window. Like the one visible lighthouse and its invisible twin of memory and desire, Mrs. Ramsay is both in here and out there, both absent and present, near and far ("For sometimes quite close to the shore, the Lighthouse looked this morning in the haze an enormous distance away" [271]).

Without Mrs. Ramsay, but with her own vision and her determined assault on the empty canvas, Lily finishes her painting at the finish of the novel. The probability is that this work will not be "virginal" (77), as she felt the earlier unfinished project to be, dreading anyone's eyes to penetrate its deficiencies; nor will it be "skimpy," as both she (149) and the unsubstantial works of other holiday painters are described (24). It will, in short, not merely be more Lily.

And it will be much more than she has so far depicted, more than her attachment to Mrs. Ramsay and all it has encompassed. For Lily has been struggling throughout the novel to fit something else into her painting. Mrs. Ramsay is not the only absent object that Lily must include in her art; no sooner has she had her vision than she goes to the edge of the lawn and scouts her surroundings for another, albeit only temporary, missing object: "Where was that boat now? And Mr. Ramsay? She wanted him" (300). And although she had never been able completely to ignore him, not until now has she been ready to accommodate him into the total vision of her painting. But, after all, the person who has always filled her thoughts before has been Mr. Ramsay's wife, known to us only by her married or husband's name. And he, too, is part of the enigmatic other lighthouse, for he is the one who once withheld it and now reaches it, even as Lily completes her painting with that final "line there, in the centre," which may stand for him or it, or both.

The actual lighthouse, beginning with Mrs. Ramsay's offering it to her son and ending with Mr. Ramsay's bringing the same son to it, encompasses the Ramsay relationship: "Directly one looked up and saw them, what she [Lily] called 'being in love' flooded them. They became part of that unreal but penetrating and exciting universe which is the world seen through the eyes of love." The couple consolidates the artist's creative romance: "The sky stuck to them; the birds sang through them." And Lily felt "how life, from being made up of little separate incidents which one lived one by one, became curled and whole like a wave which bore one up with it" (72–73).

But "their relation" (62), or "the thing she had with her husband," eludes Lily through the early scenes. "So that is marriage, Lily thought, a man and a woman looking at a girl throwing a ball" (110). But that is not marriage, and they are at best only the "symbols of marriage, husband and wife" (111), and have no dynamic impact on Lily's art. She is openly ambivalent toward Mr. Ramsay, the negative side of which stems from his being perceived as a rival for Mrs. Ramsay. But her "vision" must encompass the counterpoints of her initially spoken "Yes" and his initially spoken "But."[18]

In fact, in a world largely contained by Mrs. Ramsay's abundance of beauty and love, it is not surprising that her husband is generally perceived ambivalently, as a tyrant or a hypocrite, by several within and without his family, though most tellingly by his six-year-old son, James, as "the beak of brass, the arid scimiter of his father, the egotistical man," who "plunged and smote, demanding sympathy" (60). Mrs. Ramsay, too, considers "the sterility of men" (126), and, when she is gone, Lily cringes from his "insatiable hunger for sympathy" (226) and pictures him as a "lion seeking whom he could devour" (233).

These collectively negative reactions have tended to bias readers and critics alike against Mr. Ramsay, and Mitchel Leaska has judiciously pointed out the tendency to "ignore many of Mr. Ramsay's redeeming qualities, the most conspicuous of which are his devotion to his children and the unconditional love he bears his wife."[19]

Insofar as Mrs. Ramsay responds to her experiences with intuitions and feelings, Mr. Ramsay meets his head-on with "facts uncompromising" (11). And if "Nature has but little clay ... like that of which she moulded" Mrs. Ramsay (46–47), Mr. Ramsay is clearly aware of how "his own children sprung from his loins" (11). This reintroduces the question of origins that the family romance had succeeded in temporarily reworking, at least from Lily Briscoe's perspective. But her family romance with the Ramsays does not relieve her mind of the problem of human origins, even though her fascination with Mrs. Ramsay eventuates in creativity and individuation. Early on, Lily senses that creativity is fraught with tension and makes the "passage from conception to work as dreadful as any down a dark passage for a child" (32). Is the child, by any chance, feeling her way along a dark passage toward her parents' bedroom? And, if so, what will she encounter there—a shocking activity, an incomprehensible riddle about the mysteries of conception? Of course, such an elliptical novel as this has very little explicitly to say about sexuality, although a great deal is inferred from being left unsaid. But other deep readers of literary texts emphasize that from the very outset the novel explores the primal scene as the mystery of "parental influence," which the child senses through the electric "tensions between mother and father" that are so puzzling and disturbing.[20] Examining how the male enters and rends the female space while the female envelops the male's negativity, Martin Gliserman suggests that from the opening sentence, the novel can be read as a "symbolically sexual interaction."[21]

Pull her skirts about her as she may before Mr. Ramsay's lionly advances, Lily herself is not immune to sexual queries; only, like every other emotional issue in her life, they are dealt with aesthetically: "It was a question, she remembered, how to connect this mass on the right with that on the left." She is thinking of her painting, of course. "But the danger was by doing that," she quickly considers, is that "the unity of the whole might be broken" (82–83). This unity appears to be based on the mother-child bond, Mrs. Ramsay and James, which would be—indeed, has been—broken by introducing another mass, Mr. Ramsay, the oedipal father, who vetoes the trip to the lighthouse.

But despite his supposedly devouring needs for sympathy or praise, Lily in her fashion also idealizes him, though with none of the fervor reserved for his wife. She is especially impressed by his works of the intellect, though they make her think of a large kitchen table.

> It was Andrew's doing. She asked him what his father's books were about. "Subject and object and the nature of reality," Andrew had said. And when she said Heavens, she had no notion what that meant. "Think of a kitchen table then," he told her, "when you're not there." (38)

"Subject and object and the nature of reality" sound ominous, if not exactly bearing on sexual matters; the concepts are as abstract as the fairy tale about the fisherman and his wife Mrs. Ramsay reads to James is elliptical. Yet later on, when Lily is at the table and in her own abstract aesthetic way is puzzling over how two masses might be connected on canvas, she thinks, "Yes, I shall put the tree further in the middle; then I shall avoid that awkward space." And to remind herself, "she took up the salt cellar and put it down again on a flower in pattern in the table-cloth" (128). This relieves her uneasiness, but it does not really resolve the issue, even on aesthetic grounds, for the picture remains unfinished for ten years.

Then, upon her return, it suddenly comes back to her.

> While she had sat there last ten years ago there had been a little sprig or leaf pattern on the table-cloth, which she had looked at in a moment of revelation. There had been a problem about a foreground of a picture. Move the tree to the middle, she had said. She had never finished that picture. She would paint that picture now. It had been knocking about in her mind all these years. (220)

So it is owing to the recovery of a memory that the creative process is revived, but with that recovery other associations are also released, seemingly unrelated to the task at hand. "She had been looking at the table-cloth, and it had flashed upon her that she would move the tree to the middle, and need never marry anybody, and she had felt an enormous exultation" (262). Thus we are offered another way in which creative processes may be overdetermined by deeply emotional or, as here, by sexual issues.

As blank, receptive surfaces, canvas and tabletop are easily associated; a further object not mentioned may also have crossed Lily's mind as she looks at the tablecloth: namely, the marriage bed itself, the mention of which may be said to be avoided, as the prospect of reaching it is likewise rejected. The saltcellar, associated with candlelit meals at the Ramsays, with salt in the sea and in Lily's eyes, is a movable object on a plane of reality, one that may stand for a tree, but also may put us in mind of another, immovable object, the lighthouse.

The images of lighthouse, saltcellar, rose, and bed as, so far, only obscure allusions to the sex act coalesce in an earlier sequence involving Mrs. Ramsay and link with the present series by the evocative word *stroke*. Elsewhere, it is used for Lily's nervously active brush strokes against the canvas; here, it is the light beam that has waked Mrs. Ramsay in the night, and she has seen it "bent across their bed, stroking the floor . . . as if it were stroking with its silver fingers some seabed vessel in her brain whose bursting would flood her with delight" (99). But it is not now night, and Mrs. Ramsay had just "looked out to meet that stroke of the Lighthouse, the long steady stroke the last of the three, which was her stroke" (96); here she is identified with the lighthouse as an objectivization of the inward beacon of self-searching that she allegedly conducts on herself: "She looked up over her knitting and met the third stroke and it seemed to her like her own eyes meeting her own eyes, searching as she alone could search into her mind and heart, purifying out of existence that lie, any lie" (97). The passage is not free of ambiguities, since this flattering version of Mrs. Ramsay has been called into question;[22] but it is perplexing, also, because the significance of the lighthouse begins to shift from a self-objectifier to a quasi-erotic partner. Perhaps it is not so completely in her control as she believes—a statement generally true about herself and her relationships, as Lily gleefully points out later in regard to Mrs. Ramsay's ill-fated matchmaking propensities. Above all, she does not control the erotic sphere. And in the midst of her reveries, an untoward association process is stirred: "there curled up off the floor of the mind, rose from the lake of one's being, a mist, a bride to meet her lover" (98). And, thereafter, the light assumes increasing sexual power, until a orgasmic climax is reached:

> It silvered the rough waves a little more brightly, as daylight faded, and the blue went out of the sea and it rolled in waves of pure lemon which curved and swelled and broke upon the beach and the ecstasy burst in her eyes and waves of pure delight raced over the floor of her mind and she felt, It is enough! It is enough! (99–100)

Whatever else is made of this passage, it clearly functions to dislodge Mrs. Ramsay from her earlier complacency of praising "herself in praising the light, without vanity, for she was stern, she was searching, she was beautiful like that light." Perhaps the light simply brings out her own unfulfilled sexual longings; perhaps it is part of a sexual scene in which the stimulus or other partner is only symbolically rendered. It may be Mr. Ramsay, or it may be someone else, perhaps a child who would like to do more than the actual lighthouse does— that is, merely look on—and actively engage the parent in some obscurely sexual way.

Clearly there is, so far, no place here for Mr. Ramsay, with his "beak of brass" and "arid scimitar." The two masses, as Lily has noted, have not been connected; yet the Ramsays, as everyone can see clearly, are connected, are in love with each other. This is the puzzle that underlies the technique of the novel; it is related to Erich Auerbach's famous observation that Virginia Woolf is not so much interested in a particular act or occasion, but in what the occasion releases, things which are not seen directly but by reflection, which are not tied to the present of the framing occurrence which releases them."[23] If this passage were radically revised into a psychoanalytic context, it might suggest that the interest is not so much in what the parents do when they sleep together as in the effects their total sexual/emotional relationship has on their children, real or adopted, and on others. Yet the other interest, the need to be clear about origins, to know where and how one came to be, is not so easily subdued by technique alone and lays a claim on content, if only by indirection and displacement. For insofar as the table has been linked with the marriage bed, then it follows that thinking of the one "when you're not there" is almost like trying to unravel the primal scene of your own origins when you're not there; it is a "world without a self," or "a house full of unrelated passions" (221). The immediate problem seems to be that the child's uncertainty over what takes place is mixed up with misgivings over the paternal function. There is, in other words, more to the lighthouse than a maternal beacon; there is a towering, stroking energy as well—frightening and awful.

For as he appears so hatefully in his son's eyes, Mr. Ramsay is also a dramatically intensified alien and instrusive presence for almost everyone. His offhand refusal to permit the family outing to the lighthouse is one of those seemingly minor lapses of concern that gradually assumes greater resonance and consequence as events unfold. It is overdetermined in its effects, and, for James at a crucial moment in his development, it crystalizes his conflicts with his father (the way the lighthouse itself concentrates light to a single point) and blocks the path to identification, until it is cleared ten years later by his father's equally offhand praise for his steering to the lighthouse. The incident then encapsulates the oedipal conflict: "he hated the twang and twitter of his father's emotion which, vibrating around them, disturbed the perfect simplicity and good sense of his relations with his mother" (58). James's immediate reaction to his father's refusal, his withholding of the lighthouse as a highly prized object in the child's mind, is also remarkably Freudian: "Had there been an axe handy, or a poker, any weapon that would have gashed a hole in his father's breast and killed him, there and then, James would have seized it" (10).

But unlike Oedipus and like the good modern child he is, James does not turn his aggression onto his father; instead he nurses a grievance against tyrants until the original tyrant becomes more humanized. Meanwhile, the picture of his inner world, not presented in his own language but assisted by the omniscient narrator, has dramatically altered: into "this delicious fecundity," which he shares with his mother, "this fountain and spray of life, the fatal sterility of the male plunged itself, like a beak of brass, barren and bare." It "smote mercilessly, again and again

and James, as he stood stiff between her kness, felt her rise in a rosy-flowered fruit tree laid with leaves and dancing boughs into which the beak of brass, the arid scimitar of his father, the egotisitcal man, plunged and smote, demanding sympathy. (60)

Our close attention to these passages may be rewarded in several ways. First, James "stiff between his mother's knees," dramatizes his precarious oedipal position and, by rendering himself the mother's phallus, denies castration. Second, we glimpse where James's unacted aggression went: it is displaced onto the father, who now attacks mother as the son would like to attack him. Third, we can see how James's rage colors his perception of the parental relation, distorting it into a violent assault on the female by the male. It is this oblique rendering of the primal scene, the parental sexual relation, through the phallic drives of the six-year-old son James—which appears to operate on the novel as a whole and certainly biases the reader against the paternal role.

To bring these issues into closer alignment with the theoretical concerns of this study, it might be said that this comprehension of the primal scene, both of human origins and of adult sexuality, is so far deficient. The male is aggressive—in oral and phallic ways—and takes rather than gives; never mind that he is the father of eight—(or that Virginia's own father, Leslie Stephen, was pathetically dependent on his wife and daughters)—Mr. Ramsay is, in this light, a sterile tyrant. Lily believes that Mrs. Ramsay "pitied men always as if they lacked something—women never, as if they had something." In psychoanalytic terms, castration is a male affliction; the breast is valued over the penis and, indeed, is substituted for it. Mr. Ramsay's "little light" is merged in "some bigger light" (56), which is the other lighthouse, as determined by the female principle.

And it is as if the novel as a whole is also strongly swayed by these predilections for what has been associated with the feminine, the subjective, and the preoedipal, only catching its balance occasionally, as when Lily rushes to catch a sight of Mr. Ramsay nearing the lighthouse. Otherwise it is up to the lighthouse itself to symbolize something in the male principle mostly denied Mr. Ramsay, nominal father of eight and largely disregarded in the novel, at least up to the very end, when he conducts James and Cam to the lighthouse.

But before then, at least once Mr. Ramsay's presence is felt in a gentle, positive, and obliquely sexual way. It is toward the end of the first section, when the Ramsays find themselves reading in the library. Mrs. Ramsay is concerned to find out her husband's reactions to Minta Doyle's engagement, but bides her time and is soon lulled into a dreamy state by a volume of poetry—"swinging herself, zigzagging this way and that, from one line to another, until a little sound roused her—her husband slapping his thighs" (179).

It is a minor gesture to be sure, like many of the insignificannt facts and gestures and actions of the day that gradually light up larger vistas of meaning. It is enough, perhaps, to recall for the reader the fertile thigh of another tyrant, the Greek weather god, Zeus, and to be reminded of those fertile loins that fathered eight. So, somewhere Mr. Ramsay must be fitted into the picture for the sake of balance or harmony or simple justice; and, in fact, it is the direction taken by Lily in the final section, once she has worked through some of her feelings for Mrs. Ramsay.

It is also the overall direction of the novel, which begins with Mrs. Ramsay's holding up the promise of the lighthouse to her son and ends with Mr. Ramsay's ultimately taking him there. A great deal has been written about the ambiguity of the lighthouse, which signals land from the sea but is not quite part of either. A piece of biography may further elucidate the intricate reworking of origins that became this novel. While Virginia's mother was carrying her, Virginia's father discovered on a walking tour Saint Ives and found Talland House to let.[24] Thus her origins are linked with her father through the setting of her blissful summer holidays. By distancing herself from this intensely emotional site and choosing Scotland for the novel, she succeeds only in strengthening the bond with her father, for one of his favorite authors was Sir Walter Scott, whom he refers to as "that manly companion." Moreover, prior to the crucial scene of conjugal affection between the Ramsays cited above, Mr. Ramsay reads a chapter from Scott's *The Antiquary*. Thus, through Virginia Woolf's elliptical method, a chain of associations is forged that acknowledges masculine reality, touches on authorship and antiquity (by inference, origins), and further connects land with male, as ocean had already been linked with female. Hence the unitive power of the lighthouse, standing on land out in the sea.[25]

Whatever else the lighthouse may stand for, it clearly represents the Ramsay marriage; and the unity the lighthouse achieves by harnessing such opposites as inner and outer reality, distance and proximity, motion and stillness, light and dark, vessel and beam, is also emblematic of the human sexual unity that is seen and felt by those who come in contact with the Ramsays. It is the invisible, but completed, primal scene of their marriage, and thus, like the Sphinx, an enigmatic source of life—creative as well as destructive. Like the Medusa's head, it is both a blinding and an illuminating source of power. As its beam looks out from isolation and creeps into the parental bedroom, it is also the child born of the primal scene, product of the mutual efforts of mother and father—and in this respect the artist, as well, who in her bisexuality retains the male/female ambience of the lighthouse. It is finally a self-symbol that by holding together the parents would also hold together oneself.

By structuring her novel so that the emotional sequence runs from maternal attachment to paternal recognition, and by maintaining an aesthetic parallel that presents an androgynous ideal of art, Virginia Woolf also permits a psychoanalytic reading that discovers the creative process as oscillating between a subjective pole signified as the family romance and an objective pole signified as the primal scene. This blending of illusion and truth through the creative process emerges as the distinctive reality that is art.

Returning to this chapter's epigraph, readers may now perceive Lily Briscoe as the creative embodiment of the "profound, if irrational, instinct in favour of the theory that the union of man and woman makes for the greatest satisfaction, the most complete happiness.''[26] The Ramsay marriage, the elusive primal scene of childhood, is re-created when the two sexes in the mind corresponding to the two in the body are united insofar as the androgynous artist can allow "his mind [to] celebrate its nuptials in darkness.''[27] The blinding / illuminating lighthouse beam, the repressed procreative activity, and the artist's gesture of creative mimicry / mastery are all conveyed in the single overdetermined word—*stroke* (99, 235).

By now the dynamic polarities of creativity may be pretty well established as being influential in the process as well as embedded in the work. After these chapters, the plunge into literary creativity levels out. The next chapters consider language origins and mythic dimensions within the polarity context. Thereafter, science, and especially writings on science, will enter the evolving theories, until in the final sections a cultural synthesis will be explored.

9
An Ontogeny of Language

The Greeks made the Muses goddesses of poetry and the arts, who lived on mountains such as Helicon, Aganippe, or Pieria. It was the liquid from these springs which inspired the poets, and thus the myth admirably supports the theory that poetry stems from an oral level of the unconscious.

—Arthur Wormhoudt

1

"The Muses may be taken as pre-genital mother symbols," Wormhoudt continues, in what today we may gag at as blissfully simplistic equations: "The mountains as breast symbols and the springs as milk which issues from the breast." Sounds are profoundly connected with liquids in Wormhoudt's study of poetry; hence his title, "The Unconscious Indentification: Words = Milk."[1] Yet, however we may view this equation, its literalness need not dissuade us from granting: (1) empirical data informing us that language, nursing, and mother love all proceed simultaneously during the first year of life; and (2) psychoanalytic formulations affirming the interchangeability of words and things in the infant's developing mind.[2]

More to the point, Greenson demonstrates the intimate bond between oral sounds and oral object.[3] The one sound, he notes, which the infant can produce to express pleasure and contentment while the maternal nipple is in his month is that of *mmm* (the bilabial nasal [m]). When the nipple is withdrawn, the vowel approximation of *a-a-h* is uttered. Thus the retention and release of the nurturing object is symbolized linguistically in the culturally reinforced expression for mother: *mm-a-ah*. It is not possible that the infant's *m-ah* (or *w-ah*) sounds are intentional, semantic, or communicative in the earliest period; but as distress sounds they automatically signal the loss of the nipple. What advances things is the mother's clear grasp of the signal, the meaning of which is relayed to the infant through her responsiveness as she *directionally* echoes the cries of distress. *Ma-ma* is right here, she says reassuringly and in so doing treats the distress sound as a signal, one that she reinforces by echoing and modifying in such a way that, before long, the infant gets an inkling of the feeding session being hooked into certain prescribed signals.

This modified echoing of the infant's inchoate sounds should be emphasized, because the neat symmetry encountered between sound and name in Romance and Germanic languages, with all their maternal *m*'s, is not sufficient to make a claim for a biologically grounded universality of congruence between primary sounds and primary object.[4] As we observe throughout human evolution: biology proposes, culture disposes. Nevertheless, among the four thousand languages invented by *Homo sapiens sapiens,* many "all over the world have phonetically similar words for 'mama.'"[5] Perhaps the close fit between sound and object in *mah*-for-mother languages suggests a parental disposition to meet the infant on its own phonetic ground. But in view of the fact that two other bilabial + low front vowel combinations [pa-, ba-] are also universal early phonemes, the matchup of [ma-] is not simply genetic, accidental, or learned.

Yet if even the most adroit of linguists would be hard pressed to convey to the infant that its first utterances coincide with two phonemes [m, a] to double and form a morpheme [mama], this is what occurs in English: vocal sounds, beginning as a mix of pleasure and distress, are uttered, echoed, reinforced, and modified into linguistic signals that gradually acquire semantic validity. To summarize, the phoneme [m] is the nipple-in-mouth hum, hence conveying a presence; the phoneme [a] is the response to the nipple withdrawn, hence conveying an absence. Combined, the morphene *mama* verbally "represents" the present/absent object.

But as the infant's first signifier, what precisely does *mama* signify? Certainly not the mother as others know her (i.e., the referent), but rather as a less-than-human yet larger-than-life source of well-being and fullness, of pain and aching emptiness, of wholeness and connectedness or fragmentation and loss, and so forth. To be faithful to Greenson's genetic sequence, we would have to infer that the word is uttered before the mental capacities for memory and representation have developed. But before long, the signified is all those important partial representations of self and other that psychoanalysis has made us aware of. The child's comprehension of the more elusive referent (the actual mother) entails such developmental processes as cognizance of her as a whole object (a person), object-constancy (a degree of consistency in the relationship), and separation-individuation (development of a subsistent self). But in the beginning, due to its capacity for need-gratification, security, and self-containment, *Mama* may be considered an instinctually charged, life-affirming but, so far, pleasure-bound "for" word, or yes.

René Spitz has suggested a connection between the infant's appetitive rooting for the nipple with the acquisition of the first word of the ego's repertoire: *No*—what he terms an "against" word.[6] Before learning to integrate head shaking with the semantic sound *No*, however, the infant passes through an intermediate phase in which the rooting reflex is summoned to terminate nursing. This refusal is a "change in function" that conduces to the later deliberate *No*. That is, primordially, no-breast, then a no to the breast; later, a no to the child's own incessant oral demands, as internalization proceeds. *No* is thus the fitting opposite of *yes*, both being reinforced by a whole world of preverbal experiences. Among linguists, Jesperson held that words originally stood for whole experiences. And if true for the species, why not for the individual? More recently Slobin has reported on research that suggests "one-word utterances express underlying relational notions."[7]

Because phonetic segments [m-n-p-b-g-d-a-o] and the child's earliest sounds [ma-, pa-, ba-] emerge from this primary bond, one may wonder whether they retain resonances from the earliest period of life. Can such primal sounds be deeply allied with those earliest sensations and internalized pleasures that form representations of one's self?[8] Perhaps these sounds carry with them early sensations not only of well-being but also of grandiosity and perfectionism, any of which can be drawn on later as the dual-unity of symbiosis yields to the necessary miscues, ruptures, and lapses that accompany weaning, the separation-individuation process, and the child's establishing the good inner mother among the building blocks of its emerging self. Humming may be soothing; babbling may counteract feelings of abandonment. The mother's echoing of nonsense sounds while introducing semantic units, just like her mirroring of the child's pleasurable feelings of well-being around a feeding session in her smiling response, initiates the human dialogue. As words soon fill the widening spaces between the two and provide a sense of presence to fill an absence, we enter Winnicott's "area of intermediate experiencing," and we recognize that language, along with other transitional phenomena, thrives in a subjective/objective ambience of reality/illusion.[9]

But as language proficiency proceeds exponentially in the second year of life, it soon departs from and quickly surpasses its earlier image-bound functions. Consequently, only certain words or expressions retain "imagenic" features or promise a latent content. Language rapidly assumes its proper life, supported by its own arbitrary and conventional signifiers that loop together signifieds and referents. Thus the word *tree* (signifier) suggests the notion of tree (signified) and may be referred to the actual tree (referent). But while these relations may be consistent, they have never been proportional, for, as we have seen, the infant's earliest signifiers for mother had preceded its capacity to frame more than a prepersonal need-gratifying object, partly inside and partly beyond, as the nipple and breast are initially experienced, or as the mother is partly within its control and partly beyond it. And, no doubt, the more the mother seems to recede as she is perceived to be independent of the infant's magical wishes, the more language comes to the rescue as a more realistically acceptable vehicle for regulating need and managing demand. Derivatives of this weaning process portray the person who is signified mother as encompassing affective states enveloped in symbiotic fusion, Edenic harmony, oceanic feeling, and the like. It follows that the earliest sound that became the Logos, the earliest word, was necessarily steeped in illusion, archaic fantasy, and unforeseen arbitrariness. It also follows that language itself is to be embedded in ambiguity. No wonder Freud was struck by "The Antithetical meaning of Primal Words," as his 1910 paper was called. For the infant's first word can signify not only a host of conflicting notions,—not only is *mama* both a presence and an absence, but the exercise of *no* is really a *yes* to self-development, just as the exercise of *yes* may be a *no* to self-control.

Such overdeterminism takes us beyond the accepted view that no Logos is ever self-sufficiently itself but always a stand-in for something else (be it an idea or thing). The presence of language affirms the absence of the other, as French linguists and analysts remind us (though I suspect their emphasis on castration as the ubiquitous unstated signified is too narrow, if not also phallocentric). In any case, the infant's primal paradise is being lost even as language is being gained (the fire is dying as we approach it, but the embers speak volumes); and, as we inevitably learn, one prospect of recapturing those states is by empowering language with imagery through such mediums as the visual and the verbal arts can provide—paradise lost being recaptured in Milton's epic.

A genuinely psychoanalytic understanding of language acquisition, then, must take into account at least three fundamentals: (1) motivational sources closely allied to tension reduction and the pleasure principle; (2) the dynamic aspects of one's mediated striving for self-survival and relatedness; and (3) a susceptibility to overdeterminism.

2

Accordingly, and despite the distance just traveled, the naive over-determinism in the words = milk equation may still have its uses. As concrete sounds, as pleasurable rhythms, as emanations from what Spitz termed the "primal cavity," words may be expected to keep alive archaic memory traces with the source of oral sustenance; and in the flowing, often gushing effect of some prose, whether it be from Rabelais, Thomas Wolfe, Anaïs Nin, or Henry Miller, the reader may easily feel engulfed, soaked, or sucked into a refusion with omnipotent sources of life evocative of the oral period.[10] Like the figure in "Kubla Khan" who has "fed on honey-dew," has "drunk the milk of paradise," and envisioned a "damsel with a dulcimer," the poet will be inspired to "revive" within himself "her music and song."[11]

Cued by linguists' designation of certain sounds as "liquids" [l, r,], we can consider words as the child's active, oral creations, for the child, in naming what psychoanalysis may designate as cosmic object, holding environment, or primary care-giver, is "creating" mother. It is a momentous act of illusory omnipotence. While this preexisting but newly created object is only one's alpha and omega in the mythopoeic sense of mother-earth as womb/tomb, it is interesting that in reviewing Samuel Beckett's characters, one discovers that their names consistently begin or end with *m*, effecting their own kind of alpha-omega:

Murphy	Bem
Malloy	Pim
Malone	Bom
Watt (upside-down M)	Krim
Moran	Kram
Mahood	Pam
Macmann	Prim
Mollose	Ham
Me, *moi,* M	I'm
May (character's and	
Beckett's mother's name)	

In his novel *The Unnamable* (1955), that undifferentiated stump of a character's last creation is Worm, which asks a question about change and reversal in its spelling: *W* or *M*? *M* is the thirteenth and central letter of a twenty-six-letter alphabet; Beckett dates his own birth as Good Friday, 13 April 1906, which, as it turns out is another of his fictions.[12] In his minimalist art, [*m*] is the minimal phoneme, comparable to Murphy's association with the Greek root, *morphē,* "shape" or "form": the figure whose ground is the canvas, the chessboard, ultimately Being or the Void, and, more proximately, the totality of language or silence, which individual utterance briefly interrupts. The *mm-a* that denotes the absence of mother also marks the beginnings of self, and, as Beckett's limbless Unnamable might imply, a primitive (bodily) self not yet differentiated from or independent of the anonymous (maternal) care giver—or a phoneme in search of a morpheme. Implications of Beckett's resorting to French as stemming from an unwillingness to write in and be read by his country's as well as his mother's native tongue have not been lost on his critics and biographers; and it is possible to see his phonetic games as tracing his origins and separation from an individual and cultural matrix.[13]

Certain archaic utterances such as charms, spells, riddles, vows, curses, and incantations still occupy an omnipotent substratum of language. Northrop Frye connects charms to magical controlling devices "by compelling a certain course of action or by stopping action altogether."[14] The "primary associations" of charms are "music, sound and rhythm"; the aim of reciting powerful names in certain charms is to expel evil and to "cleanse and protect the space that the enemy has vacated." Charms may also create order out of chaos as the word of God or the use of love. Spells are the native form of charms, and their function is expressed by our word *spellbound.* Thus, words in their primitive phylogenetic uses may have an analogy with the ontogenetic properties of words to bind primary-process thinking into the secondary processes of cultural modes. Are not the infant's distressful utterances that summon its mother construed as magically producing and controlling her—hence, the basis for the magic formula or incantation that later conjures the sun, charms the crops, dispels the disease.

Also meant to be magically controlling is the curse, the verbal complement of spitting: a primitive projective gesture that aims at eliminating a "bad" parental image and restoring self-esteem while treating a piece of the environment with contempt.

Riddles, according to Frye, operate in the opposite direction, where the purpose is to unbind or loosen the spell, often within "some kind of enmity-situation or contest." The riddle has "pictorial affinities," complementing the charm's musical ones. Both are "psychologically very close together," and may be taken as "generic seeds or kernals, possibilities of expression sprouting and exfoliating into new literay phenomena." However, Levi-Strauss concludes from his work with North American Indian myths that riddles are the "grammatical equivalent of committing incest," since they join to things otherwise meant to remain separate.[15] This ingenious application is cited by Patrick A. McCarthy, whose study of *Finnegans Wake* discloses that "both incest and riddling relate to the Fall of Man and the theme of forbidden knowledge."[16]

In sum, charms may blend positively into lullabyes, negatively into sleeping or siren songs, while riddles may depict scenes of escape or rescue, or conceal forbidden wishes whose gratification entails mental acumen. The riddle's emphasis on mastery may foster the separation-individuation process and already anticipate responses to the dilemmas of triadic relationships, although the alliance with the nonsensical suggests more primitive mental processes. More obviously apropos is that type of babbling referred to in religious contexts as speaking in tongues, where one slides free of syntax and semantics regressively toward manic fusion states. On the other hand, the puns, neologisms, "schizophrenese," Blakean mystical flights, and lingusitic virtuosity of a James Joyce reproduce a dedifferentiated playfulness dissolving all sorts of boundaries. Words taken in their singular and incantatory power offer clues to how the writer may return to—that is, recreate a semblance of—oral-stage origins.

3

It is not surprising that a far greater amount of psychoanalytic scholarship has been devoted to symbol-formation than to language-acquisition and that the former is easily associated with the more archaic processes found in dreams and hallucinations, while the latter lends itself to the secondary mental processes of the ego's efforts to mediate consciously and rationally between inner reality and the environment. All the same, it should not be overlooked that symbol-formation serves integrative functions and that language may be disintegrated into such archaic modes as schizophrenese, where the key to communication has been buried in the well of psychosis. It may also help a little to distinguish symbols as a medium of representation favoring the concrete and / or pictorial from language as a system of signifiers favoring the abstract and conceptual. But psychoanalysis claims that all phases of mental life are potentially overdetermined and that while we may be able to stretch the rational and the irrational operations of language as opposite points on a scale, overlapping and interpenetration are to be expected. Moreover, from a developmental perspective, both symbol-formation and language-acquisition answer the child's vital needs for internal organization and boundary setting. Toward the end of the child's first year, during what may be called the oral stage of language activity, his / her first constructions suggest elementary relations: *mommy here, mommy away, me and mommy, my teddy,* and the like. The child employs what learning psychologists call pivot grammar, a simple word-pairing system. This recalls Freud's example of a child's play with a spool representing mother, the *fort-da* game of loss and return.[17] A rudimentary syntax begins during the second year, but the ability to use language for expressing oneself in relation to an environment in three-to-five-word sentences, really gets going from twenty-four to thirty months, that is, during the early triadic phase and the onset of oedipal issues, when he / she really begins trying to put their expanding world together.[18] *Daddy and Mommy sleep in their bed, and [but, while] me and teddy sleep in my bed. Daddy looks angry when Mommy holds me [gives me extra desserts, naps with me, etc.];* or more directly: *Daddy may hurt me for wanting Mommy,* or for the girl: *Mommy looks hurt [angry, jealous, unhappy] when Daddy bounces me*—as well as countless other similar thoughts revolving around a deep structure of oedipal ideation that may underly the child's accelerated rush into complex grammatical constructions after two and a half. Henceforth, reality is ineluctably oedipal, and children need an elaborate syntactical grasp of language to enable them to express their place in this new, triadic order of things. If Chomsky linguists are correct in maintaining that learning a language owes more to innate cognitive structures (or " 'cognizing' modules") than to the stimulus / response model, then the child is creating his / her language as well as imitating what is heard.[19] And if syntax is learned in an allegedly conflict-free sphere of the personality, its emergence in the child's mental life at the triadic stage may naturally dispose it to represent unconscious oedipal conflicts and to serve as a medium for mastery. Around this time oedipal issues are voiced in questions of origins, riddles, and jump-rope rhymes.

Where the present dynamic model of language-acquisition departs from most linguistic theories is in the emphasis on language as a preexisting system adopted as an emotional vehicle for the child to see that its needs continue to be met and as a means for overcoming potential conflicts in the sphere of separation and autonomy. To summarize from a psychoanalytic viewpoint: words are orally tinged; sentences are oedipally tinged. Words that are assigned to the self and parts of the early environment may be either simple tags and labels or more resonant images, depending on the child's "dispositional tendencies" and the quality of early care.[20] For example, the child who is encouraged to linger at the mother's breast and play with her hair, face, fingers, and the like, may continue a playfully free attitude toward toys, alphabet, and the exercise of speech.[21]

But as sounds are enlisted or conscripted to serve as words, so words are soon given their marching orders and assigned a grammatical positions in syntax to serve rudimentary sentences. Similarly, earliest attitudes or meanings may be orally derived from states of pleasure and frustration, but a new set of complex relationships dictates a fatedness to words and meanings when the oedipal child finds its speech must reside in sentences, however innate the language capacity may be. The laws that govern syntax are as relational, sequential, and logical as the restrictions placed on one's emotional life. There may also be pleasures of mastery, but along with them the child discovers that the language he/she would claim for him/herself is, in fact, the prior possession of others. Put in extreme terms by Jacques Lacan, the toddler soon enters the Symbolic Order, that of rules, commands, and taboos, condensed in Lacanian terms as the partriarchal supremacy of *le-nom-du-père*.[22] From atop Mt. Sinai descends Moses bearing stone tablets of SYNTAX.

Through syntax is the voice of the superego heard, modulated, and internalized in various ways that would hardly qualify as conflict-free; yet the nature of these acompanying conflicts has typically been construed along male-oedipal lines. In Harold Bloom's theories of poetic origins, mastery denotes the inevitable discovery of belatedness by the younger poet who sees but would deny that the admired strong father poet has already slept with his beloved muse.[23] The exposure of sexual biases in Bloom and Lacan by feminists and other critics suggests not only that the male = norm/female = other mind-set is deeply rooted but that literary composing is easily construed as male initiation rites geared toward oedipal resolution. The analogy here would be with the tradition in English private schools of initiating boys into advanced study via Latin.[24] All the same, it is doubtful that language itself is as two-dimensionally patriarchal as some feminists have argued: usually overlooked in uncovering its sexist biases are its maternal origins. First and foremost, as the Latin informs us, language enters our childhood via the mother's tongue (the primal *lingua*); subsequently, as the child emerges from the dyad and advances to a triangulation of relationships, a patriarchal culture not only intervenes but historically has sent the sexes down different paths of linguistic development, with socially privileged males moving in directions that favor creativity as well as the professions. Conditions began noticeably changing in the eighteenth century, when the rising English novel performed as an equal-opportunity employer, for not only did it thrive in the vernacular but it bridged women's domestic labors and the marketplace. While language-acquisition can no longer be examined without including gender, the subject itself has become too complex for a study that is seeking common features.

Certainly, belatedness cuts across gender lines. "Each one who enters," so reflects Joyce's Bloom on getting into bed with Molly, "imagines himself to be the first whereas he is always the last term of a preceding series" (*Ulysses,* 731). And Joyce, through his other self-character, Stephen Dedalus, had also realized, "the language in which we are speaking is his before it is mine . . . will always be for me an acquired speech" (*Portrait,* 189). Where imperial English is the norm, colonial Anglo-Irish is the other. For Virginia Woolf, it is to be strapped to the procrustean bed of the "masculine sentence."[25] And for D. H. Lawrence in *Lady Chatterley's Lover,* it meant returning to his father's Yorkshire dialect and integrating his lowly dialect with the "high" literary prose learned from his mother. Yet despite these awkward accommodations, language is our passport to the commonwealth of the real.

If words once resonated with the liquid sounds of the oral-stage pleasure-ago, sentences accompany and bear witness to the influence of the superego, which will never again freely allow words their primal autarchy or anarchy. To oversimplify a bit, words are possessed before sentences are shared. For prospective writers, the only hope is to master the demands of syntax and, through this mastery, to gain occasional triumphs by means of outwitting or other tactics. With Flaubert, many come to accept that "Language is like a cracked kettle on which we beat out tunes for bears to dance to, while all the time we long to move the stars to pity."[26] But when writers abandon syntax for calligraphy or concrete poetry, they have already joined the ranks of graphic artists; painters like Stuart Davis and other moderns have been more successful in freeing words from syntax, dislodging letters from meaning, and, in general, liberating the alphabet for purely visual pleasures.

For the child, often a letter or monosyllable serves as a sign of the self, while for the writer the sentence has often been viewed as a signature of the self: a distinctive style he/she displays in putting oneself into prose. There are, for examples, the rambling Jamesian obsequiousness, the unadorned democratic thrust of Hemingway, Faulkner's high-blown rhetoric. With the Beckett sentence, which suffers entropy and runs down toward the end, as does this one from *Company*—"I am alone in the crib in the dark"[27]—a complete vision of reality briefly materializes. There is also the Lawrencean sentence, with a sting in its tail, and the kind favored by Virginia Woolf, which holds on to the reader and doesn't want to let go, or that breaks over one like a succession of waves and pulls the reader down.

4

But with Joyce, whose sentences are mimetic of everything imaginable, from lungs that heave in and out to printing presses that go "sllt" in the day, the question is much more intriguing. He may write the characteristic Irish sentence ("The flow of the language it is" [*Ulysses,* 152]); the one that refracts other writers' themes ("The longest way round is the shortest way home," [377]), or that parodies their style; the highly wrought Joycean sentence per se, as elucidated by Anthony Burgess: "Perfume of embraces all him assailed" [168] and the ambient idioms, ferreted out by Hugh Kenner, of contemporary Edwardian style that grow visible only to post-Edwardian readers ("Stephen suffered him to pull out ... a handkerchief" [4]).[28] No doubt the Joycean sentences are intended to be as prolific and protean as the creation they imitate.[29] But while the syntax of *A Portrait* ranges from simple to complex, from intimate to oratorical, pedestrian to rhapsodic, it is, on the whole, much more conservative than that of *Ulysses*. The former deals essentially with childhood conflicts over emotional injuries and a flight from origins to realize a mythic sonship (though that of Icarus to Daedalus is but one of Stephen's many heroic self-images). The more positive emphasis is on mastery through word-sound associations like "suck," "kiss," the Virgin's "Tower of Ivory," Eileen's "cool white hands," and so forth, which are carried out so that "by thinking of things you could understand them" (*Portrait,* 43). But sexual questions are not placed in a context of mastery: sitting at his father's old anatomy class desk, Stephen is troubled by the isolated word *Foetus* carved on its surface, and can find neither a context nor a syntax for himself. He has reached the point where confronting the vulgar primal scene of origins would jeopardize his lofty family-romance revision, and he backs away. It is only in *Ulysses* that syntax and sexual cognition begin working in tandem to address origins and create a new order of meaning.

In *The Art of Joyce's Syntax,* Roy Gottfried has shown that Joyce's "language is characterized by a tacit acceptance of the ordering rules of syntax while using those same rules to twist sentences into new images."[30] *Ulysses* is "a creative disordering within a syntactic structure" to bring about "an appropriate reordering." Throughout its writing, Joyce, for all his radical originality, "needs the normal order of syntax" and depends on the reader's acceptance of it: he "draws attention to syntactic rules in one sentence in order to defy them in the next." It is a "freedom within bounds," a freedom that takes its definition "from the order it makes free with." Or to rephrase in a more suitable spirit: because language springs from bedrocks of accepted definition, Joyce is able to turn words into shamrocks. In so doing, he manages to enclose a world of meaning in a single word (Peter is the "rock" of the Roman Catholic Church, Patrick as the head of the Irish church is a "shamrock" [*Ulysses,* 80], the plant that was his device for illustrating the Trinity as three in one, etc).

To illustrate how Joyce's dialectics of "order and appropriate disorder" are interdependent, Gottfried quotes Joyce's description of Bloom and Molly in bed: their positions are determined "relatively to themselves and to each other" (737). Poised on the brink of fascinating new terrain, Gottfried only lingers before returning to his proper business. But the almost-made connection can be completed by the reader, with only a slight nudging. Joyce experiments with sexual combinations and positions within a predetermined order in ways precisely analogous to his playful subversions and affirmations of syntax, so that the two modalities of sexual congress and syntactical order acquire a latent but powerful affinity. Granted, Bloom masturbates while Molly commits adultery, and if Bloom's florid perversities are freely played out in the Nighttown sequence, it is only in a hallucination of reality, a temporary *Walpurgisnacht* license. In actuality Bloom returns to Molly to drift off to sleep, his head to her feet, a change of positions but not of persons, nor, as Joyce seems to imply, of commitment (the bit of foot fetishism notwithstanding). What doesn't happen is any outright sexual exchange between Stephen and Bloom, a dangerous possibility the novel flirts with but, as scholarship has elucidated through Stephen's wary Nighttown apprehension of Bloom as "Black Panther Vampire," manages to circumvent.[31] And it is, curiously, not through syntax that Stephen protects himself but through the more primitive and even magical ritual of naming, suitable to his regression to grandiose gestures as well as to the surrealistic mode of "Circe"; his names, moreover, are in part hallucinatory, for they are his demons and fears that he is vocalizing. But where Stephen is constrained by the vampiristic nature of pederasty and, despite his intellectual perorations, he founders through an echo chamber of syntax that traps him within a solipsistic trinity of self ("I, I and I, I." [190]) not shared by Joyce.

Indeed, through experiments with time and stream-of-consciousness techniques, Joyce manages to end the novel in admirable compliance with such superego strictures typically expressed in psychoanalysis as "dissolution of the Oedipus complex" and acceptance of "genital primacy." Molly's final *yes* is not only recurringly liberated through syntactical compliance but is overdetermined, responding as equally to Bloom's present request for breakfast as to her menstrual flow, but also to former lovers, who materialize only to recede before she recollects Bloom's proposal as they first made love on Howth Head, and so to orgasmic mutuality. Her *yes* realistically celebrates marital, genital sexuality—the flesh's ruling syntax, which establishes, subordinates, and entertains a host of creative deviations. If, as Freud notes, "we never discover a 'No' in the unconscious," then her *yes* is an instinctual as well as an instinctive *for* response to life.[32]

In sum, words and sounds may be orally derivative or, at least, orally synchronous and maternal in origin; syntax and sentences may be oedipally affiliated and parental in significance, observing a degree of superego compliance—but also a measure of deviance. Gertrude Stein's sentences would like to do away with traditional syntax—would they also like to do away with traditional heterosexuality? Is she drawing a parallel between verbal monotony and sexual monogamy? Is there some buried connection between Oscar Wilde's sexual and verbal inversions? He aspired to write a play that would be all witty conversation without stooping to plot, and nearly succeeded in *The Importance of Being Earnest,* which is a play on words (in every way imaginable, including Uranist) that inverts plot into parody. But plot and narrative are relentlessly oedipal, according to Roland Barthes, because eventually they must deal with origins: "Doesn't every narrative lead back to Oedipus?" he asks in *The Pleasure of the Text* (47). Barthes's own search for a narrative-free text led to that "book of the self," his autobiography (*Roland Barthes by Roland Barthes*). Wilde's foundling in a handbag mocks both oedipal origins and the family romance, because while he played with both, he was earnest about neither. And one of his most familiar inversions from *Earnest*—"Divorces are made in heaven"—suggests undoing as well, of monogamy, if not explicitly of the parental union.

But to return to what may well be deliberate analogies between syntactical arrangements and sexual variations in *Ulysses,* we recall that Bloom and Molly are overdetermined characters, both in a literary sense, where they take on mythic dimensions, and in the psychological sense, where they are a revision of the primordial sexual pair. While their ultimate composition must stem from their "fabulous artificer" Joyce himself, for his self-character Stephen, they represent a response to his quandary of "bride-bed, childbed, bed of death," and so are a solution to his immersion in the primal scene of origins. Molly's eternally recurring *yes* signifies both her impatience with the restraints of syntax and her acceptance of procreative adult sexuality, which allows the race to survive, despite the accumulated repertory of conflict, pain, betrayal, and residual perversions that render homeward journeys wide-ranging divagations. Beyond Stephen's immediate reach though her *yes* may be, it need not be beyond the reader's, who is also a kind of wandering Ulysses. Finally, her *yes* is the original oral word around which the sons and daughters of the earth weave their syntactical journeys. Not by accident, her last word becomes Mrs. Ramsay's first word in *To the Lighthouse:* "Yes, of course, if it's fine tomorrow"—a qualified yes to what she will not live to see fulfilled, due only in part to Mr. Ramsay's opening word: both intrusive and contrary, "But—."[33] It will be many years before his son will forgive him for butting in on that occasion.

By connecting subject with predicate and adding modifiers, syntax initiates tales and makes more complex narrative forms possible. The practice of observing the rules while disordering and reordering their manifestations also applies to the literary tradition Joyce "jocoseriously" invokes. Like syntax, the language of Homer and other literary prototypes (Dante, Shakespeare, etc.) accord with the preexisting material of the child's environment, that is, Winnicott's transitional objects and phenomena, which Joyce as artist must accept in order to carry out his relatively original reshaping and reordering operations, since, as Stephen will not let us forget, only God creates *ex nihilo.* If the Joycean creator cannot mingle with the goddesses like a child in blissful symbiosis, he can appropriate the language that bears the echoes of early harmony and well-being by holistically condensing worlds into words, by the fusion of puns, and by self-begetting neologisms; if he cannot create language out of nothing or overcome his own belatedness and undo the painfully impinging effects of the primal scene, he can recouple the copulatives and rearrange the parts of the sentences until he has conceived his own, more acceptable, connections. If there is a mixture of early pain (e.g., through maternal loss due to younger siblings, as in Joyce's case) plus such dispositional tendencies that favor mastery through language and creativity, then early interchanges with the mother form positive self-representations. These may be joined syntactically into variations on the deep structure of family-romance fantasy, which is the artist's distinctive expression of early family relationships: (latent feeling) *I feel neglected; I feel like an orphan;* (manifest form) *I am an adopted child but of true exalted parentage.* This core fantasy of the artist will strongly influence how he / she will eventually create the syntax of his / her art. Rudiments of this fantasy first begin peeking through the fissures in the painful pair words of *Mommy away:* the absent Mommy who disappoints (abandons) is replaced by the exalted queen mother who gratifies (reclaims).

Fantasy, undoubtedly adhering all along in varying degrees to language-acquisition, comes to the fore in narrative, whether it be in conventionalized or idiosyncratic forms (most likely a combination), to provide the inner coherence for an appealing as well as plausible sequence of events that mediates between principles of pleasure and reality. This suggests that syntax in narrative performs a dual role. It hosts the imaginary, but in sentences that embody established systems of rules and authority, ultimately involving a more-or-less formal traditon, even if it be one of oral storytelling: *Once upon a time a royal child was abandoned in the bulrushes, and found—.* The authority of narrative form may alert the child / artist, especially the male, to the incursion of authority in his own emotional development, of his belatedness, of quandaries over his origins, or the mysterious parantal act of excited union. He then is led toward mastery and further modification at various levels—either to protect the self-enhancing family-romance fantasy or to balance the demands imposed by reality with the urges aroused by curiosity. Tensions between relatively more subjective and objective versions of origins spur an investment in creative mastery.[34]

5

How the literary self emerges through language and "by fancies that are curled / Around these images" (T. S. Eliot, "Preludes") is found perhaps most graphically rendered in passages from Wordsworth's two versions of *The Prelude* (1805, 1850), where the poet is actively and visibly engaged in the self-remaking powers inherent in language.[35] Drawing on the Romantic view of poetry as "soul-making," Robert Langbaum has, in his latest treatment, favored self over soul.[36] It was Keats, Langbaum tells us, who first deemed this world a "vale of Soul-Making" in reaction to the mechanistic psychologies of Locke, Hartley, and Hume. And while Langbaum convincingly details how Wordsworth played off Associationist theories of the mind as a blank tablet against Platonism, in order to blend sensations with innate ideas, it required an assimilation of Freudian psychology before the critic opted for the more modern and inclusive "self."

Soul, moreover, is traditionally assigned a female gender or is inscribed as anima, and its use could only lead to anomalous results. It is the total self, with both male and female components, that Wordsworth's poem traces the making of, and that enterprise no writer had attempted before nor would attempt thereafter for another hundred years, till the opening pages of Joyce's *A Portrait*.

Let us note in passing Bion's distinction between quantity and quality in the infant's oral experiences: overemphasis on the former may promote a tendency toward greed or materialism, while achievement of the latter may bestow value on existence.[37] Clearly, Wordsworth, whose poem takes us back to "that first time / In which, a Babe, by intercourse of touch / I held mute dialogues with my mother's heart," is always careful to build in quality and to establish thereby the terms for the artist's creative romance with the world, as in these following lines: "the fairest of all rivers loved / To blend his murmurs with my nurse's song, / And . . . sent a voice / That flowed along my dreams" (Wordsworth, *Prelude*, 1.270–74).[38] Here, as Langbaum shows, are apparently rational sensations that overlay a prerational experience, but their effect, going far beyond Rationalism, produces an original "bond of union between life and joy" (1.1.558). Not only does childhood continue to intertwine the "passions that build up our human soul" for the poet (who lost his mother at eight and his father at thirteen), as the rich association of nursing, the nurse's song, and the river's flow "make ceaseless music that composed" his thoughts, but they also suggest an interchangeability in which each may represent the other. Should one be lost—for example, the nursing mother—the associated memories of song or river can be summoned. The joyous sources of life are preserved, at least in part, through the creative-romance-with-the-world fantasy, which enlivens the nature associations and rises over a family romance that denies the final pain of loss.[39] So effectively sealed together are mother and the maternal features of nature that one could speculate about the relative absence of repression over the poet's infantile period. Certainly this hopeful prospect of connectedness explains much of the power of Romantic poetry. But Wordsworth does not finally avoid loss so much as search for a way to withstand it. What may occur in his aesthetics of "emotion recollected in tranquility" is less a return of the repressed, as in neurosis, than a return to the repressed via nature, and through nature (even in its privative conditions, as figured in the leech-gatherer) to a recovery of early self-experience that can be rounded into new wholes. His reliance on Plato's mythical views of spiritual preexistence allows Wordsworth to extend his imagination beyond the psychoanalyst's "veil of amnesia," which renders early childhood inaccessible; and his appropriation of Associationism allows him to exceed the verbal games of his scientific peers by injecting a dynamic component to associations, as happens in the analytic session.

Wordsworth relies more on memories than on dreams, but, as psychoanalysis informs us, our memories are also reconstructions. If the actual early memories are not recoverable through the self-making process in poetry, their equivalents are. Langbaum is right to see "those first-born affinities" of the poet as forming, in psychoanalytic terms, early self / other representations. Complementing the feminine components of song and river in the formative self are the embedded sensations of fearsome shadows from towers and ruined feudal monuments that fall on his breast and waken him to male reality. "The composite experience of rivers and towers—which might be understood as an experience of female and male principles—stands behind the experiences of beauty and fear described in the rest of Book 1, which are composite experiences of natural and moral power" (that the river is curiously referred to above as male suggests a retrospective reordering of formative imagery to sexually balance his origins or to bolster a yet-to-emerge male self).[40] Ultimately, the ideal of nature absorbs these primal female / male images into a unified life principle, to which the poet, by reason of his internalized "affinities," may return. This happens after an upsurge of oedipal conflicts has been represented through the poet's engagement in the French Revolution (during which he fathered a child), its cruel excesses, and disillusioned aftermath. During this period, nature is the ambivalent mother who leads her unwitting son into history, where he seeks for a continuation of sympathy and sustenance in the world of man.[41] But history turns out to be a ruthless castrator, as evidenced by the revolution's invention of the guillotine, and so the weary but hopeful adult's revulsion for the "mean and vulgar works of man" (1.408) and his return for a new beginning amid the original surroundings of nature. Although an enormous amount of psychic as well as political territory has been telescoped by this precis, it will be sufficient to perceive the child's early images of beauty and fear as extended to the oedipal figures signified by nature and history.

If this poet's empathic transforming of Associationism leads him to self-experience and meaning, it may be added that the images impart significance through words.[42] And if the song the infant heard at his nurse's breast is not named, it can be inferred that the old tune was inseparable from the oral feast, from the river's flow, and from other male-solar regions that bestow a "field of light" on its (female) waters; and it can also be inferred that without this male / female confluence, the self-making processes would not advance. Such a recaptured merger experience (and others as when "What I saw? / Appeared like something in myself" [2.351–52]) must remain elusive, because the observer is part of the observed, just as dreamer becomes his dream through, in Freud's words, "an identity of perception."[43] Perhaps, in the same way, the poet is the memories he creates.

An indefinite diction is required to preserve the boundaries of inner / outer, self / other, as nonspecific and flexible. In his study of Wordsworth's language, Donald Davie has found that the "nouns are not concrete; but the verbs are" (e.g., "the face of things," "spots of time"; "see," "touch," "call").[44] But other verbs, like "molded," "joined," "abstracted," "endowed" (14.83), are invoked to mediate differences, lessen distance, and affirm affinities between the creative forces of nature and those of the imagination. Both simple and yet sublime, direct and yet indefinite, Wordsworth's poetic diction discovers the language of the self as revealed in its needs to preserve and maintain itself through a natural and powerful creative environment that, being both similar and different, functions as a subjective-object, as Winnicott referred to things in the transitional sphere of experiencing. (Beckett's sentences also speak the language of the self, but in diametric opposition: toward its disconnecting, dismantling, and extinction.) But here, the Romantic poet's simple diction may fit the "common range of daily things" (2.176); while his syntax of dynamic associations allows him to "build up greatest things / From least suggestions" (14.101–2).

Davie's view would support Langbaum's, that the self-as-process implies indefinite changes through particular actions. Wordsworth's lifelong self-making process is recorded in this poem; but in comparing the 1805 and 1850 versions of a familiar passage (2.235–54), Davie prefers the former for its active, energetic verbs and for maintaining a consistent viewpoint "from inside the child's mind"; while the latter version emphasizes the "frailty of the child, his weakness," and shifts perspectives to include the mother and the reader. Critical preferences to one side, it is clear that the two versions represent stages of the poet's growth away from an initial idealizing and single angle: clear evidence that the self-in-creativity is an ongoing, corrective, and shaping process. Consider, for example, the shift from grandiosity to empathy in the contrast between the infant (in 1805) who "Doth gather passion from his mother's eye!" to the infant (in 1850) "who with his soul / Drinks in the feelings of his mother's eye!"[45] It is through empathy that "those first-born affinities" awaken and words begin to encompass a world of experience. Empathy is relational, as the child's simplest word pairings also are. And through the imaginative power of recollection, "visionary things," "lovely forms," and "sweet sensations" are recalled, but made nonreferential and nonspecific, probably through a compromise with repression, and then are permitted to "almost make remotest infancy / A visible scene, on which the sun is shining" (1.631–35).[46]

The survival of empathy *for*—rather than attachment *to*—the early maternal object favors the cultivation of a medium and the recourse to symbolic displacements over a more personal relationship. When empathy bestows quality and value on early oral experiences, it facilitates adaptation, and it sustains for the artist the creative romance with the world when he/she must eventually face up to experiences of loss, conflicts over rivalry, and problems of origins. So if I appear to have doubled back to Wormhoudt's caption, I have also qualified the implied regression in the oral material. Moreover, empathy imparts dimensionality to relationships and creative work alike, advancing my interpretations well beyond equations of overdeterminism and defenses of displacement.

It may further be inferred that the compulsive return to idealized oral fusions—the signal theme in Romantic poetry, according to Kauvar, who rides hard on the defenses of regression and splitting—can be balanced somewhat by the appreciation of the conceptual and syntactical mastery that points to these poets' integrative functions in the triadic spheres most of us inhabit.[47] Although psychic determinism is a valuable tool for inference, it stands mute before our relative freedoms and those afforded by art.

6

... for the words which we use in our everyday speech are nothing other than watered-down magic.

Sigmund Freud (1905)

The act of creation, the actual writing of a poem, takes place, as Derrida's ingenious gloss on the mystic writing pad reminds us, only after repression, when, for example, the Wordsworthian soul remembers how but not what she felt (2.315–36).[48] Writing requires, for Derrida, that "there be neither a permanent contact nor an absolute break between [psychic] strata: the vigilance and failure of censorship." Dreams, Freud had written, are a kind of writing in which "the dreamer invents his own grammar" (Derrida's gloss), but which in turn must submit to an accepted verbal syntax to be understood. But for the writer to represent thinly disguised oral content, he/she need not be regressed to an oral level, where one presumably relives oral conflicts. Whether the scene of writing is also a reproduced (and fantasied) primal scene, as Derrida implies, is speculative, at best, but what is certain is that the act of writing, in common with other mental acts, is overdetermined. It may be inspired as much by the family romance as vehicle for unconscious fantasy, as by the primal scene as parental reality felt through the pressures of the superego, while the beleaguered ego mediates the actual writing. As a writer, Wordsworth suffered a painful inhibition "connected with the act of holding a pen," as he wrote in an 1804 letter to DeQuincy;[49] the symptom is clearly a sign of the overdetermination of writing, but the signified remains unknown.

What is known is that writing can be overdetermined because both language acquisition and linguistic functions are overdetermined. In support of this view, I would turn not to writers' histories but to cultural phenomena. An opportunity was afforded me in 1978 to observe the enormous representative power of native language (the mother tongue) when unrelated European groups felt themselves besieged by foreign powers and resorted to acts of violence and terrorism. In Wales a television tower was bombed and a kidnapping was staged by the Welsh Language Society in order to dramatize their demands for Welsh television and compulsory language instruction in the schools. "To restore the Welsh language," claimed their spokesman, Saunders Lewis, "is nothing less than a revolution." In France, the south wing of the Palace of Versailles was bombed by the Breton Republican Army, because, as the notes of these schoolteachers-turned-terrorists proclaimed, "the Breton language and culture are denied and destroyed by the imperialist French power." And south of the border, one of the issues in the more-complex Basque separatist movement is the demand to have the ancient Euskera (allegedly Celtic) language replace Spanish in the schools. Ideological goals have clearly been fueled by linguistic ideals; it would not require inordinate ingenuity to find a parallel with the legendary band of brothers coalescing around an allegiance to the mother tongue, nursing their grievances, and rising up against patriarchal oppression: the imperial tyrant to be replaced by the more remote, idealized ancestor. Far more than a merely acquired tool of verbal communication in these three instances, language was rediscovering its primitive visceral counterpart in the violent actions perpetrated on its behalf. Whatever else it achieves, terrorism in the service of language succeeds in returning the verbal to its preverbal origins.

Putting it mildly, literary creativity operates rather differently. The mastery of language, syntax, and form encountered in Romantic poets and Moderns, like Joyce, may record the way in which difficult early conflicts have been extended to a somewhat later period, where language mediates to alleviate those earlier conflicts via displacement, mastery, and whatever it is that passes under the rubrics of sublimation. All the same, these writers are also revolutionaries, whose explosions look implosive until their delayed effects on human consciousness are registered.

Consequently, I would conclude that theories of language development that rely mainly on behavioristic or cognitive modes run the risk of separating language from the dynamic field of drives and emotions that constitute childhood. If I read aright Robert Graves's reconstructions of the mythical acquisition of the alphabet, it is exceedingly conflictual: nothing less than the heroic exploits of Perseus confronting the horrors of Medusa.[50]

In one version of the origin of the Greek alphabet, the ruler Palamedes assisted the triple-headed goddess (i.e., the Fates, Muses, or Graces) in its composition. Since the alphabet presumes a commitment to language and knowledge, it may be that the Greeks perceived its inception like the joint sexual act of conception. The child-hero must endure arduous labors to locate, retrieve, and master its secrets. Similarly, though stemming from different occasions, the alphabet was invented by Hermes after witnessing the flight of cranes that make letters when they fly (that is, the chevron) and that arrange their fish in a circle. Cranes or storks and similar ancient birds like the ibis have been traced back to fertility goddesses and androgynous deities and have retained in the popular mind the role of baby bringers.[51] The bag that Perseus fills with the alphabet twigs clipped with his lunar-shaped sickle is made of craneskin. According to Graves, it is only the gorgon's mask on the outside cover of the bag that Perseus carries, and the real contents are the Greek letters inside. Whatever else one may make of Graves's mythological data, it is evident that language-acquisition is fraught with danger: it involves secrets, violence, theft, scenes of horror, and, perhaps, a defense against, or mastery of, that both ancient and modern castration complex. The frightening powers bestowed by language enable us not only to speak our names and express our desires, but to utter what we know.

10
A Phylogeny of Myths

> Ontogenesis, or the development of the individual, is a short and
> quick recapitulation of phylogenesis, or the development of the tribe
> to which it belongs, determined by the laws of inheritance and
> adaptation.
> —Ernst Haeckel, *The History of Creation*

Of course things don't work out as consistently as Haeckel's elegant analogy
supposes, but it remains a useful means of organizing and relating complex
fields of thought. For example, phylogenetically, *Homo sapiens* may be said
to have existed long before it became human in a cultural sense;
ontogenetically, the infant may live biologically for some time before it
becomes human in a psychocultural sense. "Like the newborn marsupial that
crawls over its mother's damp fur to her pouch, there to spend up to six
months completing its development, the human newborn is only half-
formed."[1] And to paraphrase Margaret Mahler, the birth of the human
organism and that of the human self may correspond, but they do not not
coincide: the latter really gets underway during the second month of life and
runs to about the thirtieth, as the toddler hatches out of maternal symbiosis.
Analogies also arise between *Homo sapiens*'s prehistorical era and *Homo
infans*'s preverbal phases, both of which are scientifically available through
direct observation (e.g., the !Kung foragers / gatherers; infant nursery schools)
and from after-the-fact reconstruction.

Further analogies arise within the cultural context: myth on the phylogenetic
side and art on the ontogenetic side are also about becoming human and what
it means to be human. As conditions, cycles, or crises in humanity's evolving
self-awareness, both myth and art are, however, imagined versions meant to
be experienced and not to be taken literally. Assuming this sounds obvious,
we also assume that at some point both must withstand the tests of time and
truth, that is, less as verifiability than as plausibility, in accord with humanity's
evolving reality sense. For although scientists must submit their hypotheses to
the scrutiny of others and have them tested by direct observation, those who
study myth and art apply a different sort of critical validation when they find
enduring meaning, for example, in such Greek myths as Orpheus and
Eurydice.

But that is the long view, which results in judgments of value, while the present view has been the near one, not of product and purpose but of process and becoming. Along with subjective and objective creative regulators deriving from origins, artists also operate within the larger framework of cultural phylogeny. Every artist has a shared mythic heritage that serves as paradigm or counterpoint for the creative drive; for Western artists the currents flow mainly from Greek mythology and the Bible, with periodic tappings into the Orient, usually by way of the occult. But every artist must undergo ontogeny processes of individual development as well, and these stages anchor his/her creative drives in other ways. This dual anchorage can be broken down as follows (relying for convenience's sake mainly on the Greeks and being only suggestive rather than encyclopedic):

I. Early Symbiotic Phases

Phylo (Mythic)	Onto (Individual)
A. Chaos: a "void, an abyss ... unlimited darkness, unformed hallucinatory matter."[2]	Early post-natal "primitive disorientation," "primary narcissism," "objectless"; physiological reflexes that aim at homeostasis, "fleeting responsivity to external stimuli."[3]
B. Gaia (Gē): earth goddess located in caves and clefts in the earth, worshipped as life source.[4]	Preobject state: mother and infant as a "dual unity within one common boundary" dim awareness of the "need-satisfying object" signified by the "unspecific smiling reponses."(44) Gratifications lead to: a pleasurable (good) quality and a painful (bad) quality of experience. Inner bodily sensations, but little differention between inside and outside, as libido and aggression are similarly mixed.

There are light and darkness, noise and silence, contacts and sensations; chaos is differentiated into a "unified situational experience" involving parts of the infant and mother; out of the inchoate void Isakower phenomena may begin to loom and to take shape as the infant introjects the breast and turns it into his dream screen. On the positive side, a dawning primal romance with the cosmos begins to appear; on the negative side, the still-fragmentary experiences constitute Melanie Klein's "schizoid-paranoid" positions of unassimilated part-objects and wishes.[5] Artists may recapture a sense of this hectic period through the dedifferentiating[6] stage of creativity when they return, in Yeats's phrase, to the "foul rag and bone shop of the human heart," or, in D. H. Lawrence's, to "the seething cauldron of lower life," the "core of chaos" as "quintessentially chaotic and fierce with incongruities,"[7] or, via synaesthesia, as commended in Baudelaire's "Correspondences," where one finds "perfumes as cool as childern's flesh/sweet as oboes."[8] Never a primitive medium for long, literature nonetheless seeks ways to contain and express the primordial. And so episodes within major works may capture a sense of this early tumultuous world. Eminent examples include: the *Walpurgisnacht* of Faust; the Nighttown episode in *Ulysses*; many portions of *Finnegans Wake*; the Marabar caves episode in *A Passage to India*; the devastations of nature that ravage Lear on the heath or eclipse the human presence in the middle section of *To the Lighthouse*; and Beckett. But, being verbal, literature is always constrained by a definiteness that music, modern sculpture, and painting can circumvent; it becomes all but impossible to encounter directly anything so primitive as the infant's preobject state (i.e., pre–whole person state) without soon discovering part-objects and in them a synedoche of whole objects.

Exposures to substances, fluids, textures, rocking motions, and the like in the early environment may mark an advance in the artist's unfolding romance with the cosmos and provide precursors of rhythm, rhyme, and color patterns as Winnicott's transitional sphere shortly comes into play. The words = milk equation, though not as simple as it once looked, may still be useful.[9] As concrete sounds, as pleasurable rhythms, as oral products, words can keep alive archaic memory traces with the source of oral sustenance; and in the flowing, often gushing effect of some prose, whether it be out of Rabelais, Thomas Wolfe, or Henry Miller, the reader may easily feel engulfed, drenched, or sucked into fusion with omnipotent sources of life evocative of the oral period. In this context, recall Greenson's discovery of the nursing infant, *mm*-ing blissfully away until the breast is withdrawn, and how the subsequent *mm-ah* sound in our culture is associated with and reinforced by the object who becomes the person denoted as "Ma."[10] And as we have seen, many archaic utterances, such as charms, spells, riddles, vows, curses, and incantations, retain an omnipotent substratum of language even as they assume cultural forms.

II.   Dyadic Phase

Tellus Mater: Earth-goddess and mother of vegetation, accompanied by her divine child, either as the female Korē, the androgynous Dionysus; or, in his	Part-object to the whole object: Now the intertwined processes of individuation (evolution of autonomous ego functions) and of separation (distancing

theriomorphic capacity, as a snake who reverts in winter to the mother's womb. Now there appears a second mother, Persephone, goddess of the underworld, of darkness, death and the winter side of Tellus Mater, mother as springtime and growth. Mother earth as sole source of life has so far been paramount, but now she gives way a bit. Another life principle soon begins to be felt. This may be the fertilizing rays of the sun, or Boreas the north wind. Or perhaps the world is hatched from a universal egg in which the night is articulated as a black-winged bird and the earth-goddess is transformed into a dove or seagull.[11] Persephone's descent to the underworld, where she is reunited with her mother, Demeter, provides a pattern for women's creative interest in questing for the mother within.

(In biblical terms, Eve, the mother of mankind, is the "bad" mother of original sin, to be balanced by Mary, the virgin mother of the Savior.)

boundary formation and disengagement from mother) move ahead rapidly but not always in tandem. The partial representations of the mother as gratifying and frustrating (the good and the bad breast) must be assimilated, as libido fuses with aggression. The stage of concern over damage to loved objects from ruthless drive-discharge is reached. A stabilized body image forms. In Mahler's terms, "the world is the junior toddler's oyster"; his "love affair with the world" comes into full play (71).

The hatching-out process has begun. While the child is forming and blending images of the mother into a whole person, it is also experiencing mother as cosmic object or holding environment through surroundings that are enlivened and articulated by transitional objects. We enter the animistic world that envelops fairy tales, beast fables, pastorals, cartoons, and some nature poetry.

But the hatching-out may be experienced as one's suddenly being pushed from within, or as being provoked from without by some strange giant or dwarf—complications are never lacking. A seed is then buried that may eventually germinate into an orphaned plant. The artist may expand and develop this notion, among countless others, into a full-fledged fantasy so strong that it, too, along with the positive nurturing and mirroring experiences, becomes a kernel of the self, or even, temporarily, a second self. If the personal mother should disappoint (e.g., become depressed, disloyal, or vanish to return with a younger sibling), then the environmental mother ("collective substitute object")[12] may be preserved as preferred partner in a creative romance with the world, as the morning star, Venus, was for Emily Brontë. "A real mother may be prone to disappear," writes Stevie Davies, "Mother Nature cannot."[13] The dual unity may be reshaped by self-wounds, fantasy, and splitting. The processes of separation may lag, while those of individuation may accelerate. But now there are the makings for a second set of parents, more noble and more worthy of the child's intense needs. Along with good and bad images of the mother, portrayed as goddess and witch, fairy godmother and vampire, come ambivalence and the split of the family romance into positive and negative forms.

Gilbert Rose has applied the irredentist principle of politics (the wish to return lost territory within one's boundaries) to the artist's wish to regain the "original dual unity with the mother" and "separate out anew."[14] When the artist succeeds in accord with "his ego ideal of perfection, he achieves a temporary reconciliation between his ego and his superego," approximating the "original sense of oneness with the mother." But his elation soon gives way to anxieties over loss of separateness through merging, and, in Rose's view, new creative processes are aroused that continue the separation-individuation process through its fluctuations of "distance and closeness, rapprochement and detachment." These ideas Rose illustrates in the art of Samuel Beckett, which explores "the shores of the earliest sense of self."

It is also at the dyadic phase that philosophers, as Rose notes, have long labored "to reconcile the infinite variety with unity, the many and the one, the endless forms of becoming with the fundamental, indivisible being"—issues that also underlie Beckett's fiction as well as the concerns of poets, from Edmund Spenser to T. S. Eliot and Yeats, who struggle to harmonize mutability and constancy, the dancer with the dance.

III. Triadic Phase   Oedipal/Genital

Magnus Mater: earth-goddess associated with the sowing of seed, the springing crops, the harvest, and, above all, with the sacred marriage to her divine son, who has matured with the seasons. The year-god (Zeus) retains his affinity to the year-mother in his marriage to Hera (from *horos,* "year"). Identity traces with earlier stages persist:	Oedipal period: the fulfilment of the oedipal wish contained in the sacred marriage is granted only to the gods, tragically denied to mortals. Out of the double-bind situation, in which the child faces castration by furthering a libidinal claim on either parent, a withdrawal of cathexis and identification with the opposite-sex parent leads to the formation

from the vegetable realm, associated with grain and grape (wine); from the animal realm, hooves and furry hind legs. At other times he may be androgynous, or a handsome young man. His sexual development and acquisition of a human body image go hand in hand with agricultural knowledge; mastery is acquired about the latter, greater awareness is expressed about the former. The love between Eros and Psyche provides a basis for exploring the ambiguities of erotic passion from either sex's point of view. Amazons and female monsters, like the Sirens, the Sphinx, and the Medusa, materialize to threaten or disrupt the male's developmental journey, and, although these are creations of Greek patriarchy meant to serve as warnings against wild nature, they may be revised by women artists to affirm female autonomy outside marriage, as in the case of Amazons.[15] (In Christianity, crucifixion and pietà motifs often represent the negative side of the oedipal conflict as submission to the father or an oedipal triumph of reclaiming mother.[16])

of a new psychic agency, the superego. The wish to have a child, in all its possible forms, which comes to the fore in the girl's early oedipal stages, may also figure in the boy's negative oedipal phase, and be important for both sexes in developing creative interests.

The triadic phase's accommodation of myth to cultural advances in cognition needs to be pursued. Chaos has been further divided to include an underworld (Tartaros), where certain famous sinners suffer eternal punishment. These are the Titans (e.g., Tityos, Tantalos, Sisyphos, and Ixion), those giants of prehistory who introduce guilt into our past by their punishment for oedipal crimes either for having laid claim to a wife or daughter of Zeus or "for having revealed the 'secrets of the gods.'"[17] It is probable that their increase in physical size and strength concretizes their increase in mental ability. The secrets, as Caldwell notes, "are in fact the secrets of the parents, specifically the secrets of parental sexuality": primal scenes. It is at this point that the defensive aims of the family romance begin to give way, though we remain in a specifically mythic context of semihuman giants, gods and goddesses, numphs and heroes.

It is also here in myth and in art that other, more primitive repressed content may find representation. Thus, the oedipal mother sexually fused with the father in the Sphinx overlays the early terrifying mother of the oral sadistic stage, hinted at by the etymology of the name (sphincter, strangler[18]) and by the poetic justice of the Sphinx's plunge into an abyss when her riddle has been solved.

The well-known genealogy of Zeus traces the shift in generative power and identificatory alliance from mother to father, but it may be worth reviewing for its further contributions to origins.[19] Uranus fathered the Titans on Mother Earth, but for his having cast the rebellious Cyclopes into the Underworld, she aroused the Titan Cronos to castrate Uranos while he slept. The blood from the genitals is generative (as menstrual blood was traditionally believed to be by many primitive peoples) and, accordingly, it fertilized Mother Earth, who bore the Furies, avengers of patriarchy. Cronos recondemns the luckless Cyclopes, and marries his sister, Rhea; of their children, the third born is Zeus, who is given over to Mother Earth and hidden in one of her caves (a return to Gē). He is suckled by nymphs in a golden cradle and enjoys all the accoutrements of the family romance, reverting to a serpent form at one point in order to hide from Cronos. Cronos swallows a stone, believing it to be Zeus, and when Zeus serves him a potion of salt and mustard, Cronos vomits up the stone, followed by Zeus's elder siblings, whom Cronos had swallowed (oral birth fantasies?). Zeus then proceeds to gather support among the Cyclopes and the Three-hundred-handed Ones to conquer Cronons and the Titans, who are sent into exile. Following this, Zeus weds Hera, an earth-goddess, and rules supreme from atop Mount Olympus. Thereafter, the gods and goddesses, often in animal shapes, perform in countless sexual scenes, some among mortals; all of these may be viewed between the proscenium columns of the primal scene and the family romance.

The artists who are remaking themselves, at least in part, by revising their origins will also pass under this proscenium arch, where these mythic prototypes will be available as cues, models, dangers, and reflecting images. Whether the artist has an actual bisexual disposition or sensibility, or else an intuitive-creative ability to enter into the lives of both sexes at various stages of development—like Virginia Woolf, D. H. Lawrence, and James Joyce, among the moderns I can best vouch for—creative processes are well served by encompassing both hemispheres of human sexuality.[20] The work of art, like Dionysus, is always twice born, first from its mother and the natural environment she represents, then from the cultural thigh of tradition. Feminist scholars have portrayed women writers as hampered, confined, penned in—or, perhaps most aptly, corseted by patriarchal myths. Accordingly, women writers either revise patriarchal myths (as in Stevie Davies's reading of *Wuthering Heights* as a "female vision of genesis" and the myth of eternal return), or draw on the "female" myth of Demeter/Persephone as the daughter's quest for reunion with her mother.[21] The feminist view, however, needs some qualifications in light of practice. Many women writers adapt comfortably to patriarchal myths; Eros/Psyche has been used in accord with its original spirit, for example, with great success by Margaret Drabble and Iris Murdoch. Also, men and women writers alike have freely adapted the partriarchal mythology of the Greeks and Hebrews. In fact, the Greek tragedies were revisions of mythic and epic versions of such heroes as Oedipus and Agamemnon. Art is almost always vision and (male) revision before becoming (female) re-revision, none of which lays *a priori* claims to superior power. Consequently, works of art emerge from a mixed parentage, which may begin in compliance with an archetypal sequence of nature (female)/culture (male) but mixes and modifies so freely along the way that any signifiers of gender become arbitrary. Up to a point it may be true that when either side is emphasized by the relative exclusion of the other, the results may be exotic and appealing in their own right, but the work itself may fail to stir our reality sense and, in the end, may suffer from the lack of balance or ripeness classically associated with maturity.

The psychological equivalent of maturity in art owes something to the awareness of mutuality in the sex relation between man and woman and to the decisive connection between copulation and procreation, an individual and cultural achievement that makes the structuring of undifferentiated primitive material intelligible. "Out of Void (Chaos) came Darkness and black Night," writes Hesiod in the *Theogony,* "and out of Night came Light and Day, her children conceived after union in love with Darkness."[22] Human sexual processes thus serve as a key to cosmic origins. While the value of binding chaotic instinctual energy, mastering helplessness, and establishing relatedness is indisputable, one cannot help noticing that mental processes are still under the influence of the mirroring mode of narcissistic perception; or, at best, they are beholden to an elaborate system of correspondences to self and world. To some extent natural forces cooperate—seed planting, fertilizing rains, sun rays, and so forth. But after a certain point art and science must be allowed to move in separate directions, and it becomes an increasingly arduous task for artists to bring their representations back into alignment with objectively defined reality. They are particularly vulnerable to the Romantic temptation to live entirely within the constructs of the family romance; consequently, the sense of balance provided by an objective pole of sexual knowledge may become increasingly elusive.

And, in fact, excessive subjectivity is inherent in the danger of finding oneself as the answer to the Sphinx's riddle, which, in effect, was the case with

Oedipus, who uncovered the secret both to humanity's and his own origins when he said that Man is the being who crawls on four legs in the morning of his life, strides on two at his noontime, and hobbles with a cane on three into his own twilight; he could have said, me—I am the answer to the riddle of parental coitus—and thereby turned the riddle into a prophecy by hobbling off into blind exile at the end. Certainly it is his self-inflating pleasure at the powers of his own "mother wit," as he later says, that blinds him to his own mother, although outwardly he is merely avoiding the oracle and pursuing the allurements of his family romance, which lead him to wed the queen mother, who is also his own. The male apparently cannot continue to have both his primal-scene mastery and his family-romance fantasy, for one will destroy the other; it is up to creativity to fill the gaps or repair the damage, just as the blinded Oedipus must return to the darkness of primordial chaos and gather up the pieces of his life for one more drama.

It is also at the triadic level that myths begin to represent biparental rebirth fantasies. In the most celebrated of these, Dionysus is first born from his earth-mother, Semele, and, after being stolen away and sewn in the thigh of Zeus, he is second born from his Olympian father. Aware of the implications of procreation, the Greeks were never able to agree on who was the chief parent. The gods may have professed it to be the father, but the playwrights seemed to have known better. Exploring how these issues extend far beyond biology and are still very much with us today will be the burden of future sections.

11
Steps Toward an Integration of Origins into Culture

> It would be as difficult for [children] to throw off their belief in God, as for a monkey to throw off its instinctive fear and hatred of a snake.
>
> —*The Autobiography of Charles Darwin*

Inadvertently, Freud blueprinted a bridge from the arts to the sciences when he outlined the three "severe wounds" by science to the "general narcissism of man, the self-love of humanity."[1] The first blow was the cosmological one struck by Copernicus in "destruction of the narcissistic illusion" that man and his planet resided in the center of the universe. The second was the biological blow struck by Darwin when he notified man that, far from being unique among creation with his superior reason and immortal soul, he had a far greater kinship with the animal kingdom than he realized. The third and psychological blow was delivered by Freud himself against the final illusion that, if nowhere else, man was entitled at least to feel "himself to be supreme in his own soul." The discoveries that the sexual drives cannot be wholly restrained and that mental processes are unconscious warned us that "the ego is not master in its own house." It seems that narcissistic blows generate acts of large-scale self-recovery along several routes which may be broadly creative, as in the arts, or mainly inventive, as in the sciences, but which are implicitly reparative as well—as, most recently, ecology and the new physics seek to rebind humanity into new wholes.

Each of the painful alterations in humanity's self-perceptions involves origins—cosmic, racial, personal. But while the above scenario assigns the scientist an objective role in origins, I shall soon propose that questions of origins tend to place even scientists in unwonted subjective roles. That is to say, a dual perspective is necessary in order to begin opening up the subjective side of science. Sensitive to my being less qualified to write about the science that scientists do than about how they write about it, I shall be emphasizing what their various disciplines tell us—directly and indirectly—about ourselves and our world. For it seems that scientists in writing about science reveal something of their less-than-totally scientific minds as well. Let it be also emphasized that examining the subjective dimensions of science no more discredits its worldview than laying bare the wishful illusions of worshipers tells us anything about divine nature (which lurks like a snake in the grass to surprise monkey-man, in Darwin's extraordinary analogy). Our interest then narrows to how scientists create science and how they use language when they recreate their scientific contributions on the page.

The scientific revolution of the seventeenth century cast doubt on the divine authorship of the cosmos and, by implication, on man's divine sonship. New theories of origins for the universe were required to fill the vacuum left by the old theology, even if it meant a newer heliocentric theology. As the idea of cosmic abandonment proved intolerable, belief systems, held together in part by a collective, self-recentering, and long-standing family romance, began undergoing various forms of revision. None of these, though, anticipated the upheavals loosed by the retiring, mild-mannered Charles Darwin, for he quietly made the most unmistakable and repugnant connections between human and animal origins, which every child perhaps suspects but deeply represses in order to become a respectable member of society. His erstwhile adversary Richard Owen hit the "crazy" irrationality of Darwin by subscribing to the notion "that his great-great-great-etc. grandfather was a Baboon, and that his great-great-etc. grandmother was a Chimpanzee."[2]

The reader can see what I am suggesting about Darwin in his *Origin of the Species*: he reminded us implicitly of our individual origins, which had once been glimpsed terrifyingly in the distorting mirrors of primal-scene fantasy of observation and then shut away, one had hoped, forever. Then unexpectedly, Darwin smashed our idealizations about uniquely existing halfway between fallen angels and risen apes, turns upside down our worship of madonnas, pre-Raphealite or otherwise, and shows us nakedly beholden to a nature "red in tooth and claw." He might as well have said humans are begotten by animals and had done with it for all the cool lucidity with which his message was received and debated.

Not that he was always careful to mince his terms. In *The Descent of Man* he was quite explicit that sexual selection is but a less rigorous extension of natural selection. During breeding times the struggle for survival of the fittest becomes a "struggle between males for the possession of the females," who select not only the strongest and best armed but discriminate to a degree among the most vigorous and attractive. And, so, in spite of his "god-like intellect which has penetrated into the movements and constitution of the solar system," Darwin concludes, "Man still bears in his bodily frame the indelible stamp of his lowly origin."[3] No wonder his detractors concluded that our ancestors evolved from baboons mounting chimps.

Rearguard (no doubt in more than one respect) campaigns are still being waged against Darwin by fundamentalists and others of a mystical bent. What the earlier attacks on him suggest is that he was promulgating more than a revolutionary hypothesis about evolution, certain ideas of which were already being broadcast less systematically through his cultural milieu, and that he was also wounding more than our narcissism over no longer being, as Mark Twain aptly said, the "Creator's pet." He was stripping off yet one more veil of a collectively cherished family romance, which, as the obsessive themes of those early debates reveal, protected the cherubic side of our natures from noticing the coital ape.

To affirm that nature is violent, blind, driven, and often brutal is to represent something about human sexual impulses, which individually undergo a complex development, encompassing deviations as well as education, before they actually perform their traditional procreative function. Not only did he connect biological nature to our origins, though; he also masculinized it in the most aggressive fashion—at least this is how his message was received, and it is not surprising that the responses were often hysterical fright or obsessive rage. In popular fantasy, the ape-man battled (before he was recast as Tarzan) with club or claw to survive in a jungle, which replaced the eighteenth-century pastoral of the noble savage reclining on mother nature's bosom. And as the benevolent Father-creator of immutable essences dissolves from view, a new disturbing image emerges of "Dame Nature . . . wilfully cruel."[4] Now not only does life lack divine order and hierarchy, it is out of control, for behind the raging ape-man is the savagely all-powerful mother-goddess, hideous and demonic.

Darwin's cultural impact may then be understood as reintroducing to social consciousness repressed sexual impulses along with derivatives of primal-scene phenomena. He was telling us deeply disturbing things about our personal origins, which Freud was to make even more unbearable in his theories of infantile sexuality. These collectively tell us that not only are we the issue of sexual drives that have undergone peculiar histories in each of our parents, but that we are also involved in their ongoing sexual activities as we unconsciously recreate them into our own primal scenes, where we grapple for our own sexual knowledge and identity. The various stages through which collective family romance constructions have shielded humanity from bonafide truths about its origins can be gauged by the outcry over the collapse of illusion that accompanies the addition of a new truth.

Consider, then, that Darwin's theories met with the same resistance in society that primal scene fantasies are met with in the individual: that is, the encroachments of alien data on the child's emerging self-autonomy are comparable to the scientists' assaults on society's most sacredly held beliefs about itself and its capacity to support and maintain our institutions. Today we may be resigned into accepting that our origins are more bestial than celestial, but the biological affinities between humans and other primates in the act of copulation do differ in an important respect: contrary to the practice of humans, animals mostly prefer to mount front to rear. However, in the child's mind, due to either animal observation or to a combination of the cathexis of bodily zones preceding the genital and an ignorance about the facts of adult sexuality, the animal paradigm may easily take root in the mind's deeper (i.e., more elusive) regions and serve for the adherence of perverse drives and representations whose repression may be far more urgent than tenuous ideas about copulation per se. In his study of the Wolf-Man, Freud speculates that since coitus *ā tergo* is "phylogenetically the older form," it survives as racial inheritance and is reactivated in individual primal scenes. But the older is also the barred, and Darwin's nation has not hesitated to declare "buggery" between men and women as well as among men a criminal offense.

The implications for individual and racial development are similar. On the phylogenetic scale, the turning around of the female partner is such an evolutionary breakthrough as to be associated with bipedalism and, thus, the ability to hunt, to use weapons and tools, to farm and divide labor, and, ultimately, to devise differentiated sex roles and stable pair-bonds. Ontogenetically, this *volte-face* marks the emergence of sexual awareness and accentuates the psychological consequences of anatomical distinctions. The consequences are manifold and far-reaching. Genital functioning becomes a mutual exchange, but in human development a gap appears, signaled by castration anxiety, and attempts to bridge it have produced more than a few philosophical and scientific theories. For the present we will stick with the evolutionary context. Elaine Morgan, for instance, establishes in the reader's mind a "pair of aquatic apes," with the "female presenting her posterior to him in the gesture of sexual invitation employed by primates for millions of years." But since "in the field of frontal sex . . . there must have been a first time," on a certain occasion she selected a pioneer, an innovative type, who, "instead of responding in a proper and friendly fashion . . . threw her on to her back." What follows may be designated as the primal rape: the female emits "piercing shrieks," thinking "he had gone berserk and was aiming to disembowel her." But the rape is also transformed by a Ring Lardner sense of humor. " 'Shut up!' he explained, clobbering her a bit and trying patiently to flatten out her knees, which she had locked into a panic-stricken fetal crouch." [5] Thus may our ontogenic knowledge or fantasies be applied to a phylogenic problem, for the violent nature of this primal rape directly corresponds to the child's perception of the primal scene as brutal act.

Likewise our historical vantage point invites asking if Darwin's scheme of combative sexual selection was either subjectively overdetermined or unduly influenced by prevailing psychological and cultural issues of his day. Stanley Edgar Hyman shows that Darwin used the struggle-for-existence idea in his earliest writings before he made it a conscious metaphor to dramatize his observations about evolution. Ardrey believes that Darwin's apologists, Herbert Spencer and Thomas Huxley, exaggerated the violent side and the individual aspect respectively,[6] although Darwin himself wrote that "all male animals which are furnished with special weapons for fighting, are well known to engage in fierce battles": for example, "male seals fight, both with their teeth and claws, during the breeding season," their hides becoming covered with scars. By whatever vehicle, the association of sex with violence was unmistakably suggested to the Victorian mind in the evolutionary hypothesis. And Ardrey's characterization meant as a *reductio ad absurdum* of a "caveman contest, a shadowing prize-fight, club against skull, with a shrinking woman in the dim cavern's reaches clutching a wailing babe," may be fairly apt in capturing the affective tone of the message. In any case, the terrified babe completes the primal scene picture.

Darwin himself was explicit in his conclusion to the *Origin* that "from the war of nature, from famine and death, the most exalted object which we are capable of conceiving, namely the production of higher animals, directly follows." Thus the war of nature is continued in the human bedroom. Hyman takes "the war of nature" as the archetypal image of the *Origin* and concludes that "Man is always on Darwin's mind as he talks of the lower orders."[7] Like Freud, Darwin was implying that the achievement of a genital level of sexual functioning presumes a history of prior stages, stages that do not disappear, stages to which one might return or, were the truth known, still be at. But for all their objective powers, Darwin's theories of origins, along with those of many evolutionists who came after, appear one-sidedly masculinist in light of women's recent contributions to anthropology and primatology. "Many scientists are reluctant to relinquish their cherished image of the male's monopoly on courtship behavior and sexual drive."[8] The fact that female primates are also assertive/aggressive reveals the old patriarchal fantasy of owing something to the boy's handling the primal scene threat by identifying in primitive fashion with the male role of overpowering the female. But the current sociobiological efforts to correlate cultural traits with genes, the altruistic over the egoistic approach, and the revisionist bent among some feminist scientists to emphasize cooperation over competition have been regarded by Stephen Jay Gould as a type of "Panglossian adaptationsim" that, among other things, looks at function while overlooking structure.[9] The wishful element in the notion that evolution reassures us that we live in the best of all possible worlds opens onto intriguing subjective tangents that cannot be pursued here.

Better to agree on the likelihood that all theories of origins, cosmic or individual, are going to be affected by the inescapable relativity that everyone suffers as observer-fantasist at the sexual scenes which first enlisted his or her curiosity and interest in self-origins at a time of heightened curiosity when he/she was unequipped to respond to it in a nondistorting way. Here is Heisenberg's principle of uncertainty with a vengeance: the primal scene profoundly disturbs the calm, neutral space between the observer and observed when the terrifying and exciting events the child is interpreting are key to his/her own origins. For *particle/wave,* substitute *person/act.* Although the impartial observer has already been discredited within most scientific circles, that figure has not so far been compromised at the levels introduced here.

In general it should not be surprising to find that scientific theories, like works of art and all other mental acts, can be overdetermined, that there are shaping fantasies (such as the belief in progress, human perfectibility, fittedness, or, more subtly, hidden agendas) with manifest and latent content, even within the core of the hardest sciences. Richard Sennett, for example, finds that B. F. Skinner's "beliefs have overtaken his theories" in *Beyond Freedom and Dignity* when they reveal a "man desperately in search of some way to preserve the old-fashioned virtues associated with nineteenth century individualism in a world where self-reliance no longer makes sense."[10] In the beginning was not the theory or principle, the Word or divine Logos, but, as Faust discovered: "In the beginning was the Deed." Ideas, words, theories scramble to keep up. But the primal deed, however we construe it, exists outside mental space. So, as *Finnegans Wake* has it, "In the buginning was the void." The theories, which may or may not bug us, be "insectuous," or include buggery, come later to rationalize the deed or avoid the void, which may be overdetermined by maternal absence or by that other presence of an absence signified in castration.

Even our most cherished philosophies can be affected. One such beginning for Western thought is concentrated in the philosophical myth of Plato's cave. There, men sit fettered in darkness, staring at the indistinct shadows cast on the cave wall by human and animal images, which are mere copies of forms but are nonetheless taken as reality. On the one hand, this mere shadow play made by copies of reality is harmless; on the other hand, it is a terrifying state of ignorance, folly, and madness, wherein the unreal is made real.[11] But this articulation of chaos, with its evocation of a dream screen, is also an expression of human origins, specified by Plato as "the world of being born," and, so, what is being suggested is "children in the darkness of the bedroom, seeing the shadows, and hearing echoes of parental intercourse." The shadow play is not meaningless at all, then, but filled with disturbing implications about our heritage. But the task of the philosopher, as opposed to that of the poet (whom Plato would banish), is to rescue man from this spectacle, to turn him away from it as one turns from a firelit cave to sunlight, rather than to interpret it as both analysis and art can enable us to do.

It was left to Plato's star pupil, Aristotle, to reverse the upward, sublimating tendency by finding more substantial forms than mere apparent copies of copies. And it is interesting that the kind of thinking we call reflection has been traced by Rappaport to originally one's reflecting on images, derived ultimately from the earliest mirroring transactions.[12] Another kind of thinking referred to as speculation also derives from the mirroring process, since *speculum* means mirror; but, as seen earlier, the mirror has ambiguous capacities, and the meaning of those shadows may not have been altogether lost to Plato or clear to Aristotle.

Nonetheless, the mirror of the Platonic mind ultimately reflects those lofty and marvelous but altogether speculative entities in the world of pure forms. The artist, on the other hand, never quite leaves the cave of human origins;

or, using Ehrenzweig's terms, he/she carries it within as creative womb. At their best, artists remind us that "all dreams of the soul/End in a beautiful man's or woman's body." So from Yeats; from D. H. Lawrence: "Everything that has beauty has a body, and is a body;/everything that has being has being in the flesh:/and dreams are only drawn from the bodies that are."[13]

The purpose of the last chapter's scaling the creative process in terms of mythic prototypes was not to suggest that there is necessarily an ideal phylogeny which the ontogeny of every artist recapitulates. But such a scale does have the value of marking the developmental path every individual more or less charts in moving from maternal to paternal attachments and beyond or back. As this shift occurs, it is accompanied by developing theories of origins that start out in an exclusively matriarchal setting and gradually introduce partiarchal elements. Extreme positions, for example, monosexual theories of origins that affect creativity, are available at any step of the total process.[14] But if artists can follow their creative demons far enough back to recover at least the semblance of chaos, they may allow the shadowy outlines of primal-scene configuration to emerge as a male/female enterprise; by working with them in whatever mysterious ways suitable, artists may emerge from this fertile inner darkness with a new and compelling vision of reality.

Philosopher, scientist, psychoanalyst, poet—so diverse and specialized in their outlook and method, we say; yet all share such a common interest in origins that their works may, more often than we think, criss-cross, overlap, and collide. It remains to follow several of these leads to further stages of generalization and to add along the way one more member to our party, someone who is also deeply invested in origins within everyday life and, so, may be named Everyman (or Everyperson). Without the inherent creative capacities within every human being, origins would never find reverberating chords of response. This capacity in everyone can be examined next as natural creativity.

12
The Three Stages of Natural Creativity

It is only our natural prejudice, and that arrogance which made our forefathers declare that they were descended from demigods, which leads us to demur to this conclusion.

—Darwin, *The Descent of Man*

In consequence of the special character of our discoveries, our scientific work in psychology will consist in translating unconscious processes into conscious ones and thus filling in the gaps in conscious perception. ... "

—Freud (1938; where his last piece of writing broke off)

While everyone creates, not everyone is an artist. We speak loosely of creative living, creative teaching, of psychotherapy or loving as an art, and it is not only because *creativity* or *art* have become consumer items or cant words. In fact, each individual has been creative in some fundamentally valid sense and retains a capacity to respond to actual artworks or new thought patterns. This capacity makes itself known in three critical phases of early development when everyone exercises creativity not artistically, to produce a work, but psychologically, to produce a self. Though drawn to more specialized goals, the artist-to-be also struggles through these phases; consequently, they may be viewed as crucial links binding human beings together irrespective of divergent talents and aspirations.

These steps of indigenous or natural creativity spring from the three areas already noted—those of the self, early dyadic ties, and triadic relationships.[1] Our adult vantage point assures us that parents are the progenitors of children, but we may be overlooking the fact once the diametrically opposite position obtained. Children become human by creating their parents or, more precisely, by creating themselves through their parents. For at the start of life, each one of us performs a prodigious creative act: we produce out of sheer necessity something that is rather cryptically referred to in analytic shorthand as a "breast" (or primary care-giver). Winnicott, for example, refers to "primary creative activity," in which the "breast is created by the infant over and over again out of the infant's capacity to love or (one can say) out of need. A subjective phenomenon develops in the baby which we call the mother's breast."[2] This internalized good breast or inner mother, along with the mirroring response and myriad other early responses, sensations, and

186

transactions between mother and infant, contributes to a nuclear core of the self, which, as has been seen, facilitates the dissolution of symbiosis. Adapting Roy Schafer's action language, one would say that in primary creativity infants begins making themselves out of their inner world and primary attachments, and they continues this process of self-making by adapting, correcting, identifying, building, and rebuilding, until, as Sheldon Bach suggests, the self emerges as something of a work of art: hence, natural creativity.[3]

Because the second stage of natural creativity parallels the first when viewed from a different angle, it can be considered more explicitly dyadic. It is here that contradictory drives, and self/other representations begin to be integrated. "The human infant," says Winnicott, "cannot accept the fact that this mother who is so valued in the quiet phases is the person who has been and will be attacked in the excited phases."[4] Yet the infant begins sensing that she is indeed that same person. Now the object it has created and destroyed, repeatedly built up and torn asunder in fantasy, must be restored, made whole again, all in order to allow the child to undergo a "moral teething" and enter Winnicott's humanly precious "stage of concern." Guilt, reparation, and distant glimmers of responsibility facilitate self-binding functions, and many fragmentary self-images and split-off drives soon may be reintegrated in processes that form the second step of natural creativity. Here begin inklings of mutuality, when the child apprehends that its drives shape the images of its world. The mother, having emerged as its first creation, remains to be discovered as the handiwork of her own self-creation. If the child's earliest calling and naming seem to have summoned her into being, her linguistic powers continue to attune and advance the primary human dialogue. The child's efforts toward creating a mother ensure greater inner harmony and autonomy on the one hand and initiate object-constancy in relating on the other. Out of all these manifold partial representations, mainly set by the child's needs, he/she eventually creates mother not only as a whole object (person) but creates its own inner boundaries and separateness as well, acquires a mediating yes/no between good/bad divisions in self or surround, and, in the crucial in-between spaces, creates transitional objects. Since these objects preexist and the child's creation of them is more an act of investing the inanimate with life qualities, of transforming things through meaning and relatedness, he/she enters not only the family but culture.[5]

If the child engages culture through play, he/she has not yet become fully committed to cultural modes until, through the exercise of language and the adoption of symbols, a new psychic agency is created at the triadic stage. As parental prohibitions and social norms are internalized, the superego takes command over the inner world. Within its sphere of operations, Peter Blos connects the "positive" trends of the Oedipus complex as affirming the child's needs to identify with the same-sex parent, whom he/she envies and admires, and the "negative" trends as indicating that the child loves the parent he/she wants to be.[6] If the superego as heir to the positive Oedipus complex manages internalized hostile wishes, the ego-ideal as heir to the negative Oedipus complex draws on primary narcissism within the self and may become attached to idealized figures/images of the same sex until these are assimilated through various adolescent crises into principles, goals, and ambitions. The operations of the superego, which militate against incest, castration dread, loss of love, and the like, seem almost part of our basic biological wiring and exercise an unmodified force against nature; but the operations of the ego-ideal, which will be explored in the final section, are far more susceptible to fluctuating cultural influences, and so extend through and beyond natural creativity at the triadic stage. Thus, while we may get our marching orders from the superego, it is the ego-ideal that sets us marching to a different drummer, be it to feminism, Fabianism, Esalen, or purely private endeavors.[7]

The third aspect of natural creativity, usually subsumed under superego development, underscores the distinctive problems faced in the triadic sphere. After the child has established a cohesive self and a *modus operandi* for relating to the environment, what remains, as his/her curiosity and cognition expand exponentially, is to re-create the parental sex relation. Internalized, the primal scene becomes "the inner scene where the taking into possession of, and giving form to one's own sexuality is staged."[8] This step poses a unique challenge in more ways than one. Not only must a second person after the primary care-giver be created—that should not be so difficult after the momentous achievement of integrating maternal images—but now no facilitating or reciprocating person in the environment exists. Previously, the infant's hunger-based needs had their counterpart in the maternal breast; its fragmentary (libidinal/aggressive) images of mother could be unified around the whole person, who also negotiated its anal-phase drives with toilet training and a primitive ("sphincter") morality. But the early genital phases are launched with no corresponding organ or person in the environment to match one's needs, since even anatomically the child's immature genitals are not suited to either parent's organs.[9] Nor will the boy or the girl be able to perform in a genital fashion for another decade; in the meantime, father and mother happily possess and deploy their own superior organs exclusively for their own pleasure. In searching for a solution to their as-yet-unformed sexuality and in desiring to participate in the "world of the parents and caring adults," children develop fantasies of sharing in adult relationships for purposes of self-identity and sexual organization.

However, the child's inevitable estrangement from the adults' sexual activities is self-wounding and results in a preoccupation among all children with themes of inclusion/exclusion (whether or not an adoption fantasy is installed).[10] Considerations of narcissistic rage and subsequent distortions regarding the parental act address the question of why the child not only internalized what cannot otherwise be mastered but also why he/she must create the primal scene. The radical reason for this is that his/her emotionally charged responses have symbolically destroyed the parents. Not only is mother being torn and mutilated, but father is being engulfed and castrated. These damaged but primary love-objects of the child's emotional life must be made whole and functional again in the child's internal representations. Thus, there are destructive forerunners to both natural or self-creativity as well as to artistic creativity that stimulate developmental processes and then get easily overlooked: it's called repression.

What sustains the child during all the tumult of primal-scene assimilation? Along with good-enough parenting there must be a protected illusion of one's invulnerability, perhaps of omnipotence, and I would hypothesize that a conviction of heroic origins is the sustaining fantasy of choice for creative individuals especially, but probably for everyone, to a lesser degree. Thus from the present perspective, the family romance performs as an internal holding environment or self-container while the individual grapples with strangely exciting and profoundly disruptive sexual stimuli. Thus may Saint George hope to slay the dragon of sexual turmoil.

Among the factors that diffentiate children's responses, the strongest may well be gender. The boy becomes aware of woman's great reproductive powers around the time he is distancing himself from mother. It suddenly appears that the object of his curiosity, the vessel of life's deepest secrets, is destined to be at a certain remove from him. He soon finds that he must embark on torturous quests for mysterious grails or hidden treasures, solve sphinxes' riddles, unravel strange mysteries—all while the girl comes to realize that she is the goal and grail, the guardian and broker of precious gems, the sphinx and mysterious source of life. Compounding the boy's difficulties and highlighting distinctions between the sexes, in Greenacre's view, is the girl's more "secretiveness regarding her [imaginative] fantasy, with a lesser need to act it out openly"; it is concerned "more with romanticizing on the basis of personal emotional involvements." The boy apparently has greater needs "for externalization, of testing, of development of precision."[11]

But these views may seem arbitrary today, and if psychoanalysis has only begun catching up in its understanding of early female development, it has hardly begun addressing the issues of woman's creativity. Evidently, masculinity for boys poses a more demanding sequence of natural creativity than does femininity for girls, whose core gender identity begins to emerge from the early identifications with the procreative mother of the reproductive process.[12] Boys are confronted with the psychic import of anatomical difference before they have instituted a masculine core of identity, so the experience is rife with castration implications; but when girls look down the fatal crossroads of gender, they already have feminine identifications with mother in the dyad to fall back on, and their defense against castration will classically take the form of protecting against loss of love objects, a gender-enhancing strategy. Consistent with these views is Seymour Fisher's findings that the fantasy life of boys is filled with damage to the body (not so with girls, who may represent their conflicts over separation/individuation through eating disorders).[13] These differences may help explain why boys deploy greater energies toward mastery and self-repair in both natural creativity and other cultural outlets, though this deeper investment need not imply greater capacity or quality of result.

Fair to say, then, that boys and girls respectively undergo the threefold process of natural creativity and distinctively create their primal scenes. Apart from the triadic sphere's decisive influence on gender and gender roles in shaping identity, the boy may go deeper (or is it only more obsessively?) into the primal-scene quandary than the girl, since greater demands are made on his natural creativity than on those of the girl, whose prospect of future procreative powers has historically foreclosed a more sustained immersion in natural creativity at the triadic stage.

Among other things, gender analysis reveals that insofar as both natural and artistic creativity involve some degree of reworking origins, they also involve a reworking of both sexes, and not just one's own with an eye toward gender role. How writers depict the sexuality of opposite-sex characters may inform us of the primal scene's relative importance and the manner of its mastery, which may in turn tell us something of the quality of the appeal of the work, if not also of its maturity. There is an enormous amount of research being published in all areas affected by gender, and the present study of creativity was interrupted at this point for three years to pursue a project involving fieldwork of a kind (surveying and interviewing British women writers of fiction) in order to do more justice to the underlying questions of sexual differences manifested in literary work. The results can be touched on only in a general way here.[14]

Both sexes draw freely on the family romance repertoire, since its sources often predate the triadic stage and stem from narcissistic issues of common import. However, in her survey of psychoanalytic literature, Nancy Chodorow concludes that mothers do not experience "infant daughters as separate from them as do mothers of infant sons."[15] Following her lead, Carol Gilligan and other feminist psychologists have concluded that the sense of oneness and continuity is stronger with infant daughters, and that their mothers' experience of them as self-extensions or doubles emphasizes narcissistic elements.[16] These findings suggest that the maternal loss/recovery processes that are frequently activated in creativity may be weaker under most circumstances in women writers than in their counterparts. Many women's great interest in romances suggests that the adoption fantasy is negotiated less in terms of exalted parents and protracted heroic quests for selfhood than of an exalted marriage. Primal-scene influences are felt in an incorporative tendency to include the "odd girl out" and to attend with great assiduity to the pairing off and matching up of characters—a trend that persists from Jane Austen to the present.

To the three women writers previously examined in some depth, male sexuality can be likened to the arrival of Mr. Ramsay and his children at the lighthouse, which Lily can view only from afar—a distant shore neither reachable nor necessarily desirable. George Eliot employs various distancing devices, flashbacks, or an equivocal word (*valvae / vulva*) in a medical text to convey a dawning awareness in her sexually accomplished male (Lydgate). And Emily Brontë whisks Heathcliff off to Europe for his sexual coming-of-age (about which a separate novel has been written). Thus, in these three instances art overcomes gaps in perception. But more noticeably than the others, Emily Brontë also substitutes the first step (narcissistic injury) and the second step (reparation as "moral teething") of natural creativity for the third stage of phallic-genital sexuality. Meanwhile, among some recent women writers, feminist ideology has militated against taking men too seriously, the implications of which have been cited by Joyce Carol Oates: "by denying subtlety and humanity to roughly one half the population, and by delineating Maleness in place of specific human beings who happen to be male, the writer with feminist interests severely jeopardizes her power to create imaginative literature."[17] Hardly a vanishing species, men for their part are continually, almost obsessively, writing about women, but perhaps no one has broken the gender barrier as successfully as James Joyce did in Molly Bloom.[18] And while the fiction of Isak Dinesen, Iris Murdoch, Joyce Carol Oates, Joan Didion, and Anne Beattie, among many others, contains creditable male portraits, the empathically rendered male often seems as rare in women's fiction as the liberated female in men's.

The capacity for female characterization, shared by both sexes, derives psychologically from the preoedipal involvement of every child's primary attachment to mother, before loyalties are substantially reshuffled at the triadic stage. By then boys have "disidentified" with mother, and girls have shifted their libidinal focus toward gender's farther shore. The absence of male genitalia (i.e., its perceived absence in women making it a dangerous possibility for men) is a subjectively construed incompleteness that, however biologically unquestioned, is far from uninteresting. Among others, Thomas Ewens distinguishes between the literal organ (penis) and its affective symbolic representation (phallus); the fear is not so much over an actual loss as the sense of a "radical lack in what had hitherto been the self-sufficiency of the child's phallic narcissism."[19] This "lack" is not described or defined for the child, but it "signifies something which remains enigmatic and mysterious." Ewens then makes a distinction between objects of instinctual drives that are "fixed by heredity or programmed in the biological organism and the indeterminate objects of desires." For Freud, "human sexuality has no fixed object or aim or naturalistic evolution; it is rather a personal history, and it is inseparable from the risks, vicissitudes, and conflicts that mark the odyssey of any human desire and stem from the lack of any adequate object." Thus, "if men and women knew what they wanted sexually, there would be no problem, but they don't," and their "desires are haunted by a lack; human sexuality remains an enigma."

However, the psychological import of anatomical sexual differences (which leads to concern over castration) appears to be more decisive among males. What is for a boy a fatal crossroads is for a girl a temporary disruption or detour to be overcome in part through her prior core gender identity. But fatal crossroads or not, castration does signify a triangulation in both sexes' affective ties and opens the way for an array of new emotions to complicate one's inner world—these include jealousy, betrayal, envy, rivalry, competitiveness: a new mode of desire, a different fear of loss. Because there is greater psychic distance covered in boys' development of a masculine self-identity, there may also be greater reliance on creative or scientific mastery, greater displacements to nonbiological spheres, a literature that carries adventuring heroes across seas, over deserts, through battles, and into jungles, where manhood is belatedly conferred or withheld and the womanly prize won or lost. Because for girls womanhood is in many respects less an achievement than an endowment, there are fewer protracted quests for heroic selfhood and more willingness to affirm community, continuity, and accommodation through romance, matching up, and mothering. Whether universal and inevitable or not, such "tendencies" have been so thoroughly appropriated by patriarchal society (which we all, for better or worse, inhabit) that it is virtually impossible to pinpoint where nature leaves off, psychology begins, and culture takes over. To whatever its extent, the masculine creation of culture that intends (or at least functions) to distance the male from the maternal matrix in his quest for identity is perceived by feminists as oppressive to woman, which, indeed, is the effect if not the motive; for in the long run, the aim of masculine-based culture is a return to, or rapprochement with, the female, which has its positive benefits for both sexes if it is not perpetrated in phallocentric terms (a big *if*).

In any event, and male = norm / female = other scenarios to the contrary, it is firmly established that the boy undergoes a two-step sequence in identity formation, but one step in object choice (if it is heterosexual); whereas the girl takes a one-step identity formation, but a two-step object choice sequence (again assuming a heterosexual outcome). These reciprocal differences affect the ways each gender confronts and internalizes the primal scene. But both sexes are affected by castration as a break in psychic continuity with threefold consequences: an indeterminancy of sexual drives; a not-unusual incompleteness of satisfaction in the sexual relation; and an uncertainty that carries over into many of our mental and cultural endeavors. Significantly, it is in the triadic sphere that open-ended desire replaces biologically programmed need.

Returning to the previous context, it is not surprising to find children seriously exercising imaginative powers for the first time during this period. Their curiosity leads toward the mysteries of sex: "the dark at the top of the stairs" (in William Inge's play); the "cries and whispers" in the next room (in Bergman's film); inevitably to the parental sex-relation; through primal-secne fantasies around, again, to their own origins; and, finally, on to their uncertain sexual futures. This quest may amount to the most difficult task of all, for here we have seen that the child is not adequately guided by drive zones or by "good-enough objects" (care-givers).

For the infant, a sense of meaning first dawns in the mother's responsiveness to its wishes, and it may feel meaning is being created as it "creates" the breast. Bion finds that the "emotional experiences" at the breast are later represented by such terms as love, understanding, and meaning; it is there the child "first acquires (or puts to use) the capacity to learn."[20] Disillusionment is administered in small but regular doses, while security objects, play, and fantasy enter the widening spaces between infant and gratifying object, all of which go to balance meaning between sheer illusion and blunt reality. But, at the risk of repeating, mental faculties are given a radically different challenge at the triadic crisis.

And this is why psychoanalysis holds that the child creates its own primal scene according to its needs, prior exposures, distortions, and fantasies, as well as in accord with the demands of adaptive learning and accelerated cognition. Even Harlow's celebrated apes could not perform coitus if they had not first been exposed to it. In writing "On the Sexual Theories of Children" (1908), Freud, for perhaps the first time, drew on direct observation to complement the reconstructions from psychoanalysis.[21] These theories often build on the child's connections between mother's changed shape and the subsequent arrival of a young sibling. The question of origins may first be phrased as, 'Where did this particular tiresome child come from?' Here the initial aim of curiosity may be to prevent a repetition "of an event so greatly feared," but the mental activity soon turns into investigations independent of the original stimulus. The effort may further build on the role of the penis (phallus) as fitting in somewhere, but the (male child's) "inquiry breaks off helplessly" due to "ignorance of the vagina" as invisible, and, so presumably, nonexistent. B. D. Lewin notes that when his (male) patients refer to "reality" (as in, I have to face reality) or to "nothing," their associations always lead to the female genitalia.[22] The immediate outcome of the impasse noted by Freud is the child's cloacal theory or birth, with variations later, on the navel or splitting open of the stomach as in Little Red Riding Hood, until genital awareress is integrated. The more primitive theory is the primal fantasy referred to earlier, based on a denial of sex differences, in attributing a penis to mother. The third basis for children's sexual theories, which may draw on any of the other fanciful notions, is the actual witnessing of parental intercourse as a sadistic event that the "stronger person inflicts on the weaker by force."

The child's "constructions," writes Aaron Esman in a summary of psychoanalytic thinking about the primal scene, "are applied to the data not only of actual observations, but also to the hints and suggestions that come from childhood gossip . . . and to the child's own efforts to solve the mysteries of procreation, childbirth, and male-female relations. In the course of his development, therefore, every child will form some notion, expressed in conscious as well as unconscious fantasy, of the primal scene irrespective of any exposure to the actual event.''[23] The primal scene may be thought of as forming part of the child's origins drama, often played out within an oedipal framework. And no matter how it is played and how it turns out, the results are likely to bring about crucial identifications; a direction for future gender identity; a withdrawal of libidinal ties from both parents; and new self-structures.

For the primal scene functions internally as a major organizing fantasy of the self. Accordingly, it assumes a certain form or structure, and Edelheit's formulation of "primal scene schema" allows us to treat it as if it were a fundamental mental structure, hence not contingent on motive. "We use our parents like recurring dreams," reflects Doris Lessing, "to be entered into when needed.''[24] A provocative image. It suggests that we, who were once our parents' dreams, have made them over into our own. But dreams have an inner dynamic, a way of arising at their—not our—bidding, and the many messages of the primal scene likely remain unconscious.

The three steps of natural creativity may be restated:

1. Primary creativity of a nuclear and bounded self;
2. Dyadic creativity of the primary parent and of transitional objects;
3. Triadic creativity of the male / female sexual relation.

From each step stem various organizing fantasies that enter into the construction of the self. "At the heart of creativity," writes Kurt Schlesigner, "lies the human capacity to construe.''[25] It is this capacity that accounts for the "subjective sense of self" we identify as being human. It is the personal, often idiosyncratic ways each of us has of making sense or no sense of the sum of our earliest sensations and relationships, our images of our self and others, along with the ways in which our deepest wishes and imaginings come to be represented to consciousness.

An interesting paper by Anne Gourevitch on "Origins: The Impact of Parental Background" conveys some of the ongoing ways in which children rework and create themselves out of their parents' total lives (including worldview, prejudices, etc.)[26] From sampling two generations of lower-middle-class Jewish immigrants, she uncovers some general truths about our upwardly mobile, success-oriented society. The felt poverty, narrowness, and clannishness of the parents' background are often repressed by their children—that is, internalized but denied—as they struggle for status and prestige, unaware that they are overcompensating and neglecting needs for self-respect and identity. The danger is that the individual aggrandizes himself as a self-made person and minimizes the importance of his / her background, severing continuity with the past, or that he / she idealizes and beautifies the parents' past. Either way, the task of self-creation is short-circuited. "People who repudiate the impact of their parents' past remain prisoners of the parents' reality." Covering up or concealing their parents' background, these people experience embarrassment and shame while pretending to be oblivious of the parental past. They may, as in the Kris material cited earlier, freeze their past into a personal mythology. The alternative, as Gourevitch makes clear, is not an easy one. "One must confront the frustrating experiences, restrictions, and often humiliations in one's own or one's parents' past, understand these feelings, have compassion for those who suffered them, resolve to resist injustice wherever one sees it, without letting this deteriorate into self-pity or cheap sentimental identification with the underdog." Her descriptions and clinical vignettes rapidly take on lucid sociological visibility, and comparable portraits could be drawn from other social strata to further illustrate individuals' shaping their past to facilitate their emergence from it.

We are familiar with the tendency to mythologize American origins through such holidays as Thanksgiving and the Fourth of July, which perpetuate images of false racial harmony or of one-sidedly benevolent militarism. There is also the quaint reconstruction of diverse places of origins into a mythological Old Country. Catering to this fantasy are theme parks built by breweries and the Disneyland people, where the fantasy-land can be revisited; our readiness to bifurcate our parentage easily fosters a collective family romance, where one chooses which illusion—the mythic Old Country or the land of the American Dream—to invest with emotional reality. Finally, among certain religious and ethnic groups who oppose birth control and abortion, sexual behavior is patterned after very circumscribed primal-scene derivatives in which parental intercourse is legitimized in the eyes of the offspring for its reproductive functions only. The splitting-off of breeding from sensual indulgence is reinforced by ancient Catholic tradition and a modern pope who cautions husbands against lusting after their wives. The upshot of such misguided idealism is the madonna/whore culture, along the lines of that found in Italy. The primal fantasy, which becomes church policy and a guide to adult sexual behavior, affirms the narcissism of the child. It says, in effect, that mothers engage in intercourse not because it gives them satisfaction or fosters adult mutuality, but because it gives them children—that is, women do it only to beget us. Similarly, the inclination of the church fathers to intrude into the most intimate details of married life evokes the child's compulsive wish to witness.

But I would not want to leave the impression that all the processes stemming from origins, even those at the close of adolescence, are predominantly cultural and conscious. Rather, cultural modes, with their observable economic, racial, and ethnic features, are often vehicles that enable more obscure sexual feelings and positions toward the parents' sexual life to ride along like stowaways or contraband. For children extrapolate about sexual behavior from nonsexual phenomena, letting one represent the other, with consequent feelings of shame and embarrassment, or of alienation and rage, often beneath a veneer of indifference or nonchalance—all of which feeds into the representation of the past. For as we remold the past, it is also molding us.

And in general, everyone sets up internal authority systems and internal need-supplying systems modeled on early transactions with parents. Everyone of us re-creates our parents internally according to our needs and strengths. We idealize them when that fills the bill, downgrade them when that suits our purposes. We may even, in the long run, humanize them, perceiving them as an independent and separate couple—though seldom do we abandon those first titles of authority and endearment to address them by their familiar names.

13
The Creation of Origins through Evolution

Car ce fait l'homme, c'est d'avoir une enfance.
—Roland Barthes

We have evolved our massive brains largely by the evolutionary process of neoteny: the slowing down of developmental rates and the consequent retention in adulthood of traits that mark the juvenile stages of our ancestors.
—Stephen Jay Gould

The three steps of self-creativity are taken by everyone.[1] Their importance may be illuminated by reconsidering more fully the intrusion of creativity into scientific theories of human origins. Ever since Darwin called attention to the human embryo's donning a fur coat between the sixth and eighth month, scientists have been curious about the interplay of ontogeny and phylogeny. Often the one is invoked to elucidate the other, but investigators in biological development have been less attentive to a parallel revealed in psychoanalysis. Though arising from discrete sources, the common element is an adaptive sexual change. Biologically, it is the shift from rear-mounting coital patterns to frontal sex, which apparently accompanied the upright posture and use of tools/weapons, which took place well over three million years ago as primates began deserting their arboreal paradise for savannas. Psychologically, the fall from paradise is marked by the child's response to disparities between the sexes and the prohibitive quality of adult sexuality. What makes the phylo/biologic and the onto/psychic more intriguingly analogous is that the child's cognitive shift from a cloacal concept of coitus to genital awareness "recapitulates" the actual shift of early man and woman from rear to frontal mounting. Roughly speaking, the child's developing mind, as much as its growing body, corresponds to (or recapitulates) the evolutionary sequence.

The problem is that we don't quite know how the latter came about: there is a gap in phylogeny. While genuine, this gap is also informative. For in re-creating humanity's origins through language, the most hard-core empiricists must stretch their thinking beyond available data and thereby become susceptible to drawing on whatever resources may individually appear to be equivalent—in short, they extrapolate. In the absence of direct evidence, they speculate from indirect and related—or seemingly related—evidence, of which even the most subjective should not be automatically excluded. Far from being reprehensible, this practice may be unavoidable, since to be human is to extrapolate. Perhaps to extrapolate is to become human, as well. Scientists, for example, may unwittingly invoke natural creativity at the triadic stage to fill the gaps in their knowledge—less, perhaps, out of childhood's need to resolve basic issues than to consolidate these within a viable professional identity: the answers, whether negative or positive, inevitably tend to validate the basic assumptions of the field.

My reasons for such an inference stem first from wide divergences in the interpretation of data among members united under a common empirical banner, and, second, from their invariable misreadings of Freud, whose contributions reveal nothing so much as the overdeterminisms of mental life. The fact that his method also doubled back to allow a reading of his own overdeterminisms is a story still being told, for the principle of over-determinism also explodes the very scientific model he aspired to.[2] All the same, a corrective for the tendency to err has been built into the core of psychoanalytic practice (if not always its theory) by means of the counter-transference concept, and it is probable that the hard sciences need more than independent corroboration when they extrapolate from their data to deliver sweeping pronouncements on the human condition. For, finally, no system of thought is fail-safe, and even psychoanalysts have been known to nod when their "even-hovering attention" was most in order.

Yet one would suppose that scientists who must meticulously decipher and explain obscure or fragmentary "texts" of nature dating from millions of years ago would have little trouble reading a text before their own eyes and printed in their own language; this seldom turns out to be the case, however, for the Freudian text apparently arouses too many anxieties, and misreadings abound when behaviorists, stretching their data to fit human culture, encounter the problematics of psychoanalysis. While the few scientific writers to be singled out may or may not be representative, they at least enjoy a degree of prominence within their fields as well as fairly high cultural visibility outside them; but as they articulate far-reaching views, they also may harbor unstated inner paradigms. All the same, I have found their writings to be absorbing, enriching, informative, and often totally persuasive on various levels. My placing them in a context not of their making does not diminish my respect.

We may begin with the evolutionary scenario of Desmond Morris, where the key to survival for the species forced from their arboreal Eden into competition for open-country game was to "greatly increase brain power."[3] From this task everything else follows. The (male) hominid needs to become a better hunter, but for his brain to develop and store learning he has to invest in a more extended period of childhood and affiliate with the "all-male groups" that hunt. Thus, even while permanent pair-bonding is being formed, a marked divergence in sex roles is being forced on the species: "he had to hunt if he was to survive"; she "had to stay put and mind the babies." These changes, along with the need for males to learn cooperation on the hunt, provide "all the ingredients necessary to make up our present sexual complexity." In sum, the mainstream of our species expresses its pair-bonding character in its "most extreme form, namely long-term monogamous marriage."

In the beginning, according to Morris's book of Genesis, was the patriarchal nuclear family, as it is now and as it shall be, world without end (amen). And he may be partly right. The hunt for game persists, at least among scientists, as the hunt for data (about the original hunts, as it often turns out). And the perennial male hunt for gamesome women perpetuates stereotypes about female passivity. The one-sidedness of this hallowed scenario, therefore, has not escaped the notice of other scientists, not the least being women: "So, while the males were out hunting, developing all their skills, learning to cooperate, inventing language, the poor dependent females were sitting back at home base having one child after another," writes Sally Slocum, "and waiting for the males to bring home the bacon."[4] Ingenious as Morris's thesis is, "it gives one the decided impression that only half the species—the male half—did any evolving."

Yet Morris does state that the female "had to develop a pairing tendency." She had to learn the art of loving, backward and forward, as it were, for nothing seals the pair-bond like sexual relations, in and out of season. "Specialized organs such as the lips, ear-lobes, nipples, breasts and genitals are richly endowed with nerve-endings and have become highly sensitized to erotic tactile stimulation."[5] By the end of this lushly detailed passage, woman's frontal anatomy has been stretched out like the Las Vegas strip on a sultry summer eve, beckoning the evolutionary gamester home for the crucial score. In this scheme of sexual complementarity, man's brain evolves in tandem with woman's body: the hunt at home culminates in the discovery of female genitalia. The rewards for becoming a pair-bonded hunter are an enriched protein diet and face-to-face sex on a regular basis.

All of which may have come about in much the way Morris says, but, apart from its one-sidedness, the trouble is that the scientist's vantage point is not just that of the modern urban male but of the adult male, for once neoteny is included in the evolutionary scheme not only do hominids acquire a childhood, they also acquire a highly compacted personal history. One has to wonder how well zoologists like Morris have thought through their material, for the adult perspective presumes paternal absenteeism then, as it often still does today, from what is happening among other members of the family— women and children—while the men are away evolving on the hunt. But if the aboriginal ape should not be blamed, believing that survival and progress rested on his shoulders—literally, in his expanding cranium—the same need not apply to his latter-day spokesman, Desmond Morris.

His figure of the naked ape recalls the "tjurunga," or reincarnated ancestor of primitive imagination who represents the tribal life source, as a primal parent rather than as a mutual partner in humanity's in primal scene.[6] Morris's link between the brain and the genitals is forged with no missing links allowed in between. This position is analogous to an early one taken by Freud in seeking the etiology of the "actual neuroses," which he attributed to conflicts in the area of genital sexuality before having fathomed the depths of infantile sexuality, a discovery Morris appears not yet to have made. He dismisses psychoanalysis for deriving its findings from an exotic subgroup known as patients, those troubled individuals whose emotional conflicts Freud had very early recognized were but exaggerations of the conflicts that existed in so-called healthy individuals.[7] And although Morris was writing in 1966 and not in 1906, he appears innocent of the psychoanalytically based fieldwork in anthropology as well as the more obvious fact that psychoanalytic training institutes have been analyzing for years the very kinds of healthy and well-attired apes (of both genders and usually physicians) Morris would expect to find at the forefront of evolutionary advance. With Freud out of the picture—not so much misread as misplaced—Morris is able to be surprised at his own discovery that the "advance of civilization has not so much moulded modern sexual behavior, as that sexual behavior has moulded the shape of civilization."[8] This will not be the last time that the eclipse of Freud paradoxically bestows on the behaviorist a fresh glow of discovery.[9]

A view of the same evolutionary sequence not seen through the naked ape's adult eyes may reveal that "food sharing and the family developed from the mother-infant bond."[10] According to Slocum, the females among modern hunter-gatherers can usually support themselves and their families. The "techniques of hunting large animals were probably much later developments, after the mother-children family pattern was established." And here comes the interesting twist: the hunter returning from a big hunt "would share food not with a wife or sexual partner, but with those who had shared food with him: his mother and siblings."

What this leads to, of course, may be exactly what Morris's plan was trying to avoid—not matriarchy, but incest. Not that he ignores this issue, but neither does he quite faced up to it, because the zoologist needs both his neoteny (prolonged childhood) for brain development and his autonomous hunter, as well. But both he cannot reasonably have. The incest taboo merely draws attention to the dilemma. Morris's solution to the "sexual rivalry between fathers and sons" is to equate the ladder of sexual development with that ring of sexual behavior manifested at puberty, a time when the offspring can "develop a home-based 'territory' of their own," where the parental pattern can be repeated.[11] Morris allows that "the hunting ape became an infantile ape," but then disallows him infantile sexuality. The naked ape has no Oedipus complex.

Or does he? So long as we are going to give our hominid an expanding childhood, we cannot deny him a strong attachment to mother as well—the incest taboo derives its prohibitive power from the equally strong power of desire. This taboo between mother and son is presumed to be humanity's oldest, and the myth of Orpheus may illustrate the manner in which it came about.[12] This Greek solar figure fell in love with Eurydice, associated with the goddesses of earth. The lovers' erotic relations turn on a miming of diurnal cycles. Darkness marks her descent into the underworld; morning, her reawakening in sunlight. At evening the sun dips below the horizon and follows her into the underworld, where their cosmic union is sexualized, as Orpheus pursues and recovers the Eurydice he had lost on earth. His permanent recovery of her is contingent on his leading her out and not looking at her face until dawn. If he violates this taboo, he will lose her; and he will, as the sun will certainly rise, for it must separate from earth for day to break. But the narrative introduces uncertain tensions of ambivalence. Why should looking upon the face of one's beloved be equated with loss? Without answering the question, the myth plays out the tragedy. Orpheus sees and loses Eurydice. Turning around is fatal.

In the myth it is the male who turns; in prehistory it was the female who turned around. But the discovery and its consequences are the same: loss of love object. The change is portrayed in terms of time because what is feasible in the hominid twilight is not possible in the early dawn of humanity. If recognizing the love-object renders it forbidden, then the interpretation of choice is the incest threat.[13] Identifying one's love with mother cancels her as a future object of desire and ensures the eventual founding of a new family. Behind the myth, as well as through it, the shift from rear to frontal sexual practices that make the awareness of one's partner unavoidable may be discerned. However gradual or abrupt, that shift concretizes the inception of incest taboos. The suspension of sexual claims on mother, that is, the interruption of drive development and its internal diversion into fantasy, ultimately brings about a protracted childhood during which parents and the parental relation are internalized to form a new psychic structure (superego) for the emerging person. Orpheus is not just an unhappy lover but a joyous musician with a mythical childhood, tutored in the arts by his mother Calliope the muse, and a culture hero, who by highlighting the face in the erotic relation downplays the aggressive component in the anonymous, promiscuous practice of rear mounting.

So it often seems that the more acquainted one is with individual development the better one is able to entertain other hypotheses than those confined by biological-behavioristic considerations. Robert Ardrey,[14] for example, also wants to retain his neoteny and his territorial instinct, but the individual development that occurs during *Homo*'s expanded childhood is, in part, the internalization of boundaries, so that the territorial impulse of primates is modified, redirected, and transformed by *Homo* into the realm of internalized representations and values.[15] When these are threatened, *Homo* may more avidly go to war to defend them than out of any vestigial territorial reflex. In sum, the psychological birth of the individual that occurs during neoteny creates a whole new world of its own, a fundamental reorganization of biological life.

Homo sapiens sapiens, then, is twice-born, like the fertility god Dionysus: first from his earth-mother, Semele; a second time from the fertile thigh of father Zeus—first from nature, second from culture. And unless these dual origins are taken into account, scientists may unknowingly stretch out the biological to aid in reconstructing what has evolved into the psychological. The unconscious, or a piece of inner reality, then becomes externalized, like the Bermuda Triangle of popular pseudoscience, or else reified, like the territorial mechanism observable in other species and then grafted onto sapient *Homo.* Vietnam wars may be fought out of the folly and madness that is fueled by mistaken idealism or out of fears from internal threats perceived as emanating from outside; but it seems unlikely that they could be waged by a biologically programmed, territorial imperative, as "one ancient, animal foundation for war," for which the citizens of a modern democracy need feel little responsibility. In Vietnam not only did the meanings of territory and boundary dissolve, but, in the end, so also did the external enemy.

Rather like the motivations for waging war, scientific paradigms have proven more shifting than one likes to believe, and scientists themselves are often prone to idealistic thinking, perhaps as a reward for or respite from extensive periods of carefully controlled observation. As a self-made scientist, Ardrey offsets his predatory picture of man by an older, "far more deeply buried" vision of "the instinct for order—shadowy, mysterious, indefinable"—something like the Holy Ghost, one surmises. The orderly behavior of most species—up to that nest-fouler, out-of-season mater, man—is clearly observable; the instinct for order in man becomes this mysterious, elusive force principally because, when you come down to it, nothing of the kind is present in him. The instincts that organize animal behavior have, in K. R. Eissler's exquisite words, been degraded into drives.[16] The absence of dependable instincts and the "comparative freedom of drives" mean that humankind has to learn order; the effort is lifelong and may be accumulative. But it has to be newly acquired on an individual basis, and it starts in the area of primary creativity wherein the infant first learns something about the repeated arrival and departure of a need-gratifying system not his own. It is further adumbrated in the peek-a-boo games with his blanket or with the toy that comes and goes (Freud's *fort-da* game), but proceeds in earnest only during toilet training. At the breast, through neoteny, and beyond, the uses of order (and tolerance for disorder) are gradually developed individually in each new generation. Neither innate nor mysterious, this achievement is the work of natural creativity.

Two of the compelling assumptions in behaviorism that enhanced the appeal of works like Ardrey's and Morris's are that the surface behavior speaks for the whole and that the lower form elucidates the higher. Behaviorism draws its great strength from attending to those things that actually happen, which is one reason why the incest taboo occupies an uneasy position in this school; whereas psychoanalysis, arising from Freud's discovery of "psychic reality," concerns itself with things that haven't happened but might happen or happen only inwardly. Human evolution plays no favorites here, for it did happen, yet it might have happened this way or that or still another way. It has to be recreated in our still-evolving minds through reasonable hypotheses, and the required intellectual effort has to draw on many unlikely, subjective resources. Evidence that the Leakeys and Donald Johanson began turning up from East Africa in the 1970s and is still being assimilated reduces many formerly firm theories to quicksilver as the origins of *Homo* recede ever further into prehistory.

As Freud noted, the need for certainty is a vestige of the absolutes once provided by religious faith, itself a continuation of the child's need to feel protected by perfect, omnipotent parents. And so it is interesting to find him on one occasion yielding to the trolls of literalism when he took a cue from Darwin that the "primitive form of human society was that of a horde ruled over despotically by a powerful male" and constituted via actual primal parricide by the exiled band of brothers.[17] Rieff observes that in Freud's own "origins myth, all history is divided, by the act of parricide, into two stages." The primal horde gives way to the "political stage—submission characterized by guilt."[18] At this point empiricists have been able to correct a psychoanalytic misconstruction, without its spokesmen necessarily being in internal agreement. Ardrey holds that in primate society the maturing male encounters not the "tyranny of a dominant father," but a hierarchical class of dominant fathers; while Morris emphasizes the evolution toward monogamous pair-bondings heading toward the nuclear family. Closer to psychoanalysis, Derek Freeman has termed the Darwin-Freud hypothesis "projected fantasy," about which Freud soon began to harbor doubts but never took the trouble to abandon.[19]

It may be that Freud's origin myth, stressing the parricidal motif, served to reinforce his dual-instinct theory (eventually to be designated Eros and Thanatos) as well as the role of defenses such as repression and identification. The two classes of instincts were first specified on the model of hunger and love, as the self-preservative and the sex instincts, the latter being singled out in the etiology of neuroses. Later, the self-preservative group was reclassified as the death instinct taken over by the ego in order to allow the organism to die naturally, while either externalizing other aggressive components or internalizing them via the superego onto the ego in the form of prohibitions, restraints, and feelings of guilt. By asserting that the "aim of all life is death," Freud, too, lapsed into accounting for the higher by recourse to the lower: even the aggressions of the superego must find their resounding echo in biology. And because he maintained that the Oedipus complex was the nuclear conflict for human and cultural development, it is clear why he wanted to establish the origins of both culture and the individual through analogous processes. His scientific speculation becomes an act of natural creativity drawn from the triadic stage and aimed at reinforcing *onto* by alignment with *phylo*. The fact that the smaller and internal design does not project perfectly onto the larger and external is no argument against the individual relevance of oedipal reality, even though current trends within psychoanalysis have been to place it along a continuum rather than at center stage. Freud's final excursion into phylogeny, when he identified himself with Moses leading modern culture out of the id's bondage on to the ego's promised land, may be seen as an example of his natural creativity performing within the area of the self.

But if Freud's patriarchal leaning shows up in his emphasizing parricide, repression, and its disguised return in patriarchal religions as the watershed of cultural evolution, it must be allowed that Ardrey's concept of primordial instincts for order and territory has not been confirmed as inherited biological tendencies through the many studies of infant/child observation.[20] And his dismissal of psychiatry's tinted way of viewing human nature through the "ruddy hues of sex" can be offest by fellow empiricist Morris's observation that "clearly the naked ape is the sexiest primate alive."[21] Sex means for Morris, an elaborate grid of learned physiological signals and responses that have favored natural selection. And, like Morris, Ardrey misses the implications of Freud's revolutionary disclosures of infantile sexuality by treating sex as a genital phenomenon with no previous history: the primal father "has sons, and the sons mature, and their awakening sexual drives find as its object the mother."[22] This is meant as a summary of Freud, but it comes out backward: first the sons mature and then sexual drives are awakened; in Freud's scheme it is just the reverse, and there is no basis in *Totem and Taboo* or elsewhere in the Freudian canon for Ardrey's misconstructions. The supposed exile of the brothers until they mature or find a superior weapon, as Freud guessed, occurs after the libidinal attachment to mother (and sisters) has taken hold and spans the latency period—neoteny—until puberty; but if repression of drives occurs with available parental figures for identification, then the exile is simply a metaphorical way of putting repression into spatial terms, just as killing and eating the father is a way of literalizing the incorporation of the father-image as guilt-inflicting superego. But Ardrey was obviously entranced with the reified scenario of his mentor, Raymond Dart, who imagined our ancestors as rapacious carnivores that "seized living quarries by violence, battered them to death," tearing and dismembering as they went in order to slake "their ravenous thirst with the hot blood of victims."[23] Here the primal scene of origins has been rendered as the primal orgy of the oral cannibalistic phase, and Dart is but one of a long line of Victorian anthropologists whose speculations about man in the so-called savage state sound all too clearly like the displaced return of civilized man's own disavowed drives. Cannibalism itself has been called into question by Arens, whose skepticism, if not prevailing, is succeeding in boiling down the substantial body of data to remarkably few tidbits; what is steamed away is largely the adipose of projected fantasy.[24]

Cannibalism not entirely to one side, a more blatant behavioristic misreading of Freud occurs in *Cannibals and Kings: The Origins of Culture* (1977), where Marvin Harris first disregards Freud's dual instinct theory by asserting, "Freud claimed that aggression is a manifestation of the frustration of the sexual instincts during childhood." He next unwittingly rephrases the Oedipus complex in Adlerian terms as a power struggle—"boys compete with their father for sexual mastery of the same woman"—the key words here being *sexual mastery*. He then depicts the resolution as consisting in the "boy's learning to direct his aggression away from his father toward socially 'constructive' activities (which may include warfare)."[25] Psychoanalysis, of course, maintains just the opposite. It is truly astonishing that any reader of Freud can overlook the passage in *Civilization and Its Discontents,* where he states that the "most important" fate of aggression in man is for it to be "introjected, internalized; it is, in point of fact, sent back to where it came from—that is, it is directed toward [one's] own ego ... in the form of conscience."[26] Perhaps it is true, as the title, *Social Amnesia,* of Russell Jacoby's book suggests, that Freud's actual views suffer the same fate as the early instinctual drives about which he wrote: namely, forgetting, a benign amnesia—ultimately, repression (an equally convincing case could be made in the spirit of Harold Bloom's anxiety of influence theory for a defensive misreading of the strong father's text). In any case, externalized aggression is what catches the eye of the behaviorist, not the less visible, internalized kind experienced as guilt, masochism, or concern. But between the two there is a world of difference, and the cultural implications are immense.

Having reversed Freud's thinking, Harris proceeds to suggest that while "Freud was definitely on to something," his "causal arrows were running backwards." In brief, Harris asserts that human cultures—specifically, the "male supremacy complex"—rather than human nature cause the "oedipal situation."[27] And while he is shortly bound to admit that "this may sound like a hopeless chicken and egg problem," he adds, "there are excellent scientific reasons for rejecting the Freudian priorities."[28] But first there are even more excellent scientific reasons for establishing those priorities.

Consequently, a well-founded skepticism emerges from one's attention to the attempts of behaviorists—and not only those in the life sciences—to include Freud in a synthesis of human evolution and culture. For example, a recent, sophisticated reading of Freud as beholden to "Newtonian psychology" appears in *The Turning Point,* by the Viennese-born physicist, Fritjof Capra. Freud's concepts of drives and defenses are compared to the actions and reactions of forces in Newton's laws of mechanics. This analogy leads to the statement that instinctual drives striving for discharge are met by "various counterforces that inhibit and distort them."[29] And, so, it follows that the "skillful analyst will concentrate on eliminating the obstacles that prevent the direct expression of the primary forces." If this sounds logical and persuasive to the reader, let him/her recall that those "primary forces" are not without content: incredibly, the analyst in this scenario is portrayed as freeing his patients to carry out parricide and incest, for they are the primary forces of psychoanalysis whose goal is not their release, but their dissolution through understanding.

It is true, however, that Freud never dissociated himself from nineteenth-century physics, that he associated the theory of relativity with anarchy, and that his model of psychic functioning can be read mechanistically: drive and defense at its crudest level were once potrayed by Bernard Meyers as a chassis-model of the mind.[30] But Freud's systems involved much more than an internalized behaviorism of (instinctual) stimulus/response reflexes. There were radical warps and distortions built into the evolving mental apparatus, cued by such terms as return of the repressed, dualistic drive (Eros and Death), and so forth, that have nothing in common with the scientist's Cartesian dualism; indeed, the more recent contributions of object-relations further destabilizes any residual Newtonianism in psychoanalysis and decentralizes it along lines comparable to Einsteinian physics.

In a narrower context it should be noted that not all male scientists in the field of evolution locate the key to human ancestry in male aggression, or in what Stephen Jay Gould labels as "cerebral primacy."[31] Obviously, reproductive proficiency as a key to survival leads to far more subtle concepts than the old predatory picture allows. The importance of genes and of securing their safe transmission to future generations opens on the one side to the sweeping claims about human nature that have arisen in sociobiology, but on the other side to the emphasis drawn by C. Owen Lovejoy and others on birth spacing, parental care, and maternal IQ. Lovejoy's extrapolations from the nature of locomotion in primates led him to speculate that bipedalism frees the hands for food gathering and carrying but also for holding on to the young.[32] With the finding of "Lucy," bipedalism among hominids is pushed back to 3.5 million years, long before any extant tools or enlarged brain. The earlier stimulus-response hypothesis of migration to the savannas, accompanied by bipedalism, hunting, and brain expansion, is less tenable if not totally discredited.

For these reasons it is possible to speculate that bipedalism accompanies a shift in reproductive strategies (especially for the female). If this includes pair-bonding as one means of preserving essential genes in the young, then bipedalism also implies a psychosexual shift from rear to frontal positions, from scent to sight, from anal to genital, from anonymous mating (which serves well enough the male's need to widely distribute his gene pool) to more affectionate intimacy that would foster pair-bond and paternal investment in the fewer offspring bearing the mother's genes). Therefore, insofar as it favors the female, bipedalism can be related to sexual dimorphism; if this is the case, then the origins of the incest taboo as coinciding with bipedalism may also have had female as well as male input. Since bipedalism is considered a biological adaptation and incest taboos are a social prohibition based on a condition of emotional ambivalence, the two phenomena have previously seemed unrelated.

It remains to be comprehended how such a conjunction of factors contributed to our becoming human. This takes us to the border where biological evolution begins crossing over to cultural evolution. "If social organization had a beginning," writes Levi-Strauss, it "could only have consisted in the incest prohibition," since it is "a kind of remodeling of the biological conditions of mating and procreation."[33] Accordingly, it is sensible to concur with Gould that the overemphasis on brain enlargement has been a "powerful cultural prejudice imposed on nature" and that bipedalism was "the great punctuation in human evolution."[34] Such a prejudice may serve a defensive role, for if bipedalism signifies incest taboos, both the biological modification and the social phenomenon continue their influence over individual development when the psychic consequences of anatomical differences are registered, especially for boys, as dread of castration, or for both sexes as the demise of the cloacal theory of sex/birth.

In order to avoid polarizing the diverging emphases in human evolution between brain/intelligence and sex/social organization, I would like to examine the enlightened proposition that "we are not the helpless subjects of evolution—we are evolution."[35] Such a view can be taken is various ways, but the key that unlocks its meaning for me is *internalization.* Culture is the internalization of evolution in at least three major ways. As Anna Freud has pointed out, what may have once been for early humanity a protective system of defenses against external dangers—flight, avoidance, camouflage, and so forth—have become gradually internalized as a defensive system against internal dangers stemming from instinctual urges (the id being the extension of the natural world into the human realm).[36] Similar to this process is the way in which the child overcomes its early fears of helplessness and the loss of its early attachments by internalizing the relationships and making them part of the self—superego being the new regulatory agency that arises from ties to the same-sex parent. Third, in the area of learning: what took place over many thousands of years between the generations—gradual modification to changing environmental forces—takes place within individuals' lives as they learn from experience, through trial and error, through others, through logical reasoning, and so forth.

This last capacity returns us to the importance of the human brain—"the most complicated object science has ever tried to understand."[37] Because the uniquely human cerebral cortex comprises ninety percent of our brain's total mass and seventy percent of its wired circuitry, it may well be the neurophysiological zone where natural creativity is processed.

Along this line, an appealing blend of scientific and dramatic imagination appears in Carl Sagan's *The Dragons of Eden;* a glimpse at his theses will further clarify natural creativity in biological science, while returning us to the familiar polarities by which this study was launched.[38] Sagan's book is subtitled *Speculations on the Evolution of Human Intelligence,* and his vehicle for understanding human origins is the triune brain, whose evolution documents, or concretizes, the three major steps of human evolution. The oldest, reptilian, or R-complex, "plays an important role in aggressive behavior, territoriality, ritual, and the establishment of social hierarchies."[39] We share our limbic system with mammals and find in it the seat of many emotions, altruism, religion, memories, olfactory sensations, and important sexual functions. The neocortex is associated with vision, upright posture, regulation of action, rational abstract thought, and most other higher mental functions. Sagan accepts the proposition that each "new step in brain evolution is accompanied by changes in the physiology of the pre-existing components," but believes these earlier segments are "still perfroming as they did in our remote ancestors."[40] The idea that the brain does reorganize itself as it accretes nevertheless removes Sagan from the more literal-minded approach taken by Arthur Koestler, who attributes a split between "archaic, emotion-based beliefs" in the old brain and the "marvelous potentialities" of the new brain to the vestigial "horse and crocodile which we carry inside our skulls."[41]

Like others before him, Sagan borrows the metaphor of Eden and the myth of the Fall, but for the singular purpose of conveying brain advances. Later we will have an opportunity to consider whether the power of these figures exceeds the prerogatives of the borrower. For Sagan, the serpent's handing Eve the "fruit of the knowledge of good and evil" is "[like] the R-complex tempting the limbic system to accept the 'abstract and moral neocritical functions' which will round out the triune brain.[42] Reptiles do not dream, Sagan hypothesizes, because something like repression has not yet occurred; their normal state of consciousness is a waking dream. Mammals hate reptiles and dream, as do primates, along with other naked apes; thus, in the "nighttime stirring of the dream dragons, we may each of us be replaying the hundred-million-year-old warfare between the reptiles and the mammals."[43] The following passage presents Sagan's speculative imagination at its freest:

> The pervasiveness of dragon myths in the folk legends of many cultures is probably no accident. The implacable mutual hostility between man and dragon, as exemplified in the myth of Saint George, is strongest in the West. (In chapter 3 of the Book of Genesis, God ordains an eternal enmity between reptiles and humans.) But it is not a Western anomaly. It is a world-wide phenomenon. Is it only an accident that the common human sounds commanding silence or attracting attention seem strangely imitative of the hissing of reptiles? Is it possible that dragons posed a problem for our protohuman ancestors of a few million years ago, and that the terror they evoked and the deaths they caused helped bring about the evolution of human intelligence? Or does the metaphor of the serpent refer to the use of the aggressive and ritualistic reptilian component of our brain in the further evolution of the neocortex? With one exception, the Genesis account of the temptation by a reptile in Eden is the only instance in the Bible of humans understanding the language of animals. When we feared the dragons, were we fearing a part of ourselves? One way or another, there were dragons in Eden.[44]

The neocortex expansion, however, also spelled out more of the consequences of eating the apple of abstract thought: woman's pelvic girdle could evolve only so fast, and, henceforth, alone among creation shall she bring forth children in pain. The advances in weapon-use means that mankind, as Ardrey had claimed before, descended from Cain the killer. But in the long run it is all worthwhile, because the neocortex can create civilization as Zeus had created Athena from his fertile brow (although to find that the evolutionary future leads to computers and chemotherapy was a letdown to this hopeful reader).

The leap to brainier computers is also the culmination of Robert Jastrow's lucid gloss on human evolution, *The Enchanted Loom*. His intriguing approach to the evolutionary stations that determine the operations of the triune brain raises the question of subjectivity in a different light. The program of the old reptile brain— "search for food, the pursuit of a mate, and flight from a predator"—are augmented by the mammalian brain, which emerged with increased circuitry for smell, smaller litters, warm-bloodedness, and parental care.[45] These instinctive behaviors are still active within us, even though they have been smothered by the neocortex overlay, which infuses human behavior with reason. The "inherited programs of the old brain" are sometimes pitted against "the flexible responses of the new one."[46] Thus a psychological-conflict model is rooted in the human brain. And even though "parental feelings are the source of some of the finest human emotions," their location in the old brain subordinates them to the higher rational functions of the cerebral cortex.[47]

Two inferences may be drawn from this line of reasoning. One: evolution is a hierarchical process, just as each of the layers of the brain fold over the other— reptile ⟩ mammal ⟩ man. And just as man is "higher" than mammals, so it follows that rationality is higher than parental care or emotional bonds; otherwise, computers would not be next in line to supplant us as they are in Jadstrow's vision. However, this view diverges from Jantsch's that we are evolution, since Jastrow's supposes that we are really only a stage in evolution toward something else.[48] The second inference, following from commonly held cultural assumptions about gender, renders Jastrow's evolutionary scenario every bit as androcentric as Desmond Morris's. Our hominid forebear "was a skillful hunter who competed with the other carnivores of his time, and held his own against the lion and the giant hyena": "his weapon was his brain."[49] These early "men, working with the theorists, created running strategies for the hunt, and effective weapons for felling game; they brought home the bacon. They and their offspring flourished." And while capturing the bacon, they originated language, which "coordinated the complex maneuvers of the hunting band," paving the way "for social cooperation" and the "tradition of learning."[50] It follows that if men can accomplish so much alone they will succeed in creating living computers, as Jastrow suggests.

And I would suggest that the inner model for this scenario of male dominance is implicit in the triune brain's composition of the rational (male) cerebral cortex over the irrational (female) mammal-fold, just as in the sexual act the male affirms dominance by imposing the missionary position. This hierarchical brain structure uncannily resembles the child's stereotype of the "good" primal scene.

Less androcentric but no less fanciful in Sagan's vista is the juxtaposition of Eden and dragons, because, whatever else they mean, they return us to a consideration of those two polar lines of individual descent. The Edenic version is divine and subjective; it awakens the family romance theme of supernatural parentage, the "demigods" that Darwin had banished from his evolutionary hypothesis. On the other side are those monsters, either as actual companions in the phylogenetic consciousness or as simply the productions of mythopoeic imagination. Like Freud, Sagan would seek a phylogenetic feedback for his speculations.

The American feminist Robin Morgan wrote a poem about her toddler catching sight of her in the buff and saying "Monster"—a response the poet attributes to the influence of the television tube.[51] Yet we know that chidren frequently associate sexuality with monster imagery, reinforced by fairy tales, like "Beauty and the Beast," and we often trace composite mythological beasts—chimeras, medusas, sphinxes—to either the primal parent or the primal parental act. What distinguishes dragons from other mythological creations is not that they may have existed in Eden but that the root meaning of *dragon* owes something to eyes—from the Greek *drakos* and Indo-European *drek, drak,* "to look" or "to glance"— and, hence, in Partridge's definition a "huge serpent, so named because of its quick-glancing, terrible eyes." Hence its monster nature owes something to the act of terrified witnessing.[52]

And so we come around full circle when we discern through a brilliant scientific mind that evolution may be represented as paradise threatened by reptilian monsters. The scientist's phylogeny is every child's ontogeny. East of Eden he / she will be occupied in creating him / herself out of his / her primal scene as the (once-monstrous) parents had earlier created him / her through it. As re-creations of origins become part of the self, he / she may even write a book about it.

14
Cosmic Origins, Lives of Scientists, Returns to Pseudosolutions

Cosmogonies, one could say, represent unconscious metaphors of human reproduction.

—Jacob Arlow (1982)

Those strange and mystical transmigrations that I have observed in silk-worms turned my philosophy into divinity.

—Sir Thomas Browne, *Religio Medici*

1. Parallels in Artistic and Scientific Creativity

Every artist, just as every individual, will pass through the three stages of natural or self-creativity in the most widely varying ways imaginable. Most likely a family-romance route—whether it be primarily in an asexual form emphasizing the mother as "cosmic object" (a term used by the psychoanalyst John R. Love), earth-goddess, muse, or the like, or in a sexual form employing rescue or marital motifs—will be taken by the artistically creative individual. And he/she will abide the riddles of sexuality and origins only when they can be appropriately represented within the framework of one's developing art. As Freud said, the artist "molds a new vision of reality," to which others are able to respond, having created their own selves and primary personal attachments, their origins fantasies and oedipal dramas.

For the artist-creator, family romance and primal scene have been proposed as correlative intrapsychic working models that may offer extreme versions of origins to be drawn on for molding newer and more acceptable modifications. To some extent these models reside in everyone, just as their derivatives appear widely throughout culture. The artist is distinguished by investing more in the imaginative possibilities of the family romance as adaptive not to "reality" but to his/her creative tasks. Within the same creative ambience he/she may adapt an internalized primal scene by assigning lofty titles to the male and female generative principles and enlisting them into the creative process that brings forth—not a newly born child—but a newly remade version of self and world, existing in the adopted medium of art. In other words, the inner dynamics of primal-scene revision may include such id material as the impregnation by mother as earth-goddess or Muse, her impregnation by the young god, or her reunion with a daughter; or, just as likely, the impregnation by father as Olympian or as one of the exalted patriarchs of the poet's art-tradition. On the other hand, we might expect the scientist, being more invested in what Melanie Klein refers to as the "epistemophilic instinct," to gravitate toward the objective pole of origins the better the master his/her sexual quandaries—a good working hypothesis, but the division is far from clear-cut and, in key instances, absent.

The primal scene begins as adult sexuality refracted through the child's perspective, a subjective/objective mix, shaped by distortions and colored by anxious excitement. As part of our mental world it gets mixed up with other primal fantasies, but, better than the others, it can point us in the direction of reality, because it uniquely discloses how our past is also our future. The work of art at its most mature surpasses both creative models when its aesthetic pleasures also appeal to our developed reality sense. And for the work to go through primal-scene restructuring at the triadic stage is for it to undergo further the remolding, differentiation, distancing, and inwardness begun during the two earlier stages.

Underlying artistic and scientific endeavors, the three stages of natural creativity may be compared to the evolution of the triune brain, where at every step there is not just adding on but reorganization and restructuring. What, for present purposes, renders human development as species-specific is that it involves more than mere growth, change, and adaptation: natural creativity is a self-making process that draws on the total environment—that is, parents, history, cultural objects of all kinds, works of art, scientific treatises in pure or diluted forms, and just about anything one can come up with in that mixed-media, living collage we discover through the interplay of inner worlds and outer surroundings. It is a continually active and reactive, distorting and transforming process, and it thrives beyond the oedipal triadic stage into the regrouping and consolidations of latency and on into adolescence, where idealizations acquire a sense of objectivity by seeming to be rediscovered in the environment, where new ones are formulated, and where all are relatively assimilated within the ego-ideal's maturing value systems.

Caught up in this mixed milieu, the scientist proceeds like the artist in several respects. In what might be termed the Freudian curve of creativity, I have privileged one scenario for the artist-in-the-making, who—out of some felt deficit, injury, or blow to self-esteem emanating from interplay with the early human environment—turns from painful reality to an inner world where investment in play, healing, mastery, and self-reconstitution through displacement onto the creative enterprise can proceed. The scientist, too, from whatever similar or still obscure motive, turns away from everyday social reality to retreat into the lab, journey into a remote field, or immerse him/herself in data, where he/she becomes emotionally invested in the conventions and traditions of the present enterprise, until sufficient mastery enables a return to society with some new formula, system, or discovery. A case in point is Freud's own period of "splendid isolation." Descartes spent two years of his late adolescence totally incommunicado, when he allegedly studied mathematics in the environs of Paris. And the dreamy-childhood picture of Newton may have been overdrawn by early biographers, but not greatly. Storr writes that during "the thirty-one years of his residence in Cambridge, he was a recluse; the very archetype of the absent-minded solitary scholar."[1] Darwin's nearly five-year journey on the *Beagle,* along with his later hermetic life-style, conforms to this schema. Further inklings of the scientist's tendency to withdraw appear in the distrust shared by Descartes, Newton, and Einstein in the value of the physical senses: all three preferred the abstract precision of mathematics.[2]

Feuer's study emphasizes another feature shared by the artist and the scientist in Einstein's references to " 'combinatory play,' and 'associative play' with images" and in Kepler's writing that science was play: "as God the Creator played, so he also taught nature, as his image, to play the very game which he played before her."[3] Recalling that play begins in the transitional sphere, where preexisting objects are appropriated and invested with great emotion, I would like to build on a study of Darwin's wedged hammer. Ralph Colp traces a most curious evolution of this fourteen-pound instrument in whose company Darwin recalls never having spent a "more delightful three weeks, than . . . pounding the NW mountains."[4] "Some of his most vivid *Beagle* recollections would be of using his hammer," his " 'usual companion' " with whom " 'most delighful hours' " were spent. It is worth noting that the instrument combined male aggressive properties with a female configuration, and, perhaps, more than coincidental that the woman he courted and married was his cousin, Emma Wedgwood, whose name and large dowry may have suggested to Darwin that he was a "Wedging force" in respect to his relations. As Darwin did less actual hammering in his middle years, so do descriptions of the activity disappear from his writings, although the *wedge* as a figure of speech reappears. "Nature," he wrote, "may be compared to a surface covered with ten thousand sharp wedges . . . all packed closely together and all driven in by incessant blows."[5] Nature favored the thrusting-in species, disfavored the thrusting-out species. By marriage and by tenaciously sticking with his new theories, Darwin was becoming one of the favored, thrusting-in species. Thus he was "probably, mainly unconsciously, identifying himself with nature" (which, like the hammer, possesses male/female properties).[6] In addition, the "imagery of a wedging force may have come to symbolize Darwin's assertion of himself in the areas of work, sex, money, and resistance to opposition."[7] When he "imagines an overall force which is timeless, nonhuman, and almost autonomous," he calls it the wedge, and, in so doing, he identifies himself with his theories of evolution.[8] In this respect, the scientist, like the artist, draws on transitional objects and initially operates in the transitional sphere of play, just as the wedge-shaped hammer is internalized as idea, metapor, identity, ideal. In its sexual associations with the genitals and his wife's family name, there may be more than a hint that the acceptance of evolutionary theory presumed an acceptance of his sexual and social desires.

In further rounding this creative curve, we may find the modern scientist ultimately less isolated than the artist and either less at the mercy of subjective impulses or less equipped to handle them; for the scientist is initiated into an alternate reality inhabited by fellow professionals and is protected from the kinds of dangerous regression to which artists are liable, though artists, too, have developed supportive traditions and communal styles, if less consistently. Allowing for these variations, the curve of creativity does bind— through relative isolation, play, and transitional phenomena—the artistic and the scientific processes. A second parallel arises in the indirect manner in which family-romance goals are expected to be achieved. For the artist it is especially gratifying to have one's work adopted by a patron, sponsor, or responsive public; for the scientist, as sociologists like Robert Merton have shown, it is no less gratifying to have one's name adopted, through discovery of a new law, rule, or phenomenon, into the official canon of scientific knowledge.

Along with these parallels, the other factor that makes possible a yoking together of literature, science, and psychoanalysis as they deal with varieties of origins is their common dependence on language. *Homo* alone verbalizes. *Homo* alone is preoccupied with origins and destinies. But their intermediate mode of representation is through language, and language lays claim to its own depths, its own histories, and its own origins. Nevertheless, the fact that the most recondite scientist must also nibble the fruit of the alphabet tree when he/she wants to communicate beyond mathematical formulae makes it possible, if only in passing, for me to include along with racial and individual origins a glimpse into those of the cosmos. For even this most rarefied area of radio astronomy, subatomic-physics, and astrophysics is made more humanly intelligible by invoking metaphors of galaxies' giving birth to stars, or their nurseries for growing stars and their nursing homes for aging stars. Like human society, galaxies evolve, are young or old, grow more healthy or fall ill.[9] At the center of certain galaxies are those provocative and invisible devouring mouths called black holes, and beyond them the quasars and supernovae, of more radiant antiquity. At the center of most scientific hypotheses about origins is the assumption, no doubt valid as well as overdetermined, that the past unlocks the present.

Apparently teleology has regained a dialectical position in this area, and as one scientist has expressed it, "the Modernist view of the universe ... as a gigantic machine cranking away for some reason totally unrelated to human life" has made room for the "Anthropic view ... that the dominant fact about the universe is that it produces intelligent life."[10] It falls well beyond my own competence to do more than estimate how far theories about our cosmic origins also draw on natural creativity, though it seems at least possible that they must do so as soon as they are put into words. Neither is it possible to do more here than wonder whether the three theories of the universe's origins might draw respectively on the three phases of natural creativity. Certainly the first of these, now all but abandoned, which envisions shifting gases and floating dust clouds gradually forming into bodies, has some resemblance to chaos and the early formation of internal / external boundaries within the area of self. The expanding / contracting hypothesis may have something in common with the separation / rapprochement processes of the dyadic phase. It then befalls the big-bang theory to serve as the orgasmic begetting associated with the triadic phase. One wonders, would a woman scientist have worded differently the big-bang theory?[11]

Less farfetched is the suggestion that in looking out into space we are looking back in time, and that microwave radiation from the "primeval fireball" of the universe takes us almost back to the scene of our own cosmic begetting thousands of millions of years ago, though it never goes quite the whole distance.[12] Here the analogies with individual and racial origins are tantalizing, to say the least: always the gaps in perception, the missing links, the sucking black holes in space that would lure us into strange new dimensions, the elusive fireball intimations of inner as well as outer voids. Yet even cosmic origins upholds that "human nature," according to Sir Bernard Lovell, "is itself intertwined with the primal state of the universe." Just as changes in climate affected our evolution and unique circumstances attended our conceptions, so in the universe, had there been "slight changes in the rate of cooling," for example, then "no galaxies, no stars, no life would have emerged." Ten seconds, or the time required for anyone's begetting, could have made all the difference. And when scientists speculate that chemical precursors of organic life, such as amino acids, bombarded planets from floating dust clouds, one senses an implicit analogy with earth as ovum and fertilizing chemicals as randomly chosen spermatazoa.

Reading contemporary scientists, one also infers that some of the damage done by the three historical blows to human narcissism—loss of geocentric placement, loss of separate creation, and loss of rational autonomy—is being undone to a measurable degree by anthropic, or "self-organizing," universe hypotheses. Perhaps we humans can tolerate being excluded from center stage only for so long, and then we must recreate our own central position in every drama from the family to the cosmos. The fact that certain heavy elements have passed from star to star until at last lighting on earth to become part of our bodies has inspired Preston Cloud in his *Cosmos, Earth, and Man* (1979), to declare that "stars have died that we might live."[13] Literary critics might call this the "pathetic fallacy," but so far the only foundation for life that biochemists can come up with is DNA; yet DNA demands carbon, and carbon results in processes that require billions of years in time and billions of light years of extent. And since carbon leads to DNA ⟩ to life ⟩ to brain cells, the question arises whether it makes any sense to "speak about a universe unless that universe contains intelligent beings."[14] A nice argument, and every bit as circular as the riddle of the Sphinx, whose answer becomes the same: *Homo*. The ultimate cosmic question may be like a Buddhist koan: What was the universe like before it began?

Since cosmic dimensions of origins are the most abstract, it is not surprising that the most brilliant modern thinker in this field, Albert Einstein, is discussed by Anthony Storr within the context of schizoid creativity. Apparently it was necessary for Einstein to disengage himself from his organism's gravity, from the proximity and claims of others, and from the planet itself in order to imagine "how the universe would appear to an observer travelling at the speed of light"; and far from welcoming the relativity of man to the objects he observes, his theories aimed at excluding the relative, the perturbations and variables introduced by the observer.[15] In this light, his creativity may have operated largely within the area of the self and sought a rationally predictable world to reinforce and conincide with his ideal mental one.

But Feuer, who prefers to emphasize the transformation of schizoid detachment into libertarian autonomy,[16] suggests that Einstein clung to the misnomer of his theory rather than opting for the principle of invariance or covariance because of the revolutionary fervor shared within his circle for socialism.[17] Relativity "conveyed that the scientific inquirer approached the problems of interpreting the physical facts with emotional longings which he shared with his friends and associates, social, political, and ethical rebels." In this perspective, they were, along with cubist and abstract artists, in rebellion against establishment dogmatism. "Einstein in particular" sought the "over-throw of absolute time and space," the idols and basic axioms of Newtonian physics. Thus, the scientific arena, Feuer suggests, was a displacement and sublimation of generational motives, forces springing from the triadic oedipal stage. Einstein may be seen as more revolutionist than relativist, after all, for he seems to have been driven by the demon of certainty as much as Marx's revolution sought not change, but the end of change, the replacement of history by a dictatorship of the proletariat—homeostasis.

Alongside his tapping into natural creativity stands Einstein's devotion to the king and queen of Belgium, his idealization of whom points toward a more directly enacted family romance. As a child he had not begun to speak until he was three, by which time he had a one-year-old sister. Such a dislocation of narcissistic centeredness by a sibling could have spurred cognitive mastery of the child's unfolding world. According to Jeremy Bernstein, he accounted for the genesis of his scientific ideas when, at four or five, his father showed him a compass. "That this needle behaved in such a determined way did not at all fit into the nature of events" as he had believed them to be: "effect connected with direct 'touch.'"[18] The phallic implications of this memory passage are apparent, and we need only equip ourselves with Freud's observation that "the thirst for knowledge seems to be inseparable from sexual curiosity" to read further into Einstein's development. The "deep and lasting impression" left by that experience implied to him that "something deeply hidden had to be behind things.''[19] In another passage he very nearly connects scientific discovery with the child's discovery of parental sexuality: ''The aspect of knowledge which had not yet been laid bare gives the investigator a feeling akin to that experienced by a child who seeks to grasp the masterly way in which elders manipulate things.''[20]

The special value of the compass lay in the fact that while, in a sense, it came from the father, it was actually a shared object, with a needle like the one owned by father, symbolically speaking, but which was under neither father's nor son's conscious control (''touch''). It was suggestive more of a ''deeply hidden'' reality accessible through science, since the compass, apart from its needle symbolizing a bodily organ, is a preexisting scientific object. Accordingly, it belongs, along with Darwin's hammer, to that order of transitional objects Winnicott investigated as part of an ''intermediate area of experiencing.'' If, moreover, the phallic needle of the compass was poised within a round glass container, we may have intimations of feminine enclosure. Although the needle of the compass is directed by laws of gravity, Einstein draws attention to its manifestation of an invisible principle in contrast to the child's ordinary observation of falling bodies. At the very least, without setting too much store by the above line of interpretation, I would suggest that the laws of sexual attraction and those of physical gravity are not clearly distinguished in a child's mind, and the one set may readily represent, replace, or commingle with the other in such ways to overdetermine the scientific process. In any case, I am not yet prepared to make a case for scientific creativity strictly comparable to the polar theory advanced for artistic creativity. Certain parallels, however, can be acknowledged in passing.

2. Science before Science

Although our century began with the prospect of a science of mythology, realized in great part by Frazer's multivolume study, *The Golden Bough,* it is only toward century's end that a mythology of science is being realized. The scientific enterprise was once—may still be—hedged about with spirits and goddesses no less than that of the artist. Leibniz notes in reference to Descartes's lost *Olympia* that ''God implants in the soul-womb the first seeds of wisdom for the scientist to bring to fruition by his reason,'' as the artist does by his imagination.[21] Thomas Kuhn's *The Structure of Scientific Revolutions* (1962), which revealed the gulf of subjectivity inherent in the shifting of scientific paradigms, is a recognized milestone in scientific self-understanding. Such critiques as Robert Ornstein's on the lopsided Western reliance on the left brain, along with the explorations in physics conducted by Gary Zukav (*The Dancing Wu Li Masters*) and Fritjof Capra (*The Tao of Physics* and *The Turning Point*), have further eroded the once solid empirical base from which scientific man operated, by injecting paradigms drawn from Eastern mysticism.

Moreover, the motives of early scientists, as we now know, were not purely scientific. Ideologies both implicitly and explicitly exerted powerful influences. Male chauvinist that he was, Francis Bacon envisioned science as the child born of the marriage between (masculine) mind and (feminine) nature.[22] When he spoke in the opening pages of *Novum Organum* (1620) of a nature to be "subdued" by the power of inductive knowledge and of the necessity "to penetrate the more secret and remote parts of nature," we get a preview of the overdetermined scientific paradigm whose inner agenda still operates in many quarters today. Kepler's ideologies were closer to the surface. He was less interested in exploring the irregularities of the new Copernican system than in forcing it to conform to Pythagorean and Christian models of perfect circles; and, rather like his contemporary, Milton, Newton wanted to justify the ways of God to Man by establishing the fundamental laws governing the universe.

But it is in the area of pre-science that a study of the mythology of science should properly begin. The geo (ego) centric model of the astrologer may now be recognized for the act of predominantly narcissistic creativity that it is; likewise, the early botanist believed plants and herbs corresponded to parts and organs of the body. As an overcharged play at chemistry, alchemy in its more blatant manifestations highlights the tendency of overdeterminism in all mental operations. As a perilous balancing act between the magical and the practical, alchemy has been traced from Aristotle via Gnostics and Arabics through the medieval world of learning—its notorious superstar being Doctor Faustus.[23] But by the Renaissance, alchemy had become, according to a source in Crombie, the domain of Free masons, tinkers, parish clerks, and glassmakers. Throughout its history, however, was the overriding aim of transmuting bases metals into gold, with the more subjective underlying aims of purification and regeneration. Like much of the literature of the time, alchemy was an allegorical quest for self-renewal through quasi-divine reparenting.

Jung devoted many years of his life—some would call it an excessive absorption—to this subject, which he viewed not so much as a series of poorly controlled experiments but as, in Storr's words, "a process of inner, psychological development in the alchemist himself"—the search for gold being a lived-out metaphor for individuation or sublimation.[24] In other words, Jung construed this pseudo-science as a facilitator of self-creation. Be that as it may, alchemy has other intriguing aspects that bear directly on this study. Certainly, there was a confusion in the alchemist between what was going on inside his mind and what was taking place in his laboratory, and there remains for us the problem of how literally to take his formulations—as concretions of psychic material or as analogies and metaphors for elusive processes that language had not yet caught up with. As Storr writes, the "combination of two dissimilar substances was described as a 'marriage,' and the production of a third thereby as a 'birth.'" Thus, processes involving origins and self-remaking were transpiring in the alchemical mind. Chemical

The alchemical death. From I. Bernard Cohen, *Album of Science, from Leonardo to Lavoisier, 1450–1800.* By permission of the Department of Rare Books & Special Collections, Memorial Library, University of Wisconsin.

elements were personified: the "king or Sol may stand for either 'sophic sulpher' or gold, and the queen or Luna for 'sophic mercury' or silver."[25] The "metallic union of gold and silver, or of the king and queen," runs Cohen's text beneath a graphic of feudal royalty, was part of a purification process leading to the philosophers' stone (see belows). In my own formulations, knowledge, or the birth of a self, emerges from the intricate mix of the primal scene (marriage) and the family romance (royalty). Even more revealing of these historical preoccupations with the rubrics of this study is a set of four plates in Cohen's text, which portrays The Alchemical Death. Plate 1 depicts a king and queen (Sol and Luna) bedded together under a tree that supports some drapery. Two stellar faces look on. Next, the corpses of the amorous pair are entombed and overseen by Death and Pluto. They then reverse positions, lying head to toe, and decompose. But, finally, on a raised tomb and exposed to renewing mist and dew, they begin to revive, although now it is no longer the same couple, but a hermaphroditic offspring. The four tableaux reveal the persistence of psychological concerns. It appears that the witnessed parental sex act results in their death, that is, the child's loss of the early idealized relation; it is followed by an assimilation of the parents as the newly regenerated self.

The "First Key" of Basil Valentine. From I. Bernard Cohen, *Album of Science': from Leonardo to Lavoisier, 1450–1800*. By permission of the Houghton Library, Harvard University.

That this overdetermined alchemical sequence externalizes not only the processes of self-creation out of the parental milieu, but also parallels the creative process of the artist, is evident. Does it say anything about the continuation of such primal fantasies within the scientific sphere proper? A mythology of science is needed before firm conclusions can be reached. Meanwhile, it can be inferred that scientific creativity is likely to owe something to all three stages of natural creativity, insofar as they are also unavoidable human steps.

3. Two Pioneers Anatomized

By working from available evidence toward larger reconstructions, one may hope to discern certain steps standing out in sharper relief than others. For example, Newton, with his laws of objects acting and reacting against one another, may have functioned principally in the dyadic area; Storr speaks of a split in this celibate scientist's object-realtions, "with the result that other human beings are either idealized as wholly good and unequivocally devoted to the subject, or else seen as wholly bad and intent on doing him injury"— wholly attracting or wholly repelling, so one may infer.[26] On a similarly primitive emotional level, he devoted thirty years to the alchemist's pursuit of the philosophers' stone—the magical transmutation of metals—which Manuel sees as a "longing for the abstract, for the ineffable, for what he never cast eyes upon"—a blend of the "father whom he never saw and the mother whom he possessed with such intense emotion."[27] The persistence of alchemical aims into the scientific area may indicate continuing primary creativity in the area of the self and thwarted forays into the triadic.

Newton scholars agree that the scientific genius cannot be separated from the suffering man. His "personality so influenced his thought, writings, and scientific behavior," Cohen wrote, "that the mark remained on the life of science as a whole for more than a hundred years."[28] Going further, Manuel declares, "When Europe adopted Newtonianism as its intellectual model, something of his character penetrated to the very marrow of the system."[29] His personal history becomes important for what it can tell us about the spurs that drove his genius, the manner and direction it took, and the bearing it has on the principal themes of this study.

Newton suffered from the puritan's overly scrupulous conscience, and it may be that reliance on the equally strict mathematical certainties of the new science opened up for him a healthier prospect of reality where the overdetermined reproaches of a guilty conscience could not afflict him—for the person who emerges from Manuel's *A Portrait of Sir Isaac Newton* was undoubtedly plagued with irrational or neurotic guilt. In his religious writings, which served as one outlet for his inner conflicts, Newton is a closet Unitarian, antitrinitarian in spirit; in his grandiose origins fantasy, "he was the only son of God and could not endure the rivalry of Christ."[30]

Had he been born in a later era, Newton's voice might have been added to Existentialism, since, like Sartre and Camus, he grew up fatherless and deprived of personal contact with the kind of authority that humanizes tradition. As it happened, both the Bible culture of his provincial mulieu and his own allegiance to reason saved him from confronting the absurdist's abyss. Both his "father, a yeoman, and his paternal grandfather were dead before Isaac Newton's premature birth on Christmas Day, 1642."[31] It is unfortunately true, as Manuel claims, that "the central figure in his life" is his mother, for in his critical third year, she remarried, this time a sixty-three-old clergyman, who was more over than twice her age. During the eight years of this marriage a second family arose, while young Isaac was left behind in the care of a maternal grandfather. When his stepfather died, his mother returned with three sibling rivals to resume a family life with a son who could hardly have felt kindly toward her. Not surprising, except in their naive candor, are two sins Newton cites at age twenty: "threatening my father and mother Smith to burn them and the house over them"; "wishing death and hoping it to some." Combine such hostile impulses with a religious psyche, and one comes up with an obsessional spur to thought in which a confusion arises between actual and fanciful causality, especially in respect to harm done to relatives. Thus it may be inferred that Newton shied away from a resolution by marriage of the oedipal conflict and turned regressively or, perhaps better, negotiated a series of trade-offs between regressive and progressive urges in the mental realm of mathematical science. There, relief (from the guilt of hostile wishes being fulfilled) could be experienced in a more neutral sphere, where causality was strictly observed and controlled.

The desire to burn down the parental home points to an attack on the primal scene, to undo and redo origins, while his concurrent boyhood interest in model building, clocks, and a mill into which he set a mouse to work may also represent undoing as well as a displacement of his sexual curiosity about how things work onto mechanical models in the transitional sphere of play. That he was effectively orphaned by his mother's second marriage is patent, and that he was deeply preoccupied with issues radiating from origins is amply documented in Manuel's study. Most of these strongly suggest family-romance themes, and since they are so similar to what one encounters in uncovering the lives of the artist, a summary may be given. Religious motifs are pronounced: (1) the son's biblical name of Isaac, the mother's of Hanna, who surrendered her son to the Lord as Newton's mother sacrificed her son to the scholarly life at Cambridge; (2) his birth on Christmas day; moreover, the prematurity of it denoted something miraculous involving divine intervention, while as a posthumous child, he was superstitiously endowed with healing powers; and (3) his Unitarian leaning, as noted, emphasized his special status, and in a list of alchemical writings he "inscribed the anagram of his name, Issaacus Neuutonus—*Jeova sanctus unus.*" Manuel goes on to mention that he was "absorbed in genealogy" and gave himself strange ancestors, "among them a Scottish lord.'' Among the "sources of genealogies of the gods and of the kings of all nations'' in Newton's historical papers, Manuel wonders if there was not a fantasy of royal birth, an "unconscious search for a line of ancestors.'' His rooms in later life were decorated entirely in royal crimson. Finally, Manuel speculates about the conflicts of traumatic separation and attraction in respect to the Edenic overtones of gravity's apple falling in his mother's garden, where he sat as a young man meditating.

The underside to these royal fantasies is, of course, emotional loss and narcissistic injury. Deprived of a real father, he lost his mother to an aged usurper at the onset of his own oedipal claims. Born prematurely, he was reminded by her that he was small enough to fit into a quart pot. He had to wear a bolster to support his neck, may have had difficulties nursing, and was smaller than his peers. Was the mouse, which he played with scientifically but also cruelly, a self-representation? Was his investment in reason and mathematics, as was the case with Descartes, a rejection of the body in order to conduct a project of self-reconsitution in a conflict-free sphere? Were his experiments in alchemy an attempt to recombine the ideal parental elements so that he could manipulate the primal scene more positively and feel less deprived of something basic to every child's development—the sense of being centered between loving parents? In short, was the alchemist in him striving to produce the perfect parental combination through which he would be better reproduced? To answer more than tentatively these questions and to pose others about interpreting his scientific work, along with the relevance of natural and polar creativity to the sciences, a great deal more collateral research would be required.

Both the promising and the prohibitive factors in such a project are highlighted by the life of the father of empiricism, René Descartes. For he attributes his vocation to the "admirable science'' of mathematical reasoning neither to a revolt against ecclesiastical authority nor to intellectual discipline but to a dream sequence he had on 10 November 1619, at age twenty-three, following certain scientific discoveries. Over the centuries proportionately little attention by philosophers has been paid to these dreams, which were summarized by his biographer, Baillet, in 1691, although the Catholic philosopher Jacques Maritain devoted an essay to the subject, hinting darkly and gleefully at Rosicrucian influences.[32] And, in fact, the momentuous dreams did occur at Ulm, a "center for Lutheran alchemists, seers, and prophets, including the Rosicrucians.''[33]

Psychoanalysts, on the other hand, have dealt with the implications of the dream, though, as Karl Stern points out, Freud himself was on this occasion uncharacteristically reticent. It is a lapse that Stern more than compensates for. But what is known of the circumstances of Descartes's origins are, if anything, more intriguing than his dreams. Baillet refers to his "blighted birth,'' which almost cost him his life, due to chest ailments, and stirred dour predictions that he would not live past age twenty. His mother, from whom he believed he had inherited his poor health, died in giving birth when René was just over a year. He was so firmly convinced that the wet nurse had saved him at birth and effected his later cure that he permanently endowed her out of gratitude. Stern discerns a subsequent split in Descartes's attitude toward women along spiritual/sexual lines. Maternal deprivation led him to relationships with "remote, lofty non-carnal women with whom he experienced spiritual exchange and challenge" as extensions of the real mother, "who left him cold."[34] Consequently, in Stern's view, the philosopher's sense of reality is founded on loss and uncertainty: doubt is the basis for all inquiry. His confident *Cogito* is a denial of loss based on a defensive splitting and isolation between mind and body. The defenses of the ego are reborn as the values of the new science (connections with which we are familiar, especially in Norman O. Brown's section on negation in *Life against Death*).

But while Stern's interpretations are a bit general and more than a bit polemical, they remain valuable for probing the psychic undercurrents during a turning point in history. Clearly pertinent to this study is the inescapable narcissistic injury in Descartes's infancy, instanced by the actual loss of his mother and bodily illness. Stern believes he emerged with a "neurosis of destiny" that made him a motherless, roaming spirit and led him "inextricably into the hands of the Anti-Mother," Queen Christina of Sweden, who lured him with an admiral's escort to her royal court. There, deprived of the "maternal triad, warmth and sleep and the proper food," he died after five months. Without needing to ratify this cogent, if somewhat pat, hypothesis, the reader can begin to discern the outline of a fatal family romance pattern with the ice queen, or, in Stern's words, *"une dame sans merci."*

More recent analysis by Roberta Recht of Descartes via his celebrated dreams supports the family-romance motif in the philosopher felicitously named René (reborn), who wished to revise his birth and who suffered from fears of sudden death without salvation (after his night of turbulent dreaming, he vowed a pilgrimmage to the shrine of our Lady of Loretto, which he fulfilled five years later). Another, not so literal kind of journey is pertinent here. Recalling his probable interest in the Rosicrucian journey to truth, in which the hero is born sickly and walks with a limp, Recht links René's need to surmount the conditions of his "blighted birth" and the popular superstitions "that infirmity at birth was the Devil's doing"—a view, she adds, that "certainly haunted" him.[35] Thus doubts are cast on the nature of his origins, and in his dreams the young philosopher is anxious to establish that they emanate from above, that is, are divinely inspired, as opposed to visitations from below—Satan's work. Moreover, his quest for mental certainty through a foolproof method is overdetermined by fears and doubts about the significance of his physical afflictions. In his third dream, he envies and longs to be in the company of poets whose bodies are "firm and erect," and, so the dream's reference to a *Corpus poetarum* is a pun that reveals a wish to possess a sturdier and more handsome—ideally, immortal—body.

As we have seen, in the emotional life of the artist narcissistic injury prompts wishes for rebirth that rise to the surface of consciousness as fantasies of exalted adoption. Recht recalls that as a philosopher Descartes wanted to be in no one's debt—a self-begetter—and in his *Discourse on Method,* he proposed to demolish the house of tradition that provided his education and to build his thought on a foundation wholly his own. But if such desires would sever the bond to the mortal mother who left him in the cold, they would not lay to rest his immortal wishes for the queen mother or the virgin mother of his faith, for these wishes, not to be denied, took their fatal and, apparently, hyperborean twist. And since the focus here is on the origins of modern science as well as on its originators, it is striking how some of the coldness of the fantasy that he defended himself against so convincingly with his clear and distinct ideas, may have attached itself to his celebrated method. From the cold-blooded nature of scientific inquiry that Descartes legitimized, scientists are only now beginning to thaw themselves out.

Yet the man was always more complicated and more interesting than his method. Because of the creative potential of the family romance, especially among those of unusual mental gifts, the scales may have tilted the father of scientific method perilously close to artistic vocation, as the third dream implies. For in it he discovers two books: one a dictionary, which he interpreted as the "interconnectedness of all sciences," according to Baillet; beneath it lay an anthology of poetry, which he would shortly decide connected philosophy with wisdom. In attempting to locate a poem beginning with "Est et Non" (Yes or No), he discovers "several small portraits in copper engravings," and the question posed through the dream, as was seen above, pivots on the desire to join the company of immortalized, dead poets.[36] Meanwhile, the dictionary has disappeared and reappeared, although no longer complete, and the anthology of poetry turns out to be a different edition. Amid these absences or gaps in resolution, the dreamer interprets the dream without fully waking. And since the first dream had begun with frightening phantoms out of the past, it is finally an abstraction, the spirit of truth, which eventually wins the day and presides as a quasi-religious ideal over the philosopher's future.

Having encountered family-romance patterns in Descartes's life, one may wonder how the opposite pole of origins might fit in. If such expectations sound unrealistic, it is not surprising. But to locate traces of primal-scene phenomena one need only return to the dreams and their published analyses.[37] The philosopher is awakened in the second dream by a peal of thunder and sees sparks everywhere in the room. Schonberger notes that in Descartes's own associations, he refers to "wisdom, which resides in the hearts of all men, like the sparks of fire latent in stones." Drawing on clinical and mythological sources, the analyst concludes that a spark is produced by the impact of two stones and that the "collision of two objects symbolized parental intercourse." Seeing the sparks is equivalent to the "sight of the performance of a sexual act," or, in the words of another analyst, the child's pleasure in seeing forbidden things was repressed, symbolically, in the dream by the thunder, and is experienced consciously "as a compromise formation in the guise of the sparks."[38] The second dream thus connotes orgasmic excitement connected with knowledge and fright. "According to Descartes," writes Schonberger, "the spark that is within is wisdom itself; and in the light of preceding considerations we may assume that wisdom is parental intercourse, something within us, that we have introjected."

In the first dream, in which he saw phantoms while walking down the streets and is buffeted by a fierce wind, sexual conflicts are also connoted; his taking refuge in a college chapel along with being handed a melon by a stranger suggest his regressively seeking safety through reassuring maternal objects— holy mother church, mother nature, the good breast, and the like. The wind and the thunder are then likely to be threatening male, that is, paternal elements, arousing castration fears and their symptomatic threat of impotence. In other words, the polarities so prominent in the dream may be derived from the above-mentioned introjects.

So much for earlier analytic readings. If we now attempt an analysis of the dreams in their dreamed sequence, we can establish a plausible progression: (1) walking down the streets signifies a questing—the awakening of sexual interests and curiosity (interrupted by buffeting oedipal fears); (2) the orgasmic sparks signify an answer to questions of sexual origins, but in a disguised or inhibited form; and (3) the discoveries of two books—the sciences contained in the dictionary, the arts contained in the *Corpus poetarum*— continue the dreams' dual or binary concerns (yes/no, right/left, above/below as divine/demonic, assertive/submissive, reason/enthusiasm, male/female) and harmonize them under the spirit of truth. But the question of origins aroused by anxiety over destiny (i.e., the dream question, What path shall I pursue?) is not resolved. Rather, overdetermined mental processes, viewed as a state of uncertainty, substitute for a path a method of ratiocination, whose one aim is certainty. Thinking becomes an assertion of the self, the present, and consciousness over the claims of authority, the past, a disturbing unconscious. The Cartesian *cogito ergo sum* is a triumph insofar as it is self-validating; it is a defeat insofar as it denigrates real mastery over the world of which the self is but a part. And, so, while thinking may have its adaptational plus in preserving components within the self and in maintaining a mental tie to the spiritualized mother, the scales are tilted too far inward toward an abstract subjectivity and—whether interpretations stress maternal loss, castration fears, the seductively soothing appeal of philosophical musing, or a fatal family romance—the Cartesian model weaves its fabric from the polar modes of origins more than one would have thought, and its peculiar self-affirmations continue to exert a dominant influence on Western science.

Although too much need not be read into the similar ways artists and scientists draw on the polar versions of origins, the parallels may look more promising than clinching. It will be sufficient to conclude that the deeper psychological struggles of Newton and Descartes within established polarities and through the steps of natural creativity have left indelible imprints on their character and work. For all their differences, they shared radical doubts and uncertainties over the nature of their origins and expressed violent wishes to destroy their ties to a personal or cultural past. A splitting in their emotional lives stemming from frustrations and conflicts with primary figures in their childhood evidently affected, by way of a counterswing, their undying allegiance to reason and science as a guarantee of certainty or a matrix of fundamental laws. How they reacted to their own pasts has deeply affected humanity's future. It is also fairly clear that for both of these bachelor scientists, science was a medium for mediating the contrary demands of originality and relatedness. The former raises issues of preserving a nucleus of grandiose self-sufficiency—discernible in Newton's obsessively holding the cosmos more strictly accountable to the mind's need for absolute causality than has been proven the case, and in Descartes's willfully triumphant *cogito*—over narcissistic injuries and precipitate parental loss. Relatedness they ultimately found not so much through persons as through their scientific medium—like many artists.

4. We're It versus We're not Alone

Is it paradoxical that narcissistic injuries may intensify narcissism rather than loosen its hold on our lives? In any case, while Newton nurtured his personally quarrelsome, misanthropic side and Descartes, his ontological affirmation of the thinking self at the center of all rational inquiry, neither of these heirs to Renaissance humanism would be likely to dispute the anthropic view of nature. And, despite science's historic assault on it, this view has proven as tenacious as it is arbitrary, since it poses questions beyond the perimeters of science. And as the extraordinary efforts of these two geniuses to protect a rational centeredness are conceded, they point to the next turn in this inquiry.

Ordinarily, we would expect that the notions of purpose in the universe—teleology—and of directional natural selection in evolution would be reinforced by one's basic sense of being wanted as a child, that the parental act of one's own begetting was intentional, not inadvertent, random, or undesired. In *The Facts of Life* (1976), R. D. Laing has addressed the painfully uncertain gropings of his own childhood, during which he had to create himself out of the condition of being unwanted. This sense of being unnecessary may have first been dramatized in the dilemma faced by that elderly adolescent, late of Wittenberg University, Prince Hamlet the Dane. His most jarring realization, apart from his father's probable murder, is how well the kingdom in the hands of his regal uncle and queen mother is getting along without him. While they are blithely proceeding with their state purposes, he alone must root out causes and return to origins. We think of him as a modern—perhaps the first modern—hero.

Teleology, the sense of order, the observance of law—these are correlative to the infant's first creation of meaning in his interactions with the nurturing parent; it is reasonable to hold that this phase makes all subsequent ones viable. Conversely, the sense of futility cancels the prospect of futurity. Our century has been called the accidental century, and W. T. Stace, among others, has noted the modern age's emphasis on causality over purpose, process over product, and existence over essence, to which one might add Robert Jay Lifton's concept of protean lifestyles over fixed character.[39]

By being out of step with his time, Hamlet was also ahead of his time, and it was not until the early Romantic characterizations of young Werther and the Byronic heroes that literature began to catch up with historical dislocations of the individual. By then the Industrial Revolution had driven the point home: the mastery of natural cases and their practical application are far more profitable than adherence to ultimate purposes. The sense of human irrelevance first took hold in nineteenth century Russia with Turgenev's *The Diary of a Superfluous Man* (1850) and Dostoevsky's *Notes from Underground* (1864), followed by the Ivanovs and Vanyas of Chekhovian drama. The transition into the present century was easily accomplished by T. S. Eliot's Prufrock, Kafka's K, Musil's Ulrich, and the evolving generations of existential and absurdist heroes down to the present in Joseph Heller's *Catch-22* and Antonioni's films on the eclipse of the individual.

Creative artists' first reaction against superfluity was to make the artist culturally central, as in the prophetic utterances of Blake or in Shelley's "Defence of Poetry" (1821); later in Baudelaire's and Wilde's Dandy, in Joyce's and Rilke's self-important portraits of the artist; and, ironically, in Rilke's and Picasso's saltimbanques: those homeless and tragic performers who create useless beauty on the fringes of industrial civilization. In this enterprise the polar underwriters of creativity are felt. For as the primal scene poises us on an axis of exclusion/inclusion, so the family romance absorbs feelings of abandonment and grandiose adoption; in the perilous modern balance between narcissism and irrelevance, art favors the former, protests against the latter, and science assumes the hero's ambiguous power as art is marginalized.

States of feeling unwanted, of being superflous, of extreme dissociation, and existential aloneness, so characteristic of our century, are usually represented in a triadic mode where the impact of destructive historical forces are anchored in the child's feelings in relation to the exclusive nature of the parental relationship (usually signified by anonymous, indifferent others). But when fundamental issues of meaning and relatedness are questioned, as in the tradition of the Absurd, then natural creativity at the primary and dyadic phases is also engaged, both in originating the works and in our ability to respond.

One need not be a disciple of Jean-Paul Sartre to recognize that he was onto something fundamental for our time when he claimed in *Saint Genet* (1963) that we are what we make of what has been made of us. The mostly missing sense of any ultimate purpose to bind individuals and communities together results not just in the fragmentations of contemporary living but in vacuums that leave us susceptible to increasing pressures to form, concoct, or adopt ad hoc value systems, often through conversion to precooked belief systems, born-again religions, occult doctrines, utopian projects, "crisis cults," or recourse to short-term movements of self-help or reform. Mircea Eliade noted in a press interview that his students "want unconsciously to find something meaningful but don't want to look in their own traditions." To be reborn one must first locate a new set of parents. Billy Graham wrote the first how-to book on this subject, entitled, not surprisingly, *How to Be Born Again* (1977).

While it is unlikely that science could develop apart from the forces of natural creativity, it does seem that from its early deflection into causes and origins science has begun angling back to purposes and goals. Or perhaps it has never really left them, for where we have been tells us where we may be heading, as in Eliot's celebrated lives, "What we call the beginning is often the end / And to make an end is to make a beginning"—and this possibility reopens the mysteries of teleology.[40] The playful "happenings," action paintings, improvised theatre, and experiments such as those by John Cage, intending to allow chance a central role in the creative process, may have been misdirected attempts to emulate operations in a universe that now appears less and less accidental: God does not throw dice, after all. The universe seems to have come about through a series of fortuitous or, to put it more paradoxically, necessary chances. "The universe evolved like life and thought," speculates Timothy Ferris, and is "as subject to chance just as our lives are," an analogy he finds that deepens our sense of having a "rightful place in nature."[41] Humanity's deeply rooted sense of being willed would then be rooted in the cosmos. The artist expresses this as an embeddedness through fate and traditional womb / tomb imagery, the scientist, as a wedding of consciousness to the universe. But as each of us recreates himself as descended apes, exiled angels, existential loners, or born-again believers, a measure of freedom is also being created.

At its simplest level of operation on the world, natural creativity resulted in the ancient doctrines of micro/macrocosm correspondence. Pre-sciences, like astrology, were attempts to remake the universe in terms of the self. "All imaginative thought attempts to bridge the gap between man and what is outside him," writes Leonard Barkin: "One method of bridging this gap is to see these two points of reference as fundamentally similar."[42] Carl Sagan notes the human tendency over the centuries to project patterns of hope and fear onto the stars: hunting cultures saw "hunters and dogs, bears and young women." Seventeenth-century European sailors cast "toucans and peacocks, telescopes and microscopes, compasses and the sterns of ships" onto the heavens.[43] As science's maturing emphasis on reality testing and exact measurement recreated the universe in terms of *it*self rather than *our*self, the narcissistic mode may have been "injured" or abandoned, but the old astrology was not so much obliterated as driven underground, to be reborn and preserved in the occult, where it remains available for filling subjective gaps in the imaginative creation of art and the self.

We may all be Cartesians to the extent that the first necessary step in thinking is directed toward self-creation, which undergoes continual modification through the discovery of the otherness of experience. Yet "as human beings," Michael Polanyi warns, "we must inevitably see the universe from a centre lying within ourselves."[44] Truth is always personal.[45] Without a "healthy narcissism," writes K. R. Eissler, man "would be crushed by the infinities that surround him."[46] It isn't surprising, then, to find man's place in the universe debated within a narcissistically acceptable framework. The one position, simply put as the We're It hypothesis, encourages belief in the uniqueness of our populated planet throughout the universe, roughly equivalent to the religious belief in special creation: truly, we are one of a kind and might just as well have been fashioned by an omnipotent being. The other position, the We're Not Alone hypothesis, opens the prospect of other populated planets in our own or other of the myriad galaxies abounding. This theory, which began with the "plurality of worlds" speculations of the pre–Socratic Greeks, seems to have opened the floodgates of fantasy and, consequently, may be subtly influencing the direction of scientific work.[47] Signs can be taken for wonders. Intelligent beings on earth can imagine superintelligent superbeings on other earths, and before scientific speculation shades into science fiction, certain longings, certain wishes, as stowaways among these soaring thought rockets, may be discernible.

For without exception, what scientific speculation and science fiction share is the assumption that outer-space inhabitants are more highly advanced than we, less organic, less planet-bound, and, for whatever reasons, they are out there exploring and looking about in our direction. We are wanted by them, but why? Usually, it is to share science, compare notes on our relative achievements—but the motive is not always clear. They are mainly out there looking around for us, and we are signaling to the effect, We're over here. Land and rescue us. Reveal the secrets of life, especially those of rebirth, immortality—that's what we need to know. We want to be born again, preferably to live forever, preferably somewhere else, for we are like the person in Yeats's poem, "fastened to a dying animal," and surrounded by "dying generations." We would sail to a Byzantium in the stars, become "an artifice of eternity," and fulfil our deepest family-romance yearnings.

The bottom line of We're Not Alone reads: we are lostlings, waiting to be found, adopted, or reclaimed by those phantasmagoric parents of early childhood who stirred up in us patterns of perfection before disappearing into our past, read: outer space. In this scenario, UFOs performing rescue missions are the return of the repressed. Since family-romance needs are emotional as well as subjective, it is unlikely that speculative science will be able to work through these emotional issues toward a postoedipal vision of reality, as art sometimes manages.

One solution to the primal scene as epitomizing the riddle of origins emerges in Carl Sagan's drawing of the anatomically correct couple as part of a symbolic communication system with outer-space visitors. For what he has conveyed is the origin of life as it is humanly understood. And the assumption is that they—whoever they may be—will also understand, but only, one fears, insofar as they are the original parents idealized onto a distant star seeking to rediscover their lost earthlings and return home. Another scientist, Francis Crick, who shared the Nobel Prize for solving the DNA riddle, has fantasied in *Life Itself* (1982) that (mother) earth was seeded with spores from an interstellar rocket; similarly, Chandra Wickramasingh and Fred Hoyle in *Evolution from Space* (1982) imagine the earth as having been bombarded with cosmic genes from a higher intelligence. Everyone is entitled to his private jokes and mental extravaganzas, but if the poet's dreams should end in responsibilities, to adapt a line from Yeats, then certainly the scientist's dreams should end in evidence. If, on the other hand, We're It, the family romance itself may have to be abandoned for the colder consolations of objective awareness.

5. Pseudo-Solutions (Three Cases)

Though poised on the razor's edge between science and fantasy, most scientists undoubtedly know where they are standing. The same may not be said of the redoubtable Erich von Daniken. Since science regains its interest as fantasy when it forfeits its claim on facts and logic, von Daniken's fanciful theories are remarkable for being the most brazen attempt so far to replace Darwinian evolution with a pseudoscientific family romance. "I claim," he writes, "that our forefathers received visits from the universe in the remote past." These "strangers annihilated part of mankind existing at the time and produced a new, perhaps the first, *Homo sapiens.*"[48]

Chariots of the Gods? appeared in 1968, followed by a sympathetic NBC documentary and more von Daniken books. It was not until nearly a decade later, by which time the fantasies had captured the popular imagination, sequels had been written, and von Daniken had been made wealthy, that serious rebuttals in English began to appear. The most devastating of these is by Ronald Story, who mentions von Daniken's devout Roman Catholic childhood, his intense "vision" at nineteen, and his subsequent falling-out with church authorities. In the fall of 1979, a *Nova* documentary came to conclusions similar to Story's, and Carl Sagan has, on various occasions, cancelled the space-gods' visas; yet their tenacity among people who should know better would be difficult to explain without reaching beyond rational explanations of ignorance and considering the powerful gravitational pull of family-romance hopes deeply grounded in the self.[49]

Extraneous to genuine scientific inquiry, von Daniken's appeal is exclusively psychological, or, it could be said, religious, for we have often been reminded, since the mid-1960s that we are living in a religious age. Religious sensibilities have their own visions of cosmic origins, and, so, one or two more examples of the manner in which they are structured by fantasy will round out this survey.

When early humanity achieved sufficient distance from its origins to worship them as divine, they retained an ambisexual nature. Historians of religion, like Mircea Eliade, have noted that new-year rituals among primitive people deploy transvestite dancers to invoke the primordial unity-totality of life at its inception; among Indians of the Americas the androgyne is sacred.[50] Elaine Pagels's work on the Gnostic gospels discloses that the notion of both masculine / feminine components in the godhead was suppressed in favor of the patriarchal tradition and the male-progenitor sequence, with which we are familiar: from mud God molded Adam; from Adam's rib molded He Eve, and so forth.[51] Consistent with patriarchal values and policies, the New Testament contributes an Immaculate Conception, a Virgin Birth, and a physical Resurrection leading to a religion in which Paul promises adopted sonship and life everlasting. Thus does the gentle veil of a divinely sponsored, family-romance descend and conceal a restructuring of human origins.

This deep involvement of religion in sexuality may stem from an underlying concern with issues of fertility / renewal / immortality, the proximity of the superego (as heir of our earliest libidinal attachments) to the id, or as part of a more general warping process of nature exacted by culture. Humankind appears as unable to get the primordial scene of human origins off its collective mind as we are incapable of dealing directly with our own individual begetting.

Thus it is no surprise to find that the founder of a famous religious cult, the Reverend Sun Myung Moon, is intensely absorbed in matters sexual. Not only does he choose marriage partners for his Moonie converts and conduct mass marriages, but he has rewritten Scripture to draw it more closely into a sexual orbit and has succeeded in twisting it a bit more in the direction of primal-scene concerns.[52]

The manner in which the Reverend Moon has emended Scripture tempts one to draw parallels between his pseudoreligion *vis à vis* the real article and Von Daniken's pseudoscience *vis à vis* science. While this analogy may hold up for someone working within an estabished religious tradition, the problem is not so symmetrical for someone analyzing the fantasy structures out of which religions in general are comprised.

What is clear is that both Reverend Moon's appeal and his threat reside in the family, for he offers the prospect of readoption and reparenting into an extended and perfected family founded less out of Christian doctrine than out of the family romance and constructed less out of fear of Satan than out of the primal scene, though we may as well retain the theological categories until they give way.

In Reverend Moon's scenario, God originally was ambisexual but tended to favor his masculine potency as "positive essentiality," his complementary feminine aspect as "negative essentiality"; while His creating "the universe as His external feminine object" maintains a universal condition of divided polarities.[53] In the Garden, the tree of life represents Adam's perfected nature, while the tree of knowledge, nominally representing good and evil, stands for Eve, and, more likely, carnal knowledge. What prevented our primal parents from having children and achieving a perfected fourfold family with God as the beneficent grandfather at the pinnacle was that Eve committed fornication with a disgruntled archangel; that is, she was seduced by a superior being, one from a higher order—or in human terms, from an older generation—before she had reached the maturity to mate with Adam. Thus she incorporates the archangel's evil and transmits it to Adam, seducing him as she had been seduced before. The primal crime in this version of the Fall from paradise was adultery.[54] In other words, the meaning of the primal act of sexual intercourse as betrayal is consistent with the child's observation of the mother's "unfaithfulness" with a sexual rival, the father. The unreadiness for this awareness, it seems, is transferred from the child to the mother, as is the guilt, in blaming Eve for introducing sin into the world.

Whence the call for a replacement of the primal and sinful pair: "Jesus and the Holy Spririt came as the True Parents in place of Adam and Eve to give rebirth to mankind."[55] This is necessary because, patriarchal mythology notwithstanding, "a father alone cannot give birth to children. There must be a True Mother with the True Father, in order to give rebirth to fallen children of goodness. She is the Holy Spirit."[56] But the Holy Ghost is hardly a woman, though that may be the point—in effect, Moon's "solution" is removing the dangerous female from the primal scene of origins.

As the family-romance solution for Moonies begins unfolding in a scripted context, recall that the theme of orphan adoption is played out in a living context when the Moonies, like homeless beggars, panhandle adults and bring their day's earnings home to the grateful father of their adopted family. Thus the divisiveness that belies the name of Unification Church, involving a well-documented brainwashing of initiates, is in effect but a "necessary" stage in the reparenting process.

The primal scene and the family romance converge in the head of the Unification Church as its members are prepared for the coming of the true parents, who are symbolized by the sun and the moon and are explicitly evoked in the name of the messenger-messiah himself: Sun Myung Moon. His unifying operations neatly combine reparenting (family romance) with arranging his members' marital couplings (primal-scene revision) in a quasi-divine mimesis of primordial creation.

The Moonie brand of religiosity may be seen either as anomalous to "true" religious pursuits or as an extreme instance that merely highlights a short-circuiting of the normal human need to recreate oneself as a person separate and independent from one's family of origins. Liabilities reside in any ready-made system that deprives the individual of initiative and freedom in this difficult task. Religion on the other hand, can—historically has—responded to the individual need for self-renewal with a mixed assortment of results. But should one then assume valid cultural functions for religion when it is not entirely devoted to overcoming feelings of helplessness, reinforcing splits in the superego between divine and diabolical, or balancing self-esteem against rage and injury, or fostering grandiosity, idealizations, messianic hopes, and the like? In contrast to the cultist vogues of the seventies reaching their apex of sheer madness and violence in the 1978 tragedy of Guyana, and in contrast to snake handling, faith healing, babbling in tongues, instant conversions, and public witnessing, there is the traditional, mystical way, grounded in human experience. As propounded in modern times by Evelyn Underhill, the mystical way involves an arduous inner process of disciplined stages: "these involve an awakening; a purging of the self; illumination; the dark night of the soul, which amounts to an eclipse or death of one's former self, accompanied by feelings of abandonment; and finally the unitive way."[57] And there is also the religious ideal of service that implicitly acknowledges human helplessness but responds in more appropriate care-giving ways while minimizing a dogma of divine adoption or a theology of salvation. As transitional phenomena, both preexisting and individually created, religions need be no more deeply entrenched in illusion than other cultural products.

Although one would have to think twice (or doublethink) before accusing scientific accounts of origins—be they from Darwin, Einstein, or Freud—of amounting to the kind of ordinary reality encountered in the European intellectual world, this is the implicit judgment made by Carlos Castaneda after his initiation into the nonordinary sorcerors' world of his Yaqui Indian master, Don Juan. The accounts, now running into several volumes, have fascinated readers in the scientific world as well as the general public ever since the publication of *The Teachings of Don Juan* in 1969. This amazing incursion of relatively undiluted ancient shamanism into a sophisticated soft science like anthropology as well as into the secular academic world warrants consideration as a conversion experience every bit as mentally intoxicating as the Moonies find theirs spiritually gratifying.

But it is difficult to attain an objective picture of Castaneda because, as one of his commentators observes with uncritical approval, "to compensate for his growing image and legend," he "erases his personal history and deliberately withholds information that would destroy the anonymity he needs."[58] If there is a better way to keep a curious world on one's scent, it has not been found;

while nothing, as Howard Hughes well knew, is quite so demystifying as visibility and factual answers. The advice seems to have come from Don Juan, who explained to his troubled pupil that "if you have no personal history, no explanations are needed; nobody is angry or disillusioned with your acts. And above all no one pins you down with their thoughts."[59]

Yet respective personal histories are essential to understand shaman and scientist as individuals as well as to grasp their interlocking relationship. Fortunately, this task has been carried out with meticulous care and understanding in three studies by M. D. Faber.[60] This scholar examines his subjects in a context of transference and countertransference in order to fathom the underlying reason for their ultimate failure. "What Castaneda experiences during the course of his apprenticeship with Don Juan is an overwhelming reactivation of long buried pain, anxiety, and terror inextricably bound up with bad maternal introjection," writes Faber. Consequently, "Don Juan becomes for Castaneda not simply a parental transference figure but a sexually ambiguous and therefore disguised recreation of the seductive, rejecting, confusing mother."[61] Suffering a deeply repressed split in the internalized mother image, Carlos places himself under Don Juan's control in order to gain the benevolently powerful early mother, only to have Don Juan, for reasons of his own, play out a sadistic game that effectively activates the malevolent side of Carlos's early mothering experience. Subsequently, Castaneda's inner world is split apart, the relationship is ruptured, and other anthropologists acquainted with Castaneda have personally conveyed the impression that his writing are attempts to master and work through the traumatic experience.[62]

Granted that this version is several degrees below the heady accounts Carlos gives of flying over the desert as a crow, I can only urge readers at all suggestible to such flights to read the Faber studies. They are as far from the ordinary as from the fanciful. This study must content itself with a brief consideration of our subjects' personal histories and how they might interlock with the evolving, familiar themes. Carlos was born circa 1938 in Brazil and, after a period in Argentina, came to California, where he studied anthropology in Los Angeles. In his writings he reveals an important period in his childhood—age six, to be exact—when his mother abandoned him. Orphaned, he states that he spent "the most hellish years of my life circulating among my mother's sisters" and his twenty-two cousins, who surrounded him "like enemies" and with whom he "waged a desperate and sordid war" before "subduing" them.[63] While Faber emphasizes maternal abandonment, I would note the conditions for a family romance of exalted adoption to shamanist father in order to heal the countless wounds to his basic self.

For his part, Don Juan had recently lost a son due to a horrible road-construction-site accident (laying the ground for a father-son odyssey); more importantly, he, too, suffered early maternal loss. "What I remembered the most is the terror and sadness that fell upon me when the Mexican soldiers killed my mother.''[64] They beat him, and they allowed his father to die later of his wounds. Perhaps this violent scene from Don Juan's past actually occurred as he claims it did. Carlos clearly takes the older man at his word and Faber, too, goes along with the account. Whether it happened as reported or whether it was an instance similar to those accounts of childhood violation and seduction that Freud's patients related and that he eventually questioned en route to discovering the unconscious side of the mind, is at least worth asking. If not fanciful, it may at least bear screen memories and buried affects that would take us into the child's unconscious, where derivatives from the primal scene could be further explored.

In any case, Carlos's willingness to be adopted and reparented by Don Juan suggests both something about the younger man's inclination to live out a family romance, even if it entails breaking with ordinary reality, and something about the older man's need to realize such a fantasy through another as it may or may not have once been realized within his sorcerer's profession. That hysterical suggestibility which appears in such shamans may have facilitated and no doubt intensified these not very edifying excursions into nonordinary reality need not be surprising;[65] but what is both surprising and dismaying is the aura of legitimacy and respectability provided by those on the near—or ordinary—side of reality.[66]

In sum, both Carlos and Don Juan are drawn to those primal poles of origins most deeply and thoroughly explored by the creative artist; and these two mind-adventurers, also like the artist, turn away from mundane reality. But whether they complete the process and return with a new vision that will contribute to our evolving reality depends on the way we read the texts—that is, as documents of science or as fabulations of fiction. For the whole enterprise, including the very existence of a Don Juan, has been called into question. The case against Castaneda brought by Richard de Mille and other scholars argues compellingly for a verdict of hoax.[67] Even the author's myth-making faculty has been deemed second-rate, and what remains are the fantasy structures analyzed above.

6. Three-Steps of Natural Creativity in Synthesis

Hoaxes like the Piltdown Man and the kind of garden-variety chicanery exposed by Martin Gardner in *Science: Good, Bad, and Bogus* (1981) or the more lethal mischief flushed out by Stephen Jay Gould's *The Mismeasure of Man* (1981) may be exceptions; but they are valuable in highlighting the subjectivism endemic to science that nourishes fantasies within the prevailing paradigm of objectivity.

Yet science and art, while clearly distinguishable as well as overlapping, need not be polarized. The one records the truths of our experience in the world; the other our deepest responses to those truths. "The mind knows in part, in part and parcel, with full stop at every sentence," wrote D. H.

Lawrence in his *Apocalypse*. "But the emotional soul knows in full, like a river or a flood." [68] What it tells us is that "we and the cosmos are one. The cosmos is a vast living body, of which we are still parts." The image of the cosmos is the "great divine dragon," not the kind that Carl Sagan portrays as disrupting our transition from the arboreal Eden, but a twofold being. The great crisis of prehistory, according to Lawrence, was the "conquest of the *inimical* serpent and the liberation within the self of the gleaming bright serpent of gold, golden fluid life within the body, the rousing of the splendid divine dragon within a man, or within a woman." (*Apocalypse,* 145). This inner dragon connects humanity for man with the other dragon in the vast cosmos of the stars, which

> writhes and lashes ... and makes the wonder of the night, it is the full rich coiling of his folds which makes the heavens sumptuously serene, as he glides around the guards the immunity, the precious strength of the planets, and gives lustre and strength to the fixed stars, and still more serene beauty to the moon. (145)

Of course, this is but an instance of the artist's creative romance with the cosmos, and Lawrence was, technically speaking, wrong to reject science and evolution. Yet he was not naively wrong: he knew what he was up to when he asserted, "the quick of the universe is in us."

Through language we re-create the visions of ourselves born out of science and art, different as they may be. However complex this process of comprehension and assimilation may become, the phases of natural creativity provide certain common, irreducible features:

1. At the primary level we ask (implicitly) is the substance there—and if so, edible/intelligible? Can it be taken in? A basic issue of suitability and meaningfulness has to be faced. It either provides intelligibility, or we soon become bored, distracted, withdrawn, and leave off feeding. Later we will furrow our philosophical brow and ask, Why is there something instead of nothing?

2. At the dyadic level, we ask (implicitly) is it in here/out there; pleasurable/painful; for/against, that is, a good or bad object? Is it alive, whole within itself, or dead, partial, extreme, one-sided (e.g., propaganda, not art)? Whose idealization is it? How can it be shared?

3. At the triadic level we begin asking, where did it come from?—what is it for? These are questions of origins, causes, and purposes; they are also sexual (or sexually tinged). What are respective genital organs for? What makes babies happen? Why do parents share sleeping? Why should I be? Questions of motive also come into play. The two earlier phases make themselves felt: does the sexual thing have meaning?—is it good or bad, human (high) or bestial (low)? Along with these quandaries and the emerging autonomy of mental functions, we begin seeking answers in a wide spectrum

of immediate, displaced, and remote areas. The answers like the questions will likely be overdetermined.

When the proffered solutions have become overdetermined—as in the three illustrative cases of von Daniken's pseudoscience or mythology, of Rev. Moon's pseudoreligion or cultism, and of Castaneda's pseudotherapy or mysticism—I wonder whether we are not witnessing, in these returns of the repressed, new remedies to old dilemmas or merely new symptom formations?

15

The Holes in Being that Reveal Our Selves

> Freud's genius makes it difficult to separate the artist from the scientist, and the attempt to set them apart does violence to a deeper understanding of the creative stream in Freud's personality.
> —Ernest S. Wolf

While the strands may stretch in various directions, human origins would seem to bind scientific and artistic reativity into a common knot. Perhaps on closer analysis there is, rather, a network of knots that our mental fingers grope for in the dark of the past, and it is not always clear which knot— personal, biological, cosmic—we come upon and begin unraveling. There- after, the tension-reducing satisfactions in sheer unraveling may also reduce our powers of discrimination.

In constructing his archetypal tragedy of the band of brothers rising up to slay the primal father in order to redistribute the tribe's libidinal resources, Freud was, in effect, playing the dramatist with his scientific imagination. But artistic creativity plus scientific speculations could no more do the work of the dramatist than Shakespeare could write *On the Origin of the Species*. Although Freud had modestly said that "I have suppressed my habit of conscious speculation as radically as possible and have absolutely forsworn the temptation to 'fill in the gaps in the universe,'"[1] he was not able to resist filling in the gaps in his oedipal-origins drama when he wrote *Totem and Taboo* (1913). Derek Freeman suggests that the "discovery" of an actual historical crime in man's archaic past may have lessened the burden of guilt Freud felt for the repressed wishes discovered in his own past: I desire to do only what others have actually done. This reconstruction is convincing, and what is about to be considered, while adding another motivational lead, should be of further interest in highlighting the interplay between creativity in the service of scientific truth and creativity in the service of aesthetic truth.

The fact is that the drama that Darwin hinted at and Freud framed a scenario for had already been composed and performed to near perfection by Shakespeare, without benefit of evolutionary hypothesis, in his tragedy *Julius Caesar*. On the Elizabethan stage, the band of brothers are the Roman senators, who indeed address themselves as brothers while locking arms in sworn conspiracy. Their envy of Caesar's powers is legitimized as opposition to tyranny, and their bathing their hands "up to the elbows" in his blood is the totem feast that ritualizes their crime and dilutes their individual guilt. In the end they recognize the futility of their oedipal transgressions and turn their swords against themselves in gestures of punishment and symbolic identi- fication with the father/victim that affirm the primacy of the suprerego, the acceptance of guilt, and the continuity of culture.

In other words, Shakespeare had worked out the crime of regicide/ parricide—not only in this play but in *Macbeth, Hamlet,* and *Richard III* among others—and therefore must have worked over the ambivalent meanings of the complex in the wholeness of his creative imagination. He had unshackled the events from history as recorded by Plutarch and had unlocked its deep emotional significance from the unconscious; in so doing, he placed his work in the transitional sphere not of children's play but of adult theater, where it could be experienced in dramatic coherence. It is probably naive to hold that because things were not put into so many words before Freud and Ernest Jones psychoanalyzed drama that previous audiences did not know within themselves more than they committed to speech or page. In fact, Freud maintained that the durability of *Oedipus Rex* is beholden to profound recognitions.[2] But as more than dramatized wishes and cathartic release, these tragic conflicts have been worked through in the creative process at least to the extent that their released energies engage others in the art medium.

Freud displayed exemplary candor in writing to his contemporary, Arthur Schnitzler, that "when I become absorbed in your beautiful creations I always believe I find behind the poetic appearance the presuppositions, interests, and results that are already known to me as my own."[3] But with Shakespeare, Freud's conflicts must have been more resistant, because he permitted himself to accept the least probable theory of Shakespearean creativity: that the bard's plays were not his own. At this point an intriguing parallel between mankind's and the bard's origins presents itself. In both instances the material available for Freud was meager, and yet he "responded to the poor historical documen- tation as a challenge to his psychological skill.[4] But for once it is not Freud's psychological skill that was revealed, for there is no scintilla of doubt that Shakespeare wrote the poems and plays attributed to him. Nor was there really much basis for the anti-Stratfordian position when Freud was writing, as Harry Trosman's careful study demonstrates. What was being revealed, then, was Freud's own psychology. For a time he had entertained the Bacon hypothesis and that of multiple authorship, but, finally, as Trosman shows, he was persuaded by the crackpot theories of the appropriately named J. T. Looney, to wit, that the real author was the Earl of Oxford, Edward de Vere. Freud and the anti-Stradfordians apparently shared the conviction that the "untutored son of the provincial citizen of Stratford, who attained a modest position as an actor in London," in Freud's words, could not have authored the supreme masterpieces of Western literature. Trosman discerns a need among the antibards to rescue an unknown aristocrat from behind Will's name, someone more commensurate with their exalted estimate of the works.

But how could Freud have aligned himself with this crew of amateurs? Trosman's answer takes us into the heart of this study. Freud exhibited symptoms here of what he himself discovered elsewhere as the family romance. Its basis lay partly in his sense of early public neglect and the reactive "partiality toward an unrecognized author who also worked in 'splendid isolation,'" whom he could rescue by identifying and so reveal the true origins of the masterworks. Beyond that were questions of paternity, with which Freud had wrestled as a young man, and a need for a nobler, more aristocratic father than the otherwise adequate one he had. "I have found love of the mother and jealousy of the father in my own case too, and now believe it to be a general phenomenon of childhood," he wrote Fliess on 15 October 1897, adding parenthetically, "Similarly with the 'romanticization of origins.'"[5] The task of relinquishing his own romantic origins was apparently negotiated through a compromise: the conflicts were displaced onto his double, Shakespeare, who, since he also stemmed from common lineage and knew too much about oedipal issues, needed to be discarded and replaced by the hidden aristocratic parent Freud had denied himself. "The dramatist's life-giving' power is a manifestation of the paternal generative power, deposed and unattributed until a suitable hidden and distant aspirant is found," writes Trosman: "The discovery of the creator is a rediscovery of the original idealized father of early, preoedipal childhood now cast in a new light and projected into the arena of history." Thus as the Greeks endowed the Olympian gods with the immortality they felt they were denied, so the author of the Shakespeare oeuvre is endowed with an exalted parentage Freud felt he was denied. Moreover, the Earl of Oxford qualifies because he had lost a father in his own early youth and had resented his mother's remarrying.[6] Thus Freud appears to be reifying an actual oedipal source for a later oedipal play as he had sought an actual historical crime of the brothers against the primal father. But in so proceeding, Freud in the one instance inadvertently undermines the power of psychic reality and in the other, also perhaps unwittingly, downgrades the powers of imagination whose generative powers he so admired and envied.

Freud said he avoided Schnitzler "out of a kind of shyness at the thought of seeing my double."[7] The affect of shyness accompanies family-romance fantasies, which Freud may have feared another artist would see through.[8] The double feared by Freud may have been the poet he could have turned into had he gone deeper into the family-romance subjectivism instead of analyzing it and displacing its residue onto the bard of Avon. In sum, Freud's scientific powers faltered in two reconstructions when his mental fingers mistakenly worried the personal knot of his own origins instead of the impersonal ones he believed himself to be unraveling. Perhaps, in addition, his preoccupations with the poet's origins distracted him from noticing that the Elizabethan had already dramatized the origins conflict that he (Freud) was striving to reproduce from evolution, because that would have meant that Shakespeare had gotten there first—a case of belatedness apropos the "anxiety of influence."[9]

Having found traces of the poet's family romance in Freud, one is encouraged find to other features as well, such as the spur of narcissistic injury. And, in fact, Ernest Wolf touches on a "gap left in [Freud's] psychological structure following the loss of his alter ego Fliess whom he had embellished with imaginary qualities."[10] This loss is overcome by his "creating a [scientific] work of artistic beauty," such as "The Aetiology of Hysteria." It follows that his writing of major texts was precipitated by personal losses: *Interpretation of Dreams* (1900) follows the death of his father (1896); *Totem and Taboo* (1912), the breakup with Jung over questions of incest; *The Problem of Anxiety* (1926), the split with Rank over the birth trauma.

Although artists are privileged with far greater latitude than scientists in subjective interweavings, the former likewise must eschew the handier personal design for the one demanded of their art. That such lapses into something on the order of the Romantics' "egotistical sublime" occur all too frequently does not mean they are readily discernible or can be objectively validated. A good example of the difficulty of this task as well as the possibility of succeeding in it can be found in Leon Edel's investigation of what went wrong in Willa Cather's *The Professor's House* (1925): the incomplete development of the professor is attributed to his being tied in too directly to a projection of her own feelings of depression.[11] Yet there are other gaps, apparent inconsistencies and oversights, in the creative arts that uniquely permit us to participate, to feel we complete the work, and to discover our own meanings, tragic or otherwise.

The subject of tragedy may repay lingering over a while longer. Is it redundant to state that this form is intensely oedipal? If we make allowances for grandiose aspirations, for dyadic-stage splitting of objects, is it still fair to find tragedy by and large oedipal and therefore peculiarly triadic? In any case, the light from this assumption need not expand beyond the few observations I want to make. Tragedies often gain their sense of completeness by representing within the life cycle a paradoxical sense of incompleteness.

Shakespeare's tragedies best illustrate those moments, usually late in the action, when the protagonists have acted upon their strongest impulses and are now gazing upon their anticipated triumphs. These moments let in the void. The hero gives vent to his inner sense of despair or purposelessness, the hollowness of his aspirations, the failure to mold vital relationships or a valid sense of self. Most memorably, this is evident in the "Tomorrow" speech of Macbeth; Lear's embrace of the Fool in the absence of his daughters; and the grim awareness among Caesar's assassins that in killing him—in abolishing the tyrant-father—they have created their own deaths:

> *Brutus.* That we shall die, we know; 'tis but the time
> And drawing days out, that men stand upon.
> *Casca.* Why, he that cuts off twenty years of life
> Cuts off so many years of fearing death.
> *Brutus.* Grant that, and then is death a benefit:
> So are we Caesar's friends, that have abridg'd
> His time of fearing death.
> (*Julius Caesar,* 3. 1. 99–105)

Death, death, death—it is as if for the first time they see beyond the object that has so far enlisted all their energies. It is the sudden aftermath of the oedipal struggle, and they are facing their own future. But instead of exulting in their triumph, they have already seen beyond to their own destiny, and their imminent celebrations can only ring hollow. To isolate this moment psychologically is to get in touch, if only fleetingly, with the sense one has at the triadic stage of no-object-being-there, either to respond to or to meet one's needs. Here it happens to occur on the heels of violence, yet it is more likely the crest of an anxiety force that began swelling with the first sense of castration (envy, ambition to defeat a rival, a fiery plague, or a sense of rottenness may be its signifiers). And it is only when the detested oedipal object is removed that the anxiety peaks into despair, hopelessness, or ennui—as befits a tragic denouement.

Tragedy is the form *par excellence* for putting us in touch with the enduring or recurring sense of uncertainty, of incompleteness, of an absence that surrounds us and encroaches even on our most hopeful scientific and cultural endeavors. In the end it is mainly tragedy that reminds us that the void remains—more elusive, greater than our capacities to fill in the missing gaps, links, of otherwise most ingenious reconstructions or careful unravelings. In tragedy, we learn how we create our own deaths.

16
Homo Undulans

Fortune, that serpentine and crooked line whereby He draws those actions His wisdom intends in a more unknown and secret way.
—Sir Thomas Browne, *Religio Medici*

Thus the unfacts, did we possess them, are too imprecisely few to warrant our certitude, the evidencegivers by legpoll too untrustworthily irreperible.
—James Joyce, *Finnegans Wake*

On his most rudimentary level, Einstein has taught us that, even more than vacuums, nature abhors straight lines. At least Relativity abhors them.

A straight line we do not very well see. It may not really exist, except ideally, mentally; or it may only appear to exist, as in Philip Slater's example of looking at a coin edgewise, whereas "in actuality, the midpoint is nearest our eye, with the line bending away from us in both directions."[1] So a straight line put under pressure, as it were, of scientific observation is recreated as a curve. Does the awareness of curvature also mark the beginning of creativity? One can be grateful, in any case, to Einstein for locating in the bending of light and the curving of space some faint correspondence to that "vain, diverse, and undulating object" that Montaigne described as man, adding, "tis hard to find any constant and uniform judgment on him."[2] And now we find that the universe is not so uniform either, for Einstein addresses for us all over again the dilemma over straightness as norm, curvature as deflection.

In "The Nature of the Gothic," John Ruskin had maintained that the best in us "cannot manifest itself but in company with much error." To err means to go astray, to divagate, to wander; but an errant knight is on a quest; and an errand bespeaks a message to deliver. In Ruskin's view, straight lines are best made by tools, but "men were not intended to work with the accuracy of tools, to be precise and perfect in all their actions." Granted, "you can teach a man to draw a straight line, and to cut one ... but if you ask him to think about any of those forms to consider if he cannot find any better in his own head, he stops; his execution becomes hesitating; he thinks, and ten to one he thinks wrong. ... But you have made a man of him for all that."[3]

Freedom—what Ruskin is talking about—is a deviation, and he finds it supremely manifested in the Gothic: "examine once more those ugly goblins, and formless monsters, and stern statues, anatomiless and rigid; but do not mock at them for they are signs of the life and liberty of every workman who struck the stone.'' But these childlike artisans who invented the Gothic let one suppose that children in their elastic sense of time and space might also inhabit a world less obsessively rational than the world of their parents—that Einstein's vision, in effect, restores to us our childhood sense of wonder and weirdness.

In any case, it is not so bad to find the universe just a trifle more gothic than the uniformity of Newton's machinery would have it to be. Curves, bends, warps, whirlpools, and spirals endow it with a sort of independent creative life apart from our own straight-mindedness, which now looks more deviant than normative.[4] Not surprisingly, it was Descartes himself who, most earnestly desiring to distinguish "the true from the false" in order "to discriminate the right path in life," turns away from the world of objects to the relationships of geometry "subsisting between straight lines." Yet his dreams blew him back and forth, as we have seen, from left to right, between their own phantoms; and Recht finds in the first dream a "fear of leftsidedness with its connotations of coldness, whiteness," sinfulness, and death.[5] Breaking with Cartesian duality, the Sartrean hero in *Nausea* (1938) prefers the rooted existence in the "great wrinkled paw" of an exposed chestnut tree root to the rational essence of a "circle" that "does not exist."[6]

A psychoanalyst, having referred to the concept of working through as linear, expressed his discomfort with it.[7] The process of a person struggling over the rough-and-tumble terrain of his psychic landscape is anything but a forward-plowing line. Rather, the analyst suggested the metaphor of the double helix, and the term working-over, a repeated upward / downward spiraling—closer to Montaigne's undulating humanity. Instead of confronting the patient with an upright, "authoritative interpretation," as Grunbaum seeks in his scientific critique of psychoanalysis, an analyst confesses, "In truth, I grope together with the patient, from guess to guess, from one tentative formulation and question to another one. A typical question on my side: 'Might it be that . . .' is responded to by the patient with his own, usually much better and more felt interpretation. And, as we go on, this stands or falls again, is modified, but into a broader context, and so forth."[8] "I have drawn my figures vacillating, disintegrated, a blend of the old and new," writes Stindberg in his Foreword to *Miss Julie* (1888). They are "conglomerations of past and present stages of civilization, bits from books and newspapers, scraps of humanity, rags and tatters of fine clothing, patched together as is the human soul," adding even a "little evolutionary history by making the weaker steal and repeat the words of the stronger."[9] yet the characters prove to be accurately drawn, and the play itself is beautiful and true.

Light, Einstein tells us, has an irregular past due to influences of celestial bodies it passes along its bending path toward us. The evolutionary counterpart for this deviation is man's deflection into protracted childhood, the deceleration of development, a lingering, bending, or even doubling back on one's origins, which, no matter how scientists rationalize it as adaptationally valuable, interrupts the linear process of growth, setting *Homo* apart. The equivalent to relativity in human evolution, then, is neoteny. In understanding individual development, the historic moment came when Freud first began to notice that "hysterics mainly suffer from reminiscences."[10] They have been bent into subjectivity, we would later learn, by the influences, or mutual attractions, of certain key figures encountered early on the trail of development. Their imaginary seductions led the patients to construct new reality systems, new protective fields of influence and resistances, which, under certain conditions, might come to the fore again, when for example, the psychoanalytic method allowed the analyst to assume the same gravitational force as the earlier influencial bodies. The past is created, relived defensively, reconstructed as memory, interpreted through the transference phenomena.

Evolutionists pay little attention to the adaptive plus of *Homo*'s ability to relive his past, but this unique endowment must surely arise from neoteny, which permits fantasy, play, experimenting, daydreaming—"back returning," as Emily Brontë puts it—in brief, the errant knight in each of us, to begin or resume our wayward quests. Imagination, then, is the internal continuation of neoteny. The quest represents our quintessentially human journey through life, for the quest is a creative mode and culture is a straying from biology, due, in K. R. Eissler's view, to an excess of narcissism and aggression in the human species, though he may as well have rounded out the picture by including an excess of libido.[11] Culture throws evolution into a cocked hat, because the process goes inward and then shoots off in untold directions more or less at once. If the continuationist school of biological evolution were right, Stephen Jay Gould writes, "life would move in a single direction and humans on top, would be properly analyzed in biological terms as the improved inheritors of all that came before." The perennial figure of the great chain of being would be reaffirmed, "but evolution is a copiously branching network, not a ladder." Similarly the straight thinking of anthropologists like Robin Fox and sociobiologists like E. O. Wilson, who would close the gaps between biology and society by finding a gene for every behavioral trait of man, fail, according to Gould, to appreciate how "human cultural evolution proceeds along paths outstandingly different from the ways of genetic change" and thus "needs laws of its own."[12] Yet while culture creates laws, those which create culture remain obscure.

Nature appears to be following suit. For in the paradoxical, ambiguous, and surrealist world of particle physics and quantum mechanics, we are told that substance is an illusion:[13] the ultimate stuff of the universe, writes Gary Zukav, is energy: "where what is = what happens, and where an unending tumultuous dance of creation, annihilation and transformation runs unabated within a framework of conservation laws and probability."[14] The collisions of subatomic particles are not material events so much as interactions betweens fields. Thus the materialism of modern physics loops back through the eighteenth-century immaterialism of Bishop Berkeley, whose *esse percipi* (to be is to be perceived) irrevocably bound the known to the knower.[15] It is only a short step to claim the universe exists to be perceived by humans.

For its part, psychoanalysis has parted company with the nineteenth-century physics that Freud had approvingly invoked and has entered more elusive interactive fields: "One can only judge it a failure of the analytic attitude to encounter an analyst speaking of what something really means," writes Roy Schafer. "To discern *further* meaning, *weightier* meaning, *more disturbed* meaning, *more archaic* meaning, or *more carefully disguised* meaning . . . does not justify the claim that one has discovered the ultimate truth that lies behind the world of appearances, the real' world."[16] But Freud himself forfeited his scientific edge when he confessed, "Our theories are our myths" and portrayed analysis in more personal, relativistic terms than had been supposed. According to Ornston, Strachey's standard translations of Freud consistently emphasize distinction and distance between subject (analyst) and object (analysand); whereas Freud often used the same verb (*erraten*) to depict their efforts as well as the reader's to guess, "puzzle and peer / guess and discern / intuit," what is going on in the unconscious—*to err* is to become human.[17]

Similar in spirit to both particle / wave theory and psychoanalytic practice, the postmodernist criticism of Harold Bloom and others, seeks for "meaning" that "is always wandering around between the texts."[18] But if diverse disciplines express parallel concerns, one may still stumble over real differences. And one does not have to accept Zukav's extrapolations from physics to psychology, via energy and visionary experiences, to value his main emphasis on the receding core of existence, be it of humanity or of the universe. For there is something infinitely elusive about the human urge to create oneself out of the dance of creation that comprises our origins, since our actual beginning, that moment of our begetting when two fields of forces interacted decisively, can never be recovered. Ever receding, it promises to offer the ultimate reality behind all metaphors of origins, be they of light and energy or of the mystic's vision of the face of God. In a difficult but valid sense, "God" is the act of parental begetting at the moment that time begins for each one of us—the mysterious primum mobile that we never see no matter how long or how far we may search. Thus in early mid-Eastern and Mesoamerican religions, God was the combined male / female sex: deep inside we know, we have always known, that the act of creation requires both sexes—the single self is always partial. Wandering between two texts, we are the meaning we can't quite decipher.

Divine or material, the cosmic puzzle, along with our evolutionary hopscotch and psychic swerves, echoes our experimental incompleteness, our existential dread, our psychological uncertainty, and continues to resound through the abyss which philosophy, science, and art strive to render bearable, intelligible, and communal.

Art may reconcile us to irregularity, as in the last word and opening line of *Finnegans Wake,* "[the] riverrun, past Eve and Adam's, from swerve of shore to bend of bay, brings us by a commodius vicus of recirculation back to Howth Castle and Environs."[19] But attendance at the *Wake* may also decenter our reading of ourselves through texts by suppressing words' primary meanings in order to entertain a host of peripheral significations that are at best strangely familiar. Art may keep alive our sense of discontinuity, as in Eliot's anxious verses—"Between the idea/And the reality/Between the motion/And the act/Falls the Shadow—" which measures the shadow of our fall from an Anglican, not an evolutionary, angle.[20] For Lawrence, who also didn't care for continuationist evolution ("like a long string hooked on to a First Cause"), the gaps suggest something positive and sexual to his aboriginal hunter. "So when the fire is extinguished, and the moon sinks, the man says to the woman: 'Oh, woman be very soft, be very soft and deep towards me ... Let me come into the deep, soft places, the dark, soft places deep as between the stars.'"[21] Scientific causality for Lawrence, like twice 2 = 4 for Dostoevsky's underground man, is a closed, claustrophobic system, while the mythic imagination allows one to breathe freely, create new—or recreate the old—organic connections, which are neither linear nor mental. It is really with the linear, the literal and monist mentality, that the modern artist has conducted his quarrel, gone underground, relied on "silence, exile, and cunning," or shown the features of madness, but Einstein seems to have thrown him a curve, low and inside across the plate, for a clean strike (although the second pitch may produce a Joycean Homer).

In fact language, with its inherent capacities for tropes, paradoxes, inversions, oxymorons, double entendres, and the turnabouts of puns, has never been a linear system for direct transmission of messages between two points; and in some ways these rich resources in language, which everyone draws on, may compensate (or overcompensate) for our sense that direct communication is so often insufficient. Paul Davies's depicting the scientific universe as paradoxical, ambiguous, and surrealistic, evokes Jacques Derrida's deconstructing a literary text. And when Joyce writes in *Finnegans Wake* (209), "arundgirond in a waveny line aringarouma she pattered and swung and sidled," and continues pretty much in this vein for 628 pages, he conducts the first verbal tour of that universe.

That this indefiniteness is not entirely a bad thing, that it may be a *felix culpa* ("foenix culprit" [*Wake*, 23]; "ferax culpa," [606] connecting fall with rebirth and fertility), is suggested by Peter Blos's account of adolescent development, and it is here that the interplay may be discerned between the two kinds of ceativity, artistic and natural. The artist, as portrayed by Edmund Wilson, in "The Wound and the Bow," suffers and draws his strength from an injury. Philoctetes is both the "victim of a malodorous disease from a snakebite on his foot, which renders him abhorrent to society and periodically degrades him and makes him helpless," and "also the master of a superhuman art [his bow whose arrows never miss] which everybody has to respect and which the normal man finds he needs." His wound motivates society to ostracize him, but his magic bow renders him essential for victory over the Trojans. Wilson perceives him as a fusion of opposites—the organic and the divine—and as an image of the artist.[22]

Blos turns to another Greek hero, Achilles, to illustrate his concept of "residual trauma." Trauma, he writes, "is an inevitable injurious experience of the infantile period"—one of the "noxious jolts to psychological growth." Even Achilles when he is dipped as an infant into the "river Styx to fortify him against mortal injury" is not perfectly protected an invulnerable. Such physical disabilities as the heel of Achilles, the wound of Philoctetes, the blindness of Teiresias, and the clubfoot of Oedipus may represent otherwise invisible psychological trauma. This is easily agreed upon, but Blos takes the notion into a new direction. "That aspect of trauma that is never resolved or resolvable, far from being a lamentable impediment, is a universal predicament that provides a driving impetus to mastery." It "propels the late adolescent into a more or less definitive set of commitments of a personal as well as an impersonal nature."[23] The wound to the self, represented by myth through a bodily organ, becomes allied with those characterological strengths born of mastery. We have considered this in the narrower sphere of artistic creativity as the narcissistic wound that stimulates reparative, self-remaking energies, but Blos includes it in a larger sphere of natural creativity. "The residual trauma serves as an organizer which promotes the consolidation of the adult personality and accounts for its uniqueness." Philoctetes discovers by his return to the ranks of the Greek warriors, that his wound is indeed healed as prophesied (it is his arrow that slays Paris). But, presumably, healed wounds remain sensitive to the touch and in general are favored by a distinguishing limp.

The point of this apparent digression is that in the psychological sphere, the abnormal (trauma)—like the bend of light particles, the swerve of evolution into neoteny, the narcissistic blow in the artist's early years, the gaps and uncertainties of natural creativity at the triadic phase—can all be entertained as indigenous to the normal curves of our human nature—or so I think, not wanting to exempt myself from the wavering principle of uncertainty.

Better to try another tangent. If a straight line is mental and ideal, it is the geometrical equivalent to the family romance, a daydream spun of ideal lineage straight to the gods, and one aimed at correcting the felt errors of the parents that seem to have jolted one off the normal course of development. But a line that seems to err, to wander astray, is crooked. Such a line, our etymology informs us, is deformed, as in *crookback,* also *devious, knavish, tricky;* somehow of a lower descent, it stems from a wayward linguistic line including Medieval English *krok* and Old Norse *krokr*: a hook (as in a road), but also from Old French, *crochet* (hooked needle) and, so, the English *crotch,* a fork in the road, or in the body—where the genitals are located, the true progenitors of that undulating line of errant knights and lovely ladies who stoop or bend to conquer, and collectively comprise our human family.

And so what John Ruskin was implicitly preserving in those gothic gorgons and gargoyles was the rich lore of infantile sexual schema through the pagan world's intruding on, and balancing off against, the soaring spires of Christianity's family romance with God the father and Mary the virgin mother. But those grotesque figures, while expelled, were never really excluded from the total design, for like terrified children their deformity bore witness to what they had seen.

If a line *per se* arises in the area of primary creativity, it may reach to infinity and so be unbounded, grandiose, altogether perfect, pure, and endless. Add two points, and an object is visibly helping to establish the boundaries of the dyadic phase. Prometheus is now bound—until the Romantics untie him. But the fork or crotch in the crooked line is tied to the triadic. It is the point where three roads meet that Oedipus killed his father and went on to marry his mother. Did he take the right or the left, *dexter* or *sinister*, route? Since right is associated with both righteous or straight (and narrow), and left with evil, some credence may be given to a still tentative but intriguing position among some psychoanalysts that left implies incest, right its avoidance.[24]

No doubt poor Oedipus took the sinister bend in the road: by erring becoming human. In a clinical paper on "The Significance of the Trifurcation of the Road," two psychoanalysts review (male) oedipal implications of the forked road as it represents the upside-down Y and, hence, the female figure, the genitals, castration, and the figure 3—all of which have a well-established background in psychoanalytic interpretation.[25] But they also emphasize the importance of the forked road as a point of decision and, thus for so entailing the kind of uncertainty already noted as inhering in the triadic stage of natural creativity. Before its forward propulsions rises the specter of incest, blocking a dangerous drift leftward and yet not confiding that the rightward course may entail a looping back around the poles of origins.

But, like Oedipus, humankind may have found it incumbent to go left to get right, to deal with incest en route to turning onto a safer road. Out of misguided wishes for incest/parricide arises superego/civilization: to err is to become human. Oedipus has come to signify the triadic along with the tragic. Like triangle, *triad* derives from Greek *treis*, "with the sense that a third person is a witness to an interaction between two others."[26] The witness testifies, as Teiresias did against Oedipus. *Testicles*, also of the same root, testify to virility.[27] *Testis* is, accordingly, a root signifier for both witness and testicles. Teiresias lost his testicles when he bore testimony to the disguised primal scene of two love-joined snakes and, interjecting his staff where it did not belong, was converted into a woman—thus he could testify to castration—but witnessing the same scene seven years later, Teiresias was restored to his original gender—thus he/she could uniquely testify to virility (and much more). The blind seer's subsequent dramatic testimony reminds Oedipus that he, too, is a third party, testifier to the primal scene (the Sphinx), and that his virility, too, is inseparable from castration (Oedipus means "lame"). Confirming Teiresias, Oedipus blinds himself as testimony to his crimes. His self-inflicted exile immediately following enacts the final terrible and repressed meaning of the primal scene at the far end from triumphantly unriddling the mystery of origins: the child's necessary and painful exclusion from adult/parental sexuality. Leaving Thebes, blind Oedipus wanders along the right path at last: once cursed, he will end blessed.

Carl Sagan and others have connected these opposites with the governing hemispheres of the human brain: law = *le droit* = right; left = Satan = rebellion, from Latin *sinister*, and so forth.[28] It is James Joyce's evenhanded position that the artist encompasses these polarities, and so he designates *Ulysses* as a jocoserious left/right-handed work of "sinister dexterity" (not ambidexterous, which, it has been pointed out, means two right hands). The curve made by Ulysses is the equivalent of birth/departure/return: the O of Odysseus, the all-round man, as Joyce's adaptation of the Homeric *polytropon*: "that man skilled in all ways of contending, the wanderer."[29] The circle ambivalently suggests that to get right eventually one must go left initially, desire the impossible, wander off course, divagate, err, bend around. Like light.

17

The Third Birth

The assumption of responsibility for one's own life and its conduct
is in psychic reality tantamount to the murder of the parents.
—Hans Loewald

1

But surely this assumption is tantamount, as well, as to their internal
metamorphoses and eventual reconstitution as prelude to the further stage
toward which this study has been tending and may be called the individual's
third birth. Axiomatic is the notion that we are twice born. Through our
biological origins we affirm our participation in the animal kingdom and
compliance with the laws of organic maturation. Through
our second birth we instigate self-creativity and, via the family, enter
psychocultural fields of more complex development by reason of our
evolutionary swerve into neoteny. Virtually all known societies are
programmed for us to be born out of mother's body into father's world.
Surrounding these two births, a dialectics of maturation and development
with distinct but interlocking agendas is played out over a lifetime.

The second birth, among other things, conditions the direction and extent
to which one can unravel the mysteries of sexual procreation and come to
terms with oneself through origins. In ancient Egypt a child grew up amid a
rich assemblage of hieroglyphs and symbols through which he/she could
decipher origins along prescribed lines. In Christian countries one is adopted
through baptism into an desexualized heavenly family. Such as idealization
perpetuates family-romance veilings that obscure origins and foster an
unworldly attitude toward organic/instinctual processes, collectively making
a virtue out off nonpenetration. But most cultural initiations aim not so much
at reality mastery as at allaying anxiety, reducing uncertainty, and anticipating
curiosity, for almost all societies incorporate their members into a framework
based on already-arrived-at solutions to questions of origins. Presumably,
once *Homo* began to question origins, he became Oedipus, a tragic signifier
of the ambivalent consequences of such questing. In the aftermath of his
anguish, the individual pain of such discoveries has been culturally

ameliorated: despite our unquenchable curiosity, we learn from experience to repress certain questions.

The exploration of a third birth carries us beyond biology and family to culture proper. Drawing on self-creativity but exceeding the reconstituted parents, it can best be defined by the examination of certain exemplary lives, selected by no means scientifically, but in part owing to the convenience of working where abundant biographical and scholarly data are available—and in part owing to the gravitational pull of these lives on the compass needles of human possibility. The fact that they are mostly males may reflect a patriarchal hegemony in our culture, but they should not be otherwise viewed as narrowly exclusive, for I hope it is less their monopoly over gender than their portion of humanity that magnetizes our attention. This is not to say that we ever really leave gender behind or that inequity implies inevitability, much less desirability. It is mainly a culturally skewed recognition of the way things have been.

Inevitably, at this third stage of self-creation, both sexes draw on available models but in respectively different ways. The most apparent contrast is that while women participate in a predominantly male culture they may draw sustenance from distinctively female traditions (stressed, for example, in Elaine Showalter's term, *A Literature of Their Own*, and promoted in such radical feminist writings as Mary Daly's and Susan Griffin's). Women nevertheless draw on (are affected by) both male / female exemplars; whereas men are more likely to draw exclusively on male models, since they have disidentified with the female in their quest for masculine identity, for which the female exists less as model than as reward. Anaïs Nin's diaries, for example, which chart her self-creation process, may or not be valuable to other women, but they are almost totally neglected by men. On the other hand, the influence of male thinkers on women is pervasive and often profound, as instanced by Rousseau's influence on George Sand, Feuerbach's on George Eliot, Herbert Spencer's on Olive Schreiner, T. S. Eliot's on Virginia Woolf, Marx's and R. D. Laing's on Doris Lessing. Insofar as "Culture is male," as Joanna Russ once wrote,[1] it functions to support male needs for reinforcement of gender-bound identity, which the male cannot establish as well in nature or in early maternal identifications as the female can. If a female-separatist tradition encourages a version of personal evolution via the single-sex process of the female parent ("Thinking back through our mothers"),[2] so can one distinguish a distinctively male counterpart in a Nietzschean version of self-begetting—but one would not mistake his *Übermensch* scenario for a norm. More normative is the gifted individual's struggle to balance parental / self components is some new blend that fosters a cultural advance. And, rather incongruently, what operates as a spur to change in the male examples to be cited is not so much the presence of patriarchy as the absence of an actual or psychologically valid father. Culture seems to advance in certain ways when the father must be created afresh by a new generation; and when the mother is belatedly rediscovered she may be reincorporated under a male guise, as Eros for Freud, or as in our first example.

John Stuart Mill begins instructing us as to how a culture-advancing third birth may come about. Once born (1806) of his mother (whose marginal early influence was vanquished from the *Autobiography* [1873], in large part due to his wife's eager red pencil), he was twice born of his father, that is, of the man's ideas into a partriarchal world of scientific rationalism. The second paragraph affirms this lineage: "I was born ... the eldest son of James Mill."[3] Somewhere around age three, his father began tutoring him in Greek and drenched him in the classics: while the boy studied, the father wrote in the same room. John's indoctrination continued with a series of walks, during which James delivered lectures on political economy. It was during this time that the stern laws of necessity and cause-and-effect underlying Utilitarianism were imbibed. In 1823, the younger Mill writes, "my professional occupation and status for the next thirty-five years of my life, were decided by my father's obtaining for me an appointment from the East India Company, in the office of the Examiner of India Correspondence, immediately under himself" (*Autobiography*, 50). At this time his cultural models were the eighteenth-century *philosophes,* and his goals were the general improvement of the world (94). All very rational, very compliant, and most praiseworthy.

But he would awaken from all this, he writes, as from a dream. Finding himself in a "dull state of nerves in the autumn of 1826," he asks: would he be joyful were all his goals accomplished? An irrepressible and distinct *no* greeted his quandary. And with that, the foundation of his life collapsed. In the next two years of his dejection ("mental crisis"), Mill reports two events that temporarily sustained him. One was in the discovery of music; the other was in the reading of *Marmontel's Memoirs* when he came to "the passage which relates his father's death, the distressed position of the family, and the sudden inspiration by which he, then a mere boy, felt and made them feel that he would be everything to them—would supply the place of all they had lost. A vivid conception of the scene and its feelings came over me, and I was moved to tears. From this moment my burden grew lighter" (85).

In "British Fathers and Sons, 1773–1913: from Filial Submissiveness to Creativity," Howard Wolf draws attention to how "the facts of Mill's life make plausible a harbored anger against the father which could be released in this imaginative way."[4] It is, therefore, the peculiar form in which the delayed oedipal crisis was manifested: the tearful catharsis at the prospect of losing and replacing a father who did not lack feeling so much as emotional availability.

And so Mill can truthfully assert, "I never turned recreant to intellectual culture, or ceased to consider the power and practice of analysis as an essential condition both of individual and social improvement" (101). But the real changes were on a much more personal level, and they were not resolved until, two years into his malaise, he came upon the poetry of William Wordsworth. Already he had acquainted himself with Byron, but found the world-weary state of a man "who had worn out all pleasures" too much like his own; moreover, the romantic-rebel image would hardly fit. And although Wordsworth's "love of rural objects and natural objects" attracted him, Scott could do landscapes better. Wordsworth's poetry expressed, however, not mere outward beauty, but states of feeling and of thought colored by feeling, under the excitement of beauty.

> In them I seem to draw from a source of inward joy, of sympathetic and immaginative pleasure, which could be shared in by all human beings; which had no connection with struggle or imperfection, but would be made richer by every improvement in the physical or social condition of mankind. From them I seem to learn what would be the perennial sources of happiness, when all the greater evils of life shall have been removed. And I felt myself at once better and happier as I came under their influence. (89)

Wordsworth legitimized Mill's latent emotional life. "I needed to be made to feel that there was real, permanent happiness in tranquil contemplation ... in the common feelings and common destiny of human beings" (89). It may be said that Wordsworth freed Mill's feminine-passive side, or introduced the Jungian anima into his psychic mandala, or returned to him the mother who had been negated in life as she would be suppressed from his *Autobiography*.[5] The joyful tears that had accompanied the awareness of the father's death may even be seen as the inner mother, who cares and sympathizes, awakening within him and thereby enabling him to complete his internal primal scene.

But the more noticeable consequences, along with the emergence from his "habitual depression," was that he integrated a "new way of thinking," and achieved a "separation from those of my habitual companions who had not undergone a similar change" (90). In other words, something near to a new self was created out of this third birth, and it is not a superficial shift of attitude or allegiance but an apparently fundamental change arising from the depths of his being. Yet if he transformed the little "manufactured man" (93) into a feeling person who elevated sympathy and admiration to equal standing with Utilitarian principles, it came about within a limited psychic economy. In a technical sense, Mill's mechanistic cause-and-effect variety of superego was modified through the poet's validating an inherent sense of self-worth. His new ideals could then undergird his sympathy for women's rights and individual liberties. Less positively, Kowalewski's study has revealed Mill introducing emotion into the political arena but also binding his own emotional allegiance to his wife, whom he idealized as an oedipal surrogate. In the end, the inner liberation was genuine but restrictive, profound but narrow.

More to the point is Loesberg's study, which proposes several new hypotheses about Mill's life. The most radical of these is that the *Autobiography*, begun in 1853, attempted to deal with the father's death in 1836 by transposing its impact onto the mental crisis of 1826–28. Unable either to rebel outright against the father's ironclad system or to adopt an alternative one (e.g., intuition) that would better accommodate feelings and free will, Mill "opened a space in his father's psychology theory" that included a "place for self-consciousness" and inner freedom. He fills this hole with his *Autobiography*, which is at once veiled philosophy, a psychological critique of his father's Associationism, and a highly selective narrative—in sum, a record of self-creation.

Wordsworth could legitimize this self-creative process because "he too had similar experience to mine," Mill writes (90). The poet "also had felt that the first freshness of youthful enjoyment of life was not lasting . . . but had sought for compensation, and found it, in the way in which he was now teaching me to find it." These thoughts mark the juncture at which the artist's capacity for self-remaking becomes available, as exemplary act or as shared vision for others to draw on as part of their self-creation. Through Wordsworth, Mill completes himself and returns to his own mental disciplines: he does not assume the identity of a nature poet. The poet's creativity is able to nourish the thinker's natural or self-creativity because both occur in culture where the self resembles a transitional object—both preexisting and created anew. But we do not become our transitional objects: we become ourselves through them.

Culture obviously conditions the manner or mode in which this self-creation can occur at any given point in history. If Mill had lived two generations earlier, thereby predating Wordsworth, there would be no *Autobiography*—at least not one with the kind of self-creativity that could leap to us beyond its time frame. According to John Morris, no one had quite written about the inner life of the self before Wordsworth attempted *The Prelude*.[6] Far from being valued for its own sake, private experience was seen in Samuel Johnson's time as a likely source of error and an easy refuge for the intellectual scoundrel, even though Boswell viewed him as subject to hypochondria, "dejection, gloom, and despair, which made existence misery."[7] Such a crisis of despondency then might acquire significance as a precursor to religious conversion, as was the case for Johnson, who left the work of self-creation up to his Creator and to his dedicated biographer. But Wordsworth and Mill learned through their crises and the insights gained therefrom that the "world and life had meaning only in their experience of it, and that depended on the vigor of the self." The self could die, taking the world with it, and recovery would then be a "rebirth to a new world."[8]

Although the crusading journalist Harriet Martineau (1802–76) found Mill "overrated" and his changeability a deplorable weakness, she was an exact contemporary whose autobiography records a nearly diametrically opposite movement.[9] Though born into an enlightened family of radical, dissenting Unitarians, she describes a grim childhood surrounded by compulsively dutiful readers at home and an overzealous nurse, whose training turned her into a "absurd little preacher," eagerly soliciting and copying down moralistic maxims.[10] Her secular salvation came through Necessitarianism and Comtian Positivism—an ostensibly objective view of behavior according to due cause and effect, uncannily similar to the Rationalism the younger Mill spurned in the elder. Unhappily resigned to religious doctrines of divine Providence as accounting for human hardship and evil, she encounters at twenty the "doctrine of Necessity," and undergoes a profound emotional and intellectual conversion:

> The moral effect of this process was most salutary and cheering. From the time when I became convinced of the certainty of the action of laws, of the true importance of good influences and good habits, of the firmness, in short, of the ground I was treading, and of the security of the results which I should take the right means to attain, a new vigour pervaded my whole life, a new light spread through my mind, and I began to experience a steady growth in self-command, courage, and consequent integrity and disinterestedness. ... Life also was like something fresh and wonderfully interesting. (*Autobiography,* vol. 1, 109–10)

That Martineau construed Mill's changes not only as weak but also as unmanly is clear from her complaint that "he was deplorably weak in judgment, with the weakness, so damaging to a man, of being as impressionable as a woman."[11] Whatever else this remarkable attitude from a feminist who never married suggests, one can at least infer that her self-creation entailed the implantation of masculine traits. Thus, when Peterman notes that the *Autobiography* achieves "an evenness of tone and almost scientific detachment," the work may be "revolutionary" stemming from a woman's hand but, of course, also from being measured by nineteenth-century male norms.[12]

More comparable to Mill, Aurore Dupin (George Sand) in her *Histoire de ma vie* (1854–55) re-creates her origins from the male side, linking her paternal relatives "and thus herself, firmly to France and French history."[13] Moreover, Sand not only rewrites the letters of the father she lost at four, but also, according to Crecelius, "substitutes her words for his" and thus recreates him "according to her own image of him, indeed according to her self-image as well."[14] This "dashing, distant" military figure becomes the source both of her family romance, which she keeps more within the original family than do most artists, and of her identity. In thus overcoming loss by creating her self through an ideal father, she exercises a blend of natural and artistic creativity. As Crecelius remarks, in Sand's making her father "*le véritable auteur de l'histoire de ma vie,*" she is making his story hers and claiming him to authorize her life as an author.[15] Just as her family romance is contained within the family, so the "novels are built on incestuous, or at the very least overdetermined, relationships, where cousins intermarry, husbands are viewed more as fathers, and characters use *brother, sister, mother, son* as terms of endearment," which are more properly oedipal scenarios than family romances.[16]

2

Less dramatic and less documented cases of self-creation occur throughout the nineteenth-century, not without excesses and negative consequences, such as when, during the earlier *Sturm und Drang* period, more than one sensitive young reader of Goethe's *Sufferings of Young Werther* fatally recreated himself in that hero's image and ended his life. Still under the spell of romantic revolt, young men later in the century fashioned themselves after Ibsen's sexually blighted Oswald in *Ghosts*. But in England the two most interesting variations on the Mill pattern are Edmund Gosse (1849–1928) and Samuel Butler (1835–1902), who recorded their mental crises in eloquent auto-biographies. Both also detail the castastrophic effect of Darwinian ideas on clerical families and the price exacted on their children. Although highly gifted in language, neither of these authors became major creative writers, as, in the next generation, would another pair of young men, Lawrence and Joyce, whom the former influenced. But Gosse and Butler, while not plunging as deeply into fantasy as the artist, further legitimized the important task of self-remaking for those who would take a "human being's privilege to fashion his inner life for himself."[17]

Gosse's natural creativity threads its way through a pair of images: the sea and the tower. His father's character dangerously blended a marine zoologist with a Plymouth brother. So fundamentalist a sect was his that when he duly wrote his anti-Darwin tract favoring the "fixity of the species" over their mutability, its contemptuous reception left him so bitter and depressed that he never fully recovered. Gosse's mother was a fervent puritan who died while he was small but whose injunctions against such worldly pleasures as reading novels were transmitted posthumously through her husband. Gosse found himself in his father's eyes hardly a flesh-and-blood creature at all, but rather "a sapling in the Lord's vineyard" (*Father and Son*, 25), "the child of many prayers" (212), and an "*âme d'élite*, a being to whom the mysteries of salvation had been divinely revealed and by whom they had been accepted" (108). After his momentous public baptism, the central event of his childhood (129), father and son alike expected momentarily to be wafted into heaven. But as Linda Peterson's reading reveals, Gosse's narrative employs parody to protect and distance him from the parents' religious excesses.[18] In fact, during the several years between his father's bereavement and his securing a second wife, young Edmund was treated as a substitute spouse—hence his recourse to imagery of trapped maidens in lonely towers.

His education at his father's hands was relentlessly religious, for the fanatical churchman "did not observe the value of negative education, that is to say, of leaving Nature alone to fill up the gaps which it is her design to deal with at a later and riper date" (64). His father, like a jealous god, would usurp the feminine role as well as perform the masculine one.[19]

But the gaps through which a separate self might be created appeared all the same—even helped along by the father's love for the sea and perhaps by some unacknowledged germ of paganism buried in him. "My great desire," writes Edmund of his Devonshire boyhood, "was to walk out over the sea as far as I could and then lie flat on it, face downwards, and peer into its depths" (73). This inchoate curiosity and absorption with the unknown was gratified in his eleventh year. He was anxiously questioning his father about the Caribbean Islands, when the man, "by an indulgent act for the caprice of which I cannot wholly account, presently let in a flood of imaginative light" (141). He took down a book from atop the bookcase a "wild masterpiece" called *Tom Cringle's Log,* with a "glow and gust of life through the romance from beginning to end which was nothing if it was not resolutely pagan." The sea became alive as a sort of text of another life beyond his own, one filled with "long adventures, fighting and escapes, sudden storms without and mutinies within ... upon the fiery blue," over which he, too, might escape (143). For he saw himself at this time as an imprisoned maiden. "My soul was shut up, like Fatima, in a tower" (144) where it (or she) might otherwise have starved without that "picaresque romance," which became a "window" and a "telescope." The shift via the images of sea and tower indicates an important transition from a regressive downward peering to an outward scanning. Moreover, he began to see with an imaginative vision in opposition to his father, whose "very absence of imagination" aided him in his zoological collecting and observing.

Having already clung to a "hard rut of individuality deep down in my childish nature" (140), the youth now began to nourish a second self, which would be encouraged by the reading of Shakespeare and the Elizabethans, by pictures of Greek gods and the romantics, until he could eventually rescue himself by escaping to London and fashioning his own "inner life." Yet he was not so free of his father or his times to embrace such outspoken moderns as Joyce, whose talent he nonetheless foster-fathered.[20]

Richard Ellmann has shown how the world of Renaissance art and architecture enabled the Victorian scholar John Ruskin to re-create his origins and inspire a movement in tune with the cataclysmic fall of Venice, which he somewhat capriciously assigned to 8 May 1418: "four hundred years to the day before his own conception—the act so impossible for him to meditate on with equanimity."[21] It marked the fall of the medieval Madonna and the rise of Pre-Raphaelite fantasy, a family romance whose purity could not survive the act of begetting. Renaissance architecture stemmed from a "state of concealed national infidelity, and of domestic corruption," he wrote in the *The Crown of Wild Olive.* Ruskin, in effect, reshapes his cultural environment to accommodate his origins, as Pope shaped his garden. In later attempts at a "revision of his character," according to Ellmann, Ruskin would recognize a robust masculine element in art. But other repressed conflicts were to return as symptoms. In a forthcoming study, Laurie Schneider examines the trial that grew out of Ruskin's harsh strictures against the flamboyant dandy, Whistler, as a neurotic conflict in which each defended himself by attacking unacceptable traits projected onto the other. And although the two exhibited antithetical life-styles, their underlying attitudes to painting were similar.[22] Ruskin painted with words, while Whistler libidinized the creative process by portraying color as a "bold whore" unless controlled by a firm, masculine line. Such blending and balancing of male and female elements apparently allowed him to synthesize the primal scene along aesthetic lines. Significantly, it was his painting *Fireworks on the Thames* that drew Ruskin's ire and his overdetermined response. Schneider refers to numerous primal-scene fantasies that grew to delusional proportions as Ruskin slipped toward insanity in his last years. Most frightening were images of darkness, especially a storm cloud threatening England, associated in Ruskin's mind with going blind (like his mother) and losing his faculties. Thus in his prepsychotic state, Ruskin may have responded to Whistler's painting as a violation of his own taboos against viewing and depicting the primal scene. In the end we are faced with the paradox that as he slipped into madness his third birth was a posthumous child: the Pre-Raphaelite Brotherhood.

Having begun with an artificial reproduction of the Frankenstein monster, the nineteenth-century's fascination with demonic will and self-creation culminated in Nietzsche's vision of Zarathustra, a profoundly destabilizing figure beyond good and evil, a prophet who mocks his role, a philosopher's bachelor daydream of sexual self-sufficiency. Though Nietzsche found his creation such a difficult act to follow that he went mad instead, a later generation would drag the unlikely *Übermensch* into a fascist nightmare from which we are still awakening.

3

Arriving at the end of the nineteenth century and devoting his life to an analytic mode of self-remaking, Freud initiated a revolution while drawing on such cultural predispositions as Romantic subjectivity, nineteenth-century philosophy, and Darwinism. From today's vantage point, however, his originality produces a reverse effect as the step-by-step progression of psychoanalytic techniques are being recapitulated in the modern psychotherapy movement. Thus his early experiments with cocaine, his study of hypnosis, and especially his provisional acceptance of cathartic experience are revived in more sophisticated forms as hynotherapy, guided fantasy, the abreactions of gestalt therapy and the primal-scream techniques of Arthur Janov. Where these "new" therapies fail to take into consideration Freud's emphasis on resistance, transference/countertransference reactions, and the arduous process of working through unconscious conflict, they drift away from his revolution. Along with neo-Freudians and other revisionists, they fail the Harold Bloom test to resolve their "anxiety of influence" dilemmas and, hence, represent, in the view of historian Russell Jacoby, a reversion to conformist psychology.[23] Indeed Freud anticipated the cultural revisionists and humanists to come when he wrote in reply to Ludwig Benswanger's wish that psychoanalysts be supplemented by contributions from philosophy and religion. The "most cultivated types of homo natura think" that one need merely change "one's viewpoint" to see the upper stories and desert the ground floor and basement, but "in that," Freud concluded, "you are the conservative, I am the revolutionary."[24]

In any case, a distinction should be upheld between the opportunities for self-making via psychoanalysis and those via some form of psychotherapy or corrective emotional experience. The goal of therapy is to heal and may cease with symptom alleviation; a corrective emotional experience often involves only the internalizing of healthy elements from the therapist (a new, improved model of the original superego). But as analysis, therapy, or corrective experience, the field of mental health encompasses at least overlapping areas and countless gradations of self-creation.

Freud's own self-creativity, which he once addressed as an intention to "mould himself into a 'new species of himself,' "[25] draws on all three stages of natural creativity and carries them forward to a third birth. In the area of the self it plays off against four nodal points or archetypes: like Faust, he was driven to discover answers even if it meant a liaison with powers from the underworld; like Oedipus, he tragically uncovered the fate of instinctual drives in the infantile period and suffered the guilt of taboo violation; like Leonardo, he sublimated the greater part of his libido into an urge for research and balanced his interests in art and science; and, like Moses, he became the Sinai lawgiver of a new ethos and the Pisgah visionary of a promised land beyond the bondage of the id and the domination of the superego.[26] There is ample evidence that Freud treated Leonardo and Moses and self-objects in his studies of them and in the self-defining aspects of creating himself. "Much of what Freud said when he penetrated into Leonardo's personality," writes Jones, "was at the same time a self-description."[27] The Faustian urge tended to blend with his self-representation as one of the *conquistadores,* while the identification with Oedipus had multiple unconcious roots. When his adherents presented him on his fiftieth birthday with a medallion of Oedipus solving the Sphinx's riddle, he became quite agitated. The Greek inscription, *Who divined the famed riddle and was a man most mighty*, was identical to what he had imagined, as an adolescent walking the court of the University of Vienna, would someday be inscribed under his own bust. One who, like Oedipus, solves the riddle of origins becomes the tragic hero in experiencing guilt—not for doing but for knowing. By discovering the oedipal son within, he creates himself as father of the Oedipus complex.

If, as we have seen, Freud also managed both to play out variations on a family romance and to penetrate its meaning, his early analytic sessions placed human origins in a new light: in effect, he verbally reproduced sexual scenes with his patients on the couch in order to understand the meanings of the primal scene as one of the major disturbances of childhood. These fertile collaborations became, in turn the primal scene, delivery room, and nursery for a new body of thought: psychoanalysis. He first began using the term *Urszenen* in 1897 to specify original instances of infantile trauma "which are organized into scenarios or scenes," but did not restrict the term to the child's exposure to parental sexual activity until the Wolf Man case twenty-one years later. [28] In his later writings, he considered the original psychic event to be as elusive as the headwaters of the Nile.

As spiritual father of the modern psyche, he, too, would recede from center stage. In his *Autobiographical Study* (1925), it is the fledgling movement he founded that commands our attention. For Freud, as Ernest Jones more than hints, this offspring must be protected by those trustees into whose hands it was passing lest if suffer the fate of Freud's younger sibling Julius, whose untimely death Freud feared came about through his fantasy attacks against the child still in the womb.[29] If Freud accomplished the third birth via natural creativity that has been discussed here, it was of himself as the first psychoanalyst or oedipal parent, and then in collaboration with his patients and early disciples as parent of the psychoanalytic movement. By uniquely drawing on his patients to establish the primal scene, he was able to understand its central import in human development. Curiously and coincidentally, at the same time he was grappling with their *Urszenen* he was experiencing his somewhat overstated "splendid isolation," comprised of obscurity and exclusion from the respectable ranks of his profession; in his chapter, "The Myth of the Hero in the Psychoanalytic Movement," Sullowey shows how he fitted his own heroic fantasies to a family romance mode.[30] These evidently reinforced his masculine sense of identity as the defiant hero of his celebrated epigraph to *The Interpretation of Dreams* (1900): "If I cannot bend the gods, / I will stir up Acheron" (*Aeneid* 7, 312). And they may well have paved the way for him to assume the fatherly role of adopting a new generation of sons (and a few daughters) into his growing movement. But as Louis Breger has also shown, Freud "struggled free from the male-centered perspective" toward a belated acceptance of Eros as a "referent for mother-love, for suppressed femininity, for sexuality, for the female-maternal principle." With Eros on the side of civilization, whose real enemy is aggression, certain "depreciated feminine qualities have received a new valuation" in Freud's later work.[31] Such corrective labors may have arisen from the rebalancing of his own internal primal scene.

It is thus possible to observe the three steps in Freud's natural creativity. His dreambook was completed only after he succeeded in the analysis of his own dreams—call it primary creativity in the area of the self. His four archetypal identifications, reinforced by his heroic image of lonely defiance, also belong in this area. About the role of his mentor and alter ego, Wilhelm Fliess, the Berlin nose-and-throat specialist with whom he shared many private "congresses" as well as his path-breaking ideas, much has been written, notably by Heinz Kohut, who sees him functioning for Freud via an idealizing transference (or, one could infer, following Winnicott, via a holding environment or transitional object).[32] In any case, this unlikely midwife to a movement and exalted partner in Freud's scientific development best exemplies natural creativity in the dyadic sphere; the illusory aspect of the relationship was evident when the two soon permanently drew apart. More enduring collaborations with his patients in extracting workable hypotheses about unconscious processes mark an advance into the triadic sphere. There, I have suggested, a symbolic primal scene was enacted in the dual quest for origins of conflict and origins of mind that converged in psychoanalysis.

A promising tangent to the innovative projects of psychoanalysis points to the manner in which its practioners-to-be, during their training analyses, may also re-create themselves in the images of their founder. While Freud has been designated as history's most analyzed person, thus presuming a continual breaking down and assimilation of both his thought and his personality, he may nevertheless loom as a potent image in the analyst's mind rather than be conceptualized as the analytic ideal. One sometimes encounters among analysts attempts to trace a line of apostolic succession leading via family romance pathways all the way to the primal scene of psychoanalysis at 33 Bergrasse, in old Vienna.

Thus, in this latter-day Genesis, Freud analyzed Ferenczi, who analyzed Melanie Klein, who supervised Donald Winnicott, and so forth. Hence the conflict of legitimacy between object-relations and ego-psychology. For on the other side, Erik Erikson was analyzed by Anna Freud, who was analyzed by her father. The bone of contention between the two wings became, not surprisingly, the question of child analysis. Miss Freud said no; Mrs. Klein, yes. But the deeper dispute was over the "true heir of Freud."[33] In a different context, Erikson himself was taken to task in the *New York Times* literary pages for suppressing his Jewish origins and re-creating himself along more acceptable American gentile lines. Likewise, Helene Deutsch has been criticized by feminists for too thoroughly identifying with a masculine bias in the field, presumably due to her merger with the primal father, Freud. The danger of a one-sidedly partriarchal descent is evident in the autobiographical account given by Robert Jay Lifton in *The Life of the Self* (1976). In reviewing his origins he refers to his first-generation parents, but, like John Stuart Mill, elides his mother from the account. He turns to the role of his father's "myth of American emergence"; the "father-son conflict"; his initiation into male-dominated psychiatry, which leads to protracted discussions in order to trace his lineage through Freud and Erik Erikson and to assert his separateness from them as if his very interesting work on symbolic immortality had somehow brought psychiatry to a third stage, which he alone had parented.[34]

If on the one hand, then, Freud's legacy is the exalted father image of the family romance (an analytic commonplace), the analyst may also look upon treatment as, in Jacob Arlow's words, a "prolonged initiation into sexual knowledge by a knowing, benevolent adult figure."[35] Recalling the emotional issues of exclusion / inclusion as stemming from primal-scene phenomena, we can see that for the analyst, the practice of psychoanalysis offers a resolution (which must be worked through) and that for the analysand the psychoanalytic situation also offers an opportunity for resolution. Inexorably, as the family romance will lead to the primal scene, there duly occurs in analysis a criss-crossing of the same poles that have proven so propitious for the study of creativity. Even though the respective goals of the creative process and the analytic process may not coincide, they do complement and overlap. Exposure to one process is likely to stimulate the self-creative energies of the other. The discovery of Freud in early modern times by, so to speak, uninitiated readers would often prove as efficacious as Mill's discovery of Wordsworth had been: an entirely new but strangely familiar inner world is revealed, new identifications are formed, Psychological Man is constituted.[37]

4

The publication of solid biographical and psychoanalytic work on Jean-Paul Sartre (1905–1980) along with his childhood memoir makes it possible to glimpse the threefold operations of natural creativity in this prodigious philosopher, artist, and biographer.[38] The conditions of Sartre's origins enlist the resources of natural creativity while also putting its theories to the test. The first condition, an existential one, was the father's death during his own infancy; the second, more psychological, was the relative indifference of the young woman who bore him to fulfilling the mother's role; the third, more cultural, was his human emergence via the formidable family library and the presence of his very literary grandfather.

The existential crisis is figured in a flippant sentence: "In 1905, at Cherbourg the young naval officer, who was already wasting away with the fevers of Cochin-China, made the aquaintance of Anne Marie Schweitzer, took possession of the big forlorn girl, married, begot a child in quick time, me, and sought refuge in death."[39] Promptly, his mother's milk dried up, and he was put out to nurse, nearly dying of enteritis himself. How, under such unpropitious circumstances, is a child to create his mother, his father, and himself?

For soon the young widow became a "minor again, a stainless virgin." He and his mother are the "children" in his grandparents' home. "A young girl's bed has been put into my room. The girl sleeps alone and awakens chastely. I am still sleeping when she hurries to the bathroom to take her 'tub.' She comes back all dressed. How could I have been born of her?" (*Words*, 11–13). Moreover, her *eau de cologne* rubdowns must have encoded certain messages;

in any case he absorbs her troubles and promises "to marry her to protect her." But her own remarriage occurs just beyond the closing pages of *The Words*, and neither paradise lost not paradise regained is ever written.

Extrapolating from Sartre's philosophical texts, Douglas Kirsner finds they represent themes derived from difficulties in the early oral period. "Commitment means engulfment. The self as shell remains by not being engulfed, for neither symbiosis nor aloneness is a viable alternative." In *Being and Nothingness*, "all human relationships are seen as being of a "mutual devouring kind," as in this passage: "While I attempt to free myself from the Other, the Other's trying to free himself; while I seek to enslave the Other, the Other seeks to enslave me"[40] The child's primitive oral anxiety over devouring the breast, thus destroying the object and being destroyed in turn, is so strong that relatedness as such becomes dangerous, if unavoidable. For good reason, then, in *No Exit* is hell "other people." But others only menace a self uninhabited by valid value systems in ways that his own was uncontained by a father; yet the existential self must still attempt to create itself through significant action. For if personal commitment threatens self-abnegation, political commitment promises self-liberation.

But political solutions to personal dilemmas may not avail if drive development is thwarted, basic trust impaired, splitting persists, and the mother is created less as a whole person than as a phantom sister:

> At about the age of ten, I read with pleasure *Les Transatlantiques*, which tells about a little American boy and his sister, both of them very innocent. I identified myself with the boy, and through him loved Biddy, the little girl. I thought for a long time of writing a story about two lost children who were discreetly incestuous. Traces of this fantasy can be found in my writings: Orestes and Electra in *The Flies*, Boris and Ivich in *The Paths of Freedom*, Frantz and Leni in [*The Condemned of*] *Altona*. The last-named are the only ones who go the whole way. What attracted me about this family bond was not so much the amorous temptation as the taboo against making love: fire and ice, mingled delight and frustration; I liked incest if it remained platonic. (*Words*, 34)[41]

To cast himself and his mother-sister in the exalted roles of Orestes and Electra suggests a family-romance style polarizing of the creative process; but although Sartre has left behind at least three memorable creative works (*Nausea, The Flies, No Exit*), he tended to abandon this side of his genius before he fully parented it. At the beginning of his ninth year, he thrived in a family-romance ambience that allowed him to be both "a prince and a shoemaker" (130), but while he could not maintain the magic of this other self, he did enjoy the magic off his young mother's companionship. Perhaps his mother, whose virginity he reinscribed, permitted an approximate living out of the fantasy and lessened a polarizing of origins in the objective primal-scene mode. If so, the urge toward mastery on which creativity draws would be reduced or offset in his possibly shared fantasy of being his mother's lover, kissing her, and sharing her bed like other bonafide lovers, at least until his thoughts reached an impasse: "I knew nothing more, but beneath the luminous surface of the idea I sensed a hairy mass" (34).

By a similarly oblique sexual curiosity, he is drawn to books as "boxes which split open like oysters, and I would see the nudity of their inner organs, pale, fusty leaves, slightly bloated, covered with black veinlets, which drank ink and smelled of mushrooms" (26). He acquires two books and places them on his mother's lap, ignorant as to their potent contents. She reads, and the sentences emerge like centipedes, the sounds swarm and vibrate through him. He quickly masters the alphabet and ability to read. So doing, he is born into a new world, asserting, "I began my life as I shall no doubt end it: amidst books" (25). If his first books were female sexuality caught in a text, his grandfather's "library was the world caught in a mirror" (31). In books he "encountered the universe: assimilated, classified, labeled, pondered" (32). Books were his transitional objects, they preexisted, yet passed through mother's lips: real, yet packed with illusion; they were his to possess, to mold, to enter the world of culture by ("the playing at culture cultivated me in the long run"), and, so, finally were they there to mold him.

The emphasis has shifted from the early dyadic sphere to primary creativity within the self. Before words were to become the building blocks of his self, he enjoys a privileged status within the family. His childish remarks are repeated and made to sound grown-up. He is a prodigy. He clowns, and his clowning becomes generosity. He draws himself out of "nothingness" and assumes the "disguise of childhood so as to give" a childless couple the "illusion of having a child" (19). He is hidden in a room to surprise his grandfather and "do him the favor of being born." He need not love and so knows nothing of hating. "Suis-je donc un Narcisse?" ("Am I therefore a Narcissus? Not even that. Too eager to charm, I forget myself") (25). "Je ne casse de me creer; je suis le donateur et la donation" ("I keep creating myself, I am the giver and the gift") (20). With reading, his imagination creates himself where his body left off. After a while he becomes too good at it: "I faked," he confesses, regarding his celebrated feats in the library: "I would spring to my feet, put Musset back in his place and standing on tip-toe, would immediately take down the heavy Corneille" (44).

Commenting on the darker side of these performances, Kirsner writes, "He was treated as a doll, a cute exhibition piece, an object—but never as a worthwhile person in his own right who had real and valid feelings of his own. The young Sartre's internal reality was systematically invalidated: his being became his being-for-others. Sartre felt his true self to be in the hands of the adults. Feeling empty, he was an impostor playing the part he understood was expected of him by adults."[42]

Thus the inner creation of the self has become problematic, just as the early tie with mother had left its ambivalence toward others. And the narcissistic issues would be settled in a singularly Sartrean manner: "I found myself by opposing myself" (71). Issues are even more complex at the triadic stage, where there is no father to murder and create, no surviving sign of male influence in his origins: "Rather than the son of a dead man, I was given to understand that I was a child of miracle" (12). Had he lived, his father would "have lain on me at full length and would have crushed me" (11). As it is, his father is "not even a shadow, not even a gaze" (12). Lacking a father, he believes he also lacks a superego. "I knew nothing of violence and hatred; I was spared the hard apprenticeship of jealousy. Not having been bruised by its sharp angles, I knew reality only by its bright unsubstantiality" (16). Against whom should he rebel? From whom should he acquire rules, duties? His grandfather is but a benign patriarch beaming down on a cloudless paradise.

Self-opposing strategies notwithstanding, the child must create a progenitor to generate himself. He would attempt this in the transitional sphere, where he was already creating a world for himself through the mirrors of words in books. He would author himself. Thus the ultimate triumph in his threefold writing career may be as biographer, though of whom is not always evident. His study of the blighted nineteenth-century poet and dandy Baudelaire, appears in 1950. As the poet had lost his mother at seven to a second marriage four years before Sartre had similarly lost his, "a loss from which he [Sartre] never fully recovered,"[43] the narcissistic-injury spur to creativity also sheds light on the choice of biographical subject. As Hayman comments, Sartre's biographies are best (if not truest) when written autobiographically.[44] There follows the absorption in the perverse bastard and inspired playwright Jean Genet, who created himself by accepting the identity (thief, criminal) assigned him by others. In 1963, Sartre more directly essays to create himself by re-creating his childhood in *The Words*. But it is in the final volumes on Flaubert that the processes of self-creativity most reveal themselves. Flaubert is a carefully chosen subject. "Sartre has had a life-long obsession with Flaubert whom he sees as opposing everything he himself holds, yet who bears so many similarities to Sartre that he may well represent Sartre's alter ego."[45]

Being both like him and unlike him, and so both subjective and objective, Flaubert resembles the Sartrean self and the male parent; he is, in effect, a self-object, preexisting yet amenable to reshaping. Both cultural father and familial son, Flaubert is also the consubstantial unity between the two, the Holy Ghost in a trinity not unlike the one outlined by Joyce between Stephen and Bloom in *Ulysses*. In reconstituting himself through Flaubert, Sartre achieves both brilliantly objective insights and perpetrates jarringly subjective distortions. He corrects his own childhood of bourgeois compliance, redesigns Flaubert's father after his own grandfather, and accuses Flaubert's mother of wanting the girl-child his own mother desired.[46] If Flaubert's fiction was as he claimed, "the response to a deep and always hidden wound," Sartre will joyfully "take up the challenge"—not of discovering the wound but of healing his own childhood afflictions.[47] He loses his eyesight if not his way, and instead of creating himself as an artist, he ends creating himself through an artist.

His greater accomplishment is that in the process of fathering himself he has succeeded—if not exactly in fathering a modern movement, as Freud did— then in midwifing and legitimizing a distinctive modern consciousness inform- ing us that as history's orphans we are condemned to father ourselves by creating our own freedom to be. Such is the emotional underpinning of a paradoxical philosophy predicated on: "I am *abandoned* in the world" and am "responsible for everything."[48] In a universe lacking parenthood, man is condemned to adopt himself.

A neat trick, to be sure, but now part of our basic human repertoire. Extrapolating from these examples, it appears that the third birth does not so much signify creating oneself through culture as creating culture through oneself—and often despite oneself.

The other major strand of French Existentialism is also knotted around the problematic place of the female when the murderous antihero finds he is being condemned not for killing an Arab but for lacking mother love. In his first important novel, *The Stranger* (1942), Albert Camus (1913–1960) creates a self without the internalized father that normally forms the psychic agency Freud designated superego. Meursault is a stranger to the pious and hypocritical mores of a society that can overlook his act of gratuitous murder yet strangely enough will not forgive his indecorous behavior at his mother's funeral. But Meursault is also a stranger to his own feelings, fantasies, and destructive impulses. His withdrawal of affect, aimless eroticism, emptiness, and susceptibility to explosive rage, as when he shoots an Arab on the beach, combine to form one of the most compelling portraits in modern literature of what psychiatry has encoded as the borderline personality.[49]

Conceivably, Meursault's superego deficiencies predispose him to act out the oedipal crisis by killing a symbolic rival, forcing society to impose its sentence of execution by guillotine as the ultimate act of castration, affirming his guilt and, by implication, his humanity, which indeed emerges only after his sentencing. The trial also allows for his more primitive aggressions associated with hostility toward the mother to be aired, and, as the novel strongly implies, it is for his symbolic matricidal behavior (smoking and joking at her wake, going out with Marie) that he is being punished—anyone might kill an Arab, but the sacred maternal ties are inviolable. In Julian Stamm's psychoanalytic reading of the text,[50] the Arab's murder stems from a "homosexual struggle," while Charles Hofling emphasizes the displacement of rage against the girlfriend, Marie, onto the Arab: "Meursault kills the Arab- mother to avoid killing Marie-mother (although the Marie relationship is also killed by the act.)"[51] Slochower claims that Meursault's "surface indifference toward his mother constitutes symbolic matricide."[52] Clearly both deeds are overdetermined, and these various readings could be reconciled by evoking the clinical profile of the borderline personality.

But the present more modest purpose is to examine the biographical connections between the existential artist and the existential character. Obviously Camus is not to be equated with either his antihero or with psychiatry's borderline personality. Yet Hofling has noted that in Camus's mother's absence from home, in her incommunicativeness (she was partly deaf and had a speech disorder), and in his grandmother's cruelty "one finds reasons" for Meursault's "deep hostility toward women."[53] Moreover, Camus's mother had a lover, and when her son was a young man residing in the vicinity, she was attacked by an Arab. That this early work is deeply personal is further evidenced by Camus's having earlier adopted the pen name of "Meursault" and placed Meursault's living quarters on his own street in Algiers.

As a self-character and as containing much of the author's emotional autobiography, Meursault tells us that Camus was intimately involved in the self-remaking process of creativity. His earliest attempts to deal with his childhood appear in the essays published in *L'Envers et L'Endroit* (1937), but as his biographer notes, "he would attempt to deal with his family's specific dramas again and again, and he still hadn't finished the job at the time of his death."[54] He had, in fact, written the first part of an ambitious novel that aspired to give definitive form to the world of his origins and childhood. It was to be called *Le Premier Homme* (*The First Man*).

If it was tragic for Camus to have been killed in an automobile accident en route to Paris with the first 175 pages of this project in manuscript form and to be prevented by destiny from completing his life task of self-creation through literature, the tragedy is compounded by events at the beginning of his life. For the first man in Camus's own life, whom his last work essayed to revive, namely his own father, was killed in the Battle of the Marne when Albert was not yet a year old.

Camus's existentialism, as well as the direction of his self-creation, then, owes as much as did Sartre's to the condition of fatherlessness. While lacking the narcissistic props of a luscious young mother and a doting grandfather, Camus did grow up in an extended family with an adequate male adult on hand, his maternal uncle, Etienne, who worked as a barrel maker. Moreover, the child's charm and brightness was not lost on his teachers, and the harshness of his poverty was somewhat softened as he entered school and after a bout with tuberculosis at seventeen decisively turned toward the life of letters. Otherwise, the parallels between the two outstanding existentialists is indeed intriguing.

There is another irony springing from Camus's painful origins and premature death. It has to do with his lack of success in learning about his father's side of the family, despite several attempts and despite the relatively easy time his biographer had with the same task. Could Camus, who was something of a womanizer, have been hindered by ambivalence about his quest? Was his writing and the continuation of his self-creating labors predicated on *not* coming to terms with paternity, especially its internal features of prohibitive superego?

In any case, the son's felt deficiencies in the mother relation and his own physical illness (from which he never completely recovered) would readily have served as motivators for the self-healing and restorative processes of creative work, while the absence of the father set the stage for the existential direction of the content. The image of the self as stranger is closely enough allied to orphan/foundling fantasies to evoke a distinctively existential family romance. As a youth Camus had been "particularly struck by one phrase" from a book by his early mentor, Grenier: "I have often dreamed of arriving alone in a strange city, alone and stripped of everything. I should have lived humbly, even miserably. Above all I should have kept the secret"—the secret, that is, of his true identity, perhaps of his noble parentage or divine parentage, for the echoes are messianic: "he came unto his own, and his own received him not."[55] But the fantasy yields, along with Sartre's royal sibling-orphans, to the more courageous creation of the human condition as one of fatherlessness.

5

If any of Sartre's contemporaries could have been more immersed in language than Camus, it would have to be Roland Barthes, the father of modern semiology, who had for many years dwelt in compliant opposition to the signs and mythologies of contemporary speech, until an automobile accident in the spring of 1980 tragically removed him from both literature and life (see chapter 4). Like Camus and especially like Sartre, Barthes never knew his father (who was a World War I casualty), and he similarly complains: "no father to kill, no family to hate, no milieu to reject: a great oedipal frustration!"[56] Hence, a Laius in language must be created, for, as he told a biographer, an "Oedipus with no Laius to kill will invent one." It will be the inimical put impersonal "doxa" of popular opinion, the "petit bourgeois consensus," whose clichés and rigidly held stereotypes would find their home in Flaubert's *Dictionnaire des idées reçues* (in *Bouvard et Pecuchet*, 1881). Writing becomes a mode of cultural alignment via studies of Racine and Balzac but mostly a vehicle of self-creation: "I am writing a text, and I call it R. B." *Roland Barthes by Roland Barthes*, drawn in part, as has been seen, from his family album adapted as his "image-repertoire" or "phantasmic," abolishes the referent and fuses the signifier with the signified: "I myself am my own symbol, I am the story which happens to me: freewheeling in language, I have nothing to compare myself to."

Somewhere, however, in this dazzling tautology is the recognition that with no father as model, rival, or other, there can be no origins quest, no Sphinx, ultimately no arrative: "If there is no longer a Father, why tell stories? Doesn't every narrative lead back to Oedipus?"[57] If one cannot find oneself through creating fictional tales, one must invoke a different strategy, devise another kind of analogy, and eventually succumb to the Lacanian model of the mirroring process as his mode: "through the Mother, present next to the Mirror" emerges in its new form: through the author, present next to his text.

Yet such a beguiling modernist strategy as this honors a great French tradition dating from Montaigne, who launched his *Essays* (1580) proclaiming, "je suis moy-mesmes la matière de mon livre" (I myself am the subject my book). Such self-conscious writing Barthes called *"la flaubertisation de l'écriture"*[58] (The Flaubertisation of literature).

And indeed, Flaubert, who did not lose his father until well into his twenties yet never became one himself, portrayed his self-development in the several versions of *A Sentimental Education* (1869) and pitted himself against bourgeois values no less fervently than Sartre or Barthes. Flaubert did not marry, withdrawing from active life and living with his mother (as did Barthes, while Sartre had Simone) from the time of her widowing until her death. Flaubert also strived to heal his "deep and always hidden wound" by creating himself through language. "My active, passionate, emotional life, full of contradictory movements and multiple feelings, ended at age 22," so he wrote his mistress, Louise Colet: "The one who is alive now and is me does nothing but contemplate the other who is dead." In his adolescent diary he wrote that writing is the "process of feeling one's thought being born, growing up, living and raising itself up on its pedestal and remaining there always!"[59] And years later he aspired to write "a book about nothing, a book dependent on nothing external, which would be held together by the internal strength of its style," as gravity holds together the earth suspended in a void. Since *le style est l'homme*, such an enterprise would conflate subject with object and so realize the self in its purest form: *"l'écrivain ne doit laisser de lui que ses oeuvres"* ("the writer should leave nothing of himself but his works").[60] Barthes would approve.

But if Flaubert came of age in the presence of a living father, this was in many important aspects a father who was no father. Being read to from *The Temptation of Saint Anthony* (1874), the older man dozed as his son continued, then awoke and left the room without comment. As a boy, Gustave had spied on his surgeon-father's autopsies, often performed on a naked woman's body. These would readily mingle with primal scenes and intensify a sadomasochistic attitude toward sexuality, as has been shown by Charles Baudry's study of the author's adolescent love and the manifest fantasies in his early writings.[61] Flaubert, Baudry writes, "suffered from nightmares in which he was attacked by a group of men holding bleeding knives in their mouths." But if Flaubert seems to have unconsciously identified with the female victim, he also consciously assumed surgical roles that would carry over to his writings, as he wrote to a friend in 1838, "I dissect ceaselessly; I enjoy this especially when I come upon an element of corruption in something I generally considered pure and when I discover gangrene in 'nice' places, I raise my head and laugh."

"It is not surprising that throughout his life one of Flaubert's greatest dreads was of becoming a father," observed Baudry, who includes the author's bisexuality, narcissism, introspection, and working-through as features of his creativity. To return briefly to the polar regulators of creativity, one finds a developed family romance in Flaubert's "The Legend of St. Julian the Hospitaler" (1877), and, since the primal scene has been mentioned, I will conclude by considering how its perverse messages and injurious impact may have affected his literary ambition "to compose a page so lascivious and erotic that if it were pasted on walls, the walls would be in heat and men and women would have intercourse on the street like dogs and pigs" (that is, not like human adults, but like beasts, according to a child's primal fantasy).[62]

Flaubert stands out today as one of the first self-conscious moderns who recognized the dislocations between language and reality, whether it be the mental or the external world. In his *Intimate Notebook* (1840–41), he observes that he could relate all his reveries and the reader would know nothing of them, because words do not so much render as distort thought.[63] And so inevitably, to succeed in recreating oneself through language is to succeed in creating something else. Going a step further, Oscar Wilde remarks that "one should either be a work of art, or wear a work of art."[64] It may also be clear now why he insists in another epigram, "The more we study Art, the less we care for Nature."[65] And why, given the view that "all art is at once surface and symbol," those who go beneath the one or read the other "do so at their own peril."[66]

Only women can bring forth life in nature: men traditionally turn to culture, the arts, and the sciences to reproduce themselves—no wonder our sampling is top heavy with logocentric males obsessed with a semblance of immortality. In Yeats's "Sailing to Byzantium," an old man would trade his body for a bird such as "Grecian goldsmiths make / Of hammered gold and gold enamelling" to sing "of what is past, or passing, or come." But even allowing for differences, the self is everyone's work of art fashioned to sing of life in all its stages and ages. Both real and illusory, the self is the work of art that we wear and become.

6

The fact that individuals are not only capable of significant self-modification (a more modest way of addressing the third birth) but indeed may have an autopoietic drive requires a few qualifiers. From Mill to Barthes, the changes wrought through self-creativity may be thought of as *directional*, that is, as fostering certain favorable shifts or advances within culture. In fact, it is largely because they are so valued that their self-documentations remain to be read. But all manner of self-creativity need not be culturally directive in a sense analogous to directional evolution; equally possible, self-creativity may succeed in fostering cultural change while failing to secure the goals of the individual who initates the process. And, finally, although culture itself changes through constant interplay with self-creating individuals, only a precious few will leave any imprint on culture at all. Thus, while self-creativity may be directional, cultural, and influential, it may also be random, obscure, and incidental; moreover, cultural changes may be responses to countless forces of which self-creation is but one. In sum, if the overwhelming arbitrariness of cultural data curtails overconfidence on the one hand, one need not, on the other, be stunned into silence.

Two recent trends appear contradictory: (1) the return to building religious components back into the human equation and (2) the shift away from a literary culture for sources of self-creativity toward a technological-electronic culture less for a rewriting than a rewiring of the self. Today we are born into an age of scientific technology and materialism, which, however advanced and enlightened in some respects, still manages to complicate if not obscure the quest for self-knowledge about origins. The current modes of obfuscation are often more subtle than those of myth and religion. A clearly observable tendency to attribute to either technology or materialism the powers to satisfy virtually all our human needs suggests the myth of Sleeping Beauty to Rollo May, and to me that the family romance of previous generations has not been dissolved so much as displaced and diffused. Many have noted in recent years the shift from a production-based to a consumer-based economy. This has also meant a national shift from independence to dependence; it is perhaps not accidental that the rise of consumer-rights groups in the seventies has been accomplished by the rise of children's-rights advocates. As consumers, our children wear clothes proclaiming brand names, and we are perhaps all the children of our charged-up economic system who must learn all over again boundaries and disciplines of self-control and conservation.

Meanwhile, the shrinking individual flinches before the hovering giants of materialism and technology, which in an important sense lack a past because they have no human history. Or else the past, such as it is, continually dissolves into a transitory present for a better tomorrow. While consumerism defines one of the roles for other-directed persons in mass culture, it merely signals a deeper malaise for such contemporary writers as Alexander Mitscherlich (*Society without the Father*, 1970) and Christopher Lasch (*The Culture of Narcissism*, 1979); and while psychoanalysts have begun treating the superego as an endangered species, feminists and other have celebrated the liberation from patriarchal constrictions. The philosopher Edith Wyshogrod discerns the outlines of a new mythology to replace patriarchal social organization, or perhaps an old one reemerging: "that of the autochthonous origin of human life, the generation of men and women not from the union of opposite sexes but from earth itself ... coming from the soil without parentage."[67] The Gaia movement in England, which holds that "the earth is influenced by life to sustain life, and that the planet itself is the core of a single, unified, living system,"[68] is named after the pre-patriarchal Greek goddess. Similar approaches have been taken in the radical feminism of Susan Griffin *inter alias,* the various Green movements, New Age religions, and the systems theory of universal interconnectedness.[69] The physicist Fritjof Capra, for example, suggests in *The Turning Point* that the astronauts dramatically revived this ancient myth of the earth as a living organism by their portrait of our planet as more than an oasis in the wastes of space but "an organism— Gaia, a living planetary being."[70]

The danger that Wyschogrod perceives in this revision lies in the sense that the "children of earth are all related to another in a great chain of peers." But instead of leading to constructive ideals, autochthony "allows for transferred allegiance to new leadership, such as the nation-state loyalties claimed by Chairman Mao," or to the blurring of age and sex difference in a unisex society of peers.[71] The inclusion of real, biological fathers, on the other hand, is here portrayed positively in Western man's "understanding of himself as a historical being, upon whose continuity the future of culture depends."[72] Thus, Wyshogrod implicitly emphasizes the importance of primal-scene mastery when she writes that by "denying or repressing the sexual role of the father, a society without relation to past or future is created."[73] The result is a self primarily interested in itself: narcissism, the unhealthy kind. And the newly risen autochthonous man: "ready to serve the nation-state placing himself in the service of its technological appurtenances."[74] But, while utopian, the Gaia and Green movements do not fit this scenario so well as the ethos of consumerism does.

That Freud had already considered these tendencies was cited by Christopher Lasch at the 1980 meeting of the American Psychoanalytic Association, where the superego as a threatened species played like a leitmotiv through his and other sessions. In *Moses and Monotheism* (1939), Freud contrasts nature cults and matriarchy with the spiritually more advanced Mosaic religion, and draws some remarkable inferences about respective mental activities within matriarchal and patriarchal societies, which if not taken too literally may direct us into the area of self-creativity begun earlier regarding the differences between matrilinear and patrilinear descent. "Since maternity is proved by the senses whereas paternity is a surmise based on a deduction and a premise," Freud argues, "the emphasis on the thought-process over the sense-perception" is evolutionary in the directional sense. Paternity is seen as opening a "new realm of spirituality where conceptions, memories, and deductions became of decisive importance."[75]

Here is yet another way of conceiving the dialectics of self-creativity—from the viewpoint of that neglected agency of the self, the superego. Different orders of descent then demand different kinds and degrees of mastery, but since every individual in historic times must account for the sexual contributions of the female as well as the male in human origins, there is no need to reduce Freud's insight to sex stereotyping. Rather, he guarantees a legitimate future for a society with fathers. What the feminist movement has taught us is that the more intimately involved fathers are in their family's well-being, the more valuable they are (the more detached, the more potentially abusive).[76]

Moreover, children without fathers are not—as may be thought—delivered from oedipal dilemmas or castration fears, but because the absence of father is often experienced as a self-deficit or a magical oedipal victory, these sons have been depicted in psychoanalytic literature as less assertive and competitive. They may be relieved from, but they are also deprived of, the valuable intrafamilial struggle for self-mastery that consolidates masculine identification. Thus, while it is easy to be impressed by the cultural achievements of a Sartre or a Barthes who expand the boundaries of self-creativity, it is not so easy to balance their contributions against the psychological struggles as unqualified triumphs—but that is the sociocultural position. If we can suspend cultural allegiances and tune into the purely psychological struggles as unqualified triumphs—but that is the sociocultural position. If we can suspend cultural allegiances and tune into the purely psychological, a better sense can be gained of how valued cultural products record the more private processes of self-creation.

Just as gender is constructed, so paternity is created, if not within the family, then in displaced cultural spheres. And in a study of creative (male) thinkers from the seventeenth century to the present, focusing on the persistent presence of parental abandonment, I have been persuaded that the child's loss is the culture's gain, though often a mixed one. The major psychological motif among these thinkers is less a flight from woman than a quest for father, that is, an ambivalent quest for fatherhood often undercut by an escape from father.[77]

7

Because cultural innovators like Sartre, Camus, and Barthes literally enter society without fathers and with a burden of narcissism, they assume an added contemporary interest; but because they attempt to master deficits through traditional literary means, they also assume an antiquarian aura today. In their Janus position, they greet us coming and going. But artists as well, insofar as they orphan themselves figuratively and must negotiate a mode of creative adoption and self-reconstitution, also speak to us of a society without fathers or, more accurately, of one without our biological parents.

Our first two creations—the one from biology, the other into family—are outside our control. They condition and make possible the third birth, which is at least partially within our control. This remaking of the self is most clearly discernible in creative spheres, where the imagination can operate between subjective and objective poles. As part of our human endowment, it is most fully represented in the works of artists—hence, the many foregoing studies—but it appears as well to be a general human tendency. It is in the creative sphere, or through our introspective, analytical capacities, or out of our interactions with others directly or indirectly through their works, that we are most active and most self-responsible in the enterprise of self-making.

Messianic cults, charismatics, Oriental hybrids like the Rajneeshies, born-again religions, self-transforming technologies, many of the human potential movements from Esalen to Scientology, a vast physical culture industry—all appeal to our autopoieic urges in various ways. The alternate culture movements are at their best when they emphasize the self-healing properties of the organism and the self-responsible capacities of the individual.[78]

During a recent visit to California, I listened, over a grain-fortified meal, while a psychologist explained that we create our own chemistry: two individuals at the same table, the one dining on red meat, the other on legumes, are actually steering their lives at different accelerations. I was astonished at this very concrete rendering of my interests in the individual's capacities for self-creation. But it is true that at the third stage of self-creativity, the charge of continuing the creation of one's own physical being is handled over to us. And surely a cultivation of jogging, aerobics, yoga, and diet is more than a symptom of the culture of narcissism. Like it or not, ingestion and exercise have replaced heredity and environment as fad or fate.

On the other hand, the purely physical or biochemical emphasis runs the risk of misplaced concretion. This danger becomes apparent when the brain psychologists extrapolate extensive cultural modes of behavior from an alleged Western overcultivation of the left hemisphere, thus implying that the vast treasures of Eastern wisdom are waiting to be tapped in the neglected right hemisphere, or in better communication lines between them via the corpus callosum. The belated attempt by Robert Ornstein in *The Psychology of Consciousness* (1972) to rebalance the overconceptualizing left hemisphere with Sufi riddles and parables is but a scientifically embellished continuation of Mill's discovery of his greater self through Wordsworth. Meanwhile, recent evidence has tended to support the view that both hemispheres are engaged in more complicated and reciprocal ways than previously held (so the Orient and the West have always been mixed together). False polarities and habits of dichotomous thinking unfortunately go hand in hand. Nonetheless, every new generation feels the need to redefine its yin/yang complements.[79] The earlier enthusiasms among the psychedelic generation were epitomized by Timothy Leary on the East coast and Michael Murphy at Esalen on the West coast, both of whom promised that LSD could switch on a billion-watt powerhouse of untapped visionary potentials inside our very skulls; yet while the drug may have imparted visions and created elation, none of the grandiose visions were grounded in a significant new work of art or theory of human or cosmic nature.[80]

Misplaced concretion often leads to displaced enthusiasm. A further instance of this fallacy presented itself through a San Francisco talk show on which Irving Oyle, author of *The New American Medicine Show* (1979) and a leading proponent of alternative medicine, imparted free medical advice to listeners who called in. He took it upon himself to diagnose and prescribe to strangers he could not see nor would ever hear from again. Moreover, the tone of his voice was one of manic excitement, buoyed by a kind of autocratic assurance. One despondent woman described a troublesome cataract. Believing that the human body is "being recreated from instant to instant by the vibration of subatomic particles beamed to the earth from the sun, and which vibrate back and forth between energy and matter," Dr. Oyle simply pointed out that the cells and tissue that produced the cataract were regenerated every twenty-four hours; therefore, this problem was something the patient was creating for herself.[81] He advised her to figure out why she had to create that cataract and just stop doing whatever it was. End of consultation. That the woman could have been left with anything other than guilt and helplessness, compounded by resentment over the omniscient expert, is difficult to imagine. So there is something to the self-intoxication and simplemindedness others have pointed out among the alternative cultures that must be weighed against their often refreshing approaches.

Irving Oyle's enthusiasm for the body as though it were a children's magic show; the enthusiastic behaviorists who would eliminate depression with a drug; the intrepid journeys through the inner body by medical technology; and the utopianism of the brain/mind contingency represented in Marilyn Ferguson's *The Aquarian Conspiracy* (1980) all share a common preference for an unconscious of raw potential, an "amazing brain," whose possibly interconnecting cells exceeds the "number of atoms in the universe," a gene pool, or a "somatic unconscious," as preferred variations to the dynamic unconscious encountered in psychoanalysis.[82] Theirs is located in the genes, the cells, the brain tissue, but not in the psyche. The implications for this increasingly dominant position are enormous. For if our consciousness is to change, the sources, as everyone would agree, must come from somewhere outside or beyond the conscious mind. How that elsewhere is conceptualized and located has direct bearing on who and how the change is being conducted. Being passive, the potential or somatic unconscious is either directly controlled by experts, consciousness, or the evolutionary will; but such pliant or mystical models of the unconscious do not allow for the value of working through one's resistances to change and to the indispensable spaces created by self-understanding that thereby accrue.

The paradigmatic self-creations of Butler and Gosse in their period entailed smashing the shackles of formal religion between the hammer and anvil of scientific enlightenment. Today it is the shackles of scientific materialism that many feel must be smashed; perhaps amid all the varieties of self-creation now available, the truly paradigmatic ones appear in such autobiographies as Thomas Merton's *Seven Story Mountain* (1948) and Paul Zweig's *Three Journeys* (1976). These worthy pilgrims renounce the technological fruits of science in favor of a quest for spiritual enlightenment. Their journeys embody the realization once again that secular progress can neither cure emotional emptiness nor satisfy spiritual longings. The malaise of modernism infected Merton amid his bohemian circle in New York as gravely as it did Zweig among his coterie in Paris. After Zweig has discovered that his life so far is a blank, he journeys into the Sahara, "to model my interior spaces to its prompting."[83] Like a preexisting transitional object to be individually reshaped, the desert becomes a self-object, real and illusory, objective and subjective, a piece of psychic geography. "When I was not equal to the task, the desert would be replaced by dull, dusty spaces. It could become a desert in another, more terrible sense." But Zweig remains pitched between "worry and vision," and it is not to be in this vast transitional sphere that his self-creation will proceed, but rather in an enclosure on Manhattan's Upper West Side, near the site of Merton's anguished conversion, which led him in time to the interior deserts of a Trappist monastery and eventually to the mountains of northern India. For Zweig, also, the step is both religious and mystical. A friend introduces him to her guru. The interchange between this holy man and a troubled follower trips a hammer in Zweig's own psyche: the effect is mesmerizing, uncanny, cathartic, binding. Later he will invoke psychoanalysis to account for this second introjecting of an unconditionally loving parent, who presides as "Baba, the father of my second birth." But the appropriation of psychoanalysis—which may hint at its future role in the self-creation process—is not to provide the understanding that will lead one to separation and further individuation, but to reinforce actions taken, to validate the need for reclaiming the beloved other. At the end of his third journey Zweig is clinging for all he is worth to his new transitional object, the beloved yet somehow impersonal Baba, with the mix of reality and illusion still mostly unsorted out. From this and comparable journeys of the spirit in our time it seems that early twentieth-century man has reaped the bitter fruits of going it alone and his descendants of today have had enough of alienation, dread, and perhaps painful insight as well.

As late twentieth-century man and woman re-create themselves, they seek for a connected selfhood, with mixed and uncertain consequences. It cannot be overlooked that traditional modes of self-understanding that can deepen and enrich our lives, often at a painful price, require a marked degree of psychic structuring. The exercise of insight issues from one's passage through the triadic sphere. We are most free and in touch with ourselves when we through insight are able to ripen our humanity. But in recent years, awareness is to be heightened or consciousness is to be raised either by getting in touch with the body or by getting involved in social causes—both beneficial enterprises, but also incomplete and often oversold, with an inevitable eggs-in-one basket disillusionment. More disturbing is the virtual eclipse from cultural discourse of the primacy of self-knowledge and its replacement by some variant of self-rebirth, which, if not accompanied by other mental activities, readily takes on the magical and wishful characteristics of the earlier dyadic phases. Self-creativity then becomes diverted into self-obscurity. What is most often obscured is the role of aggression, epitomized by the caption of parental murder, and the recognition of needs to initiate internal repair: we murder to create.

Yet for well or ill, almost everyone is drawn to some form of third-birth pangs leading to self-creation. And the fact that many are finding themselves irresistibly caught up in it keys the fundamental trend that underlies all the others. In previous societies, except in bohemian quarters and among aristocratic classes, the work of self-creation was neither widely nor directly experienced: it was transmitted to future generations. Children were instructed, not always in so many words, to correctively recreate their parents' lives for them, though ostensibly for a mutually cherished better tomorrow, while at the same time the younger generation were expected to realize their own destinies in accord with chosen models. These often double-binding projects of sequential creativity and familial continuity are increasingly being supplanted by varieties of internal and simultaneous self-creation by the present generation, often to the detriment of the next generation.

However, to label the dust clouds arising from these processes as a kind of noxious narcissism would be premature, although economically exploitative or narcissistically derived energies no doubt are fueling many of these endeavors. Yet the mutations of the third-birth stage may be adaptive responses to cultural crises we will only be able to delineate when the dust has begun to clear in the near or remote future. For the present, we can affirm that the third birth draws on processes that can be subjected to analysis. In our first birth the scales were tilted toward mother as primary caretaker, inevitable source of life and extension of the natural world. In the second, the scales were tilted toward father, traditional embodiment of and spokesman for cultural modalities that tend ubiquitously to be patriarchal. The third birth stems from the necessary assimilation of the first two, as there emerges a nuclear self with the relative capacity for shaping and reshaping itself through life.

The third birth of the individual, when it takes place, is not like the other two, being neither biologically bound nor psychologically attuned to the emergence from symbiosis. It may center on the ego-ideal, as the writings of Peter Blos indicate; but it will involve all the psychic agencies and systems. While it is species-specific to *Homo* it is phase-specific to nothing quite predictable. And while it may come about with the suddenness of conversion, it is not intrinsic to any of the adolescent phases. It may just as well be gradual, recurrent, and lifelong. To say that one may at some level be creating oneself upon arising in the morning may sound flippant but need not be dismissed out of hand; certainly under the devastation of loss, everyone is sooner or later and maybe repeatedly charged with self re-creation in the aftermath of mourning. At bottom, the process is mysterious.

Yet it is real. The multiplicity and variety of human life bespeaks a degree of indeterminate organization and personal freedom. But it is far from certain whether this process will be dictated more by the dehumanizing fads and pressures of the culture than by the self-responsible energies of our very complex, still unfolding feedoms.

Appendix A.
Fantasy and Preverbal Sources of
Literary Creativity and Literary Mode

Fantasy is part of the individual's effort to deal with inner reality.
It can be said that fantasy and daydreams are omnipotent
manipulations of external reality. Omnipotent control of reality
implies fantasy about reality. The individual gets to external reality
through the omnipotent fantasies elaborated in the effort to get away
from inner reality

—D. W. Winnicott, "The Manic Defence"

1

Although the intimate interplay between fantasy and art has a well-established psychoanalytic tradition—from Freud's 1908 paper on "The Relation of the Poet to Daydreaming" to later investigations by Rank, Kris, Greenacre, Holland, Eissler, Ehrenzweig, Rothenberg, Storr, and Skura—the creative enterprise still eludes precise formulation.[1] True, fantasy has shed its earlier onus as part of a reality-denying mechanism and has been accorded vital adaptive functions for the ego;[2] all the same, creative adaptations of fantasies, considered early (infantile) instinctual representations, may just as easily substitute for as assist in what are optimistically called the processes of normal development toward that elusive goal of genital primacy. But if one does not yet find a psychoanalytic consensus that creative adaptation has shaken loose the shackles of pathology, at least the earlier aversions (e.g., romantic subjectivity as morbid) and the patronizing gestures (e.g., Dostoevsky as a great psychologist) have diminished. Likewise, those factitious debates between art and neurosis have also pretty much been laid to rest; yet the artist still draws into psychoanalytic range by dint of anomaly rather than normality, and drawing the line is far from easy.[3] However, from the amount of serious attention paid in recent years, a measure of advance in understanding has accrued.

Still, many questions persist. Those to which this project addresses itself center on how to explore creativity within the rich resources of psychoanalysis without, on the one hand, resorting to regressive modalities, such as the dream model or other models of conflict and illness that circumscribe response by highlighting pathology, yet without, on the other hand, settling for vapid abstractions that recognize only the positive, or so-called life-enhancing, benefits. Recently, a wealth of reader's-response and Lacanian contributions to applied analysis has led down new avenues of inquiry, but *a priori* positions of textual and linguistic autonomy presuppose creativity without a creator. The enduring challenge is to remain faithful both to Freud's revolutionary theories, which first really opened up the realm of early (preverbal) development, and at the same time later integrative forces within the self, so that creativity may inhabit the total human continuum and not be allocated only the infantile or the adult portions. More precisely, the task is to legitimize creativity as a human process in its own right, but at the same time as one that may be comprehended by psychoanalytic concepts. The relation of preverbal mental processes to the verbal product is far from simple, and the about-to-be proposed correlations, which underpin the polarity theories, must remain tentative. Thus this inquiry addresses basic issues, but in a more technical context than suits the study's mainline.

If fantasies from very early phases of development not only persist but also enter and influence creative processes, are there then correlations between particular types of fantasies and literary genres or modes? Ostensibly not, because fantasy is simply too fluid, ubiquitous, and polymorphous. And so despite its central, overdetermining role in mental life and evident influence on creativity, current trends in applied psychoanalysis would bypass it. This is unfortunate, for even in the family romance, wherein the child fundamentally reconstructs his/her origins, we find not just, as the title of Marthe Robert's study, *The Origins of the Novel*, suggests, but the rich substratum of all art, whether it be myth, poetry, or fiction. So ancient and widespread is this fantasy that it can flow in and out of consciousness and, seemingly at random, into various periods and conventions or endow the artist's own endeavors with motive and form just as readily as it can come into play at significant moments of anyone's development from early childhood into adolescence. The need then arises to further specify fantasy by locating it in image and symbol as micro-units for processes operating in the literary work as a whole. After that, the problem of mode can be addressed.

2

"I'm not the milk and the milk's not me! I'm Mickey!"
—Maurice Sendak, *In the Night Kitchen*

In a Donald Barthelme story, the object named in the title appears at the outset as a given.[4] "The balloon, beginning at a point on Fourteenth Street ... expanded northward all one night, while people were sleeping, until it reached the Park. There I stopped it" ("The Balloon," 15). This is perhaps the best opening of a story since Kafka's Gregor Samsa woke up one morning to find he had turned into an enormous cockroach, and the brunt of the satire likewise is Kafkaesque—absurd, elliptical, and diffuse, rather than transparently clear in focus and aim. The balloon, while being imminently present and real enough in its own terms, is, like so much of modern experience, elusive, or like a Beckett or Ionesco play, seemingly quite clear in its own terms, yet resistant to established canons and categories. "It was agreed that since the meaning of the balloon could never be known absolutely, extended discussion was pointless" (16).

In effect it becomes part of the urban condition, like smog or uncollected garbage, or the partial demolition of some huge building, which until then had been a magnificent hotel and permanent landmark. Suddenly there appears the wrecker's ball. No one asks why. And then a boarded-up chasm. People walk around it and peep in through the slits. It doesn't pay to ask too many questions. Someone must know what's happening. Meanwhile, one adapts. A degree of satire on urban dwellers' capacities for living with anything begins to emerge.

But the fantasy, like the balloon over midtown Manhattan, continues to hover: "green and blue paper lanterns" are hung from its "warm gray underside," or messages are written on the surfaces, some of them obscene invitations. Children jump from buildings on it, while the critics treat it with mixed reviews, like any other recent opening. Gradually it is woven into everyone's language and experience. "People began, in a curious way, to locate themselves in relation to aspects of the balloon" (20). Soon it is integrated into the environment, where man and balloon and building all may meet at various intersections. Finally, it comes to offer the "possibility, in its randomness, of mislocation of self, in contradistinction to the grid of precise, rectangular pathways under our feet" (21).

The reference to "our feet" reminds the reader that an "I" seemed to have been in control of this operation from the outset. And in the final paragraph the narrator returns to the fore. "I met you under the balloon, on the occasion of your return from Norway; you asked if it was mine; I said it was." The balloon is a "spontaneous autobiographical disclosure, having to do with the unease I felt at your absence, and with sexual deprivation." The beloved's return having rendered the balloon superfluous, it is hauled away in trailer trucks to be stored in West Virginia.

So the balloon turns out to be a lover's fantasy, concocted to fill the vacuum of his beloved's absence. But what a bizarre sort of fantasy.

The step from balloon to psychonanalytic explanation seems a simple one, but let Jonathan Swift make it for us. On Gulliver's second voyage he encounters a man as "tall as an ordinary spire-steeple" and finds himself a captive of the gigantic Brobdingnagians. In the course of his adventures he witnesses a girl nursing from a "monstrous Breast, which I cannot tell what to compare so as to give the curious Reader an idea of its Bulk, Shape and Colour. It stood prominent six Foot, and could not be less than sixteen in Circumference. The Nipple was about half the Bigness of my Head, and the Hue both of that and the Dug so varified with Spots, Pimples and Freckles, that nothing could appear more nauseous."[5] Swift, among other things, is having fun with conventions of beauty and with science's recent enthusiasm over distorting lenses. But by now one may have begun to wonder whether Barthelme has not also greatly magnified his object in order to find a suitable comparison for the "curious Reader."

In a later episode the hapless Gulliver is set astride one of the girl's nipples, and although he is at various times poisoned, squashed, dropped, suffocated, and nearly drowned, he is never quite absorbed by the monstrous thing.

That experience is reserved for David Alan Kepesh, the central sufferer in Philip Roth's novella, who wakes up one morning to find he has turned into a "breast of the mammalian female" due to a "massive hormonal influx" within his body between midnight and four A.M.[6] He is informed that he is "now an organism with the general shape of a football or a dirigible" with a "spongy consistency" about six feet in length. At one end he is "rounded off like a watermelon"; at the other he terminates "in a nipple, cylindrical in shape, projecting five inches" and "perforated at the tip" The "wrinkled, roughened skin of the nipple—which admittedly, is exquisitely sensitive to touch like no tissue on the face, including the mucous membrane of the lips—was formed out of the glans penis" (*Breast*, 14–15).

Thus this "volcanic secretion from the pituitary of 'mammogenic' fluid" sets in operation a satiric fantasy capable of moving in almost any direction. The regression in the comic conversion of phallus to nipple sets up the reader for a send-up of polymorphous perversity, whether it be of the Norman O. Brown type or of the 1960s youth-culture variety. There is a suggestion of regaining the fountain of life. Opportunities for milking gags (pun permitted) from the meetings with his mistress and his psychoanalyst abound. And indeed Roth does allow his "Breast" to rise to a few such occasions, but, as he stated in an interview, he preferred to go against both the obvious Kafkaesque opportunities as well as apparently those of his own manic talents. Rather, he wanted to see his hero's plight as a human problem: one must still—even under these trying circumstances—evolve a strategy for getting on with life.

But despite his hero's insistence that the Breast is he and he is the Breast, one comes away with the feeling that he is still himself, speaking to us from inside the Breast. He talks more like another Portnoy than a Breast.[7] Perhaps the manic flight, once launched, is stronger than Roth can manage, and critics have been generally disappointed either that he did not do more with his fantasy or that he did anything with it at all. The consensus seems to be that what was needed least from this talented writer was a Breast, especially one with a professor of English inside it. But Roth had his reasons, and unlike his fellow breast-fantasists, he eschews either the family romance or the rescue fantasy as logical props. For Kepesh, the Breast is here to say, and he may as well cut his losses and make the best of things—like Mickey *In the Night Kitchen*, diving down to the bottom of a gigantic milk bottle and singing, "I'm in the Milk and the Milk's in me. God Bless Milk and God Bless Me!"[8]

3

Balloons are employed in fantasies and games as symbolic of the
mother's body or breasts.
                                  —D. W. Winnicott, "The Manic Defence"

We now have the three items laid out—or rather looming—before us. There
appear to be great similarities in this blending of breast fantasy and satire.
Disproportions of size between the male figure and the female gland are
consistent, as are the figures' mingling of helplessness and omnipotence,
pleasure and repugnance. A deeper coherence remains to be found.

In 1938 a Viennese psychoanalyst published some findings based on rather
unusual material drawn from his patients and others.[9] he related his material to
hypnagogic phenomena—mental states preceding sleep. The problem seems to
reside in the vivid yet apparently unrelated sensations of his subjects. A few
examples may suffice: (1) lying on something crumpled, but the crumpled
feeling is also in the mouth; (2) a floating, sinking, giddiness; (3) something
jagged, sandy, and dry felt by the mouth and the whole body, a lump that
can't be swallowed; (4) visually, something shadowy and indefinite, generally
round, that swells as it approaches and threatens to crush the subject before
shrinking down to nothing. And, yes, in one account, "it's like a balloon."

The analyst notes that falling asleep entails a withdrawal of interest and
cathexes from the outside world. Certain ego functions break down and
differentiations diminish. Most of the sensations center on the oral cavity, and
with the regressive pull toward sleep an "archaic phase of development" is
revived. He concludes that the imprints reported are "mental images of
sucking at the mother's breast and of falling asleep there when satisfied."

It remained for B. D. Lewin to name these memory traces "Isakower
Phenomena," after their discoverer, Otto Isakower, and to carry the
investigation forward, notably in "Reconsideration of the Dream Screen."[10]
He also enriched the data and confirmed the original conclusions. A colleague
reported that floating before him was a "round mass, dark in color, with
granulations"; another described a "vaporish white cloud or looming mass."
The frequently overwhelming, thick, gigantic, visual component may be in its
more primitive aspect an endless wall, which one may be both inside and
against, while later memory traces add form, that is, curvature, and collect
details: it becomes "pink, studded with roses, and contains erectile tissue" as
the emphasis shifts from the "whitish expanse of breast" to the areola and
nipple. Thus the brown and gray lines of Barthelme's balloon are
particularized by Roth's "rosy pink" nipple.

Lewin hypothesized that the large visual mass as a mental picture of the
breast becomes the dream screen onto which the infant, as he falls asleep after
nursing, projects his earliest dreams. The dream screen came to represent the
"breast and also sleep at the breast." Lewin had earlier predicted a triad of

oral wishes that are engaged in nursing: to eat, to be eaten, to sleep.[11] Objects that may stand for the dream screen range from rubber balls, balloons, sand hills, blackboards, film, and other more fluid objects. For one patient the dream screen "curved over backward, rolled up, and then rolled off in the distance." Sometimes other details of the experience bring out differences in nursing: thus rubber may refer to the nipple on the baby bottle for a non-breast-fed child.

Spitz recognized the importance of these phenomena because they preserve traces of the I—not I experience of self-differentiation.[12] Blurring distinctions between different regions of the body is also common and is illustrated in Roth's Kepesh. Swiftian disproportions in size also pertain, as do the powers of the Balloon to induce a dislocation of self and compel new adaptations. Further, in Lewin's oral triad as the baby settles down to sleep, he may have "fantasies of going to sleep within the mother's belly." Thus, if one may so infer, to be eaten at the breast is to regain entrée to the womb. Hence, we are in the realm of oceanic feelings—the deepest, but, paradoxically, not the most deeply repressed, layer of the mind—and their representations in the blank dream. This Lewin refers to as an elusive state of mind: vague, like a pure emotion, and one that may bring forth ecstasy or orgastic discharges. Oceanic feeling may equally entail a dedifferention of ego functions along with manic fusion. Thus Gulliver embarks on a literal ocean for his travels, leaving behind the structured order of his family and English society. His abduction in a box by an eagle and his being dropped at sea prior to his rescue serve as a rebirth into functioning reality.

Finally, since all of Lewin's points cannot be summarized, I will close with his expanded list of Isakower Phenomena, which include not only the dream screen and the blank dream but "psychic structures, such as hallucinations, depersonalizations, daydreams" and various others.[13]

One of which might well involve creative processes. Certain parallels have already been noted. It may also be recalled that hypnagogic states in general (whether they coincide with Kris's "regression in the service of the ego." Weissman's "dissociative function," Eissler's "Doxaletheic function," or other, more complicated steps in the creative process) are related to that phase of wise passivity, of loafing and inviting one's soul, which is the necessary prerequisite for awakening creative energies.[14] Barthelme's balloon appeared at night while "people were sleeping." There is also the summoning of the good, stable breast as a backdrop for one's excited, agitated arousal of erotic or aggressive fantasy. Lewin notes that the dream screen may later be summoned to block painful primal-scene stimuli—a point elaborated by Ralph B. Little in reporting on Sputnik emerging from the "white billowing clouds" of his patient's dream screen—and one that I hope to return to later.

Being in intimate rapport with the good breast, whether one is astride its nipple, beneath its looming ambience, or safely tucked inside, is also conducive to stirrings of omnipotence. It may not be accidental that Gulliver acquires the power of language from the good nurse Glumdalclicth, who rescues him from the farm girl's traumatic act of feeding, that the "I" magically summons the massive balloon over Manhattan, dictating as well its withdrawal, and that Philip Roth remarked in an interview that being turned into a part-object is somehow related to a primitive and magical but everyday exercise of language. "I'm a p__. She's a c__! My partner is an a__!" Alan David Kepesh is the word made flesh—though the omnipotence is in his author, not in himself. Yet there is in his new condition the kind of protection from depression, homosexual fears, and oedipal conflicts that one achieves by manic flight—the fusion of ego and superego, ultimately based on that of infant and breast (as metonymy for primary care-giver). It is a timeless state, when the infant's thoughts, gestures, and utterances, "control" the mother, and to control her means to control the universe.

One also discerns in each instance a certain downgrading of the actual breast. Gulliver perceives it as a repugnant, nauseous monster, invoking olfactory associations that suggest anal attacks. Perhaps he would like to treat it as the graffiti-smearing New Yorkers do the balloon, though, of the three, Barthelme seems most alive to his object's range of adaptive possibilities. One has the impression his balloon is more the transitional object—a medium for perceiving the greater outside world—than the fetish born of fixation or overdependence. And when the still-mysterious but whole woman returns, the part-object is packed away for another day.

Bradley has reported on the widespread tendency within psychoanalysis and society in general to substitute the breast for the nipple.[15] While Barthelme's balloon is nippleless and Swift's nipple is hugely grotesque, it is left for Roth to man the breast and absurdly strive to phallicize its tip. Id-analysis might reveal that the nipple stirs up associations of the wished for, but dangerous, phallic mother, dangerous because the phallus—fantasied either as her own or as the paternal phallus in intercourse—is castrative. Thus regressive literary journeys through time or space may be guided by the primal fantasy of the woman with a penis, but they often tend to get lost in the stormy seas or cast on the rocks of castration anxiety.

For Kepesh, the breast is both somehow an insult to his manhood, as though it were an emanation of a repressed feminine identification returning, and also a fundamental fact of life. For Roth, *The Breast* seems to be both an irresistible opportunity for redonning one's early ego skin and also a trap laid for psychoanalytic investigations of art, so one resists the temptation of being sucked too far in.[16]

4

Externally, a good breast is one that having been eaten waits to be reconstructed. In other words, it turns out to be ... the mother holding the situation in time.

—D. W. Winnicott

If not from our rather resistant examples, then at least from Isakower Phenomena, it may appear by now that the child's first images from the outside world derive from interaction with the breast, that they persist, and, at the very minimum, they may be seen to perform a role in creativity. "I look at this white sheet of paper lying on my desk. I perceive its shape, its color, its position," is the way Sartre's brief philosophical account of the image begins.[17] How many other writers have not also begun by reducing their attention to blank paper before projecting onto it? The screen derivative of the early breast endows the infant's *tabula rasa* with fundamental meaning and reference to another being. Writing is tinged with the magical gestures of finding, incorporating, repelling. Breast imagery, however, remains relatively simple. It has its limitations and can carry one's imagination only so far; yet the absent breast is the first hole in being (to paraphrase Sartre), and the intolerable vacuum is filled by primitive oral fantasy.[18] Following object-relations theory, creativity begins in the depressive position, the child's reparative efforts to replace or repair the hole made by its "instinct love."[19] But as these examples show, creativity can also play on the manic defense—a fusion with the breast based on a denial of aggressive love, guilt, and the need for reparation.

At a somewhat later stage of development the child is exposed to—or entertains a fantasy of—a more complex configuration of the outside world, arising from the mother's other fundamental relationship. One way or another, the child comes upon or fantasizes about the primal scene, comprised of the sexually combined parents. Like the child's mastery of the breast by fusing his/her aggressive/libidinal drives, the "dynamic power of the [primal] scene is so great that it can only be mastered by introjection."[20] And like the child's manic defenses, the primal scene also fosters a denial of reality and stimulates an investment in fantasy.[21] The results are varied and complex. Bisexual identifications may be precipitated. Cannibalistic fantasies may be aroused as well as distortions of anal attack, phallic beatings, and the like, because the child "inevitably will react in accordance with his libidinal phase of development at any given time."[22] In allegiance with denial, the family romance may be summoned to lower a veil on those "bestial" or "disloyal" activities. Other fantasies involving the archaic world of oceanic bliss may be ruptured and dislocated. In the children's book, the disturbing nighttime sounds that awaken Mickey are only the benevolent cooks in the somewhat mysterious night kitchen. But, inevitably, earlier breast-face equations are disfigured by the intrusion of genital functions as the virgin goddess of yore becomes a bit of a whore. Yet it is the persistence of denial (the "banishment of intolerable external stimulation ... in favor of the acceptance of instinctual wishes") that threatens to steer art into the treacherous straits of pathology, unless concepts of playfulness, mastery, and working through are introduced.[23]

Denial and play, the collision of family romance with primal scene, Bradley's association of bees' ability to suck or sting with conflicting oral wishes,[24] Lewin's oral triad, and a host of fantasy material related to the subject of this study are all present in John Barth's story, "Ambrose His Mark."[25] Suitably, the mode blends satire and farce to produce its manic effects. The nameless infant, "Honey," is being nursed by his voluptuous mother. "Cradled against her by the sag of the hammock, I drank me to a drowse; and she too, just as she lay—mottled by light and leaf-shadow, lulled by my work upon her ... soon slept soundly" ("Ambrose," 23–24). As a portrait of the artist as a young nursling, the story blends the acquisition of identity by naming with Margaret Mahler's psychological birth of the human infant as part of the separation-individuation process. So long as he is at his mother's breast, he is simply "Honey," a pleasurable extension of her substances. The nearby grape arbor and the golden swarm of bees evoke the child's dawning creative romance with the world. In this dyadic stage, the father's absence is accounted for by his removal to an asylum following "his mad invasion of the delivery room," ostensibly to deny his paternity; and the symbiotic bond with the mother is reinforced by an erotic current powered by the child: "A nerve or something," the mother boasts, "runs from here right to you-know-where" (16).

Suddenly a swarm of bees from a neighbor's yard forms a "roaring gold sphere" above the sleeping mother and infant. "Ten thousand, twenty thousand strong they clustered. Her bare bosoms, my squalling face—all were buried in the golden swarm" (25). Nursing pleasures have got out of control: an oral assault is accompanied by dangers of smothering and engulfment. Once again, a phallic presence is summoned, this time to ward off manic fusion. In a comic melee involving a shotgun-wielding neighbor and a grandfather wildly spritzing his garden hose (like a primal scene memory disrupting blissful innocence), the rapturous dyadic phase and its disruption by an instinct-storm of swarming oral impulses is finally resolved by phallic awareness.

It is soon decided that the child will be named after the bees and the beelike birthmark near his eye: Ambrose (ambrosia). By way of adding a reaction-formation and consolidating the family romance, the inspiration stems from Saint Ambrose, who as a baby had bees swarming "on his mouth while he was asleep in his father's yard, and everyone said he'd grow up to be a great speaker" (33). As to his mother, who received a bad sting on the "fount" of the infant's "sustenance," she offers her breast no more. Indeed as the story appears at least in part to be a weaning fantasy and rite of passage from dyadic to triadic reality, it fortuitously includes the polarities of creativity.

Followers of Lacanian analysis will find in the child's naming his induction into Symbolic Order via *le nom du père*. In reacting against Lacan's phallocentrism, Kristeva arrives at a distinction congenial to the present line of exploration when she assigns the semiotic to the feminine, the symbolic to the masculine—signs being associated with the image, the dyad, the preoedipal; symbols with patriarchy.[26]

In contrast to images of the breast, representations of the primal scene, though stemming from developmentally more advanced stages of childhood, are often more obscurely disguised and encoded in culturally neutral forms. Such unlikely guises are the caduceus, the gammadion (swastika), the bullfight, the Crucifixion, the zodiac, the Sphinx, and many other mythic or real monsters.[27] In other studies of creativity, I have found the six-legged spider to be an obsessive symbol in Ingmar Bergman's films, and the rainbow, phoenix, and plumed serpent to be related to memory traces of primal scenes in the works of D. H. Lawrence.[28]

While breast representations are relatively simple (pleasure / unpleasure, presence / absence), those of primal scenes are always complex. The progression is from hanging fruit to the hanged god; from the oceanic paradise to the infernal machine.[29] The former class tends to have a basic, though obvious enough when once understood, point of reference. But the latter tends to rely on a high degree of condensation and displacement, often radiating into remote and mysterious meanings. The former may be under the sway of the pleasure principle, the latter of the reality principle, for it may be inferred that although the message printed on the dream screen by the primal scene may be spelled out as conflict and castration, the emotional import is exclusion, the poignant meaning is separation and a sense of mortality.

A symbol may then be considered an overdetermined image, one that has, so to speak, lost its innocence. This distinction leads into dream analysis, where all "images" are loaded up with symbolic inferences. Hence the double reference of typical dream symbols: the snake as phallus, life-giving powers, and knowledge, but also as castration (not to mention manifold untypical references for the dreamer). A symbol is an image hiding a rich latent content. Generally speaking, the dream symbol shrouds a primitive structure of reality, which in a traditional psychoanalytic context is the "self [the body or any of its parts] and intimate blood relatives, or the phenomena of birth, love, and death."[30] Art is never so consistent. Thus a balloon image may stand for the breast, but what would the breast image itself stand for—something else more primary? Hardly. Surrealistic playfulness to the contrary, the process of art is not to be identified with the process of dream.[31] What is primary in the one is not always so in the other. In art there may be images that are mental representations of real things and little more, though from the total context they may acquire an enriched significance, notably, the balloon. Similarly, several images may enrich a single symbol.

For present purposes, images fall into three categories: (1) the literary image: a unit of representation; (2) the dream "image": a piece of autobiography; (3) the archetypical image: a bond between the individual and the cosmos (the great mother, the tree of life, omphalos, phoenix, etc.). What appears to happen in the creative process (as distinct from but partly analogous to the dream process) is that symbolization distorts, wounds, or somehow alters an image into greater meaning. More precisely, the image may distort and so individualize objects of our experience or the world, but the symbol may express object-penetration. While the image may enclose a simple condition of being, the literary symbol, like the myth, may often enwrap minidramas. We may retain images of paradise, but we rely on symbols and myths to tell of the Fall. Or consider the different responses between a tower and a ruined tower. A symbol is a ruined image.

If we take a large fish and turn him white, give him battle scars, a violent history, associate him with Leviathan, the White Goddess, *vagina dentata,* and so forth, the simple image of whale is transformed into Moby Dick, a creature of limitless speculative import. There are countless ducks, tame and wild, but when an Ibsen character, due to waning vision, wounds one wild duck, thereby sending it into the undergrowth of the sea, where it hides until, retrieved and adopted, it serves as the occasion for the same hunter's illegitimate daughter (also going blind) to shoot herself—then we have a literary symbol around which the whole work is unified.

Likewise Chekhov's seagull is turned into a dramatic symbol by being shot and associated with the destructive flight of Nina. A bird in flight may summon associations with immortality, but the bird of paradise has no feet and must fly until he falls to his death. The pelican punctures her breast to feed her young. The phoenix is consumed on a nest of flames to be reborn from its ashes. These birds are endowed with rich, mythic histories and function as archetypal symbols.

Symbols that do not embody injury may inflict injury on others, as the Sphinx or Virginia Woolf's lighthouse. One way or another, the symbol becomes a part of ourselves. Shot down, it is worn around our necks.[32] Symbols show the natural world painfully humanized. The human image is also wounded into painful meaning. Oedipus, the lame king and tragic sufferer, is but one of a long line;[33] Prometheus, with his stomach attacked by vultures, is another. Then there are Achilles,' heel, Philoctetes's noisome yet potent wound, the pierced parts of Christ, Samson's cut hair, John the Baptist's head on a platter, Orpheus and all the dismembered fertility heroes and gods—instances are ubiquitous once one starts looking.

It would seem that artists have themselves been pierced by reality at some profound level of consciousness beyond or despite the manic phase or manic defense. Symbols are associated with mourning; they are in fact the internalizations of lost love objects but often with the record of one's struggle to retain them imbedded in their very matrix.[34] I am persuaded that in many instances the precipitant of this conflict has been the primal scene, which dramatizes so poignantly not only the threat of castration but the inevitable loss of the breast (as maternal Eden) as well—the two great sources of anxiety in early life.

Thus symbols may be seen as combined images with indefinite meanings. Symbols are able to compress great spans of individual history and cultural prehistory. The Sphinx is composed of disparate parts, including a woman's head, a lion's body, and large wings, sometimes a tail. It represents the riddle of life's origins in the sexually combined parents, but it means literally "sphincter," made menacing as strangler, and it swallows those who fail to solve its riddle. Psychoanalytic scholarship has succeeded in locating the very early and terrifying great mother as often lurking beneath the primal scene representation.[35]

The next step is from the universal to the particular. Oscar Wilde's poem, for example, begins with a "beautiful and silent Sphinx" watching a twenty-year-old student in his study.[36] A "curious cat" and "monstrous" muse, she is the object of the student's wide-ranging interrogation. "Come forth," he invites the "exquisite grotesque" creature of a "thousand weary centuries," who has "read the Hieroglyphs on the great sand-stone obelisks," come forth and reveal your sexual secrets: "were you standing by when Osis to Osiris knelt? / And did you watch the Egyptian melt her union for Antony . . . ?" ("Sphinx," 713). If this "loathsome mystery" has witnessed sexual scenes and serves as a virtual memory bank of polymorphous perverse sexuality, she has also been privy to the "Jewish maid who wandered with the Holy Child." Eventually as her own own royal "bedfellow" the "Great Ammon" lies with her "beside the Nile," a royal sexual scene is evoked. (716). If we then ask who is this temptress Sphinx, "half-woman and half animal," the answer on one level would be Oscar Wilde himself (713). The poem is dedicated to Marcel Schwob, a young French symbolist Wilde had been attracted to: "In writing the poem, Wilde the seducer / Sphinx confronted the reticent student / Schwob with Schwob's own thinly repressed desires."[37] One of the themes around which the exotic fantasies are wrapped is that of innocence / experience, fall / redemption, and, in the final verses, the crucifix's "pallid burden, sick with pain, watches the / world with wearied eyes, / And weeps for every soul that dies, and weeps for / every soul in vain" (722). If it is asked what are the unconscious fantasies (now that we have a notion of the conscious ones), an analyst might be intrigued by the Sphinx's phallic imagery: "curving claws of yellow ivory," a tail like a "monstrous Asp," "curious rock crystal breasts, the "tongue like a scarlet snake," and so forth, and might wonder about fetishes and phallic mothers as encoding a homosexual-style of female aversion (713). But in returning to the world-weary redeemer on the crucifix, one may note a synthesis of the creative process that had swung between the innocence of the Holy Family and the carnality the sexual pair via the Divine Son, who has witnessed all the Sphinx has. Thus while the Wildean Sphinx is highly particularized, its composition is true to the general principles of polar creativity.

One last example: The image of swans floating on a lake looks simple enough. Should Yeats be on hand when they take flight, he would be—and was—reminded of the passage of seasons at Coole Park and of his own transitoriness in contrast to their eternal return. Yeats had also been under the bountiful and protective wing of Lady Gregory during this period. Perhaps her classical grace and ideal of beauty are also figured in the swans, which arrive and depart in a pattern both seasonal and nurturing. Mallarmé's famous swan is quite different.[38] His swan neglected to depart with the season and so is discovered on a snowy mountain, frozen half into the lake. It flutters its wings bravely, futilely, but significantly. One senses a radical split in nature, a painful dualism between flesh and spirit, matter and idea, security and freedom. The moment is dramatic. The poem records a conflict of tragic ambivalence. The swan is a representation of terrified union with a clenching, unyielding object. Its wings create excited anxious movement—the wish for flight while yet being coldly immobilized. It is particularly this aspect of the swan that imparts the child's traumatized response to witnessing a forbidden sexual scene—almost entirely repressed, one may feel, in the poem—yet which releases key primal-scene details (as well as expanding into archetypal memories of the violent sexual ecstasy bound up in Yeats's "Leda and the Swan").[39]

The primal scene, then, it seems to me, stands for the inevitable junction that the serious artist must cross if he/she is to deal with adult sexuality. It is where in a strictly Freudian context the "incitement premium" of "fore-pleasure" gives way to the "final pleasure" afforded by the artist's finding his way "back to reality."[40] The dream screen, like the family romance, offers the artist necessary flexibility for bringing the imagination into full play. Overinvestment in the family romance can lead to its deification in the marvels of the occult, the lure of alternative realities, such as the phallic woman (mother), who appears in demonic or femme fatale forms.[41] Overinvestment in the primal scene can underwrite the Strindbergian motto: "Sexual love is conflict."[42]

On the other hand there may be an art that can transcend conflict, that can look back on it in reverie, an art that may resemble the blank dream in its evocation of pure emotion, mystical fusion, or oceanic feeling: "far, far down the intricate galleries of sleep, to the very heart of the world ... beyond the strata of images and words, beyond the iron veins of memory, and even the jewels of rest, to sink in the final dark like a fish, dumb, soundless, and imageless, yet alive and swimming."[43]

In Western art such states are rarely more than fleeting glimpses—beatific or apocalyptic though they may be. One discovers instead, and probably prefers as well, Joyce's brilliant but entirely mundane punning. This word coupling, though suggested by Norman O. Brown as what results when "two words get on top of each other and become sexual"[44]—seems rather to be sudden, surprising moments of manic fusion between the reader's single self and the *unus mundus,* which in Jungian terms might be the great mother and in Kleinian terms the good breast.[45] The sense of profound underlying order and connectedness is a rare quality embedded in only the supreme works of art, yet it can be forged in the smithy of Joycean puns.

5

It is just when we are manic-defensive that we are *least likely to feel*
as if we are defending against depression.
                    —D.W. Winnicott, "The Manic Defence"

If literary wordplay advances the manic mode, there is also the depressive
mode, immortalized on the one hand by Samuel Beckett, whose dour tributes
to Joycean punning ("In the beginning was the pun") are rendered spare and
harsh, and popularized on the other hand by Kurt Vonnegut, who, like Swift,
distorts space by traveling through time. As the obverse of manic self-
affirmation, Beckett's Malone spurns his prospect for identity with, "To speak
for example of the times when I go liquid and become like the mud, what good
would that do?"[46] A Vonnegut persona, Kilgore Trout, confides to his only
companion, a parakeet named Bill, that "humanity deserved to die horribly,
since it behaved so cruelly and wastefully on a planet so sweet.[47] Both
modern authors lean to understatement and a flatness of affect that suit a
monosyllabic minimalism (*How It Is,* "So it goes"), and both have as much
difficulty relinquishing their benighted characters and obsessive themes as
depressives have in releasing old love objects.[48] Yet out of their apparent
deficiencies come brilliant metaphysical ruminations and amazing flights of
fancy. Their deadpan art passes beyond satire and depression into the ironic
mode.[49] What greater tribute has any artist ever paid to the "absent object"
and the "depressive position" of at-times frantic ennui than *Waiting for
Godot*?—an absurdist compression, so say critics, of (Balzac's) Godeau, God,
and gestapo—to which may be added the good object (or breast).

But our earlier writers eschew any ironic solution to the depressive position.
Kepesh's inner flight becomes his chemically rationalized plight; whereas
Beckett's disabled and atrophied figures—such as the limbless Unnamable in
the glass jar—simply exist. In the ironic, depressive mode, conflicts stemming
from loss are introjected; in the satiric, manic mode, they are projected. The
one shows the skeleton enclosing the vibrant heart; the other sets the skeleton
dancing. In the one loss is inevitable or lamentable; in ther other, avoidable
or tolerable.

For these writers, breast fantasy also subordinates oceanic feeling, mystical
fusion, and the family romance to the soundly traditional ends of the manic
mode of satire. Satire (in its root, "to be full of variety, saturated") presumes
one has swallowed great portions of the outside world and not only at the
breast. Satire is also quite obviously a verbal form of splitting, eliminating,
smearing, desecrating—hence, an outward flow of aggressvie, creative energy;
irony, turning inward preparatory to a more complex, symbolic rebuilding of
self / world than the satiric mode allows for. In the above examples the breast
is perhaps summoned by means of the dream screen in a hypnagogic, creative
state, but memories of later stages of development intrude and permit the

pleasures of utilizing the breast as content while circumscribing its emotional significance.[50] Finally, like the Grail Chalice and the Crucifixion, the breast and the primal scene are not exclusive, but hold each other in dynamic perspective. The one engenders loss; the other, loneliness. As reconstituted by the artist, the one may be the primal image; the other may be the primal symbol. We have only begun to examine their creative import.

To summarize, after a cursory look at the question of whether literary forms or modes may have consistent psychological correlations via fantasy, attention narrowed to the more modest and manageable area of certain basic units of fantasy. While the entry of imagery and symbolism into psychoanalysis under the heading of "indirect representation" in dreams effectively lowered a drawbridge onto the field of literature, the two terms are often either poorly distinguished or used interchangeably, if not indiscriminately, as well. By working from literary examples and from clinical material, I have striven to establish between image and symbol a genetic (or temporal) sequence that can be discerned in latent content and degree of complexity. In classical analytic terms, the image may contribute more to forepleasure, the symbol more to final pleasure, with its bending and harmonizing the demands of reality. In the evolving theories of this study, there appears to be a correspondence of image and symbol to family romance (as dyadic fantasy) and primal scene (as triadic reality). By these polar origins, art is not so much determined as overdetermined.

Appendix B.
A Note on Polar Creativity in the Visual Arts

Christian painting, iconography, and illuminated texts represent in countless variations on polar versions of origins not only by subject matter but by means of opposing murals, diptychs, or marginalia. All together, the phenonema warrant a separate study, but a few examples may serve here. Cathedral vestibules often display opposing murals or paintings—one of the Holy Family, either in a stable setting or in the carpenter shop, on the right, while on the left is displayed the slaughter of the innocents ordered by Herod at the time of Christ's birth. Here one sees a miracle of birth juxtaposed with its violent opposite. Soldiers are mercilessly swinging swords at helpless women, who are either sacrificially offering up their infants or protecting them with their own bodies. Each picture represents a version of origins—one divine and sexless, guarded over by the cherub of religious fantasy; the other a terrifying distortion of primal-scene violence. Unavoidably, the human families entering the church to worship pass between these extremes.

The Book of Hours within one design displays the double motif of the Holy Family fleeing Egypt, while below, Herod's men attack mothers and children. In illuminated manuscripts a scene like the Annunciation, when the Holy Ghost appears as a dove to impregnate Mary through her ear with the Word of God to be made flesh, is bounded by marginalia from pagan mythology—sphinxes, nymphs, fawns, centuars, and the like—sufficient to add what looks to the modern eyes like a cryptic and ironic commentary on our bestial origins, before they were revised by religious ideals. Similarly, gorgons, hyenas, or other mythical beasts are often frozen in the posture of expulsion from a sacred edifice, and even the carved capitals of columns, archways, and pilasters in cloisters, where the sacred otherwise dominates, one encounters similar primal-scene reminders of our animalistic origins. These must have nicely counterpointed a nun's patiently praying over the mysteries of her rosary. As the family-romance version of origins is molded by religious themes of the Immaculate Conception and the Virgin Birth, primal scene reminders are retained in art by subordination and symbolic submersion through more archiac pagan forms, wherein animal instincts and human origins grotesquely converge. As Freud knew, nothing is given up by the mind, but the modes of retention very widely, and often the veils of religious repression are more numerous than Salome's, though no less charming.

Traditional Christian art protects the Virgin Mother by holding her separate and aloof from sexual ideas of any sort, at least if we defer to the artist's conscious intentions, while the loss of the mother image is always associated with awakening sexuality, be it with the serpent crushed beneath her feet or as the *mater dolorosa* contemplating her Son's crucifixion or in a pietà configuration.[1] As noted, crucifixion fantasies have served as the basis for Edelheit's "primal scene schema."[2]

But to the poles of creative endeavor the visual arts offer no more outstanding parallel than *The Garden of Earthly Delights* by Hieronymous Bosch. The vividly surrealistic imagery of the tryptich has excited viewers over the centuries as much as it has confounded critics. It seems to fit into the schemes neither of art history nor of Christian orthodoxy. Not the least of the painting's fascination occurs when the two side panels are closed over the wider center panel and another painting appears. This is the earth itself, a globe in gray tones, harking back, supposedly, to the dawn of creation, to a sphere of primodial unity.[3] The act of opening it then leads one to the next stage of creation, the garden of earthly delights. In other words, when the cosmogonic whole is penetrated, it divides, and out of the pair emerges a third: the meaning of the pair is the coitally joined parents, and of the third, the creation of new life. Creation, like sexual awareness, is both an awful awakening and a fall into a condition of dividedness.

As the eye travels over this brave new world of man and woman in various activities—from praying to sexual playing, bathing to witnessing, along with grotesque scenes of torture and bestialism—one encounters not only the polymorphous perverse phrases (cannibalism, anal eroticism, sadism, satyriasis) up to the genital, but also the larger patterns of humanity from the morning to the evening of our life, from the sunlit bosom of paradise through the dark bowels of damnation.

During the Renaissance, sexual scenes became both explicit and humanized after gaining the right of entry to consciousness in large part by dint of historical and mythological distancing. In Titian's (1477–1576) *Sacred and Profane Love*, critics note that there is little to distinguish "between the two female groups except that one is draped and the other is not"; and Panovsky concluded that the nude actually personified the higher love.[4] In Titian, the voluptuous reclining female, nude or suggestively draped, is usually Venus; her partner is Mars, Adonis, Cupid, a lute player, or the like. Also present on the scene with quivers of arrows are cherubic cupids, bearing witness to the act as well as embodying its consequences. When less threatening shepherds pair off in pastoral innocence, cupids nestle complacently on a nearby bank. Myth also licenses the other side of naturalized sex in the animalistic *Rape of Europa*. In the portrayal of sex as a violent stabbing in his *Tarquin and Lucretia,* a third figure is peeping through the drapery.[5] *The Nymph and the Satyr,* attributed to the Fontainebleau School, features a lusty bearded male with horns and furry flanks coming upon a sleeping nude; as he is about to

Titian, *Tarquin and Lucretia*. Fitzwilliam Museum, Cambridge, England.

remove her hand from her genital area, a frightened cupid raises his arm, apprehensive that once his sleeping beauty awakens to sexuality he will loss her forever. Another painting that plays on the "psychical consequences of anatomical differences" is Tintoretto's *Venus and Mars Surprised by Vulcan*. A bearded Mars is in the process of removing a cloth from Venus's crotch as Vulcan peeks out from under a clothes rack, while Cupid appears to doze in the corner. What he sees, however, with his inner eye is cleverly depicted by a round mirror to his left, a magnified externalization of the eye. Venus herself is already wide awake and with her left arm compliantly lifting her robes. With the child both as issue and witness to parental sex, the primal scene is here most completely rendered.

The combination in many such Renaissance paintings of pagan gods, goddesses, and cherubic offspring who suit family-romance revisions of origins on the one side, with explicit sexual themes whose anlage appears to suit primal-scene versions of origins on the other, is at first perplexing. It had been earlier proposed that family romance and primal scene conflations occur principally in ancient myths and psychotics, but that as culture evolves, the two diverge along separate paths as the mysteries of sex are mastered and the revisions of origins fuel the imagination for purposes of art. Therefore, the conflation of the ideal and the carnal in Renaissance painting would call into question this scenario. But I suspect that since the polar versions of origins thrive within the imagination as inseparable from the psyche, they can be summoned in versatile ways. More specifically, I would interpret these conflations as follows: the copresence of polar versions of origins (the exalted and the lowly, the divine and the mundane) suggests that the intrusion of explicit sexual material in a sublime context overpowers the family romance and may lead to its dissolution as a consequence of primal-scene recognition. That this cryptically recorded advance in sexual cognition should occur along with other advances in the sciences is congruent with the period.

A somewhat more disguised manner in which content evokes primal-scene associations occurs in depicted performances—opera, theater, circus, and the like. W. H. Brown's *Bareback Riders* (1886) depicts a handsome couple gracefully astride a cantering black steed, while in the lower left a dismayed clown looks on helplessly, and on the right a gentleman in formal attire holds a whip. Here the inner theme appears to be the child's envy and admiration for the father's phallic prowess in balancing himself on one foot and the beautiful lady, her face averted, on his knee. Some conflations may merely be visual puns playfully and prankishly daring us to see more in them. Duchamp's application of a mustache to the *Mona Lisa* and Beardsley's androgynous icon (female bosom, male genitalia) for the cover of Wilde's *Salome* manage willy-nilly to elicit a sexual scene by putting the man on the woman—but sometimes a joke is just a laugh.

As opposed to conflation of content, conflation of creative process is uniquely preserved in painting, as earlier drafts of a given work sometimes

W. H. Brown, *Bareback Riders*. National Gallery of Art, Washington D.C., gift of
Edgar William and Bernice Chrysler Garbisch. (See also Seurat's *Circus*.)

survive not only independently but as palimpsests to enrich texture and
subject. In some instances, it appears that the subjective phases of creativity
as a process involving separation-individuation are also preserved and can be
studied. Three examples can be cited. At an exhibition of Andy Warhol's
portraits of friends and celebrities, I was struck by the fact that while most of
them were doubles, mirror images with subtle differences, the exceptions were
four monumental canvases of Chairman Mao, an "Olympian Big Brother,"
as the catalogue reads, and a single portrait of Warhol's mother, Julia
Warhola. There was no self-portrait, but the more one gazed at the mother the
more closely she resembled the son, the original mirror image for his
differentiating self. Look long enough at her image and the son rises almost
to the surface because it is the same basic face or matrix.[6] A computer
analysis of the *Mona Lisa* reveals the same process in reverse order: the painter
began with himself and externalized the other.[7]

The great English painter, J. M. W. Turner (1775–1851) troubled his
enthusiastic apologist, John Ruskin, for never having drawn *"one .. beautiful
... human ... form,"* and David Gervais notes that Turner is "possibly the
greatest painter never to fully articulate his feelings for what was once the
greatest of all subjects, the human body."[8] Adrian Stokes's account is

helpful on several scores, telling us that from an unfinished portrait of his mother, there are strong facial resemblences (when Turner was twenty-five his bad-tempered mother was taken to Bethlehem Hospital and released uncured a year later, to die in an asylum four years later).[9] Taking Stokes's principle inference that the painter's "inner life" was "projected onto Nature," Gervais concludes that his "only way of painting the human form was to paint it as landscape itself."

Turner's *Upper Falls of the Reichenbach: rainbow* supports these views and a good deal more. On the left a vast cascading falls plunges beyond the minute presence of a peasant girl with a lamb; on the mountainside beyond are more sheep grazing. If one peers long enough at this scene, another figure emerges: the precipice directly above the grazing sheep is a huge, backward-tilted chin; below the sheep and a rainbow necklace are two swelling breasts only partially included; around the tip of the chin are pursed lips. It is a woman's head tilted back in agony or ecstasy, recalling (or additionally conflating) both Bernini's Saint Teresa and the Sphinx (both figures of stone). The mustard yellows that Turner favored in many of his canvases render the rocky terrain in near flesh tones. Is this figure, then, Winnicott's "environment mother," who legitimizes her child's creative romance with the world? Is it the mother in the pangs of childbirth, or in sexual pleasure? Or being lost through madness or death? The painting dates from 1806, two years after her actual death. Is it, then, the primary love object lost to consciousness, mourned, and creatively restored?

Stokes addresses Truner's well-established obsession with fire and water (floods, steam, smoke, etc). Via a color link between flame and urine, these fuse in an image of *scalding,* which Stokes associates with the mother/son relation (the mother being scalded as a dire fulfilment of childish fantasy, or the son's being scalded as punishment for his wishes). Stokes is a bit more hesitant and unclear than one could want in this passage,[10] but if the half-buried image of the mother in the landscape is one of pain from burning or scalding, then the falls offer an appropriate counterpoint—a reaction-formation of dowsing the fire one has caused with a torrent of liquid (accompanied by a rainbow promise of no widescale flooding). We also have a novel way of thinking about putting paint onto the canvas as assuaging and reconstituting a burned object: the painter's cool yellows soothe and undo the yellow flames of primitive rage, thus restoring a destroyed object. The motif of upward tilted chin and supine features appears in several of the artist's landscapes, including *The Great Saint Bernard Pass* (1803) and *The First Bridge above Altdorf* (1845).

As another rendition of the creative process, Degas's scenes of dancing lessons and ballet rehearsals with the interplay of feminine grace and masculine preponderance, of stillness and motion, of light and dark, are structurally suggestive of the counterbalancing of male/female principles in art's sublimated mode. But so complete in themselves are these works that to infer more is to risk overdeterminism in the eye of the beholder.

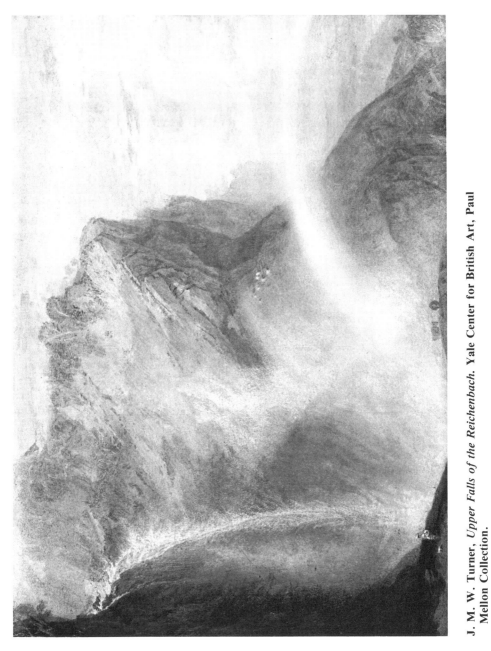

J. M. W. Turner, *Upper Falls of the Reichenbach*. Yale Center for British Art, Paul Mellon Collection.

Although Freud shied away from the lure of Surrealism, with its conscious captivity of the unconscious, one of his successors has probed the cryptic textures of Max Ernst's painting to discern the primal scene's profound imprint.[11] Although, as Berman notes, his mother is all but elided from his autobiography, it begins with an origins fantasy that centers the female and excludes the male: "Max Ernst hatched from an egg which his mother had laid in an eagle's nest and over which the bird had brooded for seven years."[12] Out of these mythical origins emerges the bird Loplop, dream image, self-representation, creative genius, and artistic motif.[13] In Berman's analysis, the artist externalized his childhood fears and sexual quandaries onto furniture or surrounding surfaces, and ultimately derived pleasure from a kind of projected looking. Later he describes how he would voluntarily "provoke hallucinations ... in looking obstinately at wood-panels, clouds, wallpapers, unplastered walls, and so on to let his 'imagination' go." In recalling how he had initiated frottage (rubbing), he describes himself gazing excitedly at a wood-grained floor at an inn: "I then decided to explore the symbolism of this obsession, and to assist my contemplative and hallucinatory faculties, I took a series of drawings from the floorboards by covering them at random with sheets of paper which I rubbed with a soft pencil ... I was surprised at the sudden intensification of my visionary faculties and at the hallucinatory succession of contradictory images being superimposed on each other with the persistence and rapidity of amorous memories." After further explorations, his "eyes perceived human heads, various animals, a battle ending in a kiss."[14] And in that "battle ending in a kiss," he evidently discovered a truer version of origins than being hatched by a magnificent bird.

Appendix C. A Tale of Two Knights, or a Variant on the Heroic Birth Theme in *The Seventh Seal* and *Camino Real*

What these two works[1] have to tell us about the creative process is both interesting and similar up to a point. Both began as one-act plays early in their authors' careers. Not only are they Everyman dramas, but the interweaving of symbols, characters, and events takes on the overdeterminism and irrational logic of the dream.

Their similarities are indeed remarkable. Inherently decent heroes find themselves embarked on a nonspecific quest through a nightmarish world where evil, corruption, and depravity abound. Bergman's Antonius Block is returning from a crusade to find his homeland devastated by a plague. Williams's Kilroy (the name given to GI's in Europe toward the end of the war) is trapped in a Central American town. Their days of masculine glory behind them, they conduct foredoomed skirmishes with a heartless opponent: the monastic chess player, Death, in Block's drama; the fascist hotel manager, Gutman, in Kilroy's.

Along with scenes of cruelty and torture are psychological motifs that point to a sadomasochistic construct of reality. A current of aversion toward women and sexuality in general runs through the works. The heroes are chaste: both having bid farewell to heterosexuality along with their spouses, they seek or settle for male companionship. An equation of sexuality and death is explicit in Kilroy's heart condition (we are warned that "a real hard kiss would kill" him, and indeed an unspecified sexual episode with Esmeralda, the Gypsy's daughter and a forbidden sister, does). And the Knight, having heard that the source of the plague lies between a woman's legs, finds death awaiting him in his wife's castle. Kilroy notes the cruel death of the Baron du Charlus for carrying his perversions to extremes, and the Knight, who wants to solve the riddle of evil in a divinely created world, watches as a hair-shorn girl is burned for witchcraft. For these goodly questers there is something deadly about the female sex.

While there are oblique primal-scene referents in both works, the stronger messages that emerge in the sex = death formula are psychological fears of incest/castration. But it is in respect to the family-romance motifs that the works take us in new directions. As a feudal lord, Block has a castle with a faithful lady awaiting his return, but this embodiment of heroic fantasies is shattered by his homecoming, presided over by Death and followed by the memorable *danse macabre*. The Knight's chivalric romance with his Redeemer extends beyond the grave. But the motifs of exalted parentage and adoption also shape the film more immediately. For it is a traveling family of circus performers who do not adopt the Knight so much as he, by making their safe passage through the night into his own cause, seems to have adopted them. The family includes a juggler given to visions and riddles, his wife, and their small child. Their names (Jof and Marie) and their aura of luminous innocence clearly connect them with the Holy Family. In a radiant scene that stands outside time as a moment of sacramental communion, this family and the Knight share a bowl of wild strawberries and cream. Then the Knight returns to his obsessive chess game with the scythe-bearing monk of Death; and the film ends with a juxtaposition of the Holy Family, epitomizing mankind's sacred origins, seen escaping form the forest of plague and death, while the Knight and his entourage are silhouetted in an apocalyptic procession. Obviously this powerful sequence awakens various meanings for viewers, and I would only suggest here that the modern artist-hero, even while bargaining with his mortal destiny, adopts a family romance vision of reality as the Knight adopts the Holy Family. Ostensibly, the Knight's action affirms the possibility of miracle amidst divine malice; but, more subtly, it is the power of creative imagination that delivers the hero from despair in our modern world of random atrocities and casual cruelties that the film allegorizes.

The Knight's comical sidekick gives the pair a certain quixotic air, and Williams's play is explicitly the dream of a weary old Don Quixote who announces upon his arrival at the Camino Real, where the real is also, in Spanish, *real,* that is, regal—hence, where romatic heroes' dreams and real experiences intersect—that he is seeking a companion to share his journey through *terra incognita.*

Like Block, Kilroy (his oedipal claims implicit in the origins of his name kill-*roi,* i.e., the king)[2] is relentlessly pursued by the Streetcleaners of death, employed by Mr. Gutman, whose sadism evokes World War II Nazis, like the original Gutman, played by Sidney Greenstreet in *Casablanca.* Many of these captive denizens, like the aging lovers, Jacques Casanova and Marguerite Gautier, want to escape, but Kilroy, unable to be of service, instead finds himself initiated into the hapless brotherhood of male cuckolds. This and his fatal encounter with Esmeralda (a forbidden "sister" whose perfume has the scent of "Tabu") prepare Kilroy for his rebirth out of Don Quixote's dream and into that ageless knight's company. Together the two devoted romantics head for the distant mountains, where the violets of higher romance will finally burst through the rocks of brute reality.

The adoption theme here is interesting for being worked out along purely male lines. In traditional myth, the male is twice born, first into nature from the goddess of the earth, second into culture from the god on Olympus, giving the son a bisexual ambience and a rich assortment of goddesses to perform their roles in his adoption. But in these works females are dangers to be avoided, while senior males are split into cruel/kindly portions; and in Williams's play, at least, the rebirth of Kilroy and his adoption by Don Quixote signify a latter-day romantic artist's homosexual resolution to the riddle of origins. Quixote's dream issues from the fertile male womb and reproduces its own kind in the quixotic Kilroy.[3] For his part, Antonius Block, by assuming the role of self-sacrificing redeemer for the Holy Family, is transformed through death into his own Christ-like ideal, and his redemption depends on the kind of faith one brings to the experience. The family romance, then, need not for all male writers lead through primal scene mastery to the strategic "adoption" of adult heterosexuality, as was the preferred route for Joyce and Lawrence.

Appendix D. Shaw and Kafka: The Interplay of Psychological Norms and Literary Values

To advance the issues raised in the introduction and pursued piecemeal thereafter, I would begin by requesting that the reader indulge me in a piece of intellectual history.

For several years I had read Shaw and tried to understand his work in relation to his life. I then wrote a book detailing this understanding.[1] But only after several more years did I begin to understand the book itself. The reason for this cognitive lag is that only in this present study have I been able to formulate the theoretical dimensions toward which the earlier work was groping to locate itself. Fitting the family romance onto my sight like a close-up lens had enabled me to perceive dual motifs working their way through the Shavian material. These were self-images and self-characters, within the orphan / fondling ambience on the one hand, and, on the other, a transformation of the early idealized and deficient mother into the everlasting life force, in constant need of heroes and heroines to guide her forward, either to produce the remade self as the superman or the rebuilt environment through creative evolution. All of those concepts could be poised neatly between the life and the works, and shed light in either direction.

This was all to the good, but I was increasing concerned about Shaw's undeniable sexual troubles—his prolonged virginity, his pattern of attraction to women in their forties (the closer to the age of his mother when she abandoned the family the better), and, finally, his own sexless marriage. These peculiarities were matched with a trend in his creative work following the triumphant synthesis of *Man and Superman* (1903). His goal, after dealing with problems within his society, was to chart the workings of the Life Force, to imagine the process of creative evolution.

But here I encountered contradictions that only now seem resolvable. For while Shaw, in plays like *Back to Methuselah* (1920) and *Farfetched Fables* (1948), had concentrated his evolutionary zeal on human reproduction, his concern for the future reverted to an obsession with the past, and his aims revealed themselves as attempts to revise the whole sexual relationship between man and woman. His ideal of a mental orgasm was more than a witty riposte to romantic enslavemant to the pleasure principle: he really wanted to abolish the sex act. To support and rationalize this aim he placed sexuality on an evolutionary scale. Matriarchal parthenogenesis, discussed by his Don Juan, is the form of reproduction first selected by the life force in its search for fulfilling its purpose. In *Back to Methuselah* time has been projected ahead some twelve centuries, and by now the Life Force, in its unending quest for more perfect forms, has forsaken those sexual practices most common to mankind, but most repellent to Shaw, in favor of oviparity. This hatching process also served to reduce the period of infantile dependency. Beyond that token reliance on matter are the Disembodied Races, currently operating as Thought Vortexes, which penetrate existing forms with evolutionary schemes.

Thus the long-evolved act of human reproduction must continue to "evolve" and be mentally refined until it is finally vaporized into nonexistence. Only in this way can the family romance, as Shaw's creative love affair with the maternal life force, thrive. But the actual primal scene of human origins is precisely what Shaw had been unable, through no fault of his own, to create, hindered as he was by a disfunctional alcoholic father and a headstrong mother, and so he never recreates heterosexual love in the sense of bringing his artistic vision in line with it. Apart from an intellectual model of the philosopher helmsman steering the ship of state fueled by female energy, he either goes behind heterosexuality to presexual patterns or completely passes it by. Hence, in very important ways his art does not return to reality, at least according to present hypotheses and to generally held attitudes toward "reality." Is this valid? On the one hand, my impression was confirmed that despite the brillant Shavian talkathons, important considerations were excluded; on the other hand, all art is supposedly a matter of sublimation and the notion of "return to reality" may enclose hidden agenda—psychological norms overshadowing aesthetic ideals.

Looked at differently, this demonstrable imbalance between the poles of origins makes one wonder whether there may not be a counterbalancing harmony of mature art, analogous to the balancing of male and female psychic components within the artist. Perhaps Platonists, Romantics, and Shavians tilt the scales toward the early idealization of the family romance; and perhaps on the other side, moderns like Franz Kafka are overly burdened by the dehumanizing, alienation powers of the primal scene. Gregor Samsa, who wakes to find himself a giant cockroach, is on one level perhaps responding to the proximity of parental sex relations:

> With his last conscious look, he saw ... his mother in her underbodice ... rushing toward his father, leaving one after another behind her, on the floor, her loosened petticoats, stumbling over her petticoats straight to his father and embracing him, in complete union with him—but here Gregor's sight began to fail—with her hands clasped round his father's neck she begged for her son's life.[2]

His sight fails literally as his comprehension fails psychologically. He sees that the parental act concerns him, which is true insofar as he is its issue, but the sadomasochistic portrayal twists it away from mastery and renders him overwhelmed. Flat on his back, with his numerous thrashing legs, he is both an internalized primal scene and its dehumanizing impact. In his gloss on this passage, John White writes, "The mother is punished (castrated) for her attempt to save the son from the threatening (castrating) father" who "can only possess the mother by eliminating the jealous son."[3]

Kafka's brilliant vignette, "Up in the Gallery," conveys in more human terms the impasse of the child who, having observed the parental relation, would like to turn it into a rescue fantasy in the first paragraph, but seems in the second to recognize the hopelessness of his outsider's status and weeps in resignation.

> If some frail, consumptive equestrienne were to be forced by a merciless, whip-swinging ringmaster to ride on a swaying horse before an insatiable audience for months without a break round and round in the arenas, whizzing along, throwing kisses, swaying at the ceaseless roar of the orchestra and the ventilators into the eternally opening gray future, accompanied by the ebbing and renewed swelling of clapping hands, which really are steam hammers—perhaps then a young visitor to the gallery might race down the long stairway through all the of seats, rush into the arena and cry: Stop! through the fanfares of the always responsive orchestra.
>
> But since that is not so; since a beautiful lady, white and red, flies into the arena through the curtains which the proud grooms open before her; since the ringmaster, devotedly seeking her eyes, breathes toward her in an animal posture; carefully lifts her onto the dapple-gray horse, as if she were his most beloved granddaughter about to start on a dangerous journey; cannot decide to signal with the whip for the performance to start; finally, conquering his apprehension, cracks it; runs alongside the horse, openmouthed; follows the leaps of the rider with a sharp eye; can barely comprehend her artistic skill; attempts to warn with English exclamations; furiously exhorts the hoop-holding grooms to utmost attentiveness; before the great somersault implores the orchestra with raised arms to be silent; finally lifts the girl from the trembling horse, kisses her on both cheeks, and considers no ovation from the audience sufficient; while she herself, supported by him, on the tips of her toes, in a cloud of dust, arms outstretched, head thrown back, attempts to share her fortune with the entire circus—since that is so, the visitor to the gallery lays his head on the railing and, submerging into the closing march as if into an oppressive drama he weeps, without being conscious of it.[4]

The deeper motive for the impasse, the inability to achieve a positive oedipal victory by means of rescuing the mother, is clouded by making her a "consumptive equestrienne." For in so doing he assigns her his own illness and to that extent identifies with her position, the passive feminine one of the negative oedipal conflict. And it is this dilemma that extinguishes both the family romance's rescue variant as well as the prospect for a successful unraveling of the primal scene and finally turns adult sexuality itself into an alien, negative experience. Gabriel Josipovici has articulated this impasse in nonclinical prose. "Kafka's art," he writes, continues his "rebellion against the father. . . . But almost at once he finds the father installed in the very heart of writing itself," that is, in the need for plot, organization, and forward movement. "The rejection of the father thus turns into a rejection of himself not just as businessman, or father, but as writer."[5] Yet his writing draws on this alienation and derives its distinctive power from it. "In the night it became clear to me, as clear as a child's lesson book," he wrote in a 1922 letter, that writing "is a reward for serving the devil."[6]

> This descent to the dark powers, this unshackling of spirits bound by nature, these dubious embraces and whatever else may take place in the nether parts which the higher parts no longer know, when one writes one's stories in the sunshine. Perhaps there are other forms of writing, but I know only this kind; at night, when fear keeps me from sleeping, I know only this kind.

Ultimately, his alienation and self-abasement are converted into an image of inverted heroism in which the writer is the "scapegoat of mankind." Yet paradoxically (again) his apparent failure to work out the sexual equation is indissolubly bound up with his creative distinction. If we are content that he has articulated the modern experience, especially of those elusive borderline states as lucidly as Strindberg has rendered schizophrenic ones, then we need not ask anything more of him.[7] For both authors have thereby extended our human bounds.

But perhaps despite one's sexual preferences, it is possible for everyone to express gratitude for other modern writers who, like Yeats, Joyce, D. H. Lawrence, and Virginia Woolf, have grappled with these problems and taken us some distance down the road in the direction of daylight. It is evident that when Joyce expresses the view that Nora made a man of him, he is also allowing for the opening up of pathways which will lead his art toward greater maturity. Lawrence, for his part, insisted that the male be fertilized by the female, and strove to his last breath to get the sex relation straight and out in the open—no longer "a chamber of horrors." And it is interesting to read in light of the territorial contests over Virginia Woolf's legacy that in 1937 she feels "overcome with happiness. ... Can't bear to be separate. ... an enormous pleasure being wanted: a wife. And our marriage so complete."[8]

But the argument finally is not for heterosexual art, much less for heterosexual artists; rather it is for the significance of an art that partakes of a mutuality derived from male as well as female positions, an art that struggles with its sphinx in order to balance off the unavoidable facts of origins with the alluring alternatives of fantasy. If these become criteria for an art for adults, they are necessarily incomplete and exclusive, for to love art is to love exceptions. But given their limitations, may not these human ideals acquire a validity as yet unrecognized, and a status not unworthy of respect?

Since Winnicott has legitimized a transitional sphere of culture in which everyone resides and carries on the processes of sorting out inner and outer reality, Freud's early formulations about artists' finding their way back to reality can stand an internal revision, for even their writings enter the Winnicott sphere of cultural phenomena. Thus it would be more precise to say that while the artist is finding his / her way to our reality, that is, one that may be valued and shared with others, we are also engaged in finding our way to *his / her* reality. In other words, art entails a dual task; the onus of reaching reality does not fall entirely on artists' shoulders: we must meet them halfway in order to continue the journey together.

Appendix E. The Interfusion of Art and Science; The Creation of Death

"[A blacksmith] will tell you that the bar will dissipate itself away by degrees if you persevere with the hard wallops. Some of the atoms of the bar will go into the hammer and the other half into the table or the stone or the particular article that is underneath the bottom of the bar."

"That is well-known," I agreed.

"The gross and net result of it is that people who spent most of their natural lives riding iron bicycles over the rocky roadsteads of this parish get their personalities mixed up with the personalities of their bicycle as a result of the interchanging of the atoms of each of them and you would be surprised at the number of people in these parts who nearly are half people and half bicycles."

—Flann O'Brien

All the arts and sciences are simply different dialects of the same language, all contributing towards an attitude of life.

—Lawrence Durrell

1. Science Completing Art?

Art has always been deeply involved in the science and philosophy of its time, though once upon a distant time these disciplines were known as magic. Today, we may admire the ritual dancers' carved masks, but behind them the dancers are seriously drawing the gods of rain or thunder or sunlight into their communal orbit. We may be awed by the weird faces stacked up on a totem pole, but it stands there to repulse evil. We may discover hidden gems of fantasy in a cosmogonic myth, but to the tribe it is literal history. We may be dazzled by the patterns that sprinkle out of a Navajo medicine man's fingers to make his exquisite sand painting, but his purpose is curative. Because primitive art has practical or profound functions for its people, we may hazard guesses about the supernatural realm it opens onto—but the distinctions remain our own. It is in our minds that we separate art from magic because we know that in some early cultures this separation actually evolved.

The development of art forms from primitive to modern may be minimal from the perspective of design, but from that of function the changes are substantial. At some point, perhaps comparable to the shift to frontal sex practices, the axis was tilted by beauty away from the primacy of power to that of pleasure. But art as a mimesis of seasonal patterns retains its base in regeneration. In primitive societies it is the magic art of the tribe that ritually creates and renews itself; in modern societies the artist remakes himself and his world in such a way that others may participate in this renewal. A vestige of primordial magic adheres to the art process as a healing, integrative force that contributes to self-revitalization and the binding of disparate individuals into a larger community. Its shocks of recognition, as Melville noted, are transmitted round the globe.

As creativity assumes greater individuation and autonomy in early communities or as their members place greater demands on originality and inventiveness, primitive chants, myths, and tales develop into narrative or dramatic form. But they retain the prevailing cosmology of their time, which, until the seventeenth century in the West, was a peculiar geocentric mix of astrology and observation derived from Ptolemy. This pseudoscientific system provided the superstructure of philosophy and theology for centuries, and, along with them, of art. It is a system both hierarchical and peculiarly poetic, as Northop Frye observes.[1] Its netherworld and upper worlds were charted by Dante under the lantern of Thomism. Milton was the last to retain the classical cosmos as pure poetry. After the new sciences "called all in doubt" and the "circle of perfection" was broken, Romantics like Blake and Moderns like Yeats and Lawrence had to create afresh new systems out of occult sciences and mystical doctrines, for the imagination could neither feed on the bread of empiricism nor be left to starve.[2] Likewise, Joyce and Eliot reshaped universal myths of grail quests and eternal recurrence by means of parallel, paradox, and parody.

Shakespeare and his contemporaries worked with a schematic psychology of chemical elements (earth, air, fire, water) transformed into four basic humors or temperaments (blood—sanguine, choler—choleric, black bile—melancholy, yellow bile—phlegmatic) and did quite well. In *Darwin's Plots,* Gillian Beer has traced the influence of evolution on Victorian fiction; and, among Americans, Jack London, Frank Norris, and Theodore Dreiser used Darwinian motives of natural selection and the struggle for survival to account for social and individual behavior. Shaw turned to Lamarck for his plays about creative evolution.[3] Eugene O'Neill tried to imagine modern family tragedy through the filtering lens of Freud, botching the job in such plays as *Mourning Becomes Electra* and *Strange Interlude* until he relied on the tragic family in his own unconscious for *The Iceman Cometh* and *Long Day's Journey into Night.* In his essay on "Freud and the Future" (1936), Thomas Mann was among the first to explore three bonds between the psychoanalytic and the creative impulse: love of truth, the understanding of disease, especially as an instrument of knowledge, and how penetration into the childhood of the individual soul opens onto the primitive, mythical life of mankind.[4]

Like the spirit world of Primitive art, thought systems enter later stages of art and literature and make themselves felt. But it would be mistaken to conceive of art and science as tap dancing in tandem to provide a compatible understanding of our world.[5] This need is usually satiated by one of the better varieties of science fiction but doomed if it extends further. And regardless of the final form assumed by the work of art, the elements of science are pulled into the artist's creative mix along with everything else he can pluck from the inner world and outer surround. They may become additional "collective alternates" for a family romance to invest with unpredicted meanings, or serve as links or barriers in his/her creative romance with nature;[6] they may bridge a private abyss only to be burned down or blown up later; they may solve technical or tactical problems unforeseen in their home science. In *Ulysses,* scientific ideas are refracted through Leopold Bloom's mind less to inform the reader of the state of science on that June day in 1904 than to formulate the state of Bloom's mind.

Joyce invokes the astronomical term *parallax* to hint at the Einsteinian dimension of his characters (Bloom and Stephen), who are in relatively altering relationships with each other in reference to a third character (Molly). But he allows mythic and scientific perspectives to coexist impartially. Thus, the pre-Copernican universe of our senses informs us that the sun rises from the bed of earth and journeys across the skies till its evening return, like Odysseus leaving and finding his way back to Penelope, or like Bloom leaving "bedsteadfast" Molly for his modern odyssey. Consequently, Joyce's astronomy and astrology are part of a framework "which further enlarges and universalizes the epic scope of the book."[7]

But as often as not the scientific influence on art bears little resemblance to what the scientific mind may want to reclaim as its own. Lawrence Durrell and Samuel Beckett can be cited as two moderns who take modern science in divergent directions.

Durrell, according to John Weigel, composed his *Alexandrian Quartet* after certain ideas from Einstein's physics, which are alluded to by his characters, expressed as metaphors, or exerted on the structure.[8] Justine catches her reflection in five mirrors and exclaims, "Look! five different pictures of the same subject. Now if I wrote I would try for a multi-dimensional effect in character, a sort of prism-sightedness."[9] And when Darley, the narrator-observer on his island, begins the task of writing, he realizes "that each person can only claim one aspect of our character as part of his knowledge. To everyone we turn a different face of the prism." The reader may find such signals intrusive, and the critic may conclude that they are only a fancy way of advancing the traditional business of writing novels. Following Durrell's prefatory note to *Balthazar,* Weigel observes that the first three works of the quartet "relate to space; the fourth to time." Specifying the manner in which humans warp time, Darley wishes to "record experiences, not in the order in which they took place—for that is history—but in the order in which they first became significant to me." Not exactly a radical innovation, and critics like George Steiner have found the "narrative style" ultimately to be "baroque."[10] Yet regardless of how smooth Durrell's integration of science and art ends up—whether Einstein is felt to be an invited guest or an alien ghost—it is certainly one of the more ambitious attempts in this area, though the likelihood that a nuclear physicist might read the *Quartet* with greater awareness than a layman remains an untested hypothesis. And readers who find Durrell's approach too programmatic may turn to critics like Joseph Frank, who has explored the reader's journey through a text as including a linear/temporal flow of words with an expanding "spatial format" of "images, patterns, leit-motivs, analogy, and contrast." That is, the text draws the reader into its own flowing, expanding, contracting space-time continuum. Spatial form is seen as disrupting "pure causal/temporal sequence"; when this happens, the "reader must work out a new [syntax] by considering the novel as a whole in a moment of time."[11] Similarly, Picasso arrived at the simultaneity of cubism without recourse to science but by, among other things, directly observing the rooftop patterns of villages in the Pyrenees.

Certainly the intrusion of a scientific spirit world into the work of Samuel Beckett feels less programmatic and more subtly at home. Beckett is familiar to modern ears as the relentless voice of age and decay, of deterioration and lessness. "As one reads the novels in sequence one notes a tendency to deprive the protagonist more and more of possessions and attributes which are not essential to the central life of a human being," goes a commentary by G. C. Barnard, who concludes that this process is ultimately a search for a central self usually believed by the characters to be exterior but which may be and needs to be interior—a nuclear self, which would arrest the schizophrenic process of deterioration. Barnard continues:

> Murphy abandoned his bourgeois social position and practically all his possessions, except the rocking chair which helped him to close his eyes to the outer world and retire within his mind. Watt abolished the normal 'real' world and lived a life of phantasy. Moran, living at first an inhibited, methodical, middle-class life, bounded by his possessions, house and garden, was driven by his voices to abandon all and wander into the 'Molloy country,' where that physical deterioration commences which ended in Molloy with his two stiff legs and his lack of toes. Molloy's possessions, like Malone's, were reduced to a minimum, a few intrinsically worthless remnants which, nevertheless, had value for their possessor. And in Mahood we reach the limit of denudation; a trunk and head, limbless, with no possessions and no power of speech. Thus rescued he seems as close to 'unaccommodated man' as he could possibly be and yet live.
>
> Yet Beckett goes further, and deprives his protagonist, M, of the whole physical body and of all perception of, and relationship with, the external physical world. But M, still animated by the Will, is impelled to clothe his essential Self with images, the last of which is Worm. To realize Worm imaginatively he necessarily has to attribute to it some signs of existence, such as hearing or movement; but these immediately negate it as a transcendent being; they are 'lendings' which obscure 'the thing itself'. There is no issue from this impasse.[12]

Not only are characters deteriorating, losing bodily parts and mental functions, but the self-supportive systems of logic, reason, and language, as well, are breaking down. The conditions that begin in the microcosm as atrophy radiate outward to the macrocosm as entropy. To paraphrase Barnard, a malignant regressive process within the individual brings about a withdrawal of the ego's cathexis to the external world, representable as a quest for an inner core—corner may be more apt—of the self safe from the bombardment of stimuli from the environment, silent, immune to change or disruption (not unlike Storr's view of Einstein's efforts); ultimately it is toward a womblike nirvana, in positive terms; in negative terms, toward a catatonic stupor or miming of death. Beckett has been considered more as party to this process than its mere spokesman.[13] To what extent this may be valid is more difficult than may be admitted. Certainly he has chosen a marginal, reclusive life-style, but he appears less mad than a schizophrenic *manqué*, who might idealize delusion and disorganization as peacefulness but is continually riveted into painful lucidity: his consciousness can't snap apart and let chaos rush in any more than his organism will permit death before its time.

But whatever the actual situation, he is remarkably well equipped to bridge the inner reality of schizophrenic deterioration and emptiness both with Spenglerian angst over the decline of the West and with sympathetic signals from a universe that, having expanded to its outermost limits, now begins to collapse back on itself. The lessening of energy available for work in maintaining systems is known as entropy; its results are disorganization and dedifferentiation—preparatory, perhaps, for a return to the primordial womb. And Beckett, too, teases at the idea of some rebirth to follow after the collapse into chaos, but most often to mock our hopes. The only game that can be played after Godot again fails to show up is Endgame, the final clearing of the board.[14] But Beckett may have jumped the scientist's gun: the universe may continue expanding indefinitely. It has been described by one scientist as a bowling ball almost at the end of the return track, slowing down as it nears the crest of the final hump: it could waver and roll back or it could make it over. The iffyness of Beckett's creation leaves open various interpretations. Perhaps it is Mother Nature receding from technological man; perhaps it is a personal mother withdrawing from her child before he has created an inner mother or nuclear self. A sadistic component in this process often makes it appear willful, as though she could return like M. Godot, tomorrow, maybe, if she so chose. Meanwhile a self has to be made out of the yawning void and the felt injustices; but for one whose motto might well be, The end is in the beginning—the self Western man labors to create is an absence.

Whether scientists are finding literary parallels to their laws and speculations in postmoderns like Beckett, there are signs of a yin-yang marriage between art and science in the tendency among neuropsychologists like Robert Ornstein to find such archaic literary forms as the Sufic parables and Buddhist koans, to be peculiarly reponsive to the right brain's mode of "holistic mentation";[15] while physicists and microbiologists are discovering corresponding echoes of their insights in Blake's infinity in a grain of sand or in Yeats's imagery of the dancer as inseparable from the dance, as well as in the aesthetics of irregualrity in Taoism and in the resurgence of interest in Gaia, the Greek earth goddess and personification of our living planet. In fact, poetic imagery is being consumed by many more scientists today than by literary pundits, who are content to diet on the meager menus of deconstructionism.

But clearly this holistic tendency in both the healing arts and the theoretical sciences is a hallmark of our time. On a subjective level, the message seems to be that not only may humankind lay claim to the mother of frustration and separation, she who signifies betrayal and provokes mastery and alienation, but we may also share the primordial mother of oneness and connectedness with whom we once shared symbiotic intimacy.[16] Is this a case of the return of the repressed as lost emotional territory formerly excluded by the restrictive rational mind? So it seems. But this mother, who, it is felt, must be reclaimed in order to ensure a sense of wholeness, has always been known to artists, who kept her alive in their creative romance with the world.

2. Or Art Completing Science?

> Art is the perfection of nature.
> —Sir Thomas Browne, *Religio Medici*

Hugh Kenner's *The Mechanic Muse* (1987) deftly details the interface of technologies and modern experimentation, but not all moderns were susceptible to the incursions of applied science—D. H. Lawrence, for instance. His works do, however, demonstrate how scientific elements can influence and alter natural as well as artistic creativity to such an extent that all three become virtually inseparable. It may be said that he encounters nature with the same pantheistic exuberance as his Romantic forbears; but when he cast a cold eye on his native colliery he saw what Blake had found in the "Satanic mills" where wheels "with cogs tyrannic/[were] moving by compulsion each other"—in short, Newtonian science at work, converting individuals into mechanisms within a cosmic machine.[17] Beyond social compromise, Lawrence's human beings are "carried along by either currents of life energy or currents of death energy."[18] The death-energy system is paradoxically adaptive to the present industrial order. Ursula in *The Rainbow* (1915) observes her schoolmistress with her uncle Tom and thinks that his "real mistress was the machine" and that Miss Inger "worshipped the impure abstraction, the mechanisms of matter" where she was "free from the clog and degradation of human feeling."[19] And in the sequel, *Women in Love* (1920), Gerald, the strong-willed mining magnate, represents to Gudrun the "terrible bondage of this tick-tack time, this twitching of the hands of the clock, this eternal repetition of hours and days."[20]

A machine has no personal history and, as Bersani notes, "no connections beyond its own system of organized motion." It epitomizes the deathlike efficiency of absolute narcissism and the self-centered mode of "frictional sex," in which each partner, acting and reacting against the other, strives for his or her satisfaction. The orgasm is the product of this mechanical sex, or "machine-fucking," as Mellors snorts in a burst of misanthropy to Connie.[21] By such means does Lawrence wire a scientific theory and a social mode to human genitalia.

Since his colliery father was both party to and victim of industrialism, it is not accidental that Lawrence's quest for revitalizing the sex relation included the dislocations of his filial ties along with a need to revise his origins and remake himself and his world in non-Newtonian terms. Only a reimmersion in nature can begin to heal the wounds of industrialism on the body of the world. But this also entails a reconciliation with the biological father. Thus Mellors is a tough countryman who reverts to the father's dialect; and as the one was a miner who descended into the pits, the other is portrayed as a prospector who "smelt out the heaviest ore of [Connie's] body into purity" in a tender-sensual, organic mode of touch rather than brutalizing exploitation. As Mellors approaches Connie, so Lawrence views creative work as a "re-sourcing" of the sexual relation via the novel, which "can inform and lead into new places the flow of sympathetic consciousness ... and reveal the passional secret places of life."[22] The final results of artistic creativity are, of course, the works themselves. At their highest pitch, when they are works of genius, they "create a new universe that we cannot 'unthink,' which we cannot truly conceive of as not existing."[23]

Similarly in science, the final results had first begun as hypotheses that hatched into theories and laws and then grew into the systems and structures that transform our environment as well as our images of ourselves. For through the wonders of science we are also being created. We go to work to encounter our brains in computers, return home to find ourselves on electronic screens. There and in other places we see our reflections variously as space traveler, risen ape, machine with replaceable parts. Having created science, it returns the favor by recreating us and our world. Even the slabs of Stonehenge have been decoded as a primitive computer: supposedly "one mark on the long road of progress toward mincrominiaturization and the on-board computers that took Apollo spaceships to the moon," observe a pair of skeptical anthropologists who more modestly conclude the stones have more to do with pastoral life in the second millenium B.C. than with today's computer science.[24] This appropriative urge is complementary to the biologist's efforts to find a primordial, brainy ancestor who will endow his current interests with a legitimate bloodline. And, so, even when we admire science for recreating life in more validly objective terms we must make allowances for subjective, narcissistic forces to color, shape, and maintain a centripedal orbit for our inner spaceships. The longest way round is the shortest way home, goes a famous line of Homeric lineage, and it appears to have been neceesary for science to land on the moon in order to discover earth as a lonely oasis in a wasteland of space. But surely the other image of our planet, as Spaceship Earth, is illusory, for it assumes scientific man is confidently seated at the controls.

William Neiderland reminds us in a series of probing studies that the science of geography stems from *Gaia* or *Gē,* that earliest of Greek earth goddesses, and fittingly so, since geography is a continuation of exploration by the individual over a larger body begun by the infant in the sphere of preplay, when the mother's body was his universe.[25] This correspondence has suggested to Niederland that a new science of psychogeography be launched, and I have been struck by the coincidental fact that D. H. Lawrence in writing about the migrations of European peoples westward toward new centers (or nodalities), states that "place attracts its own human element, and the race drifts inevitably to its own psychic geographical pole."[26]

For Niederland the "Imago Mundi is the mental representation of the world," with unconscious sources in the dual unity of mother-infancy, and, so, "the history of geographic exploration is permeated by a multitude of fantasies, myths, superstitious beliefs, and other subjective elements."[27] He traces both the naming of America and California to an archaic belief in blissful islands (as both bodies of land appeared on early maps), referred to as *Insulae Fortunatae.* The naming of America was in some respects a misnomer, but it caught on and gained widespread acceptance in part because Americus Vesputious's name appeared on an island-shaped map of the new continent, and the name itself has linguistic affinities with Romance language words for mother. Similarly Edward Said in *Orientalism* (1979) demonstrates how far the East is a subjective creation of the West. And although he is not a psychoanalyst, it is apparent from his work that the Orient is the object of projections, centering on the female as passive, mysterious, alluring, corrupt, and promiscuous. The relinquished mother of the oedipal period may have only receded and been reestablised in the beckoning/forbidding land of the East.

It is not surprising, then, that travel often stimulates natural as well as artistic creativity in the dyadic and triadic areas, nor that the extension of any frontier is felt as a triumph over the ultimate darkness that conceals death.

3. Death as Final Self-Creation

"But better to die than live mechanically a life that is a repetition of repetitions. To die is to move on with the invisible. To die is also a joy, a joy of submitting to that which is greater than the known: namely, the pure unknown."

—D. H. Lawrence, *Women in Love*

The first results of natural creativity are a self, an unfolding identity, and a life-style. The later fruits of natural creativity are observable in the production of a family, a career or profession, the sum total of what Jung called everyone's life task. In Yeats's twenty-eight lunar phases of the soul: "Before the full / It sought itself and afterwards the world."[28] In some as yet undefined way, artistic creativity, given its head, tends to appropriate the energies of natural creativity. "The intellect of man is forced to choose / Perfection of the life, or of the work," is Yeats's stark rephrase of the scholastic antimony between the virtures of prudence and art. The comic master of the Restoration stage, William Congreve, seemed to have both recognized and surmounted the dilemma when he claimed to have put his talent into writing and his genius into living. Those who followed after and became known as dandies managed to turn their lives into works of art but left little else for us to remember them by. As medical science becomes ever more precise in predicting one's life expectancy or the duration of terminal illnesses, and as death with dignity or the right to die is widely debated, perhaps there is also a sense in which one creates one's own death—the final act of natural creativity. Creative suicide has already been made into a TV documentary.

"The aim of all life is death," Freud wrote in *Beyond the Pleasure Principle,* echoing Shakespeare, misconstruing biology, but laying out an intriguing hypothesis. Being conservative, the instincts aim to return life to an earlier state, and so the "living organism struggles most energetically against events (dangers, in fact) which might help it to attain its life's aim rapidly—by a kind of short-circuit."[29] The aim is to die *naturally.* But the situation is even more paradoxical in human organisms, for they insist on mixing free will and illusion into the base of necessity in order that even death may appear to be created. Shakespeare is perhaps kindest in allowing his tragic heroes to create their own dying—are they also dress rehearsals for our own performance? K. R. Eissler says that Freud was more indebted to Shakespeare than to biological evolution for his death-instinct theory—another case of one variety of creativity filling the needs of another.[30]

But if death is a feature of natural creativity, artists have never been hesitant in including winter within the seasonal cycle. And a few memorable characters have, in fact, set about creating their deaths. It is the implicit burden of Tolstoy's character in "Ivan Illyich." In Robert Browning's (1849) "The Bishop Orders His Tomb at Saint Praxed's Church," the secret gradually dawns on the reader that the decadent papist, "dying by degrees / Hours and long hours in the dead night," has no intention of dying or of entering a spiritual paradise.[31] He plans to "lie through the centuries" amid precious stones, the mutterings of a Mass, and the scent of incense and gradually turn himself into a work of art. The ambivalent wish to escape life into permanence is continued in Yeats's golden bird on a golden bough, which sings about the generation of the very living things it had sought to escape. Yeats came to share the Heraclitean view that "men and gods die each other's life, live each other's death," and he called this spirit tragic gaiety. By creating culture, we incorporate death and recreate it (though Ernest Becker following Otto Rank views culture as a denial of death).[32]

D. H. Lawrence captured these tensions in human life in a fragment he wrote, called "The Flying Fish."[33] He had nearly died of complications from pneumonia in Mexico City in 1926, and for the first time was faced with an irrefutable diagnosis of tuberculosis (a word he never allowed himself to use). The manuscript remains unfinished because, as he explained to friends, it was "written so near the borderline of death, that I have never been able to carry it through in the cold light of day."

It opens with Gethin Day, an Englishmen and amateur botanist being summoned home by his dying sister Lydia (the name of Lawrence's mother): "Come home else no Day in Daybrook" ("Flying Fish," 780). This family estate in the English midlands was built in the sixteenth century by another traveler, Sir Gilbert Day, who made his house an ark of continuity against the floods of time, with a flying fish on its roof. Sir Gilbert's *Book of Days* further binds the individual to time and history by the "Common day of ordinary living and the Greater Day," the Absolute, which contains everything. In Mexico, Gethin has found that the ordinary day "had cracked like some great bubble, and to his uneasiness and terror, he had seemed to see through the fissures the deeper blue of that other Greater Day where moved the other sun shaking its dark blue wings" (782). And "now, try as he might, he was aware of a *gap* [my italics here only] in his *time-space continuum*."

> Gethin Day would sit for hours at the very tip of the ship, on the bowsprit, looking out into the whitish sunshine of the hot Gulf of Mexico. Here he was alone, and the world was all strange white sunshine, candid, and water, warm, bright water, perfectly pure beneath him, of an exquisite frail green. It lifted vivid wings from the running tip of the ship, and threw white pinion-spray from its green edges. And always, always, always it was in the two-winged fountain, as the ship came like life between, and always the spray fell swishing, pattering from the green arch of the water-wings. And below, as yet untouched, a moment ahead, always a moment ahead, and perfectly untouched, was the lovely green depth of the water, depth, deep, shallow-pale emerald above an under sapphire-green, dark and pale, blue and shimmer-green, two waters, many waters, one water, perfect in unison, one moment ahead of the ship's bows, so serene, fathomless and pure and free of time. It was very lovely, and on the softly-lifting bowsprit of the long, swift ship the body was cradled in the sway of timeless life, the soul lay in the jewel-coloured moment, the jewel-pure eternity of this gulf of nowhere. And always, always, like a dream, the flocks of flying fish swept into the air, from nowhere, and went brilliantly twinkling in their flight of silvery watery wings rapidly fluttering, away, low as swallows over the smooth curved surface of the sea, then gone again, vanished, without a splash or evidence, gone. One alone like a little silver twinkle. Gone! The sea was still and silky-surfaced, blue and softly heaving, empty, purity itself, sea, sea, sea.

And it is through the sea that he discovers the Absolute, an element not his own, not a void, not entropy, but the ecstatic, rhythmic sources of life, which, glimpsed in its totality, is a perfection beyond human capacity. He

watched spell-bound, minute after minute, an hour, two hours, and still it was the same, the ship speeding, cutting the water, and the strong-bodied fish heading in perfect balance of speed underneath, mingling among themselves in some strange single laughter of multiple consciousness, giving off the joy of life, sheer joy of life, togetherness in pure complete motion, many lusty-bodied fish enjoying one laugh of life, sheer togetherness, perfect as passion. They gave off into the water their marvellous joy of life, such as the man had never met before. And it left him wonderstruck.

'But they know joy, they know pure joy!' he said to himself in amazement. 'This is the most laughing joy I have ever seen, pure and unmixed. I always thought flowers had brought themselves to the most beautiful perfection in nature. But these fish, these fleshy, warm-bodied fish achieve more than flowers, heading along. This is the purest achievement of joy I have seen in all life: these strong, careless fish. Men have not got in them that secret to be alive together and make one like a single laugh, yet each fish going his own gait. This is sheer joy—and men have lost it, or never accomplished it. The cleverest sportsmen in the world are owls beside these fish. And the togetherness of love is nothing to the spinning unison of dolphins playing under-sea. It would be wonderful to know joy as these fish know it. The life of the deep waters is ahead of us, it contains sheer to-getherness and sheer joy. We have never got there.'

There as he leaned over the bowsprit he was mesmerized by one thing only, by joy, by joy of life, fish speeding in water with playful joy. No wonder Ocean was still mysterious, when such red hearts beat in it! No wonder man, with his tragedy, was a pale and sickly thing in comparison! What civilization will bring us to such a pitch of swift laughing togetherness, as these fish have reached? (794–95)

Perhaps Lawrence failed to create death after all; or perhaps he worked through death, as did Nietzsche with his Dionysian vision of tragedy as a celebration of life, or Yeats with his vision of Irish martyrs as the birth of a terrible beauty. But certainly in his late poems like "The Ship of Death," Lawrence subtly evokes the idea of the artist's narcissistic injury and transcends it as the necessary death-blow that opens the self to the seeds of rebirth:

> Now it is autumn and the falling fruit
> and the long journey towards oblivion.
>
> The apples falling like great drops of dew
> to bruise themselves an exit from themselves.
>
> And it is time to go, to bid farewell
> to one's own self, and find an exit
> from the fallen self.[34]

The fallen self that drops into the "Greater Day" and thereby falls into cycles of mortality also has the power to create itself with memories of an arboreal Eden, of the serpent's apple in the garden, of Newton's apple of gravity, of Cezanne's apples, which are beautiful women, or of Lawrence's female pomegrante, wherein "the end cracks open with the beginning." Thus Lawrence, setting out to create the "pure unknown" of death, succumbs to the phoenix of regeneration, while Beckett, overwhelmed by mortality, strives to create nothing else: "They give birth astride of a grave, the light gleams an instant, then it's night once more.[35]

In mourning, natural creativity allows all of us to introject death and recreate it as we internalize and assimilate a relationship to a lost love-object. Our capacity to create life out of its absence is balanced by another power, that of seeing and knowing what we create. "We walk through ourselves, meeting robbers, ghosts, giants, old men, young men, wives, widows, brothers-in-law," muses Joyce's Stephen in *Ulysses*: "but always meeting ourselves" (*Ulysses,* 213). (Do we meet ourselves even in cosmic space? Is every encounter in some way a self-encounter: Dr. Frankenstein, I presume?)

Stephen's sentiments are later echoed by his counterpart and ghostly father, Bloom: "Think you're escaping and run into yourself. Longest way round is the shortest way home." The sense of home must be what makes GEography psychic.

If, as it appears, inner reality, with its potential for self-knowledge, must somehow become reflected, displaced, or projected before it can be recognized and perhaps reassimilated, then our continual recreating of works of science or of art, of our own racial or individual past, of all our various past and present relations, of our disciplines and occupations, of our shifting roles or ideals of ourselves—all form part of our unending self-creation. Sartre maintained somewhere that as knowledge must always be objective and the self always be subjective, ergo self-knowledge was unattainable. Although we all probably violate the philosopher's logic in minor ways, Freud's self-analysis stands as a major one. Yet he acknowledged the Joycean process referred to above when he wrote Fliess (14 November 1897), "I can only analyse myself with objectively acquired knowledge (as if I were a stranger)." If self-analysis were possible, he adds, there would be no illness. But stranger-analysis is both a possibility and a continuing process. We read and reread the great works of artistic and scientific imagination because we sense in some fashion they have already read us. Thus we strive toward the objectively subjective goal of self-knowledge.

Appendix F.
Royal Fantasy and Historical Interface

> The pulse of the passions assuredly beat as high, the depths and soundings of the human heart were as well understood three thousand years ago, as they are at present; the face of nature and 'the human face divine,' shone as bright then as they have ever done.
>
> —William Hazlitt

> What is now prov'd was once only imagin'd.
>
> —William Blake

Freud, whose name has become synonymous with inherent drives and inner motives, deviated from his own radical originality on two occasions when he speculated about a band of brothers, who out of sexual deprivation cannibalized their primal father and thereby started the oedipal ball rolling. The first occasion was in *Totem and Taboo,* and the second was in the recently-discovered paper, "A Phylogenetic Fantasy," which he had the prescience not to publish.[1] In this Lamarckian scenario, the sons' paranoia is generated by the fathers' actual castrations and then genetically transmitted to future generations. In her paper on insight, Anna Freud speculates more subtly that the development of one's system of defenses "may go back to phylogenesis, when men had to maintain themselves in surroundings which were more hostile and more dangerous to them than any of their own instinctual drives."[2] The flight response to an external danger then gradually becomes internalized as one learns to repress, avoid, displace, etc., dangerous internal wishes bred by the monsters within. The appeal of her shift in emphasis from drive to defense is that civilization, from a psychoanalytic point of view, is greatly contingent on the internalization and sublimation of psychic activity being prevented direct expression—hence the superego, eroticism, and guilt.

By way of analogy with the phylogenetic origin of psychic conflict, I am intrigued with the origin of imagination and those psychic polarities that fuel it. The innermost core of much imaginative energy clearly shows up as one's sense of being an orphan / foundling, which is made tolerable through a family romance and then granted infinite elaborations via the artist's creative romance with the world. But what if what has been thoroughly analyzed as humanity's (quite possibly) most ubiquitous fantasy should have once stemmed from a normal practice? What if "psychoanalytic thought" has only "minimally conceptualized the child as coping with the hatred absorbed from its disturbed parents''?[3]

Children, who have for many centuries been the objects of a brutalizing history, have only recently become its subjects. The psychohistorical investigations of Lloyd deMause, for example, trace an evolutionary line of parenting modes that approximate the rise of civilization and run from infanticidal to abandonment, ambivalent, intrusive, socializing, and most recently helping/empathic practices.[4] Support for this controversial schema comes from an independent quarter in John Boswell's *The Kindness of Strangers: The Abandonment of Children in Western Europe from Late Antiquity to the Renaissance.*[5] His exhaustive documentation established that for centuries the exposing and selling of children was a commonly accepted practice, neither proscribed by law nor discouraged by moralists. Children were simply family property, specifically the father's, to be disposed of as seen fit (only selling into slavery was frowned upon). Those born out of wedlock were given even slighter prospects of survival—drowning was commonly their fate. At best, the others would be swaddled and suspended in trees to protect them from wild animals, until a kind-hearted, affluent stranger might pass by and take pity. Later there would be church steps and discrete chutes, monasteries, convents, and orphanages to absorb the unwanted.

What was widespread in late antiquity must have also existed in earlier times, for example, whenever population growth exceeded food supplies or whenever sexual practices conspicuously violated communal taboos. Thus all children would grow up either having experienced some form of parental abandonment or having observed it in their immediate surroundings, be it done to a sibling or a neighbor. The likelihood of its being a purely subjective fantasy seems highly remote, and consequently myths about the birth of a hero or the founding of a race would have been incorporating real-life experiences. But, along with the literary works they often evolved into, the ancient narratives far exceeded the precipating deed. "The founding of the Roman state," Boswell writes, "was the happy result of the abandonment of children." A "vestal virgin who had been raped bore twin sons, and the harsh monarch ordered them abandoned on the Tiber. Left in a basket which floated ashore, they were found by a wolf and suckled by her until a shepherd took them home to his wife and the couple brought them up as their own."[6] But the actuality of abandonment has been reversed and transformed by the imagination. Historically, the abandoning parents would most likely be from the poorer classes like the shepherds, who are duly assigned foster-care roles; the danger of exposure to wild animals is converted into a maternal wolf; and the narcissistic injury is compensated for by the twins' heroic destiny as Romulus and Remus.

Thus, while abandonment could well have been an ever-present threat, imagination correctively reworks this fundamental trauma into a more tolerable form with results that inscribe the origins as well as the triumph of art. Enkidu is adopted by the royal Gilgamesh only to abandon him in death; the tale of Oedipus encompasses physical abuse, exposure, multiple parents, heroic achievement, and incest. As Boswell points out, given the prevalence of abandonment, incest with one's grown child in a brothel or elsewhere was a key source of concern.[7] For contemporaneous audiences, *Oedipus Rex* was probably a very realistic drama. Such tragedies notwithstanding, literature is generally stamped from early on with a wishful resolution to dire historical realities. In much classical drama and romance, literary convention thrives on recognition scenes in which reunion with a long-lost relation evidently served to lessen the guilt of those parents who exposed or sold their children and to sustain the hopes of siblings who have been forcibly separated. The extraordinary feats of heroes who began life as foundlings would also alleviate parental guilt. The optimistic prospects of orphans who become famous, powerful, or wealthy of course also imply attempts at undoing psychic traumas on the part of the victims, although recent studies have found a high correlation between parental loss and exceptional achievements by the orphaned children.[8] But that may largely attest to unusually strong drives toward mastery.

Indeed, the concept of abandonment has always been a composite of subjective and objective features for at least as long as children have been able to form an affective attachment to a primary care-giver. Given its high visibility in ancient times, abandonment would inevitably have been incorporated by children as a signifier of retaliation for their own hostile wishes toward the parents (arising from abuse, neglect, or exclusion from sexual activity). At that point, the prospect of abandonment became a psychic event.[9] Thus both the path of the child who had suffered actual abandonment and that of the child who had felt abandoned by emotional slights or from projection meet at the crossroads of narcissistic injury where a corrective way out of their painful conditon is sought.

The analogy here would be with Freud's seduction theory, which he set aside with the discovery of psychic reality; but while he discarded the theory of childhood seduction as an adequate key to neurosis, he never discounted the role of seduction as contributing to emotional conflict. Similarly, it is not the practice of abandonment *per se* but what the imagination does with it by way of healing inner wounds that helps account for the emergence of art. For just as psychoanalysis became a science of wishes, so did literature become a critical reenactment of wishes. Strictly speaking, both art and psychoanalysis are less beholden to deeds done than to their emotional import.

Returning to the spirit of Freud's speculations about a primordial parricide to validate the Oedipus complex, I would propose that as the fears or the effects of abandonment have been internalized for purposes of mastery, the imagination is being conceived. Its phylogenetic birth, however, entails neither a totally external event nor a purely internal fantasy, but rather a complex series of feedback loops that draw on historical abandonment, emotional loss and self-injury, fantasies of recovery, and literary convention. An additional loop would include as part of the child's struggle for mastery his/her need to establish selfhood by discovering the true parents, resolving the riddle of origins, and grasping the nature of sexuality.

The importance of this inner struggle between degrees of illusion and reality helps explain why changing historical patterns, e.g., parenting and the decline of socially-sanctioned abandonment or other external influences, go only so far in elucidating the unfolding life of the imagination. Yet inescapably, artists who perennially draw on the resources of the family romance are not only appealing to something central in everyone's emotional life but are also revealing memory-traces of very ancient practices. To modify Blake: what they freely imagine today was actually done then. Thus, while art is always changing, the core of the imagination itself does not evolve in any directional sense, possibly because historical as well as emotional truth anchors its center. Is this the artist's innermost secret that Freud felt never would be penetrated?

In any event, William Hazlitt's 1817 essay, "Why the Arts Are not Progressive," still makes provocative reading.[10]

Notes

Chapter 1. A Dialectics of Creativity

1. Sigmund Freud, *Standard Edition*, vol. 9 and 11, respectively (London: Hogarth, 1955).

2. Ernst Kris, *Psychoanalytic Explorations in Art* (London: George Allan and Unwin, 1953).

3. The classic paper on this viewpoint is Robert C. Bak's "The Phallic Woman," *The Psychoanalytic Study of the Child* 23 (1968): 15–36.

4. "Classically," writes T. A. Watters, the family romance "occurs with the child's wish to be adopted by a noble person, resulting from the nature of the child's emotional problems, his [her] imaginative resourcefulness, adroitness, plausible possibility and circumstances, such fantasy taking innumerable forms." The earlier forms include "wishing to be adopted, being adopted, or being a step-child as a release from sibling rivalry or replacement"; later forms are erotically tinged from the "unsolved disappointments and despair of the oedipal period" ("Forms of the Family Romance," *Psychoanalytic Review* 43 (1956): 204–13). Note a distinction that can prevent confusion: in the fantasy, the wish is to be adopted; in the family romance, one is adopted, but by a lowly set of parents with one's task being to recover the original royal pair, the true parents. The phrase "innumerable forms" is essential to this study. Watters also notes a gender factor: "in the prepubescent girl there is a more healthy preoccupation with romantic thoughts, whereas in the boy there may be the romantic ones, but in addition those of ambition." Feminists may find this a backhanded compliment, but imaginative works by women do favor the romantic over the ambitious, for whatever complicated psychocultural reasons.

5. Otto Rank, *The Myth of the Birth of the Hero* (New York: Knopf, 1959); *Psychoanalytic Explorations on Art*; Phyllis Greenacre, "The Family Romance of the Artist," *The Psychoanalytic Study of the Child* 13 (1958): 9–36. Although Skura defines primal fantasy with an emphasis on primary process thinking, rather than, as I do, on origins, I agree with her general approach to the subject and in particular when she states that the "true building blocks of the imagination are not daydreams but primitive fantasies," allowing that much more also goes into the building up of creative products (Meredith Anne Skura, "Literature as Fantasy: Psychic Function," in *The Literary Use of the Psychoanalytic Process* [New Haven: Yale University Press, 1981], chap. 3, p. 78).

6. William Niederland "Clinical Aspects of Creativity," *American Imago* 24 (1967): 6–34; "Psychoanalytic Approaches to Creativity," *Psychoanalytical Quarterly* 45 (1976): 185–212.

7. Jean-Paul Sartre, *The Words* (New York: Fawcett World, 1966), 121.

8. Linda Joan Kaplan, "The Concept of the Family Romance," *The Psychoanalytic Review* 61 (1974): 169–202; Heinz Kohut, *The Analysis of the Self* (New York: International Universities Press, 1971).

9. Naming his study *Idols of Perversity: Fantasies of Feminine Evil in Fin-de-Siècle*

Culture (New York: Oxford, 1986) after a Medusa *cum* halo painting by Jean Delville, Bram Dijkstra documents the pervasiveness of these images. Referring to the painting, he writes, "As a result of her instinctual affinity with the animals, woman had truly become 'the idol of perversity,' the livid-eyed, snake-encircled, medusa-headed flower of evil, whose aggressively pointed breasts were as threatening as the fangs of a devouring animal. This woman, if she were to breed at all, could only be expected to mother hordes of degenerate temptresses, treacherous sea creatures, predatory cats, snakelike lamias, harpies, vampires, sphinxes, countless other terrible, man-eating creatures" (325). A distinction could be made between the monster as projecting/threatening engulfment or as conveying castration fears; and some composite monsters, like the sphinx and medusa, contain enough male elements to invite ambivalent sexual and primal-scene interpretations as a way through the infantile morass. While the image of woman as "idol of perversity" nicely epitomizes the morbid inversion of the family romance, I am not presuming to reduce these richly complex figures, which not incidentally accompanied women's gradual emancipation, to a core fantasy, but simply to suggest that a repulsive tie is still a tie; a dark romance with a frightful goddess is still a romance. Obviously there is a repertory of preexisting forms for artists to draw on at any given time under various internal and external pressures, but they were not always preexisting, and even when reenlisted for current purposes they must to a degree by freshly re-created. For more on the subject, see Virginia M. Allen, *The Femme Fatale* (Troy, N.Y.: Whitston, 1983); Margaret Hallissy, *Venomous Woman* (Westport, Conn.: Greenwood, 1987).

10. Emily Dickinson, *The Letters*, vol. 1, ed. by Thomas Johnson (Cambridge: Harvard University Press, 1958), 306.

11. S. Freud, "A Special Type of Object-Choice Made by Men," vol. 11 of *Standard Edition*.

12. Edoardo Weiss, "The Phenomenon of 'Ego Passage,'" *Journal of the American Psychoanalytic Association* 3 (1954): 267–281.

13. S. Freud, "From the History of an Infantile Neurosis," in vol. 11 of *Standard Edition*.

14. William Niederland, "Early Auditory Experiences, Beating Fantasies and the Primal Scene," *The Psychoanalytic Study of the Child* 13 (1958): 471–504; "Clinical Aspects of Creativity," *American Imago* 24 (1967): 6–34.

15. While my own approach is transhistorical and transcultural, I am aware not only of multiple functions but also of manifold causality for the fantasies and creative motives under discussion. For an exploration of the relativizing influences on a primal fantasy, see Stanley Rosenman, "The Myth of the Birth of the Hero Revisited: Disasters and Brutal Child Rearing," *American Imago* 45 (1988): 1–44.

16. Otto Rank, *The Myth of the Birth of the Hero*; Geza Roheim, *The Riddle of the Sphinx* (London: Hogarth Press, 1934); Geza Roheim, *The Gates of the Dream* (New York: International Universities Press, 1952); Theodore Reik, *Dogma and Compulsion* (New York: International Universities Press, 1951).

17. James Clark Moloney, "Oedipus Rex, Cu Chulain, Khepri and the Ass," *Psychoanalytic Review* 54 (1967): 201–47.

18. Angel Garma (1978) explores the implications of his title, "Oedipus Was Not the Son of Laius and Jocasta." Since both sets of parents are rulers and since the family romance plays off superior against inferior, it is logical that the real parents would be more plebian, possibly the shepherds who received him from his first royal mother and passed him on to his second. The lowly shepherds may be represented by the coital Sphinx, the asexual phase of the fantasy by the Corinthian parents, and the sexual Phase by the Theban parents (*International Journal of Psychoanalytic Psychotherapy* 7: 326–25).

19. Dorothy Smith Sides, *Decorative Art of the Southwestern Indians* (New York: Dover Publications, 1961).

20. Eva Hunt, *The Transformation of the Hummingbird* (Ithaca: Cornell Universities Press, 1977). See also Gerardo Reichel Dolmatoff, *Amazonian Cosmos: The Sexual and Religious Symbolism of the Tukan Indians* (Chicago: University of Chicago Press, 1971).

21. Henry Edelheit, "Crucifixion Fantasies and Their Relation to the Primal Scene," *International Journal of Psycho-Analysis* 55 (1974): 193–204.

22. Emily Dickinson, *Letters*, Vol. 2, 508.

23. "Jack Kerouac Conference at Volo University," *New York Times*, 7 July 82, 8.

24. M. Griaule, *Conversations With Ogotemmeli* (New York: Oxford University Press, 1956).

25. William Niederland, *The Schreber Case* (New York: Quadrangle Press, 1974), 85.

26. Maurits Katan, "Schreber's Hereafter," in the Niederland study.

27. Daniel Dervin, *Through a Freudian Lens Deeply, A Psychoanalysis of Cinema* (Hillsdale, N.J.: Analytic Press, 1985).

28. Dervin, *Through a Freudian Lens Deeply*.

29. Harold Blum, "A Psychoanalytic View of *Who's Afraid of Virginia Woolf?*," *Journal of the American Psychoanalytic Association* 17 (1969): 888–903.

30. Stephen M. Weissman, "Frederick Douglass, Portrait of a Black Militant: A Study in the Family Romance," *The Psychoanalytic Study of the Child* 30 (1975): 725–52.

31. A similar family romance fate seems to have overtaken the completion of Alex Haley's *Roots* (New York: Doubleday, 1976). When questions were raised about disparities between his and others' account of the African site of origins, Haley responded, "I, we, need a place called Eden . . . I wanted to portray our original culture in its pristine state" Such a purpose, Eliot Fremont Smith comments, "owes more to Rousseau than to modern anthropology," and he proceeds to detect a tone of grandiosity in Haley's dismissal of his critics as well as in his comparison of his book to the Bible, the ultimate book of origins ("Alex Haley and the Rot in *Roots*," *Village Voice*, 30 May 1977, 82–84).

32. Marc A. Rubenstein, " 'My Accursed Origin': The Search for the Mother in *Frankenstein*," *Studies in Romanticism* 15 (1976): 165–94.

33. Leslie Fiedler's piece appeared in the *New York Times Book Review*, 9 June 1974, under the title, "Lord of the Absolute Everywhere." Martin Widzer, in a delightful study of comic-book superheroes, has connected family romance fantasies to miraculous birth scenes ("The Comic-book Superhero: A Study in Family Romance Fantasy," *Psychoanalytic Study of the Child* 32 [1977]: 565–603).

34. Virginia Woolf, *Between the Acts* (New York: Harcourt, Brace, 1941), 99.

35. Alice Miller, "The Drama of the Gifted Child and the Narcissistic Disturbance of the Psychoanalyst," *International Journal of Psycho-Analysis* 60 (1979): 47–58.

36. Ernst Kris, "The Personal Myth," *Journal of the American Psychoanalytic Association* 4 (1956): 653–81.

37. Mark Shechner, *Joyce in Nighttown* (Berkeley: University of California Press, 1974).

38. Barbara Tomasi, "The Fraternal Theme in Joyce's *Ulysses*," *American Imago* 30 (1973): 177–91.

39. D. H. Lawrence, *The Collected Letters*, 2 vols, Harry T. Moore, ed. (New York: The Viking Press, 1962) Additional references incorporated into the text.

40. *The Letters of James Joyce*, edited by Richard Ellmann (New York, 1966).

41. James Joyce, *A Portrait of the Artist as a Young Man*, edited by Chester

Anderson (New York: Viking Critical Edition, 1968); page numbers to be incorporated into my text. *Ulysses* (New York: Random House, 1961); page numbers incorporated. Julian B. Kaye, "Who is Betty Byrne?" in *Portraits of the Artist*, ed. William Morris and Clifford Nault (New York: The Odyssey Press, 1962).

42. Evert Sprinchorn, "A Portrait of the Artist as Achilles," in *Approaches to the Twentieth Century Novel*, edited by John Unterecker (New York: Thomas Y. Crowell, 1965).

43. Vincent J. Cheng, "Stephen Dedalus and the Black Panther Vampire," *James Joyce Quarterly* 24, no. 2 (1987): 143–60.

44. Ruth Bauerle, "A Sober Drunken Speech: Stephen's Parodies in the Oxen of the Sun," *James Joyce Quarterly* 5 (1967): 40–45.

45. Ernest Jones, *Essays in Applied Psycho-Analysis*, 2 vols. (London: Hogarth, 1951); Norman Holland, *The Dynamics of Literary Response* (New York: Oxford University Press, 1968), 40.

46. William Schutte, *Joyce and Shakespeare* (New Haven: Yale University Press, 1957).

47. Michael Seidel, "*Ulysses*, Black Panther Vampire," *James Joyce Quarterly* 13, no. 4 (1976): 415–27. Note, the 1984 edition of *Ulysses* (New York: Random House) corrects the above quote as follows: "Black panther. Vampire." (496).

48. In a recent paper, "Bloom Again," I have explored the role of the replacement son, which is clearly related to family romance constructions.

49. Shari Benstock, "*Ulysses* as Ghoststory," *James Joyce Quarterly* 12, no. 4 (1975): 396–413.

50. Mary Shelley, *Frankenstein* (New York: Oxford University Press, 1972).

51. Richard Ellmann, *"Ulysses" on the Liffey* (New York: Oxford University Press, 1972), 73.

52. Ibid., 162.

53. Joyce's book of personal/mythic origins begins suitably with "Once upon a time . . ." but the mildly mocking echo ". . . and a very good time it was . . ." is more ironic than innocent, since the story is by a father with a hairy face seen through a glass threateningly. This primal fantasy or reconstructed memory becomes more ironical in a Lacanian reading that would suggest the child's self comes into being as it enters the symbolic order of language already wrought into a story about a maternal moocow. Thus as the glass frames the self in the patriarchal eye, father inscribes son, and as the mother is already contained in the father's language, so the minotaur is prefigured in the maze. But while allowing for these and other overdeterminations, one needs to focus on the fact that in the very beginning it is the father's word that penetrates the son's virginal ear. If we consider the infant Stephen thus protrayed as a tabula rasa of passive receptivity, he is also in a feminine position *vis à vis* the father. In this earliest and most fundamental reconstruction of experience, we may find a paradigm both of the primal scene, with the son occupying the mother's place, and of a central recurring theme in the major works where the homosexual threat is announced by such key words as *suck*, *Christine*, and *Panther* and interpreted as a feminizing threat. Just as consistently, mastery is accomplished via the same medium through which the threat is introduced, namely language, storytelling: among the Dublin patriarchs Stephen spins the Parable of the Plums or retells *Hamlet* as a ghost story, using the aggressor's weapons in his defense against the aggressor's threat. Just as there is a darker side to the family romance, so does the primal scene's ominous aspect impinge on the tolerable compromises in the various positions of Boylan and the Blooms. But through the more personal "ghost story" that Stephen grapples with throughout the Ulysses day, this darker side intrudes via *Hamlet* as the recurring "List!" and "Remember me!" cue us to the old king's murder by a brother who pours poison into the porches of his ear—a

more lethal parallel to the father's ostensibly benign aural penetration that initiates *A Portrait*. No wonder Stephen will have none of the higher interpretations of parental conception proffered by a religion that produces a sacred pigeon to penetrate the Virgin's ear with the word of God, but no wonder, either, he has become so obsessed by it. To such idealizations Stephen must always play the heretic, even if his own alchemical sublimations do not serve him in very good stead, either.

As the father's negative force diminishes over the years of Joyce's visions and revisions, so does the heroic defiance of the family romance become less concentric and more diffuse. But as if to replace it, the primal scene becomes more central as one of the organizing principles of *Finnegans Wake* (New York: Viking Penguin, 1976), where it has two aspects that bear on present concerns. We may recall that the carefully staged scene of parental lovemaking in chapter 16 between HCE and ALP (as Mr. and Mrs. Porter) is clearly demarcated by the four voyeuristic bedposts of Mamalujo—the composite child who will not be excluded or driven into exile, where heroic fantasies could be hatched and nursed in defiance, but will rather return to sit in judgment on the primordial parental act. But in contrast to this traditional protrayal from the perspective of relative mastery, is the "insectuous" version—signified by the improper earwig that mischievously enters the mental organ through the ear's orifice. In this consistent context of representation by displacement upward, the insect is the word, and the word is any variation one chooses on incest. It is always the *seim anew*. The original seed or Logos that impregnates the son grows into a creative self, which sees in the generative secrets of mothering a distinctive species of art that announces its own autonomy when it proclaims that in the "buginning was the void." Not the father and his symbolic order, but a void out of which a new order may be created.

Out of this void comes not creation *ex nihilo*, which Joyce perforce rejected, if at times grudgingly, but a deepening and expanding awareness that all human creation is a kind of recreation following the primordial scene of human origins in Eden. On all its phylo- and ontogenetic levels, the original scene of human begetting is properly interpreted as everyone's Fortunate Fall into concrete mortal experience.

54. D. H. Lawrence, *The Man Who Died* (New York: Random House, 1953).

55. Dorothy Brett, *Lawrence and Brett, A Friendship* (Philadelphia; J. B. Lippincott, 1933). When I caught up with Dorothy Brett in Taos a few months before she died in 1977, I asked her if she was the only convert to Lawrence's utopia. She laughed, adding, "And that wasn't much." (*D. H. Lawrence Review* 11, no. 2 (1978): 191–93).

56. Phyllis Greenacre, "The Family Romance of the Artist."

57. D. H. Lawrence, *Collected Letters*, 570. For an elaboration of Lawrence's family romance and its interaction with the primal scene, see my *A "Strange Sapience": The Creative Imagination of D. H. Lawrence* (Amherst: University of Mass. Press, 1984).

58. Hillis Miller, "D. H. Lawrence: *The Fox* and the Perspective Glass," *Harvard Advocate* 137 (1952); David J. Kleinbard, "Laing, Lawrence, and the Maternal Cannibal," *The Psychoanalytic Review* 58, no. 1 (1971): 1–13; Edmund Bergler, "D. H. Lawrence's 'The Fox' and the Psychoanalytic Theory on Lesbianism," In *A D. H. Lawrence Miscellany* (Carbondale: Southern Illinois University Press, 1959); Judith G. Ruderman, " 'The Fox' and the 'Devouring Mother,' " *The D.H. Lawrence Review* 10, no. 3 (1977): 251–69; James Twitchell, "Lawrence's Lamia's: Predatory Women in *The Rainbow* and *Women in Love*," *Studies in the Novel* 11, no. 1 (1979): 23–42.

59. George H. Ford, *Double Measure* (New York: W. W. Norton, 1965).

60. Ruderman, " 'The Fox' and the 'Devouring Mother.' "

61. D. H. Lawrence, *Sons and Lovers* (New York: Viking Critical Edition, 1968), 141; further page references to be noted in text.

62. Twitchell, "Lawrence's Lamia's."

63. Charles Rossman, " 'You Are the Call and I Am the Answer': D. H. Lawrence and Women," *D. H. Lawrence Review* 8 (1975): 255–329, supports this viewpoint.

64. D. H. Lawrence, *Fantasia of the Unconscious* (New York: Viking Press, 1969), 157.

65. Ibid., 145.

66. An intermediate stage in this process occurs in the destructive oral sensuality of Ursula and Anton in *The Rainbow* (New York: Viking, 1965), 479. There it is her "beaked mouth" and her "fierce, beaked, harpy's kiss" that overpowers the hapless male.

67. D. H. Lawrence, *Lady Chatterley's Lover* (New York: Grove Press, 1959), 102.

68. Ibid., 242.

69. From D. H. Lawrence's poem "Red Herring," in *Pansies, The Complete Poems of D. H. Lawrence*, (New York: The Viking Press, 1972), 490.

70. D. H. Lawrence, "Demon Justice" in *Pansies, The Complete Poems of D. H. Lawrence*.

71. Mark Spilka, "On Lawrence's Impotence," a paper delivered at a 1979 Lawrence conference and published in *D. H. Lawrence: The Man Who Lived*, ed. Harry T. Moore and Robert Partlow (Carbondale: Southern Illinois University Press, 1980).

72. Marilyn French, *The Book as World: James Joyce's* Ulysses (Cambridge: Harvard University Press, 1976).

Chapter 2. The Subjective Phases of Creativity in Emily Brontë

1. Phyllis Greenacre, "The Family Romance of the Artist," *The Psychoanalytic Study of the Child* 13 (1958): 9–44.

2. William G. Niederland, "Clinical Aspects of Creativity," *American Imago* 24 (1967): 6–34. Simon Grolnick considers the question of maternal deficiency at the end of his study of Emily Dickinson and concludes that what one may often encounter in the lives of artists is not deficient parenting but lack of "fit" between primary caretakers and the emergent genius: "She was *Poetry* surrounded by *Prose*; there seemed to be an uncrossable abyss in between." "Emily Dickinson: The Interweaving of Poetry and Personality" was read at the Winter 1985 meeting of the American Psychoanalytic Association. In respect to the Emily of this chapter, it appears both views are valid—both a lack of fit and severe injuries to the self. The roles played by Heathcliff and Nelly in respect to maternal loss are set down in Philip Wion's "The Absent Mother in Emily Brontë's *Wathering Heights*," *American Imago* 42 (1985): 143–64.

3. Winifred Gérin, *Emily Brontë: A Biography* (Oxford: Clarendon Press, 1971). She has written on the lives of all the Brontë children.

4. Gérin, *Brontë*, 11.

5. Inklings, perhaps, of a hyperborean fantasy. Just as a legendary people were located in Greek mythology in a land of perpetual sunshine beyond the north winds, so might the mother be alive beyond the cold grave. A few years earlier, Mary Shelley, who lost her mother at birth, worked a similar fantasy into *Frankenstein*.

6. Their play also revealed their sexual curiosity and concern with origins and, accordingly, the role of primal-scene material.

7. Meredith Anne Skura, *The Literary Use of the Psychoanalytic Process*, 60.

8. Gérin, *Brontë*, 15.

9. Ibid., 40.

10. David A. Rothstein, "On Presidential Assassination: The Academia and the Pseudo-Community," *Adolescent Psychiatry* 4 (1975): 264–98. A comparable phenomenon occurred among the children in Virginia (Woolf) Stephen's family. A newspaper was initiated called the *Hyde Park Gate News*; it issued weekly from the time Virginia was nine until she was thirteen. It included both fiction and family news, and was meant to be read by the parents. See Quentin Bell's *Virginia Woolf: A Biography* (New York: Harcourt Brace Jovanovich, 1979).

11. Gérin, *Brontë*, 21, 23.

12. Fannie E. Ratchford, *Gondal's Queen: A Novel in Verse by Emily Jane Brontë* (Austin: University of Texas Press, 1955), 31.

13. Many artists employ something comparable. Traditionally in Western art, from Chaucer to Milton, there was the ready-made system of Christian religion-myth. By the time of Blake it was necessary to create one's own mythic substructure, a practice continued by Yeats. D. H. Lawrence built into his writings an elaborate theory of occultism. These preliminary creative activities provide the later products with a richly resonant sense of depth.

14. Ratchford, *Gondol's Queen*, 25–26.

15. Cf. Rosalind Miles, "A Baby God: The Creative Dynamism of Emily Brontë's Poetry," in *The Art of Emily Bronte*, edited by Anne Smith (New York: Barnes and Noble, 1976), 92.

16. Ratchford, *Gondal's Queen*, 20.

17. Gérin, *Brontë*, 54.

18. Keith Sagar, in *The Art of Emily Brontë*, 131.

19. Arnold Kettle, *An Introduction to the English Novel* (New York: Hutchinson's University Library, 1951).

20. "Their images, and especially those of the children, were unforgettably depicted in the *Illustrated London News*—starving scarecrows with a few rags on them and an animal growth of black hair almost obscuring their features" (Gérin, *Brontë*, 226).

21. Emily Brontë, *Wuthering Heights*, edited by William M. Sale, Jr. (New York, W. W. Norton 1972), 39.

22. Arnold Kettle, *Introduction to the English Novel*.

23. Lucille Dooley, "Psychoanalysis of the Character and Genius of Emily Brontë," *Psychoanalytic Review* 17 (1930): 208–39. While more impressionistic than analytical, the author does refer to family-romance motifs.

24. Gérin, *Brontë*, 10.

25. Gérin, *Brontë*, 45.

26. Byron is mentioned in Niederland's 1967 study ("Clinical Aspects") and is being further studied by Peter Hartocolis, who delivered a paper on Byron at the 1976 December meeting of the American Psychoanalytic Association, entitled "Congenital Deformity as a Factor of Artistic Creativity: the Case of George Gordon Byron." The above incident in Byron's life illustrates how a physical defect can become the basis for a narcissistic injury.

27. Ratchford, *Gondal's Queen*, 47–8.

28. Stevie Davies, *Emily Brontë: The Artist as a Free Woman* (Manchester, England: Carcanet Press, 1983), 103.

29. Brontë, *Wuthering Heights*, 38–39.

30. Keith Sagar, "The Originality of *Wuthering Heights*," 134.

31. Gérin, *Brontë*, 226. Barbara Munson Goff's major study of the novel deepens our understanding of the author's preoccupations with origins by depicting Heathcliff as the product of natural breeding with affinities to Darwin's theories of natural selection. Heathcliff embodies the creative/destructive forces of nature that civilization (via Lockwood *et al.*) would deny. Even so, he is an imaginative projection of what constitutes the natural in humanity. ("Between Natural Theology and Natural

Selection: Breeding the Human Animal in *Wuthering Heights*," *Victorian Studies* 27, no. 4 [Summer 1984]: 477–508.)

32. Joan Carson, "Visionary Experience in *Wuthering Heights*," *Psychoanalytic Review* 62 (1975): 131–52. Stevie Davies, writing that the novel "imagines the human soul as being female, seeking a lost male counterpart," (*Emily Brontë*, 97) draws on Jungian as well as other mythic models of rebirth and eternal return to understand Emily Brontë's vision of "universal forgiveness" (105) as a female response to universal pain rather than original sin. This emphasis on forgiveness and reparation (also in light of the outbursts of unbridled rage in the story), seen as working toward an incorporation of the individual into the whole, an establishment of an inclusive pattern of death and life within a universal nature, suggests that Emily Brontë was working through powerful destructive feelings deriving from maternal loss. In Davies's suggestive chapter, "The Mother Benneath the Earth," the "loss of her mother at the age of three" is "the most salient biographical fact" (155). Davies's understanding of the individual's incorporation into a larger sustaining mythic whole suggests the ultimate resolution of the great harm to the author's emergent self-outcast/orphan fantasies.

33. Dorothy Van Ghent, *The English Novel: Form and Function* (New York: Rhinehart and Co., 1953).

34. Irving H. Buchen, "Emily Brontë and the Metaphysics of Childhood and Love," in *Twentieth Century Interpretations of Wuthering Heights,* ed. Thomas A. Volger (Englewood Cliffs, N.J.: Prentice-Hall, 1968), 112.

35. Philippa Tristram, " 'Divided Sources,' " in *The Art of Emily Bronte*, 183.

36. Stevie Davies, *Emily Brontë*, 102, In her examination of how nature, the feminine, and literalness are interwoven, Margaret Homans suggests that the Brontë sisters viewed motherhood as an end to childhood and consequently an end to writing since the creative drive originated there ("Dreaming of Children: Literalization in *Jane Eyre* and *Wuthering Heights*," in *The Female Gothic*, edited by Juliann E. Fleenor, [Montreal: Eden Press, 1983]).

37. Eric Solomon, "The Incest Theme."

38. Michael D. Reed, "The Power of *Wuthering Heights*: A Psychoanalytic Examination," *The Psychocultural Review* 1 (1977): 21–42.

39. Brontë, *Wuthering Heights*, 47.

40. Arnold Kettle, *Introduction to the English Novel.*

Chapter 3. "Precious Seeing": Mirroring as a Humanizing Process; Self-Remaking as a Creative Process

1. From W. B. Yeats's poem, "An Acre of Grass," in *The Complete Poems* (New York: Macmillan, 1962), 299.

2. William Niederland, "Clinical Aspects of Creativity," *American Imago* 24, no. 1–2 (1967): 6–34; "Psychoanalytic Approaches to Artistic Creativity," *The Psychoanalytic Quarterly* 45, no. 2 (1976): 185–212; Heinz Kohut, *The Analysis of the Self* (New York: International Universities Press, 1971); *The Restoration of the Self* (New York: International Universities Press, 1977). Both analysts place a premium on narcissistic injury as a spur to aggression and to subsequent strategies of reparation and reconstitution. Although I draw on Kohut's "cohesive self" and "nuclear self," I have some misgivings about the implications of these terms and would prefer something less optimistic like nucleii of self-representations.

3. William Shakespeare, *Love's Labour Lost*, 4. 3. 327–30. References are to act, scene, and line.

4. Fannie E. Ratchford, *Gondal's Queen*, 41, "The Argument of Gondal."
5. Ibid., 41.
6. Keith Sagar, "The Originality of *Wuthering Heights*," 121.
7. Gérin, *Brontë*, 6.
8. This popularized version of *Gilgamesh* by Herbert Mason (New York: Mentor Books, 1972) both edits and expands, extrapolates and interprets, the sources that began appearing in the nineteenth century on the 7th century B.C. stone tablets. There is no complete and historically authentic version of the poem; every act of scholarly attention seems to involve a degree of reconstruction. That Mason's version is faithful both to the exigencies of history and the spirit of art is apparent to me after consulting *Assyrian and Babylonian Literature*, edited and introduced by Robert Francis Harper, containing a translation of the poem by William Russ-Arnolt (New York: Appleton, 1904); and *The Gilgamesh Epic and Old Testament Parallels* by Alexander Heidel (Chicago: University of Chicago Press, 1949). Nonetheless, Mason's tendency to make explicit what remains implicit in the poem has not been overlooked. The most complete scholarly version is by John Gardner and John Maier, *Gilgamesh* (New York: Knopf, 1984). Subsequent references to Mason's version incorporated in the text.
9. The polar versions of origins (which the present study is at pains to elucidate) can also be found in this epic. Family romance motifs enter in the creation of Gilgamesh by the gods, and are more fully developed in the later versions quoted by Otto Rank in *The Myth of the Birth of the Hero*. Here he is dropped from a castle tower lest an oracle that he will slay his royal grandfather be fulfilled; an eagle catches the falling infant and bears him away to a garden where he is raised by a second set of parents. His celebrated feat of interjecting himself between two amorous lions, slaying them, and wearing their skins has been interpreted by the psychoanalyst Henry Edelheit as representing primal-scene schema, including the child's identifications with the coital parents.
For purposes of clarification, a distinction may be made linking the present line of inquiry with Appendix A. *Breast* imagery as perhaps the most archaic group of representations is associated with the symbiotic stage and the oral needs bound up with it; *facial* imagery, while also beginning with nursing experiences and the infant's smiling response, is associated with the hatching-out phases of the second year, i.e., specifically with the individual's becoming a human being among others of his kind. Breast imagery then may be taken as symbiotic vestiges and instinctual derivatives, with regressive overtones; facial imagery accompanies the separation-individuation process. (See Michael Eigin, "On the Significance of the Face," *The Psychoanalytic Review* 67 no. 4 [1980]: 427–42.)
10. Cf. James Hamilton, "Transitional Fantasies and the Creative Process," *The Psychoanalytic Study of Society* 6 (1975): 53–70. Picasso's experimental writing, which was acclaimed by the surrealists, first appeared in *Cahiers d'Arte*, 1935, 1937. The painter turned to language as a mode of expression during a fallow period, and yet one can feel the brush strokes behind the words. Similarly, as will be seen, Pope reverted temporarily to graphics when language would not serve his turn.
11. Edith Sitwell, *Alexander Pope* (London: Faber & Faber, 1930), 19.
12. Samuel Johnson, *Lives of the Poets* (New York: Avon, 1965), 290.
13. "This longing for romance, so cruelly thwarted by the shape and sufferings of his miserable body, caused him to endow his parents with a purely mythological noble birth," writes Sitwell (*Alexander Pope*, 20–21). I would rephrase this to suggest the longings for romance were stimulated by his physical deformities for corrective aims.
14. Alexander Pope, "An Epistle to Dr. Arbuthnot," *The Poems of Alexander Pope*, ed. John Butt (New Haven: Yale University Press, 1963), 597.
15. Sitwell, *Alexander Pope*, 6–7.

16. Ibid., 28.

17. Reuben Bower, *Alexander Pope: The Poetry of Allusion* (New York: Oxford University Press, 1959), 165. For more on this subject, see Maynard Mack, *Alexander Pope: A Life* (New York: Norton, 1985) Chapter Five, "First Heroes," 88–117.

18. Sitwell, *Alexander Pope*, 35.

19. Ibid., 7, quoting from an early Preface to Pope's works.

20. William K. Wimsatt, *The Portraits of Alexander Pope* (New Haven: Yale University Press, 1965), xxiv. See also, Maynard Mack, *Pope: A Life*, 153–58.

21. Sitwell, *Alexander Pope*, quoting the same Preface, 7.

22. James Anderson Winn, *"A Window in the Bosom," The Letters of Alexander Pope* (Hamden, Conn.: Shoe String Press, 1977); for his portraits, see Wimsatt, above. Winn believes that a "similar need for an attractive social and moral appearance led to the role-playing I have described in his letters—in his use of rakish language in addressing women, his pretended aloofness to attacks from lesser writers, his elegant deference to aristocrats" (199).

23. Mack, *Pope: A Life*, 658. See also the section, "The man reborn in the poems," 719–26.

24. Pope, "An Epistle to Dr. Arbuthhnot," 601.

25. Sitwell, *Alexander Pope*, 22.

26. Maynard Mack, "Pope: The Shape of the Man in His Work," *Yale Review* 67, no. 4 (1978): 493–517. Mack studies from a psychological viewpoint similar to this one the various hardships, over-compensations, and strategies that Pope's physical body worked on the body of his poetry.

27. Sitwell, *Alexander Pope*, 28–29.

28. Ibid., 10 and 22.

29. Samuel Johnson, *Lives of the English Poets*, (New York: Avon, 1965), 338. But Johnson also allows that the poet's infirmity placed him in "perpetual need of female attendance."

30. Pope, "An Essay in Criticism," 153.

31. Ibid., 162.

32. Sitwell, *Alexander Pope*, 74.

33. Pope, quoted in Sitwell, *Alexander Pope*, 80.

34. Ibid, 74.

35. Pope, "Epistle to Dr. Arbuthnot," 602, ll. 205–6.

36. Pope, "An Essay on Man," 522.

37. Appendix B, Sitwell, *Alexander Pope*, 294.

38. Quoted by Maynard Mack in *The Garden and the City, Retirement and Politics in the Later Poetry of Pope, 1731–1743* (Toronto: University of Toronto Press, 1969), 62

39. Mack, *The Garden and the City*, 26.

40. Arnold H. Modell, "The Transitional Object and the Creative Act," *Psychoanalytic Quarterly* 39 (1970): 240–50.

41. D. W. Winnicott, "Transitional Objects and Transitional Phenomena."

42. Quoted in Mack, *The Garden and the City*, 26.

43. Ibid., 28–29. Mack quotes a contemporary source to the effect that "after his mother's death, his friend Richardson painted a picture, now lost, of Pope in a mourning gown with a strange view of the garden to shew the obelisk as in memory to his mother's Death." "Certainly the key position of the obelisk," Mack continues, "signalizes not only the gravity of Pope's loss but also, with an aptness of which he himself was probably not fully conscious, his repossession of her beyond 'the solemnity ... of the cypresses'... for she was one of the chief *dramatis personae* in that continuing drama about the meaning of life in which we may watch both the historical

Pope and the figure who speaks to us from the poems of the 30's weave in his inner consciousness."

44. Ibid., 28–29. Mack notes the traditional "associations between consciousness and caverns" which are implicit in Pope usages of the "Cave of Spleen, Cave of Poetry, and Cave of Truth."

45. Both quotes found in Ibid., 87.

46. H. F. Clark, quoted in Ibid., 60.

47. Ibid., 66.

48. William Shakespeare, *Richard II*, 4. 1. 276–88.

49. Stephen M. Weissman, "Face to Face: The Role of Vision and the Smiling Response," *The Psychoanalytic Study of the Child* 32 (1977): 421–52.

50. Sigmund Freud, *The Interpretation of Dreams*, translated by A. A. Brill (New York: Random House, 1950), 453; James Strachey's translation in the Standard Edition, vol. 5, 602, reads "perceptual identity."

51. F. Scott Fitzgerald, *The Great Gatsby* (New York: Bantam, 1946), 56.

52. Alfred Lord Tennyson, "The Lady of Shalott," *Tennyson's Poetry*, edited by Robert Hill (New York: Norton, 1972), 14, ll. 37–8; future references incorporated into the text.

53. Jerome Hamiliton Buckley, *Tennyson: The Growth of a Poet* (Cambridge: Harvard University Press, 1967), 49.

54. Tennyson, "To—, as When with Downcast Eyes We Muse," *Tennyson's Poetry*, 45.

55. Tennyson, "In Memoriam A. H. H.," 123, stanza 6, ll. 35–39.

56. "Among School Children," *Collected Poems*, 214.

57. James Joyce, *A Portrait of the Artist As a Young Man* (New York: Viking Critical Edition, 1968), 267.

58. For a feminist treatment of the pre-oedipal splits in the maternal image, see Dorothy Dinnerstein, *The Mermaid and the Minotaur* (New York: Harper and Row, 1976).

59. Bernard Green, "The Effects of the Distortion of the Self: A Study of *The Picture of Dorian Gray*," *The Annual of Psychoanalysis* 7 (1979): 391–410. For a psychobiography that touches on the Prime Scene, see Alexander Grinstein, "Oscar Wilde," *American Imago* 37 (1980): 125–79 (esp. 172–73).

60. Otto Rank, *The Double: A Psychoanalytic Study*, trans. Harry Tucker (Chapel Hill: University of North Carolina Press, 1971); Jane Simaon and Carl Goldberg, "The Role of the Double in the Creative Process and Psychoanalysis," *Journal of the American Academy of Psychoanalysis* 12, no. 3 (1984): 341–61; Robert Rogers, *The Double in Literature* (Detroit: Wayne State University Press, 1970); Karl Miller, *Doubles: Studies in Literary History* (New York: Oxford, 1985).

61. Ellen Moers, *The Dandy: Brummell to Beerhohm* (New York: Viking, 1960).

62. Karl Beckson, "Oscar Wilde and the Masks of Narcissus," *Psychoanalytic Study of Society*, vol. 10 (Hillsdale, N.J.: Analytic Press, 1984), 251.

63. Henrik Ibsen, *Peer Gynt*, trans. Rolf Fjelde (New York: NAL, 1964), 209; furture references incorporated in text.

64. Ibsen, *Peer Gynt*. Christopher Fry's translation here better captures the mother's ambivalence (*The Oxford Ibsen*, vol. 3 [New York: Oxford University Press, 1972], 262).

65. Ibsen, *Peer Gynt*, Christopher Fry translation, 421.

66. "It was Ibsen's own character that was reflected in this man," writes his biographer, Halvan Holt in *The Life of Ibsen*, vol. 2 (London: George Allen, 1931), 26.

67. *Ibsen: Letters and Speeches*, ed. Evert Sprinchorn (New York: Hill and Wang Dramabook, 1964), 65–69.

68. Jean-Paul Sartre, *Saint Genet* (New York: New American Library, 1964), 26.

69. Ibid., 15.

70. Robert Jay Lifton, "Proteus Revisited," *Adolescent Psychiatry* 4 (1976): 21–36.

71. For the Lacanian source of Genet's play, see Catherine Clément, *The Lives and Legends of Jacques Lacan* (New York: Columbia University Press, 1983), 67–72.

72. An analysis of Genet's early prose by Stanley Coen arrives at similar conclusions in "The Author and His Audience: Jean Genet's Early Work," *Psychoanalytic Study of Society* 10 (1984): 302. The "author/narrator" seeks to draw the "reader into an intensely responsive relationship, representative of loving parent and child, whose task is to provide him with affirmation, admiration, and acceptance."

73. Joyce, *A Portrait*, 252.

74. Philip Roth, *Portnoy's Complaint* (New York: Random House, 1969), 274; Bruno Bettleheim, "Portnoy Psychoanalyzed," *Psychiatry and Social Science Review* 4, no. 10 (15 August 1970): 2–9; reprinted from *Midstream* (1970).

75. *New York Times Book Review*, 25 September 1988.

76. Vivian Gornick, *Essays in Feminism* (New York: Harper and Row, 1978).

77. "Whatever Happened to Feminist Fiction?" *New York Times Book Review*, 19 August 1984.

78. Erica Jong, *How to Save Your Own Life* (New York: Holt, Rinehart and Winston, 1977), 157.

79. "Talk with Philip Roth," by Sara Davidson, *New York Times Book Review,* 18 September 1977, 52.

80. Erica Jong, *Here Comes and Other Poems* (New York: New American Library, 1975), 270.

81. Ibid., 269.

82. Ibid., 270.

83. Ibid., 15.

84. Yeats, "An Acre of Grass."

85. Niederland, "Clinical Aspects of Creativity," 23.

86. Kohut, *The Restoration of the Self*, 183; 177–79.

87. Freud, "Creative Writers and Daydreaming," 153.

Chapter 4. Roland Barthes: Self-Remaking *à la Française*

1. Jacques Lacan, "The Mirror Stage as Formative of the Function of the I as Revealed in Psychoanalytic Experience," chap. 1 of *Ecrits*, trans. Alan Sheridan (New York: Norton, 1977).

2. J. Laplanche and J. B. Pontcalis, *The Language of Psychoanalysis* (New York: Norton, 1973).

3. Catherine Clément, *The Lives and Legends of Jacques Lacan* (New York: Columbia University Press, 1983), 168.

4. John Sturrock, *Structuralism and Science* (New York: Oxford University Press, 1979), 131.

5. Roland Barthes, "The Death of the Author," *Image Music Text* (New York: Fontana, 1977) 142–48.

6. Ibid., 145.

7. Ibid., 142.

8. If there is a family romance latent in the author's sense of paternal absence and abandonment, it would be akin to Sartre's fantasy of having his books adopted by an admiring public (as examined in chapter 1).

9. Jacques Lacan, *The Language of the Self*, trans. Anthony Wilden (Baltimore: Johns Hopkins Press, 1968).

10. D. W. Winnicott, "Transitional Objects and Transitional Phenomena," *International Journal of Psycho-Analysis* 34 (1953): 89–97.

11. Roland Barthes, *A Lover's Discourse*, trans. by Richard Howard (New York: Hill and Wang, 1978), 16, additional references incorporated.

12. M. N. Evans, "Introduction to Jacques Lacan's Lecture: The Neurotic's Individual Myth," *Psychoanalytic Quarterly* 43 (1979): 386–404.

13. Eugen Bar, "Understanding Lacan," *Psychoanalysis and Contemporary Thought*, (New York: International Universities Press, 1974), 3: 473–544; Harold Blum, "Symbolic Processes and Symbol Formation," *International Journal of Psycho-Analysis* 59 (1978): 455–71. My own skepticism is set down in "Reading Freud and Returning to Lacan," *The Psychoanalytic Review*, in press.

14. Daniel Dervin, "Lacanian Mirrors and Literary Reflections," *Journal of the Philadelphia Psychoanalytic Association* 7 (1980): 129–41; Michael Eigen, "The Area of Faith in Winnicott, Lacan, and Bion," *International Journal of Psycho-Analysis* 62 (1981): 413–33.

15. D. W. Winnicott, "Mirror-role of Mother and Family in Child Development," *The Visual Behavior of Infants in the First Year of Life*, ed. P. Lomas (London: Proceedings of the Royal Society of Medicine, 55 (1968): 26–33.

16. Eigen, "Area of Faith," 413–33; Juliet Mitchell, *Psychoanalysis and Women* (New York: Random House, 1974), 40.

17. Eigen, "Area of Faith," 422.

18. Ibid.

19. There may be an allusion in this phrase to a series of Renaissance paintings of which Titian's "Venus at Her Toilet with Two Cupids" (see Appendix B, no. 7) is the most famous example.

Chapter 5. Pip and Peer

1. D. W. Winnicott, "Transitional Objects and Transitional Phenomena," *Collected Papers*, London, 1958.

2. Charles Dickens, *Great Expectations* (New York: Holt, Rinehart, and Winston, 1972); future references incorporated by page numbers in text.

3. Barbara Hardy, *The Moral Art of Dickens* (London: Athlone Press, 1970), 146.

4. For more on the fairy-tale elements, see Harry Stone, *Dickens and the Invisible World* (Bloomington: Indiana University Press, 1979). Fantasy and fairy tale may serve as bridges for the creative process to cross from the purely personal to the publicly significant.

Arthur A. Adrian writes that Dickens's "own past neglect became inseparable from the general character of the age," and he "kept returning to the theme of the delinquent parent and the homeless and alienated child in search of identity." Moreover, "prisons, impecunious fathers, exploitive mothers, violated and captive children" function in the novels as a "microcosm of nineteenth-century England" (*Dickens and the Parent-Child Relationship*, [Athens: Ohio University Press, 1984], 136). In noting the frequent child-parent reversals in Dickens's plots, which play out a "child's dedicated efforts to redeem a flawed parent through love" (130), Adrian touches on the rescue variant of the family romance, with the added quirk that the parent in need is usually father.

5. This evocative phrase has been often invoked by Sydney Smith as in "The Golden Fantasy," *Bulletin of the Menninger Clinic* 41, no. 4 (July 1977): 411–14. A few points from the summary of this paper may be noted: "In patients dominated by the 'golden fantasy,' a sense of separateness from the mother has not been achieved. These patients characteristically remember mother as unavailable during the critical period

of individuation-separation. Their fantasy is linked with an emotionally charged 'memory' of losing mother just at that point in development when the child suffered from a heightened awareness associated with separation and its consequent depression" (414). For a fuller treatment, see his "The Golden Fantasy: A Regressive Reaction to Separation Anxiety," *International Journal of Psycho-Analysis* 58, no. 3 (1977): 311–24.

While it may never be possible to determine whether early loss affected the authors considered here in such a way to account for the golden fantasy influencing their works, there were similar disruptions in their families while they were growing up. After Dickens's father was sent to a debtors' prison, he was also removed from home to work in the infamous blacking factory. Ibsen's father also perpetrated on his family the humiliation of bankruptcy, and as a result the son was dispatched to be apprenticed to an apothecary.

6. G. Robert Stange, "Expectations Well Lost," in *The Dickens Critics*, ed. George H. Ford and Lauriat Lane, Jr. (Ithaca: Cornell University Press, 1961), 294–308. The steeple-between-the-legs image may also suggest, in a strictly psychoanalytic sense, the phallus, copulation, and birth—all of which are important in the present interpretation.

7. Ibid., 304.

8. In Taylor Stoehr's study, *Dickens: The Dreamer's Stance* (Ithaca: Cornell University Press, 1965), the action is polarized around Miss Havisham's Satis House and Magwitch's Newgate Prison, giving "structural expression to the forces that battle within Pip through the major part of the novel" (129). These epitomize high and low versions of origins. In the one, "everything glitters at the surface, cold, bright, and hard as Estella's jewels; but there is no action, and what lies underneath that surface is rotting away." In Magwitch's world "everything is done in the warmth of affection or the heat of passion." These two worlds are also polarized along male/female lines and must be harmonized to comprehend origins. A third point of reference is the Forge, where Joe Gargery and Biddy live, but Stoehr maintains that Dickens "does not really believe in the Forge and what it stands for as a desirable way of life." Thus it is dropped from the narrative and is "revived only as a kind of last resort at the end." Last resort or not, it is integral to the inner theme of resolving the riddle of human origins.

9. "Pip's ambition is definable under the aspect of aggression as well as in terms of the regressive desire for passive enjoyment of life's bounty," is the position of Julian Moynahan, which he supports by viewing Pohick as Pip's demonic double (69–71). He also identifies the family romance as the base for Pope's great expectations ("The Hero's Guilt: The Case of *Great Expectations*," *Essays in Criticism* 10 [1960]: 60–79).

10. Henrik Ibsen, *Peer Gynt*, trans. Rolf Fjelde (New York: NAL, 1964), 10.

11. Henrik Ibsen, *Peer Gynt*, trans. Christopher Fry (New York: Oxford University Press, 1972), 368.

Chapter 6. Dialectical Creativity and the Self: Thomas Hardy's *The Mayor of Casterbridge*

1. Martin Grotjahn, "The Primal Crime and the Unconscious," in *Searchlights on Delinquency* (New York: International Universities Press, 1949), 306–14.

2. Thomas Hardy, *The Mayor of Casterbridge* (London: Macmillan, 1978), 272; additional references incorporated by page numbers in-text.

3. Dale Kramer, *Thomas Hardy: The Forms of Tragedy* (Urbana: University of Illinois Press, 1975), 84.

4. Ibid., 86–87.

5. Ibid., 84–85.

6. Hardy's emotional involvement in the novel impinges in this study in three areas: (1) The primal crime, wherein a male rejects a mother and daughter may have been a reversal of the author's feelings when his mother gave birth to a daughter when he was scarcely eighteen months. (2) Robert Gittings's biography, *Young Thomas Hardy* (London: Penguin, 1978), opens with a discussion of Hardy's lifelong preoccupation with his family geneology, which he called "The Hardy Pedigree." His attempts to improve his standing centered on his father's hasty marriage to a woman brought up as a pauper child on parish relief (24). As a child, Hardy was both attractive and precocious; and a childless woman, Mrs. Martin, with her family holdings of two manor houses, became "obsessively fond" of him, causing his mother great jealousy. Gittings writes that the great wealth of the Martins must have made them seem to Thomas like "creatures from another planet." Herein is a strong impetus for the adoption theme of the family romance. In addition, when Hardy was nine years old, his native town, like Casterbridge, was host to a royal visitor, Prince Albert. That this stimulated his fantasies is evident from the use he made of its in this novel (3). Of the various sexual or quasi-sexual activities that Hardy was exposed to growing up (the primal kind not withstanding), the one that made the strongest impression on his sensibilities was that of a young woman hanged publicly for the murder of her spouse. Hardy would draw on this memory for *Tess of the D'Urbervilles*. Apart from the spectacle being highly libidinized for him, one can only speculate to what extent it might also have represented either a primal scene or the fulfillment of such wishes directed toward the mother as ecompassed by the primal crime. In any case, seeing one's forbidden wishes fulfilled would also carry a significant burden of guilt and the need for self-punishment of the kind Henchard brought onto himself.

Chapter 7. George Eliot and the Paradox of Maturity; August Strindberg and the Pathology of Creativity

1. Virginia Woolf, "George Eliot," in *The Common Reader* (New York: Harcourt, Brace, and World, 1925), 171–72.

2. Ibid, 172.

3. George Eliot, *Middlemarch*, ed. Bert G. Hornback (New York: Norton Critical Edition, 1977), 64. Future page references to this edition will occur in the text.

4. For example, see Lee R. Edwards, "Women, Energy, and *Middlemarch*," in *Middlemarch* (New York: Norton Critical Edition, 1977), 683–93.

5. Gillian Beer, "Myth and the Single Consciousness: *Middlemarch* and The Lifted Veil," in *This Particular Web: Essays on Middlemarch*, ed. Ian Adam (Toronto: University of Toronto Press, 1975), 102.

6. The great crisis in Eliot's own life, linking her to Dorothea, was a loss of religious faith and a quest for a substitute in a form of secular humanism enlarged by a kind of sympathy and generosity that approached the selflessness of religious faith. For the importance of sympathy for both Dorothea as character and Eliot as creator, see Elizabeth Deeds Ermath, who writes that sympathy and constructive action arise out of the "recognition of difference: between oneself and another, or between the differing impulses of one's own complex motivation" (George Eliot's Conception of Sympathy," *Nineteenth Century Fiction* 40 [1985]: 25).

7. Richard Ellmann, "Dorothea's Husbands," in *Golden Codgers: Biographical Speculations* (New York: Oxford University Press, 1973; reprinted Norton Critical Edition, 1977).

8. Barbara Hardy, *The Appropriate Form: An Essay on the Novel* (London: University of London, Athlone Press, 1964).

9. David Carroll in *"Middlemarch* and the Externality of Fact," in *This Particular Web*, has drawn my attention to these passages, and has noted the gothic undercurrents of the novel, including *Frankenstein* ("The images of ghostly and illicit experiments multiply and parody the childbirth for which Dorothea longs"), succubi, and vampires, 85.

10. Paul Theroux, "Hapless Organ," *New Statesman*, 19 April 1974, 554.

11. Hilary Fraser, "Saint Theresa, Saint Dorothea, Miss Brooke in *Middlemarch*," *Nineteenth-Century Fiction* 40, no. 4 (1986): 400–411.

12. *The Complete Works of Saint Teresa of Jesus*, 2 vols., trans. and ed. Allison Peers (London: Sheed and Ward, 1946), 192–93.

13. *The Poems, English, Latin, and Greek, of Richard Crashaw*, ed. L. C. Martin (Oxford: Clarendon Press, 1927), 319–20.

14. Barbara Hardy, *"Middlemarch* and the Passions," in *This Particular Web*.

15. *The Collected Letters of D. H. Lawrence*, ed. Harry T. Moore (New York, Viking Press, 1962), 234; K. R. Eissler, *Goethe: A Psychoanalytic Study, 1775–1786*, 2 vols. (Detroit: Wayne State University Press, 1968), 70. While the question of Strindberg's madness has been extensively debated, it has not as yet been decided. Theodore Lidz appreciates Strindberg's ability to write *The Father* (1887) "at the height of his paranoid passion" and delusional jealousy, and maintains that in the years following the collapse of his first marriage he "crashed into full-blown insanity" ("August Strindberg: A Study of the Relationship between His Creativity and Schizophrenia," *International Journal of Psycho-Analysis* 45 [1964]: 399–406). More leniently, Anthony Storr writes, "There is no doubt that Strindberg's inner world was psychotic; but his exploration of it was deliberate and to some extent controlled." And he goes on to quote approvingly what surely must be an untenably extreme position laid out by Evert Sprinchorn, "that Strindberg created his experiences in order to write about them" (*The Dynamics of Creation* [New York: Atheneum, 1972], 209–10). Others write less conclusively that "Strindberg several times approached the abyss of schizophrenia, close enough to look searchingly into the turmoil therein but without plunging over the precipice" (Donald L. Burnham and Sven Arne Bergmann, "August Strindberg's Need-Fear Dilemma as Seen in His Relationship with Harriet Bosse," *Psychiatry and the Humanities*, vol. 1, ed. Joseph H. Smith [New Haven: Yale University Press, 1976], 73–97).

16. Maurice Valency, *The Flower and the Castle* (New York: Grosset and Dunlop, 1966), 354.

17. Evert Sprinchorn in his introduction to *The Chamber Plays* (New York: Dutton, 1962). The translation of the *Ghost Sonata* from which I will be incorporating quotes is by Elizabeth Sprigge in *Six Plays of Strindberg* (New York: Doubleday Anchor, 1955).

18. Jacob Arlow discusses the relationship between the destruction of houses and primal-scene fantasies. Specifically, Arlow refers to the burning of a house; although the house in this play collapses, Strindberg had just written a thematically similar play, called *The Burnt House*. The idea of salvaging oneself, or a part of oneself, from a collapsing structure and then being born anew only to repeat the process of reentering a collapsing house, as we find in this play, may have direct reference to Strindberg's mental collapse during his inferno period, from which he had only recently emerged. One of the most bizarre episodes during this bizarre period was the accidental burning of his hands while attempting alchemical experiments to find a formula for making gold; this led to his hospitalization and further disintegration before the reparative functions of the not entirely burned-out self were activated. He claims to have written *Ghost Sonata* with "bleeding hands," owing to a case of psoriasis. His third marriage, upon which he was shortly to enter, had already collapsed by 1907, the period of *The Chamber Plays*, and once again he was facing the inferno of disorganization (Jacob

Arlow, "Pyromania and the Primal Scene: A Psychoanalytic Comment on the Work of Yukio Mishima," *The Psychoanalytic Quarterly* 47 [1978]: 24–53). In his autobiographical novel *The Son of a Servant* (New York: Doubleday, Anchor, 1966), Strindberg explicitly connects his birth with his father's ruin ("Probably he had been an unwanted child, as his father had gone bankrupt, just before his birth, and the child first saw the light of day in a house that had been plundered and stripped" [15]); while his early childhood fears are explicitly conected with a nocturnal fire. His mother attempts to soothe him by saying that "God protects the unfortunate"; but when it is learned that two people perished, she "explains," it was "God's will" (27). The sense of being an unwanted child is related to the child's own alleged lack of will; this connection is made explicit by the father in the play of the same name: "My father and mother had me against their will, and therefore I was born without a will."

19. The Faustian motif, which many critics have noticed, provides additional underpinning for the kind of precocious sexual curiosity that leads to primal-scene awareness.

20. See Evert Sprinchorn's introduction to *The Chamber Plays*.

21. I am quoting from a study of E. Minkowski's work by R. D. Laing, "Minkowski and Schizohrenia," *Review of Existential Psychology and Psychiatry* 3, no. 3 (1963): 195–207. The principal work by Minkowski is *La Schizophrenia* (Paris, 1953). Strindberg's *To Damascus*, part 1 (1897) in *The Genius of Scandinavia Drama*, edited by Evert Sprischorn (New York: New American Library, 1964), also illustrates the insights of Minkowski.

22. The paranoid infrastructure of the play reveals human relationships determined entirely by power and dominance. At the bottom, Miss Julie, deprived of any will, is on the verge of slitting her throat with the valet's razor, while he shakes in his own boots as his master threateningly rings for his polished boots. The master is himself the victim of his wife's conniving to ruin him (another burnt house) for insurance, and she is beholden to her purely anonymous lover at the peak of this paranoid hierarchy.

23. S. Freud, *Totem and Taboo*; *Resemblances Between the Psychic Lives of Savages and Neurotics* (New York: Random House, 1946), 44.

24. For an incisive account of this concept, see James Henderson, "Exorcism, Possession, and the Dracula Cult: a Synopsis of Object-Relationns Psychology," *Bulletin of the Menninger Clinic* 40, no. 6 (1976): 603–28.

25. For the clinical tie-in, see Edward Hitschman, "Swedenborg's Paranoia," *American Imago* 6 (1949): 45–50.

26. Theodore Lidz, "Creativity and Schizophrenia," 404.

27. Freud, "The Case History of Schreber," *Standard Edition*, vol. 12; William Niederland, *The Schreber Case* (New York: Quadrangle Books, 1974). Leonard Shengold, who has studied this phenomenon in relation to Rudyard Kipling, maintains that "soul murder involves the deliberate traumatization or deprivation by an authority (parent) of his charge (child). The victim is robbed of identity and of the ability to maintain authentic feelings"—this from his synopsis of a paper, "The Problem of Soul Murder," presented at the Fall 1977 meeting of the American Psychoanalytic Association; see also his "An Attempt at Soul Murder: Rudyard Kipling's Early Life and Work," *The Psychoanalytic Study of the Child* 30 (1975): 683–724.

28. R. D. Laing, "Minkowski and Schizophrenia," 200.

29. David Carroll, "*Middlemarch* and the Externality of Fact," in *This Particular Web*.

30. Ibid., 84.

31. Ibid., 79.

32. Melanie Klein, *et al*, *New Directions in Psycho-Analysis* (London: Tavistock, 1955).

Chapter 8. The Dualistic Mode in Virginia Woolf's *To the Lighthouse*

1. Marilyn R. Farwell, "Virginia Woolf and Androgyny," *Contemporary Literature* 16 (1975): 433–51.

2. Elaine Showalter, "Virginia Woolf and the Flight into Androgyny," chapter 10 of *A Literature of Their Own* (Princeton: Princeton University Press, 1977), 265.

3. Quentin Bell, *Virginia Woolf: A Biography* (New York: Harcourt, 1972), 19.

4. Robert Gittings, *Young Thomas Hardy* (New York: Penguin, 1978), 244.

5. Bell, *Virginia Woolf*; Virginia Woolf, *To the Lighthouse* (New York: Harcourt, 1955); quotes incorporated in text by page.

6. Howard Harper, *Between Language and Silence: The Novels of Virginia Woolf* (Baton Rouge: Louisiana State University Press, 1983), 138.

7. Just as D. H. Lawrence was attemptingg to implement the visions of his imagination by founding a utopian colony while simultaneously binding them into creative form, so Virginia Woolf, in Phyllis Rose's words, sought the "idealized mother of early childhhood" in "a series of quasi-maternal figures selected from among the English aristocracy and associated with the perfection and divinity of the Venus de Milo." The wish to be reborn from an exalted parent is conveyed in the imagery Violet Dickensen evoked in her. Virginia is the diminutive wallaby wishing to be nursed by the maternal kangaroo (Violet) and sheltered in her womb-pocket (*Woman of Letters: A Life of Virginia Woolf* [New York: Oxford University Press, 1978], 115–16). The displacement of the fantasy onto actual persons has the advantage of dislodging it from the original source and allowing creativity the opportunity for mastery lest the attachments become too blind and too binding. Evidence for this reworking of origins is strikingly apparent in Virginia's letters to her sister Vanessa, the goddess/madonna whose "first-born" is Virginia. According to Angelica Garnett, Virginia's version of her sister "tended to soar into Olympian regions" (see editorial note, xxi, to vol. 2 of the *Letters*, 1912–1922, edited by Nigel Nicolson [New York: Harcourt, Brace, Jovanovich, 1976]).

A subtly probing study by Mark Spilka (*Virginia Woolf's Quarrel with Grieving* [Lincoln: University of Nebraska Press, 1980]) may have touched on the psychotic core from which Virginia's family romance was hatched. Spilka's plausible reconstructions are based on Virginia's "deathbed reactions in 1895 when she had secretly laughed at her mother's crying nurse and, on a second visit, had hallucinated a man at the edge of her mother's bed" (6). Spilka construes the man to be Herbert Duckworth, the woman's first husband, safely dead after four years of blissful marriage with Julia, and so still deeply felt within the second marriage but never discussed, and therefore susceptible to idealization whether it be by his remarried widow or by her daughter, Virginia. He is, in Spilka's terms, the robber in the bedroom, the ghostly thief of Julia's affections, the source of her melancholic preoccupations, and the enduring, if elusive, rival within the second marriage. This being the case, Virginia Woolf's art is unusually restorative; and by her reinstating the original marriage, a primal scene is implicitly evoked. But the family romance possibilities are even more apropos. Spilka quotes Virginia as saying that her mother had "cast over the figure of her bridegroom all the golden enchantments of Tennysonian sentiment"; the years with this "saintly" clergyman had been consecrated, stainless, "exalted in a world of pure love and beauty" (27). Spilka's thesis is that Virginia's laughter and her hallucination are signs that the mother's loss is being denied, that the thirteen-year-old child cannot bring herself to engage the work of mourning, partly because of the complications within the family from past, unmourned attachments. Agreeing with this speculation, I would like to add another consideration: the hallucination of the man beside the mother's bed is also Virginia, that is, her wish, delusionally realized, to take the father's place and become the mother's preferred lover. In her elaborate fantasy, Virginia would be both child and lover to the exalted love object, permitting the desires to be loved and to love both to be gratified.

When the mother's death thwarted any likelihood for fulfilment of these wishes, which had been bound within fantasy, the delusional features of the unconscious wish erupt briefly into consciousness: a wish-fulfillment through disguised visualization as in the dream.

8. Harper, *Between Language and Silence,* 296.

9. On the alphabet scale of Mr. Ramsay's philosophical pursuits, he had reached only to *Q* while the mysterious *R* eludes him. Read symbolically, the letters might imply that the *Q* that holds him fast is Mrs. Ramsay as Queen; the *R* he seeks is, as his own initial, the goal of authentic selfhood—also figured by the *R*-like lighthouse, which he does reach after the loss of *Q* the original lighthouse. The other lighthouse is even further beyond him in Harper's view: its three stroke signal equals *U* (..-), the unconscious perhaps, or the unknown (*Between Language and Silence,* 154).

10. Quention Bell contrasts Virginia's "virginal" beauty with her mother's, and the choice of name for Lily concretizes these ideas. An early but enduring nickname for Virginia was "Goat," suggesting self-images or drives at variance with ideal beauty and translatable into Lily's homeliness. As a "deputy for the author," she might also be considered a self-character, as proposed by David Daiches, *Virginia Woolf* (Norfolk, Conn.: New Directions, 1942), 84. And in respect to the view that "two rival streams dashed together and flowed confused but not harmonised in her blood," Rose (*A Life of Virginia Woolf,* 170) writes that the "rhythms of ambivalence, of attraction and rejection, dominates the book, channeled through Lily." Coping with Mrs. Ramsay's death ten years later at forty-four, Lily is the same age as Virginia writing the novel.

11. "Her death," wrote Virginia Woolf following the loss of her mother at thirteen, "was the greatest disaster that could happen" (Bell, *Virginia Woolf,* 42). The death of Mrs. Ramsay reported in parentheses in part 2 invites analogies with the above bracketed episode.

12. Harper, *Between Language and Silence,* 142. For similar interpretations of this point and others throughout this chapter, see Claire Kahane, "The Nuptials of Metaphor: Self and Other in Virginia Woolf," *Literature and Psychology* 30, no. 2 (1980): 72–82.

13. Expanding on this phrase from Margaret Mahler, Louise Kaplan writes, "The mother's presence is like a fixed light that gives the child the security to move out safely to explore the world and then return safely to harbor. She makes the world of time and space sensible and intelligible. As the child separates from the state of oneness with his mother, he continues to have an inner experience of a mothering presence which orients him in the world." This may be a signified of "the other Lighthouse" referred to after Mrs. Ramsay's death. (Louise J. Kaplan, *Oneness and Separateness* [New York: Simon and Schuster, 1978], 16) In the same mode as Mahler, Alma Bond states that "Mrs. Stephen almost certainly was not as good a mother of separation as she was of dual unity" ("Virginia Woolf: Manic-Depressive Psychosis and Genius; An Illustration of Separation-Individuation Theory," *Journal of the American Academy of Psychoanalysis* 13, No. 2 (1985): 193). See also Louise F. Strouse, "Virginia Woolf— Her Voyage Back," *American Imago* 38, no. 2 (1980): 185–202; Shirley Panken, *Virginia Woolf and the "Lust for Creation": A Psychoanalytic View* (Albany: State University of New York Press, 1987).

14. Mitchell, Leaska, *Virginia Woolf's Lighthouse: A Study in Critical Method* (New York: Columbia University Press, 1970), 71, 75.

15. Virginia Woolf, *The Waves* (London: Hogarth, 1963); for more, see James Naremore, *The World without a Self* (New Haven: Yale University Press, 1973).

16. Otto Isakower, "A Contribution to the Patho-Psychology of Phenomena Associated with Falling Asleep," *International Journal of Psycho-Analysis* 19 (1938): 331–45; Bertram D. Lewin, "Reconsideration of the Dream Screen," *The Yearbook of Psychoanalysis* 10 (1954); see app. A.

17. Philip Weisman, "Theoretical Considerations of Ego Regression and Ego Functions in Creativity," *Psychoanalytic Quarterly* 36 (1967): 37–50; Albert Rothenberg, *The Emerging Goddess: The Creative Process in Art, Science, and Other Fields* (Chicago: University of Chicago Press, 1979).

18. Harper, *Between Language and Silence* 139.

19. Leaska, *Study in Critical Method,* 97.

20. Harper, *Between Language and Silence,* 137.

21. Martin Gliserman, "Virginia Woolf's *To the Lighthouse:* Syntax and the Female Center," *American Imago* 40 (1983): 53.

22. Leaska, *Study in Critical Method,* 68–72; Bell, *Virginia Woolf,* 19.

23. Erich Auerback, *Mimesis* (New York: Doubleday, 1957), 463–88.

24. That her conception and birth are associated with her father's act of quasi-generation in discovering a summer site is evident from their appearing in the same passage in Virginia Woolf's *Moments of Being* (New York: Harcourt, 1976), 109.

25. For more on the relation of Scott to Mr. Ramsay and Virginia Woolf, see Steven Cohan, "Why Mr. Ramsay Reads *The Antiquary,*" *Women and Literature* 7 (1979): 14–24.

26. Virginia Woolf, *A Room of One's Own,* (New York: Harcourt Brace, 1929), 101–2.

27. Ibid., 108.

Chapter 9. An Ontogeny of Language

1. Arthur Wormhoudt, "The Unconsicous Identification—Words = Milk," *American Imago* 23 (1949): 234–39.

2. Lawrence Kubie, "Neurotic Distortion of the Symbolic Process," *Journal of the American Psychoanalytic Association* 1 (1953): 56–86.

3. Ralph Greenson, "About the Sound *mm* . . .," *Psychoanalytic Quarterly* 23 (1954): 234–39.

4. "Linguists have reconstructed a language, IndoEuropean, from which the Centum and Satem languages developed, the former including the Germanic as well as the Latin/Romance families. Therefore, this [m] could be reconstructed as belonging to IndoEuropean" (personal communication from Judith Parker, linguist).

5. Charles Hockett, "The Problems of Universals in Language," in *Universals of Language,* ed. J. H. Greenberg, 2d ed. (Cambridge: MIT Press, 1966), 5.

6. Rene Spitz, *No and Yes: On the Genesis of Human Communication* (New York: International Universities Press, 1957).

7. Justin Call, "Some Prelinguistic Aspects of Language Development," *Journal of the American Psychoanalytic Association* 28 (1980): 259–89; Otto Jesperson, *Language: Its Nature, Development, and Origin* (London: Macmillan, 1921); Dan Isaac Slobin, *Psycholinguistics* (Oakland, N.J.: Scott Foresman, 1979), 80.

8. Margaret Mahler, *The Psychological Birth of the Human Infant* (New York: Basic Books, 1975).

9. D. W. Winnicott, "Transitional Objects and Transitional Phenomena," *International Journal of Psycho-Analysis* 34 (1953): 89–97.

10. René Spitz, "The Primal Cavity: A Contribution to the Genesis of Perception and Its Role for Psychoanalytic Theory," *The Psychoanalytic Study of the Child* 10 (1955): 215–40.

11. Samuel Taylor Coleridge, "Kubla Khan," *Selected Poems* (Northbrook, Ill.: A. H. M. Publishers 1956), 62.

12. Deidre Bair, *Samuel Beckett; A Biography* (New York: Harcourt, Brace, Jovanovich, 1978). For more on May Beckett, see Hugh Culik, "Neurological Disorder and the Evolution of Beckett's Maternal Images." *Mosaic* 22 (1989): 41–55.

13. Personal communication from Sidney Mitchell, a Beckett scholar; Gilbert Rose, "On the Shores of Self," *The Power of Form* (New York: International Universities Press, 1980). Herself suitably named, Eileen Watts offers an answer to the riddle of Beckett's great emphasis on names: lacking relationships, his "narrators consider their sense of identity to be contingent upon their names" ("Beckett's Unnamables: Schizophrenia, Rationalism, and the Novel," *American Imago* 45, no. 1 [1988]: 85–106). As in schizophrenia, words replace reality and so reify the self. In "Beckett and Bion" (*International Review of Psycho-Analysis* 16 [1989]: 163–9), Didier Anzieu conflates Pim and Bom into "two faces of the same person," namely, Wilfred Bion, Beckett's analyst in 1934–35. For more on the remarkable exchanges between analyst and artist, see Bennett Simon, "The Imaginary Twins: The Case of Beckett and Bion," same journal, 15 (1988): 331–52. Noting Beckett's depiction of *Endgame* as a "matter of fundamental sounds," Simon elsewhere analyzes the characters as possessing "just enough 'presence' to be able to describe 'absence'" (*Tragic Drama and the Family,* [New Haven: Yale University Press, 1988], 213; 221).

14. Northrop Frye, *Spiritus Mundi: Essays on Literature, Myth, and Society* (Bloomington: Indiana University Press, 1967).

15. Claude Levi-Strauss, *The Scope of Anthropology* (London: Cape, 1967).

16. Patrick McCarthy, *The Riddles of Finnegans Wake* (Teaneck, N.J.: Fairleigh Dickinson University Press, 1980).

17. Sigmund Freud, *Beyond the Pleasure Principle,* vol. 18 of *Standard Edition.*

18. Slobin, *Psycholinguistics,* 80.

19. Ian Hacking, "Chomsky and His Critics," *New York Review of Books,* 23 October, 1980.

20. Samuel Abrams on the theory of character (Panel at the Fall 1980 Meeting of the American Psychoanalytic Associations) prefers this phrase over inheritance or temperament because it stresses the potential for development and is less neutral. Of the six aspects he has studied, the following are significant for studying the directional sources of creativity: *directedness* as a tendency to locate experience in outward or inward zones; *orientedness,* as attention given to the person, the toy, or the task; *tone,* as affective responses and accompanying mood, and *stimulus/response* as for example, the tendency to retain interest in an activity or to seek fresh stimuli. For the differences between noun/pronoun acquisition for self- and object-representations, see Bonnie Litowitz and Norman Litowitz, "Development of Verbal Self-Expression," in *The Future of Psychoanalysis,* ed. Arnold Goldberg (New York: International Universities Press, 1983), 397–430.

21. Rudolph Eckstein, "From the Language of Play to Play with Language," *Adolescent Psychiatry* 4 (1976): 142–62.

22. Jacques Lacan, *The Four Fundamental Concepts of Psychoanalysis* (New York: Norton, 1978).

23. Harold Bloom, *The Anxiety of Influence* (New York: Oxford University Press, 1973).

24. Walter Ong, *The Barbarian Within* (New York: Macmillan, 1962).

25. Martin Gliserman, "Virginia Woolf's *To the Lighthouse*," *American Imago* 40 (1983): 51–101 examines how "syntax acquires semantic significance" (79).

26. Julian Barnes, *Flaubert's Parrot* (London: Cape, 1984).

27. Samuel Beckett, *Company* (New York: Grove Press, 1980).

28. Anthony Burgess, *Joysprick: An Introduction to the Language of James Joyce,*

(London: Andre Deutsch, 1973); Hugh Kenner, *Joyce's Voices* (Berkeley: University of California Press, 1978).

29. Erwin Steinberg, "Characteristic Sentence Patterns in 'Proteus' and 'Lestrygonians,'" *New Light on Joyce from the Dublin Symposium,* ed. Fritz Senn (Bloomington: University of Indiana Press, 1972).

30. Roy Gottfried, *The Art of Joyce's Syntax in Ulysses* (Athens: Unversity of Georgia Press, 1980).

31. Michael Seidel, "*Ulysses*' Black Panther Vampire," *James Joyce Quarterly* 13 (1976): 415–27.

32. Sigmund Freud (1925), "Negation," vol. 19 in *Standard Edition,* (London: Hogarth, 1955).

33. Howard Harper, *Between Language and Silence: The Novels of Virginia Woolf* (Baton Rouge: Louisiana State Universtiy Press, 1983).

34. In *Finnegans Wake* (New York: Penguin, 1976), Joyce said he "put the language to sleep," and by "Spraken sie Djoytsch" he composed his "nightynovel" out of 130 phonemes and twenty–nine languages, of which one is English. The manifold disruptions, dislocations, violations, and amalgamations of syntax and narrative are appropriate verbal renditions of the primordial disturbance of the human family: incest. See Margot Norris, *The Decentered Universe of Finnegans Wake* (Baltimore, Johns Hopkins University Press, 1976), esp. 28–40; and Strother B. Purdy, "Mind Your Genderous: Toward a *Wake* Grammar," *New Light on Joyce,* ed. Fritz Senn (Bloomington: University of Indiana Press, 1972), 46–78.

35. T. S. Eliot, "Preludes," in *The Collected Poems,* (New York: Harcourt, 1950); William Wordsworth, *The Prelude,* ed. by I.C. Maxwell (New York: Penguin, 1971); further references incorporated into the text are to the 1850 version unless otherwise stated.

36. Robert Langbaum, *Mysteries of Identity* (New York: Oxford University Press, 1977).

37. Wilfred Bion, *Learning from Experience* (New York: Jason Aronson, 1983).

38. Phyllis Greenacre, "The Family Romance of the Artist," *The Psychoanalytic Study of the Child* 13 (1958): 9–36.

39. David Beres, "Discussion of the Family Romance," *The Psychoanalytic Study of the Child* 13 (1958): 40–42.

40. Robert Langbaum, *Mysteries of Identity,* 32.

41. Robert Onorato, *The Character of the Poet* (Princeton: Princeton University Press, 1971).

42. The manifold meanings of the Greek root, *logos,* in Lindell and Scott's *Greek Lexicon* (New York: Oxford University Press, 1968) include "report," "account," "principle," "mind," "the divine spark or governing principle of the cosmos," "the Word of God," but also (4) the "esteem, consideration, value put on a person or thing"; *logos* puts the worth in words, to reverse our poet's name. As creation incarnates the divine *Logos,* so the *logos* of the poet incarnates (not just clothes) thought (see *Wordsworth: Language as Counter Spirit,* Frances Ferguson, [New Haven: Yale University Press, 1977], introduction). Geoffrey Hartman's similarly inflected paper, "Words, Wish, Worth: Wordsworth," suggests that the poet descends from Mount Snowden in the finale of *The Prelude* bearing the renewed power of the word reunited with its sources in classical texts and natural sounds, a unity of the "power in sound and the power in light, or ear and eye, or nature and mind." "Thus Snowden is a vision of mastery," the meaning and interpretation of which remain elusive but favor the creation of light and time in Genesis over the law and precept on Sinai and thus close to the purely creative act of language like the act of God—"Let there be"—the divine *Logos* before metaphor and syntax take over (see Harold Bloom

et al, eds. *Deconstruction and Criticism* [New York: Seaburg Press, 1979]. If the power of the divine *Logos* is revealed in Genesis, the power of the individual *logos* must also stem from a genetic moment when wish, word, and deed were fused. Such is Hartman's valuable inference. But beyond the poet's sense of primordial power, the possibility of his achieving a continuing medium for the return to, or recovery of, the archaic past, one must include maternal empathy. The final verses of the poet on Mount Snowden, by reason of their invoking the power of God the father and responding to the aliveness of the natural environment, further assimilate male and female principles into poetic vision.

43. Sigmund Freud (1900), *The Interpretation of Dreams*, 453.

44. Donald Davie, *Articulate Energy: An Inquiry into the Syntax of English Poetry* (New York: Routledge and Kegan Paul, 1975).

45. Similarly, the 1798 and 1849 versions of "Anecdote to Fathers" show Wordsworth moving steadily away from a "self-centered father figure toward the creation of a poet-narrator, as he himself goes through the inevitable process from having a father to becoming father" (Laurence W. Mazzeno, "Of Fathers, Children, and Poets: Wordsworth's 'Anecdote for Fathers,'" *Psychocultural Review* 1 [1977]: 421–33). For the impact of repeated loss on Wordsworth's personality, see Joseph Griska, "Wordsworth's Mood Disturbance," *Literature and Psychology* 24 (1974): 144–52; and for a Kleinian analysis of the poet's early object-relations, see Wallace W. Douglas, *Wordsworth: The Construction of a Personality* (Kent, Ohio: Kent State University Press, 1967): for a more current psychoanalytic reading, see Barbara A. Schapiro, *The Romantic Mother: Narcissistic Patterns in Romantic Poetry* (Baltimore: Johns Hopkins University Press, 1983).

46. See "The Depth of Response," in Richard Onorato's *The Character of the Poet.*

47. Gerald Kauvar, "The psychological Structure of Romantic Poetry," *The Psychoanalytic Review* 64, no. 1 (1977): 21–40.

48. Jacques Derrida, "Freud and the Scene of Writing," *Yale French Studies* 48 (1972): 74–117. This somewhat eccentric theory of writing, which has provoked an even more eccentric response from Harold Bloom in his chapter "The Primal Scene of Instruction," in *A Map of Misreading* (New York: Oxford University Press, 1975), is allegedly from an early passage in Freud's *The Problem of Anxiety* (1926). "If writing—which consists in allowing a fluid to flow out from a tube upon a piece of white paper—has acquired the symbolic meaning of coitus," Freud writes, then writing "will be abstained from, because it is as though forbidden sexual behavior were being indulged in." The fact that Freud is illustrating inhibitions and symptoms and nowhere mentions a primal scene does not inhibit Derrida's or Bloom's intriguing but mostly free-wheeling speculations about the nature of writing.

49. Cited in Onorato, *The Character of the Poet,* 12.

50. Robert Graves, *The White Goddess* (New York: Octagon Books, 1948).

51. M. Margolis and P. Parker, "The Stork Fable—Some Psychodynamic Considerations," *Journal of the American Psychoanalytic Association* 20 (1972): 494–511.

Chapter 10. A Phylogeny of Myths

1. Ashley Montagu, "Mother's Touch," *Science Digest,* April 1981, 16.

2. From "Psychocosomogony: The Presentation of Symbiosis-Individuation in Archaic Greek Myth," by Richard S. Caldwell, whose contributions have been instrumental in shaping my own views in this section. *The Psychoanalytic Study of Society* (New York: Psychohistory Press, 1981), 9: 93–104.

3. These phrases and those following below have been drawn from chapters 3 and 4 of Margaret Mahler's *The Psychological Birth of the Human Infant* (New York: Basic Books, 1975); 41–43; future references incorporated into the text.

4. To Ludwing Drees, *Olympia: Gods, Artists, and Athletes* (New York: Praeger, 1968), I am indebted for the following breakdown in early Greek images of earth-goddesses.

5. Melanie Klein's work is familiar to most readers, a good sampling of which may be found in *New Directions in Psycho-Analysis* (London: Tavistock 1955); less familiar, but no less valuable, are Michael Balint's writings, for which, for immediate reference, one may turn to *Primary Love and Psycho-Analytic Technique* (New York: Liveright, 1965).

6. A term employed by Anton Ehrenzweig in *The Hidden Order of Art* (Berkeley: University of California Press, 1967).

7. W. B. Yeats, "The Circus Animals' Desertion," *Collected Poems,* 335; D. H. Lawrence, *Saint Mawr* (New York: Random House, 1953) and *Phoenix* (New York: Viking, 1974), 259.

8. Charles Baudelaire, "Correspondences," in *French Symbolist Poetry,* trans. by C. F. MacIntyre (Berkeley: University of California Press, 1958), 13.

9. Arthur Wormhoudt, "The Unconscious Identification: Words = Milk."

10. Ralph Greenson, "About the Sound mm ...," *Psychoanalytic Quarterly* 23 (1954): 234–39.

11. Cf. the Creation myths in Robert Graves, *The Greek Myths,* vol. 1 (Baltimore: Penguin Books, 1955); also, Marvin Margolis and Philip Parker, "The Stork Fable," *Journal of the American Psychoanalytic Association* 20 (1972): 494–511.

12. Phyllis Greenacre, "Woman As Artist," *Psychoanalytic Quarterly* 29, no. 2 (1960): 211.

13. Stevie Davies, *Emily Brontë: The Artist as a Free Woman* (Manchester, England: Carcanet Press, 1983), 20.

14. Gilbert Rose, "On the Shores of Self: Samuel Beckett's *Molloy*—Irredentism and the Creative Impulse," *Psychoanalytic Review* 60 (1973): 587–604; reprinted in *The Power of Form* (New York: International Universities Press, 1980).

15. William Blake Tyrrell, *Amazons, A Study in Athenian Mythmaking* (Baltimore: Johns Hopkins University Press, 1984). Lee R. Edwards takes the myth of Psyche as a "classic example of the female heroic paradigm," especially in its struggles to reconcile love with power (*Psyche As Hero* [Middletown, Conn.: Wesleyan University Press, 1984]).

16. Joseph Simo, "On Christianity and the Oedipal Winner," *Psychoanalytic Review* 70, no. 3 (1983): 321–30.

17. Caldwell, "Psychocosmogony."

18. Leonard Shengold, "The Parent as Sphinx," *Journal of the American Psychoanalytic Association* 11 (1963): 725–51.

19. Norman O. Brown's introduction to Hesiod's *Theogony* (New York: Bobbs-Merrill Library of Liberal Arts, 1953), 19.

20. To these may be added George Eliot. After carefully examining her early relationship with her brother Isaac, Ruby Redinger writes that "it is impossible to overestimate the importance of her bisexual identification." Redinger is also persuaded that "similar twofold identification occurs among many writers, including those of the 'highest stature,' for example, Dostoevsky and Henry James" (*George Eliot: the Emergent Self* [New York: Knopf, 1975]), 59.

21. Stevie Davies, *The Artist as a Free Woman,* 105.

22. Hesiod, *Theogony* 56.

Chapter 11. Steps Toward an Integration of Origins into Culture

1. Sigmund Freud (1917), "A Difficulty in the Path of Psychoanalysis," *Standard Edition,* Volume 17.

2. Adrian Desmond, *Archetypes and Ancestors: Paleontology in Victorian London, 1850–1875* (Chicago: University of Chicago Press, 1984), 33. In his *Autobiography* (New York: Norton, 1969), 104–5, Darwin writes that Owen "became my bitter enemy, not owing to any quarrel between us, but as far as I could judge out of jealousy at its [*Origin of the Species*] success."

3. *Darwin,* ed. by Philip Appleman, (New York: Norton Critical Edition 1970), 208. Modern readers of this work notice that for a "book mainly about sex," as Stanley Edgar Hyman notes, it "is oddly reticent in certain areas." Hyman goes on to suggest that a "good deal of the eroticism repressed in connection with human sexuality gets released in the accounts of animal sexuality." Stanley Edgar Hyman, *The Tangled Bank* (New York: Atheneum, 1974), 52–54.

4. Darwin quoted in Stanley Edgar Hyman, *The Tangled Bank*, 38.

5. Elaine Morgan, *The Descent of Woman* (New York: Stein and Day, 1980), 65–67.

6. Robert Ardrey, *African Genesis*, (New York: Atheneum, 1973), 168–69.

7. Stanley Edgar Hyman, *The Tangled Bank,* 31.

8. Evelyn Shaw and Joan Darling, *Female Strategies* (New York: Walker, 1985); Anne Fausto-Sterling, *Myths of Gender* (New York: Basic Books, 1985).

9. Stephen Jay Gould, "Cardboard Darwinism," *New York Review of Books,* 25 September 1986; the adaptationist approach under review is Bettyann Kevles' *Female of the Species: Sex and Survival in the Animal Kingdom* (Cambridge: Harvard University Press, 1986).

10. Richard Sennett, *New York Times Book Review,* 22 September 1971, 45.

11. I am paraphrasing here, as I will be quoting directly hereafter, from an excellent analysis of Plato's cave by Bennett Simon in *Mind and Madness in Ancient Greece* (Ithaca: Cornell University Press, 1978), 171–79. Plato's "Allegory of the Cave" appears in Book 7 of *The Republic*, trans. by F. M. Cornford (New York: Oxford University Press, 1963), 227–35.

12. David Rapaport, *Organization and Pathology of Thought* (New York: Columbia University Press, 1951).

13. W. B. Yeats, *Collected Poems* (New York: Macmillan, 1956), 162; D. H. Lawrence, *Collected Poems* (New York: Viking Press, 1964), 691.

14. In this larger framework the anxiety of influence, which Harold Bloom has so sensitively delineated, is defensive, in the sense that psychoanalysis sees homosexuality as a defense against maternal engulfment. (Cf. Robert Stoller, "Symbiosis, Anxiety and the Development of Masculinity," *Archives of General Psychiatry* 30 [1974]: 164–72.) In a study of Jung's anxiety over the influence of Freud, I have concluded that Jung fabricated an event out of his past that he described to Freud as a homosexual assault on him by an older man. It is clear that this warning signal was invoked at a time when the relationship between the two men was most intense, when Jung was placing himself in the position of Freud's hysterical patients and thereby subjecting himself all the more to fears of being overwhelmed by the other's stronger personality. Thus the appropriateness of his pseudomemory. Whether there was also an underlying fear of maternal engulfment remains speculative (Daniel Dervin, "A Crux in the

Jung/Freud Letters," *Bulletin of The Menninger Clinic* 41, no. 2 [1977]: 131–44).

Chapter 12. The Three Stages of Natural Creativity

1. Gilbert Rose refers to the ego's ongoing integrative functions as "normal, garden-variety creativity," and states that "growth is a form of self-creation." (Cf. "Narcissistic Fusion States and Creativity," in *The Unconscious Today*, ed. Mark Kanzer [New York: International Universities Press, 1971], 495–505.) Coming at this phenomenon from their own context, scientists like Erich Jantsch have coined the term *autopoiesis* to mean "self-production or self-renewal." See *The Self-Organizing Universe* (New York: Pergamon Press, 1980). James Henderson's use of "three areas of psychic activity" first started me thinking along the above stages of natural self-creativity ("Exorcism, Possession, and the Dracula Cult," *Bulletin of the Menninger Clinic* 40, no. 6 [1977]:603–28).

2. D. W. Winnicott, "Transitional Objects and Transitional Phenomena," in *Collected Papers* (New York: Basic Books, 1958). More precisely and more recently, Louise Kaplan has written, "*After* his physical needs are attended to, the neonate's greatest hunger is for human dialogue." By the sixth week, the "infant has begun to construct a libidinal object" ("Symposium on *The Interpersonal World of the Infant,*" *Contemporary Psychoanalysis* 23, no. 1 [1987]: 27–43).

3. Sheldon Bach, "On the Narcissistic State of Consciousness," *International Journal of Psycho-Analysis* 58 (1977): 232.

4. D. W. Winnicott, "The Depressive Position in Normal Emotional Development," *Collected Papers.*

5. Arnold H. Modell, "The Transitional Object and the Creative Act," *Psychoanalytic Quarterly* 39 (1970): 240–50. In Lacan's terms, the child enters the Symbolic Order through language, but language-acquisition occurs both earlier and from a different source than Lacan allows. And language is but one of the transitional objects by means of which individuals of both sexes enter culture.

6. Peter Blos, "The Geneology of the Ego Ideal," *Psychoanalytic Study of the Child* 29 (1974): 43–88.

7. The technical meaning psychoanalysis assigns to positive/negative as active/passive is intended to be value neutral, and in any case should not alter the inference that the superego's currency is stamped with *no,* the ego-ideal's with *yes.* The formation of the superego coincides with childhood; that of the ego-ideal extends through adolescence and beyond.

8. P. Ikonen and E. Rechartdt, "On the Universal Nature of Primal Scene Fantasies," *International Journal of Psycho-Analysis* 65 (1984): 63–72.

9. These views derive from forthcoming studies by Donald Kaplan and William I. Grossman.

10. Ikonen and Rechardt, "Primal Scene Fantasies," 64.

11. Phyllis Greenacre, "Woman as Artist," *Psychoanalytic Quarterly* 29 (1960): 208–27.

12. "A study of nursery preschool children carried out by Diane McGuinness, of the Department of Psychology at Stanford University, found boys more curious, especially in regard to exploring their environment." Richard M. Restak, *The Brain: The Last Frontier* (New York: Doubleday, 1979).

13. Seymour Fisher, *Development and Structure of the Body Image,* 2 vols. (Hillside, N.J.: Erlbaum Associates, 1986). On eating disorders as a focus for mother-daughter conflicts, see Kim Chernin, *The Hungry Self: Women, Eating, and Identity* (New York: New York Times Books, 1985). The male adolescent's disorder of choice

is imposturousness, according to Louise Kaplan in *Adolescence* (New York: Simon and Schuster, 1984) and in *The Family Romance of the Impostor-Poet Thomas Chatterton* (New York: Atheneum, 1988).

14. A portion of my study appears under the title, "Matricentric Narratives: A Report on the Psychoanalysis of Gender Based on British Woman's Fiction," *The Journal of Psychoanalytic Anthropology* 9 (1986): 393–446.

15. Nancy Chodorow, *The Reproduction of Mothering: Psychoanalysis and the Sociology of Gender* (Berkeley: University of California Press, 1978), 100–107; "Primary Femininity," in *Sexual Excitement*, by Robert Stoller (New York: Pantheon, 1979).

16. One should keep an open mind in considering these writers' preoedipal emphasis and their tendency to gloss over the girl's profound and protracted conflicts with her mother. Perhaps because maternal identification and "feminization" are the outgrowth of the girl's developmental program, her "original struggles to become a self separate from mother were more dramatic, violent, and fraught with conflict" than the boy's (Louise J. Kaplan, *Adolescence: The Farewell to Childhood* [New York: Simon and Schuster, 1984], 169).

17. Joyce Carol Oates, review of *Remember Me,* by Fay Weldon, *New York Times Book Review,* 21 November 1976.

18. For an assessment, see Bonnie Scott, *Joyce and Feminism* (Bloomington: Indiana University Press, 1984).

19. Thoman Ewens, "Female Sexuality and the Role of the Phallus," *Psychoanalytic Review* 63 (1976): 615–37.

20. W. R. Bion, *Transformations* (New York: Basic Books, 1965).

21. Sigmund Freud, *Standard Edition,* vol 9.

22. B. D. Lewin, "The Nature of Reality, the Meaning of Nothing, with an Addendum on Concentration," *Psychoanalytic Quarterly* 17 (1948): 524–26.

23. Aaron Esman, "The Primal Scene, A Review and a Reconsideration," *The Psychoanalytic Study of the Child* 28 (1973): 49–83.

24. Doris Lessing, "My Father," in *A Small Personal Voice* (London: Curtis, 1963).

25. Kurt Schlesinger, "On the Creative Process and the Human Capacity to Construe," *International Journal of Psychotherapy* 8, no. 1 (1980): 482–500.

26. Anne Gourevitch, "Origins, The Impact of Parental Background," *Contemporary Psychoanalysis* 14 (1978): 226–45.

Chapter 13. The Creation of Origins through Evolution

1. *Car ce fait l'homme, c'est d'avoir une enfance* (For by having a childhood, we become human). Roland Barthes, *"Le Grain d'une Enfance,"* a review of Jean Daniel's *le Refuge et la Source* in *Le Nouvel Observateur* (5 September 1977). Though neoteny has been singled out for reasons germane to a study of creativity, this does not mean that in the total reconstruction of human origins such phenomena as birth spacing, strong social bonds, and longevity are overlooked. Cf. C. Owen Lovejoy, "The Origin of Man," *Science* (23 January 1981), and his discussion in Donald Johanson and Maitland Edey's *Lucy* (New York: Simon and Schuster, 1981). See also Ashley Montagu, *Growing Young* (New York: McGraw-Hill, 1983).

2. Norman Holland, "Freud, Physics, and Literature," *Journal of the American Academy of Psychoanalysis* 12, no. 3 (1984): 301–20. Please note that I am not implying that Freud, when rightly read, is right, but that misreadings reveal the reader.

3. Desmond Morris, *The Naked Ape: A Zoologist's Study of the Human Animal* (New York: McGraw Hill, 1967).

4. Sally Slocum, "Woman the Gatherer: Male Bias in Anthropology," in *Toward an Anthropology of Women,* ed. Rayna R. Reiter (New York: Monthly Review Press, 1975), 36–50. See also Frances Dahlberg, ed., *Woman the Gatherer* (New Haven: Yale University Press, 1981).

5. Morris, *The Naked Ape,* 66.

6. Geza Roheim, "The Evolution of Culture," *International Journal of Psycho-Analysis* 15 (1934): 387–418; see discussion of Lebe in chapter one.

7. In *Studies on Hysteria* (1895), Freud urged his public to "keep free from the theoretical prejudice that we are dealing with the abnormal brains of *'degeneres'* and *'desequilibres'* ["degenerate and unbalanced persons"]" *Standard Edition*, vol. 2, 294.

8. Morris, *The Naked Ape*, 50.

9. Cf. Russell Jacoby, *Social Amnesia: A Critique of Conformist Psychology from Adler to Laing* (Boston: Beacon Press, 1975), for a discussion of this tendency to forget within psychology.

10. Sally Slocum, "Woman the Gatherer."

11. Morris, *The Naked Ape*, 81.

12. This subject receives more extensive treatment in my article, "Opheus and Eurydice, A Myth about Human Evolution," *The Journal of Psychoanalytic Anthropology* 6, no. 3 (1983): 277–88.

13. Marie Bonaparte, "The Fault of Orpheus in Reverse," *International Journal of Psycho-Analysis* 35 (1954): 109–12.

14. Robert Ardrey, *African Genesis* (New York: Atheneum, 1973).

15. Among hard-core scientists, Ludwig Von Bertalanffy, considered now to be one of the founders of systems theory, had suggested as early as 1956 that human beings inhabit a predominantly symbolic world, thereby alligning himself with Suzanne Langor and Ernst Cassirer (see the collected writings in *A Systems View of Man*, ed. Paul A. LaViolette [Boulder, Colorado: Westview Press, 1981]).

16. K. R. Eissler, "The Fall of Man," *The Psychoanalytic Study of the Child* 30 (1975): 589–46.

17. Sigmund Freud, *Totem and Taboo*, vol. 13 of the *Standard Edition;* see also the newly discovered paper published as *A Phylogenetic Fantasy* (Cambridge: Harvard University Press, 1987).

18. Philip Rieff, *Freud: The Mind of the Moralist* (New York: Doubleday, 1961), 214.

19. Derek Freeman, "*Totem and Taboo*—A Reappraisal," *The Psychoanalytic Study of Society* 4 (1967): 9–33; for a revival of Freud's theories see Robin Fox *The Red Lamp of Incest* (New York: E. P. Dutton, 1980), 54; reviewed by me in *The Journal of Psychohistory* 9, no. 4 (1982): 471–74.

20. "Popular treatments of territoriality such as *The Territorial Imperative* (Ardrey, 1966) have created the illusion that territory is universal among animals and, further, that humans are necessarily territorial as well." David P. Barash, *Sociobiology and Behavior* (New York: Elsevier Socientific Publishing Co., 1977), 255. See also Alexander Alland, Jr., *The Human Imperative* (New York: Columbia University Press, 1982).

21. Morris, *The Naked Ape,* 63.

22. Robert Ardrey, *African Genesis,* 162.

23. Raymond Dart, quoted by Donald Johanson and Maitland Edey in *Lucy* (New York: Simon and Shuster, 1981), 40. Ardrey's relationship to Dart is discussed on 64–68.

24. William Arens, *The Man-Eating Myth* (New York: Oxford, 1979); a review of the controversy, "Are the Horrors of Cannibalism Fact—or Fiction?" by Gina Kolata, appears in *Smithsonian,* March 1987, 151–70.

25. Marvin Harris, *Cannibals and Kings: The Origins of Cultures* (New York: Random

House, 1977), 64–65. While it may be unwarranted to consider cognitive styles like behaviorism as stemming more or less directly from the child's emerging phallic consciousness, there may nonetheless be affinities worth noting. The three areas of correspondence I have in mind are: (1) the emphasis on size, measurement, control, mastery; (2) the drive toward penetration of what is considered unknown, mysterious, etc; (3) the emphasis on external phenomena, which is the hallmark of behaviorism, with a concurrent neglect of the internal, invisible, subjective realities, which are the concerns of artists, philosophers, and psychoanalysts. To these latter groups the world of the behaviorist does not come across as wrong so much as two-dimensional, lacking in resonance, inwardness, depth. Such a felt deficiency, which does not readily lend itself to mediation, also corresponds to early feeding experiences in which the breast is perceived either largely as a surface area, a quantity, or as providing a sense of meaning and quality to experience. The prephallic basis may be one reason for avoiding hooking scientific modalities onto one gender over another. The term phallic consciousness I have borrowed from D. H. Lawrence, who means something different by it: a vital center of consciousness below the solar plexus, which has yielded historically to mental consciousness, the mode of scientific rationalism; the former relies on touch, the latter on sight.

26. Freud, *Civilization and Its Discontents, Standard Edition* 21, 123.

27. Harris, *Cannibals and Kings,* 65.

28. Ibid., 66.

29. Fritjof Capra, *The Turning Point* (New York: Simon and Schuster, 1982), 182.

30. See also Holland, "Freud, Physics, and Literature."

31. Stephen Jay Gould, "Our Greatest Evolutionary Step," in *The Panda's Thumb* (New York: Norton, 1980).

32. C. Johanson and M. Edey, *Lucy,* (1981) 320–27.

33. Claude Levi-Strauss, "The Family," in *Man, Culture, and Society,* ed. Harry Shapiro (New York: Oxford University Press, 1956).

34. Gould, *Panda's Thumb,* 131–32.

35. Erich Jantsch, *The Self-Organizing Universe* (New York: Pergamon Press, 1980), 8.

36. "Insight. . . ." Chap. 70 of *The Writings of Anna Freud* vol. 8 (New York: International University Press, 1981).

37. Robert Jastrow, *The Enchanted Loom: Mind in the Universe* (New York: Simon and Schuster, 1981), 64.

38. Carl Sagan, *The Dragons of Eden* (New York: Random House, 1977).

39. Sagan, *Dragons of Eden,* 60.

40. Ibid.

41. Arthur Koestler, *Janus: A Summing Up* (New York: Random House, 1978). For an extensive historical investigation of the development of creativity in relation to the bicameral brain, see Julian Jaynes, *The Origin of Consciousness in the Breakdown of the Bicameral Mind* (Boston: Houghton, Mifflin, 1976).

42. Sagan, *Dragons of Eden,* 138.

43. Ibid., 150.

44. Ibid., 140–41.

45. Jastrow, *The Enchanted Loom*, 34.

46. Ibid., 131.

47. Ibid.

48. Erich Jantsch, *The Self-Organizing Universe,* 8.

49. Jastrow, *The Enchanted Loom,* 114.

50. Ibid., 116–18.

51. Robin Morgan, *Monster* (New York: Random House, 1972).

52. Eric Partridge, *Origins*; for more on the dragon, see Judy Allen and Jeanne Griffiths, *The Book of the Dragon* (Secaucus, N.J.: Chartwell Books, 1979).

Chapter 14. Cosmic Origins, Lives of Scientists, Returns to Pseudosolutions

1. Anthony Storr, *The Dynamics of Creation* (New York: Atheneum, 1972), 70.

2. Karl Stern, *The Flight from Woman* (New York: Farrar, Straus, and Giroux, 1965).

3. Lewis Feuer, *The Scientific Intellectual* (New York: Basic Books, 1963), 13.

4. Ralph Colp, Jr., "Charles Darwin's Vision of Organic Nature," *New York State Journal of Medicine* 79, no. 10 (1979): 1622–1629; follow-up letter in December 1979 issue, 1979.

5. Darwin in his chapter on "The Struggle for Existence," *The Origin of the Species,* quoted by Colp, "Charles Darwin's Vision," 1628.

6. Ibid., 1627.

7. Ibid.

8. Colp, follow-up letter, 2136.

9. Timothy Ferris, "Crucibles of the Cosmos," *New York Times Magazine,* 7 January 1979.

10. From an unpublished paper by John A. O'Keefe, "On Wheeler's Cosmology", presented at the seminar of the nonrational under the auspices of the Washington School of Psychiatry, 1977. See John Wheeler, "The Universe as Home for Man," *The Nature of Scientific Discovery,* ed. Owen Gingerich (Wash. D.C.; Smithsonian Institution Press, 1975). See also his Foreword to the major study, by John D. Barrow and Frank J. Tipler, *The Anthropic Cosmological Principle* (New York: Oxford University Press, 1986).

11. Along parallel lines to these speculations are some psychoanalytic clinical data and further speculations by Carl Sagan. Robert Faguet reports a patient's associations to the big-bang theory with his own hatching-out from the symbiotic phase of infancy, a kind of "baptism of space." In addition, the expanding universe concept was the split of the maternal image into good and bad partial representations into an ever more dangerous separation unless some degree of reconciliation can occur (see "A Long Time Ago in a Galaxy Far Far Away ...," *The American Journal of Psychoanalysis* 38 [1978]: 359–60).

Carl Sagan, in yielding to his speculative bent, takes the "Steady State cosmology [as] blissful; an Oscillating Universe, in which the universe expands and contracts, painfully and forever; and a Big Bang expanding universe, in which the cosmos is created in a violent event, suffused with radiation" and connects them with "human perinatal experiences." Having made his acquaintance with Freud, this accomplished scientist has not yet made his way forward in evolving psychoanalytic thought to Margaret Mahler's work on the psychological birth of the individual; but if he ever does, I believe his speculations will be much more firmly grounded (see "The Amniotic Universe," in *Broca's Brain* [New York: Random House, 1979]).

12. Sir Bernard Lovell, "Whence—We Are What We Know about Where We Came From," *New York Times Magazine,* 16 November 1975.

13. Preston Cloud, *Cosmos, Earth and Man; a Short History of the Universe* (New Haven: Yale University Press, 1979).

14. John Archibald Wheeler, "Our Universe: The Known and the Unknown," *American Scientist* 56, no. 1 (1968): 1–20.

15. Anthony Storr, *The Dynamics of Creation,* 67; see also Albert Rothenberg, "Einstein's Creative Thinking and the General Theory of Relativity," *American Journal of Psychiatry* 136 (1979): 38–43.

16. Lewis Feuer, *The Scientific Intellectual,* 12.

17. Lewis Feuer, *Einstein and the Generations of Science* (New York: Basic Books, 1974).

18. Jeremy Bernstein, *Einstein* (New York: Viking, 1973), 16.

19. Ibid.

20. Ibid., 14.

21. Roberta Recht, " 'The Foundations of an Admirable Science': Descartes' Dream of 10 November 1619," *Humanities in Society* 4, no. 2 and 3 (1981): 203–21.

22. Quoted from Evelyn Fox Keller, *Reflections on Gender and Science* (New Haven: Yale University Press, 1985), 7.

23. A. C. Crombie, *Medieval and Early Modern Science,* vol. 1 (New York: Doubleday, 1959), 129–39.

24. Anthony Storr, *C. G. Jung* (New York: Viking, 1973), 86.

25. I. Bernard Cohen, *Album of Science, from Leonardo to Lavoisier, 1540–1800* (New York: Scribners, 1980), 32.

26. Anthony Storr, *The Dynamics of Creation,* 70.

27. Frank E. Manuel, *A Portrait of Isaac Newton* (Cambridge: Harvard University Press, 1968), 190.

28. I. Bernard Cohen, *Franklyn and Newton* (Philadelphia: The American Philosophical Society, 1956), 14.

29. Manuel, *A Portrait of Isaac Newton,* 18.

30. Ibid., 30.

31. Ibid., 23–25.

32. Jacques Maritain, *The Dream of Descartes* (New York: Philosophical Library, 1944), 11–30.

33. Roberta Recht's " 'Foundations of an Admirable Science' " undergirds the following discussion. After her reading this paper before the International Psychohistory Association in June of 1982, I explored with her the intriguing family romance implications, which we agreed were one extension of her line of inquiry.

34. Karl Stern, *Flight from Woman,* 91–99.

35. Recht, " 'Foundations,' " 206.

36. Ibid., 204–6.

37. Stephen Schonberger, "A Dream of Descartes: Reflections on the Unconscious Determinants of Science," *International Journal of Psycho-Analysis* 20 (1939): 43– 57; J. O. Wisdom, "Three Dreams of Descartes," 28 (1947): 11–17.

38. J. O. Wisdom, "Three Dreams of Descartes," 16.

39. W. T. Stace, "Man against Darkness," *Atlantic Monthly,* September 1948.

40. T. S. Eliot, "Four Quartets," 144.

41. Timothy Ferris, "Physics' Newest Frontier," *New York Times Magazine,* 26 September 1982, 70.

42. Leonard Barkin, *Nature's Work of Art: The Human Body as Image of the World* (New Haven: Yale University Press, 1975).

43. Carl Sagan, *Cosmos* (New York: Random House, 1980), 46.

44. Michael Polanyi, *Personal Knowledge: Towards a Post-Critical Philosophy* (New York: Harper and Row, 1958).

45. Arnold Modell, "The Nature of Psychoanalytic Knowledge," *Journal of the American Psychoanalytic Association* 26 (1978): 641–57.

46. K. R. Eissler, "Death Drive, Ambivalence, and Narcissism," *The Psycho-analytic Study of the Child* 26 (1971): 25–78.

47. Steven J. Dick, *Plurality of Worlds: The Origins of the Extraterrestrial Debate from Democritus to Kant* (New York: Cambridge University Press, 1982).

48. Erich von Daniken, *Chariots of the Gods?,* trans. Michael Heron (New York: Bantam, 1971), viii.

49. Ronald Story, *The Space-Gods Revealed* (New York: Harper and Row, 1976). On the credulity side, see Philip Slater, *The Wayward Gate* (Boston: Beacon Press, 1977).

50. Walter L. Williams, *The Spirit and the Flesh: Sexual Diversity in American Indian Culture* (Boston: Beacon, 1987).

51. Elaine Pagels, *The Gnostic Gospels* (New York: Random House, 1979).

52. For favorable commentary on Moon's religion, Darral Richardson, eds., *A Time for Consideration* (New York and Toronto: Edwin Mellen Press, 1978); and Frederich Sontag, *Sun Myung Moon and the Unification Church* (Nashville: Parthenon Press, 1977). For more circumspect views, see Irving Louis Horowitz, ed., *Science, Sin and Scholarship,* (Cambridge: MIT Press, 1978). For first-hand accounts, see Christopher Edwards, *Crazy for God* (Englewood Cliffs, N.J.: Prentice Hall, 1979); Allen Tate Wood, *Moonstruck* (New York: William Morrow: 1979).

53. *The Divine Prinicple* (New York: The Holy Spirit Association for the Unification of World Christianity, 1973) contains the basic testament of Reverend Moon. Future references will be incorporated by page into the text.

54. Moon, *Divine Priniciple,* 45. Lucifer's motive was threefold: "he envied God's love for Adam and Eve; he was jealous that Adam was to be Eve's future husband; and his desire was aroused" (Elizabeth Clark, "Women in the Theology of the Unification Church" in *Exploring Unification Theology.* ed. by Susau Hodges and Darrol Bryant [Toronto: Edwin Mellen Press, 1978], 148–66).

55. Moon, *Divine Principle,* 118.

56. Ibid., 215.

57. Evelyn Underhill, *Mysticism* (New York: Dutton, 1961).

58. Sam Keen, "Sorcerer's Apprentice," *Seeing Castaneda,* ed. Daniel C. Noel (New York: C. P. Putnam's, Capricorn Books, 1976), 73.

59. Carlos Castaneda, *Journey to Ixtlan* (New York: Simon and Schuster, 1972), 30.

60. "Don Juan and Castaneda," *Psychocultural Review* 1, no. 3, 4 (1977); *The Psychoanalytic Review* 64 (1977): pt. 3, 323–80.

61. Faber, *Psychoanalytic Review,* 331.

62. Bryce and Ruth Boyer, who have spent many years among the Mescalero Apaches.

63. Castaneda, *A Separate Reality* (New York: Pocketbooks, 1974), 140.

64. Ibid., 135–37.

65. Bryce Boyer, "Remarks on the Personality of Shamans with Special Reference to the Apache of the Mescalero Reservation," *The Psychoanalytic Study of Society* 2 (1962): 233–54; Bryce Boyer, *Childhood and Folkore* (New York: Library of Psychological Anthropology, 1979).

66. See, for example, the enthusiastic review by the psychoanalyst Else First reprinted from the *New York Times Book Review* in Noel's *Seeing Castaneda,* and the naive attempt at "Relating the Work of Carlos Castaneda to Psychiatry," by Bruce W. Scotton, *Bulletin of the Menninger Clinic* 42 (1978): 233–38.

67. Richard De Mille, ed., *The Don Juan Papers: Further Castaneda Controversies* (Santa Barbara, Calif.: Santa Barbara Press, 1980).

68. D. H. Lawrence, *The Apocalypse* (New York: Viking, 1969), 184; additonal references incorporated.

Chaper 15. The Holes in Being that Reveal Our Selves

1. Sigmund Freud, *The Letters,* ed. Ernst L. Freud (New York: Basic Books, 1960), 25 February 1908; inner quote is a line from Heine. It was Sartre who once referred to man as a "hole in being" because he alone of living forms could imagine his own death, his nonbeing.

2. On the vexed question of the complex's ubiquity, see Anne Parsons, "Is the Oedipus Complex Universal?" *Psychoanalytic Study of Society* 3 (1964): 278–328; and

Lowell Edmunds, *Oedipus: The Ancient Legend and Its Later Analogues* (Baltimore: Johns Hopkins University Press, 1985); Theodore and Ruth Lidz, *Oedipus in the Stone Age* (Madison, Conn.: International Universities Press, 1989).

3. Quoted by Bernd Urban, "Schnitzler and Freud as Doubles: Poetic Intuition and Early Research on Hysteria," *Psychoanalytic Review* 65 no. 1 (1978): 131–65.

4. Harry Trosman, "Freud and the Controversy over Shakespeare Authorship," *Journal of the American Psychoanalytic Association* 13, no. 3 (1965): 475–98.

5. The complete sentence: "Similarly with the 'romanticization of origins' in the case of paranoics—heroes, founders of religion," offers an ambiguity of self-including and self-distancing in light of his heroic task of founding a scientific movement. The key connecting word is *similarly. The Origins of Psycho-Analysis,* ed. Marie Bonaparte, Anna Freud, and Ernst Kris (New York: Basic Books, 1954), 223; for slightly different wording, see *The Complete Letters of Sigmund Freud to Wilhelm Fliess, 1887–1904,* ed. Jeffrey Masson (Cambridge: Harvard University Press, 1985), 272.

6. Harry Trosman, *Freud and the Imaginative World* (Hillsdale, N.J.: The Analytic Press, 1985), 82–84.

7. Quoted by Bernd Urban, "Schnitzler and Freud."

8. Donald M. Kaplan, "On Shyness," *International Journal of Psycho-Analysis* 53 (1972): 439–53.

9. Harold Bloom's phrase and title. That Freud in his private oedipal drama admitted suffering guilt for fulfilled death wishes directed toward a younger sibling who died when Freud was in his second year adds one more quirky dimension to the subject. The child's name was Julius, and Leonard Shengold refers in an analysis of Freud to "fraticide as a displacement of parricide." (Freud also had an older brother and half-brother). Thus Shakespeare's public interpretation of Freud's private parricidal drama. (Cf. Ernest Jones, *Biography of Freud,* vol. 2, and Shengold "Freud and Joseph," in *The Unconscious Today,* 1971). For Freud's own tendency to shape his life in accord with the heroic myth, see Frank Sulloway, "Freud's Personal Myth of the Hero," in *Freud, Biologist of the Mind: Beyond the Psychoanalytic Legend* (New York: Basic Books, 1979).

10. Ernest Wolf, "*Saxa Loquuntur*: Artistic Aspects of Freud's 'The Aetiology of Hysteria,'" *Psychoanalytic Study of the Child* 26 (1972), 547.

11. Leon Edel, "Psychoanalysis and Literary Biography," in *Literary Biography* (Toronto: Toronto University Press, 1957).

Chapter 16. *Homo Undulans*

1. Philip Slater, *Footholds* (New York: Dutton, 1977), 190.

2. Michel de Montaigne, *The Complete Essays,* trans. by Donald Frame (Stanford: Stanford University Press, 1965), 5.

3. John Ruskin, *Stones of Venice,* vol. 2, *Complete Works,* 8 (New York: Thomas Crowell, 1905), 161.

4. Slater takes hurricane / whirlpool as "the core metaphor for all matter"; also interesting is his idea of matter as "ambivalent energy." Ambivalence, or opposing forces, as in yin / yang, produces a stasis or balance; whereas motion requires an imbalance. Both are necessary to life. He concludes with inferences drawn from bipolar phenomena, for example love / hate: "At peak intensity and at zero intensity all emotions seem to merge. Put simply, while hate may appear to be on a straight line, it is actually curving around toward its opposite, love, if pursued far enough. Straight-sightedness is short-sightedness. The whirlpool figure, like the black hole in space and the double helix mentioned below are similar enough to one another as well as to other

geometric forms such as Yeats's interpenetrating gyres or cones to make one wonder if, along with their being images to suggest basic operations in the universe, they might also have some internal reference as mental structures. Their affinities with the "Two monstrous, lovejoined serpents," which Ovid has the bisexual Teiresias discovering, offer a mythological clue to their sexual affinity.

5. Roberta Recht, "An Admirable Science," 211–12.

6. Jean Paul Sartre, *Nausea* (New York: New Directions, 1964) 129.

7. Samuel Weiss on a panel "Conceptualizing the Nature of the Therapeutic Action of Child Analysis" (Fall 1978 Meeting, American Psychoanalytical Association).

8. Leon Wurmser, "Some Comments about Adolf Grunbaum's Criticism of 'the Validity of Hidden Motives in Psychoanalytic Theory,'" (Paper read at the Winter 1986 American Psychoanalytic Meeting). Grunbaum, who had written *The Foundations of Psychoanalysis: A Philosophical Critique* (Pittsburgh: Pittsburgh University Press, 1984), was in attendance and participated in the discussion.

9. August Strindberg, foreword to *Miss Julie*, in *Six Plays of Strindberg*, trans. by Elizabeth Sprigge (New York: doubleday, 1955), 65.

10. Sigmund Freud, *Studies on Hysteria, Standard Edition* 2, 7.

11. K. R. Eissler, "Death Drive, Ambivalence, and Narcissism," *The Psychoanalytic Study of the Child,* 1971, vol. 26, 25–78.

12. Stephen Jay Gould, "The Ghost of Protagoas," *New York Review of Books,* 21 January 1981, 42–44; Robin Fox, *The Red Lamp of Incest* (New York: Oxford University Press, 1947).

13. Paul Davies, *Superforce* (New York: Simon and Schuster, 1984), 23.

14. Gary Zukav, *The Dancing Wu Li Masters* (New York: Morrow, 1979), 213.

15. See Karl Popper on essentialism in *Conjectures and Refutations* (New York: Harper and Row, 1968), 105.

16. Roy Schafer, *The Analytic Attitude* (New York: Basic Books, 1983), 8; Norman Holland "Freud, Physics, and Literature," *Journal of the American Academy of Psychoanalysis* 12 (1984): 301–20.

17. Darius Gray Ornston, "Psychotherapy and Translation" (Paper read at the American Psychoanalytic Meeting, December 1986).

18. Harold Bloom, *Kabbalah and Criticism* (New York: Seabury, 1975), 107–8.

19. James Joyce, *Finnegans Wake* (New York: Viking/Penguin, 1976), 33; future references incorporated.

20. T. S. Eliot, "The Hollow Men," *Complete Poems,* 58.

21. D. H. Lawrence, "Pan in America," in *Phoenix,* 30.

22. Edmund Wilson, *The Wound and the Bow* (New York: Oxford University Press, 1947).

23. Peter Blos, "When and How Does Adolescence End: Structural Criteria for Adolescent Closure," *Adolescent Psychiatry* 5 (1977): 4–17.

24. Martin J. Weich, "Directions: A Hierarchy of Symbols" (presented at American Psychoanalytic Association, Fall 1978). Weich argues that the general movement of civilization is dextral. His examples of rightward activity from agricultural to writing arts also include telling time as clockwise, road travel, music notation, and calculus: "a developing society, like a developing individual, sees progress as going to the right and regress toward the left." Since left-to-right implies bad to good, immoral to moral, this directional motion suggests the "superego development of the individual and society." Cultural models affect the developing individual. Rightward behavior is reinforced; leftward behavior favors the id and leads to outlaw behaviors such as incest. Dextral curves are then reaction formations that the ego implements at the urgings of the superego.

25. Jerome Weinberger and Jules Glenn, "The Significance of the Trifurcation of

the Road: Clinical Confirmation and Illumination," *Journal of the American Psychoanalytic Association* 25 (1977): 655–67.

26. Robert D. Levine, letter to the *New York Times Book Review,* 19 October 1980.

27. Eric Partridge, *Origins, A Short Etymological Dictionary of Modern English,* (New York: Macmillan, 1959).

28. Sagan, *The Dragons of Eden.*

29. Homer, *The Odyssey*, trans. by Robert Fitzgerald (New York: Doubleday, 1963), 1.

Chapter 17. The Third Birth

1. Joanna Russ, "What Can a Heroine Do? Or, Why Women Can't Write," in *Images of Women in Fiction,* ed. Susan Koppelman Cornillon (Bowling Green, Ohio: Popular Press, 1972), 4. The view, of course, is neither fair to women's great cultural contributions, nor true. See, for example, Peggy Reeves Sanday, *Male Domination / Female Power: On the Origins of Sexual Inequality* (New York: Cambridge, 1981).

2. The often-cited phrase is by Virginia Woolf, who was extremely ambivalent toward mothers, real or literary, especially, for example, Jane Austen (*A Room of One's Own* [New York: Harcourt Brace, 1929], 79).

3. John Stuart Mill, *Autobiography,* ed. Jack Stillinger (New York: Riverside Editions, 1969); page references will appear in the text.

4. Howard R. Wolf, "British Fathers and Sons, 1773–1914: from Filial Submissiveness to Creativity," *Psychoanalytic Review* 52 (1965): 53–70. See also Bruce Mazlish, *James and John Stuart Mill* (New York: Basic Books, 1975), and Jonathan Loesberg, "Free Association: Mill's *Autobiography* as the Fiction of Philosophy," discussed below and appearing in *Interspace and Inward Sphere* (Macomb: Western Illinois University Press 1978).

5. David Kowalewski, "Politics and Emotion in the Thought of John Stuart Mill," *The Journal of Psychohistory* 7, no. 4 (1980): 403–14.

6. John N. Morris, *Versions of the Self* (New York: Basic Books, 1966), introduction. The celebrated oak tree incident that marked the conversion experience of Jean-Jacques Rousseau in 1749 also involved a catharsis of tears as well as an altered state of consciousness lasting for half an hour. The new self that Rousseau awakened into would have lasting cultural consequences, but it cannot be said to be a true self-creation, for it excluded, as Charles Kligerman has shown, the instinctual drives ("The Character of Jean-Jacques Rousseau," *Pychoanalytic Quarterly* 20 (1951): 237). Rather, this father of French romanticism gave birth to a myth in the pejorative sense as a collective fantasy, namely that of promordial innocence and the noble savage.

7. James Boswell, *The Life of Johnson,* vol. 1 (New York: Oxford University Press, 1934), 63–94, quoted in *Versions of the Self*, 20.

8. Morris, *Versions of the Self*, 29.

9. R. K. Webb, *Harriet Martineau: A Radical Victorian* (New York: Columbia University Press, 1960), 34. Future references are to *Harriet Martineau's Autobiography* in three volumes (London: Smith, Elder, 1877).

10. *Autobiography*, 1: 12. The present discussion adheres closely to chap. 5 in Linda H. Peterson's *Victorian Autobiography, The Tradition of Self-Interpretation* (New Haven: Yale, 1986), 120–55.

11. *Autobiography*, 3: 505, cited in Webb's *A Radical Victorian,* 34.

12. Peterson, *Victorian Autobiography*, 152.

13. Kathryn J. Crecelius, *Family Romances: George Sand's Early Novels* (Bloomington: Indiana University Press, 1987), 4–5.

14. Ibid., 5.

15. Ibid., 9.

16. Ibid., 2.

17. Edmund Gosse, *Father and Son* (1907; Reprint. London: Penguin, 1976), 224, additional references incorporated. Samuel Butler's *The Way of All Flesh* (posthumously published, 1903; (reprinted, New York: Penguin, 1966) has been referred to as a novel, though it is at best thinly fictionalized from life.

18. Peterson, *Victorian Autobiography*, 169–81.

19. Pearlman's excellent study points out that while young Edmund was subjected to the fanaticism of a seventeenth-century cleric, he also enjoyed the special dignity assigned children in the nineteenth-century, middle-class household. Pearlman also sorts out the child's oedipal relation with the mother, and in a synopsis of Gosses's juvenile verse drama, *King Erik*, touches on family romance material ("Father and Mother in *Father and Son*," *Victorian Newsletter*, 55 [Spring 1979]: 19–23). Peterson juxtaposes the father's and the son's account of the death scene with the mother to reveal how the son "significantly revises his father's account, making maternal love stronger than marital" (220). The mother's deathbed then becomes the location for a revision of the primal scene, in which the father is upstaged by the son.

20. Peterman persuasively expresses her doubts that Gosse achieved authentic selfhood through his autobiographical text, the biblical scripting of the parents being too formidable to be replaced by an equally formidable set of paradigms. This task would be fulfilled by Joyce through his self-character, Stephen Dedalus, with his powerful mythical-religious props. In this case Gosse becomes a John the Baptist, leading the way but seeing ahead poorly.

21. Richard Ellmann, *Golden Codgers: Biographical Speculations* (New York: Oxford University Press, 1973), 48–50.

22. For more on Ruskin, see Laurie Schneider, "Ms. Medusa: Transformations of a Bisexual Image," *Psychoanalytic Study of Society* 9, (1981): 105–54.

23. Russell Jacoby, *Social Amnesia* (Boston: Beacon Press, 1975).

24. Ernest Jones, *The Life and Work of Sigmund Freud*, vol. 3 (New York: Basic books, 1957), 204.

25. In a letter of Fliess, quoted by Stanley Rosenman, "Turning from the Dual Empire to the Inner World: Freud's Creation of Psychoanalysis," *The Journal of Psychohistory* 15, no. 2 (1987): 207–15. According to Rosenman, this "new species of himself" meant "a father in control of his emotions," in accord with the Mosaic archetype. The phrase is cited in a different context, however, by William McGrath, *Freud's Discovery of Psychoanalysis* (Ithaca: Cornell University Press, 1986), 296–7. In the original passage (28 May 1899), Freud has overcome one of the last obstacles to his dreambook, which he affirms enthusiastically: "None of my works has been so completely my own as this; it is my own dung-heap, my own seedling and a *nova species mihi* [sic!]." Since the obstacle had been one of Freud's own screen memories, *The Interpretation of Dreams* is both an act of self-creation and the generation of a new science.

26. Frank Sulloway, *Freud: Biologist of the Mind* (New York: Basic Books, 1979); for a possible split between "internalized good and bad mothers," see Jim Swan, "Mater and Nannie: Freud's Two Mothers and the Discovery of the Oedipus Complex," *American Imago* 31, no, 1 (1974): 1–64.

27. Jones, *Freud*, vol. 2 (New York: Basic Books, 1955), 432; see Joseph D. Lichtenberg, "Freud's Leonardo," *Journal of the American Psychoanalytic Assoc.* 26 (1978): 863–80; on the relation to Moses, from Philip Rieff, *Freud: The Mind of the Moralist* (New York: Doubleday, 1961) to Michael P. Carroll, "'Moses and

Monotheism' Revisited—Freud's 'Personal Myth'?'' *American Imago* 44, no. 1 (1987): 15–37.

28. J. Laplanche and J. B. Pontcalis, *The Language of Psychoanalysis* (New York: Norton, 1973), 335.

29. Jones, *Freud,* 3: 44.

30. Sullowey, *Biologist of the Mind.*

31. Louis Breger, *Freud's Unfinished Journey* (New York: Routledge and Kegan Paul, 1981), chap. 6.

32. Heinz Kohut, *The Analysis of the Self* (New York: International Universities Press, 1971).

33. Michael Ignatieff, "Freud's Cordelia," *The New York Review,* 14 October 1988, 16–19.

34. Robert Jay Lifton, *The Life of the Self* (New York: Simon and Schuster, 1976), 86.

35. Jacob Arlow, "Theories of Pathogenesis" (paper read at American Psychoanalytic Association Meeting, Winter 1980).

36. P. Ikonen and E. Rechardt, "On the Universal Nature of Primal Scene Fantasies," *International Journal of Psycho-Analysis* 65 (1984): 63–72.

37. The title and theme of a collection of papers edited by Robert Boyers (New York: Harper and Row, 1975). See also Philip Rieff, *Triumph of the Therapeutic* (New York: Harper and Row, 1968).

38. On the works, see Charles Hanly, *Existentialism and Psychoanalysis* (New York: International Universities Press, 1980).

39. Jean-Paul Sartre, *The Words,* trans. Bernard Frechtman (New York: Fawcett, 1966), 9. Further references included in text.

40. Douglas Kirsner, *The Schizoid World of Jean-Paul Sartre and R. D. Laing* (Atlantic Highlands, N.J.: Humanities Press, 1977), 52. The quotation from Jean-Paul Sartre, *Being and Nothingness* (1943), trans. J. E. Barnes (New York: Washington Square Press, 1966), 474–5.

41. Apparently in her own way, his mother reinforced the bond of sisterhood by "bringing up her son as if she were a girl," according to Ronald Hayman in *Sartre: A Life* (New York: Simon and Schuster, 1987), 33.

42. Douglas Kirsner, *Schizoid World,* 46.

43. Hayman, *Sartre: A Life,* 40.

44. Ibid.

45. Douglas Kirsner, *Schizoid World,* 43. Annie Cohen-Solal is more specific. In 1943 the decision was made; by 1956 he had filled twelve notebooks; after more delays, he worked daily on the project throughout the 1960s (*Sartre: A Life,* trans. Anna Cancogni (New York: Pantheon, 1987), 467–86.

46. Hayman, *Sartre: A Life,* 414–5.

47. Ibid., 413.

48. Jean-Paul Sartre, *Being and Nothingness* (New York: Washington Square Press, 1966), 710.

49. .Charles K. Hofling, "Notes on Camus's *L'Étranger*," in *The Human Mind Revisited,* ed. Sydney Smith (New York: International Universities Press, 1979), 159–204. Also see Reference 301 83, Borderline Personality Disorder in Diagnostic Criteria *DSM-111*: (1) impulsivity or unpredictability; (2) a pattern of unstable and intense relationships; (3) inappropriate intense anger or lack of control; (4) identity disturbance; (5) affective instability; (6) intolerance of being alone; (7) physically self-damaging acts. (*Diagnostic and Statistical Manual of Mental Disorders*, third edition [Washington D.C.: American Psychiatric Association, 1987].)

50. Julian Stamm, "Camus' *Stranger*: His Act of Violence," *American Imago* 26 (1966): 281–290.'

51. Hofling, "Notes," 185.

52. Harry Slochower, "Camus' *The Stranger*: The Silent Society and the Ecstasy of Rage," *American Imago* 26 (1966): 291–95.

53. Hofling, "Notes," 198.

54. Herbert R. Lottman, *Albert Camus* (New York: Doubleday, 1979), 19.

55. Stephen Olayon touches on a family romance dimension to the novel in stating that when Meursault "is near the sea and the sun," he is "cuddled by his Cosmic parents" and feels a sense of unison and innocence. But the sun is ambivalently rendered as "mutilator" and "negative imago of the father" the afternoon of the killing. Lacking a real father, Meursault projects the archaic "phylogenetic" paternal image onto the sun. Since his name implies sea-salt and his mistress is Marie (*mère, mer*), his lovemaking is an oedipal crime that the guillotine will cancel. Meursault is also seen as a Christ figure by Olayon ("Camus' *The Stranger*: The Sun-metaphor and Parricidal Conflict," *American Imago* 40 [1983]: 189–205). However, the oceanic affinities between Maria and Meursault strongly suggest the dangers of symbiotic engulfment (*à la* Sartre) and the need to separate-differentiate from the maternal matrix *sans père*.

56. *Roland Barthes by Roland Barthes*, 45.

57. Roland Barthes, *The Pleasure of the Text*, 47.

58. Philip Thody, *Roland Barthes: A Conservative Estimate* (New York: Macmillan, 1977), 10.

59. Gustave Flaubert, *The Letters of Gustave Flaubert*, trans. Francis Steegmuller, 2 vol., (Cambridge, Mass: Belknap Press, 1980).

60. Gustave Flaubert, *Carnets de travail*, ed. Pierre-Marc de Biasi (Paris: Balland, 1988): reviewed by Julian Barnes, *Times Literary Supplement*, 7–13 October 1988, 1090–2.

61. Flaubert, *"Un Parfum à sentir,"* a piece composed at fifteen, quoted by Francis Baudry, "Adolescent Love and Self-Analysis as Contributors to Flaubert's Creativity," *The Psychoanalytic Study of the Child* 35 (1980): 398.

62. The French scholar Marthe Robert advances a psychoanalytic reading of the novel and Flaubert in particular that is in remarkably accord with the present in the sense that the same two concepts—family romance and primal scene—are invoked, though not dynamically opposed or fused into a theory of creativity. In *Origins of the Novel* (Bloomington: Indiana University Press, 1980), pt 3, chap. 2, Flaubert is viewed through two types featured in fiction and apparently rooted in each author's creative imagination: the bastard and the foundling. The former term is applied to Flaubert's response to a primal scene in which the male parent following a drunken orgy, is sexually seduced by the female—the bastard being the unwanted issue of bestial passion. The foundling coincides with the family romance scenario of Flaubert's "dreams of being admitted to the highest social circles and of making his mark there" (215).

63. Flaubert, *Intimate Notebook, 1840–1841*, ed. and trans. Francis Steegmuller (New York: Doubleday 1967), 50.

64. Oscar Wilde, *Complete works*, edited by Vyvyan Holland (London: Collins and Glasgow, 1966), 1206.

65. Oscar Wilde, *Complete Works*, 970.

66. Ibid., 17.

67. Edith Wyschogrod, "Sons Without Fathers: A Study in Identity and Culture," *Journal of the American Academy of Psychoanalysis* 16 (1978): 249–62.

68. James E. Lovelock is the founder of this movement according to "Britain's

Whole Earth Guru,'' *New York Times Magazine,* 23 December 86. He has written *The Ages of Gaia, A Biography of Our Living Earth* (New York: Norton, 1988).

69. Carl A. Raschke, *The Interruption of Eternity: Modern Gnosticism and the Origins of the New Religious Consciousness* (Chicago: Nelson Hall, 1980); Fergus M. Bordewich, ''Colorado's Thriving Cults,'' *New York Times Magazine*, 7 May 1988.

70. Fritjof Capra, *The Turning Point*, 285.

71. Wyschogrod, ''Sons without Fathers,'' 251, 256.

72. Ibid., 251. While I am sympathetic to a positive role for fathers, I would not subscribe to any implied or hidden agenda that might he construed as antifeminist or neo-conservative.

73. Ibid., 252.

74. Ibid., 261.

75. Sigmund Freud, *Moses and Monotheism, Standard Edition*, 23.

76. See the conclusions of Judith Lewis Herman's *Father-Daughter Incest* (Cambridge: Harvard University Press, 1981).

77. Daniel Dervin, ''Abandonment: A Dominant Pattern in the Development of Creative Writers, Philosophers, and Scientists Since the 17th Century,'' *Journal of Psychohistory* 15, no. 2 (1987): 153–88.

78. Two of the positive contributions noted by Stephen Appelbaum, a psychoanalyst from the Menninger Foundation, in the course of his extensive survey of these new therapies, societies, movements, and lifestyles: *Out in Inner Space* (New York: Doubleday, 1979).

79. For living discussions of these issues see *Brain/Mind Bulletin* (Los Angeles: Interface Press).

80. Although now mainly forgotten or recalled in nostalgic reveries about the sixties, it was the commonly expressed view among Leary and fellow LSD revolutionaries that not only did the hallucinogenic agent produce profoundly religious, transcendental experiences but it freed the brain to play over again inside the user's head the cataclysmic origins of the universe. In other words the intracranial light-and-energy show was interpreted as a recapitulation not of individual origins, for personal history was bypassed, but of cosmic origins, stored among the vast memory bank of the brain. For an early attempt to validate these hypotheses in a quasi-scientific manner, see Timothy Leary, ''The Religious Experience: Its Production and Interpretation,'' *Psychedelic Review* 1, no. 3 (1964): 324–46; and for fuller treatment, Timothy Leary, *High Priest* (New York: College Notes and Texts, 1968). Future historians of the period may trace from the Alan Watts–Timothy Leary–Richard Alpert nucleus a first legitimization and popularization of the need for instant mystical and magical self-renewal experiences that were to span in countless directions through the seventies. It would then be a matter, as one of the Moonie commentators writes, of damning the heretic (Leary was exiled, jailed) and adopting the heresy: transcendental renewal for all.

81. Quoted by Appelbaum, *Out in Inner Space*, 116.

82. Robert Ornstein and Richard F. Thompson, *The Amazing Brain* (Boston: Houghton Mifflin, 1984), 21.

83. Paul Zweig, ''Against Emptiness,'' in *Three Journeys: An Automythology* (New York: Basic Books, 1976).

Appendix A. Fantasy and Preverbal Sources of Literary Creativity and Literary Mode

1. Otto Rank, *The Myth of the Brith of the Hero*, ed. Philip Freund (New York:

Knopf, 1959); Ernst Kris, *Psychoanalytic Explorations in Art* (London, Allen and Unwin Ltd., 1953); Phyllis Greenacre, "The Family Romance of the Artist, "*The Psychoanalytic Study of the Child* 134 (1958): 9–44; Norman Holland, *The Dynamics of Literary Response* (New York: Oxford University Press, 1968) and *The I* (New Haven: Yale University Press, 1985); K. R. Eissler, *Goethe: A Psychoanalytic Study*, 2 vols. (New York: International Universities Press, 1968) and *Discourse on Hamlet and "Hamlet"* (New York: International Universities Press, 1971); Anton Ehrenzweig, *The Hidden Order of Art* (Berkeley: University of California Press, 1967); Albert Rothenberg, *The Emerging Goddess* (Chicago: University of Chicago, 1979); Meredith Skura, *The Literary Uses of Psychoanalysis* (New Haven: Yale University Press, 1983). For a state-of-the-art discussion of these questions and these writers, see Donald Kaplan's "The Psychoanalysis of Art: Some Ends, Some Means," *Journal of the American Psychoanalytic Association* 36 (1988): 259–93. In pointing out that the fit subject for psychoanalytic practice is a "version of neurosis," he considers all other subjects entertained by the analyst as analogical. Analogy is primarily a similarity of function but also of structure (homology). Art, along with sexology, child development, and other cultural fields is designated a "boundary problem." Applied psychoanalysis "is always, at best, a piecemeal and unresolved affair." Its findings, therefore, are hedged with uncertainty. Indeed, the method of this section is an exploration of analogy: between emotional states (manic, depressive) and literary mode (satire, irony), between breast representations and literary images, between primal scene configurations and literary symbols, ultimately between early fantasy and later imagination.

2. Phantasies (the *ph* once having a technical denotation) were considered the "primary content of unconscious mental products," by Susan Isaacs in "The Nature and Function of Fantasy," *Developments in Psycho-Analysis* (London: Hogarth, 1952), 67–119. For a more adaptive approach, see Julia Segal, *Phantasy in Everyday Life, A Psychoanalytic Approach to Understanding Ourselves* (London: Penguin, 1985).

3. "This idea is still around today," writes Charles Rycroft, "despite Freud's belated disapproval of it in 1928, when he wrote, 'Before the problem of the creative artist analysis must, alas, lay down its arms.' It owes its vitality, I suspect, to four disparate sources.' Rycroft discusses these as envy, oneupmanship, pressure on doctoral scholars to grind out more and more theses, and "the fact that there is indeed some similarity between the creative imagination and the oneiric, dream-producing faculty" ("Freud and the Imagination," *The New York Review*, 4 April, 1975, 26–30). Other thoughts on the subject may found in the symposium papers of Niederland, Eissler, et al, "Genius, Psychopathology and Creativity," *American Imago* 24 (1967); Harry Slochower, *Mythopoesis* (Detroit: Wayne State University Press, 1970), introduction; *Essays in Creativity*, Stanley Rosner and Lawrence Abt, eds. (Croton-on-the-Hudson, N.Y.: North River Press, 1974). For examples on the positive side, see Edwin I. Corbin, "The Autonomous Ego Functions in creativity," *Journal of the American Psychoanalytic Association* 22, No. 3 (1974): 568–87; and on the negative side, Lawrence Kubie, "Unsolved Problems Concerning the Relation of Art to Psychotherapy," *American Journal of Art Therapy* 12 (1973): 95–105; David Werman, "Methodological Problems in the Psychoanalytic Interpretation of Literature," *Journal of the American Psychoanalysis Association* 27, No. 2 (1979): 451–78; Aaron Esman, "Psychoanalysis and Literary Criticism—A Limited Partnership, *Psychoanalysis and Contemporary Thought* 5, No. 1 (1982): 17–25.

4. Donald Barthelme, "The Balloon," in *Unspeakable Practices, Unnatural Acts* (New York: Bantam, 1969); additional references incorporated by page.

5. Johnathan Swift, *Gulliver's Travels* (New York: Viking Critical Edition, 1961).

6. Philip Roth, *The Breast* (New York: Holt, 1972), 13; additional references incorporated.

7. Portnoy's comic-pathetic varieties of masturbation, especially when he tries self-fellatio, reveal the primordial bond with the breast, played out on the male's body. Hence Kepesh's fusion with the breast can be seen as Portnoy's wishfulfillment.

8. The alternative is shown in Woody Allen's manic satire on *Everything You Always Wanted to Know About Sex. . .* In one of skits, he is pursued by a gigantic spouting breast-on-wheels and defends himself like Saint George against the dragon. This may be an outlandish concretization of Melanie Klein's persecutory "bad breast," i.e., the projection of frustrations and basis for the manic defense.

9. Otto Isakower, "A Contribution to the Patho-Psychology of the Phenomena Associated with Falling Asleep," *International Journal of Psycho-Analysis* 19 (1938): 31-45.

10. B. D. Lewin, "Reconsideration of the Dream Screen," *Psychoanalytic Quarterly* 22 (1953): 174–99.

11. B. D. Lewin, *The Psychoanalysis of Elation* (London: Hogarth, 1951).

12. Rene Spitz, "Some Early Prototypes of Ego Defenses," *Journal of the American Psychoanalytic Association* 19 (1961): 626–51.

13. Lewin, "Dream Screen," 201–2.

14. Ernst Kris, *Psychoanalytic Explorations in Art* (London: Allen and Unwin, 1953); Philip Weissman, "Theoretical Considerations of Ego Regressions and Ego Functions in Creativity," *Psychoanalytic Quarterly* 36 (1967): 37–50; K. R. Eissler, *Discourse on Hamlet and "Hamlet"* (New York: International Universities Press, 1971), 519–53; Edwin Corbin, "The Autonomous Ego Functions in Creativity" *Journal of the American Psychoanalytic Association* 23 (1974): 568–87.

15. Noel Bradley, "Notes on Theory-Making, on Scotoma of the Nipples, and on the Bee as Nipple," *International Journal of Psycho-Analysis* 54, no. 3 (1973): 301–14.

16. Manic absorption is one of art's current and desperate strategies to reach audiences preoccupied with their own affairs. One thinks of the wrap-around sound of electronic music, see-through/walk-through sculpture, and the audience-enveloping innovations of environmental theater. But manic fusion is only a phase of creativity according to Anton Ehrenzweig, *The Hidden Order of Art* (Berkeley: University of California Press, 1967).

17. Jean-Paul Sartre, *The Psychology of the Imagination*, trans. Bernard Frechtman (New York: Philosophical Library, 1948).

18. Jean-Paul Sartre, "The Hole," *Existentialism and Human Emotions* (New York: Philosophical Library, 1957).

19. D. W. Winnicott, "The Depressive Position in Normal Development," *Collected papers,* 262–77 1958), 270. This term is Melanie Klein's for the critical stage in early development when the child begins to grasp the urgency of reconciling his/her libidinal and destructive urges as they are sensed to be converging on the same object, mother. Elsewhere, Winnicott prefers the "stage of concern." A regressive response becomes the manic defense.

20. Geza Roheim, *The Riddle of the Sphinx* (London: Hogarth, 1934), 225.

21. Phyllis Greenacre, "The Primal Scene and the Sense of Reality," *Psychoanalytic Quarterly* 42 (1973): 10–41.

22. Ibid., 17. For additional applications, see Raymond Tarbox, "Blank Hallucinations in the Fiction of Poe and Hemingway," *American Imago* 24 (1967): 312–43.

23. "The Primal Scene and the Sense of Reality," 19.

24. Greenacre; Bradley, "Notes on Theory-Making."

25. John Barth, *Lost to the Funhouse* (New York: Grosset and Dunlap, 1969), 14–34; quotes cited in the text.

26. Julia Kristeva, *A Kristeva Reader* (New York: Columbia University Press, 1986).

27. Henry Edelheit, "Mythoposiesis and the Primal Scene," *The Psychoanalytic*

Study of Society 5 (New York: International Universities Press [1972] 5: 212–33; Noel Bradley, "Primal Scene Experience in Human Evolution and Its Phantasy Derivatives in Art, Proto Science and Philosophy," *The Psychoanalytic Study of Society* 4 (New York: International Universities Press, 1967): 725–51.

28. On spiders, see two papers by Kenneth Alan Adams, "Love American Style," *Journal of Psychoanalytic Anthropology* 4 (1981): pt 1 and 2, 157–97; *Journal of Psychohistory* (1983), 10: 409–62.

29. From "The Ceremony of innocence, is drowned" first stanza to the "rough beast" with its lions head and man's body in the second stanza. For the applicability of Yeats's "Second Coming" to my thesis, I am greatful for the analysis by Richard P. Wheeler, "Yeats's 'Second Coming': What Rough Beast?" *American Imago* 31, (1974): 233–51.

30. Ernest Jones, "The Theory of Symbolism," in *Papers on Psycho-Analysis* (Boston: Beacon, 1967), 102.

31. In Guillaume Apollinaire's play, *Les Mamelles de Tirésis* (1917), balloons float out of the bisexual prophet's bosom.

32. When the albatross was first psychoanalyzed by a man (David Beres, "A Dream, A Vision, A Poem," *International Journal of Psychoanalysis* 32 [1951]: 97–116), it turned out to be the "ambivalently loved mother"; but when psychanalyzed by a woman (Mary Jane Lupton, "The Rime of the Ancient Mariner: the Agony of Thirst," *American Imago* 27 [1970]: 140–59), it turned out to be a "supernatural totem animal," a "father-bird." This is what is meant by a symbol being *overdetermined*.

33. Peter L. Hays, *The Limping Hero* (New York: New York University Press, 1971).

34. This object-relations approach is epitomized by Hanna Segal, "On Symbolism," *International Journal of Psycho-analysis* 59 (1978): 315–19.

35. Leonard Shengold, "The Parent as Sphinx," *Journal of the Psychoanalytic Review* 11 (1963): 725–51.

36. "The Sphinx," *The Works of Oscar Wilde,* edited by John Gilbert (London: Spring Books, 1963), 712–22; additional references incorporated.

37. Regenia Gagnier, *Idylls of the Marketplace, Oscar Wilde and the Victorian Public* (Stanford: Stanford University Press, 1986), 45.

38. Stéphane Mallarmé, *"Plusiers Sonnets,"* vol. 2 in *Poems.* Trans. C. F. MacIntyre (Berkeley: University of California Press, 1965), 82–3.

39. This is not to deny that there might be—and probably is—buried autobiography in Mallarmé's swan—specifically, ambivalent feelings about being reunited with his mother whom he lost to the grave at five. For more, see Charles Mauron, *Introduction to the Psychoanalysis of Mallarmé* (Berkeley: University of California Press, 1963), 154–6.

40. Freud, "Creative Writers and Daydreaming."

41. For the influence of this figure in Yeat's development, see Yeats's 'A Bronze Head': A Freudian Investigation," F. A. C. Wilson, *Literature and Psychology* 22 (1972): 5–12. The literary history of this fascinating figment, mentioned earlier, has yet to be written. The phallic mother may either represent the child's wishful assumption that the early mother admits of no imperfections, translated in his mind to mean: no missing parts, ergo. . .or it may come to represent the paternal phallus in coitus. Hence the former view may fit into a family romance scheme; while the latter view may be the child's effort to deal with the primal scene.

42. August Strindberg, *The Father*, in *Six Plays*, 42.

43. D. H. Lawrence, "Glad Ghosts," *Complete Stories*, vol. 3 (New York: Viking, 1968), 697–8.

44. Norman O. Brown, *Closing Time* (New York: Random House, 1973).

45. Judith Hubback, "Uses and Abuses of Analogy," *The Journal of Analytical Psychology* 18, no. 2 (1973): 81–104.

46. Samuel Beckett, *Malone Dies* (New York: Grove, 1958), 225.

47. Kurt Vonnegut, *Breakfast of Champions* (New York: Dell, 1973).

48. Samuel Beckett, *How It is* (New York: Grove: 1970); "So it goes" is the ironic refrain in Kurt Vonnegut's *Slaughterhouse Five* (New York: Dell, 1970).

49. The ironic mode is Northrop Frye's term. Beckett's endless variations on the pattern of immense ground and minute figure is, however, tinged with Swiftian satire.

50. Ralph B. Little in "Behind the Dream Screen," *Psychoanalytic Review* 57 (1970): 137–42, examines primal-scene phenomena lurking in the dream screen. Norman Holland, who has devised a workable psychoanalytic theory of literature as an "introjected transformation" by the reader of core fantasies in the text, touches briefly on satire as reaction-formation (*The Dynamics of Literary Response* [New York: Oxford, 1968], 311, 315). To pursue a bit further the notion of satire, not reduced to the manic mode but sharing affiliations with it, I would assign the defensive process of *splitting* (of self/other as well as good/bad properties inside and outside the self) as an accepted convention of satire. The unstated assumption of the satirist is that with the good breast safely tucked inside, he (and most satirists are male) is at liberty to disparage, reject, assault the bad breast in various cultural embodiments. Hence satire's classical orgins introduce a misogynist strain with Archilochus, Simonides, and Juvenal that persists through Molière and Thurber. Adding to this picture is another event in early childhood when the infant at around eight months, having established an image of the original care-giver, is disturbed by perceptions of a non–care-giver, resulting in stranger-anxiety. In attempting to eliminate or drive off this alien object, who may be affixed to the bad breast, we may locate the seedlings of a satiric adaptation. Needless to say, in the triadic stage the stranger and the bad object are mixed in and confused with the sexual intruder in the primal scene. The counterpart in preliterature societies is the expulsion of the *pharmakos*, or scapegoat. Finally, as satire owes a substantial debt to the dyadic phase, it normally occupies a subordinate position in major works or else dissolves into ambiguity, paradox, irony, etc, by undergoing triadic shaping.

Appendix B. A Note on Polar Creativity in the Visual Arts

1. For representations, see Samuelle Olivieri, ed., *The Life of the Madonna in Art* (Boston: Daughters of St. Paul, 1985); for a cultural study, see Marina Warner, *Alone of all Her Sex: The Myth and the Cult of the Virgin Mary* (New York: Random, 1983); for a psychoanalytic study, see Michael P. Carroll, *The Cult of the Virgin Mary* (Princeton: Princeton University Press, 1986).

2. Henry Edelheit "Crucixion Fantasies and Their Relation to the Primal Scene," *International journal of Psycho-Analysis* 55 (1974): 193–204.

3. Mircea Eliade, *The Myth of the Eternal Return* (Princeton: Princeton University Press, 1954).

4. Robert Melville, *Erotic Art of the West* (New York: Putnam, 1973), 154.

5. He is the slave whom Tarquin had threatened to kill unless Lucretia submitted. Ian Donaldson sees him as "a fellow conspirator, holding back the curtains" and as a voyeur who compromises the moral force of the subject (*The Rapes of Lucretia* [Oxford: Clarendon Press, 1982], 13–20).

6. Daniel Dervin, "Hopper and Warhol at the Whitney: The Self in the Artist, the Self in the Art," *Psychoanalytic Review* 68 (1981): 293–300.

7. Lillian Schwartz, "Leonardo's Mona Lisa," *Art and Antiques* January 1987, 50–54. More a fragmentation than a conflation of mother/child images is Titian's

Venus at Her Toilet with Two Cupids. As a nude Venus demurely scrutinizes her visage in a narrow mirror held by one cupid, another cupid attempts to crown her with a wreath. The sequence from right to left is cupid, Venus image, cupid, Venus. Although less than half the goddess's face is reflected in the mirror, the technique of doubling/dividing evokes both Lacan's "mirror stage" and Winnicott's mirroring. The psychological meaning is not too difficult to establish. The child with a wreath is close to mother, touching her and eyeing her with rapt devotion. Like hers, his hair is blond and curly, while the other child's is dark and cropped. Since this one is also larger and farther away from mother, one can conclude that the two boys are stages of the same child's development. Accordingly, the larger boy's mirror image of the mother is diminished: he has already begun to hatch out, to stand alone, to disidentify. There may also be a symbolism in the positioning of the mother's hands: one is over the robes covering the genital area, lest a precocious sexual awakening occur; the other is across one breast while leaving the other available, perhaps for the younger, unweaned child by whom she is still properly worshipped.

8. David Gervais, "On the Figures in Turner's Landscapes," *Cambridge Quarterly* 14 (1985): 20–50; the Ruskin quote is from his *Complete Works* edited by E. T. Cook and A. Wedderburn, 1903–1912, vol. 36, 270, cited by Gervais.

9. Adrian Stokes, "Turner," *The Image in Form* (New York: Harper, 1972), 211–35.

10. Ibid., 225.

11. Leon E. A. Berman, "The Role of the Primal Scene in the Artistic Works of Max Ernst," in *Psychoanalytic Perspectives on Art*, ed. Mary Matthews Gedo, vol. 3 (Hillsdale, N.J.: Analytic Press, 1988), 147–60.

12. Max Ernst, "Some Data on the Youth of M. E. as Told by Himself," *The Autobiography of Surrealism*, ed. Marcel Jean (New York: Viking, 1980), 401–403.

13. In the same volume as Berman's study, see Charlotte Stokes, "Sisters and Birds: Meaningful Symbols in the Works of Max Ernst."

14. Quoted by Luck R. Lippard, *Surrealists on Art* (Englewood Cliffs, N.J.: Prentice-Hall, 1970), pp. 120–21.

Appendix C. A Tale of Two Knights, or a Variant on the Heroic Birth Theme in *The Seventh Seal* and *Camino Real*

1. *The Seventh Seal* by Ingmar Bergman appears in *Four Screenplays* (New York: Simon and Schuster, 1960); Tennessee Williams, *Camino Real* (New York: New Directions, 1953).

2. For more on the psychological import of the name, see Clyde H. Ward, "Kilroy Was Here," *Psychoanalytic Quarterly* 31 (1962): 80–91.

3. Elsewhere I have studied these authors and their works: see "The Spook in the Rainforest, the Incestuous Structure of Tennessee William's Plays," *The Pyschocultural Review* 3–4 (1979): 153–84; "From Spider-god to Spider-artist, the Spinning of an Identity in Ingmar Bergman's Films," *Through a Freudian Lens Deeply* (Hillsdale, N.J.: Analytic Press, 1985).

Appendix D. Shaw and Kafka: The Interplay of Psychological Norms and Literary Values

1. Daniel Dervin, *Bernard Shaw: A Psychological Study* (Lewisburg, Pa.: Bucknell University Press, 1975).

2. Franz Kafka, "Metamorphosis," in *The Penal Colony* (New York: Schocken Books, 1948).

3. John S. White, "Psyche and Tuberculosis," *The Psychoanalytic Study of Society* 4 (1967): 204.

4. The translation of "Up in the Gallery" is by Claus Reshke and another one may be found in *The Complete Short Stories*, ed. Natham Glazer (New York: Schocken Books, 1946). Compare this vignette with the painting, *Bareback Riders*.

5. Gabriel Josipovici, "Linearity and Frgamentation," in *The Lessons of Modernism* (Totowa, N.J.: Rowman and Littlefield, 1978).

6. Franz Kafka, *Letters to Friends, Family, and Editors*, trans. Richard and Clara Winston (New York: Schocken Books, 1977), 332–35.

7. For an interesting psychoanalytic use of Kafka's parables, see Manuel Ross, "The Borderline Diatheseis," *The International Review of Psycho-Analysis* 3, no. 3 (1976): 305–21.

8. Virginia Woolf, *The Diary*, vol. 5, edited by Anne Olivier Bell (New York: Harcourt Brace Jovanovich, 1984), 115; see the "Critical Response" between Quentin Bell and Jane Marcus, *Critical Inquiry* 11 (1985), 486–501.

Appendix E. The Interfusion of Art and Science; The Creation of Death

1. Northrop Frye, *Anatomy of Criticism* (Princeton: Princeton University Press, 1957).

2. Quotes taken from John Donne's "The First Anniversary," in *The Complete Poetry* (New York: Modern Library, 1941), 171, and Marjorie Hope Nicolson's *Breaking the Circle* (Evanston Ill.: Northwestern University Press, 1950), 34. Coleridge's incomplete struggles toward a synthesis of science, art, and philosophy have been examined in Trevor H. Levere, *Poetry Realized in Nature: Samuel Taylor Coleridge and Early Nineteenth Century Science* (New York: Cambridge University Press, 1981); and Ron Harre, "Davy and Coleridge: Romanticism in Science and the Arts," in *Common Denominators in Art and Science*, ed. Martin Polloch (Aberdeen: Aberdeen University Press, 1983).

3. Gillian Beer, *Darwin's Plots: Evolutionary Narrative in Darwin, George Eliot, and Nineteenth Century Fiction*, (New York: Routledge and Kegan Paul, 1984); George Levine, "Darwin and the Evolution of Fiction," *New York Times Book Review*, 5 October 1986.

4. Thomas Mann, *Essays* (New York: Knopf, 1958), 303–24.

5. For recent developments in the interplay between modern physics and the novel, see Robert Nadeau, *Readings from the New Book on Nature* (Amherst: University of Massachusetts Press, 1981); and on related subjects, Paul C. Vitz and Arnold B. Glincher, *Modern Art and Modern Science: the Parallel Analysis of Vision* (New York: Praeger, 1984); L. J. Jordanova, ed., *Languages of Nature: Critical Essays on Science and Literature* (New Brunswick: Rutgers University Press, 1986); Peter Morton, *The Vital Science; Biology and Literary Imagination, 1860–1900* (London: Allen and Unwin, 1984); L. J. Joranova ed., *Languages of Nature, Critical Essays in Science and Literature,* (New Brunswick N.J.: Rutgers University Press, 1986); J. Clifton Albergotti, *Mighty Is the Charm: Lectures in Science, Literature, and the Arts* (Wash. D.C.: University Press of America, 1982).

6. Phyllis Greenacre, "The Family Romance of the Artist," *Psychoanalytic Study of the Child* 13: (1958): 9–36.

7. Mark E. Littman and Charles A Schwerghauswr, "Astronomical Allusions: Their Meaning and Purpose in *Ulysses*," *James Joyce Quarterly* 2, no. 4 (1965): 238–45.

8. John A. Weigel, "*The Alexandrian Quartet* as Experiment," in *Lawrence Durrell* (New York: Twayne English Authors Series, 1965), 86–7.

9. Lawrence Durrell, *Justine* (New York: Dutton, 1961), 27.

10. Durrell, *Justine*, 115; George Steiner, "Lawrence Durrell, the Baroque Novel," in *The World of Lawrence Durrell*, edited by Harry T. Moore (New York: Dutton, 1964), 15.

11. Jeffrey Smitten in his preface and introduction to *Spatial Form in Narrative* (Ithaca: Cornell University Press, 1981) 13–20. New Criticism, predicated on the text as a discrete entity, may owe something to the subject/object split in traditional, Newtonian science. Postmodernist literary theories, for example of intertextuality, imply an Einsteinian advance, yet the elision of the author perpetuates a split-off approach.

12. G. C. Barnard, *Samuel Beckett: A New Approach* (London: Dent, 1970), 67. Barnard uses a false-self/true-self Laingian vocabulary; the use of nuclear self is my borrowing from Heinz Kohut.

13. Russell Meaves, "Beckett, Sarraute, and the Perceptual Experience of Schizophrenia," *Psychiatry* 36 (1973): 61–69; and earlier cited studies by Didier Anzieu & Bennett Simon.

14. Samuel Beckett, *Endgame* (New York: Grove, 1953).

15. Robert Qrnstein, *The Psychology of Consciousness* (New York: Harcourt Brace Jovanovich, 1972).

16. This conceptual context stems from Louise Kaplan's *Oneness and Separateness* (New York; Simon and Schuster, 1978).

17. Quotes are from William Blake's preface to "Milton" and "Jerusalem," plate 15, *Complete Writings* (New York: Oxford University press, 1966), 481, 635–36.

18. Leo Bersani, "Lawrentian Stillness," chap. 6 of *A Future for Astyanax, Character and Desire in Literature* (Boston: Little, Brown, 1976), 164.

19. D. H. Lawrence, *The Rainbow* (New York: Viking, 1965), 349.

20. D. H. Lawrence, *Women in Love* (New York: Viking, 1960), 456.

21. D. H. Lawrence, *Lady Chatterley's Lover* (New York: Grove, 1959).

22. *The Complete Letters of D. H. Lawrence* ed. Harry T. Moore, 2 vols. (New York: Viking, 1962), 23 April 1915; Lawrence, *Lady Chatterley's Lover*, 117.

23. K. R. Eissler, "Remarks on an Aspect of Creativity," *American Imago* 35, no. 2 (1978): 59–76.

24. Through a careful reconstruction of the cultural milieu of Europe at the time of Stonehenge's construction, Leon Stover and Bruce Kraig in *Stonehenge: The Indo-European Tradition* (Chicago: Nelson Hall, 1978), attempt to understand how the monument was created by a "Nonliterate chiefdom society, to represent their technology, their society, their politics, and their mental processes: not those of our own. The authors demonstrate that over the centuries man has re-created Stonehenge in his own image or according to his chief concerns; the last of these, the one that transforms the Wessex Warriors into protoscientists, is G. S. Hawkins, *Stonehenge Decoded* (New York: Doubleday, 1965).

25. William Niederland, "The History and Meaning of California: A Psychoanalytic Inquiry," *Psychoanalytic Quarterly* 40 (1971): 485–90; "The Naming of America," in *The Unconscious Today*, ed. Mark Kanzer (New York: International Universities Press, 1971). The prospect of a new field of study, called psychogeography, was introduced at the December 1977 meeting of the American Psychoanalytic Assocation. For a related approach, see Barbara Maria Stafford, *Voyage into Substance, Art, Science, Nature, and the Illustrated Travel Account* (Cambridge: MIT

Press, 1984); and Howard Stein, *Developmental Time, Cultural Space: Studies in Psychogeography*, (Norman: University of Oklahoma Press, 1987).

26. D. H. Lawrence, *The Symbolic Meaning* (Arundel, England: Centaur Press, 1962), 20.

27. Niederland, "Naming of America" 460–61.

28. W. B. Yeats, "The Phases of the Moon," in *Collected Poems* (New York: Macmillan, 1956).

29. Sigmund Freud, *Beyond the Pleasure Principle*, Standard Edition, 18.

30. K. R. Eissler, *Discourse on Hamlet and "Hamlet"* (New York: International Universities Press, 1971), 20.

31. Robert Browning, *Poetical Works, 1833–64*, edited by Ian Jack (New York: Oxford, 1970), 432.

32. Ernest Becker, *The Denial of Death* (New York: Free Press, 1973).

33. D. H. Lawrence, "The Flying Fish," *Phoenix* (New York: Viking, 1972), 780–98; additional references incorporated.

34. D. H. Lawrence, *Collected Poems*, (New York: Viking, 1971), 716–20.

35. Samuel Beckett, *Waiting for Godot* (New York: Grove, 1954), 58.

Appendix F. Royal Fantasy and Historical Interface

1. Sigmund Freud, *A Phylogenetic Fantasy* (Cambridge: Harvard, 1987).

2. Anne Freud, "Insight: Its Presence and Absence in Normal Development," *The Writings of Anna Freud,* vol. 8 (New York: International Universities Press, 1981), 145.

3. Stanley Rosenman, "The Myth of the Birth of the Hero Revisited: Disasters and Brutal Child Rearing," *American Imago* 45, no, 1 (1988): 8.

4. Lloyd deMause, *Foundations of Psychohistory* (New York: Creative Roots, 1982), 136.

5. John Boswell, *The Kindness of Strangers* (New York: Pantheon, 1988), 76–79.

6. Ibid., p. 76.

7. Ibid., 107–9.

8. Marvin Eisenstadt, et al, *Parental Loss and Achievement* (Madison, Conn.: International Universities Press, 1989).

9. For abandonment to become an inner dread, Gregory Rochlin cites three conditions: the child's need for a responsive caregiver, the caregiver's absence, the child's inability to provide its own comfort and inner stability *(Grief and Its Discontents*, Boston: Little, Brown, 1965), 13–14. In *Tragic Drama and the Family*, Bennett Simon notes that the transition from epic to tragedy entails a "shift in emphasis from warfare outside the family to warfare within the family" where themes of guilt related to sacrifice and scapegoating come to the fore (26). The communal or familial rationalization that the individual must sacrificed, i.e., abandoned for the greater good is played out and undermined.

10. William Hazlitt, *The Round Table* (New York: Dutton, Everyman's Library, 1964), pp. 160–64.

Glossary / Primer

Some of these definitions have been paraphrased from LaPlanche and Pontcalis, *The Language of Psycho-Analysis*, where fuller discussions of the terms may be found (with the exception of the *Self* to which I have devoted an essay in *Dictionary of Literary Themes and Motifs* [Greenwood, 1988] under "Psychoanalysis of the Self").

CATHEXIS. Strong emotional investment in or attachment to an idea, a thing, a part of the self, or another person.

FAMILY ROMANCE. The realized fantasy of heroic, royal, or divine parentage through birth, rebirth, reunion, marriage, or any variation on the orphan / adoption theme. It springs from a sense of disappointment in the parents' not perfectly reciprocating the child's needs to love and be loved, from felt blows to early self-esteem, from a poor fit between child and parent, and / or from actual parental failures and abuse. The wish to be adopted, reborn, etc., is a desire to recenter the self by reinstating or achieving an ideal early state of parental affection. The essential structure is the self and two contrasting sets of parents, the prevalent mode is adoption or marriage, the basic aim is self-restoration via an elevated status. As it bestows inner spaces between the emergent self and biological origins, it favors the creative process and the artist's creative romance with the world. It is a pervasive phenomenon that cuts across time and cultures. Given its essential core and countless variants, it can be modified by the artist's sexual identity and orientation. The present study examines how it can also be *displaced* and *inverted*. The former addresses an indirect fulfilment of the fantasy via an adoption of the work by an illustrious patron or grateful public; the latter locates an inversion of the romance theme via demonic figures. Also examined is the family romance in scientific endeavors. The point of departure is its function as an imaginary creation of one's origins.

HYPNAGOGIC STATES refers to the return of primitive mental stages, involving pictorial and sensory content, prior to falling asleep. It is a normal state wherein regression can be observed and studied. Isakower connects these experiences to the child's original nursing experiences, and Lewin connects them with the *dream screen*, from the child's visual memory traces of the breast.

MENTAL PROCESSES. Freud distinguished two modes of mental functioning, *primary* and *secondary,* which roughly parallel the pleasure and the reality principles, id and ego, the unconscious and conscious areas of the psyche. The distinction grew moore complicated as Freud shifted from a typographical to a structural model of the psyche, allowing for, among other things, unconscious operations in the ego. In general, *primary process* thinking is more mobile, fluid, imagistic, oneiric, less bounded by time, space, and logical constraints that accrue through reality testing and are consciously mediated through *secondary process,* which is more rational, conceptual, etc.

METHOD is a mixture of strategies. Though neither clinical nor rigorously empirical, it borrows from both and relies on language as a vehicle of meanings for coherence. It is *inductive* insofar as it draws from a wide range of samples to arrive at general inferences; it is *psychoanalytic* when it interprets textual data according to overdeterminism of motive or multilayeredness of structure. And by *reconstructing* larger blocks of meaning from smaller units, the purpose is less to reconstitute a figure's life than to formulate the human mind. *Analogies* between principles of creativity in the arts and the sciences comprise the ultimate, indispensable method.

NARCISSISM refers in a technical sense to the libidinal cathexis of (i.e., strong emotional attachment to) the self. It may be *primary* (original, part of the symbiotic dyad with the mother) and so equated with the early months of life, or *secondary* (persisting, part of one's sense of esteem and self-worth); and so modified by later developmental periods. It is permissible to speak of a healthy narcissism as well as a pathological kind, which may be manifested as excessive preoccupation with one's emotional needs as corrective attempts at overcoming early deficits in primary relationships. *Narcissistic injury* refers to damage to one's sense of self or wounds to self-esteem, in which some loss is experienced; it is a spur to creativity.

The OBJECT is the child's subjective construction of however much he/she knows about the primary care giver at a given point in development. The *object* is usually parent(s) before they are perceived as person in their own right. The term does not denote objectivity, therefore, but rather the opposite in order to take into account how the other is recreated by need, desire, etc, as in "love object." More technically, then, the *object* is that through which the drive seeks to attain its aim.

OVERDETERMINISM may refer to a plurality of causal factors as well as a multiplicity of unconscious segments, each susceptible to coherent interpretation while constituting a greater whole.

PRIMAL SCENE refers narrowly to the child's direct witnessing of parental intercourse or to his fantasies about it—often a combination of the two, with ample allowance for subjective distortions colored by, or refracted through, the child's psychosexual stage of development at the time (ranging from the oral through the oedipal periods). More broadly, the term encompasses childhood theories about the nature of adult sexuality, one's subjective impressions of the total parental relation, and where one fits in. So universal is this experience of childhood—or some variation on it—that it is seen as having become built into our deeper mental structure. As a quasi-objective version of origins, it constitutes this study's other point of departure.

SELF may refer to the whole person or to a separate center of initiative within the person (separate, that is, from primary caregivers). The self is a subjective sense of ourselves, comprising self-representations and object-representations; the former may draw on bodily sensations, the latter on personal relationships. While one's *identity* may state one is Mr. So-and-so, our self informs us that we are alive (not numb or dead), whole and cohesive (not fragmented), centered (not diffuse), and, finally, capable of reflecting, symbolizing, feeling, and providing a sense of continuity and connectedness with our surroundings. *Self-character* functions as a stand-in for the author in his/her created world; a self-representation given independent standing; a core of autobiographical affects, memories, attitudes, or desires; an alter ego.

TRANSITIONAL OBJECTS AND PHENOMENA is D. W. Winnicott's way of addressing what he calls the child's "first not-me possessions": i.e., the blankets, dolls, toys, etc. which preexist and are neither part of the child's person nor belonging to the parents. As they appear during weaning and thrive in the widening spaces between the child and his mother—almost between mouth and nipple—they inherit some of the emotional significance originally directed to the mother and hence retain a richness of illusion balanced off by their own preexisting reality. These objects are eventually abandoned, but the process itself continues in cultural spheres, especially the arts, humanities, and also, it seems now, the sciences. These original possessions are also referred to as *subjective-objects* or *self-objects*, by way of addressing their duality and ambiguity. The process begun in the transitional sphere, according to Winicott, continues as the lifelong task of sorting out reality from illusion, inner from outer, subjective from objective. Usually, transitional objects refer to "objects" in the everyday sense of "things," but they may also encompass individuals and systems such as language, literary tradition, etc. Our capacity for free play with ideas, forms, images, hypotheses strongly suggests that creativity of all types occurs in the transitional sphere.

Bibliography

Adam, Ian, ed. *This Particular Web: Essays on Middlemarch.* Toronto: University of Toronto Press, 1975.

Adams, Kenneth Alan. "Arachnophobia: Love American Style," Part 1, *The Journal of Psychoanalytic Anthropology* 4 (1981): 157–97; Part 2, *Journal of Psychohistory* 10 (1983): 409–62.

Adrian, Arthur. *Dickens and the Parent-Child Relationship.* Athens: Ohio University Press, 1984.

Alland, Alexander, Jr. *The Human Imperative.* New York: Columbia University Press, 1982.

Allen, Judy, and Jeanne Griffiths. *The Book of the Dragon.* Secaucus, N.J.: Chartwell Books, 1979.

Allen, Virginia M. *The Femme Fatale.* New York: Whitson, 1983.

Anzieu, Didier. "Beckett and Bion." *International Review of Psycho-Analysis* 16 (1989): 163–69.

Appelbaum, Stephen. *Out in Inner Space.* New York: Doubleday, 1979.

Appleman, Philip, ed. *Darwin.* New York: Norton Critical Edition, 1970.

Ardrey, Robert. *African Genesis.* New York: Atheneum, 1973.

Arens, William. *The Man-Eating Myth.* New York: Oxford, 1979.

Arlow, Jacob. "Pyromania and the Primal Scene: A Psychoanalytic Comment on the Work of Yukio Mishima." *Psychoanalytic Quarterly* 43, no. 1 (1978): 24–53.

———. "Theories of Pathogenesis." Paper read at American Psychoanalytic Association Meetings, Winter 1980.

———. "Scientific Cosmogony, Mythology, and Immortality." *Psychoanalytic Quarterly* 51 (1982): 191.

Auerbach, Erich. *Mimesis.* New York: Doubleday, 1957.

Bach, Sheldon. "Narcissistic Fusion States and Creativity." In *The Unconscious Today,* edited by Mark Kanzer. 495–505. New York: International Universities Press, 1971.

———. "On the Narcissistic State of Consciousness." *International Journal of Psycho-Analysis* 58 (1977): 209–33.

Bair, Deirdre. *Samuel Beckett : A Biography.* New York: Harcourt Brace Jovanovich, 1978.

Bak, Robert, C. "The Phallic Woman." *Psychoanalytic Study of the Child* 23 (1968): 15–36.

Balint, Michael. *Primary Love and Psycho-Analytic Technique.* New York: Liveright, 1965.

———. *The Basic Fault.* London: Tavistock, 1968.

Bar, Eugen. "Understanding Lacan." In *Psychoanalysis and Contemporary Science,* edited by Leo Goldberger and Victor Rosen, 3: 473–544. New York: International Universties Press, 1974.

Barash, David P. *Sociobiology and Behavior.* New York: Elsevier Scientific Publishing Co., 1977.

Barkin, Leonard. *Nature's Work of Art: The Human Body as Image of the World.* New Haven: Yale University Press, 1975.

Barnard, G. C. *Samuel Beckett: A New Approach.* London: Dent, 1970.

Barnes, Julian. *Flaubert's Parrot.* London: Cape, 1984.

Barrow, John D., and Frank J. Tipler. *The Anthropic Cosmological Principle.* New York: Oxford, 1986.

Barth, John. *Lost in the Funhouse.* New York: Grosset and Dunlop, 1969.

Barthelme, Donald. *Unspeakable Practices, Unnatural Acts.* New York: Bantam, 1969.

_____. *Sixty Stories.* New York: Putnam, 1981.

Barthes, Roland. *The Pleasure of the Text.* New York: Farrar, Straus, and Giroux, 1975.

_____. *Roland Barthes by Roland Barthes.* New York: Hill and Wang, 1977.

_____. *Image Music Text.* New York: Fontana, 1977.

_____. Review of *"Le Grain d'une Enfance." Le Nouvel Observateur,* 5 September 1977.

_____. *A Lover's Discourse.* New York: Hill and Wang, 1978.

Baudelaire, Charles. "Correspondences." *French Symbolist Poetry.* Translated by C. F. MacIntyre. Berkeley: University of California Press, 1958.

Baudry, Francis. "Adolescent Love and Self-Analysis as Contributors to Flaubert's Creativity." *Psychoanalytic Study of the Child* 35 (1980): 377–416.

Bauerle, Ruth. "A Sober Drunken Speech: Stephen's Parodies in the Oxen of the Sun." *James Joyce Quarterly* 5 (1967): 40–45.

Becker, Ernest. *The Denial of Death.* New York: Free Press, 1973.

Beckett, Samuel. *Waiting for Godot.* New York: Grove, 1954.

_____. *Malone Dies.* New York: Grove, 1958.

_____. *How It Is.* New York: Grove, 1970.

_____. *Company.* New York: Grove, 1980.

Beckson, Karl. "Oscar Wilde and the Masks of Narcissus." *Psychoanalytic Study of Society.* Vol 10. Hillsdale N.J.: Analytic Press, 1984.

Beer, Gillian. "Myth and the Single Consciousness: *Middlemarch* and the Lifted Veil." In *This Particular Web: Essays on Middlemarch,* edited by Ian Adam, 91–116. Toronto: University of Toronto Press, 1975.

_____. *Darwin's Plots: Evolutionary Narrative in Darwin, George Eliot, and Nineteenth Century Fiction.* New York: Routledge and Kegan Paul, 1984.

Bell, Quentin. *Virginia Woolf: A Biography.* New York: Harcourt Brace Jovanovich, 1974.

Benstock, Shari. "*Ulysses* as Ghoststory." *James Joyce Quarterly* 12, no. 4 (1975): 396–413.

Beres, David. "A Dream, A Vison, A Poem," *International Journal of Psycho-Analysis.* 32 (1951): 97–116.

Bergler, Edmund. "D. H. Lawrence's 'The Fox' and the Psychoanalytic Theory of Lesbianism." In *A D. H. Lawrence Miscellany,* 49–55. Carbondale: Southern Illinois University Press, 1959.

Bergman, Ingmar. *Four Screenplays.* New York: Simon and Schuster, 1960.

Berman, Leon. "The Role of the Primal Scene in the Art of Max Ernst." In *Psychoanalytic Perspectives on Art,* edited by Mary Matthews Gedo. Vol. 3. Hillsdale, N.J.: Analytic Press, 1988.

Bersani, Leo. *A Future for Astynax: Character and Desire in Literature.* Boston: Little, Brown, 1976.

Bettelheim, Bruno. "Portnoy Psychoanalyzed." *Psychiatry and Social Science Review* 4, no. 10 (15 August 1970): 2–9; Reprint *Midstream* (1970).

Bion, Wilfred. *Transformations*. New York: Basic Books, 1965.

_____. *Learning from Experience*. New York: Jason Aronson, 1983.

Blatt, Sidney J. *Continuity and Change in Art*. Hillsdale, N.J.: Erlbaum, 1984.

Bloom, Harold. *The Anxiety of Influence*. New York: Oxford University Press, 1973.

_____. *Kabbalah and Criticism*. New York: Seabury, 1975.

_____. *A Map of Misreading*. New York: Oxford University Press, 1975.

Blos, Peter "The Geneology of the Ego Ideal." *Psychoanalytic Study of the Child* 24 (1974): 43–88.

_____. "When and How Does Adolescence End: Structural Criteria for Adolescent Closure." *Adolescent Psychiatry* 5 (1977): 5–17.

Blum, Harold. "A Psychoanalytic View of *Who's Afraid of Virginia Woolf?*" *Journal of the American Psychoanalytic Association* 17 (1969): 888–903.

_____. "Symbolic Processes and Symbol Formation." *International Journal of Psycho-Analysis* 59 (1978): 455–71.

Bonaparte, Marie. "The Fault of Orpheus in Reverse." *International Journal of Psycho-Analysis* 25 (1954): 109–112.

Bond, Alma. "Virginia Woolf: Manic-Depressive Psychosis and Genius: An Illustration of Separation-Individuation Theory," *Journal of the American Academy of Psychoanalysis* 13, no. 2 (1985), 191–210.

Bordewich, Fergus M. "Colorado's Thriving Cults." *New York Times Magazine,* 1 May 1988.

Boswell, James. *The Life of Samuel Johnson*. New York: Oxford, 1934.

Boswell, John. *The Kindness of Strangers: The Abandonment of Children in Western Europe from Late Antiquity to the Renaissance*. New York: Pantheon, 1988.

Bower, Reuben. *Alexander Pope: The Poetry of Allusion*. New York: Oxford University Press, 1959.

Boyer, Bryce. "Remarks on the Personality of Shamans with Special Reference to the Apache of the Mescalero Reservation." *The Psychoanalytic Study of Society* 2 (1962): 233–54.

_____. *Childhood and Folklore*. New York: Library of Psychological Anthropology, 1979.

Boyers, Robert, ed. *Psychological Man*. New York: Harper and Row, 1975.

Bradley, Noel. "Primal Scene Experience in Human Evolution and Its Phantasy Derivatives in Art, Proto Science and Philosophy." In *Psychoanalytic Study of Society,* edited by Werner Muensterberger and Bryce Boyer, 4: 725–51. New York: International Universities Press, 1967.

_____. "Notes on Theory-Making, on Scotoma of the Nipples and on the Bee as Nipple." *International Journal of Psychoanalysis* 54, no. 3 (1973): 301–14.

Breger, Louis. *Freud's Unfinished Journey*. New York: Routledge and Kegan Paul, 1981.

Brett, Dorothy. *Lawrence and Brett, A Friendship*. Philadelphia: J. B. Lippincott, 1933.

Brontë, Emily. *Wuthering Heights*. Edited by William M. Sale, Jr. New York: Norton, 1972.

Brown, Norman O. Introduction to Hesiod's *Theogony*. New York: Bobbs-Merrill Library of Liberal Arts, 1953.

_____. *Closing Time*. New York: Random House, 1973.

Bryant, Darrol and Herbert Richardson, ed. *A Time for Consideration*. New York and Toronto: Edwin Mellen Press, 1978.

Buchen, Irving H. "Emily Brontë and the Metaphysics of Childhood and Love." In *Twentieth Century Interpretations of Wuthering Heights,* edited by Thomas A. Volger. Englewood Cliffs, N.J.: Prentice–Hall, 1968.

Buckley, Jerome Hamilton. *Tennyson: The Growth of a Poet.* Cambridge: Harvard University Press, 1967.

Burgess, Anthony. *Joysprick: An Introduction to the Language of James Joyce.* London: Deutsch, 1973.

Burnham, Donald, and Sven Arne Bergmann. "August Strindberg's Need-Fear Dilemma as Seen in His Relationship with Harriet Bosse." In *Psychiatry and the Humanities,* edited by Joseph Smith, vol. 1. New Haven: Yale University Press, 1976.

Caldwell, Richard S. "Psychocosomogony: The Presentation of Symbiosis-Individuation in Archaic Greek Myth." In *Psychoanalytic Study of Society,* 9: 93–104. New York: Psychohistory Press, 1981.

Call, Justin. "Some Prelinguistic Aspects of Language Development." *Journal of the American Psychoanalytic Association* 28 (1980): 259–89.

Capra, Fritjof. *The Turning Point.* New York: Simon and Schuster, 1982.

Carrol, David. "*Middlemarch* and the Externality of Fact." In *This Particular Web,* edited by Ian Adam. Toronto: University of Toronto Press, 1975.

Carroll, Michael. *The Cult of the Virgin Mary.* Princeton: Princeton University Press, 1986.

Carson, Joan. "Visionary Experience in *Wuthering Heights.*" *Psychoanalytic Review* 62 (1975): 131–52.

Casteneda, Carlos. *Journey to Ixtlan.* New York: Simon and Schuster, 1972.

———. *A Separate Reality.* New York: Pocketbooks, 1974.

Cheng, Vincent J. "Stephen Dedalus and the Black Panther Vampire." *James Joyce Quarterly* 24, no. 2 (1987): 143–60.

Chodorow, Nancy. *The Reproduction of Mothering: Psychoanalysis and the Sociology of Gender.* Berkeley: University of California Press, 1978.

Clark, Elizabeth. "Women in the Theology of the Unification Church." In *Exploring Unification Theology,* edited by Susan Hodges and Darrol Bryant, 148–66. Toronto: Edwin Mellen Press, 1978.

Clément, Catherine. *The Lives and Legends of Jacques Lacan.* New York: Columbia University Press, 1983.

Cloud, Preston. *Cosmos, Earth, and Man: A Short History of the Universe.* New Haven: Yale University Press, 1979.

Coen, Stanley I. "The Author and His audience: Jean Genet's Early Work." *Psychoanalytic Study of Society.* Volume 9. New York: Psychohistory Press, 1984.

Cohan, Steven. "Why Mr. Ramsay Reads *The Antiquary.*" *Women and Literature* 7 (1979): 14–24.

Cohen, I. Bernard. *Franklyn and Newton.* Philadelphia: The American Philosophical Society, 1956.

———. *Album of Science, from Leonardo to Lavoisier, 1540–1800.* New York: Scribners, 1980.

Cohen-Solal, Annie. *Sartre: A Life.* New York: Pantheon Books, 1985.

Coleridge, Samuel Toylor. *Selected Poems.* Northbook, Ill.: AHM Publishers, 1956.

Colp, Ralph, Jr. "Charles Darwin's Vision of Organic Nature." *New York State Journal of Medicine* 79 (September, December 1979): 1622–29, 2136.

Corbin, Edwin I. "The Autonomous Ego Functions in Creativity." *Journal of the American Psychoanalytic Association* 22, no. 3 (1974): 568–87.

Crashaw, Richard. *The Poems: English, Latin, and Greek.* Edited by L. C. Martin. Oxford: Clarendon Press, 1927.

Crecelius, Kathryn. *Family Romances.* Bloomington: Indiana University Press, 1987.

Crombie, A. C. *Medieval and Early Modern Science.* Vol. 1. New York: Doubleday, 1959.

Culik, Hugh. "Neurological Disorder and the Evolution of Beckett's Maternal Images." *Mosaic* 22 (1989): 41–54.

Daiches, David. *Virginia Woolf.* Norfolk, Va.: New Directions, 1942.

Darwin, Charles. *Autobiography.* New York: Norton, 1969.

Davidson, Sara. "Talk with Philip Roth." *New York Times Book Review,* 18 September 1977, 52.

Davie, Donald. *Articulate Energy: An Inquiry into the Syntax of English Poetry.* New York: Routledge and Kegan Paul, 1975.

Davies, Paul. *Superforce.* New York: Simon and Schuster, 1984.

Davies, Stevie, *Emily Brontë: The Artist as a Free Woman.* Manchester, England: Carcanet Press, 1983.

deMause, Lloyd. *Foundations of Psychohistory.* New York: Creative Roots, 1982.

De Mille, Richard. *The Don Juan Papers: Further Castaneda Controversies.* Santa Barbara, Calif.: Santa Barbara Press, 1980.

Derrida, Jacques. "Freud and the Scene of Writing." *Yale French Studies* 48 (1972): 74–117.

Dervin, Daniel. *Bernard Shaw: A Psychological Study.* Lewisburg, Pa.: Bucknell University Press, 1975.

_____. "A Crux in the Jung/Freud Letters." *Bulletin of the Menninger Clinic* 41, no. 2 (1977): 131–44.

_____. "The Spook in the Rainforest: The Incestuous Structure of Tennessee Williams' Plays." *The Psychocultural Review* 3–4 (1979): 153–84.

_____. "Lacanian Mirrors and Literary Reflections." *Journal of the Philadelphia Psychoanalytic Association* 7. (1980): 129–141.

_____. "Hopper and Warhol at the Whitney." *Psychoanalytic Review* 68 (1981): 293–300.

_____. "Orpheus and Eurydice: A Myth about Human Evolution." *Journal of Psychoanalytic Anthropology* 6, no. 3 (1983): 277–88.

_____. *A "Strange Sapience": The Creative Imagination of D. H. Lawrence.* Amherst: University of Massachusetts Press, 1984.

_____. *Through a Freudian Lens Deeply: A Psychoanalysis of Cinema.* Hillsdale, N.J.: Analytic Press, 1985.

_____. "Matricentric Narratives: A Report on the Psychoanalysis of Gender Based on British Women's Fiction." *Journal of Psychoanalytic Anthropology* 9 (1986): 393–446.

_____. "Abandonment: a Dominant Pattern in the Development of Creative Writers, Philosophers, and Scientists since the Seventeenth Century." *Journal of Psychohistory* 15 (1987): 153–88.

Desmond, Adrian. *Archetypes and Ancestors: Paleontology in Victorian London, 1850–1875.* Chicago: University of Chicago Press, 1984.

Dick, Steven J. *Plurality of Worlds: The Origins of the Extraterrestrial Debate from Democritus to Kant.* New York: Cambridge University Press, 1982.

Dickens, Charles. *Great Expectations.* New York: Holt, Rinehart, and Winston, 1972.

Dickinson, Emily. *The Letters.* Edited by Thomas Johnson. 3 vols. Cambridge: Haruard Univesity Press, 1958.

Dijkstra, Bram. *Idols of Perversity: Fantasies of Feminine Evil in Fin de Siècle Culture.* New York: Oxford University Press, 1986.

Dinnerstein, Dorothy. *The Mermaid and the Minotaur.* New York: Harper and Row, 1976.

Donaldson, Ian. *The Rapes of Lucretia.* Oxford: Clarendon Press, 1982.

Donne, John. *The Complete Poetry.* New York: Modern library, 1941.

Dooley, Lucille. "Psychoanalysis of the Character and Genius of Emily Brontë." *Psychoanalytic Review* 17 (1930): 208–39.

Douglas, Wallace. *Wordsworth: The Construction of a Personality.* Kent, Ohio: Kent State University Press, 1967.

Drees, Ludwig. *Olympia: Gods, Artists, and Athletes.* New York: Praeger, 1968.

Duchen, Claire. *Feminism in France.* London: Routledge and Kegan Paul, 1986.

Durrell, Lawrence. *A Key to Modern British Poetry.* Norman: University of Oklahoma Press, 1952.

_____. *Justine.* New York: Dutton, 1961.

Eckstein, Rudolph. "From the Language of Play to Play with Language." *Adolescent Psychology* 4 (1976): 142–62.

Edel, Leon. "Psychoanalysis and Literary Biography." In *Literary Biography.* Toronto: Toronto University Press, 1957.

Edelheit, Henry. "Mythopoiesis and the Primal Scene." In *The Psychoanalytic Study of Society,* vol. 5: 212–233. New York: International Universities Press, 1972.

_____. "Crucifixion Fantasies and Their Relation to the Primal Scene." *International Journal of Psycho-Analysis* 55 (1974): 193–204.

Edmunds, Lowell. *Oedipus: the Ancient Legend and Its Later Analogues.* Baltimore: Johns Hopkins University Press, 1985.

Edwards, Lee R. "Women, Energy, and *Middlemarch.*" New York: Norton Critical Edition of *Middlemarch,* 1977.

_____. *Psyche As Hero.* Middletown, Conn.: Wesleyan University Press, 1984.

Edwards, Christopher. *Crazy for God.* Englewood Cliffs, N.J.: Prentice Hall; 1979.

Ehrenzweig, Anton. *The Hidden Order of Art.* Berkeley: University of California Press, 1967.

Eigen, Michael. "On the Significance of the Face." *The Psychoanalytic Review* 67 (1980): 427–42.

_____. "The Area of Faith in Winnicott, Lacan, and Bion." *International Journal of Psycho-Analysis* 62 (1981): 413–33.

Eisenstadt, Marvin, et al. *Parental Loss and Achievement.* Madison, Conn.: International Universities Press, 1989.

Eisenstein, Hester. *Contemporary Feminist Thought.* Boston: G. K. Hall, 1983.

Eissler, K. R. "Genius, Psychopathology and Creativity." *American Imago* 24 (1967): 35–81.

_____. *Goethe: A Psychoanalytic Study.* New York: International Universities Press, 1968.

_____. "Death Drive, Ambivalence, and Narcissism." *Psychoanalytic Study of the Child* 26 (1971): 25–78.

_____. *Discourse on Hamlet and "Hamlet."* New York: International Universities Press, 1971.

_____. "The Fall of Man." *Psychoanalytic Study of the Child* 30 (1975): 589–646.

_____. "Remarks on an Aspect of Creativity." *American Imago* 1–2 1978: 59–76.

Eliade, Mircea. *The Myth of the Eternal Return.* Princeton: Princeton University Press, 1954.

Eliot, George. *Middlemarch.* Edited by Bert G. Hornback. New York: W. W. Norton, 1977.

Eliot, T. S. *The Collected Poems.* New York: Harcourt, Brace, 1950.

Ellmann, Richard. *"Ulysses" on the Liffey.* New York: Oxford University Press, 1972.

_____. *Golden Codgers.* New York: Oxford University Press, 1973.

_____. *Oscar Wilde.* New York: Knopf, 1988.

Ermath, Elizabeth Deeds. "George Eliot's Conception of Sympathy." *Nineteenth Century Fiction* 49 (1985): 23–42.

Ernst, Kris. *Psychoanalytic Explorations in Art.* London: Allen and Unwin, 1953.

Esman, Aaron. "The Primal Scene, A Review and a Reconsideration." *The Psychoanalytic Study of the Child* 28 (1973): 49–83.

_____. "Psychoanalysis and Literary Criticism—A Limited Partnership." *Psychoanalysis and Contemporary Thought* 5, no. 1 (1982): 17–25.

Evans, M. N. "Introduction to Jacques Lacan's Lecture: The Neurotic's Individual Myth." *Psychoanalytic Quarterly* 43 (1979): 386–404.

Ewens, Thomas. "Female Sexuality and the Role of the Phallus." *Psychoanalytic Review* 63 (1976): 615–37.

Faber, M. D. "Don Juan and Castaneda." Parts 1–2. *Psychocultural Review* 1 (1977): 3–4. Part 3. *The Psychoanalytic Review* 64 (1977): 323–80.

_____. "Relating the Work of Carlos Casteneda to Psychiatry." *Bulletin of the Menninger Clinic* 42 (1978): 233–38.

Faguet, Robert. "A Long Time Ago in a Galaxy Far, Far Away ..." *The American Journal of Psychoanalysis* 38 (1978): 359–60.

Farwell, Marilyn R. "Virginia Woolf and Androgyny." *Contemporary Literature* 16 (1975): 433–51.

Fausto-Sterling, Anne. *Myths of Gender.* New York: Basic Books, 1985.

Ferguson, Frances. *Wordsworth: Language as Counter Spirit.* New Haven: Yale University Press, 1977.

Ferris, Timothy. "Crucibles of the Cosmos." *New York Times Magazine,* 7 January 1979.

_____. "Physics' Newest Frontier." *New York Times Magazine,* 26 September 1982.

Feuer, Lewis. *The Scientific Intellectual.* New York: Basic Books, 1963.

_____. *Einstein and the Generations of Science.* New York: Basic Books; 1974.

Fiedler, Leslie. "Lord of the Absolute Everywhere." *New York Times Book Review,* 9 June 1974.

First, Ruth, and Ann Scott. *Olive Schreiner.* London: Deutsch, 1980.

Fisher, Seymour. *Development and Structure of the Body Image.* 2 vols. Hillside, N.J.: Erlbaum, 1986.

Flaubert, Gustave. *Intimate Notebook, 1840–41.* Edited and Translated by Francis Steegmuller. New York: Doubleday, 1967.

_____. *The Letters of Gustave Flaubert.* Edited by Francis Steegmuller. 2 vols. Cambridge Mass.: Belknap Press, 1980.

_____. *Carnets de travail.* Paris: Balland, 1988

Ford, George H. *Double Measure.* New York: W. W. Norton, 1965.

Fox, Robin. *The Red Lamp of Incest.* New York: Oxford University Press, 1947.

Fraser, Hilary. "St. Theresa, St. Dorothea, Miss Brooke in *Middlemarch.*" *Nineteenth Century Fiction* 40 (1986): 400–411.

Freeman, Derek. "Totem and Taboo—A Reappraisal." *The Psychoanalytic Study of Society* 4 (1967): 9–33.

French, Marilyn. *The Book as World: James Joyce's Ulysses.* Cambridge: Harvard University Press, 1976.

Freud, Anna. "Insight: Its Presence and Absence as a Factor in Normal Development." In *The Writings of Anna Freud,* vol. 8. New York: International Universities Press, 1981.

Freud, Sigmund. (1895). *Studies on Hysteria.* In vol. 2 of the *Standard Edition,* London: Hogarth, 1955.

_____. (1900). *The Interpretation of Dreams.* In vols. 4 and 5 of the *Standard Edition.*

_____. (1905). "Psychical (or Mental) Treatment." In vol. 7 of the *Standard Edition.*

_____. (1908). "Creative Writers and Day-Dreaming." In vol. 9 of the *Standard Edition.*

_____. (1909). "Family Romances." In vol. 9 of the *Standard Edition.*

_____. (1911). "Formulations on the Two Principles of Mental Functioning." In vol. 11 of the *Standard Edition.*

_____.(1911). "A Special Type of Object-Choice Made by Men." In vol. 11 of the *Standard Edition.*

_____. (1911). The Case History of Schreber. In vol. 12 of the *Standard Edition*.

_____. (1912); *Totem and Taboo*. In vol. 13 of the *Standard Edition*.

_____. (1917). "A Difficulty in the Path of Psychoanalysis," In vol. 17 of the *Standard Edition*.

_____. (1918). "From the History of an Infantile Neurosis." In vol. 17 of the *Standard Edition*.

_____. (1920). *Beyond the Pleasure Principle*. In vol. 18 of the *Standard Edition*.

_____. (1925). "Negation." In vol. 19 of the *Standard Edition*.

_____. (1925). *An Autobiographical Study*. In vol. 20 of the *Standard Edition*.

_____. (1926). *Inhibitions, Symptoms, and Anxiety* (also titled *The Problem of Anxiety*). In vol. 20 of the *Standard Edition*.

_____. (1930). *Civilization and Its Discontents*. In vol. 21 of the *Standard Edition*.

_____. (1939). *Moses and Monotheism*. In vol. 23 of the *Standard Edition*.

_____. *The Origins of Psycho-Analysis*. New York: Basic Books, 1954.

_____. *The Letters*. Edited by Ernst L. Freud. New York: Basic Books, 1960.

_____. *The Complete Letters of Sigmund Freud to Wilhelm Fliess*. Edited by Jeffrey Moussaief Masson. Cambridge: Harvard University Press, 1985.

_____. *A Phylogenetic Fantasy*. Cambridge: Harvard University Press, 1987.

Frye, Northrop. *Spiritus Mundi: Essays on Literature, Myth and Society,* Bloomington: Indiana University Press, 1967.

Gagnier, Regenia. *Idylls of the Marketplace: Oscar Wilde and the Victorian Public.* Stanford, Calif.: Stanford University Press, 1986.

Gardner, John, and John Marier. *Gilgamesh*. New York: Knopf, 1984.

Garma, Angel. "Oedipus Was Not the Son of Laius and Jocasta." *International Journal of Psychoanalytic Psychotherapy* 7 (1978): 316–25.

Gedo, John. *Portraits of the Artist*. New York: Guilford, 1983.

Gérin, Winifred. *Emily Brontë: A Biography*. Oxford: Clarendon Press, 1971.

Gervais, David. "On the Figures in Turner's Landscapes." *Cambridge Quarterly* 14 (1985): 20–50.

Gittings, Robert. *Young Thomas Hardy*. London: Penguin, 1978.

Gliserman, Martin. "Virginia Woolf's *To the Lighthouse:* Syntax and the Female Center." *American Imago* 40, no. 40 (1983): 51–101.

Goff, Barbara Munson. "Between Natural Theology and Natural Selection: Breeding the Human Animal in *Wuthering Heights*." *Victorian Studies* 27 (1984): 477–508.

Gornick, Vivian. *Essays in Feminism*. New York: Harper and Row, 1978.

Gosse, Edmund. *Father and Son*. London: Penguin, 1976.

Gottfried, Roy. *The Art of Joyce's Syntax in Ulysses*. Athens: University of Georgia Press, 1980.

Gould, Stephen Jay. *The Panda's Thumb*. New York: Norton, 1980.

_____. "The Ghost of Protagoras." *New York Review of Books,* 21 January 1981.

_____. "Cardboard Darwinism." *New York Review of Books,* 25 September 1986.

Gourevitch, Anne. "Origins: The Impact of Parental Background." *Contemporary Psychoanalysis* 14 (1978): 226–45.

Graves, Robert. *The White Goddess*. New York: Octagon Books, 1948.

_____. *The Greek Myths*. New York: Penguin, 1955.

Green, Bernard. "The Effects of the Distortion of the Self: A Study of *The Picture of Dorian Gray.*" *The Annual of Psychoanalysis* 7 (1979): 391–410.

Greenacre, Phyllis. "The Family Romance of the Artist." *Psychoanalytic Study of the Child* 13 (1958): 9–42.

_____. "Woman as Artist," *Psychoanalytic Quarterly* 29 (1960): 208–27.

_____. "The Primal Scene and the Sense of Reality." *Psychoanalytic Quarterly* 42 (1973): 10–41.

Greenson, Ralph. "About the Sound mm. . . ." *Psychoanalytic Quarterly* 23 (1954): 234–39.

Griaule, Marcel. *Conversations with Ogotemmeli.* New York: Oxford University Press, 1956.

Grinstein, Alexander. "Oscar Wilde." *American Imago* 37 (1980): 125–37.

Griska, Joseph. "Wordsworth's Mood Disturbance." *Literature and Psychology* 24 (1974): 144–52.

Grolnick, Simon. "Emily Dickinson: The Interweaving of Poetry and Personality." Paper presented at the meeting of the American Psychoanalytic Association, Fall 1985.

Grotjahn, Martin. "The Primal Crime and the Unconscious." In *Searchlights on Delinquency,* edited by K. R. Eissler, 306–14. New York: International Universities Press, 1949.

Hacking, Ian. "Chomsky and His Critics." *New York Review of Books,* 23 October 1980, 47–49.

Hallissy, Margaret. *Venomous Women.* Westport, Conn.: Greenwood, 1987.

Hamilton, James C. "Transitional Fantasies and the Creative Process." *The Psychoanalytic Study of Society* 6 (1975): 53–70.

Hanly, Charles. *Existentialism and Psychoanalysis.* New York: International Universities Press, 1980.

_____. *The Moral Art of Dickens.* London: The Athlone Press, 1970.

Hardy, Barbara. *The Appropriate Form: An Essay on the Novel.* London: Athlone Press, 1964.

Hardy, Thomas. *The Mayor of Casterbridge.* London: Macmillan, 1978.

Harper, Howard. *Between Language and Silence: The Novels of Virginia Woolf.* Baton Rouge: Louisiana State University Press, 1983.

Harper, Robert Francis. *Assyrian and Babylonian Literature.* New York: Appleton, 1904.

Harre, Ron. "Davy and Coleridge: Romanticism in Science and the Arts." In *Common Denominators in Art and Science,* edited by Martin Pollock. Aberdeen, Scotland: Aberdeen University Press, 1983.

Harris, Marvin. *Cannibals and Kings: The Origins of Cultures.* New York: Random House, 1977.

Hartman, Geoffrey, ed. *Deconstruction and Criticism.* New York: Continuum, 1987.

Hartocolis, Peter. "Congenital Deformity as a Factor of Artistic Creativity: the Case of George Gordon Byron." Paper read at the December 1976 meeting of the American Psychoanalytic Association.

Hawkins, G. S. *Stonehenge Decoded.* New York: Doubleday, 1965.

Hayman, Ronald. *Sartre: A Life.* New York: Simon and Schuster, 1987.

Haynal, André. *Depression and Creativity.* New York: International Universities Press, 1985.

Heidel, Alexander. *The Gilgamesh Epic and Old Tetament Parallels.* Chicago: University of Chicago Press, 1949.

Henderson, James. "Exorcism, Possession, and the Dracula Cult: A Synopsis of Object-Relations Psychology." *Bulletin of the Menninger Clinic* 40, no. 6 (1976): 603–28.

Herman, Judith Lewis. *Father-Daughter Incest.* Cambridge: Harvard University Press, 1981.

Hesse, Hermann. *Pictor's Metamorphoses.* New York: Farrar, Straus, and Giroux, 1982.

Hill, Robert W., ed. *Tennyson's Poetry.* New York: W. W. Norton, 1972.

Hitschman, Edward. "Swedenborg's Paranoia." *American Imago* 6 (1949): 45–50.

Hockett, Charles. "The Problems of Universals in Language." In *Universals of Language,* edited by J. H. Greenberg. 2d ed. Cambridge: MIT Press, 1966.

Hofling, Charles K. "Notes on Camus' *L'Étranger.*" In *The Human Mind Revisited,* Edited by Sydney Smith. New York: International Universities Press, 1979.

Holland, Norman. *The Dynamics of Literary Response*. New York: Oxford University Press, 1968.

———. "Freud, Physics, and Literature." *Journal of the American Academy of Psychoanalysis* 12, no. 3 (1984): 301–20.

———. *The I*. New Haven: Yale University Press, 1985.

Holt, Halvan. *The Life of Ibsen*. London: George Allen, 1931.

Homans, Margaret. "Dreaming of Children: Literalization in *Jane Eyre* and *Wuthering Heights*." In *The Female Gothic,* edited by Juliann E. Fleenor. Montreal: Eden, 1983.

Homer. *The Odyssey*. Translated by Robert Fitzgerald. New York: Doubleday, 1963.

Horowitz, Irving Louis. *Science, Sin and Scholarship*. Cambridge: MIT Press, 1978.

Hubback, Judith. "Uses and Abuses of Analogy." *The Journal of Analytical Psychology* 18, no. 2 (1973): 91–104.

Hunt, Eva. *The Transformation of the Hummingbird*. Ithaca: Cornell University Press, 1977.

Hyman, Stanley Edgar. *The Tangled Bank*. New York: Athenium, 1974.

Ibsen, Henrik. *Peer Gynt*. Translated by Rolf Fjelde. New York: NAL, 1964.

———. *Peer Gynt*. Translated by Christopher Fry. New York: Oxford, 1972.

———. *Letters and Speeches*. Edited by Evert Sprinchorn. New York: Hill and Wang, 1964.

Ignatieff, Michael. "Freud's Cordelia." *New York Review of Books,* 14 November 1988.

Ikonen P., and E. Rechardt. "On the Universal Nature of Primal Scene Fantasies." *International Journal of Psycho-Analysis* 65 (1984): 63–72.

Isakower, Otto. "A Contribution to the Patho-Psychology of Phenomena Associated with Falling Asleep." *International Journal of Psycho-Analysis* 19 (1938): 331–45.

Isaacs, Susan. "The Nature and Function of Fantasy." In *Developments in Psycho-Analysis*, edited by Joan Rivière. London: Hogarth, 1952.

Jacoby, Russell. *Social Amnesia: A Critique of Conformist Psychology from Adler to Laing*. Boston: Beacon Press, 1975.

Jantsch, Erich. *The Self-Organizing Universe*. New York: Pergamon Press, 1980.

Jastrow, Robert. *The Enchanted Loom: Mind in the Universe*. New York: Simon and Schuster, 1981.

Jaynes, Julian. *The Origin of Consciousness in the Breakdown of the Bicameral Mind*. Boston: Houghton Mifflin, 1976.

Jean, Marcel, ed. *The Autobiography of Surrealism*. New York: Viking, 1980.

Jesperson, Otto. *Language: Its Nature, Development, and Origin*. London: Macmillan, 1921.

Johanson, D., and M. Edey. *Lucy*. New York: Simon and Schuster, 1981.

Johnson, Samuel. *Lives of the English Poets*. New York: Avon, 1965.

Jones, Ernest. *Essays in Applied Psycho-Analysis*. 2 vols. London: Hogarth, 1951.

———. *The Life and Work of Sigmund Freud*. 3 vols. New York: Basic Books, 1957.

———. *Papers on Psycho-Analysis*. Boston: Beacon, 1967.

Jong, Erica. *Here Comes and Other Poems*. New York: NAL, 1975.

———. *How to Save Your Own Life*. New York: Holt, Rinehart and Winston, 1971.

Jordanova, L. J., ed. *Languages of Nature: Critical Essays on Science and Literature*. New Brunswick, N.J.: Rutgers University Press, 1986.

Josipovic, Gabriel. "Linearity and Fragmentation." In *The Lessons of Modernism*. Totowa, N.J.: Rowman and Littlefield, 1978.

Joyce, James. *Ulysses*. New York: Random House, 1961.

———. *The Letters of James Joyce*. Edited by Richard Ellmann. New York: Viking, 1966.

_____. *A Portrait of the Artist As a Young Man.* New York: Viking Critical Edition, 1968.

_____. *Finnegans Wake.* New York: Viking / Penguin, 1976.

Kafka, Franz. *The Complete Short Stories.* New York: Schocken, 1946.

_____. *Letters to Friends, Family, and Editors.* Translated by Clara Winston. New York: Schocken Books, 1977.

Kahane, Claire. "The Nuptials of Metaphor: Self and Other in Virginia Woolf." *Literature and Psychology* 30, no. 2 (1980): 72–82.

Kaplan, Donald. "On Shyness." *International Journal of Psycho-Analysis* 53 (1972): 439–53.

_____. "The Psychoanalysis of Art: Some Ends, Some Means." *Journal of the American Psychoanalytic Association* 36 (1988): 259–93.

_____. "Some Technical Aspects of the Oedipus Complex." Unpublished paper.

_____. Kaplan, Donald, and William I. Grossman. "Three Commentaries on Gender in Freud's Thought: A Prologue on the Psychoanalytic theory of Sexuality." *Fantasy, Myth and Reality*, edited by Harold Blum, *et al*, New York: International Universities Press, 1989.

Kaplan, Linda Joan. "The Concept of the Family Romance." *Psychoanalytic Review* 61 (1974): 169–202.

Kaplan, Louise. *Oneness and Separateness.* New York: Simon and Schuster, 1978.

_____. *Adolescence.* New York: Simon and Schuster, 1984.

_____. *The Family Romance of the Impostor-Poet Thomas Chatterton.* New York: Atheneum, 1988.

Katan, Maurits. "Schreber's Hereafter." In *the Schreber Case*, edited by William Niederland New York: Quadrangle Press, 1974.

Kauvar, Gerald. "The Psychological Structure of Romantic Poetry." *The Psycho-analytic Review* 64, no. 1 (1977): 21–40.

Kaye, Julian B. "Who is Betty Byrne?" In *Portraits of the Artist,* edited by William Morris and Clifford Nault. New York: The Odyssey Press, 1962.

Keen, Sam. "Sorceror's Apprentice." In *Seeing Casteneda,* edited by Daniel C. Noel. New York: C. P. Putnam's, Capricorn Books, 1976.

Keller, Evelyn Fox. *Reflections on Gender and Science.* New Haven: Yale University Press, 1985.

Kenner, Hugh. *Joyce's Voices.* Berkeley: University of California Press, 1978.

_____. *The Mechanic Muse.* Oxford: Oxford University Press, 1987.

Kettle, Arnold. *An Introduction of the English Novel.* New York: Hutchinson's University Library, 1951.

Kevles, Betty Ann. *Female of the Species: Sex and Survival in the Animal Kingdom.* Cambridge: Harvard, 1986.

Kirsner, Douglas. *The Schizoid World of Jean-Paul Sartre and R. D. Laing.* Atlantic Highlands, N.J.: Humanities Press, 1977.

Klein, Melanie, *et al.* *New Directions in Psycho-Analysis.* London: Tavistock, 1955.

Kleinbard, David J. "Laing, Lawrence, and the Maternal Cannibal." *Psychoanalytic Review* 58 (1971): 1–13.

Kligerman, Charles. "The Character of Jean-Jacques Rousseau." *Psychoanalytic Quarterly* 20 (1951): 237–52.

Koestler, Arthur. *Janus: A Summing Up.* New York: Random House, 1978.

Kohut, Heinz. *The Analysis of the Self.* New York: International Universities Press, 1971.

_____. *The Restoration of the Self.* New York: International Universities Press, 1977.

Kolata, Gina. "Are the Horrors of Cannibalism Fact—or Fiction?" *Smithsonian,* March 1987, 151–70.

Kowaleswki, David. "Politics and Emotion in the Thought of John Stuart Mill." *Journal of Psychohistory* 7 (1980): 455–66.

Kramer, Dale. *Thomas Hardy: The Forms of Tragedy.* Urbana: University of Illinois Press, 1975.

Kris, Ernst. *Psychoanalytic Explorations in Art.* London: Allen and Unwin, 1953.

_____. "The personal Myth." *Journal of the American Psychoanalytic Association* 4 (1956): 653–81.

Kristeva, Julia. *A Kristeva Reader.* Edited by Toril Moi. New York: Columbia University Press, 1986.

Kubie, Lawrence. "Neurotic Distortion of the Symbolic Process." *Journal of the American Psychoanalytic Association* 1 (1953): 59–86.

_____. "Unsolved Problems Concerning the Relation of Art to Psychotherapy." *American Journal of Art Therapy* 27, no. 2 (1979): 451–78.

Kuhns, Richard. *Psychoanalytic Theory of Art.* New York: Columbia University Press, 1983.

Lacan, Jacques. *The Four Fundamental Concepts of Psychoanalysis.* New York: Norton, 1978.

_____. *The Language of the Self.* Translated by Anthony Wilden. Baltimore: Johns Hopkins University Press, 1968.

_____. (1949). "The Mirror Stage as Formative of the Function of the I as Revealed in Psychoanalytic Practice." Chap. 1 of *Écrits,* translated by Alan Sheridan. New York: W. W. Norton, 1977.

Laing, R. D. "Minkowski and Schizophrenia." *Review of Existential Psychology and Psychiatry.* 3, no. 3 (1963): 195–207.

Langbaum, Robert. *Mysteries of Identity.* New York: Oxford University Press, 1977.

Langor, Elinor. "Whatever Happened to Feminist Fiction?" *New York Times Book Review,* 19 August 1984.

Laplanche, J., and J. B. Pontcalis. *The Language of Psychoanalysis.* New York: W. W. Norton, 1973.

Lawrence, D. H. *Saint Mawr* and *The Man Who Died.* New York: Random House, 1953.

_____. *Lady Chatterley's Lover.* New York: Grove Press, 1959.

_____. *The Collected Letters.* New York: Viking, 1962.

_____. *The Symbolic Meaning.* Arundel, England: Centaur, 1962.

_____. *The Rainbow.* New York: Viking, 1965.

_____. *Sons and Lovers.* New York: Viking, 1968.

_____. *The Apocalypse.* New York: Viking, 1969.

_____. *Fantasia of the Unconscious.* New York: Viking, 1969.

_____. *Complete Poems.* New York: Viking, 1972.

_____. "The Flying Fish." In *Phoenix: The Posthumous Writings.* New York: Viking, 1972.

Leary, Timothy. "The Religious Experience: Its Production and Interpretation." *Psychedelic Review* 1, no. 3 (1964): 324–46.

_____. *High Priest.* New York: College Notes and Texts, 1968.

Leaska, Mitchell, *Virginia Woolf's Lighthouse: A Study in Critical Method.* New York: Columbia University Press, 1970.

Lessing, Doris. *A Small Personal Voice.* London: Curtis, 1963.

Levere, Trevor. *Poetry Realized in Nature: Samuel Taylor Coleridge and Early Nineteenth Century Science.* New York: Cambridge University Press, 1981.

Levi-Strauss, Claude. "The Family." In *Man, Culture, and Society,* edited by Harry Shapiro. New York: Oxford University Press, 1956.

_____. *The Scope of Anthropology.* London: Cape, 1967.

Levine, George. "Darwin and the Evolution of Fiction," *New York Times Book Review,* 5 October 1986.

Lewin, B. D. "The Nature of Reality, the Meaning of Nothing, with an Addendum on Concentration." *Psychoanalytic Quarterly* 17 (1948): 524–26.
_____. *The Psychoanalysis of Elation.* London: Hogarth, 1951.
_____. "Reconsideration of the Dream Screen." *Psychoanalytic Quarterly* 22, no. 2 (1953): 174–99.
Lichtenberg, Joseph D. "Freud's Leonardo: Psychobiography and Autobiography of Genius." *Journal of the American Psychoanalytic Association* 26 (1978): 863–80.
Lidz, Theodore. "August Strindberg: A Study of the Relationship between His Creativity and Schizophrenia." *International Journal of Psycho-Analysis* 45 (1964): 399–406.
Lidz, Theodore, and Ruth Wilmanns Lidz. *Oedipus in the Stone Age.* Madison, Conn.: International Universities Press, 1989.
Lifton, Robert Jay, "Proteus Revisted." *Adolescent Psychiatry* 14 (1976): 21–36.
_____. *The Life of the Self.* New York: Simon and Schuster, 1976.
Lippard, Lucy R. *Surrealists on Art.* Englewood Cliffs, N.J.: Prentice-Hall, 1970.
Litowitz, Bonnie and Norman Litowitz. "Development of Verbal Self-Expression." In *The Future of Psychoanalysis,* edited by Arnold Goldberg. New York: International Universities Press, 1983. 397–430.
Little, Ralph. "Behind the Dream Screen." *Psychoanalytic Review.* 57, no. 1 (1970): 132–42.
Littman, Mark, and Charles Schwerghauser. "Astronomical Allusions: Their Meaning and Purpose in *Ulysses.*" *James Joyce Quarterly* 2, no. 4 (1965): 238–45.
Loewald, Hans. "The Waning of the Oedipus Complex." *Journal of the American Psychoanalytic Association* 27 (1979): 751–75.
Loesberg, Jonathan. "Free Association: Mill's *Autobiography* as the Fiction of a Philosophy." In *Interspace and Inward Sphere,* edited by Norman A. Anderson and Margene E. Weiss. Macomb: Western Illinois University Press, 1978.
Lottman, Herbert. *Albert Camus.* New York: Doubleday, 1979.
Lovejoy, C. Owen. "The Origin of Man." *Science,* 23 January 1981.
Lovell, Bernard. "Whence—We Are What We Know About Where We Came From." *New York Times Magazine,* 16 November 1975.
Lovelock, James E. *The Ages of Gaia: A Biography of Our Living Earth.* New York: W. W. Norton, 1988.
Lukacher, Ned. *Primal Scenes.* Ithaca: Cornell University Press, 1986.
Lupton, Mary Jane. "The Rime of the Ancient Mariner: The Agony of Thirst." *American Imago* 27 (1970): 140–59.
Mack, Maynard, *The Garden and the City: Retirement and Politics in the Later Poetry of Pope, 1731–1743.* Toronto: University of Toronto Press, 1969.
_____. "Pope: The Shape of the Man in His Work," *Yale Review* 67, no. 4 (1978): 493–517.
_____. *Alexander Pope: A Life.* New York: Norton, 1985.
Mahler, Margaret. *The Psychological Birth of the Human Infant* New York: Basic Books, 1975.
Mallarmé, Stephane. "*Plusiers Sonnets.*" In *Poems,* translated by C. F. MacIntyre. Berkeley: University of California Press, 1965.
Mann, Thomas. *Essays.* Translated by H. T. Lowe-Porter. New York: Vintage Books, 1958.
Manuel, Frank E. *A Portrait of Isaac Newton.* Cambridge: Harvard University Press, 1968.
Margolis, Marvin, and Philip Parker. "The Stork Fable." *Journal of the American Psychoanalytic Association* 20 (1972): 494–511.
Maritain, Jacques, *The Dream of Descartes.* New York: Philosophical Library, 1944.
Mason, Herbert. *Gilgamesh.* New York: Mentor, 1972.

Mauron, Charles. *Introduction to the Psychoanalysis of Mallarmé.* Berkeley: University of California Press, 1963.

Mazlish, Bruce. *James and John Stuart Mill.* New York: Basic Books, 1975.

Mazzeno, Laurence. "Of Fathers, Children, and Poets: Wordsworth's 'Anecdote for Fathers.'" *Psychocultural Review* 1 (1977): 421–33.

McCarthy, Patrick. *The Riddles of Finnegans Wake.* Teaneck, N.J.: Fairleigh Dickinson University Press, 1980.

McGrath, William J. *Freud's Discovery of Psychoanalysis.* Ithaca: Cornell University Press, 1986.

Meaves, Russell. "Beckett, Sarraute, and the Perceptual Experience of Schizophrenia." *Psychiatry* 36 (1973): 61–69.

Melville, Robert. *Erotic Art of the West.* New York: G. P. Putnam's Sons, 1973.

Miles, Rosalind. "A Baby God: The Creative Dynamism of Emily Brontë's Poetry." In *The Art of Emily Bronte,* edited by Anne Smith. New York: Barnes and Noble, 1976.

Mill, John Stuart. *Autobiography.* New York: Riverside, 1969.

Miller, Alice. "The Drama of the Gifted Child and the Narcissistic Disturbance of the Psychoanalyst." *International Journal of Psycho-Analysis* 60 (1979): 47–58.

Miller, Hillis. "D. H. Lawrence: 'The Fox' and the Perspective Glass." *Harvard Advocate,* December 1952.

Miller, Karl. *Doubles: Studies in Literary History.* New York: Oxford University Press, 1985.

Mitchell, Juliet. *Psychoanalysis and Women.* New York: Random House, 1974.

Modell, Arnold H. "The Transitional Object and the Creative Act." *Psychoanalytic Quarterly* 39 (1970): 240–50.

———. "The Nature of Psychoanalytic Knowledge." *Journal of the American Psychoanalytic Association* 26 (1978): 641–57.

Moers, Ellen. *The Dandy: Brummell to Beerbohm.* New York: Viking, 1960.

Moloney, James Clark. "Oedipus Rex, Cu Chulain, Khepri and the Ass." *Psychoanalytic Review* 54 (1967): 201–47.

Montaigne, Michel de. *The Complete Essays.* Translated by Donald Frame. Stanford, Calif.: Stanford University Press, 1965.

Montagu, Ashley. "Mother's Touch." *Science Digest,* April 1981.

———. *Growing Young.* New York: McGraw Hill, 1983.

Moon, Sun Myung. *The Divine Principle.* New York: The Holy Spirit Association for the Unification of World Christianity, 1973.

Moore, Harry T., ed. *The Complete Letters of D. H. Lawrence.* New York: Viking, 1962.

———. ed. *The World of Lawrence Durrell.* New York: Dutton, 1964.

Morgan, Elaine. *The Descent of Woman.* New York: Stein and Day, 1980.

Morgan, Robin. *Monster.* New York: Random House, 1972.

Morris, Desmond. *The Naked Ape.* New York: McGraw Hill, 1967.

Morris, John N. *Versions of the Self.* New York: Basic Books, 1966.

Moynahan, Julian. "The Hero's Guilt: The Case of *Great Expectations.*" *Essays in Criticism* 10 (1960): 60–79.

Mujeeb-ur-Rahman, Md., ed. *The Freudian Paradigm: Psychoanalysis and Scientific Thought.* Chicago: Nelson-Hall, 1977.

Nadeau, Robert. *Readings from the New Book on Nature.* Amherst: University of Massachusetts Press, 1981.

Naremore, James. *The World Without a Self.* New Haven: Yale University Press, 1973.

Niederland, William. "Early Auditory Experiences, Beating Fantasies, and the Primal Scene." *Psychoanalytic Study of the Child* 13 (1958): 471–504.

_____. "Clinical Aspects of Creativity." *American Imago* 24 (1967): 6–34.

_____. "The History and Meaning of California: A Psychoanalytic Inquiry." *Psychoanalytic Quarterly* 40 (1971): 485–90.

_____. "The Naming of America." In *The Unconscious Today,* edited by Mark Kanzer. New York: International Universities Press, 1971.

_____. *The Schreber Case.* New York: Quadrangle Press, 1974.

_____. "Psychoanalytic Approaches to Artistic Creativity." *Psychoanalytic Quarterly* 45 (1976): 185–212.

Norris, Margot. *The Decentered Universe of "Finnegans Wake."* Baltimore: Johns Hopkins University Press, 1976.

Oates, Joyce Carol. Review of *Remember Me,* by Fay Weldon. *New York Times Book Review,* 21 November 1976.

O'Keefe, John A. "On Wheeler's Cosmology." Paper read at Washington School of Psychiatry, Seminar on the Nonrational, 1977.

Olayon, Stephen. "Camus' *The Stranger*: The Sun metaphor and Parricidal Conflict." American Imago 40 (1983): 198–205.

Olivieri, Samuelle. *The Life of the Madonna in Art.* Boston: Daughters of St. Paul, 1985.

Ong, Walter. *The Barbarian Within.* New York: Macmillan, 1962.

Onorato, Robert. *The Character of the Poet.* Princeton: Princeton University Press, 1971.

Ornstein, Robert, and Richard F. Thompson. *The Amazing Brain.* Boston: Houghton Mifflin, 1984.

Orston, Darius Gray. "Psychotherapy and Translation." Paper read at the American Psychoanalytic Meeting, December 1986.

Ovid. *Metamorphoses.* New York: NAL, 1958.

Pagels, Elaine. *The Gnostic Gospels.* New York: Random, 1979.

Panken, Shirley. *Virginia Woolf and the "Lust of Creation."* Albany, N.Y.: State University of New York Press, 1987.

Parsons, Anne. "Is the Oedipus Complex Universal?" *Psychoanalytic Study of Society* 3 (1964): 278–328.

Partridge, Eric. *Origins, A Short Etymological Dictionary of Modern English.* New York: Macmillan, 1959.

Pearlman, E. "Father and Mother in *Father and Son." Victorian Newsletter* 55 (1979): 19–23.

Peterson, Linda H. *Victorian Autobiography, The Tradition of Self-Interpretation.* New Haven: Yale University Press, 1986.

Pinter, Harold. *The Homecoming.* New York: Grove, 1965.

Plath, Sylvia. *Collected Poems.* New York: Harper and Row, 1981.

Plato. *The Republic.* Translated by F.M. Cornford. New York: Oxford University Press, 1963.

Polanyi, Michael. *Personal Knowledge: Towards a Post-Critical Philosophy.* New York: Harper and Row, 1958.

Pope, Alexander. *The Poems of Alexander Pope.* Edited by John Butt. New Haven: Yale University Press, 1963.

Popper, Karl. *Conjectures and Refutations.* New York: Harper and Row, 1968.

Purdy, Strother. "Mind Your Genderous: Toward a *Wake* Grammar." In *New Light on Joyce,* edited by Fritz Senn. Bloomington: University of Indiana Press, 1972.

Rank, Otto. *The Myth of the Birth of the Hero.* New York: Knopf, 1959.

_____. *The Double: A Psychoanalytic Study.* Chapel Hill: University of North Carolina Press, 1971.

Rappaport, David. *Organization and Pathology of Thought.* New York: Columbia University Press, 1951.

Raschke, Carl A. *The Interruption of Eternity: Modern Gnosticism and the Origins of the New Religious Consciousness.* Chicago: Nelson Hall, 1980.

Ratchford, Fannie E. *Gondal's Queen: A Novel in Verse by Emily Jane Brontë.* Austin: University of Texas Press, 1955.

Recht, Roberta. "'The Foundations of an Admirable Science': Descartes' Dream of 10 November 1619." *Humanities in Society* 4 (1981): 203–21.

Redingen, Ruby. *George Eliot: The Emergent Self,* New York: Knopf, 1975.

Reed, Michael D. "The Power of *Wuthering Heights:* A Psychoanalytic Examination." *The Psychocultural Review* 1 (1977): 21–42.

Restak, Richard. *The Brain: The Last Frontier.* New York: Doubleday, 1979.

Rieff, Philip. *Freud: The Mind of the Moralist.* New York: Doubleday, 1961.

_____. *The Triumph of the Therapeutic.* New York: Harper, 1968.

Robert, Marthe. *Origins of the Novel.* Bloomington: Indiana University Press, 1980.

Rochlin, Gregory. *Grief and Its Discontents.* Boston: Little, Brown, 1965.

Roheim, Geza. "The Evolution of Culture." *International Journal of Psycho-Analysis* 15 (1934): 387–418.

_____. *The Riddle of the Sphinx.* London: Hogarth, 1934.

Rose, Gilbert. "On the Shores of Self: Samuel Beckett's *Molloy*—Irredentism and the Creative Impulse." *The Psychoanalyic Review* 60 (1973): 584–604.

_____. *The Power of Form.* New York: International Universities Press, 1980.

Rose, Phyllis. *Woman of Letters: A Life of Virginia Woolf.* New York: Oxford University Press, 1978.

Rosenman, Stanley. "Turning from the Dual Empire to the Inner World: Freud's Creation of Psychoanalysis." *Journal of Psychohistory* 15 (1987): 207–15.

_____. "The Myth of the Birth of the Hero Revisited: Disasters and Brutal Child Rearing." *American Imago* 45 (1988): 1–44.

Rosner, Stanley, and Lawrence Abt, eds. *Essays in Creativity.* Croton-on-the-Hudson, N.Y.: North River Press, 1974.

Ross, Manuel. "The Borderline Diatheseis." *International Review of Psychoanalysis* 3, no. 3 (1976): 305–21.

Rossman, Charles. "'You Are the Call and I Am the Answer': D. H. Lawrence and Women." *D. H. Lawrence Review* 8 (1975): 255–329.

Roth, Philip. *The Breast.* New York: Holt Rinehart and Winston, 1972.

Rothenberg, Albert. "Einstein's Creative Thinking and the General Theory of Relativity." *American Journal of Psychiatry* 136 (1979): 38–43.

_____. *The Emerging Goddess.* Chicago: University of Chicago Press, 1979.

Rothstein, David A. "On Presidential Assination: The Academia and the Pseudo-Community." *Adolescent Psychiatry* 4 (1975): 264–98.

Rubenstein, Marc A. "'My Accursed Origin': The Search for the Mother in *Frankenstein.*" *Studies in Romanticism* 15 (1976): 165–94.

Ruderman, Judith G. "'The Fox' and the 'Devouring Mother.'" *The D. H. Lawrence Review* 10 (1977): 251–69.

Ruskin, John. *Stones of Venice,* vol. 2 *Complete Works.* New York: Thomas Crowell, 1905.

Russ, Joanna. "What Can a Heroine Do? Or, Why Women Can't Write." In *Images of Women in Ficiton,* edited by Susan Koppelman Cornillon. Bowling Green, Ohio: Popular Press, 1972.

Rycroft, Charles. "Freud and the Imagination." *The New York Review of Books,* 3 April 1975, 26–30.

Sagan, Carl. *The Dragons of Eden.* New York: Random House, 1977.

_____. *Broca's Brain.* New York: Random Huse, 1979.

_____. *Cosmos.* New York: Random House, 1980.

Sagar, Keith. "The Originality of *Wuthering Heights.*" In *The Art of Emily Brontë,* edited by Anne Smith. New York: Barnes and Noble, 1976.

Sartre, Jean-Paul. *The Psychology of the Imagination.* Translated by Bernard Frechtman. New York: Philosophical Library, 1948.

_____. *Saint Genet.* New York: NAL, 1952, 1964.

_____. *Being and Nothingness.* New York: Washington Square Press, 1956.

_____. *Nausea.* New York: New Directions, 1964.

_____. *The Words.* Translated by Bernard Frechtman. New York: Fawcett, 1966.

Schafer, Roy. *The Analytic Attitude.* New York: Basic Books, 1983.

Schapiro, Barbara. *The Romantic Mother: Narcissistic Patterns in Romantic Poetry.* Baltimore: Johns Hopkins Press, 1983.

Schlesinger, Kurt. "On the Creative Process and the Human Capacity to Construe." *International Journal of Psychotherapy* 8, no. 1 (1980): 482–500.

Schonberger, Stephen. "A Dream of Descartes: Reflections on the Unconscious Determinants of Science." *International Journal of Psycho-Analysis* 20 (1939): 43–57.

Schutte, William. *Joyce and Shakespeare.* New Haven: Yale University Press, 1957.

Schwartz, Lillian. "Leonardo's Mona Lisa." *Art and Antiques,* January 1987.

Scott, Bonnie. *Joyce and Feminism.* Bloomington: Indiana University Press, 1984.

Segal, Julia. *Phantasy in Everyday Life.* London: Penguin, 1985.

Seidel, Michael. "*Ulysses'* Black Panther Vampire." *James Joyce Quarterly* 13 (1976): 415–27.

Shakespeare, William. *The Riverside Edition.* Boston: Houghton Miffiin, 1974.

Shaw, Evelyn, and Joan Darling. *Female Strategies.* New York: Walker, 1985.

Shechner, Mark. *Joyce in Nighttown.* Berkeley: University of California Press, 1974.

Shelley, Mary. *Frankenstein.* New York: Oxford University Press, 1972.

Shengold, Leonard. "The Parent as Sphinx." *Journal of the American Psychoanalytic Association* 11 (1963): 725–51.

_____. "Freud and Joseph." In *The Unconscious Today,* edited By Mark Kanzer. New York: International Universities Press, 1971.

_____. *Soul Murder.* New Haven: Yale University Press, 1989.

Showalter, Elaine. *A Literature of Their Own.* Princeton: Princeton University Press, 1977.

Sides, Dorothy Smith. *Decorative Art of the Southwestern Indians.* New York: Dover Publications, 1961.'

Simo, Joseph. "On Christianity and the Oedipal Winner." *Psychoanalytic Review* 70, no. 3 (1983): 321–30.

Simon, Bennett. *Mind and Madness in Ancient Greece.* Ithaca: Cornell University Press, 1978.

_____. "The Imaginary Twins: The Case of Beckett and Bion." International Review of Psycho-Analysis 15 (1988); 331–52.

_____. *Tragic Drama and the Family.* New Haven: Yale University Press, 1988.

Sitwell, Edith. *Alexander Pope.* London: Faber and Faber, 1930.

Skura, Merideth Anne. *The Literary Use of the Psychoanalytic Process.* New Haven: Yale University Press, 1983.

Slater, Philip. *Footholds.* New York: Dutton, 1977.

_____. *The Wayward Gate.* Boston: Beacon Press, 1977.

Slobin, Dan Isaac. *Psycholinguistics.* Oakland, N.J.: Scott Foresman, 1979.

Slochower, Harry. "Camus' *The Stranger*: The Silent Society and the Ectasy of Rage." *American Imago* 26 (1966): 291–95.

_____. *Mythopoesis.* Detroit: Wayne State University Press, 1970.

Slocum, Sally. "Woman the Gatherer: Male Bias in Anthropology." In *Toward an Anthropology of Women,* edited by Rayna R. Reiter. New York: Monthly Review Press, 1975.

Smith, Anne. *The Art of Emily Brontë.* New York: Barnes and Noble, 1976.

Smith, Eliot Fremont. "Alex Haley and the Rot in *Roots.*" *Village Voice,* 30 May 1977.

Smith, Sydney. "The Golden Fantasy: A Regressive Reaction to Separation Anxiety." *International Journal of Psycho-Analysis* 58 (1977): 311–24.

Smitten, Jeffrey. *Spatial Form in Narrative.* Ithaca: Cornell University Press, 1981.

Solomon, Eric. "The Incest Theme in *Wuthering Heights.*" In *Twentieth Century Interpretations of Wuthering Heights,* edited by Thomas A. Volger. Englewood Cliffs, N.J.: Prentice-Hall, 1968.

Sontag, Frederich. *Sun Myung Moon and the Unification Church.* Nashville, Tenn.: The Parthenon Press, 1977.

Spector, Jack J. *The Aesthetics of Freud.* New York: Praeger, 1973.

Spilka, Mark. "On Lawrence's Impotence." In *D. H. Lawrence: The Man Who Lived,* edited by Robert Partlow and Harry T. Moore. Carbondale: Southern Illinois University Press, 1980.

_____. *Virginia Woolf's Quarrel with Grieving.* Lincoln: University of Nebraska Press, 1980.

Spitz, Ellen Handler. *Art and Psyche.* New Haven: Yale University Press, 1985.

Spitz, René. "The Primal Cavity." *Psychoanalytic Study of the Child* 10 (1955): 215–40.

_____. *No and Yes: On the Genesis of Human Communication.* New York: International Universities Press, 1957.

_____. "Some Early Prototypes of Ego Defenses," *Journal of the American Psychoanalytic Association.* 19 (1961): 626–51.

Sprinchorn, Evert. Introduction to *The Chamber Plays by August Strindberg.* New York: Dutton, 1962.

_____. "A Portrait of the Artist as Achilles." In *Approaches to the Twentieth Century Novel,* edited by John Unterecker. New York: Crowell, 1965.

Stace, W. T. "Man Against Darkness." *Atlantic Monthly,* September 1948.

Stafford, Barbara Maria. *Voyage into Substance, Art, Science, Nature, and the Illustrated Travel Account.* Cambridge: MIT Press, 1984.

Stamm, Julian. "Camus' *Stranger:* His Act of Violence." *American Imago* 26 (1966): 281–90.

Stange, Robert. "Expectations Well Lost." In *The Dickens Critics,* edited by George H. Ford and Lauriat Lane, Jr. Ithaca: Cornell University Press, 1961.

Stein, Howard. *Developmental Time, Cultural Space: Studies in Psychogeography.* Norman: University of Oklahoma Press, 1987.

Steinberg, Erwin. "Characteristic Sentence Patterns in 'Proteus' and 'Lestrygonians.'" In *New Light on Joyce from the Dublin Symposium,* edited by Fritz Senn. Bloomington: University of Indiana Press, 1972.

Stern, Karl. *The Flight from Woman.* New York: Noonday, 1965.

Stoehr, Taylor. *Dickens: The Dreamer's Stance.* Ithaca: Cornell University Press, 1965.

Stokes, Adrian. *The Image in Form.* New York: Harper and Row, 1972.

Stoller, Robert. "Symbiosis, Anxiety, and the Development of Masculinity." *Archives of General Psychiatry* 30 (1974): 164–72.

_____. *Sexual Excitement.* New York: Atheneum, 1979.

Stone, Harry. *Dickens and the Invisible World.* Bloomington: Indiana University Press, 1979.

Storr, Anthony. *The Dynamics of Creation.* New York: Atheneum, 1972.

_____. *C. G. Jung.* New York: Viking, 1973.

Story, Ronald. *The Space-Gods Revealed.* New York: Harper and Row, 1976.

Stover, Leon, and Bruce Kraig. *Stonehenge: The Indo-European Tradition.* Chicago: Nelson Hall, 1978.

Strindberg, August. *The Chamber Plays.* New York: Dutton, 1962.

_____. *The Son of A Servant.* New York: Doubleday, 1966.

Strouse, Louise F. "Virginia Woolf—Her Voyage Back." *American Imago* 38 (1980): 185–202.

Sturrock, John. *Structuralism and Science.* New York: Oxford University Press, 1979.

Sulloway, Frank. *Freud, Biologist of the Mind: Beyond the Psychoanalytic Legend.* New York: Basic Books, 1979.

Swan, Jim. "Mater and Nannie: Freud's Two Mothers and the Discovery of the Oedipus Complex." *American Imago* 31 (1974): 1–64.

Swift, Jonathan. *Gulliver's Travels.* New York: Viking Critical Edition, 1961.

Tarbox, Raymond. "Blank Hallucinations in the Fiction of Poe and Hemingway." *American Imago* 24 (1967): 312–43.

Theroux, Paul. "Hapless Organ." *New Statesman,* 19 April 1974.

Thody, Philip. *Roland Barthes: A Conservative Estimate.* New York: Macmillan, 1977.

Tomasi, Barbara. "The Fraternal Theme in Joyce's *Ulysses.*" *American Imago* 30 (1973): 177–91.

Tristram, Philippa. "'Divided Sources.'" In *The Art of Emily Brontë,* edited by Anne Smith. New York: Barnes and Noble, 1976.

Trosman, Harry. "Freud and the Controversy over Shakespearean Authorship." *Journal of the American Psychoanalytic Association* 13 (1965): 475–98.

_____. *Freud and the Imaginative World.* Hillsdale, N.J.: The Analytic Press, 1985.

Twitchell, James. "Lawrence's Lamias: Predatory Women in *The Rainbow* and *Women in Love.*" *Studies in the Novel* 11, no. 1 (1979): 23–42.

Tyrrell, William Blake. *Amazons: A Study in Athenian Mythmaking.* Baltimore: Johns Hopkins University Press, 1984.

Underhill, Evelyn. *Mysticism.* New York: Dutton, 1961.

Urban, Bernd. "Schnitzler and Freud as Doubles: Poetic Intuition and Early Research on Hysteria." *Psychoanalytic Review* 65, no. 1 (1978): 131–65.

Valency, Maurice. *The Flower and the Castle.* New York: Grosset and Dunlop, 1966.

Van Ghent, Dorothy. *The English Novel: Form and Function* New York: Rhinehart, 1953.

Vitz, Paul, and Arnold B. Glincher. *Modern Art and Modern Science:The Parallel Analysis of Vision.* New York: Praeger, 1984.

Von Bertalanffy, Ludwig. *A Systems View of Man.* Edited by Paul A. LaViolette. Boulder, Colo.: Westview Press, 1981.

Von Daniken, Erich. *Chariots of the Gods?* New York: Bantam, 1971.

Vonnegut, Kurt. *Slaughterhouse Five.* New York: Dell, 1970.

_____. *Breakfast of Champions.* New York: Dell, 1973.

Ward, Clyde. "Kilroy Was Here." *Psychoanalytic Quarterly* 31 (1962): 80–91.

Warner, Marina. *Alone of All Her Sex: The Myth and the Cult of the Virgin Mary.* New York: Random House, 1983.

Watters, T. A. "Forms of the Family Romance." *Psychoanalytic Review* 43 (1956): 204–13.

Watts, Eileen. "Beckett's Unnamables: Schizophrenia, Rationalism, and the Novel." *American Imago* 45 (1988): 85–106.

Webb, R. K. *Harriet Martineau: A Radical Victorian.* New York: Columbia University Press, 1960.

Weich, Martin J. "Directions: A Hierarchy of Symbols." Presented at American Psychoanalytic Association, Fall 1978.

Weigel, John. *Lawrence Durrell.* New York: Twaynes English Authors Series, 1965.

Weinburger, Jerome, and Jules Glenn. "The Significance of the Trifurcation of the Road: Clinical Confirmation and Illumination." *Journal of the American Psychoanalytic Association* 25 (1977): 655–67.

Weiss, Edoardo. "The Phenomenon of 'Ego passage." *Journal of the American Psychoanalytic Association* 3 (1954): 267–81.

Weiss, Samuel. *"Conceptualizing the Nature of the Therapeutic Action of Child Analysis."* Presented at the meeting of the American Psychoanalytical Association, Fall 1978.

Weissman, Philip. "Theoretical Considerations of Ego Regression and Ego Functions in Creativity." *Psychoanalytic Quarterly* 36 (1967): 37–50.

Weissman, Stephen M. "Frederick Douglass, Portrait of a Black Militant: A Study in the Family Romance." *The Psychoanalytic Study of the Child* 30 (1975): 725–52.

———. "Face to Face: The Role of Vision and the Smiling Response." *Psychoanalytic Study of the Child* 32 (1977): 421–52.

Werman, David. "Methodological Problems in the Psychoanalytic Interpretation of Literature." *Journal of the American Psychoanalytic Association* 27, no. 2 (1979): 451–78.

Wheeler, John Archibald. "Our Universe: The Known and the Unknown." *American Scientist* 56 (1968): 1–20.

———. "The Universe as Home for Man." In *The Nature of Scientific Discovery,* edited by Owen Gingerich. Washington D.C.: Smithsonian Institution Press, 1975.

Wheeler, Richard. "Yeats' 'Second Coming': What Rough beast?" *American Imago* 31 (1974): 233–51.

White, John. "Psyche and Tuberculosis." *The Psychoanalytic Study of Society* 4 (1967): 204.

Widzer, Martin. "The Comic-book Superhero: A Study in Family Romance Fantasy." *Psychoanalytic Study of the Child* 32 (1977): 565–603.

Wilde, Oscar. *The Works.* Edited by John Gilbert. London: Spring Books, 1963.

———. *The Complete Works.* Edited by Vyvyan Holland. London: Collins and Glasgow, 1966.

Williams, Tennessee. *Camino Real.* New York: New Directions, 1953.

Williams, Walter L. *The Spirit and the Flesh: Sexual Diversity in American Indian Culture.* Boston: Beacon, 1987.

Wilson, F. A. C. "Yeats' 'A Bronze Head': A Freudian Investigation." *Literature and Psychology* 22 (1972): 5–12.

Wilson, Edmund. *The Wound and the Bow.* New York: Oxford University Press, 1947.

Wimsatt, William K. *The Portraits of Alexander Pope.* New Haven: Yale University Press, 1965.

Winn, James Anderson. *"A Window in the Bosom": The Letters of Alexander Pope.* Hamden, Conn.: Shoe String Press, 1977.

Winnicott, D. "Transitional Objects and Transitional Phenomena." In *Collected Papers*. New York: Basic Books, 1958.

_____. "Mirror-role of Mother and Family in Child Development." In *The Visual Behavior of Infants in the First Year of Life*, edited by P. Lomas. London: Proceedings of the Royal Society of Medicine 55 (1968): 26–33.

Wion, Philip K. "The Absent Mother in Emily' Brontë's *Wuthering Heights.*" *American Imago* 42 (1985): 143–64.

Wisdom, J. O. "Three Dreams of Descartes." *Internatioal Journal of Psycho-Analysis* 28 (1947): 11–17.

Wolf, Ernest S. "*Saxa Loquuntur:* Artistic Aspects of the Aetiology of Hysteria." *Psychoanalytic Study of the Child*, 26 (1971): 535–54.

Wolf, Howard R. "British Fathers and Sons, 1773–1913: From Filial Submissiveness to Creativity." *Psychoanalytic Review* 52 (1965): 53–70.

Wood, Allen Tate. *Moonstruck*. New York: Morrow: 1979.

Woolf, Virginia. *The Common Reader*. New York: Harcourt Brace, 1925.

_____. *To the Lighthouse*. New York: Harcourt Brace, 1927.

_____. *A Room of One's Own*. New York: Harcourt Brace, 1929.

_____. *Between the Acts*. New York: Harcourt Brace, 1941.

_____. *The Waves*. London: Hogarth, 1961.

_____. *The Letters of Virginia Woolf*. Edited by Nigel Nicolson vol. 2, 1912–22. New York: Harcourt Brace, Jovarovich, 1976.

_____. *The Diary*. Edited by Anne Qlivier Bell. Vol. 5, New York: Harcourt Brace Jovanovich, 1984.

Wordsworth, William. *The Prelude*. Edited by I. C. Marwell. New York: Penguin, 1971.

Wormhoudt, Arthur. "The Unconscious Identification Words = Milk." *American Imago* 23 (1949): 234–39.

Wurmser, Leon. "Some Comments about Adolf Grunbaum's Criticism of the Validity of Hidden Motives in Psychoanalytic Theory." Presented at the American Psychoanalytic Meeting, Winter 1986.

Wyschogrod, Edith. "Sons Without Fathers: A Study in Identity and Culture." *Journal of the American Academy of Psychoanalysis* 16 (1978): 249–62.

Yeats, W. B. *Collected Poems*. New York: Macmillan, 1956.

Zukav, Gary. *The Dancing Wu Li Masters*. New York: Morrow, 1979.

Zweig, Paul. *Three Journeys: An Automythology*. New York: Basic Books, 1976.

Index